P9-DIB-525

Fodor's

MAINE COAST

3rd Edition

Where to Stay and Eat
for All Budgets

Must-See Sights
and Local Secrets

Ratings You Can Trust

Fodor's Travel Publications   New York, Toronto, London, Sydney, Auckland
www.fodors.com

FODOR'S MAINE COAST

Editors: Debbie Harmsen, Carolyn Galgano

Editorial Contributors: Neva Allen, Stephen Allen, Bethany Cassin Beckerlegge, Mary Ruoff, Laura V. Scheel, George Semler, Sarah Stebbins, Michael de Zayas

Production Editors: Jennifer DePrima, Carrie Parker
Maps & Illustrations: Mark Stroud and David Lindroth, *cartographers;* Bob Blake, Rebecca Baer, *map editors;* William Wu, *information graphics*
Design: Fabrizio La Rocca, *creative director;* Guido Caroti, Siobhan O'Hare, *art directors;* Tina Malaney, Chie Ushio, Ann McBride, Jessica Walsh, *designers;* Melanie Marin, *senior picture editor*
Cover Photo: (Schoodic Point, Acadia National Park): Susan Cole Kelly
Production Manager: Amanda Bullock

3rd Edition

ISBN 978–1–4000–0424–9

ISSN 1554–5830

SPECIAL SALES

This book is available at special discounts for bulk purchases for sales promotions or premiums. Special editions, including personalized covers, excerpts of existing books, and corporate imprints, can be created in large quantities for special needs. For more information, write to Special Markets/Premium Sales, 1745 Broadway, MD 6-2, New York, New York 10019, or e-mail specialmarkets@randomhouse.com.

AN IMPORTANT TIP & AN INVITATION

Although all prices, opening times, and other details in this book are based on information supplied to us at press time, changes occur all the time in the travel world, and Fodor's cannot accept responsibility for facts that become outdated or for inadvertent errors or omissions. So **always confirm information when it matters,** especially if you're making a detour to visit a specific place. Your experiences—positive and negative—matter to us. If we have missed or misstated something, **please write to us.** We follow up on all suggestions. Contact the Maine Coast editor at editors@fodors.com or c/o Fodor's at 1745 Broadway, New York, NY 10019.

PRINTED IN THE UNITED STATES OF AMERICA

10 9 8 7 6 5 4 3 2

Be a Fodor's Correspondent

Your opinion matters. It matters to us. It matters to your fellow Fodor's travelers, too. And we'd like to hear it. In fact, we need to hear it.

When you share your experiences and opinions, you become an active member of the Fodor's community. That means we'll not only use your feedback to make our books better, but we'll publish your names and comments whenever possible. Throughout our guides, look for "Word of Mouth," excerpts of your unvarnished feedback.

Here's how you can help improve Fodor's for all of us.

Tell us when we're right. We rely on local writers to give you an insider's perspective. But our writers and staff editors—who are the best in the business—depend on you. Your positive feedback is a vote to renew our recommendations for the next edition.

Tell us when we're wrong. We're proud that we update most of our guides every year. But we're not perfect. Things change. Hotels cut services. Museums change hours. Charming cafés lose charm. If our writer didn't quite capture the essence of a place, tell us how you'd do it differently. If any of our descriptions are inaccurate or inadequate, we'll incorporate your changes in the next edition and will correct factual errors at fodors.com immediately.

Tell us what to include. You probably have had fantastic travel experiences that aren't yet in Fodor's. Why not share them with a community of like-minded travelers? Maybe you chanced upon a beach or bistro or B&B that you don't want to keep to yourself. Tell us why we should include it. And share your discoveries and experiences with everyone directly at fodors.com. Your input may lead us to add a new listing or highlight a place we cover with a "Highly Recommended" star or with our highest rating, "Fodor's Choice."

Give us your opinion instantly at our feedback center at www.fodors.com/feedback. You may also e-mail editors@fodors.com with the subject line "Maine Coast Editor." Or send your nominations, comments, and complaints by mail to Maine Coast Editor, Fodor's, 1745 Broadway, New York, NY 10019.

You and travelers like you are the heart of the Fodor's community. Make our community richer by sharing your experiences. Be a Fodor's correspondent.

Happy Traveling!

Tim Jarrell, Publisher

CONTENTS

Be a Fodor's Correspondent 3

1 EXPERIENCE THE MAINE COAST 7
  What's Where 8
  Maine Coast Planner 10
  Maine Today 11
  Quintessential Maine Coast 12
  Maine Coast Top Attractions 14
  Top Experiences 16
  If You Like 18
  Great Itineraries 21
  When to Go 25
  On The Calendar 26

2 THE SOUTHERN COAST 27
  Orientation and Planning 28
  Southern and Inland York County 32
  The Yorks, Ogunquit, and Wells 39
  The Kennebunks 60

3 GREATER PORTLAND 73
  Orientation and Planning 74
  Exploring Portland 78
  Where to Eat 84
  Where to Stay 87
  Nightlife and the Arts 89
  Shopping 91
  Sports and the Outdoors 93
  Side Trips from Portland 94

4 THE MID-COAST REGION 105
  Orientation and Planning 107
  From Brunswick to Wiscasset . . 111
  Boothbay and Pemaquid Peninsulas 130
  Cushing and St. George Peninsulas 143

5 PENOBSCOT BAY 153
  Planning and Orientation 154
  Rockland Area 157
  Rockport, Camden, and Lincolnville 167
  Belfast to Bangor 181

6 THE BLUE HILL PENINSULA . . 199
  Orientation and Planning 200
  Blue Hill and Environs 203
  Deer Isle and Stonington 213

7 ACADIA NATIONAL PARK AND MOUNT DESERT ISLAND 219
  Orientation and Planning 221
  Gateways to Mount Desert Island 224
  Bar Harbor 229
  Acadia National Park 241
  Around Mount Desert Island . . . 250
  The Outer Islands 260

8 WAY DOWN EAST 263
  Orientation and Planning 264
  Eastern Hancock County 267
  Steuben to Cherryfield 278
  Columbia Falls to Cutler 280
  Cobscook and Passamaquoddy Bays 289

TRAVEL SMART MAINE
COAST.................... 302
  Getting Here and Around...... 303
  Essentials 306
INDEX..................... 314
ABOUT OUR WRITERS 320

MAPS

What's Where................. 8–9
The Southern Coast............. 36
Portland 76
Around Greater Portland 96
The Mid-Coast................. 112
Penobscot Bay 159
Rockport and Camden.......... 168
Blue Hill Peninsula............. 207
Bar Harbor 230
Acadia National Park and Mount
Desert Island 244
Way Down East 269
Campobello Island 293

ABOUT THIS BOOK

Our Ratings

Sometimes you find terrific travel experiences and sometimes they just find you. But usually the burden is on you to select the right combination of experiences. That's where our ratings come in.

As travelers we've all discovered a place so wonderful that its worthiness is obvious. And sometimes that place is so unique that superlatives don't do it justice: you just have to be there to know. These sights, properties, and experiences get our highest rating, **Fodor's Choice**, indicated by orange stars throughout this book.

Black stars highlight sights and properties we deem **Highly Recommended**, places that our writers, editors, and readers praise again and again for consistency and excellence.

By default, there's another category: any place we include in this book is by definition worth your time, unless we say otherwise. And we will.

Disagree with any of our choices? Care to nominate a place or suggest that we rate one more highly? Visit our feedback center at www.fodors.com/feedback.

Budget Well

Hotel and restaurant price categories from ¢ to $$$$ are defined in the opening pages of each chapter. For attractions, we always give standard adult admission fees; reductions are usually available for children, students, and senior citizens. **AE, D, DC, MC, V** following dining and lodging listings indicate when American Express, Discover, Diner's Club, MasterCard, and Visa are accepted.

Restaurants

Unless we state otherwise, restaurants are open for lunch and dinner daily. We mention dress only when there's a specific requirement, and reservations only when they're essential or not accepted.

Hotels

Hotels have private bath, phone, TV, and air-conditioning, and operate on the European Plan (aka EP, meaning without meals), unless we specify that they use the Continental Plan (CP, with a continental breakfast), Breakfast Plan (BP, with a full breakfast), Modified American Plan (MAP, with breakfast and dinner), or are all-inclusive (AI, covers all meals and most activities). We list facilities but not if there's a charge for them.

Essentials

Please see the Travel Smart section in the back of the book for travel essentials for the entire Maine Coast; city- and area-specific basics are in each chapter.

Many Listings

★	Fodor's Choice
★	Highly recommended
⊠	Physical address
⊹	Directions or Map coordinates
✆	Mailing address
☎	Telephone
🖷	Fax
⊕	On the Web
✉	E-mail
🎫	Admission fee
⊙	Open/closed times
Ⓜ	Metro stations
🖃	Credit cards

Hotels & Restaurants

🏨	Hotel
⇆	Number of rooms
⚲	Facilities
⑂	Meal plans
✕	Restaurant
🍴	Reservations
🏛	Dress code
⌇	Smoking
🍷	BYOB

Outdoors

🏌	Golf
⛺	Camping

Other

☏	Family-friendly
⇨	See also
⊠	Branch address
☞	Take note

Experience the Maine Coast

WORD OF MOUTH

"As you'll see on the park map, Acadia is a little bit of a patchwork of donated lands. If you don't want to drive you can take the free Island Explorer shuttle to all the best spots, and around the park loop road. One nice idea is to hop off at one location, hike to another location and hop back on. If you want to rent bikes to explore the Carriage Trails you can do that in Bar Harbor. When you arrive be sure to go to the park info center and get info on all that you can do and then decide on your plans."

—cindyj

WHAT'S WHERE

The following numbers refer to chapters.

2 The Southern Coast. Stretching north from Kittery to just outside Portland, this is Maine's most-visited region. The towns along the shore and miles of sandy expanses cater to summer visitors. Old Orchard Beach and York Beach feature Coney Island–like amusements, while Kittery, the Yorks, and the Kennebunks have much to offer of historical interest.

3 Portland. Maine's largest and most cosmopolitan city, Portland deftly balances its historic role as a working harbor with its newer identity as a center of sophisticated arts and shopping, innovative restaurants, and stylish accommodations.

4 The Mid-Coast Region. North of Portland, from Brunswick to Monhegan Island, the craggy coastline swirls and winds its way around pastoral peninsulas. Dozens of lighthouses stand watch atop rock-strewn bluffs. Its villages boast maritime museums, antiques shops, and beautiful architecture.

5 Penobscot Bay. This region combines lively coastal towns with dramatic natural scenery. Camden is one of Maine's most picture-perfect towns, with its pointed church steeples, antique homes, and the famed historic windjammer fleet.

6 Blue Hill Peninsula. Art galleries are far more plentiful here than shops selling lobster T-shirts and lighthouse souvenirs. The entire region is ideal for biking, hiking, kayaking, and boating. For many, the Blue Hill Peninsula defines the silent beauty of the Maine Coast.

7 Acadia National Park and Mount Desert Island. Travelers come by the millions to climb (mostly by car) the miles of 19th-century carriage roads leading to Acadia National Park's stunning peaks and vistas of the island's mountains. Bar Harbor is more of a visitor's haven, while Southwest Harbor and Bass Harbor offer quieter pleasures.

8 Way Down East. This is the "real" Maine, some say, and it unfurls in thousands of acres of wild blueberry barrens, congestion-free coastlines, and a tangible sense of rugged endurance. It is the vulnerability of the land here to the winds, the winters, and the immense tides that makes the area so strikingly beautiful.

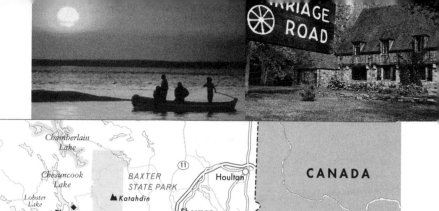

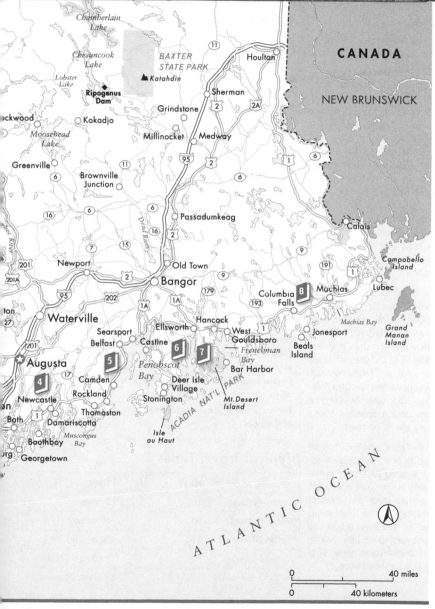

CANADA

NEW BRUNSWICK

Chamberlain Lake

Chesuncook Lake

BAXTER STATE PARK

▲ Katahdin

Houlton

11

Sherman

2

2A

Lobster Lake

Ripogenus Dam

Grindstone

ckwood

Kokadjo

Millinocket

Medway

2

95

2

6

1

6

Moosehead Lake

Greenville

6

Brownville Junction

11

Passadumkeag

Calais

16

6

6

16

9

201

15

Dead River

2

Campobello Island

Newport

7

Old Town

9

191

1

Lubec

201A

95

202

Bangor

179

Columbia Falls

8

Machias

ton

1A

193

Machias Bay

Grand Manan Island

27

Waterville

1A

Hancock

West Gouldsboro

Jonesport

Searsport

Ellsworth

Frenchman Bay

Beals Island

201

Belfast

Castine

6

7

Bar Harbor

Augusta

5

Penobscot Bay

Mt. Desert Island

17

Camden

Deer Isle Village

ACADIA NAT'L PARK

4

Rockland

Newcastle

Thomaston

Stonington

Kennebec River

Bath

1

Damariscotta

Muscongus Bay

Isle au Haut

Boothbay

rg

Georgetown

ATLANTIC OCEAN

0   40 miles

0   40 kilometers

MAINE COAST PLANNER

Getting Here and Around

Maine has two major international airports, Portland International Jetport and Bangor International Airport, to get you to or close to your coastal destination. Manchester-Boston Regional Airport in New Hampshire is about 45 minutes away from the southern end of the Maine coastline, so that would also be a viable option. Boston's Logan Airport is the only truly international airport in the region; it's about a 90-minute drive north to the Maine border.

Amtrak offers regional service from Boston to Portland via its Downeaster line that originates at Boston's North Station and makes four stops in Maine: Wells, Saco, Old Orchard Beach (seasonal), and finally Portland. Greyhound and Concord Trailways also offer bus service from Boston to many towns along the Maine coast.

All that being said, once you are here the best way to experience the winding backroads of the craggy Maine coast is in a car. There are miles and miles of roads far from the larger towns that no bus serves, and you won't want to miss discovering your own favorite ocean vista while on a scenic drive.

Touring the Coast

Organized bus tours can be a great way to cover a lot of ground and hit the highlights of the coast, but here are a few alternative tours that allow you to see Maine in a whole new way.

If you are a cycling enthusiast hoping to explore Mt. Desert Island, look into Maine Coast Bicycle Tours (⊕ www.mainecoastbicycletours.com). This outfit offers diverse cycling adventures for every level of fitness that come complete with luxury dining and accommodations, top-notch equipment, and the ultimate in local knowledge.

Another great way to experience the coastline of Maine is sailing the high seas. Maine Windjammer Cruises (⊕ www.mainewindjammercruises.com) takes cruising to another level by offering vacations sailing on historic working schooners. Cruises leave from Camden, and can be anywhere from a weekend-long to a weeklong trip. Two of the tall ships in their fleet, the **Grace Bailey** and the **Mercantile**, are National Historical Landmarks.

If you are looking for a water adventure that keeps you a bit closer to the shore, try a sea kayaking tour with Kayak Excursions of Kennebunk (⊕ www.southernmainekayaks.com). Whether you are an experienced paddler or a complete novice, the registered Maine guides will tailor the trip to your needs. In addition to daytime outings to places like Goose Rocks Beach and Cape Porpoise, Kayak Excursions offers sunset and full-moon tours.

For more tours, see Travel Smart Maine Coast at the back of the book.

Typical Travel Times

	Miles	Time
Boston–Portland	108	2 hours
Kittery–Portland	50	50 minutes
Portland–Freeport	17	20 minutes
Portland–Camden	80	2 hours
Portland–Bar Harbor	175	3 hours, 20 minutes

MAINE TODAY

The Politics

Like so many other Americans, Mainers are dealing with issues at the forefront of the news: how to fix the health-care system, how to deal with the current economic issues, and how best to provide clean, sustainable energy for the future. The issue of health care has brought national attention to one of Maine's elected officials, Senator Olympia Snowe. At the time of this writing, she is working as a member of a bipartisan commission to hammer out the details of health-care reform. As a moderate Republican, Senator Snowe's support for health-care-reform legislation has become increasingly important to the Obama administration as it attempts to build enough consensus across party lines to get the reform bill passed. With public opinions heating up over what health-care reform will actually mean for the American people, Olympia Snowe has placed herself at the influential center of the debate by helping to craft this legislation. Only time will tell whether the finished bill actually gains her support.

The Economy

With the country trying to pull itself out of an economic slump, Maine is facing its own unique set of issues. The lobster fishing industry, which is a main component of Maine's economy, is in crisis. Since lobster is generally viewed as an expensive delicacy, demand for the product in tough times has decreased dramatically. Between 2005 and 2009 lobster prices dropped nearly two dollars a pound, putting a financial squeeze on the industry as fuel and equipment costs have risen. One can only hope that better economic times will reverse this trend, but that remains to be seen.

One bright spot for the state's economy has been the widespread recognition of the culinary scene in Portland. National publications like *Bon Appétit* and the *New York Times* are picking up on what the locals have known for some time: that the level of sophistication Portland-area chefs are bringing to the table is sky-high. This national attention has generated great interest in the Harvest on the Harbor food festival held in October, and the festival and the restaurants that inspired it will continue to be a boon to the local economy.

The Environment

Producing clean and sustainable energy is another issue that Maine is tackling head-on. As of this writing, Maine produces 95% of the wind energy in New England through two major wind farms; an additional three farms are currently under construction, and many more are in development. While Gov. John Baldacci travels to Europe to promote Maine's wind industry and attract investors, questions are being raised back home about the possible location of test wind turbines off the shores of the artists' colony of Monhegan Island or the protected island of Damariscove. Harnessing the power of the wind off the Maine coast may be a way to bring new jobs and revenue to the state, but it will be a delicate balancing act between sustainable energy and sustaining the coastal environment that draws so many visitors to Maine's shores.

QUINTESSENTIAL MAINE COAST

Lighthouses

Maine's long and jagged coastline is home to more than 60 lighthouses, perched high on rocky ledges or on the tips of wayward islands. Though modern technology in navigation has made many of the lights obsolete, lighthouse enthusiasts and preservation groups restore and maintain many of them, and often make them accessible to the public. Some of the state's more famous lights include Portland Head Light, commissioned by President George Washington in 1790 and immortalized in one of Edward Hopper's paintings; Two Lights, a few miles down the coast in Cape Elizabeth; and West Quoddy Head, on the United States' easternmost tip of land. Some lighthouses are privately owned and others accessible only by boat, but plenty are within easy reach and open to the public, some with museums and tours.

Fishermen

Fishermen are to Maine as farmers are to the Midwest. Commercial fishing is a big part of the state's economy, and much of it is driven by hardy individuals or small family outfits who often go to work in the wee hours of the morning. It's a tough gig—working conditions vary with the weather; boats, traps, and nets require a lot of care; regulations must be met; and the catch can either be feast or famine. Yet the rugged men and women who ply the coast live their heritage with pride and determination. The lobster boat is beautiful in its simplicity, a classic study in form following function, and it's the working waterfront of coastal towns and villages that makes a visit to the Maine Coast worthwhile, but most of all, memorable.

Counting all its nooks, crannies, and crags, the Maine Coast would stretch for thousands of miles if you could pull it straight. All that space hides great heritage, food, and ideal places for relaxation.

Shellfish

Maine will forever be famous for its delectable lobsters, but it would be a shame to visit the state without trying one of its other, equally delicious shellfish. Maine shrimp are smaller than the more familiar cocktail variety, yet sweeter and perfect in a salad. A variety of clams, including the perennial favorite littleneck, is readily available in waterfront markets such as Portland's Harbor Fish Market. Steam them in large pots until they open, then dip in drawn butter. A cousin to the clam, mussels are sweet enough to eat without butter. Scallops here are especially tender. Try them fried and dipped in tartar sauce or sautéed as an appetizer. Crabmeat is best eaten in a toasted hot-dog roll with a minimum of mayonnaise and a leaf of green lettuce.

The Idyllic Shore

A large sign greets drivers coming into the state as they cross over from New Hampshire: MAINE: THE WAY LIFE SHOULD BE. Indeed. Though the suburbs are growing, life for the most part along the coast is far removed from the chaotic crowd scene of large urban areas. This simple-life vibe is especially apparent along the water's edge. Imagine standing on the shore, waves washing the sand rhythmically, as seagulls float and cry above. From offshore comes the clang of bell buoys, keeping time with the waves, as a lone lobstermen pulls his traps one by one into his chugging boat. The breeze carries the scent of salt mixed with a hint of diesel fuel and brine-soaked wharf wood. With a little luck, there's a weathered Adirondack chair nearby to plunk down into for the remainder of the day, and a B&B behind it for the night's stay. What more could one ask for?

MAINE COAST TOP ATTRACTIONS

Acadia National Park

(A) Hosting more than two million visitors annually, this jewel of the Maine coast was the first national park to be established east of the Mississippi River. Take a drive around Mt. Desert Island's 20-mi Park Loop Road to acquaint yourself with the area and indulge in spectacular views of the mountains and the sea. Head to the top of Cadillac Mountain for amazing 360-degree views, or bike the scenic 45-mi carriage-road system, inspecting each of the 17 stone bridges along the way.

The Beaches

(B) What can we say? One of the most attractive things about the Maine Coast is the coastline itself! Though swimming in this neck of the woods is truly for the hardiest of souls (summer ocean water temps hover around 55 degrees), Maine has a beach to suit everyone's taste. From Old Orchard Beach's 7-mi strip of sand complete with shops, pier, and amusements to the quieter sugar-sand horseshoe of Pemaquid Beach, you can find just the right spot to while away a warm summer day.

L.L. Bean

(C) This iconic Maine retailer specializing in clothing and equipment for outdoor living was founded in 1912 by Leon Leonwood Bean. Nearly one hundred years later, this one-man operation has morphed into a billion-dollar business that still sells a version of the product (the Maine Hunting Shoe, now the L.L. Bean Boot) that started it all. The flagship store in Freeport sits in the same location where Leon started his business years ago, and now, in addition to merchandise, offers lessons in everything from archery to snowshoeing to fly fishing through its Outdoor Discovery Schools. The store is open 24 hours a day, 365 days a year.

The Farnsworth Museum

(D) In Rockland, the Farnsworth is one of the most important small museums in the country, housing a comprehensive collection portraying Maine's influence in American art. Particularly of note is the Wyeth Center, which has extensive holdings from the three generations of Wyeth artists: N.C., a turn-of-the-20th-century illustrator; his son Andrew, one of the most famous American artists; and Andrew's son James, also an accomplished painter.

Fort Knox State Park/Penobscot Narrows Bridge and Observatory

(E) The largest fort in Maine, Fort Knox was constructed from 1844 to 1869 to defend Maine from a British naval attack. Though the fort never saw any real fighting, it was used as training ground for soldiers during the Civil War and Spanish-American War. The structure is one of the best-preserved fortifications in Maine. In a striking juxtaposition of old and new, the Penobscot Narrows Bridge next door rises above the landscape with its architectural cable-stayed design. It has the tallest public bridge observatory in the world; the 360-degree view from the top is breathtaking. From late May through October you can take the fastest elevator in Maine up 420 feet to the observatory, where placards identify the mountains, cities, and lakes you can see from the top.

Portland Head Light

(F) One of the most-photographed lighthouses in the nation, the historic Portland Head Light was commissioned by George Washington, and completed in 1791 for the whopping sum of $2,250. Positioned at the southwest entrance of Portland harbor, Portland Head Light was first lit with 16 whale-oil lamps; it now features an automated beacon that can be seen from 16 mi away. It is the state's oldest lighthouse.

TOP EXPERIENCES

Perfection on a Bun

It's hard to think of Maine without thinking of lobster, and there's good reason for that. With the state's most famous food available at nearly every stop along the coastline, it would be nearly impossible to escape a Maine Coast vacation without sampling the goods. So if seafood's your thing, why not enjoy a delectable search for your favorite lobster roll? In Maine, lobster with just a touch of mayo and a lettuce leaf nestled in a buttery grilled hot-dog bun is the standard "lobster roll" preparation, so it's hard to go wrong. We can say that you're most likely to find the best rolls at a lobster shack, and the most authentic ones are right next to the water with beautiful unobstructed views of working lobster boats in a scenic Maine harbor. Ask the locals (nicely), and you may enjoy a heavenly lunch at a secret spot that even the best tour books can't find!

Sailing the Coast

The coastline of Maine is a sailor's paradise, complete with hidden coves, windswept islands, and picture-perfect harbors where you can pick up a mooring for the night. With nearly 3,500 mi of undulating, rocky shoreline, you could spend a lifetime of summers sailing the waters off the Maine coast and never see it all. If you're not one of the lucky few with a sailboat to call your own, there are many companies that offer sailboat charters, whether for day trips or weeklong excursions. It might sound like an expensive getaway, but since meals and drinks are usually included, an overnight sailing charter might not cost any more than a seaside hotel room. Plus, you have the advantage of an experienced captain to provide history and insight along the voyage.

Wild Maine Blueberries

They may be tiny, but the wild blueberries of Maine pack a flavorful punch, and barely resemble their generic bloated cousins at the grocery store. If you are visiting Maine when they are in season (sometimes starting in late July and lasting until early September), take every opportunity to savor them, whether in pie, muffin, or pancake form, and you'll understand their legendary culinary status. In August and September, you can even pick your own blueberries at Staples Homestead, a family farm that has been in operation since 1838.

Sunrise on Cadillac Mountain

At 1,530 feet, Cadillac Mountain in Acadia National Park is the tallest mountain along the East Coast of the United States, so what better place to view a magnificent sunrise? Drive the winding and narrow 3.5-mi road to the summit and be one of the first faces in Maine to feel the summer sun's rays. While you're at the summit, hike the .3-mi trail around the top, where on a clear day you'll have excellent views of Frenchman Bay and the Porcupine Islands. Make sure to plan a visit during summer months, as the road up the mountain is generally closed from the end of October through March.

Finding That Perfect Souvenir

Artists and craftspeople abound along the Maine coast, meaning that finding the perfect souvenir of your vacation will be an enjoyable hunt. Whether you choose a watercolor of a picturesque fishing village, a riotously colorful piece of hand-painted pottery, or a handcrafted piece of jewelry, you'll be supporting the local economy while taking a little piece of Maine home with you.

The Sweet Stuff

Summer vacations in Maine go hand in hand with sweet treats; it would be hard to walk through Boothbay's shopping area without trying the homemade fudge at one of the candy stores, buying an ice cream for your sweetie, or bringing home some saltwater taffy to share with the folks back at the ranch. In York, you must visit The Goldenrod, where they've been making their famous taffy since 1896. The whoopie pie is another a must-try when touring the coast. Made from two chocolate circles of cake with vanilla cream filling in between, the whoopie pie is a delectable Maine tradition. Try the hamburger-sized ones at Moody's Diner on Route 1 in Waldeboro—they are particularly delish!

Communing With Nature

One of the best aspects of a coastal Maine vacation is the opportunity to get up close and personal with nature. While moose and bear sightings are relatively rare close to the ocean, there are numerous chances to observe birds, seals, and whales. An excellent Web site that provides interactive coastal maps to show the best bird-watching locales and also tells where you can catch a tour to see those adorable puffins is ⊕ *www.mainebirding.net*. There are numerous outfits along the coast that offer whale-watches; check out ⊕ *www. visitmaine.com* for listings of tours in Wells, Boothbay, and Acadia National Park. The tours head to the whale feeding grounds about 20 mi offshore, where the majestic animals are so numerous, some tours may offer a money back guarantee if you don't see one! The journey is also a great chance to see seals and seabirds.

Doing Everything

The Maine coast has so much to offer that it would be easy to fill every day of your trip with activities from morning until night. Fitness enthusiasts have endless biking, hiking, and kayaking opportunities; sailors will love exploring the coastal islands; history buffs can visit historic forts and myriad museums; kids will be begging to return to the amusements at Old Orchard Beach or the waterslides of Aquaboggan in Saco. If you have a family that's always on the go, planning vacation activities to suit all your tastes will be a breeze in Maine.

Doing Nothing

But then again, coastal Maine is the perfect destination for those who want to rest, relax, and get away from it all. What could be better than a comfortable seat on a porch and a picturesque harbor view? Or a leisurely stroll along the beach after an afternoon of napping in the sun? Visiting in the spring or fall, when the tourist season isn't at its peak, will guarantee you a quieter trip; you can soak up the spring blooms or fall foliage along the craggy coast in blissful (near!) solitude.

IF YOU LIKE

Art

Inspired by the state's quiet graces, artists for generations have been migrating to the Maine Coast. This has made art a cottage industry of sorts here. Painters such as Winslow Homer, Edward Hopper, and the Wyeths have put Maine scenes on their most famous canvases, while the functional beauty of the state's pottery is among the best anywhere.

■ **Portland.** The coastal city has some excellent repositories for art. In the **Portland Museum of Art** hang two of Homer's best-known coastal Maine paintings. The museum also owns or displays more than 20 works from the artist, as well as pieces by Monet, Picasso, and Renoir. Unique in New England is the **Museum of African Culture,** also in Portland, devoted exclusively to sub-Saharan African tribal arts. Its collection includes wooden masks and bronze figures.

■ **Rockland.** Situated at the center of this revitalized city, the Farnsworth Art Museum is home to an extensive collection of American art that relates to Maine. Bequeathed by Lucy Copeland Farnsworth, the daughter of a wealthy lime merchant, the museum opened in 1948, and at the time housed works by George Bellows, William Zorach, and Andrew Wyeth. In addition to the more than 10,000 works of American art, the museum also has a dedicated space, the Wyeth Center, devoted to collecting, researching and exhibiting the works of three generations of the Wyeth family: N.C., Andrew, and James.

■ **The Maine Art Trail.** This association encompasses seven of Maine's leading art museums, including the Portland Museum of Art and Farnsworth Art Museum, mentioned above. Two other museums included in the art trail that are located along the Maine Coast are the Ogunquit Museum of American Art and the Bowdoin College Museum of Art. The Ogunquit Museum, about 40 mi south of Portland in Ogunquit, is dedicated solely to the exhibition and preservation of American art and is situated on the scenic edge of Narrow Cove. Bowdoin College Museum of Art, on the college's campus in Brunswick, has one of the oldest collections in the nation, dating back to 1811. The museum now houses a diverse collection of more than 15,000 objects, with ancient, European, American, non-Western, and contemporary holdings. For more information on the Maine Art Trail, visit ⊕ *www.maineartmusuems.org.*

■ **The Coastal Islands.** Visitors who come to Maine to create their own art have plenty to paint or photograph. **Monhegan** and **Vinalhaven** islands are well-known destinations for painters attracted to the power exhibited where land meets sea. Photographers flock to the region during foliage season in the fall; at other times of the year they focus their lenses on classic New England architecture, colorful lobster buoys, and the mighty windjammers.

Beachcombing

There is nothing at all fancy about beachcombing. All you need is a pair of comfortable shoes, a relaxed gait, and an appreciation for the simple things in life— a trio most any visitor to the Maine Coast has in abundance.

■ **Where.** Plenty of secluded coves and rocky beaches on Maine's famously rugged coastline await exploration. **Popham Beach** and the sandy expanse at nearby **Reid State Park** are two especially good choices. Farther south, don't miss **Old Orchard Beach.**

■ **When.** The best time to wander is after the tide has gone out, when the retreating water has left behind its treasures. Early spring is an especially good time to see sand dollars washed up on beaches.

■ **What to Look For.** The best part of beachcombing is that you never quite know what to expect to find at your feet. Sea glass—nothing more than man-made glass worn smooth from its seaward journeys—is a common find. Weathered glass in shades of blue is a prized find, as that color is the most rare. You'll also find shells in abundance: blue mussels, tiny periwinkles, razor, or "jackknife" clams, ridged scallops, and oysters with their rough outside shell and lovely mother-of-pearl interiors.

■ **Before You Go.** One thing to note is that some beaches have restrictions on whether you can take away shells and other flotsam and jetsam. Keep an eye out for posted rules, or ask a local what you can or cannot take home with you.

Bicycling

Long-distance cyclists have long favored Maine's byways for their terrain, stunning vistas, and ease of navigation. Biking in Maine is especially scenic in and around Kennebunkport, Camden, Deer Isle, the Penobscot Bay area, and the Schoodic Peninsula. But most any town offers easy access to windy, hilly, and often tree-lined roads that meander through towns and villages that you might otherwise pass by. It's a great way to see small working farms and classic New England architecture.

■ **Acadia.** The carriage paths in **Acadia National Park** are especially ideal for cycling, with many miles of off-road trails providing finer and more intimate views than the roads open to traffic. For a cardio workout, ride the road to the top of

Cadillac Mountain and then gaze out in every direction to the surrounding coast, islands, and bays.

■ **Mid-Coast.** For more adventurous riders, many ski resorts, such as **Camden Snow Bowl** (⇨ Chapter 5), allow mountain bikes during the summer months.

■ **Portland.** If your stay in Maine includes Portland, put your wheels to the paved **Eastern Prom** Trail (⇨ Chapter 3). It extends from the edge of the Old Port to East End Beach, then to Back Bay for a 6-mi loop, before returning.

■ **All Along the Coast.** U.S. 1, the major road that travels along the Maine Coast, is only a narrow two-lane highway for most of its route, but it is still one of America's most historic highways, a sort of Appalachian Trail on a highway. As a result, this road is very popular in spring, summer, and fall with serious long-distance bike riders. Bicyclists should ride carefully and look out for motorists who may be looking out for a glimpse of the sea.

■ The Maine government publishes many maps and routes for cyclists; printable versions of these maps, as well as general cycling information, are available on the Web at *www.exploremaine.org/bike*.

Shopping

The Maine Coast has a surprisingly vibrant shopping scene, running the gamut from lobster T-shirt tourist traps to fine-art galleries, from local pottery studios to high-end and world-famous furniture makers. Many small-town main streets have been rejuvenated, thanks to storefronts that cater to tourists. Be advised that the best shopping areas tend to be concentrated in the corridor from Kittery to Bar Harbor.

■ **Freeport.** The world headquarters of **L. L. Bean** put the town of Freeport on the shopping map, and it's now shopping central for the state. There are plenty of stores to check out, many of them factory outlet stores, including big names like Coach, J.Crew, and Brooks Brothers. For fine-furniture aficionados, there's world-renowned Thos. Moser Cabinetmakers.

■ **Portland.** The Old Port, the heart of downtown Portland, is filled with specialty shops and assorted galleries in the area of Exchange Street, while more touristy stores proliferate along the waterfront's Commercial Street. Independent bookstore lovers will revel in the stacks of Longfellow Books; fashionistas will love the selection at Hélène M.

Whale-Watching

Few things speak of the great deep blue unknown like a whale, and any sighting of these magnificent creatures is dramatic and not soon forgotten. Fortunately, the cold waters off the Maine Coast are the perfect summer feeding ground for a variety of whales, including finbacks, humpbacks, minkes, and even the occasional rare blue whale and the endangered right whale.

■ **When.** The whale-watching season varies by tour skipper, but generally runs between the months of April and October.

■ **Where.** No matter which part of the coast you visit—even the far east (called "Down East"), near New Brunswick, Canada—there is a tour available from a not-too-distant port.

■ **What's It Like?** Tour lengths vary typically from two to five hours, as boats chug within 20 mi of the coast. Whale-watching vessels have plenty of open deck space for photo ops, plus covered areas for inclement weather or those with underdeveloped sea legs. Most also offer basic meal items and bottled drinks.

■ A whale sighting is not always a sure bet, though some skippers boast good track records, but there are other things likely to be seen, including seals, dolphins, and various oceangoing birds. No matter; the experience of being on the sea is a good way to spend a few hours during your coastal tour.

■ **Where to Find a Tour.** A few companies to sign on with for spotting these mighty creatures are **Cap'n Fish's Boat Trips** (⊕ *www. boothbayboattrips.com*) in Boothbay Harbor, which has both whale- and puffin-watching adventures; **Bar Harbor Whale Watching Co.** (⊕ *www.barharborwhales. com*), with its three-hour excursions via catamaran; **Old Port Mariner Fleet,** (⊕ *www. oldportmarinefleet.com*) based in Portland and also offering fishing trips; and **Island Cruises** (⊕ *www.bassharborcruises. com*), which departs from Bass Harbor and allows passengers to spot whales while aboard a lobster boat.

GREAT ITINERARIES

HIGHLIGHTS OF THE MAINE COAST

Much of the appeal of the Maine Coast lies in its geographical contrasts, from its long stretches of swimming and walking beaches in the south to the cliff-edged, rugged rocky coasts in the north. And not unlike the physical differences of the coast, each town along the way reveals a slightly different character. This sampler tour will provide you with a good taste of what the Maine Coast offers; allow the individual chapters to invite you along other trails on the way.

Day 1: The Yorks

Start your trip in York Village with a leisurely stroll through the seven buildings of the Old York Historical Society, getting a glimpse of 18th-century life in this gentrified town. Spend time wandering among the shops or walking the nature trails and beaches around York Harbor. There are several grand lodging options here, most with views of the harbor. If you prefer a livelier pace, continue on to York Beach, a haven for families with plenty of entertainment venues. Be sure to plan for a stop at Nubble Light. ⇨ *See The Southern Coast, Chapter 2.*

Days 2 and 3: Ogunquit

For well over a century, Ogunquit has been a favorite vacation spot for those looking to combine the natural beauty of the ocean with a sophisticated environment. Take a morning walk along the Marginal Way to see the waves crashing on the rocks. In Perkins Cove, have lunch, stroll the shopping areas, or sign on with a lobster-boat cruise to learn about Maine's most important fishery—the state's lobster industry supplies more than 90% of the world's lobster market. See the extraordinary collection at the Ogunquit Museum of American Art, take in a performance at one of the several theater venues, or just spend time on the beach. ⇨ *See The Southern Coast, Chapter 2.*

Day 4: The Kennebunks

Head north to the Kennebunks, allowing at least two hours to wander through the shops and historic homes of Dock Square in Kennebunkport. This is an ideal place to rent a bike and amble around the back streets, head out on Ocean Avenue to view the Bush estate, or ride to one of the several beaches to relax awhile. ⇨ *See The Southern Coast, Chapter 2.*

Days 5 and 6: Portland

You can easily spend several days in Maine's largest city, exploring its historic neighborhoods, shopping and eating in the Old Port, or visiting one of several excellent museums. A brief side trip to Cape Elizabeth takes you to Portland Head Light, Maine's first lighthouse, which was built in 1790–91. The lighthouse is on the grounds of Fort Williams Park and is an excellent place to enjoy a picnic. Be sure to spend some time wandering the ample grounds. There are also excellent walking trails (and views) at nearby Two Lights State Park. If you want to take a boat tour while in Portland, get a ticket for Casco Bay Lines and see some of the islands that dot the bay. ⇨ *See Greater Portland, Chapter 3.*

Day 7: Bath to Camden

Head north from Portland to Bath, Maine's shipbuilding capital, and tour the Maine Maritime Museum or have lunch on the waterfront. Shop at boutiques and antiques shops, or view the plentitude of beautiful homes. Continue on U.S. 1 north through the towns of Wiscasset and Damariscotta, where you may find yourself pulling over frequently for outdoor flea markets or intriguing antiques shops. ⇨ *See The Mid-Coast Region, Chapter 4.*

Days 8 and 9: Camden

Camden is the picture-perfect image of a seaside tourist town: hundreds of boats bobbing in the harbor, immaculately kept antique homes, streets lined with boutiques and specialty stores, and restaurants serving lobster at every turn. The modest (by Maine standards, anyway) hills of nearby Mt. Battie offer good hiking and great spots to picnic and view the surrounding area. Camden is one of the hubs for the beloved and historic windjammer fleet—there is no better way to see the area than from the deck of one of these graceful beauties. If you're an art lover, save some time for Rockland's Farnsworth Art Museum and the Wyeth Center. ⇨ *See Penobscot Bay, Chapter 5.*

Days 10 and 11: Mount Desert Island/Acadia National Park

From Camden, continue north along U.S. 1, letting your interests dictate where you stop (or head south to explore the Blue Hill Peninsula, ⇨ *see Chapter 6*). Once you arrive on Mount Desert Island, you can choose to stay in Bar Harbor, the busiest village in the area, or in the quieter Southwest Harbor area; either way, the splendor of the mountains and the sea surround you. Several days are easily spent exploring Acadia National Park, boating or kayaking in the surrounding waters, and simply enjoying the stunning panorama. ⇨ *See Acadia National Park and Mount Desert Island, Chapter 7.*

GREAT ITINERARIES

MAINE MARITIME HISTORY TOUR

Maine's maritime leanings extend well back into the early 17th century, and while many things have changed, the sea—via lobstering, fishing, and tourism—is still the backbone of the state's economy and culture. This tour gives the traveler a glimpse of how the sea has influenced the people, towns, and industries along the coast of Maine to create the delightful and diverse region it is today. ■ TIP➔ **You can squeeze the Bath-to-Rockland portion into one day, and Searsport into one day as well if you want to do the trip in just six days.**

Days 1 and 2: Portland

A thriving, working harbor since the 17th century, Portland has maritime history written all over it. Take a step back in time at the Fish Exchange, where the day's catch is unloaded and auctioned off to worldwide markets just as it was centuries ago. For a more refined maritime experience, head to the Portland Museum of Art to see the impressive collection of sea-inspired art by such greats as Edward Hopper and Winslow Homer. Lighthouses still play an integral role in keeping Maine's coast safe and navigable. Visit Fort Williams Park and Two Lights State Park, in Cape Elizabeth, to see the area's most famous lighthouses. For a more intimate view of the sea, try a boat cruise from Portland to the nearby islands in Casco Bay. ⇨ *See Greater Portland, Chapter 3.*

Days 3 and 4: Bath to Rockland

From Portland, head north to Bath, Maine's present shipbuilding capital. The Bath Iron Works, which once built tall-masted wooden schooners, now builds destroyers for the U.S. Navy. Spend some time at the Maine Maritime Museum and Shipyard to get a sense of the area's previous prowess in the shipping industry. Wander the streets of Bath to see the grand mansions of 19th-century sea captains (many of which are now elegant B&Bs).

Head north on U.S. 1 to Wiscasset, a village that gained great wealth in the shipbuilding industry as evidenced by its stunning array of grand sea captains' and merchants' homes. Tour the Nickels-Sortwell house (1807) to get a glimpse of the wealth these seafaring businessmen enjoyed. Continue on to Damariscotta, another town that found success in shipbuilding. From here, take a detour down Route 130 to the Pemaquid Peninsula. At the end of Route 130, Pemaquid Point Lighthouse has stood watch since 1827. Adjacent to the light is the Fishermen's Museum, which has a fascinating display illustrating Maine's 400-year-old fishing industry. ⇨ *See The Mid-Coast Region, Chapter 4.*

Days 5 and 6: Rockland/Camden

Make your way north from Damariscotta to Rockland, where you can tour the Farnsworth Art Museum and Wyeth Center, an excellent place to see maritime-inspired artworks. The fascinating Maine Lighthouse Museum, also in Rockland, displays many lighthouse and Coast Guard artifacts as well as other maritime curios. You can—and should—take a one-day or overnight cruise on a historic windjammer from either Rockland or nearby Camden. Sailing aboard one of these graceful schooners is the ideal way to see the coast. ⇨ *See Penobscot Bay, Chapter 5.*

NEW HAMPSHIRE

Searsport

Camden

Penobscot
Bay

Blue Hill
Bay

Rockland

Wiscasset

Damariscotta

Bath

Muscongus
Bay

Portland

Fishermen's
Museum

Pemaquid Point
Lighthouse

ATLANTIC OCEAN

Days 7 and 8: Searsport

Farther up U.S. 1 is the town of Searsport, Maine's second-largest deepwater port and a haven for both maritime history buffs and antiques treasure hunters. The relationship between the two is not accidental—world-traveling 19th-century sea captains, a good many of whom made their homes here, constantly brought back goods and gifts from Europe to fill their houses. You never know what kind of gem you can find in one of the multitude of antiques shops and outdoor flea markets.

A treasure of another sort exists here as well: the Penobscot Marine Museum is a multibuilding complex brimming with fascinating sea history. Several hours can be easily spent here. ⇨ *See Penobscot Bay, Chapter 5.* ■TIP→ **Weekend traffic heading to the Maine Coast along its feeder roads, I-95 and U.S. 1, can be brutally frustrating, especially at the tollbooths. If you travel midweek instead (or outside of peak season), you won't find yourself nearly as stymied.**

WHEN TO GO

Despite long winters, Maine's dramatic coastline and pure natural beauty welcome visitors of all tastes year-round. Be aware that black-fly season, from mid-May to mid-June, can rile even the most seasoned outdoorsy-folk. Also note that many smaller museums and attractions are open only for high season—from Memorial Day to mid-October—as are many of the waterside attractions and eateries.

Memorial Day is the start of the migration to the beaches and the mountains, and summer begins in earnest on July 4. This is the high season for the Maine Coast, when many smaller inns and hotels from Kittery on up to the Bar Harbor region fill up early on weekends. Larger hotels will have more vacancies, but it's still a good idea to book in advance in some of the more popular locales.

Fall, with its fiery foliage, is when many inns and hotels are booked months in advance by leaf-peeping visitors. As green disappears from the leaves of deciduous species, a rainbow of reds, oranges, yellows, purples, and other vivid hues appears. The first colors emerge in mid-September in northern areas; "peak" color occurs at different times from year to year. Generally, it's best to **visit the northern reaches in late September and early October** and move southward as October progresses.

All leaves are fallen by Halloween, and hotel rates drop significantly until ski season begins around Thanksgiving. Late October until late November is the hunting season for deer (using firearms) in most areas; those who venture into the woods should wear bright orange clothing.

Winter (November–April) is the time for downhill and cross-country skiing. Maine has several major ski resorts as well as numerous smaller mountains. Along the coast, bed-and-breakfasts that remain open will often rent rooms at far lower prices than in summer.

In spring, the fourth Sunday in March is designated as Maine Maple Sunday, and farms throughout the state open their doors to visitors not only to watch sap turn into golden syrup but to sample the sweet results.

Climate

In winter coastal Maine is cold and damp; inland temperatures may be lower, but generally drier conditions make them easier to bear. Snowfall is heaviest in the interior mountains, up to several hundred inches per year in northern Maine. Spring is often windy and rainy. Coastal areas can be uncomfortably humid in summer, though nights are usually cool. Autumn temperatures can be quite mild in southerly areas well into October, but northern areas can be quite cold by Columbus Day. A period of unseasonably mild weather sometimes occurs in late October and early November.

The following are the average daily maximum and minimum temperatures for Portland.

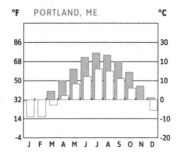

°F   PORTLAND, ME   °C

ON THE CALENDAR

WINTER	
January	Warm up with chili, hot cocoa, and toasted marshmallows next to a bonfire at **WinterFest** (late January) in Stonington, then chill out while ice-skating.
March	Held the fourth Sunday of the month, **Maine Maple Sunday** is when syrup producers throughout the state open their doors to share the spring rite of syrup making with the public.
SPRING	
May	Birders flock to Whiting every spring for the **Down East Spring Birding Festival** during Memorial Day weekend.
June	Stately old tall ships parade the bay during **Windjammer Days** (late June) in Boothbay Harbor. Climb aboard one of these fine sailing vessels during the grand sail parade.
SUMMER	
July	Guests can participate in the **Great Schooner Race** (July 1–6) in Penobscot, when more than two-dozen tall ships and their skippers compete against one another. Celebrate an important part of coastal Maine's heritage at the **Native American Festival and Maine Indian Basketmakers Market** in Bar Harbor (see ⊕ *www.maineindianbaskets.org* for exact date). Blues bands from around the country converge in Rockland for the **North Atlantic Blues Festival** (early July). One of the most beautiful of all wooden sailing boats is celebrated during **Friendship Sloop Days** in Rockland (see ⊕ *www.fss.org* for exact dates), during which you can watch sloop and rowboat races. Enjoy clams fried, steamed, and in clam cakes at the immensely popular **Yarmouth Clam Festival** (third Friday in July).
August	Ten tons of Maine's most famous crustacean are prepared and consumed at the **Maine Lobster Festival** in Rockland (see ⊕ *www.mainelobsterfestival.com* for exact dates), where the Maine Sea Goddess, a prom queen of sorts, receives her crown. Held Way Down East in Machias, the **Wild Blueberry Festival** (see ⊕ *www.machiasblueberry.com* for exact dates) has pie-eating and baking contests, music, and food courts.
FALL	
September	Catch Maine's windjammer fleet at the **WoodenBoat Sail-in with Maine Windjammers** (mid-September) in Brooklin, when the harbor fills with these wonderful old schooners.
November	The **Maine Literary Festival,** in Camden the first weekend of November, celebrates authors who write about Maine.
December	Santa arrives by boat during **Christmas by the Sea,** in Camden, Rockport, and Lincolnville the first weekend in December.

The Southern Coast

WORD OF MOUTH

"Ogunquit has a small-town atmosphere. I loved going to Perkins Cove, taking a walk along the Marginal Way and sitting by the cove watching the fishing boats—very scenic. Also, there are some great restaurants and shops in Perkins Cove."

—mmouse52

By Laura V.
Scheel

Maine's southernmost coastal towns—Kittery, the Yorks, Ogunquit, the Kennebunks, and the Old Orchard Beach area—reveal a few of the stunning faces of the state's coast, from the miles and miles of inviting sandy beaches to the beautifully kept historic towns and carnival-like attractions. There is something for every taste, whether you seek solitude in a kayak or prefer being caught up in the infectious spirit of fellow vacationers. The Southern Coast is best explored on a leisurely holiday of two days—more if you require a fix of solid beach time.

North of Kittery, long stretches of hard-packed white-sand beach are closely crowded by nearly unbroken ranks of beach cottages, motels, and oceanfront restaurants. The summer colonies of York Beach and Wells brim with crowds and ticky-tacky shorefront overdevelopment, but nearby, quiet wildlife refuges and land reserves promise an easy escape. York evokes yesteryear sentiment with its acclaimed historic district, while upscale Ogunquit tantalizes stylish and sporty visitors with its array of shops and a cliffside walk.

More than any other region south of Portland, the Kennebunks—and especially Kennebunkport—provide the complete Maine Coast experience: classic townscapes where white-clapboard houses rise from manicured lawns and gardens; rocky shorelines punctuated by sandy beaches; quaint downtown districts packed with gift shops, ice-cream stands, and visitors; harbors with lobster boats bobbing alongside yachts; rustic, picnic-tabled restaurants specializing in lobster and fried seafood (aka lobster pounds in Maine lingo); and well-appointed dining rooms. As you continue north, the scents of french fries, pizza, and cotton candy hover in the air above Maine's version of Coney Island, Old Orchard Beach.

ORIENTATION AND PLANNING

GETTING ORIENTED

Although the Southern Coast makes up just a mere portion of Maine's many thousands of miles of shoreline, it offers an incredible variety of sights to discover. The best way to explore the region is by car—taking the time to sidetrack on inviting byways. Summer traffic may be demanding and an inconvenience, but the beauty and diversity of Maine is worth a little patience. (Note that Amtrak, coming from Boston, does make a seasonal stop at Old Orchard Beach, but service is infrequent.)

TOP REASONS TO GO

Time Travel. Visit the majestic late-18th-century Hamilton House and experience the great fortunes won—and lost—in the maritime trade.

Sand in Your Toes. Ogunquit and Wells provide many miles of blissful beach walking.

Sleeping Like Royalty. Stay at one of Kennebunkport's luxurious inns, like the Captain Lord Mansion or the Cape Arundel Inn.

Harvesting the Sea. Head out on a lobster-boat excursion to glimpse one of Maine's largest industries, and take home some of the catch!

Hot Diggety Dogs. Chomp into a famous frankfurter at Flo's Steamed Hot Dogs, where they've been selling their dogs since 1959.

This chapter begins just across from the New Hampshire border in Kittery, the "Gateway to Maine," and heads in a general northward direction. Many of the sites and towns are off the main thoroughfares of U.S. 1 and I–95; you can decide how quickly you want to pass from one town to the next. From Kittery a brief northwestward trip will bring you to pastoral South Berwick, then back to the coastal towns of the Yorks, Ogunquit, and Wells. The town of Kennebunk is slightly inland, while its sister town of Kennebunkport is right on the water. Old Orchard Beach is a quintessential frolicking beach town.

PLANNING

WHEN TO GO

As with most of the Maine Coast, the Southern Coast is highly popular in summer. Crowds converge and gobble up rooms and dinner reservations at prime restaurants. Even so, July, August, and September are the best months to vacation in Maine. The weather is warm, and every town has its share of summer festivals, outdoor concerts, and gatherings. In July and August most roads are extremely busy (don't expect speedy jaunts down U.S. 1), campgrounds are filled to capacity, and hotel rates are high. Midweek tends to be a little quieter than weekends.

The brilliance of fall foliage brings another round of visitors to the state; often the off-season rates revert back to their summer heights, but even then it's not quite as crowded as summer. The prime time for leaf peeping here is usually the first week of October (check the state's weekly updated site: *www.mainefoliage.com*).

Many accommodations and restaurants stay open throughout the year, though they do have limited hours come winter. In the off-season, rates are lower, and you won't be waiting in line anywhere.

GETTING HERE AND AROUND

AIR TRAVEL

If traveling to the Southern Coast by air, most visitors fly into Portland International Jetport (⇨ *see Travel Smart Maine Coast*), which is 35 mi northeast of Kennebunk. Limited air service is also available from Pease International Airport in Portsmouth/Newington, New Hampshire, 25 mi south of Kennebunkport. Visitors flying into Boston's Logan airport can rent a car and be in the Kennebunkport area in less than two hours (depending on traffic) for the 75-mi drive.

Information Pease International Airport (✉ *36 Airline Ave., Newington, NH* ☎ *603/433–6536* ⊕ *www.peasedev.org/pease/airport.asp*).

BIKE TRAVEL

A bicycle can make it easy to get around the Kennebunks, the Yorks, and the Old Orchard Beach area, but the lack of shoulders on some roads can be intimidating. Ogunquit would seem like a good place for bikes, but traffic is hectic in the high season, making it a bit tricky. Biking around town is better, safer, and far more pleasant in the shoulder seasons (early summer or after Labor Day). Two good resources are the Bicycle Coalition of Maine and the Maine Department of Transportation (⊕ *www.exploremaine.org/bike/index.html*).

BUS TRAVEL

The Shuttlebus-Zoom is a localized bus service connecting the communities of Biddeford, Saco, Old Orchard Beach, Scarborough, South Portland, and Portland.

Information Shoreline Explorer (☎ *207/324–5762 Ext 2932 (weekdays)* ⊕ *www.shorelineexplorer.com*). **Shuttlebus-Zoom** (☎ *207/282–5408* ⊕ *www.shuttlebus-zoom.com*).

For car-free travel from the Yorks to Kennebunkport and over to Sanford, the Shoreline Explorer Network connects private and public transportation venues—mainly trolleys and buses. Each segment has its own schedule and fare range, but it's easy enough to get around.

CAR TRAVEL

U.S. 1 from Kittery is the shopper's route north; other roads hug the coastline. Interstate 95 is usually a faster route for travelers headed to towns north of Ogunquit. Exits on the turnpike coincide with mileage from the border.

Route 9 goes from Kennebunkport to Cape Porpoise and Goose Rocks. Parking is tight in Kennebunkport in peak season. Possibilities include the municipal lot next to the Congregational church ($2 an hour from May through October) and 30 North Street (free year-round).

TRAIN TRAVEL

Amtrak offers rail service from Boston to Portland, with stops in Wells and Saco and a seasonal stop in Old Orchard Beach.

Information Amtrak (☎ *800/872–7245* ⊕ *www.thedowneaster.com*).

2

TROLLEY TRAVEL

Trolleys ($1–$3) serve several areas. A trolley circulates among the Yorks from late June to Labor Day. A trolley fleet serves the major tourist areas and beaches of Ogunquit in July and August. Trolleys circulate in Wells on weekends from Memorial Day to Columbus Day and daily from late June to Labor Day. Trolleys circulate through Kennebunkport to Kennebunk Beach from Memorial Day to Columbus Day; an all-day ticket is $13. Biddeford–Saco–Old Orchard Beach Transit operates a trolley that circulates through Old Orchard Beach and a bus service from Old Orchard to Portland with stops in Scarborough and at the Maine Mall.

RESTAURANTS

Maine produces well over 90% of the world's lobsters, so it's no surprise that a good portion of its restaurants feature the state's mascot on their menus. Creative chefs have gone well beyond the traditional steamed variety with seemingly endless ways to prepare the dish. Fortunately, the area's restaurants, while almost always giving a nod to the famous crustacean, do not limit themselves to it. Many places specialize in local seafood, and given that Maine has more than 5,000 miles of shoreline, there is plenty of it to choose from. Restaurants range from the casually eclectic to the formal prix-fixe—and everything in between. You won't find many international restaurants (except Asian), but most menus make explorations into the flavors of other cultures.

HOTELS

The variation in lodgings along the Maine Coast has a lot to do with individual zoning laws. Towns like the Kennebunks, York Harbor, and Ogunquit have a much higher number of small inns and bed-and-breakfasts, while York Beach, Old Orchard Beach, Wells, and Kittery seem to be filled with one hotel-motel complex after another. U.S. 1 is famous (or infamous, depending on how you look at it) for its rampant commercialism, and its lodging options usually show it. A stay in one of the restored mansions will cost you quite a bit more than a night at a sprawling hotel, but almost all lodging establishments offer off-season price reductions and special package rates. Minimum-stay requirements are common for weekends and July through Labor Day. Expect to pay the most in Kennebunkport, Ogunquit, and the Yorks.

WHAT IT COSTS					
	¢	$	$$	$$$	$$$$
Restaurants	under $7	$7–$10	$11–$17	$18–$25	over $25
Hotels	under $60	$60–$99	$100–$149	$150–$200	over $200

Restaurant prices are for a median main course at dinner, excluding sales tax of 7%. Hotel prices are for two people in a standard double room in high season, excluding service charges and 7% tax.

GREAT ITINERARIES

IF YOU HAVE 3 DAYS

A three-day trip to the Southern Coast can give you a good taste of the different flavors of the region. Start your trip in **South Berwick.** Here you can tour the historic home of author Sarah Orne Jewett and the grand Hamilton House. From South Berwick follow Route 236 east to Route 91, back to U.S. 1 in York. Take Route 1A and explore the historic sites of **York Village.** Continue the few miles to **York Harbor,** a good place to spend the night. On your second day, follow the Shore Road (Route 1A) and stop in lively **York Beach,** where you can swim, bowl, or play arcade games until after dark. Continue north on Route 1A and spend the night and the next day in **Ogunquit.** Here you can walk the Marginal Way and spend several hours exploring the shops of both Perkins Cove and the village of Ogunquit. If you're visiting in summer, save some time to relax at Ogunquit Beach.

IF YOU HAVE 5 DAYS

Start your first day in **Kittery,** an area rich in history and natural beauty, as well as a shopper's mecca. If the weather cooperates, bring a picnic, a kayak, or your walking shoes for a full day of enjoying the vistas and trails of Ft. Foster. From here, follow the three-day itinerary. On Day 5, leave Ogunquit, and continue on U.S. 1 into **Wells,** a town known for its 7-mi stretch of pristine beaches. There are several opportunities for bird- and nature-watchers at Beach Plum Farm as well as the Wells Reserve and the Rachel Carson National Wildlife Refuge. Follow scenic Route 9 to the Kennebunks, a good place to spend the night. If you have more time, visit historic homes and museums, as well as the shops in **Kennebunk-port's** busy Dock Square, or, if you like the sights and sounds of a carnival-on-the-beach atmosphere, take coastal Route 9 north from the Kennebunks to **Old Orchard Beach.**

SOUTHERN AND INLAND YORK COUNTY

KITTERY

55 mi north of Boston; 5 mi north of Portsmouth, New Hampshire.

One of the earliest settlements in the state of Maine, Kittery suffered its share of British, French, and American Indian attacks throughout the 17th and 18th centuries, yet rose to prominence as a vital shipbuilding center. The tradition continues; despite its New Hampshire name, the Portsmouth Naval Shipyard is part of Maine and has been one of the leading researchers and builders of U.S. submarines since its inception in 1800. The shipyard has the distinction of being the oldest naval shipyard continuously operated by the U.S. government, and is a major source of local employment. It's not open to the public, but those on boats can pass by and get a glimpse of its national significance.

Known as the "Gateway to Maine," Kittery has come to more recent light as a major shopping destination thanks to its complex of factory outlets. Flanked on either side of U.S. 1 are more than 120 stores, which attract hordes of shoppers year-round. For something a little less commercial, head east on Route 103 to the hidden Kittery most people miss: the lands around **Kittery Point**. Here you can find hiking and biking trails and, best of all, great views of the water. Pepperell Cove, the harbor at Kittery Point, is said to be the first commercial port in Maine to thrive in the salt cod trade. With Portsmouth, New Hampshire, across the water, Whaleback Ledge Lighthouse, and the nearby Isles of Shoals, the town of Kittery is a truly picturesque and idyllic place to pass some time. Also along this winding stretch of Route 103 are two forts, both open in summer.

ESSENTIALS

Visitor Information Maine Tourism Association & Visitor Information Center (⊠ *U.S. 1 and I-95, Kittery* ☎ *207/439–1319* ⊕ *www.mainetourism.com*).

EXPLORING

Ft. Foster. Built in 1872, this town park was an active military installation until 1949. Today the 88-acre area is ideal for picnics (barbecue grills are all over) and explorations into the rocky crevices along the beach. There are also numerous walking trails, swimming areas, and special spots from which to windsurf and kayak. ⊠ *Pocahontas Rd., Kittery Point* ☎ *207/439–3800* 🖃 *$10 per car* ☉ *Open daily, Memorial Day—Labor Day; open to pedestrian traffic only the remainder of the year.*

Ft. McClary. Built in 1690 to protect the mouth of the Piscataqua River, the fort successfully countered pirates, American Indians, the French, and the British. The fort is particularly notable for its 1812 hexagonal blockhouse (open for touring with admission to the park) and its location on a scenic harbor with ocean views. ⊠ *Rte. 103, Kittery Point* ☎ *207/439–2845* ⊕ *www.state.me.us/doc/parks* 🖃 *$3* ☉ *Memorial Day–Labor Day.*

Kittery Historical and Naval Museum. Head here for a glimpse into Kittery's three centuries (and continuing) of naval history. The museum has a curious exhibit of artifacts and photographs, and even a lighthouse lens on display. ⊠ *U.S. 1 at Rogers Rd.03904* ☎ *207/439–3080* ⊕ *www. kitterymuseum.com* 🖃 *$3; $6 family* ☉ *June–Oct., Tues.–Sat. 10–4.*

Lady Pepperell House. As it claims above the doorway, which is framed by two glorious two-story fluted pilasters, this is one of the most elegant houses in America. Set just past Ft. McClary, this house, built in 1760, was meant to be the grandest mansion in the Piscataqua Valley, as befits "a lady." The immensely rich widow of Sir William Pepperell—one of the J. Paul Gettys of his day—Lady Mary retained the honorary title bestowed on her husband's family owing to his great exploits during the French and Indian wars. Although private and not open regularly for tours, the house may be visited a few times during the year—make inquiries in town. ⊠ *Rte. 103, Kittery Point.*

NEED A BREAK?   Just shy of Kittery Harbor you'll see the market Frisbee's (⊠ *Pepperell Cove, Rte. 103* ☎ *207/439–0014*), which has stood proudly in the same spot since 1828. It's heralded as the oldest family-owned market in the country, and there are all kinds of articles and photographs inside showing the family lineage over the years. This old place has likely changed very little since those long-ago days, with its high ceilings and creaky wooden floors (apparently the very same ones that Mark Twain once trod). There's a butcher on the premises, a produce section, and a deli, plus there are baked goods—the chocolate-chip cookies are particularly tasty. There's also fresh coffee.

WHERE TO EAT AND STAY

$$
SEAFOOD

✕ **Cap'n Simeon's Galley.** The nautical-theme dining room may have one of the best views in the area. Look out to the pier, nearby lighthouses, islands, and historic forts while you sample any number of fresh seafood or steak options, from fried oysters and boiled lobster to fresh haddock and New York sirloin. It's a popular place for a hearty Sunday brunch, with everything from lobster quiche to specialty pancakes rounding out the menu. On Saturday nights there's live musical entertainment in the lounge. ✉ *90 Pepperell Rd. (Rte. 103)* ☎ *207/439–3655* ⊕ *www.capnsimeons.com* ⊟ *D, MC, V* ✆ *Closed Columbus Day–Memorial Day.*

$–$$
SEAFOOD
★

✕ **Chauncey Creek Lobster Pound.** From the road you can barely see this restaurant's red roof hovering below the trees, but chances are you can see the cars parked at this popular spot along the high banks of the tidal river. The menu has lots of fresh lobster choices and a raw bar with locally harvested offerings like clams and oysters. Bring your own beer or wine if you desire alcohol. In season, it's open daily for lunch and dinner. ✉ *16 Chauncey Creek Rd., Kittery Point* ☎ *207/439–1030* ⊕ *www.chaunceycreek.com* ⊟ *MC, V* ✆ *Closed mid-Oct.—Mother's Day.*

$$–$$$
SEAFOOD

✕ **Warren's Lobster House.** A local institution, this waterfront restaurant specializes in seafood and has a huge salad bar. The pine-sided dining room leaves the impression that little has changed since Warren's opened in 1940. Dine outside overlooking the water when the weather is nice. ✉ *11 Water St.* ☎ *207/439–1630* ⊕ *www.lobsterhouse.com* ⊟ *AE, MC, V.*

$$$–$$$$
★

▦ **Portsmouth Harbor Inn & Spa.** Renovations have added a bit more decadence to this property, formerly the Inn at Portsmouth Harbor, but the antique beauty of the place remains the same. The brick Victorian was built in 1889 on the old Kittery town green. It overlooks the Piscataqua River and Portsmouth Harbor. An easy walk over the bridge takes you to nearby Portsmouth, New Hampshire. English antiques and Victorian watercolors decorate the inn, and most rooms have water views. Special spa packages are available. **Pros:** easy walk to historic Portsmouth; most rooms have harbor and water views; spa treatments available on-site. **Cons:** rooms are on the second and third floors, up steep stairs; antique home's rooms are not huge (though bright and uncluttered, with high ceilings). ✉ *6 Water St.* ☎ *207/439–4040* ⊕ *www.innatportsmouth.com* ⇌ *5 rooms* ⅃ *In-room: Wi-Fi. In-hotel: spa, no kids under 12* ⊟ *MC, V* ⅢⅢ *BP.*

SHOPPING

Kittery has more than 120 outlet stores. Along a several-mile stretch of U.S. 1 you can find just about anything, from hardware to underwear. Among the stores are Crate & Barrel, Eddie Bauer, Jones New York, Esprit, Waterford/Wedgwood, Lenox, Ralph Lauren, and J. Crew. Find store locations, discounts, and events within the **Kittery Outlets**

2

(⊠ *U.S. 1* ☎ *207/439–4367 or 888/548–8379* ⊕ *www.thekitteryoutlets. com*) by contacting the outlet association; also, look for brochures in nearby restaurants or tourist centers. **Kittery Trading Post** (⊠ *301 U.S. 1* ☎ *207/587–6246 or 888/587–6246* ⊕ *www.kitterytradingpost.com*) rivals Freeport's L. L. Bean for camping, fishing, boating, and other types of outdoor accoutrements. In business since 1938, the company continues to grow and offers various outdoor seminars and instruction.

SPORTS AND THE OUTDOORS

With all the water around—the Piscataqua River and the Atlantic Ocean meet here—it's no wonder that outdoor recreation in Kittery revolves around marine pursuits. For a lively historical boat tour narrated by the captain himself, take a trip with **Captain & Patty's Piscataqua River Tours** (⊠ *90 Pepperell Rd. [Rte. 103], Kittery Point* ☎ *207/439–8976* ⊕ *www. capandpatty.com*). The hour-plus-long trips leave the dock several times a day; get tickets at the dock. For private off-shore fishing trips, scenic cruises, whale-watching, or scuba charters, sign up with **Seafari Charters** (⊠ *7 Island Ave.* ☎ *207/439–5068* ⊕ *www.seafaricharters.com*).

EN ROUTE

If you're continuing on to the Berwicks, take Route 101 north from U.S. 1 and relax amid farmland on your way to South Berwick. If you want to stay along the coast, skip the Berwicks and head straight to the Yorks by taking beautiful Route 103 from Kittery Point, a drive of about 6 mi.

THE BERWICKS

14 mi northwest of Kittery via Rtes. 236 (or 101) and 91.

For a brief stay or just a passing detour westward from the coast in Kittery, the several towns that make up the Berwicks—North Berwick, South Berwick, and Berwick—reveal many of the pleasant pastoral byways that originally attracted its 17th-century settlers. Most of the activity is in the little town of South Berwick, a somewhat artsy little enclave amid the farmland and just next to the border of New Hampshire (it seems that many of its residents spend more time in nearby Portsmouth than elsewhere in Maine). The main street is a busy thoroughfare and popular travel route for interstate trucks, but its sidewalks are lined with practical shops set in stately brick buildings, and its quaint layout bespeaks its New England setting. It's a great place to spend a morning or afternoon sampling some of its good restaurant offerings and exploring the nearby historic homes and state park.

EXPLORING

Fodor's Choice ★

Hamilton House. This palatial Georgian home was featured in author Sarah Orne Jewett's Revolutionary War novel, *The Tory Lover*. The mansion, with four immense chimneys, dormer windows, and a mansard roof, was built in 1785 by shipbuilder Jonathan Hamilton to receive noted guests (including John Paul Jones) in regal splendor. In 1898 Mrs. Emily Tyson and her stepdaughter purchased the home and, with the help of their friend Sarah Orne Jewett, resurrected and decorated the place in a combination of Colonial and Victorian styles. If touring the innards of old homes doesn't interest you, come here

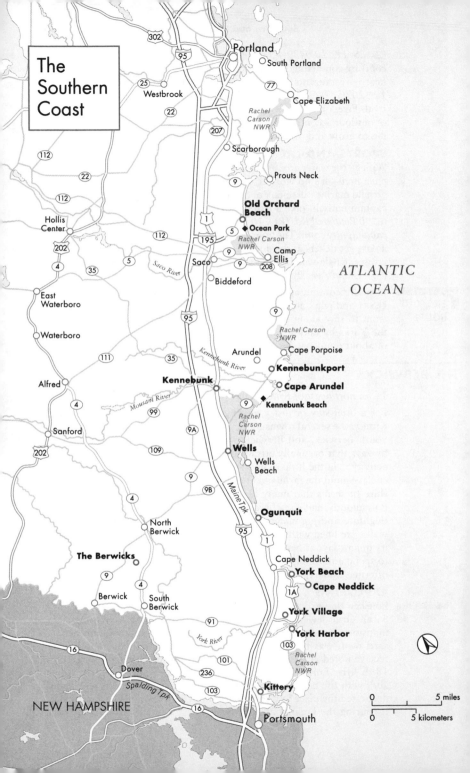

The Southern Coast

302

95

Portland

South Portland

25

Westbrook

22

77

Cape Elizabeth

207

Rachel Carson NWR

112

Scarborough

22

Prouts Neck

9

112

Old Orchard Beach

Hollis Center

1

◆ Ocean Park

202

112

195

5

Rachel Carson NWR

4

5

Saco River

Saco

Camp Ellis

35

9

208

Biddeford

East Waterboro

95

9

ATLANTIC OCEAN

Waterboro

Rachel Carson NWR

111

35

Kennebunk River

Arundel

Cape Porpoise

Alfred

Kennebunk

Kennebunkport

4

Mousam River

Cape Arundel

99

9

◆ Kennebunk Beach

Sanford

9A

Rachel Carson NWR

202

109

Wells

Wells Beach

9

4

9B

Maine Tpk

Ogunquit

North Berwick

95

1

The Berwicks

Cape Neddick

9

York Beach

4

1A

Cape Neddick

Berwick

South Berwick

York Village

91

York Harbor

York River

103

Rachel Carson NWR

16

101

Kittery

Dover

236

Spalding Tpk

103

NEW HAMPSHIRE

16

Portsmouth

0   5 miles

0   5 kilometers

Maine's Beloved Sarah Orne Jewett

"Tact is, after all, a kind of mind reading." —Sarah Orne Jewett

Maine has had its share of famous authors, resident and visiting, who have heralded both the natural and the physical spirit of the state itself in their literary works. Horror guru Stephen King makes his home in Bangor; Harriet Beecher Stowe wrote *Uncle Tom's Cabin* while living in Brunswick; and poet Henry Wadsworth Longfellow grew up in Portland. But few among Maine's literary greats are so warmly regarded as Sarah Orne Jewett, born the daughter of a country doctor and his wife in South Berwick in 1849.

Sarah Orne Jewett grew up privileged, yet not out of touch with the rural farming community of 19th-century Maine; often she accompanied her father on house calls throughout the area, and many credit her skills of quiet observation and sensitivity to these trips in the doctor's horse and buggy. Known for her sketches of rural life, Jewett is seen as a true daughter of Maine in the way that she beautifully and lovingly portrayed the intimate and poignant moments of her fellow citizens. Most famous are her novels *The Country Doctor* (1884) and *The Country of the Pointed Firs* (1896), though she published dozens of short stories and poems throughout her writing career. Nowhere else in literature are there more endearing

portraits of small-town life than in *The Country of the Pointed Firs*; within her words you can nearly smell the sea air as it mingles with the scent of pines and clearly visualize the colorful characters that populate her stories.

After she published her novel *The Tory Lover* (1901), based on the wealthy Hamilton family from nearby South Berwick, a review in the *Lewiston Journal* magazine section from that year summed up her writing skills aptly: "So strong and true are the pictures drawn of life...they come to Maine readers with a sort of familiarity, born of the tales of those troublous times handed down from their forefathers. Her readers feel a nearness to these men and women which makes them forget that more than a century separates them."

Jewett never married, though she had a long and loving friendship with the widow Annie Fields, with whom she spent many years traveling and socializing with other literary greats of the day, including Willa Cather, William Dean Howells, Henry James, Rudyard Kipling, and Harriet Beecher Stowe. A serious carriage accident in 1902 precipitated the end of her writing career and her eventual death in 1909. Sarah Orne Jewett's writing remains as a picture of the quintessential Maine known in the hearts and minds of Maine residents, both past and present.

---

to explore the grounds; they're simply spectacular. Beautifully kept gardens look out over the tidal Salmon Falls River below, where first owner Hamilton built ships, filled them with goods, and sailed straight to England from his front yard. The Embargo Act of 1807 ended his trade and, hence, his fortune quite abruptly. Picnickers and hikers are welcome on the grounds year-round from dawn to dusk, free of charge. Held within the formal gardens, **Sundays in the Garden** offers a summer concert series ranging from classical to folk music. ✉ *40 Vaughn's*

La., South Berwick ☎ *207/384–2454* ⊕ *www.historicnewengland.org* ✉ *$8* ⊘ *House tours June–mid-Oct., Wed.–Sun. 11–4.*

Sarah Orne Jewett House. This sturdy Georgian-style home dates to 1774 and reflects the shipbuilding wealth of its time. Sarah Orne Jewett was born in the house in 1849, lived elsewhere for a time, then came back to reside with her sister for the remainder of her life. The view from her desk in the top-floor hall looks down on the town's major intersection, which indeed gave her material for her novels, including *The Country of the Pointed Firs*. Now a museum, the house contains period furnishings. Jewett's bedroom remains as she left it. To reach the Sarah Orne Jewett House, follow Route 236 until you reach the center of South Berwick; at the division of Routes 236 and 4, look for signs; the home is right in the center of town. ✉ *5 Portland St., South Berwick* ☎ *207/384–2454* ⊕ *www.historicnewengland.org* ✉ *$5* ⊘ *June–mid-Oct., Fri.–Sun. 11–4.*

WHERE TO EAT AND STAY

$$$

AMERICAN

✕ **Lodge Restaurant at Spring Hill.** With a waterfront seat alongside a placid large pond surrounded by rolling countryside, this location is hard to beat. The menu mixes a good amount of meat and seafood; there's a bit of everything from salmon to filet mignon, and haddock to, yes, even Wiener Schnitzel. You may be witness to some nuptials, as it's a popular site for weddings. ✉ *117 Pond Rd., South Berwick* ☎ *207/384–2693* ▭ *D, MC, V* ⊘ *Closed Mon. and Tues. No lunch.*

$$–$$$

ECLECTIC

✕ **Pepperland Café.** Think upscale diner without the neon, chrome, and swivel chairs for this popular spot in downtown South Berwick. Brick walls alternating with walls painted a deep red add to the warmth of the scattering of tables and pillowed couches. The lunch menu gives the greatest nod to the diner culture with blue-plate favorites such as hot meat-loaf pie or bangers and mash; dinner gets a bit more sophisticated, with options like the ancho-and-cardamom-dusted grilled tuna loin. The Sunday brunch offers up a tasty mix of classics like chicken-fried steak and eggs or a crab-cake Benedict. The owners strive to use local produce and meats whenever possible. The bar is a favorite among local micro and Belgian beer fanciers. ✉ *279 Main St., South Berwick* ☎ *207/384–5535* ▭ *MC, V* ⊘ *Closed Mon. No dinner Sun.*

$

★

⌂ **Academy Street Inn.** Antiques, family photos, and a collection of sleds and snowshoes adorn the interior of this grand 1903 home, within walking distance of the historic Sarah Orne Jewett house. Inside, all is warm wood, a blending of Arts and Crafts and Mission styles, with colorful touches of rich fabrics and textiles. Its location on the New Hampshire border is convenient for exploring both southern Maine and New Hampshire. Rates include big breakfasts served in the formal dining room. Rooms are comfortably furnished and spacious; some have the added decadence of claw-foot tubs for a good soak. One of the innkeepers is also a charter captain; touring and fishing expeditions can be arranged. **Pros:** exquisite and authentic historic lodging; very reasonable rates; walk to town center. **Cons:** one room's bathroom is a few paces down the hall (though private); rooms arc upstairs (no elevator). ✉ *15 Academy St., South Berwick* ☎ *207/384–5633* ⇥ *5 rooms*

↻ In-room: no phone, no TV (some), Wi-Fi. In-hotel: no kids under 10 ☐ *AE, D, MC, V* ❘❂❘ *BP.*

NEED A BREAK?

A casual picnic on the exquisite grounds of Hamilton House or within Vaughan Woods State Park is a great way to recharge before heading farther afield. You'll find an array of tasty sandwiches—try the "Rte. 236," with garlic and herb turkey, Muenster cheese, and pesto mayo—fresh sushi, salads, and soups at Nature's Way Market (✉ *272 Main St., South Berwick* ☎ *207/384–3210*). The store is also known for its organic and gourmet selections of cheeses, meats, produce, beverages, and wine.

NIGHTLIFE AND THE ARTS

In July the Hamilton House presents **Sundays in the Garden** (✉ *40 Vaughan's La.* ☎ *207/384–2454* ✉ *$8* ⊕ *www.historicnewengland.org*), a series of Sunday afternoon concerts ranging from blues to folk and jazz. Picnicking is encouraged on the ample lawn; concerts begin at 4.

SPORTS AND THE OUTDOORS

Vaughan Woods. Many nature trails wind through pine and hemlock forests in this 250-acre preserve along the banks of the Salmon Falls River, making it the perfect place for a picnic or stroll. The river was of prime importance to early settlers, and it was here that the nation's first water-powered sawmill was built. Local legend says that among the ships that carried supplies and the harvested timber downriver and to the sea, was one called the *Pied Cow*, which unloaded the first cows to inhabit Maine in 1634. ✉ *28 Oldsfields Rd., South Berwick* ☎ *207/384–5160* ✉ *$3* ☉ *Memorial Day–Labor Day, daily dawn–dusk.*

EN ROUTE

For an appealing drive back toward the coast and the Yorks, follow Route 236 east out of South Berwick until it meets with Route 91, which branches off to the left. The less-than-10-mi winding road leads you past farmland, exquisite antique homesteads, and marshland views meandering from various tidal rivers. When you get to U.S. 1, head north to the York area.

THE YORKS, OGUNQUIT, AND WELLS

The Yorks—York Village, York Harbor, York Beach, and Cape Neddick—are typical of small-town coastal communities in New England and are smaller than most. Many of their nooks and crannies can be explored in a few hours. The beaches are the big attraction here.

Not unlike siblings in most families, the towns within this region reveal vastly different personalities. York Village and York Harbor abound with old money, picturesque mansions, impeccably manicured lawns, and gardens and shops that cater to a more staid and wealthy clientele. Continue along Route 1A from York Harbor to York Beach, and soon all the pretense falls away like autumn leaves in a storm—it's family vacation time (and party time), with scores of T-shirt shops, ice-cream and fried-seafood joints, arcades and bowling, and motor court–style motels. Left from earlier days are a number of trailer and RV parks spread across the road from the beach—in prime real estate that must have developers and moneyed old-timers in pure agony.

North of York Beach, Cape Neddick blends back into more peaceful and gentle terrain, while Ogunquit is elegant, high-spirited tourism to the hilt. With its walkable village filled with restaurants, shops, and B&Bs, Ogunquit is a prime resort destination. Farther north on U.S. 1 is Wells, a town seemingly lost in the commercialism of the main route, yet blessed with some of the area's best beaches.

YORK VILLAGE

About 6 mi north of Kittery on Rte. 103 or Rte. 1A via U.S. 1.

As subdued as the town may feel today, the history of York Village reveals a far different character. One of the first permanently settled areas in the state of Maine, it was once witness to great destruction and fierce fighting during the French, Indian, and British wars; towns and fortunes were sacked, yet the potential for prosperity encouraged the area's citizens to continually rebuild and start anew. Colonial York citizens enjoyed great wealth and success from fishing and lumber as well as a penchant for politics. Angered by the British-imposed taxes, York held its own little-known tea party in 1775 in protest. Then in the late 1700s the first cries for independent statehood from ruling Massachusetts were heard here, though these would not be answered until the next century.

The actual village of York is quite small, housing the town's basic components of post office, town hall, a few shops, and a stretch of impressive antique homes. It feels more lived in than touristed, though the various museums of the York Historical Society are well worth a visit. Sharp-eyed American history buffs may notice something amiss with York's Civil War Monument. After the war it was common for towns to erect a statue of a Civil War soldier to honor the local boys who served and died, and York was no exception. The statue sent to York, however, was most likely meant to be shipped much farther south—the image is of a Confederate soldier. Legend says that the citizens of York, acting in accordance with their frugal New England Yankee nature, refused to pay the extra money required to switch the statue for the correct one. That lost Confederate soldier still stands today in York Village, though no one seems to know where the Union statue ended up.

GETTING HERE AND AROUND
In an effort to keep traffic down, ease parking woes, and keep visitors (and locals) happy, the trolleys of the **York Trolley Company** (☎ *207/363–9600 ⊕ www.yorktrolley.com*) make daily loops through York Village, York Harbor, out to Nubble Lighthouse, and all the way to Short Sands Beach in York Beach. Route maps can be picked up nearly everywhere in York and at the chamber of commerce; fares are $1.50 one-way and $3 for the loop.

EXPLORING

York Village Historic District. Most of the 18th- and 19th-century build-ings here are clustered along York Street and Lindsay Road; seven are owned by the Old York Historical Society and charge admission. You can buy tickets for all the buildings at the **Jefferds Tavern** (⊠ *Rte. 1A at Lindsay Rd.03909*), a restored late-18th-century inn. The **Old York Gaol** (1720) was once the King's Prison for the Province of Maine; inside are dungeons, cells, and the jailer's quarters. Several times a week, costumed reenactors spin tales of why they're behind bars; these stories are based on actual, imprisoned characters from the 18th cen-tury. The 1731 **Elizabeth Perkins House** reflects the Victorian style of its last occupants, the prominent Perkins family. The Historical Society also gives guided walking tours (or simply take the self-guided tour as you go through each of the seven buildings; admission is valid for two consecutive days). ☎ *207/363–4974* ⊕ *www.oldyork.org* ✉ *All build-ings $10; $5 for one building* ☽ *Mid-June–mid-Oct., Mon.–Sat. 10–5.*

Stonewall Kitchen. You've probably seen the kitchen's smartly labeled jars of gourmet chutneys, jams, jellies, salsas, and sauces in specialty stores back home. York is the headquarters and processing center for them. The company's attractive complex houses the company store, a bustling café and take-out restaurant, a viewing area of the cooking and bottling processes, and stunning gardens. Café tables are set outside, and the store is brimming with wares that would make Martha Stewart proud. Sample all the mustards, salsas, and dressings that you can stand, or have lunch at the café. Takeout is available during store hours; lunch is served daily 11–3; Sunday is brunch day. The venture's latest addition is the cooking school, where participants can join in evening or luncheon courses that utilize local as well as national culinary talent. Reservations are recommended, though walk-ins are accepted if space allows; most classes cost in the $35–$50 range and are under two hours. ⊠ *Stonewall La. just off U.S. 1, next to information center* ☎ *207/351–2712* ⊕ *www. stonewallkitchen.com* ☽ *Mon.–Sat. 8–8, Sun. 9–6.*

WHERE TO EAT

$$$$
SEAFOOD
✕ **Foster's Downeast Clambake.** Save your appetite for this one. Special-izing in the traditional Maine clambake—a feast consisting of rich clam chowder, a pile of mussels and steamers, Maine lobster, corn on the cob, roasted potatoes and onions, bread, butter, and Maine blueberry crumb cake (phew!)—this massive complex provides entertainment as well as belly-busting meals. You can also opt to have clambake fixings shipped to your home or have a special event catered. ⊠ *5 Axholme Rd.* ☎ *207/363–3255 or 800/552–0242* ▤ *AE, MC, V.*

SHOPPING

With its eclectic showing of housewares, casual women's clothing and jewelry, baby items, and unusual tokens for the home and garden, **Daisy Trading Company** (⊠ *388 Rte. 1* ☎ *207/363–7941* ⊕ *www.daisytrading. com*) is a feast for shoppers. You can't miss the bright yellow build-ing and mélange of eye-catching products outside on Route 1, close to the entrance to York Village. Bring a basket for Saturday morning shopping at the **Gateway Farmers' Market** (⊠ *1 Stonewall Ln., just off*

U.S. Rte. 1), held at the Greater York Region Chamber of Commerce visitor center from early June until Columbus Day. Beginning at 9 AM, you'll find a variety of local fresh produce as well as flowers, artisan bread, homemade soaps, and many specialty foods. It's a good place to gather the makings for a nice beach picnic. The market also opens up on Tuesday afternoons from 2 to 5:30 beginning June 30 until September 1. Guess the theme at **Gravestone Artwear** (⊠ *250 York St. [Rte. 1A]* ☎ *800/564–4310* ⊕ *www.gravestoneartwear.com*), where you'll find items adorned with Colonial, Victorian, and Celtic gravestone-carving designs. There are also crystals, gravestone-rubbing supplies, books, and candles. Watercolors, mixed media, oils, photography, and more make up the featured art at **Village Gallery** (⊠ *244 York St. [Rte. 1A]* ☎ *207/351–3110* ⊕ *www.yorkvillagegallery.com*), where many local artists are represented.

YORK HARBOR

Approximately 3 mi north of York Village via Rte. 1A.

Just a few miles from the village proper, York Harbor opens up to the water and offers many places to linger and explore. The harbor itself is busy with boats of all kinds, while the harbor beach is a good stretch of sand for swimming. Much more formal than the northward York Beach, and much quieter, the area retains a somewhat more exclusive air.

EXPLORING

Sayward-Wheeler House. Built in 1718, the waterfront home was later remodeled in the 1760s by Jonathan Sayward, a local merchant who had prospered in the West Indies trade. By 1860 his descendants had opened the house to the public to share the story of their Colonial ancestors. The house, accessible only by guided tour, reveals both the simple decor of the 18th century and the more opulent and elaborate furnishings of the 19th century. ⊠ *9 Barrell Ln. Extension, York Harbor* ☎ *207/384–2454* ⊕ *www.historicnewengland.org* ⊠ *$5* ☼ *June–mid-Oct., 2nd and 4th Sat. of month 11–5; tours on the hr. 11–4.*

WHERE TO EAT

$$$–$$$$
SEAFOOD

✕**Dockside Restaurant.** On an island overlooking York Harbor, this restaurant is ideally situated. With the water in such close proximity, it's no surprise that there's plenty of seafood on the menu, but also such treats as beef tenderloin and duckling. Start with the rich lobster and scallop crepe or an order of local Maine oysters. ⊠ *22 Harris Island Rd., just off Rte. 103* ☎ *207/363–2722* ⊕ *www.docksidegq.com* ⊟ *D, MC, V* ☼ *Closed Mon. (except July and Aug.) and late Oct.–May.*

$$$–$$$$
AMERICAN

✕**Harbor Porches.** Eating here is actually very much like sitting on someone's porch—assuming that someone has a lot of money and can afford extravagant views over York Harbor. Wicker chairs at linen-covered tables fill the space and are surrounded by large windows. There is a lot of local seafood on the menu, as well as rack of lamb and steak. For lunch, try one of the hearty sandwiches or specialty pizzas. The Maine crab-cake appetizer is worth a try, as is the lobster bisque. Jeans and sneakers are not allowed at dinner. It is open for breakfast, lunch,

Sunday brunch, and dinner. ⊠ *Stage Neck Rd.* ☎ *207/363–3850* ▤ *AE, D, DC, MC, V* ☺ *Closed 2 wks. in Jan.*

WHERE TO STAY

2

$$$–$$$$
Fodor's Choice
★

🏠 **Chapman Cottage.** This impeccably restored inn, named for the woman who had it built as her summer cottage in 1899, sits proudly atop a swath of lawn. The luxuriant bedspreads, fresh flowers, antiques, and beautiful rugs only hint at the indulgence found here. Innkeepers Donna and Paul Archibald spoil their guests with sumptuous breakfasts, afternoon hors d'oeuvres, port, sherry, and homemade chocolate truffles, all prepared by Paul, a professionally trained chef. Most rooms have fireplaces and whirlpool tubs; all are spacious, bright, and airy. It's a five-minute walk to either York Village or the harbor, but you may never wish to leave. **Pros:** beautifully restored historic lodging; luxury appointments; attention to detail. **Cons:** no water views; most rooms on upper floors (and no elevator). ⊠ *370 York St.* ☎ *207/363–2059 or 877/363–2059* ⊕ *www.chapmancottagebandb.com* ⇆ *6 rooms* ⅋ *In-room: no phone, Wi-Fi. In-hotel: restaurant, bar, no kids under 12* ▤ *AE, D, MC, V* ¶⊙| *BP.*

$$–$$$$

🏠 **Dockside Guest Quarters.** This is the kind of place that people return to year after year. Set on its own private peninsula bordering York Harbor and the ocean, the complex consists of the main inn as well as a series of buildings that house standard rooms and suites with kitchenettes. Adirondack chairs are thoughtfully placed by twos around the spacious lawn, with plenty of space for privacy if desired. Many hours could be spent on the wraparound porch enjoying the views. Rooms are adorned with antiques and simple white bedspreads; some have fireplaces, and most have outdoor decks. **Pros:** secluded waterfront location with boating access; ample green space for strolling or lawn games. **Cons:** rooms in outer buildings not as charming as those in the main house; not an in-town location. ⊠ *Harris Island Rd.* ☎ *207/363–2868 or 800/270–1977* ⊕ *www.docksidegq.com* ⇆ *13 rooms, 6 suites, 6 studios* ⅋ *In-room: refrigerator (some), kitchenette (some), Wi-Fi (some). In-hotel: bicycles, water sports, restaurant, public Wi-Fi* ▤ *D, MC, V* ☺ *Closed Dec.–Mar.* ¶⊙| *BP.*

$$$$

🏠 **Edward's Harborside.** This turn-of-the-20th-century B&B sits on the harbor's edge and is a two-minute walk from the beach. Rooms have private baths (there are three additional rooms without baths that can be combined to make suites for families) and are spacious and have big windows to take in the water views. One room has a large whirlpool tub. There is a very homey feel here; throughout the inn are photos of the various family members' weddings and other gatherings. **Pros:** grand water views and access to deep-water dock; close to beach. **Cons:** most rooms up steep stairs; third-floor rooms are smallish and share bath. ⊠ *Stage Neck Rd.* ☎ *207/363–3037* ⊕ *www.edwardsharborside. com* ⇆ *7 rooms* ⅋ *In-room: Wi-Fi. In-hotel: no kids under 8* ▤ *MC, V* ¶⊙| *BP.*

$$$–$$$$
★

🏠 **Inn at Tanglewood Hall.** The inn's artfully painted floors, lush wallpapers, and meticulous attention to detail are the fruits of a former designation as a designers' showcase home. This 1880s Victorian "cottage," as these mansions were humbly called back in the day, is a haven of elegance and comfort, set back among trees and stunning perennial gardens. Rooms are individually decorated, though all share decadently rich coloring and fabrics, high ceilings, and many large windows; some have fireplaces. **Pros:** elegant and authentic historic lodging; serene setting amid gardens and grand trees; short walk to beaches and nature trails. **Cons:** no water views; most rooms on upper floors (no elevator). ✉ *611 York St.* ☎ *207/351–1075* ⊕ *www.tanglewoodhall.com* ⌨ *6 rooms* ⌂ *In-room: no phone, no TV, refrigerator (some), Wi-Fi. In-hotel: no kids under 12* ⊟ *AE, MC, V* ⦿ *BP.*

$$–$$$$ ⊡ **York Harbor Inn.** A mid-17th-century fishing cabin with dark timbers
★   and a fieldstone fireplace forms the heart of this inn, while several wings and outbuildings have been added over the years, making for quite a complex with a great variety of styles and appointments. The rooms are furnished with antiques and country pieces; many have decks overlooking the water, and some have whirlpool tubs or fireplaces. The nicest rooms are in two adjacent buildings, Harbor Cliffs and Harbor Hill. The dining room ($$$–$$$$; no lunch off-season) has great ocean views. **Pros:** many rooms have harbor views; close to beaches and scenic walking trails; some luxury appointments. **Cons:** rooms vary greatly in style and appeal; many rooms accessed via stairways (no elevator). ✉ *480 York St., Coastal Route 1A, York Harbor* ☎ *207/363–5119 or 800/343–3869* ⊕ *www.yorkharborinn.com* ⌨ *54 rooms, 2 suites* ⌂ *In-room: Wi-Fi. In-hotel: restaurants, bar* ⊟ *AE, DC, MC, V* ⦿ *CP.*

SPORTS AND THE OUTDOORS

Shore Walk. Take the stroll for a good beachcombing exploration and a jaunt across York's beloved Wiggly Bridge. You can start at various spots—either from Route 103 alongside York Harbor (there is minimal parking here, but you'll know it when you see the bridge) or from the George Marshall Store in York Village (140 Lindsay Rd.).

KAYAKING   Take to the water in a guided kayak trip with **Harbor Adventures** (⌂ *P.O. Box 345, York Harbor 03911* ☎ *207/363–8466* ⊕ *www. harboradventures.com*). Choose from harbor tours, full-moon paddles, half-day trips, and even a luncheon paddle; prices start around $45. There are also kayak fishing expeditions and surf kayaking trips available. Departure locations vary. Bicycle tours are also offered.

BIKING   **Berger's Bike Shop** (✉ *241 York St., No. 1, York* ☎ *207/363–4070*) rents all manner of bikes for local excursions.

FISHING   **Captain Tom Farnon** (✉ *Rte. 103, Town Dock No. 2, York Harbor* ☎ *207/363–3234*) takes up to six passengers on lobstering trips, by reservation. **Fish Tale Charters** (✉ *85 Bog Rd., York* ☎ *207/363–3874* ⊕ *www.maineflyfishing.net*) takes anglers on fly-fishing or light tackle charters in search of stripers or juvenile bluefin tuna; departure points vary. **Rip Tide Charters** (✉ *1 Georgia St., York* ☎ *207/363–2536* ⊕ *www. mainestriperfishing.com*) goes where the fish are—departure points vary, from Ogunquit to York and Portsmouth, New Hampshire. They specialize in fly-fishing and light tackle for stripers, mackerel, and bluefish. **Shearwater Charters** (⌂ *P.O. Box 472, York Harbor 03911* ☎ *207/363–5324*) offers spin or fly-casting charters in the York River and along the shoreline from Kittery to Ogunquit. Bait-fishing trips are also available. Departure spots depend on time and tides.

HIKING AND WALKING For a peek into the Rachel Carson National Wildlife Refuge, take the 2-mi **Brave Boat Harbor Trail,** which is one of the few walking trails available in the refuge. It's a prime bird-watching area. Look for Brave Boat Harbor Road just off Route 103 for trail access and parking.

EN ROUTE Continue along Route 1A from York Harbor to York Beach. The waterfront mansions eventually give way to seaside trailer parks, 1950s-style resort motels, and stunning sections of rocky shores and beaches.

YORK BEACH

6 mi north of York Harbor via Rte. 1A.

Like many shorefront towns in Maine, York Beach has a long, long history of entertaining summer visitors. Take away today's bikinis and boom-box music and it's easy to imagine squealing bathers adorned in the full-length bathing garb of the late 19th century. Just as they did back then, visitors today come here to eat ice cream, enjoy carnival-like novelties, and indulge in the sun and sea air.

York Beach is a real family destination, devoid of all things staid and stuffy—children are meant to be both seen and heard here, and that's part of what gives the area its invigorating feel. Just beyond the sands of Short Sand Beach is a host of amusements, from bowling to indoor minigolf and the Fun-O-Rama arcade.

ESSENTIALS

Visitor Information The **Greater York Region Chamber of Commerce** (✉ *1 Stonewall La., off U.S. 1, York* ☎ *207/363–4422* ⊕ *www.gatewaytomaine.org*).

EXPLORING

Nubble Light. Head out a couple of miles on the peninsula to see what is said to be one of the most photographed lighthouses on the globe. Set out on a hill of rocks, the lighthouse is still in use. Direct access is prohibited, but an information center shares the 1879 light's history. Find parking at Sohier Park, at the end of Nubble Road, as well as restrooms and plenty of benches. ✉ *End of Nubble Rd., off Rte. 1A.*

🐾 **York's Wild Kingdom.** Between the zoo and the carnival rides, it's sometimes hard to distinguish the wild animals from the kids here. The zoo has an impressive variety of exotic animals and is home to the state's only white Bengal tiger. Combination tickets can be purchased to visit the zoo and the amusement park, and discounts are available for kids under 10. There are extensive picnic areas, paddleboats, elephant shows, and plenty of other amusements. ✉ *U.S. 1 (about 2 miles from exit 7, look for the 40-foot sign), also entrance at 23 Railroad Ave. at York Beach, York* ☎ *207/363–4911* ⊕ *www.yorkzoo.com* 🎟 *$14.50 zoo only; $19.50 zoo and rides (adults)* ☉ *Late May–Sept.*

WHERE TO EAT

$$$–$$$$
AMERICAN
Fodor's Choice
★

✕ **Blue Sky on York Beach.** Making its home on the second floor of the grandly restored Atlantic House Hotel, this wide-open and inviting restaurant adds a keen sense of swanky sophistication to this casual beach town. A massive stone fireplace anchors the great room of high ceilings, exposed ductwork, and warm wood floors; unusual hanging light fixtures attract the eye and cast a gentle glow. The menu, executed by well-known chef and owner Lydia Shire, takes regional New England fare to new heights. Memorable choices include the lamb pizza appetizer and the lobster stew; the deep fried short ribs are painfully delicious and tender, as is the Biba duck with scallion pancakes. For a closer look at what happens in the kitchen, you can sit at the curved food bar, with full views of the wood-fired oven and the chefs at work. There's an additional bar menu for the lounge; be sure to try one or more of their eclectic specialty cocktails. In good weather, sit out on the large deck with views of the town below. Sunday jazz brunch is also a winner here. ⊠ *2 Beach St., York Beach* ☎ *207/363–0050* ⊕ *www. blueskyonyorkbeach.com* ⌂ *Reservations recommended* ▤ *AE, D, MC, V* ⊘ *No lunch Sept.–June.*

$$–$$$$
SEAFOOD

✕ **Fox's Lobster House.** This place is a little pricier than your average fried-seafood joint (then again, few are cheap), but its location is ideal—right up by Nubble Light and with grand views of the ocean beyond. The place gets packed, but the scenery (or the full bar) should make the wait quite bearable. You can get takeout or dine inside with table service. For the most ambitious appetite, see if you can tackle the 3-pound baked stuffed lobster. In addition to the regular offering of seafood, choose from steaks, chicken, and pasta; save room for the homemade blueberry pie. ⊠ *End of Nubble Rd.* ☎ *207/363–2643* ⌂ *Reservations not accepted* ▤ *MC, V* ⊘ *Closed Nov.–Apr.*

$–$$
AMERICAN

✕ **The Goldenrod.** If you wanted to—and you are on vacation—you could eat nothing but the famous taffy here, made just about the same way today as it was back in 1896. The famous Goldenrod Kisses—some 65 tons are made per year—are a great attraction, and people line the windows to watch the taffy being made. Aside from the famous candy, this eating place is family oriented, very reasonably priced, and a great place to get ice cream from the old-fashioned soda fountain. Breakfast is served all day, while the simple lunch menu doubles as dinner; choose from sandwiches and burgers. There is even penny candy for sale for, yes, a penny apiece. ⊠ *2 Railroad Ave.* ☎ *207/363–2621* ⊕ *www. thegoldenrod.com* ▤ *AE, MC, V* ⊘ *Closed Columbus Day–late May.*

$$$
ITALIAN

✕ **Mimmo's.** Water views can be had from some tables at this casual but very busy spot on Long Sands Beach. The menu is Italian, with lots of pastas to choose from and classics such as eggplant parmigiana. If you can't get enough seafood, try the *coastazurro,* with shrimp, haddock, calamari, and mussels sautéed with garlic. No alcohol is served, but diners can bring their own. For dinner, reservations are a good idea. ⊠ *243 Long Beach Ave. (Rte. 1A)* ☎ *207/363–3807* ▤ *AE, MC, V.*

2

WHERE TO STAY

$$$$ ★ ☷ **Atlantic House Hotel.** For years, this aged beauty sat weary and neglected smack in the middle of York Beach, caught in the mire of area zoning laws and red tape. An eyesore no longer, this 1888 hotel has returned to its former splendor with flying colors. The standard hotel rooms are awash in calming blues, greens, and creams, accented with designer fabrics, gas fireplaces, and Jacuzzi tubs. For more space, there are one- and two-bedroom suites (with surprisingly reasonable weekly rates), complete with full kitchens, laundry, and separate living and dining rooms. All spaces are uncluttered, have gleaming hardwood floors, and are blessed with ample windows to allow for plenty of natural light. Several suites have private decks. Many conveniences are also housed within the hotel: the elegant Blue Sky at York Beach restaurant, a full-service spa, Clara's Cupcake Café, a wine and specialty food shop, a children's apparel store, and a women's boutique with clothing, jewelry, cosmetics, and accessories. **Pros:** elegant, sophisticated lodging; walk to beach/town; great on-site amenities; good choice for weekly stay. **Cons:** not a beachfront location (4th floor has partial waterviews); not for budget travelers. ⊠ *2 Beach St., York Beach* ☎ *207/363–0051* ⊕ *www. atlantichouseyorkbeach.com* ➫ *7 rooms, 8 suites* ⚭ *In-room: safe, kitchen (some), refrigerator (some), DVD, Wi-Fi In-hotel: 2 restaurants, bar, spa, laundry facilities, Wi-Fi, parking* ▭ *AE, D, DC, MC, V.*

$–$$ ☷ **Katahdin Inn.** This is the kind of place that is much like visiting family: you feel at ease enough to sit on the front porch (which overlooks the ocean) in your bathing suit, settling in for an evening of board games and—not everyone's favorite thing—sharing the bathroom. Nonetheless, this vivid yellow 19th-century inn sits on the edge of a residential area (many of the neighboring homes are aged Victorian vacation beauties), faces the ocean, and is a short walk from all the action of York Beach. Most rooms—on the small side but with high ceilings—have water views, and each is adorned simply with white bedspreads and floral wall coverings. It's simple, affordable lodging at its best, where the ocean and the area attractions ought to stand out with more flourish. Coffee is served in the morning; most guests start the morning watching the sunrise over the sea. **Pros:** direct waterfront location; walk to beach and to town attractions; reasonable rates. **Cons:** most rooms share bathrooms; upper-floor rooms accessed via steep stairs. ⊠ *11 Ocean Ave.* ☎ *207/363–1824* ⊕ *www.thekatahdininn.com* ➫ *9 rooms, 2 with bath* ⚭ *In-room: no phone, no TV, refrigerator, no a/c. In-hotel: Wi-Fi.* ▭ *MC, V.*

$$$–$$$$ ☷ **Union Bluff Hotel.** Although this hotel had to be rebuilt after a devastating fire, the face of the massive, turreted structure remains very similar to its mid-19th-century beginnings. Things are quite a bit more modern these days, but its original grandeur is still evident. Spread out among three separate buildings (the newest is the giant Meeting House, complete with function hall and ballroom: think lots of weddings and business conferences), lodging styles range from standard hotel fare to more contemporary. Many rooms have endless ocean views from private balconies; those that don't are so close that you can still smell the sea air. Rooms don't have a lot of antique character, but they

feature all the amenities of contemporary hotels, with standard, comfortable furnishings. You couldn't get much closer to all the activity of Short Sands Beach, which is just steps away. The pub serves lunch and dinner daily and has a late-night menu; the restaurant ($$$) is open for breakfast and dinner. **Pros:** many spectacular, uninterrupted ocean views; right in the midst of the York Beach action. **Cons:** rooms lack any charm or character befitting of inn's origins; not for those looking for a quiet getaway. ⊠ *8 Beach St.* ☎ *207/363–1333 or 800/833–0721* ⊕ *www.unionbluff.com* ⬌ *36 rooms, 6 suites in main inn; 21 rooms in adjacent motel; 8 rooms in Meeting House* ⬧ *In-room: refrigerator, Wi-Fi. In-hotel: restaurant, bar* ⊟ *AE, D, MC, V.*

NIGHTLIFE AND THE ARTS

Inn on the Blues (⊠ *7 Ocean Ave., York Beach* ☎ *207/351–3221*) is a hopping blues club that attracts national bands.

SHOPPING

There is no shortage of souvenir shopping here. Be sure to get some Goldenrod Kisses—Maine's famous saltwater taffy, made the same way today as it has been for more than a century—at the **Goldenrod** (⇨ *see Where to Eat*). If you need new flip-flops, a sweatshirt, or a bathing suit, you'll find plenty to choose from. Route 1A is the main drag, with smaller, alleylike streets running perpendicular to it; the center of town is easily walkable.

CAPE NEDDICK

4 mi north of York Beach via Rte. 1A, just north of York on U.S. 1.

Cape Neddick is one of the more peaceful of York's villages, running from the water (and Route 1A) along U.S. 1 between York and Ogunquit. Not heavily developed, the town has many modest residential homes, with a sprinkling of businesses catering to both locals and visitors. There are a few restaurants and inns, but no distinct downtown hub. The views are a nice combination of water, pastoral, and wooded landscapes.

EXPLORING

Mount Agamenticus Park. Maintained by the York Parks and Recreation Department, this humble summit of 692 feet above sea level is said to be the highest peak along the Atlantic seaboard. That may not seem like much, but if you choose to hike to the top, you will be rewarded with incredible views that span all the way to the White Mountains in New Hampshire. If you don't want to hoof it (though it's not very steep), there is parking at the top. The Nature Conservancy has chosen the site as very significant owing to the variety of unusual natural flora and fauna. To get here, take Mountain Road just off U.S. 1 in Cape Neddick (just after Flo's Steamed Hot Dogs) and follow the signs. The area is open daily, with no charge. It's a popular place for equestrians and cyclists as well as families and hikers. ⓓ *York Parks and Recreation Department, 200 U.S. Rte. 1 S, York 03909* ☎ *207/363–1040.*

WHERE TO EAT AND STAY

$$$–$$$$ ✕ **Clay Hill Farm.** Set on 30 acres of pastoral farmland, this is a popular
ECLECTIC   place for elegant weddings. It also has a long-standing reputation for
★   excellence. If you can bear to forgo the lobster crepe—a scallion crepe
wrapped around fresh Maine lobster, caramelized onions, and spin-
ach served over toasted almond rice pilaf and drizzled with Newburg
sauce—inquire about the intriguing nightly chef's special. An extensive
wine list complements the menu, and there is a pianist in the dining
room Wednesday through Saturday nights in season. Get a table by a
window and you'll be treated with quite an avian showing—the restau-
rant property has been named a bird refuge by the National Wildlife
Federation. Jeans and sneakers are not allowed. ⊠ *220 Clay Hill Rd.*
☎ *207/361–2272* ⊕ *www.clayhillfarm.com* ⚓ *Reservations essential*
▤ *AE, D, MC, V.*

¢   ✕ **Flo's Steamed Hot Dogs.** Yes, it seems crazy to highlight a hot-dog stand,
AMERICAN   but this is no ordinary place. Who would guess that a hot dog could
★   make it into *Saveur* and *Gourmet* magazines? But there is something
grand about this shabby, red-shingle shack that has been dealing dogs
since 1959. The line is out the door most days, but the operation is
so efficient that the wait is not long at all. Flo has passed on, but her
granddaughter keeps the business going, selling countless thousands of
hot dogs each year. Be sure to ask for the special sauce—consisting of,
among other things, hot sauce and mayo (you can take a bottle of the
sauce home, and you'll want to). ⊠ *1359 U.S. 1* ☎ *No phone* ⊕ *www.*
floshotdogs.com ▤ *No credit cards* ⊗ *Closed Wed.*

$$$–$$$$ ✕ **Frankie & Johnny's Natural Food Restaurant.** If you've had about all the
VEGETARIAN   fried seafood and calories you can stand for one day, try this casual
little spot that focuses on healthy—but tasty—meals. Choose from
a variety of vegetarian dishes as well as seafood, poultry, and meat
options. The toasted peppercorn seared sushi-grade tuna, served with
coconut risotto on gingered vegetables, is excellent. You're welcome and
encouraged to bring your own libations. ⊠ *1594 U.S. 1, Cape Neddick*
☎ *207/363–1909* ⊕ *www.frankie-johnnys.com* ▤ *No credit cards* ⊗ *No*
dinner Mon.–Wed. No lunch.

$–$$$ ▥ **Country View Motel & Guesthouse.** Set back along one of U.S. 1's less
hectic sections is this appealing little motel—it looks more like an inn
than what you usually envision as a motel. There are a few rooms in the
main house, and the rest are in the adjacent motel complex. It's clean,
pretty, and in a good central location for exploring the Yorks and Ogunquit, which are just a few miles away. Suites sleep up to four people and
have full kitchens. Guests with well-behaved dogs will appreciate the
on-site pet park for exercise and play. **Pros:** central location between
Ogunquit and Yorks; ample grounds provide picnic areas and gas grills.
Cons: not an in-town location; no water views or beachfront. ⊠ *1521*
U.S. 1 ☎ *207/363–7160 or 800/258–6598* ⊕ *www.countryviewmotel.*
com ⇋ *19 rooms, 3 suites* ⚲ *In-room: kitchen (some), refrigerator,*
Wi-Fi. In-hotel: pool, some pets allowed ▤ *MC, V* ⎢⎜⎢ *CP* ⊗ *Closed*
Jan.–mid-Apr.

SHOPPING

Home furnishings with an antique feel are the specialty of **Jeremiah Campbell & Company** (✉ *1537 U.S. 1* ☎ *207/363–8499*). Everything here is handcrafted, from rugs, decoys, furniture, and lighting to glassware. The shop is closed Wednesday. Quilt and fabric lovers will delight in a visit to **Knight's Quilt Shop** (✉ *1901 U.S. 1* ☎ *207/361–2500* ⊕ *www. mainequiltshop.com*), where quilts and everything needed to make them—including instructional classes—can be found.

SPORTS AND THE OUTDOORS

FISHING Offering a host of various guided fishing trips, private casting lessons, and a summer "striper school," **Eldredge Bros. Fly Shop** (✉ *1480 U.S. 103902* ☎ *207/363–9269 or 207/363–9279* ⊕ *www.eldredgeflyshop. com*) offers fishing trips in fresh- or saltwater; kayak rentals are also available for those who wish to venture out on their own. Rod-and-reel rentals are also offered.

GOLFING For a challenging 18-hole round, head to the **Cape Neddick Country Club** (✉ *650 Shore Rd. [Rte. 1A]* ☎ *207/361–2011* ⊕ *www.capeneddickgolf. com*), where the public is welcome. Greens fees start at $58.

KAYAKING Hop on one of the regularly scheduled guided kayak trips with **Excursions/Coastal Maine Outfitting Co.** (✉ *1740 U.S. 1* ☎ *207/363–0181* ⊕ *www.excursionsinmaine.com*). You can cruise along the shoreline or sign up for an overnight paddle. Reservations are recommended; trips start at $60. Kayaks and other boats are available for rental.

EN ROUTE You have two options when continuing on to Ogunquit: travel north on Route 1A, which will merge with U.S. 1 and take you into downtown Ogunquit; or, for a slower, more winding, scenic jaunt, take a right just out of York Beach onto Shore Road. You'll pass impeccable homes and get frequent glimpses of the rocky coast before ending up just shy of Perkins Cove; continue to the village of Ogunquit by turning left at the end of the road.

OGUNQUIT

10 mi north of the Yorks via Rte. 1A and 1 or Shore Rd.

A resort village in the 1880s, stylish Ogunquit gained fame as an artists' colony. Today it has become a mini Provincetown, with a gay population that swells in summer. Many inns and small clubs cater to a primarily gay and lesbian clientele. For a scenic drive, take Shore Road through downtown toward the 100-foot Bald Head Cliff; you'll be treated to views up and down the coast. On a stormy day the surf can be quite wild here.

GETTING HERE AND AROUND

The **Ogunquit Trolley** (✎ *P.O. Box 2368, Ogunquit 03907* ☎ *207/646–1411* ⊕ *www.ogunquittrolley.com* 🎫 *$1.50 (at each boarding); kids under 10 ride free with an adult*) is one of the best things that happened to this area. Parking in the village is troublesome and expensive, beach parking is costly and often limited, and so it's often just easier to leave your car parked at the hotel. The trolley begins operation in May and stays in service until Columbus Day. Stops are numerous along the route that begins at Perkins Cove and follows Shore Road through town, down to Ogunquit Beach, and out along U.S. 1 up to Wells (where a connecting Wells trolley takes over for northern travel). Maps are available wherever you find brochures and at the Chamber of Commerce Welcome Center on U.S. 1, just as you enter Ogunquit from the south.

ESSENTIALS
Visitor Information Ogunquit Chamber of Commerce (⊠ *36 Main Street [U.S. 1] 03907* ☎ *207/646–2939* ⊕ *www.ogunquit.org*).

EXPLORING
Ogunquit Heritage Museum. For a look at Ogunquit's colorful past, including its early days as a thriving art colony and its maritime history, visit the exhibits here and in the Winn House, which itself dates to 1785 and also focuses on Colonial architecture. ⊠ *86 Obed's La.* ☎ *207/646–0296* ⊕ *www.ogunquitheritagemuseum.org* ⊠ *Donations accepted* ⊙ *June–Sept., Tues.–Sat. 1–5.*

Ogunquit Museum of American Art. The small but worthwhile museum dedicated to 20th-century American art overlooks the ocean and is set amid a 3-acre sculpture garden. Inside are works by Henry Strater, Marsden Hartley, Winslow Homer, Edward Hopper, Gaston Lachaise, Marguerite Zorach, and Louise Nevelson. The huge windows of the sculpture court command a superb view of cliffs and ocean. Look for special events on Tuesday evenings, ranging from gallery talks to readings, film screenings to music. ⊠ *543 Shore Rd.* ☎ *207/646–4909* ⊕ *www.ogunquitmuseum.org* ⊠ *$7* ⊙ *July–late-Oct., Mon.–Sat. 10–5, Sun. 1–5.*

★ **Perkins Cove.** This neck of land, connected to the mainland by Oarweed Road and a pedestrian drawbridge, has a jumble of sea-beaten fish houses. These have largely been transformed by the tide of tourism to shops and restaurants. When you've had your fill of browsing and jostling the crowds, stroll out along **Marginal Way**, a mile-long footpath between Ogunquit and Perkins Cove that hugs the shore of a rocky promontory known as Israel's Head. Benches along the route give walkers an opportunity to stop and appreciate the open sea vistas, flowering bushes, and million-dollar homes.

WHERE TO EAT
¢–$ ✕ **Amore Breakfast.** One could hardly find a more-satisfying, full-bodied
AMERICAN breakfast than at this smart and busy joint just shy of the entrance
★ to Perkins Cove. A lighthearted mix of retro advertising signs adorns the walls of this bright, open, and very bustling dining room, where breakfast is a sophisticated affair. You won't find tired standards here—the only pancakes are German potato—rather, you'll have a hard time choosing among the options. The Oscar Madison omelet combines crabmeat with asparagus and Swiss, topped with a dill hollandaise. For a real decadent start, opt for the Banana Foster: pecan-coated, cream cheese–stuffed French toast with a side of sautéed bananas in rum syrup. The offers of a half, three-quarters, or full order give an indication of this item's richness. To ease the wait for a morning table, a self-serve coffee bar is available next door at the Café Amore. You

can also pick up sandwiches, baked goods, and gift items here. ✉ *309 Shore Rd.* ☎ *207/646–6661* ⊕ *www.amorebreakfast.com* ⊟ *D, MC, V* ⊗ *Closed mid-Dec.–Mar., and Wed. and Thurs. in spring and fall. No lunch or dinner.*

$$$$
ECLECTIC
Fodor's Choice
★

✕**Arrows.** Elegant simplicity is the hallmark of this restaurant in an 18th-century farmhouse 2 mi up a back road. Expect much more than the usual here; you'll likely find delicacies such as wild sturgeon caviar paired with vodka-cured salmon on the daily-changing menu—much of what appears is dependent on what is ready for harvest in the restaurant's abundant 1-acre garden. The roasted quail with fried noodles and the escargots with summer–herb butter appetizers are also beautifully executed. Try the "Indulgence Menu," a 10-course tasting menu prepared "at the whim of the chef," for $135. Guests are encouraged to dress up; absolutely no jeans or shorts. ✉ *41 Berwick Rd.* ☎ *207/361–1100* ⊕ *www.arrowsrestaurant.com* ⚐ *Reservations essential* ⊟ *MC, V* ⊗ *Closed Mon. and mid-Dec.–mid-Apr. No lunch.*

$$$–$$$$
ECLECTIC
★

✕**Bintliff's Restaurant.** The lounge is inviting with velvet chairs and couches, but it's the food and the extensive wine list that bring people back again and again. Steaks are a specialty here, but don't overlook the other intriguing entrées. For example, you might want to try the eggplant Napoleon, which combines crispy eggplant, tomatoes, braised onions, fresh mozzarella, roasted red peppers and shallots, and marinated portobello mushrooms. Bintliff's is one of the best spots for Sunday brunch and breakfast. ✉ *335 Main St. (U.S. Route 1)* ☎ *207/646–3111* ⊕ *www.bintliffsogunquit.com* ⚐ *Reservations essential* ⊟ *AE, D, MC, V.*

$$$–$$$$
ECLECTIC
★

✕**Five-O Shore Rd.** Right on Main Street in the thick of the action, this place gets really busy, but justly so. Popular with the hip and sophisticated crowd, you're likely to see the signature "cosmotinis" topping nearly every table. The menu is inventive, using an unusual blend of ingredients for a satisfying whole; the rack of spring lamb is prepared with a curry and Eastern-spice marinade and coconut pesto sauce and served with crème fraîche thyme mashed potatoes with caramelized shallots. If you're not hungry, just go for the cocktails (a staggering menu to choose from) and the lively atmosphere. There's also a late-night lounge menu. ✉ *50 Shore Rd.* ☎ *207/646–5001* ⊕ *www.five-oshoreroad.com* ⚐ *Reservations essential* ⊟ *AE, D, MC, V.*

NEED A BREAK?

Whether you're looking for something hot or cold, stop in for a treat at Caffe Prego (✉ *44 Shore Rd.* ☎ *207/646–7734*). **With more than two dozen flavors of gelato, an intriguing roster of heavenly malted frappés, granitas, and a full espresso bar, you'll find the pick-me-up you're craving. If you're hungry, there's also a good selection of brick-oven-fired pizzas (their specialty), grilled panini sandwiches, salad, and pasta.**

WHERE TO STAY

$$–$$$

▦**Marginal Way House.** This may be the best location in all of Ogunquit if you want to be close to the water. The expansive lawn of the complex stretches down from the main 1880s house right to the banks of the tumbling Ogunquit River just as it breaks from the sea. One apartment

2

sits on that edge, as does another shingled building that houses more rooms with decks atop the raging waters. Rooms have floral wallpaper, lots of wicker, and a curious assortment of attic-style artwork—unfussy, a bit outdated, but very comfortable. Guests spend a lot of time on the back porch, where morning coffee is available, or out among the flowers in the yard. It's a two-minute walk to town and five minutes to the beach across the footbridge. Apartments are rented weekly in high season. **Pros:** overlooks both ocean and tidal river; extraordinary water views from many rooms and grounds; short walk to beach. **Cons:** rooms in main house accessed via steep stairs; some rooms are on the small side; some rooms do not have a/c. ⊠ *22-24 Wharf La.* ☎ *207/646–8801* ⊕ *www.marginalwayhouse.com* ⤳ *23 rooms, 7 suites, 1 apartment* ⚲ *In-room: kitchen (some), refrigerator, no phone. In-hotel: some pets allowed, Wi-Fi* ⊟ *MC, V* ☾ *Closed Nov.–Apr.*

\$\$–\$\$\$\$ ⊡ **Ogunquit Resort Motel.** Right along U.S. 1 about 2 mi north of Ogunquit Village, this large complex is great for families and for those who prefer larger hotels over B&Bs. Boasting the largest pool in Ogunquit, the resort also has an outdoor hot tub. Beachgoers can walk to Footbridge Beach just about a half-mile away. Choose from deluxe, superior, and luxury rooms; luxury suites have fireplaces and Jacuzzi tubs. Unusual for hotels of this size is the free continental breakfast laid out each morning. You can leave your car here and hop on the trolley to get around, saving yourself the agony (and expense) of trying to park in town or at the beach. Ask about Internet specials. **Pros:** on the Ogunquit Trolley route; good place for people traveling with kids; good-size rooms with standard large-hotel amenities. **Cons:** not an in-town location; not for those looking for the more personalized small-lodging experience. ⊠ *719 Main St. (U.S. 1)* ☎ *877/646–8336* ⊕ *www.ogunquitresort.com* ⤳ *85 rooms, 8 suites* ⚲ *In-room: refrigerator, Wi-Fi. In-hotel: pool, gym* ⊟ *AE, D, MC, V* ⑩ *CP.*

\$\$\$–\$\$\$\$ ⊡ **Rockmere Lodge.** Midway along the Marginal Way walk, this shingle-style Victorian cottage is an ideal retreat from the hustle and bustle of Perkins Cove and Ogunquit. Each room has a distinct personality and color scheme, and all but two have ocean views. Rooms are fluffed to the hilt with colorful pillows, curtains, antiques, and other objects. You'll find it easy to laze the day away on the wraparound porch or in the gardens. **Pros:** dramatic oceanfront location; easy walk to both Ogunquit and Perkins Cove; historic lodging with authentic detail. **Cons:** many rooms accessed via steep stairs; not for people traveling with small children; no in-room a/c. ⊠ *150 Stearns Rd.* ☎ *207/646–2985* ⊕ *www.rockmere.com* ⤳ *8 rooms* ⚲ *In-room: no phone, DVD, refrigerator. In-hotel: Wi-fi, no kids under 14* ⊟ *D, MC, V* ⑩ *BP.*

\$\$ ⊡ **Yardarm Village Inn.** With stenciling winding up stairs and along many of its walls and tin ceilings, this inn has been lovingly cared for since its construction in the late 19th century. Set near the now-defunct trolley bed of the same era, the peaceful home is a very short walk from the activity of Perkins Cove. Standard rooms are large, and suites have separate sitting rooms—good spots to enjoy the fruits of the inn's in-house gourmet wine and cheese shop. Those eager to get on the water can cruise with the innkeepers on their 26-foot single sail (about \$25 for two hours). A continental breakfast is offered for an extra fee. **Pros:** easy walk to Perkins Cove; comfortable historic lodging; in-house wine and cheese shop provides the means for a good picnic. **Cons:** most rooms on second and third floors. ⊠ *406 Shore Rd.* ☎ *207/646–7006 or 888/927–3276* ⊕ *www.yardarmvillageinn.com* ⟿ *6 rooms, 4 suites* ⟁ *In-room: no phone, refrigerator, Wi-Fi. In-hotel: Internet terminal* ▤ *No credit cards* ☽ *Closed Nov.–Apr.*

NIGHTLIFE AND THE ARTS

Much of the nightlife in Ogunquit revolves around the precincts of Ogunquit Square and Perkins Cove, where people stroll, often enjoying an after-dinner ice-cream cone or espresso. Because Ogunquit is popular with gay and lesbian visitors, its club scene reflects this.

Ogunquit's summer repertory company, the **Booth Theater** (⊠ *13 Beach St.* ☎ *207/646–8142* ⊕ *www.boothproductions.com*), stages performances nightly in summer at the Betty Doon Motor Hotel, ranging from Neil Simon and Stephen Sondheim to popular favorites such as *School House Rock!*. The season kicks off around mid-June and continues through August. **Jonathan's Restaurant** (⊠ *2 Bourne La.* ☎ *207/646–4777* ⊕ *www.jonathansrestaurant.com*) plays host to some well-known and up-and-coming comedians and musicians weekly—during peak season, from June to mid-October. The movies are first-run at **Leavitt Fine Arts Theatre** (⊠ *259 Main St.* ☎ *207/646–3213* ⊕ *www.leavittheatre.com*), but it's also been Maine's summer theater since 1923. Look for the grand architectural elements of that earlier era before the movie starts.

Maine Street (⊠ *195 Main St. [U.S. 1]* ☎ *207/646–5101* ⊕ *www.mainestreetogunquit.com*) has live entertainment and is a popular dance spot. One of America's oldest summer theaters, the **Ogunquit Playhouse** (⊠ *U.S. 1* ☎ *207/646–5511* ⊕ *www.ogunquitplayhouse.org*) mounts plays and musicals with well-known actors of stage and screen from late June to Labor Day.

SHOPPING

Ogunquit Village and Perkins Cove are well stocked with shops, many carrying the ubiquitous supply of Maine lobster T-shirts and tourist-type gadgets. There are also some galleries and specialty spots, selling everything from artwork to fine linens and apparel.

More than just an art gallery, the **Barn Gallery** (⊠ *Shore Rd. and Bourne La.* ☎ *207/646–8400* ⊕ *www.barngallery.org*) hosts special programs, workshops, and exhibitions by some well-known local artists. Peruse the possible treasures at the multidealer **Blacksmith's Antique Mall** (⊠ *166 Main St.* ☎ *207/646–9643*), where you probably won't find any bargains; but then again, you might. Stock up in case of rain at **Books Ink** (⊠ *Perkins Cove* ☎ *207/361–2602* ⊕ *www.booksink.com*), where you'll find an array of toys, games, and puzzles in addition to books. Besides a good collection of stained glass, the wares at **Out of the Blue** (⊠ *19 Perkins Cove Rd.* ☎ *207/646–0430*) include home and garden accoutrements, jewelry, and all things related to wine.

For a huge selection of glassworks, pottery, and jewelry, stop at **Panache Gallery of Fine American Crafts** (⊠ *1949 U.S. 1* ☎ *207/646–4878*).

2

SPORTS AND THE OUTDOORS

A great spot to stretch your legs and have a picnic is **Beach Plum Farm** (⊠ *U.S. Route 1, ½ mi north of Ogunquit village*), a 22-acre parcel of land with several barns and a house. Maintained by the Great Works Regional Land Trust, the area is open from dawn to dusk and features ocean views and community gardens. Benches and a marked path around the perimeter welcome walkers. **Ogunquit Beach,** a 3-mi-wide stretch of sand at the mouth of the Ogunquit River, has snack bars, a boardwalk, restrooms, and changing areas (at the Beach Street entrance). Families gravitate to the ends; gay visitors camp at the beach's middle. The less crowded section to the north is accessible by footbridge and has portable restrooms, all-day paid parking, and trolley service.

OUTFITTER **Liquid Dreams Surf Shop** (⊠ *731 Main St.* ☎ *207/641–2545* ⊕ *www. liquiddreamssurf.com*) rents surfing equipment—you will want the wet suit—and bodyboards; it also sells bathing suits and wave-riding supplies. If you're new to the sport, sign up for surf camp or a private lesson.

BOATING Anglers can sign on with **Bunny Clark Deep Sea Fishing** (⊠ *Perkins Cove* ☎ *207/646–2214* ⊕ *www.bunnyclark.com*), which leaves the dock twice daily from early April through mid-November. The long boat ride with **Deborah Ann Whalewatching** (⊠ *Perkins Cove* ☎ *207/361–9501*) is worth it to witness humpback and finback whales in their natural habitat out on Jefferies Ledge. **Finestkind** (⊠ *Perkins Cove* ☎ *207/646–5227* ⊕ *www. finestkindcruises.com*) operates cocktail cruises, lobstering trips, and cruises to Nubble Light. Pack a picnic for a billowy 1½- or 2-hour sail with **The Silverlining** (⊠ *Perkins Cove* ☎ *207/646–9800* ⊕ *www. silverliningsailing.com*), a 42-foot wooden sloop. She leaves the dock at Perkins Cove five times daily. For more deep-sea fishing adventures, climb aboard the **Ugly Anne** (⊠ *Perkins Cove* ☎ *207/646–7202* ⊕ *www. uglyanne.com*), for half- or full-day trips.

EN ROUTE The summer traffic isn't the only thing that may make your northern drive up U.S. 1 from Ogunquit to Wells a slow one—this stretch is an **antiques lover's paradise.** Individual shops with antiques spilling out into the driveways and lawns are numerous, as are the multidealer and multibuilding shops. You can find quilts, glassware, maritime items, aged books, and hundreds of other things on this route. Wells is also home to a great outdoor flea market, held on weekends and a few other days during the week; you can't miss it, it's on the right side of U.S. 1 as you drive by going north.

WELLS

5 mi north of Ogunquit on U.S. 1.

Lacking any kind of noticeable village center, Wells could be easily overlooked as nothing more than a commercial stretch on U.S. 1 between Ogunquit and the Kennebunks. But look more closely—this is a place where people come to enjoy some of the best beaches on the coast. Part of Ogunquit until 1980, this family-oriented beach community has 7 mi of densely populated shoreline, along with nature preserves where you can explore salt marshes and tidal pools and see birds and waterfowl.

The area is also rich in history; Wells has been a thriving community in one way or another since the mid-1600s. It's actually a little more peaceful now than it was back then—the flocks of tourists that crowd the beaches and roadsides are far friendlier than the American Indians and French who engaged in near constant warfare and attacks during the 17th century.

GETTING HERE AND AROUND

Leave your car at your hotel and take the **Wells Trolley** (☎ 207/646–2451 ⊕ *www.wellschamber.org* 🖃 *$2*) to the beach or to the shops on U.S. 1. The seasonal trolley makes pickups at the Wells Transportation Center when the *Downeaster* (the Amtrak train with service from Boston to Portland) pulls in. If you want to continue south toward Ogunquit, the two town trolleys meet at the Wells Chamber of Commerce on U.S. 1; get a route map here.

ESSENTIALS

Visitor Information **Wells Chamber of Commerce** (✑ *P.O. Box 356, Wells 04090* ☎ *207/646–2451* ⊕ *www.wellschamber.org*).

EXPLORING

Meetinghouse Museum and Library. The headquarters for both the Ogunquit and Wells Historical Society, this building holds a series of concerts, programs, tours, and exhibits. The library is a gold mine for those interested in genealogy. ✉ *938 U.S. 1* ☎ *207/646–4775* ⊕ *www.wells-ogunquithistory.org* 🖃 *Donations accepted* ☉ *Memorial Day –Columbus Day., Tues.–Thurs. 10–4; mid-Oct.–May, Wed. and Thurs. 10–4.*

ᕙ **Wells Auto Museum.** A must for motor fanatics and youngsters, this museum has more than 80 vintage cars and motorcycles, as well as lots of related memorabilia. The kids will love the antique games and music boxes they can actually play with. ✉ *U.S. 1* ☎ *207/646–9064* ⊕ *www.wellsautomuseum.com* 🖃 *$7* ☉ *Memorial Day–Columbus Day, daily 10–5.*

Wells Reserve at Laudholm Farm. Extensive trails lace the farm's 1,600 acres of meadows, orchards, fields, and salt marshes, as well as two estuaries and 9 mi of seashore. Laudholm Farm, a 17th-century saltwater farm, was a thriving home to livestock for nearly four centuries, growing its own saltwater hay in the extensive marshes. Today the site houses the visitor center, where an introductory slide show is screened and a bookstore is well stocked with publications on local and state history. Within the farmhouse are rooms with historical exhibits and information; outside in the separate ecology center are learning exhibits geared mainly for kids. In winter, cross-country skiing is permitted. ✉ *342 Laudholm Farm Rd.* ☎ *207/646–1555* ⊕ *www.wellsreserve.org* 🖃 *$3* ☉ *Grounds daily 8–5. Visitor center mid-Jan.–late May and mid-Oct.–mid-Dec., weekdays 10–4; late May–mid-Oct., weekdays 10–4, Sat. 10–4, Sun. noon–4).*

NEED A BREAK?
How would you like a doughnut—a really superior one that the same family has been making since 1955? The doughnuts from **Congdon's** (✉ *1090 Post Rd.* ☎ *207/646–4219* ⊕ *www.congdons.com*) easily rival (many say there is no contest) some of those other famous places we won't mention here.

Choose from about 30 different varieties, though the plain one really gives you an idea of just how good these doughnuts are. There's a drive-through window so you don't have to get out of the car; or you can take a seat inside and have breakfast or lunch.

WHERE TO EAT

$–$$$ ✕ **Billy's Chowder House.** Locals head to this simple restaurant in a salt
SEAFOOD marsh for the generous lobster rolls, haddock sandwiches, and chowders. Big windows in the bright dining rooms overlook the marsh. ⊠ *216 Mile Rd.* ☎ *207/646–7558* ⊕ *www.billyschowderhouse.com* ⊟ *AE, D, MC, V* ⊘ *Closed mid-Dec.–mid-Jan.*

$$ ✕ **Cafe at Merriland Farm.** There's a lot going on at this 200-year-old
AMERICAN working farm and family affair. It's a great place for breakfast (beginning at 8 AM)—homegrown berries appear in jams, jellies, crepes, pancakes, spread over Belgian waffles, and any other place they taste good. The menu is quite creative for breakfast and lunch, going well beyond the basics with treats, such as portobello Benedict, artful crepes, grilled sandwiches, wraps, and half-pound burgers. Don't miss the desserts— luscious berries in pie, shortcake, or baked crisp. This farm is a delightful beauty. You may want to hit the on-site golf greens to fight off some of the added calories. From late July until the frost hits you can pick blueberries to take home. ⊠ *591 Coles Hill Rd.* ☎ *207/646–5040* ⊕ *www.merrilandfarmcafe.com* ⊟ *MC, V* ⊘ *Closed mid-Dec.–Apr. No dinner Sun.–Thurs.*

$$ ✕ **Maine Diner.** It's the real thing here—one look at the nostalgic (and
AMERICAN authentic 1953) exterior and you start craving good diner food. You'll get a little more here—how many greasy spoons make an award-winning lobster pie? That's the house favorite, as well as a heavenly seafood chowder. There's plenty of fried seafood in addition to the usual diner fare, and breakfast is served all day, just as it should be. Be sure to check out the adjacent gift shop, Remember the Maine. ⊠ *2265 U.S. 1* ☎ *207/646–4441* ⊕ *www.mainediner.com* ⊟ *D, MC, V* ⊘ *Closed 1 wk in Jan.*

WHERE TO STAY

$$ ▦ **Beach Farm Inn.** Innkeepers Nancy and Craig painstakingly renovated and decorated this 19th-century farmhouse, and its gracious appointments are a testament to their care and good taste. Craig, also a woodworker, has made a good portion of the furniture as well as sculptures throughout the home. Decorated with a multitude of antiques, four-poster beds, ample sitting areas, and artful rugs, the home is a place of real peace among the general commotion of Wells. The appealing enclosed breakfast area is the stage for Craig's monumental breakfasts served each morning; if it's nice out, eat on the deck overlooking the pool and grounds. Winter packages include wreath-making and cooking workshops. The beach is about a half-mile walk down the country road. **Pros:** easy access to beaches and activities of Route 1; gracious historic lodging; beautiful grounds and pool. **Cons:** some rooms share a bath; not all baths are attached; rooms located up steep stairs. ⊠ *97 Eldridge Rd.* ☎ *207/646–8493* ⊕ *www.beachfarminn.com* ⤴ *8 rooms,*

6 with bath; 2 cottages � *In-room: no phone (some), no TV. In-hotel: pool, no kids under 12* ☐ *AE, MC, V* ☉ *BP.*

$$–$$$$

Fodor's Choice

★

🏨 **Haven by the Sea.** Once the summer mission of St. Martha's Church in Kennebunkport, this stunning, exquisite inn has retained many of the original details from its former life as a seaside church. The cathedral ceilings and stained-glass windows remain, all gathering and spreading the grand surrounding light. The guest rooms are spacious, some with serene marsh views. Four common areas, including one with a fireplace, are perfect spots for afternoon refreshments. The inn is one block from the beach. **Pros:** unusual structure with elegant appointments; nightly happy hour; walk to beach. **Cons:** not an in-town location. ✉ *59 Church St.* ☎ *207/646–4194* ⊕ *www.havenbythesea.com* ➥ *6 rooms, 2 suites, 1 apartment* � *In-room: Wi-Fi. In-hotel: no kids under 12* ☐ *AE, MC, V* ☉ *BP.*

NIGHTLIFE AND THE ARTS

A **summer concert series** is held in pretty Wells Harbor Park at the gazebo (Saturday nights, July through early September). Music ranges from rock to gospel, reggae to swing; concerts begin around 6:30 and are free. Look for Harbor Road just off U.S. 1 by the fire and police stations; the park is about 1 mi down Harbor Road. Also loved for its excellent sushi, **Torches Patio Pub & Grille** (✉ *757 Post Road [U.S. Route 1]* ☎ *207/646–0344* ⊕ *www.origamisushibar.net*) plays host to live acoustic music Thursday through Saturday nights, outdoor on the patio. When weather disagrees, the music moves inside. It's also a popular spot for fans of sports on the big screen; multiple televisions keep the games going.

SHOPPING

Douglas N. Harding Rare Books (✉ *2152 Post Rd. [U.S. 1]* ☎ *207/646–8785* ⊕ *www.hardingsbooks.com*) has more than 100,000 old books, maps, and prints. **Goosefare Antiques** (✉ *2262 Post Rd. [U.S. 1]* ☎ *207/646–0505* ⊕ *www.goosefareantiques.com*) is a group shop specializing in 18th-, 19th-, and early-20th-century antiques. The **Lighthouse Depot** (✉ *2178 Post Road [U.S. 1]* ☎ *207/646–0608* ⊕ *www.lighthousedepot.com*) calls itself the world's largest lighthouse gift store, with lighthouse-theme gifts and memorabilia. **Reed's Antiques and Collectibles** (✉ *1773 Post Rd. [U.S. 1]* ☎ *207/646–8010* ⊕ *www.reedsantiques.com*) is a multidealer shop filled with all manner of antiques, from advertising to glass, tools to toys. **R. Jorgensen** (✉ *502 Post Rd. [U.S. 1]* ☎ *207/646–9444*) stocks 18th- and 19th-century formal and country antiques from the British Isles, Europe, and the United States.

Thousands of 18th- and 19th-century antiques are stuffed into a 200-year-old barn at **Wells General Store** (✉ *2023 U.S. 1* ☎ *207/646–5553*).

Local farmers gather to sell their fresh goods, including organically raised lamb, herbal soaps, flowers, baked goods, eggs, fruit, and produce at the weekly **Wells Farmers' Market** (✉ *Sanford Rd. [Rte. 109], in the Wells Town Hall parking lot* ⊕ *www.wellsfarmersmarket.org*), held Wednesday afternoons from 1:30 to 5 late May to mid-October.

2

SPORTS AND THE OUTDOORS

With its thousands of acres of marsh and preserved land, Wells is a great place to spend a lot of time outdoors. Nearly 7 mi of sand stretch along the boundaries of Wells, making beach going a prime occupation. Tidal pools sheltered by rocks are filled with all manner of creatures awaiting discovery. Parking is available for a fee (take the trolley!) at **Crescent Beach,** along Webhannet Drive; **Wells Beach** (at the end of Mile Road off U.S. 1) has public restrooms and two parking areas. There is another lot at the far end of Wells Beach, at the end of Atlantic Avenue. Across the jetty from Wells Harbor is **Drakes Island Beach** (end of Drakes Island Road off U.S. 1), which also has parking and public restrooms. Lifeguards are on hand at all the beaches. Rent bikes, surfboards, wet suits, boogie boards, and probably a few other things at **Wheels and Waves** (⊠ *578 U.S. 1* ☎ *207/646–5774*).

FISHING Many fish are bound to be caught by anglers with **Captain Satch and Sons** (☎ *207/337–0800 or 207/337–0716* ⊕ *www.wellsharbor.com*). It offers two trips daily, from Wells Town Dock. In addition to boat trips, a guide can take you fishing from the shore within the Rachel Carson Reserve. Go fishing along the coast or way out in the deep with *Three Ladies* (☎ *207/337–8800*) ; departure points vary. There's also a two-hour scenic coastal cruise.

GOLFING The 9-hole golf course at **Merriland Farm** (⊠ *545 Cole Hills Rd.* ☎ *207/ 646–0508* ⊕ *www.merrilandfarm.com*) is pretty challenging and was built by owner-farmer Jim Morrison amid the blueberry and raspberry patches. The course is open daily (except Tuesday League Day) from April through October, with greens fees of $13. This 200-year-old working farm also offers blueberry and raspberry picking from late July until the berries run out.

KAYAKING **World Within Sea Kayaking** (☎ *207/646–0455* ⊕ *www.worldwithin.com*) conducts guided kayaking tours with lessons. Departure points vary.

The **Rachel Carson National Wildlife Refuge** (⊠ *321 Port Rd. [Rte. 9]* ☎ *207/646–9226* ⊕ *www.fws.gov/northeast/rachelcarson*) has a mile-long-loop nature trail through a salt marsh. The trail borders the Little River and a white-pine forest where migrating birds and waterfowl of many varieties are regularly spotted.

EN
ROUTE

Drivers have a multitude of options going north from Wells to the Kennebunks. You can travel along U.S. 1, from Wells to the town of Kennebunk, stopping at every antiques shop along the way. To go directly to Kennebunkport, take Route 9A/35, which is a fairly breathtaking route as far as Colonial and Victorian architecture is concerned. Another route to take from Wells, especially if you are visiting the Rachel Carson National Wildlife Refuge, is Route 9 toward Kennebunkport, along which are beautiful views of salt marshes, farms, and plenty of impressive homes. Route 9 will connect with Route 9A/35; follow the signs to Kennebunkport.

THE KENNEBUNKS

The Kennebunks encompass Kennebunk, Kennebunk Beach, Goose Rocks Beach, Kennebunkport, Cape Porpoise, and Arundel. This cluster of seaside and inland villages provides a little bit of everything—salt marshes, sand beaches, jumbled fishing shacks, and architectural gems.

Handsome white-clapboard homes with shutters give Kennebunk, an early-19th-century shipbuilding center, a quintessential New England look. The many boutiques and galleries surrounding Dock Square draw visitors to Kennebunkport. People flock to Kennebunkport mostly in summer, but some come in early December when the Christmas Prelude is celebrated on two weekends. Santa arrives by fishing boat, and the Christmas trees are lighted as carolers stroll the sidewalks.

From Kennebunk, Route 35 south leads to Kennebunk's Lower Village. Continue south on Beach Avenue for Kennebunk Beach. To reach Kennebunkport from the Lower Village, head east on Route 9/Western Avenue and cross the drawbridge into Dock Square—technically, you're not in Kennebunkport until you cross that bridge. Continue east on Route 9, or take scenic Ocean Avenue and Wildes District Road to quiet Cape Porpoise. To access Goose Rocks Beach, continue east on Route 9, which is now called the Mills Road. Arundel is between Kennebunk and Kennebunkport.

KENNEBUNK

Approximately 6 mi north of Wells via U.S. 1; 23 mi south of Portland via Maine Tpke.

Sometimes bypassed on the way to its more touristed sister town of Kennebunkport, Kennebunk has its own appeal. In the 19th century the town was a major shipbuilding center; docks lined the river with hundreds of workers busily crafting the vessels that would bring immense fortune to some of the area's residents. Although the trade is long gone, the evidence that remains of this great wealth exists in Kennebunk's numerous impressive mansions. Kennebunk is a classic small New England town, with an inviting shopping district, steepled churches, and fine examples of 18th- and 19th-century brick and clapboard homes. There are also plenty of natural spaces for walking, swimming, birding, and biking.

The town of Kennebunk is divided between two villages; the upper one extends around the Mousam River on Route 9, while the lower one is several miles down Route 35, just shy of Kennebunkport proper. The drive down Route 35 keeps visitors agog with the splendor of the area's mansions, spread out on both sides of the road. To get to the grand and gentle beaches of Kennebunk, go straight on Beach Avenue from the intersection of Routes 9 and 35 in the lower village.

ESSENTIALS

Visitor Information Kennebunk-Kennebunkport Chamber of Commerce (🔖 *17 Western Ave., Kennebunk 04043* 🕾 *207/967–0857* ⊕ *www. visitthekennebunks.com*).

KENNEBUNK WALKING TOURS

To take a little walking tour of Kennebunk's most notable structures, begin from the Federal-style Brick Store Museum, on Main Street. Head south on Main Street (turn left out of the museum) to see several extraordinary 18th-century homes, including the Nathaniel Frost House at 99 Main Street (1799) and the Benjamin Brown House at 85 Main Street (1788).

When you've had your fill of historic homes, head back up toward the museum, pass the 1773 First Parish Unitarian Church (its Asher Benjamin–style steeple contains the original Paul Revere bell) and turn right onto Summer Street. This street is an architectural showcase, revealing an array of styles from Colonial to Federal. Walking past these grand

beauties will give you a real sense of the economic prowess and glamour of the long-gone shipbuilding industry.

For a guided architectural walking tour of Summer Street, contact the Brick Store Museum at 207/985–4802.

For a dramatic walk along the rocky coastline and beneath the views of Ocean Avenue's grand mansions, head out on the **Parson's Way Shore Walk,** a paved, 4.8-mi round-trip. Begin at Dock Square and follow Ocean Avenue along the river, passing the Colony Hotel and St. Ann's Church, all the way to Walker's Point. You can simply turn back from here, or take a left onto Wildes District Road for a walk amid more luxury homes and trees.

EXPLORING

Brick Store Museum. The cornerstone of this block-long preservation of early-19th-century commercial buildings is **William Lord's Brick Store.** Built as a dry-goods store in 1825 in the Federal style, the building has an openwork balustrade across the roof line, granite lintels over the windows, and paired chimneys. Exhibits chronicle Kennebunk's relationship with the sea. The museum leads architectural walking tours of Kennebunk's National Register Historic District on Wednesday and Friday, typically from May to October. ⊠ *117 Main St., Kennebunk* ☎ *207/985–4802* ⊕ *www.brickstoremuseum.org* ✉ *Donations accepted; walking tours $5* ⊗ *Tues.–Fri. 10–4:30, Sat. 10–1.*

First Parish Unitarian Church. Built in 1773, just before the American Revolution, this stunning church is a marvel. The 1804 Asher Benjamin–style steeple stands proudly atop the village, and the sounds of the original Paul Revere bell can be heard for miles. It holds Sunday services, and on Tuesdays in summer tours of the sanctuary take place at 10 AM. ⊠ *114 Main St.* ☎ *207/985–3700* ⊕ *www.uukennebunk.org.*

WHERE TO EAT

$
AMERICAN

✕ **Duffy's Tavern & Grill.** Every small town needs its own lively and friendly tavern, and this bustling spot is Kennebunk's favorite. Housed in a former shoe factory whose exposed brick, soaring ceilings, and hardwood floors remain; and right outside are the tumbling waters of the Mousam River as it flows from the dam. There's a large bar with several overhead televisions (yes, sports are big here), and plenty of seating in the main room; there are more tables in a back section, but that space lacks the energy and architectural detail of the main section. Prices are refreshingly reasonable for these parts; you'll find plenty of comfortable standards here, including burgers, sandwiches, pizza, and salads, as well as an appetizer menu with lots of chicken wings and fried items. Breakfast is served on Saturday and Sunday mornings, and there's live entertainment on weekend evenings. ⊠ *4 Main St., Kennebunk* ☎ *207/985–0050* ⊕ *www.duffyskennebunk.com* ⊟ *AE, MC, V.*

$$ ✕ **Federal Jack's.** Run by the Kennebunkport Brewing Company, the
AMERICAN complex is housed in an old shipbuilding warehouse right on the water. Many different beers are handcrafted on-site, including favorites such as 'Taint Town Ale (so named because the brewery "taint quite Kennebunk and taint quite Kennebunkport) and Goat Island Light—try the sampler if you can't decide. The food is American pub style, with lots of seafood elements; the clam chowder is rich and satisfying. There's also a Sunday brunch buffet, and a late-night menu for those who get hungry while playing pool in the back room. Brew tours are available. You can find the restaurant and brewery just before the bridge into Kennebunkport. ⊠ *8 Western Ave., Lower Village* ☎ *207/967–4322* ⊕ *www.federaljacks.com* ⊟ *AE, MC, V.*

$$$–$$$$ ✕ **Grissini.** This popular trattoria draws high praise for its northern Ital-
ITALIAN ian cuisine. Dine by the stone hearth on inclement days or on the patio when the weather's fine. You can mix and match appetizers, pizzas, salads, pastas, and entrées from the menu to suit your hunger and budget. For lighter fare, choose from the "Grotta" menu with its generous selection of ciabatta sandwiches, salads, pastas, and small plates. ⊠ *27 Western Ave., Kennebunk* ☎ *207/967–2211* ⊕ *www.restaurantgrissini. com* ⊟ *AE, MC, V.*

$$$$ ✕ **White Barn Inn.** Formally attired waiters, meticulous service, and exqui-
AMERICAN site food have earned this restaurant accolades as one of the best in New
★ England. Regional New England fare is served in a rustic but elegant dining room. The three-course, prix-fixe menu ($95), which changes weekly, might include steamed Maine lobster nestled on fresh fettuccine with carrots, ginger, and snow peas. ⊠ *37 Beach Ave., Kennebunk* ☎ *207/967–2321* ⊕ *www.whitebarninn.com* ⌖ *Reservations essential, jacket required* ⊟ *AE, MC, V* ⊙ *Closed 3 wks. in Jan. No lunch.*

WHERE TO STAY

$$$–$$$$ ⌂ **Bufflehead Cove Inn.** On the Kennebunk River at the end of a winding
dirt road, this gray-shingle B&B sits amid fields and apple trees. Surprisingly, however, it's only five minutes from Dock Square. Rooms in the main house are outfitted with a funky mix of antiques, Far Eastern, and eclectic art. The Hideaway Suite, with a two-sided gas fireplace, king-size bed, and large whirlpool tub, overlooks the river. The Garden Studio has a fireplace and offers the most privacy. It's a great place to bring your kayaks or canoe for paddling trips right from the dock; or simply opt to gaze upon the river from the expansive wraparound porch. The roomy cottage, set back a ways from the main house, has a large private deck with generous water views and decadent touches like a wood-burning fireplace and a two-person whirlpool tub; a two-night minimum stay is required. **Pros:** beautiful and peaceful pastoral setting;

CLOSE UP

All About Lobsters

Judging from the current price of a lobster dinner, it's hard to believe that lobsters were once so plentiful that servants in rich households would have contracts stating they could be served lobster "no more than two times a week."

The going price for lobsters in the 1840s was three cents per lobster—not per pound, per lobster. Today Maine is nearly synonymous with lobsters, the fishery being one of Maine's primary industries. Well over 60 million pounds of lobster are landed a year in the state, making Maine, by far, the biggest supplier in the nation.

Because of the size restrictions, most of the lobsters you find in restaurants weigh 1¼ to 1½ pounds. However, lobsters can actually grow much larger and live to a ripe old age. The largest lobster ever caught off the coast of Maine weighed in at nearly 45 pounds, and was more than 50 years old!

For an authentic, Maine-style lobster dinner, you must go to a lobster pound. Finding one should not be difficult. Generally, these places are rustic and simple—they look more like fish-packing plants than restaurants. Hundreds of freshly caught lobsters of varying sizes are kept in pens, waiting for customers. Service is simple in the extreme. You usually sit at a wooden picnic table, and eat off a thick paper plate. A classic "Down East" feast includes lobster—boiled or steamed—with clam chowder, steamers, potato, and corn on the cob—and, of course, a large bib tied around your neck.

—Stephen Allen

2

ideal riverfront location; perfect for a serene getaway. **Cons:** a short drive from town. ⊠ *18 Bufflehead Cove Rd., Kennebunk* ☎ *207/967–3879* ⊕ *www.buffleheadcove.com* ⌷ *2 rooms, 3 suites, 1 cottage* ⚷ *In-room: no phone, refrigerator (some), Wi-Fi. In-hotel: public Internet, no kids under 1* ☰ *D, MC, V* ☯ *Closed Dec.–Apr.* � ⎊ *BP.*

$$–$$$
AMERICAN   ⊡ **Kennebunk Inn.** This stately brick building has quite a presence on Main Street in downtown Kennebunk. Perpetual renovation and upgrades have been giving this inn more dignity and comfort, slowly erasing the boardinghouse feel that could come from a multitude of rooms, arranged astride long, creaky corridors. Aged wood floors have been refinished, and rooms are simply decorated with antiques. There's nothing fussy about the place. The real pride here is in the dining room, where the husband-and-wife chef-owners do an incredible job with their restaurant ($$–$$$). The brasserie-style menu is nicely varied, including treats such as braised beef short ribs with corn and basil risotto, salads, and wraps. **Pros:** great in-town location; reasonable rates for the area; comfortable and spacious rooms in historic building. **Cons:** rooms are located on second and third floors; no water views or beachfront. ⊠ *45 Main St., Kennebunk* ☎ *207/985–3351* ⊕ *www.thekennebunkinn.com* ⌷ *18 rooms, 7 suites* ⚷ *In-room: no phone, kitchen (some), Wi-Fi. In-hotel: restaurant, bar, some pets allowed* ☰ *AE, D, MC, V* ⎊ *CP.*

$$$$
 ⟳   ⊡ **The Seaside.** This handsome seaside property has been in the hands of the Severance family since 1667. The modern hotel units, all with sliding-glass doors that open onto private decks or patios (half with

ocean views), are appropriate for families; so are the cottages with one to four bedrooms. You can't get much closer to Gooch's Beach. The inn supplies beach chairs; take a dip in the outdoor shower to wash off the salt and the sand. **Pros:** ideal beachfront location; lawn games available; great ocean views from upper-floor rooms. **Cons:** rooms are hotel standard and a little outdated (but fair sized); not an in-town location. ⊠ *80 Beach Ave., Kennebunk* ☎ *207/967–4461 or 800/967–4461* ⊕ *www.kennebunkbeachmaine.com* ⇆ *22 rooms, 11 cottages* ⚭ *In-room: refrigerator, Wi-Fi. In-hotel: beachfront, laundry service* ▭ *AE, MC, V* ⊘ *Cottages closed Nov.–May* ❑❑ *CP.*

$$ ▦ **Waldo Emerson House.** The home itself is a historical gold mine, made grand with unusual maritime architectural touches by a shipbuilder in 1784 and later home to the great-uncle of beloved poet Ralph Waldo Emerson (the writer spent many youthful summers in the house). It's believed that the house was also a stop on the famed Underground Railroad. Notice the sliding wooden panels in the windows, said to keep inhabitants safe from the soaring arrows of angry Indians. The elegance of the wide-plank pine floors remains, as does some remarkable original tile work around the many fireplaces. Rooms are spacious, and filled with antiques and colorful quilts, and all of them have working fireplaces. Innkeepers Kathy and John Daamen provide a shuttle to area beaches and operate the Mainely Quilts gift shop next door. **Pros:** good base for exploring both Kennebunk and Kennebunkport; authentic historic lodging; complimentary afternoon tea. **Cons:** most rooms accessed via steep stairs; no water views or beachfront; not an in-town location. ⊠ *108 Summer St. (Rte. 35), Kennebunk* ☎ *207/985–4250 or 877/521–8776* ⊕ *www.waldoemersoninn.com* ⇆ *4 rooms* ⚭ *In-room: no phone, no TV (some), Wi-Fi. In-hotel: bicycles, public Internet, no kids under 6* ▭ *AE, D, MC, V* ❑❑ *BP.*

$$$$ ▦ **White Barn Inn.** For a romantic overnight stay, you need look no
★ further than the exclusive White Barn Inn, known for its attentive, pampering service. No detail has been overlooked in the meticulously appointed rooms, from plush bedding and reading lamps to robes and slippers. Rooms are in the main inn and adjacent buildings. Some have fireplaces, hot tubs, and luxurious baths with steam showers. The inn is within walking distance (10–15 minutes) of Dock Square and the beach. **Pros:** elegant, luxurious lodging; full-service; in a historic building. **Cons:** no water views or beachfront; overly steep lodging prices; not in town. ⊠ *37 Beach Ave., Kennebunk* ☎ *207/967–2321* ⊕ *www. whitebarninn.com* ⇆ *16 rooms, 9 suites* ⚭ *In-room: DVD, Wi-Fi. In-hotel: restaurant, bar, pool, spa, bicycles, concierge, laundry service, public Internet, no kids under 12* ▭ *AE, MC, V* ❑❑ *CP.*

SHOPPING

The **Gallery on Chase Hill** (⊠ *10 Chase Hill Rd., Kennebunk* ☎ *207/967–0049* ⊕ *www.maine-art.com*) presents original artwork by Maine and New England artists. **Marlow's Artisans Gallery** (⊠ *64 Main St., Kennebunk* ☎ *207/985–2931*) carries a large and eclectic collection of crafts. **Tom's of Maine Natural Living Store** (⊠ *52 Main St., Kennebunk* ☎ *207/467–4005*) sells all-natural personal-care products.

2

SPORTS AND THE OUTDOORS

Kennebunk Beach has three parts: Gooch's Beach, Mother's Beach, and Kennebunk Beach. Beach Road, with its cottages and old Victorian boardinghouses, runs right behind them. Gooch's and Kennebunk attract teenagers; Mother's Beach, which has a small playground and tidal puddles for splashing, is popular with families. For parking permits (a fee is charged in summer), go to the **Kennebunk Town Office** (⊠ *1 Summer St. [Rte. 35]* ☎ *207/985–2102* ⊕ *www.kennebunkmaine.us* ☉ *Mon., Tues., Thurs. and Fri., 8:00–4:30; Wed. 1–4:30*).

For an unusual exploring treat, visit the **Kennebunk Plains** (⊠ *Rte. 99 west, a few miles out of Kennebunk* ☎ *207/729–5181*), a 135-acre protected grasslands habitat that is home to several rare and endangered species of vegetation and wildlife. Locally known as the blueberry plains, a good portion of the area is abloom with the hues of ripening wild blueberries in late July; after August 1 visitors are welcome to pick and eat all the berries they can find. The roads take you through vast grasslands and scrub-oak woods and by ponds. The area is maintained by the Nature Conservancy and is open daily from sunrise to sunset.

Three-mile-long **Goose Rocks,** a few minutes' drive north of town off Route 9, has plenty of shallow pools for exploring and a good long stretch of smooth sand; it's a favorite of families with small children. You can pick up a parking permit ($12 a day, $50 a week) at the **Kennebunkport Town Hall** (⊠ *6 Elm St., Kennebunkport* ☎ *207/967–4243* ☉ *Weekdays 8–4:30*) or at the Police Department on Route 9 on the way to the beach.

EN ROUTE The drive from Kennebunk to Kennebunkport will take you by the **Wedding Cake House** (⊠ *104 Summer St. [Rte. 35], Kennebunk*). The legend behind this confection in fancy wood fretwork is that its builder, a sea captain, was forced to set sail in the middle of his wedding; the house was his bride's consolation for the lack of a wedding cake. It is not open to the public.

KENNEBUNKPORT

Approximately 6 mi north of Wells via U.S. 1; approximately 22 mi south of Portland.

The area focused around the water and Dock Square in Kennebunkport is where you can find the most activity (and crowds) in the Kennebunks. Winding alleys disclose shops and restaurants geared to the tourist trade, right in the midst of a hardworking harbor. Kennebunkport has been a resort area since the 19th century, but its most famous residents have made it even more popular—the presidential Bush family is often in residence in their immense home, which sits dramatically out on Walker's Point. The amount of wealth here is as tangible as the sharp sea breezes and the sounds of seagulls overhead. Newer mansions have sprung up alongside the old; a great way to see them is to take a slow drive out along Ocean Avenue.

GETTING HERE AND AROUND

Get a good overview of the sights with an **Intown Trolley** tour. The narrated 45-minute jaunts leave every hour starting at 10 AM at the designated stop on Ocean Avenue, around the corner of Dock Square. The fare is valid for the day, so you can hop on and off at your leisure. ⊠ *Ocean Ave., Kennebunkport* ☎ *207/967–3686* ⊕ *www.intowntrolley. com* ☜ *$15 all-day fare* ☉ *Late May–mid-Oct., daily 10–5.*

Dock Square. The heart and pulse of this busy little Kennebunkport is this town center. Boutiques, T-shirt shops, art galleries, crafts stores, and restaurants encircle the square and spread out alongside streets and alleys. Many businesses close in winter, but those that stay open tend to offer nice discounts in December. Walk onto the drawbridge to admire the tidal Kennebunk River.

Nott House. Also known as White Columns, the imposing Greek Revival mansion with Doric columns is furnished with the belongings of four generations of the Perkins-Nott family. The 1853 house is open for guided tours and also serves as a gathering place for village walking tours, offered Thursday and Saturday at 11. It is maintained by the Kennebunkport Historical Society, which also runs the **History Center of Kennebunkport,** a mile away from the Nott House on North Street; the year-round center includes several exhibit buildings containing an old schoolhouse and jail cells. ⊠ *8 Maine St., Kennebunkport* ☎ *207/967– 2751* ⊕ *www.kporthistory.org* ☜ *$7 for house tours; $7 for walking tours* ☉ *July–mid-Oct., Thur. 10–4 and 7–9; Fri. 1–4, Sat. 10–1.*

☾ ★ **Seashore Trolley Museum.** Here streetcars built from 1872 to 1972, including trolleys from major metropolitan areas and world capitals—Boston to Budapest, New York to Nagasaki, San Francisco to Sydney—are all beautifully restored and displayed. Best of all, you can take a trolley ride for nearly 4 mi on the tracks of the former Atlantic Shoreline trolley line, with a stop along the way at the museum restoration shop, where trolleys are transformed from junk into gems. Both guided and self-guided tours are available. ⊠ *195 Log Cabin Rd., Kennebunkport* ☎ *207/967–2712* ⊕ *www.trolleymuseum.org* ☜ *$8.50* ☉ *Early May– mid-Oct., daily 10–5:00; reduced hrs in spring and fall, call ahead.*

WHERE TO EAT

$$–$$$$
SEAFOOD
Mabel's Lobster Claw. Mabel's has long been serving lobsters, homemade pies, and lots of seafood for lunch and dinner in this tiny dwelling out on Ocean Avenue. With its paneled walls, wooden booths, autographed photos of various TV stars (plus several members of the Bush family), and paper place mats that illustrate how to eat a Maine lobster, this place is a simple little classic. The house favorite is the Lobster Savannah—split and filled with scallops, shrimp, and mushrooms in a Newburg sauce. Make sure to save room for the peanut-butter ice-cream pie. Reservations are recommended. ⊠ *124 Ocean Ave., Kennebunkport* ☎ *207/967–2562* ▤ *AE, D, MC, V* ☉ *Closed Nov.–Apr.*

$$$
SEAFOOD
✕ **Pier 77 Restaurant & the Ramp Bar & Grille.** The view takes center stage at this dual establishment, consisting of a fine dining portion and the more casual and boisterous Ramp. Pier 77 serves up more sophisticated fare, focusing on meats and seafood; the tiny, tiny Ramp pays homage to a

really good burger, fried seafood, and other pub-style choices. The place is vibrant with live music most nights in summer and a great place for cocktails on the water. ⊠ *77 Pier Rd., Cape Porpoise* ☎ *207/967–8500* ⊕ *www.pier77restaurant.com* ▱ *AE, MC, V* ☺ *Closed Jan.–mid-Mar.*

WHERE TO STAY

$$$$ ⚑ **Cape Arundel Inn.** This shingle-style inn commands a magnificent ocean view that takes in the Bush estate at Walker's Point. The spacious rooms are furnished with country-style furniture and antiques, and most have sitting areas with ocean views. You can relax on the front porch or by the fireplace. The Rockbound complex, a later addition (1950s), doesn't have the 19th-century charm of the main house, but the rooms are large, many have fireplaces, and all have private balconies from which to take in the views. In the candlelit dining room ($$$–$$$$), open to the public for dinner, every table has a view of the surf. The menu changes seasonally. **Pros:** extraordinary views from most rooms; close to town and attractions. **Cons:** most rooms accessed via stairs; not for the budget-minded. ⊠ *208 Ocean Ave., Kennebunkport* ☎ *207/967–2125* ⊕ *www.capearundelinn.com* ⊃ *19 rooms, 1 suite* ♿ *In-room: no phone, no TV (some), Wi-Fi, no a/c. In-hotel: restaurant, bicycles.* ▱ *AE, D, MC, V* ☺ *Closed Jan. and Feb.* ⎺⎺ *CP.*

$$$$
Fodor's Choice
★
⚑ **Captain Lord Mansion.** Of all the mansions in Kennebunkport's historic district that have been converted to inns, the 1812 Captain Lord Mansion is the stateliest and most sumptuously appointed. Distinctive architecture, including a suspended elliptical staircase, gas fireplaces in all rooms, and near-museum-quality accoutrements, make for a formal but not stuffy setting. Six rooms have whirlpool tubs. The extravagant suite has two fireplaces, a double whirlpool, a hydro-massage body spa, a TV/DVD and stereo system, and a king-size canopy bed. Day-spa services are available for added luxury. **Pros:** elegant and luxurious historic lodging; in-town location; beautiful landscaped grounds and gardens. **Cons:** not for those on a tight budget; not a beachfront location. ⊠ *Pleasant and Green Sts., Kennebunkport* ☎ *207/967–3141 or 800/522–3141* ⊕ *www.captainlord.com* ⊃ *15 rooms, 1 suite* ♿ *In-room: Wi-Fi. In-hotel: bicycles, public Internet, no kids under 12* ▱ *D, MC, V* ⎺⎺ *BP.*

$$$–$$$$
Fodor's Choice
★
⚑ **The Colony.** You can't miss this place—it's grand, white, and incredibly large, set majestically atop a rise overlooking the ocean. The hotel was built in 1914 (after its predecessor caught fire in 1898), and much of the splendid glamour of this earlier era remains. Many of the rooms in the main hotel (there are two other outbuildings) have breezy ocean views from private or semiprivate balconies. All are outfitted with antiques and hardwood floors; the bright white bed linens nicely set off the colors of the Waverly wallpaper. The restaurant ($$–$$$$) features New England fare, with plenty of seafood, steaks, and other favorites. The Colony is also Maine's first environmentally responsible hotel. **Pros:** lodging in the tradition of grand old hotels; many ocean views; plenty of activities and entertainment for all ages. **Cons:** not for visitors looking for more intimate or peaceful lodging; rooms with ocean views come at steep prices; some rooms do not have a/c. ⊠ *Ocean Ave.* ☎ *207/967–3331 or 800/552–2363* ⊕ *www.thecolonyhotel.com/maine*

⚓ *124 rooms* ⌂ *In-room: no TV (some), Wi-Fi. In-hotel: restaurant, room service, bar, pool, beachfront, bicycles, some pets allowed* ▭ *AE, MC, V* ☉ *Closed Nov.–mid-May* ❢❢ *BP.*

$$$ ⌬ **Rhumb Line.** Although the rooms are standard motel fare, the facilities set this family-friendly motor lodge apart. It's on the trolley line, making getting around Kennebunk-area sites easy. Lobster bakes (extra charge) are held in the evening on weekends from late May through June, and daily from July through August. Available kitchenettes (some suites have full kitchens) make it a good bet for travelers looking to ease the meal budget. Kids love the indoor pool, especially on gray or cool days. **Pros:** reasonably priced lodging for area; spacious and comfortable rooms; plenty of activities on the property. **Cons:** not a waterfront location; rooms are very standard with little character. ⊠ *Ocean Ave., P.O. Box 3067,Kennebunkport* ☎ *207/967–5457 or 800/337–4862* ⊕ *www. rhumblinemaine.com* ⚓ *56 rooms, 3 suites* ⌂ *In-room: refrigerator, Wi-Fi. In-hotel: restaurant, pools, gym* ▭ *AE, D, MC, V* ❢❢ *CP.*

THE ARTS

Lively summer theater performances are held in a 19th-century barn Tuesday through Sunday (June through Labor Day), with some matinees, at the **Arundel Barn Playhouse** (⊠ *53 Old Post Rd., Arundel* ☎ *207/985–5552* ⊕ *www.arundelbarnplayhouse.com*).

SHOPPING

Abacus (⊠ *2 Ocean Ave., Dock Sq., Kennebunkport* ☎ *207/967–0111* ⊕ *www.abacusgallery.com*) sells eclectic crafts and furniture. **Kennebunkport Arts** (⊠ *1 Spring St., Dock Sq., Kennebunkport* ☎ *207/967–3690*) is a contemporary crafts gallery with a good selection of unusual items for the home. **Mast Cove Galleries** (⊠ *Mast Cove La., Kennebunkport* ☎ *207/967–3453* ⊕ *www.mastcove.com*) sells graphics, paintings, and sculpture by 105 artists.

SPORTS AND THE OUTDOORS

BIKING **Cape-Able Bike Shop** (⊠ *83 Arundel Rd., Kennebunkport* ☎ *207/967–4382* ⊕ *www.capeablebikes.com*) rents bicycles of all types, including trailer bikes and tandems. Guided bike and kayak tours are also available.

BOATING AND FISHING To reserve a private sail for up to six people, contact Captain Jim Jannetti of the ***Bellatrix*** (⊠ *Kennebunkport* ☎ *207/590–1125* ⊕ *www. sailingtrips.com*), a vintage racing yacht. He'll teach you the ropes if you wish. Find and catch fish with **Cast Away Fishing Charters** (⌂ *P.O. Box 245, Kennebunkport 04046* ☎ *207/284–1740* ⊕ *www.castawayfishingcharters.com*). **First Chance** (⊠ *4-A Western Ave., Kennebunk 04043* ☎ *207/967–5507 or 800/767–2628* ⊕ *www.firstchancewhalewatch. com*) leads whale-watching cruises and guarantees sightings in season. Daily scenic lobster cruises are also offered aboard *Kylie's Chance.* For half- or full-day fishing trips as well as discovery trips for kids, book some time with **Lady J Sportfishing Charters** (⊠ *Arundel Wharf, Ocean Ave. 04046* ☎ *207/985–7304* ⊕ *www.ladyjcharters.com*).

ⵣ Several scenic cruises and lobster-trap hauling trips run daily aboard the ***Rugosa*** (⊠ *Depart from Nonantum Resort, Ocean Ave.* ☎ *207/ 967–5595*).

EN ROUTE For a rewarding drive that goes into the reaches of the coastline on the way to Old Orchard Beach, head out of Kennebunkport on Route 9. Plan to do some beach walking at Goose Rocks Beach or Fortunes Rocks Beach, both ideal for stretching your legs, or just looking for shells or critters in the tide pools. Route 9 continues to wind through wooded areas, heads through the slightly weary-looking old mill town of Biddeford, across the Saco River, and into Saco, a busy town with commerce and its accompanying traffic. Once you get past Saco, Route 9 returns to its peaceful curves and gentle scenery, leaving crowded civilization behind. It winds through the charming resort villages of Camp Ellis and Ocean Park; or you could pack a picnic and spend some time at Ferry Beach State Park (look for the entrance just off Route 9 on Bayview Road). The varied landscapes in the park include forested sections, swamp, beach, and lots of dunes, all of which have miles of marked trails to hike.

It's a longer route to Old Orchard Beach but worth it for the gems to be found along the way.

OLD ORCHARD BEACH AREA

15 mi north of Kennebunkport, 18 mi south of Portland.

Back in the late 19th century Old Orchard Beach was a classic, upscale, place-to-be-seen resort area. The railroad brought wealthy families looking for entertainment and the benefits of the fresh sea air. Although a good bit of this aristocratic hue has dulled in more recent times—admittedly, the place is more than a little pleasantly tacky these days—Old Orchard Beach remains a good place for those looking for entertainment and thrills by the sea.

The center of the action is a 7-mi strip of sand beach and its accompanying amusement park, which resembles a small Coney Island. Despite the summertime crowds and fried-food odors, the atmosphere can be captivating. During the 1940s and '50s, in the heyday of the Big Band era, the pier had a dance hall where stars of the time performed. Fire claimed the end of the pier—at one time it jutted out nearly 1,800 feet into the sea—but booths with games and candy concessions still line both sides. In summer the town sponsors fireworks (on Thursday night). Places to stay run the gamut from cheap motels to cottage colonies to full-service seasonal hotels. You won't find free parking in town, but there are ample lots. Amtrak has a seasonal stop here.

ESSENTIALS

Visitor Information Old Orchard Beach Chamber of Commerce (✉ *1st St.,* ⌂ *P.O. Box 600, Old Orchard Beach 04064* ☎ *207/934–2500 or 800/365–9386* ⊕ *www.oldorchardbeachmaine.com*).

EXPLORING

Ocean Park. A world away from the beach scene lies Ocean Park, on the southwestern edge of town. Locals and visitors like to keep the separation distinct, touting their area as a more peaceful and wholesome family-style village (to that end, there are no alcohol or tobacco sales in this little haven). This vacation community was founded in 1881 by Free

Will Baptist leaders as an interdenominational retreat with both religious and educational purposes, following the example of Chautauqua, New York. Today the community still hosts an impressive variety of cultural happenings, including movies, concerts, recreation, workshops, and religious services. Most are presented in the Temple, which is on the National Register of Historic Places. Although the religious nature of the place is apparent in its worship schedule and some of its cultural offerings, visitors need not be members of any denomination; all are welcome. There's even a public shuffleboard area for vacationers not interested in the neon carnival attractions several miles up the road. Get an old-fashioned raspberry lime rickey at the Ocean Park Soda Fountain (near the library, at Furber Park); it's also a good place for breakfast or a light lunch. (☎ *207/934–9068 Ocean Park Association*)

☺ **Palace Playland.** Open from mid-April to Labor Day, this amusement park has rides, booths, and a roller coaster that drops almost 50 feet. Every week is the Fourth of July here: each Thursday night in summer, sky-watchers are treated to a fireworks display. Admission to the park is free; ride passes can be purchased individually (about $1.15 per ticket, with rides requiring 2 to 4 tickets); an all-day, unlimited ride pass is about $29. ⊠ *1 Old Orchard St.* ☎ *207/934–2001* ⊕ *www. palaceplayland.com.*

WHERE TO EAT

$$$–$$$$
SEAFOOD
✕ **Joseph's by the Sea.** Large windows frame the ocean opening up beyond the dunes at this fine restaurant, which offers outdoor dining in season. Appetizers may include goat-cheese terrine and lobster potato pancake. Try the grilled Tuscan swordfish or seared sea scallops. Breakfast is also served daily in summer. ⊠ *55 W. Grand Ave., Old Orchard Beach* ☎ *207/934–5044* ⊕ *www.josephsbythesea.com* ▤ *MC, V.*

$$–$$$
ECLECTIC
★
✕ **The Landmark.** This restaurant almost feels as if it doesn't belong here, at least not in this modern transformation of Old Orchard Beach. Tables are set either on the glassed-in porch or within high, tin-ceiling rooms. Candles and a collection of giant fringed Art Nouveau lamps provide a warm, gentle light. The menu has a good selection of seafood and meats, many treated with flavors from various parts of the globe. It's the kind of menu that encourages you to try new things, and you definitely won't be disappointed. Outside on the stone patio and sheltered by umbrellas is the "in the rough" dinner menu, with everything cooked on the adjacent grill. Choose from clambake-style meals, charbroiled and marinated skewers, and BBQ ribs. Coffee and pastries are served out here in the morning. ⊠ *25 E. Grand Ave., Old Orchard Beach* ☎ *207/934–0156* ▤ *AE, D, MC, V* ☺ *Closed late Nov.–Mar.*

$$$
SEAFOOD
✕ **Yellowfin's.** Inside this diminutive restaurant housed in an impeccably kept yellow Victorian, it is fresh, bright, and appropriately beachy. A giant tank bubbles quietly in the background, while its resident colorful fish in the tank survey the landscape of white linen–covered tables adorned with sand and shell centerpieces. White cloth panels draped along the ceiling add an enveloping sense of comfort to the lively space. Not surprisingly, the house specialty is ahi yellowfin tuna, pan seared and treated with a wasabi ginger sauce; other choices include seared scallops, lamb, and a savory seafood fra diavolo. The chicken marsala

2

is a very popular choice here. Brunch is offered on Saturday and Sunday in July and August. In Ocean Park it's BYOB—you'll have to stock up in nearby Old Orchard Beach. ⊠ *5 Temple Ave., Ocean Park* ☎ *207/934–1100* ▤ *D, MC, V* ⊙ *No lunch.*

WHERE TO STAY

$$–$$$ ⚏ **Billow House Inn.** This gracious B&B-motel complex is right behind the beach dunes. All rooms, whether in the motel-style units or within the main 1881 house, are attractively adorned with colorful quilts and ample sitting areas, and have decks so guests can take in the water views. All guests are spoiled with afternoon fresh-baked cookies in their rooms. Other useful amenities include beach chairs, umbrellas, free laundry, and outdoor grills. **Pros:** ideal beachfront location; perfect for travelers who will cook some of their own meals; set within active Ocean Park community—lots of events happening. **Cons:** not for travelers who wish to be in the thick of Old Orchard Beach activity; many rooms accessed via stairs. ⊠ *2 Temple Ave., Ocean Park* ☎ *207/934–2333 or 888/767–7776* ⊕ *www.billowhouse.com* ⇨ *10 rooms, 3 suites* ⚿ *In-room: kitchen (some), refrigerator. In-hotel: beachfront, Wi-Fi* ▤ *AE, D, MC, V* �📱*CP.*

$$–$$$$ ⚏ **Old Orchard Beach Inn.** Dating from 1730, this is Old Orchard Beach's oldest inn. Saved from impending demolition in the late 1990s, the entire place was completely renovated with great care and attention to historic detail. The spacious guest rooms are furnished with antiques, area rugs cover the pine floors, quilts brighten the beds, and lace curtains frame the windows. Many rooms have views over the town and of the shimmering Atlantic beyond. The location is ideal—quiet yet very close to the action in the town center. **Pros:** authentic historic lodging (listed on the National Historic Register), set back off the busy main drag but within short distance from all the action. **Cons:** rooms accessed via steep stairs; not a beachfront location. ⊠ *6 Portland Ave.* ☎ *207/934–5834 or 877/700–6624* ⊕ *www.oldorchardbeachinn.com* ⇨ *17 rooms, 1 suite* ⚿ *In-room: Wi-Fi.* ▤ *AE, D, MC, V* �📱*CP.*

NIGHTLIFE AND THE ARTS

In season, local performers play everything from country and oldies to reggae and rock in Town Square every Monday and Tuesday night at 7. Fireworks light the sky on Thursday night at 9:30 from late June through Labor Day. Concerts by classically trained musicians and choir groups are held most Sunday evenings in Ocean Park. Several bars in Old Orchard Beach feature live bands, dancing, and karaoke.

The community of **Ocean Park** (⊕ *www.oceanpark.org*) has a lively and varied cultural scene. Educational lectures, musical programs and concerts, storytelling, dances, and even yoga classes are offered daily throughout summer. All are welcome; check the Web site or get a copy of their summer program for an event schedule. The home of Salvation Army camp meetings (the Salvation Army has been holding these religious-based meetings in this spot since the late 1800s), the **Old Orchard Beach Pavilion** (⊠ *Union Ave. and 6th St., Old Orchard Beach* ☎ *207/934–2024* ⊕ *www.oobpavilion.org*) also hosts classical concerts including choirs, orchestras, and brass bands from throughout the New England area. Free parking is available.

SPORTS AND THE OUTDOORS

Not far from Old Orchard Beach is the Maine Audubon–run **Scarborough Marsh Nature Center** (⊠ *Pine Point Rd. [Rte. 9], Scarborough* ☎ *207/883–5100* ⊕ *www.maineaudubon.org* 🎟 *Free, guided tours begin at $5* ☉ *Memorial Day–Sept.*). You can rent a canoe and explore this natural haven on your own, or sign up for a guided trip. The salt marsh is Maine's largest and is an excellent place for bird-watching and peaceful paddling along its winding ways. The Nature Center has a discovery room for kids, programs for all ages ranging from basket making to astronomy, birding and canoe tours, and a good gift shop.

Greater Portland

3

WORD OF MOUTH

"Portland is an interesting, small city— classic, old New England architecture, working port, funky little shops, and zillions of coffee shops . . . a nice weekend trip. "

— gail

www.fodors.com/community

Updated by
Sarah Stebbins

Maine's largest city is considered small by national standards—its population is just 64,000—but its character, spirit, and appeal make it feel much larger. In fact, it is a cultural and economic center for a metro area of 230,000 residents—one-quarter of Maine's entire population. Portland and its environs are well worth at least a day or two of exploration.

A city of many names throughout its history, including Casco and Falmouth, Portland has survived many dramatic transformations. Sheltered by the nearby Casco Bay Islands and blessed with a deep port, Portland was a significant settlement right from its start in the early 17th century. Settlers thrived on fishing and lumbering, repeatedly building up the area while the British, French, and American Indians continually sacked it. Many considered the region a somewhat dangerous frontier, but its potential for prosperity was so apparent that settlers came, despite the danger, to tap its rich natural resources.

Portland's first home was built on the peninsula now known as Munjoy Hill in 1632. The British burned the city in 1775, when residents refused to surrender arms, but it was rebuilt and became a major trading center. Much of Portland was destroyed again in the Great Fire on July 4, 1866, when a boy threw a celebration firecracker into a pile of wood shavings; 1,500 buildings burned to the ground. Poet Henry Wadsworth Longfellow said at the time that his city reminded him of the ruins of Pompeii. The Great Fire started not far from where people now wander the cozy streets of the Old Port.

Despite all the calamity and destruction, the city of Portland has always had a great spirit. Each time the city has fallen, its residents have rebuilt—much like a phoenix rising from the ashes.

ORIENTATION AND PLANNING

GETTING ORIENTED

Several distinct neighborhoods reveal the many faces of a city that embraces its history as well as its art, music, and multicultural scenes. The most visited section, the restored Old Port, features a real working waterfront where emblematic lobster boats share ports with modern cruise ships, ferries, and vintage sailing yachts. In spots along Fore, Exchange, and other downtown streets, the asphalt has worn away to reveal the original cobblestones beneath. Stately homes built by ships' captains line the streets of the Western Promenade; artists, artisans, and other small businesses have taken over many formerly abandoned and now renovated redbrick warehouses. The nightlife is active here, with numerous clubs, taverns, and bars pouring out the sounds of live

TOP REASONS TO GO

Natural beauty: Take in iconic views of the rough coastline and bright white sails juxtaposed against a gray-blue sea from the lighthouse at Portland Head Light.

Adventure: Sail to Peaks Island aboard a Casco Bay Lines ferry or take a whale-watching or schooner cruise from Portland Harbor.

History: Experience the style of Colonial Maine at the Tate House, a grand 1775 home built by an English sea captain.

Art: Pay homage to Winslow Homer, Edward Hopper, Andrew Wyeth, and others at the Portland Museum of Art.

Shopping: Gear up for the outdoors at the original L. L. Bean store, which is open 24 hours a day and has everything from sweaters to ski equipment.

3

music and lively patrons. Exceptional restaurants, shops, and galleries, many with locally produced goods, abound here as well. Water tours of the harbor and excursions to the islands of Casco Bay depart from the piers of Commercial Street.

Downtown Portland has emerged from a years-long on-again, off-again funk, during which much retail commerce was lost to shopping malls in the outlying suburbs. Its burgeoning Arts District centers around a revitalized Congress Street, which runs the length of the peninsular city from alongside the Western Promenade in the southwest to the Eastern Promenade on Munjoy Hill in the northeast. Congress Street is peppered with interesting shops, eclectic restaurants, and several excellent museums.

Just beyond the Arts District is the West End, an area of extensive architectural wealth. Predominantly residential, the neighborhood is filled with stunning examples of both the city's historical and economic prominence and its emphasis on preserving this past. A handful of historic homes are open to tours.

PLANNING

WHEN TO GO

Winters are long in Maine, so the city celebrates the warmer months (roughly May through October) with a full schedule of outdoor events, including concerts, farmers' markets, and festivals. The many happenings are testament to this small city's large and lively spirit.

GETTING HERE AND AROUND

Portland is wonderfully walkable; an able-bodied explorer can easily take in the Old Port, the Arts District, and the West End. Narrated trolley tours are also available. However, to discover some of the other areas outlined in this chapter, such as Portland Head Light and Freeport (home of L.L. Bean), a car is necessary. To get to many islands in Casco Bay, hop aboard a waterfront ferry.

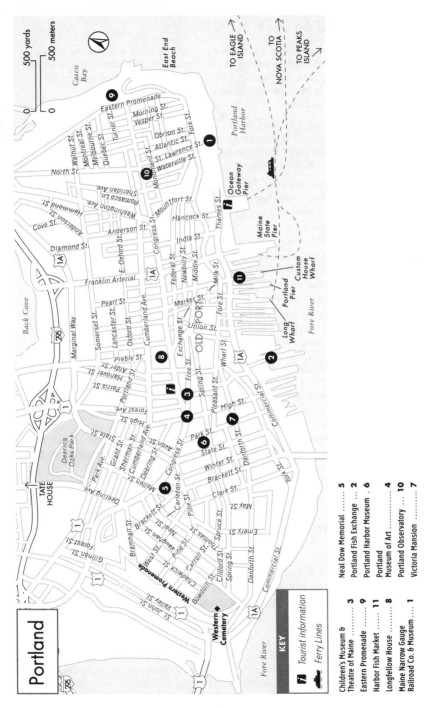

Portland

0   500 yards

0   500 meters

Casco Bay

East End Beach

TO EAGLE ISLAND

TO NOVA SCOTIA

TO PEAKS ISLAND

Eastern Promenade

Morning St.
Vesper St.

Walnut St.
Montreal St.
Melbourne St.
Quebec St.
Turner St.

Obrion St.
Atlantic St.
St. Lawrence St.
Waterville St.
Fore St.
Monument St.

North St.

Romasco Ln.
Washington Ave.
Sheridan St.

Hammond St.
Anderson St.
Cove St.
Diamond St.

Congress St.
Mountfort St.
Hancock St.
India St.

E. Oxford St.
Anderson St.

Franklin Arterial

Pearl St.

Federal St.
Newbury St.
Middle St.

Thames St.

Portland Harbor

Ocean Gateway Pier

Maine State Pier

Custom House Wharf

Portland Pier

Long Wharf

Fore River

Market St.
Union St.
Exchange St.

Somerset St.
Lancaster St.
Oxford St.
Cumberland Ave.

Back Cove

Marginal Way

Preble St.
St. Alder St.
Hanover St.

Parris St.
Portland St.
Forest Ave.

OLD PORT

Spring St.
Free St.

Wharf St.

Commercial St.

High St.

Pleasant St.

Deering Oaks Park

High St.
State St.

Grant St.
Sherman St.
Cumberland Ave.
Deering Ave.
Congress St.

Mellen St.
Carleton St.
Pine St.
Park St.
State St.
Winter St.
Brackett St.
Clark St.

Park Ave.

Bramhall St.
Vaughan St.
Neal St.

Chadwick St.
St. Neal St.
Carroll St.
Thomas St.
Clifford St.
Spring St.

May St.
Emery St.

Danforth St.

York St.

Gilman St.
Forest St.

Deering Ave.

St. John St.
Valley St.

Western Promenade

Western Cemetery

Fore River

KEY

ℹ Tourist information

⛴ Ferry Lines

Children's Museum &
Theatre of Maine **3**
Eastern Promenade **9**
Harbor Fish Market **11**
Longfellow House **8**
Maine Narrow Gauge
Railroad Co. & Museum ... **1**

Neal Dow Memorial **5**
Portland Fish Exchange ... **2**
Portland Harbor Museum . **6**
Portland
Museum of Art **4**
Portland Observatory ... **10**
Victoria Mansion **7**

AIR TRAVEL

Portland International Jetport is served by Air Tran, Continental, Delta, Jet Blue, Northwest, United, and US Airways.

Information Portland International Jetport (⊠ *Westbrook St. off Rte. 9, Portland* ☎ *207/774-7301* ⊕ *www.portlandjetport.org*).

BIKE TRAVEL

The craggy fingers of land that dominate this part of the coast are fun for experienced cyclists to explore, but the lack of shoulders on many roads combined with heavy tourist traffic can be intimidating. Two good resources are the Bicycle Coalition of Maine and the Maine Department of Transportation, which provide information on trails and bike shops around the state.

Information Bicycle Coalition of Maine (✍ *P.O. Box 5275, Augusta 04332* ☎ *207/623-4511* ⊕ *www.bikemaine.org*). **Maine Department of Transportation Explore Maine by Bike** (⊕ *www.exploremaine.org/bike*).

BUS TRAVEL

Greater Portland's Metro runs eight bus routes in Falmouth, Portland, South Portland, and Westbrook. The fare is $1.25; exact change is required. Buses run from 5:30 AM to 11:45 PM.

Bus Stations Portland Transportation Center (☎ *207/828-1151.*).

Bus Lines Concord Coach Lines (☎ *800/639-3317* ⊕ *www.concordcoachlines.com*) **Metro Greater Portland Transit District** (☎ *207/774-0351* ⊕ *www.gpmetrobus.com*).

CAR TRAVEL

Several car-rental options are available at the Portland Jetport; others are dispersed around the South Portland area, just outside the main city limits. ⇨ *See Car Rental in Travel Smart Maine Coast at the back of the book for national rental agency phone numbers.*

Congress Street leads from I–295 into the heart of Portland; the Gateway Garage on High Street, off Congress, is a convenient place to leave your car downtown. North of Portland, U.S. 1 brings you to Freeport's Main Street, which continues on to Brunswick and Bath. East of Wiscasset you can take Route 27 south to the Boothbays, where Route 96 is a good choice for further exploration. To visit the Pemaquid region, take Route 129 off U.S. 1 in Damariscotta; then pick up Route 130 and follow it down to Pemaquid Point. Return to Waldoboro and U.S. 1 on Route 32 from New Harbor.

PARKING   Metered on-street parking is available in Portland at $1 per hour, with a two-hour maximum. Parking lots and garages can be found downtown, in the Old Port, and on the waterfront; most charge $1 per hour or $8–$10 per day. If you're shopping or dining, remember to ask local vendors if they participate in the Park & Shop program, which provides an hour of free parking for each vendor visited.

TAXIS   Though sometimes bustling, Portland is still a small city, so taxis do not rush about as they do in locales that are more populous. Your best bet is to call ahead rather than wait to flag down a driver. Meter rates are $1.90 for the first 1/10 mi, 30¢ for each additional 1/10 mi throughout

Portland. There are also water taxies to get you to and from the islands of Casco Bay. Rates for one-way trips range from $30 to $110, depending on the destination.

Taxi Companies **ABC Taxi** (☎ *207/772–8685*). **ASAP Taxi** (☎ *207/791–2727*). **Elite Taxi** (☎ *207/871–7667*). **Portland Express Water Taxi** (☎ *207/415–8493*). **Presumpscot Water Taxi** (☎ *207/879–2562*).

TRAIN TRAVEL

Amtrak runs the *Downeaster* train service from Boston to Portland, with stops (some seasonal) along the coastal route.

Information **Amtrak** (☎ *800/872–7245* ⊕ *www.amtrakdowneaster.com*).

VISITOR INFORMATION

Contacts **Greater Portland Convention and Visitors Bureau** (✉ *14 Ocean Gateway Pier, off Commercial St., Portland* ☎ *207/772–5800 or 877/833–1374* ⊕ *www.visitportland.com*). **Portland Regional Chamber of Commerce** (✉ *60 Pearl St., Portland* ☎ *207/772–2811* ⊕ *www.portlandregion.com*). **Portland's Downtown District** (✉ *549 Congress St., Portland* ☎ *207/772–6828* ⊕ *www. portlandmaine.com*).

EXPLORING PORTLAND

Numbers in the margin correspond to numbers on the Portland and Around Greater Portland maps.

THE OLD PORT

Fodor's Choice ★ A major international port and a working harbor since the early 17th century, the Old Port bridges the gap between the city's historical commercial activities and those of today. It is home to fishing boats docked alongside whale-watching charters, luxury yachts, cruise ships, and oil tankers from around the globe. Busy Commercial Street parallels the water and is lined with brick buildings and warehouses that were built following the Great Fire of 1866 and intended to last for ages. In the 19th century candle makers and sail stitchers plied their trades here; today specialty shops, art galleries, and restaurants have taken up residence.

As with much of the city, it's best to park your car and explore the Old Port on foot. You can park at the city garage on Fore Street (between Exchange and Union streets) or opposite the U.S. Custom House at the corner of Fore and Pearl streets. A helpful hint: Look for the PARK & SHOP sign on garages and parking lots and get one hour of free parking for each stamp collected at participating shops. Allow a couple of hours to wander at leisure on Market, Exchange, Middle, and Fore streets. The city is very pedestrian-friendly. Maine state law requires vehicles to stop for walkers in crosswalks, and many benches allow for rest and a grand dose of people-watching.

TOP ATTRACTIONS

❶ **Maine Narrow Gauge Railroad Co. & Museum.** Whether you're crazy about
☺ old trains or just want to see the sights from a different perspective,
the railroad museum has long been delighting people with its extensive
collection of locomotives and rail coaches and tours on original narrow
gauge railcars. The three-mile jaunt takes you along Casco Bay, at the
foot of the Eastern Promenade. Theme trips include the Polar Express
ride, based on the popular children's book, a Halloween ride (wear your
costumes), and a July 4th fireworks ride. ⌧ *58 Fore St.* ☎ *207/828–0814*
⊕ *www.mngrr.org* ⌕ *Train $10, museum $2* ☺ *Trains mid-May–mid-
Oct., daily on the hr 11–4; mid-Feb.–mid-May and mid-Oct.–mid-Nov.,
weekends on the hr 11–3* PM. *Museum late-Oct.–mid May, weekdays
10–4; late May–late Oct., daily 10–4.*

❷ **Portland Fish Exchange.** For a lively and sensory-filled (you may want to
hold your nose) glimpse into the Old Port's active fish business, drop
by the 30,000-square-foot Portland Fish Exchange. Peek inside coolers
teeming with cod, flounder, and monkfish, watch fishermen repairing
their nets and prices being settled through an auction process. It's a
great behind-the-scenes view of this dynamic market. Auctions take
place Sunday at 11 AM and Monday through Thursday at noon. ⌧ *6
Portland Fish Pier* ☎ *207/773–0017* ⊕ *www.pfex.org* ⌕ *Free.*

⓫ **Harbor Fish Market.** A Portland favorite for more than 40 years, this
freshest-of-the-fresh seafood market ships lobsters and other Maine
delectables almost anywhere in the country from its location on a working wharf. A bright-red façade opens into a bustling space with bubbling
lobster pens and fish, clams, and other shellfish on ice; employees are
as skilled with a fillet knife as a sushi chef. ⌧ *9 Custom House Wharf*
☎ *207/775–0251 or 800/370–1790* ⊕ *www.harborfish.com* ⌕ *Free.*

THE ARTS DISTRICT

This district starts at the top of Exchange Street, near the upper end of
the Old Port, and extends west past the Portland Museum of Art. Congress Street is the district's central artery. Much of Portland's economic
heart is here, including several large banking and law firms. It's also
where Maine College of Art and the Portland Public Library make their
homes. Art galleries, specialty stores, and a score of restaurants line
Congress Street. Parking is tricky; two-hour meters dot the sidewalks,
but there are several nearby parking garages.

TOP ATTRACTIONS

❸ **Children's Museum & Theatre of Maine.** Touching is okay at Portland's
☺ relatively small but fun Children's Museum, where kids can pretend
they are lobstermen, veterinarians, shopkeepers, or actors in a play. The
majority of the museum's exhibits, many of which have a Maine theme,
are best for children 10 and younger. Camera Obscura, an exhibit about
optics, provides fascinating panoramic views of the city. The museum's
newest addition, Have a Ball! teaches about the science of motion,
letting kids build ramps that make balls speed up, slow down, and
leap across tracks. ⌧ *142 Free St.* ☎ *207/828–1234* ⊕ *www.kitetails.
org* ⌕ *Museum $8; Camera Obscura only, $4* ☺ *Memorial Day–Labor*

GREAT ITINERARIES

Numbers in the text correspond to numbers in the margin and on the Portland map.

IF YOU HAVE 1 DAY

Spend the morning wandering the streets and shops of the **Old Port**. Break for a harborside lunch along Commercial Street. In the afternoon, hit the museums in the **Arts District**. Architecture buffs will want to take a drive or stroll through the **West End** neighborhood. End the day with a drive up Congress Street to the **Eastern Promenade** for sweeping hilltop views of **Casco Bay**.

IF YOU HAVE 3 DAYS

Spend your first day in the **Old Port** and the Arts District. Art lovers will want several hours inside the **Portland Museum of Art ❹**; families should visit the **Children's Museum of Maine ❸**. Take an hour or so to walk the **West End** neighborhood, with its stunning Colonial Revival and Victorian homes, then head to Hadlock Field for a baseball game or spend the night downtown. On your second day, take a morning boat ride to **Eagle Island** or another to Casco Bay island. In the afternoon, drive to **Cape Elizabeth** and visit Portland Head Light and Two Lights. Return to Portland for the night. On your third day, head north to **Freeport**, where you can shop at various outlets and L.L. Bean.

IF YOU HAVE 5 DAYS

Spend your first two days in Portland. Be sure to linger in the **Old Port** and stroll through the architectural splendor of the **West End**. You can leave your car at your hotel for both days and easily get around on foot. See the islands via a Casco Bay Lines ferry, vintage schooner, whale-watch or other themed cruise, or a sportfishing adventure.

On Day 3 take a ferry to **Peaks Island** and prepare to relax. You'll have left your car in Portland; rent a bicycle on the island to explore its quiet streets; take a guided kayak trip; or sign up with a golf-cart tour. Spend a peaceful night here. On Day 4 return to Portland and head out in your car for several hours of touring, including a visit to nearby **Cape Elizabeth** to see Portland Head Light. The park is a great place for a picnic lunch. Continue your scenic drive, stopping at several state parks for hiking and beach-combing, before making your way to **Prouts Neck**. Here you can stroll along the Cliff Walk and visit Winslow Homer's home and studio. Head back to the interstate and continue north to **Freeport**. Have dinner here and spend the night—but not before midnight shopping at L.L. Bean. Spend Day 5 browsing the outlets, hiking through Wolfe's Neck Woods State Park, or taking a scenic harbor cruise.

Day, Mon.–Sat. 10–5, Sun. noon–5; day after Labor Day–day before Memorial Day, Tues.–Sat. 10–5, Sun. noon–5.

❽ **Longfellow House.** The boyhood home of the famous American poet is one of the first brick houses in Portland. It's particularly interesting because most of the furnishings, including French Rococo-Revival wallpaper, a vibrant painted carpet, and the young Longfellow's writing desk, are original. The Colonial Revival structure, built in 1785, sits back from the street and has a small portico over its entrance and four chimneys surmounting the roof. The house is part of the Maine Historical Society, which includes an adjacent museum with exhibits about Maine life and a research library. After your guided tour of the home, stay for a picnic in the Longfellow Garden, designed from period sketches. ⊠ *489 Congress St.* ☎ *207/774–1822* ⊕ *www.mainehistory. org* ⊟ *house and Maine Historical Society Museum, $8; museum only, $5; garden, free* ☉ *House and Maine Historical Society Museum: May–Oct., Mon.–Sat. 10–5, Sun. noon–5; last tour at 4. Nov. and Dec., call for hrs. Library: year-round, Tues.–Sat. 10–4.*

3

❻ **Portland Harbor Museum.** Immerse yourself in Portland's deep maritime
♨ history at this small yet thoughtfully executed museum. There's a pink room with an exhibit about Rosie the Riveter types: women who went to work as mechanics, crane operators, and electricians in the Portland shipyard during World War II. Another exhibit is devoted to the steamship known as New England's "Titanic," which sank in an 1898 storm, taking 175 people with it. You'll also find vintage postcards depicting coastal scenes, with their inscriptions transcribed on the wall, photography by local artists, and plenty of model ships, historical maps, and marine artifacts. ⊠ *510 Congress St.* ☎ *207/773–3800* ⊕ *www. portlandharbormuseum.org* ⊟ *$3* ☉ *mid-May–mid-Oct., daily 10–4; after mid-Oct., call for hours.*

❹ **Portland Museum of Art.** Maine's largest public art institution has a num-
★ ber of strong collections, including fine seascapes and landscapes by Winslow Homer, John Marin, Andrew Wyeth, Edward Hopper, Marsden Hartley, and other painters. Homer's *Weatherbeaten,* a quintessential Maine Coast image, is here, and the museum owns and displays more than 20 of his other works. The Joan Whitney Payson Collection of impressionist and postimpressionist art includes works by Monet, Picasso, and Renoir. Harry N. Cobb, an associate of I. M. Pei, designed the strikingly modern Charles Shipman Payson building. The nearby L.D.M. Sweat Galleries house the museum's 19th-century American art collection, and the 1801 McLellan House has gorgeous Federal design and interactive educational stations. ⊠ *7 Congress Sq.* ☎ *207/775–6148* ⊕ *www.portlandmuseum.org* ⊟ *$10, free Fri. 5–9* ☉ *Memorial Day–Columbus Day, Mon.–Thurs. and weekends 10–5, Fri. 10–9; Columbus Day–Memorial Day, Tues.–Thurs. and weekends 10–5, Fri. 10–9.*

❼ **Victoria Mansion.** Built between 1858 and 1860, this Italianate-style man-
★ sion is widely regarded as the most sumptuously ornamented dwelling of its period remaining in the country. Architect Henry Austin designed the house for hotelier Ruggles Morse and his wife Olive. The interior design—everything from the plasterwork to the furniture (much of it original)—is the only surviving commission of New York designer Gustave Herter. Behind the elegant brownstone exterior of this National Historic Landmark are colorful frescoed walls and ceilings, ornate marble mantelpieces, gilded gas chandeliers, a magnificent 6-foot by 25-foot stained-glass ceiling window, and a freestanding mahogany staircase. Guided tours run about 45 minutes and cover all the architectural highlights. During the Christmas season the rooms in the mansion are richly decorated by local interior decorators and florists to reflect the opulence and elegance of the Victorian era. ⊠ *109 Danforth St.* ☎ *207/772–4841*

⊕ *www.victoriamansion.org* ✉ *$15* ⊘ *May–Oct., Mon.–Sat. 10–4, Sun. 1–5; Christmas tours day after Thanksgiving—Jan. 3, daily 11–5.*

WORTH NOTING

9 **Eastern Promenade.** Of the two promenades, this one, often overlooked by tourists who flock to the western end of the city, has by far the best view. Gracious Victorian homes border one side of the street; on the other is a 68-acre hillside park that slopes down to the water. At the base of the hill are the Eastern Prom Trail, a great place for walking or cycling, and the tiny East End Beach. On a sunny day the park is a lovely spot for picnicking and people-watching. ⊠ *Congress St. and Eastern Promenade.*

5 **Neal Dow Memorial.** Now the headquarters of the Maine Women's Christian Temperance Union, this majestic 1829 Federal-style home is open for tours. The mansion, once a stop on the Underground Railroad, is filled with the Civil War general's original antiques, books, and papers on prohibition—the mission that gave him fame as the man responsible for Maine's adoption of the anti-alcohol bill in 1851. ⊠ *714 Congress St.* ☎ *207/773–7773* ✉ *Free* ⊘ *Weekdays 11–4 or by appointment.*

10 **Portland Observatory.** This octagonal observatory on Munjoy Hill was built in 1807 by Captain Lemuel Moody, a retired sea captain, as a signal tower. Moody used a telescope to identify incoming ships and flags to signal to merchants where to unload their cargo. It is the last remaining signal tower in the country, and is held in place by 122 tons of ballast. After visiting the small museum at the base, you can climb to the Orb deck and take in views of Portland, the islands, and inland to the White Mountains. ⊠ *138 Congress St.* ☎ *207/774–5561* ⊕ *www. portlandlandmarks.org* ✉ *$7* ⊘ *Memorial Day weekend–Columbus Day, daily 10–5.*

OFF THE BEATEN PATH

★ **Tate House.** This magnificent house fully conjures up the style—even high style—of Colonial Maine. Built astride rose granite steps and a period herb garden overlooking the Stroudwater River on the outskirts of Portland, the 1755 house was built by Captain George Tate. Tate had been commissioned by the English Crown to organize "the King's Broad Arrow"—the marking and cutting down of gigantic forest trees, which were transported overland to water and sent to England to be fashioned as masts for the British Royal Navy. The house has several period rooms, including a sitting room with some fine English Restoration chairs. With its clapboard still gloriously unpainted, its impressive Palladian doorway, dogleg stairway, unusual clerestory, and gambrel roof, this house will delight all lovers of Early American decorative arts. Guided tours of the gardens are held once a week from mid-June to mid-October. House tours are offered five days a week in season. Call or visit the Web site for special holiday programs during December. ⊠ *1267 Westbrook St.* ☎ *207/774–6177* ⊕ *www.tatehouse.org* ✉ *$7* ⊘ *Mid-June–mid-Oct., call for hrs.*

TAKE A TOUR

AUTO TOURS

To see the sights from land and sea, book a tour with **Downeast Duck Adventures** (⊠ *Long Wharf, 177 Commercial St.* ☎ *207/774–3825* ⊕ *www.downeastducktours.com*) Memorial Day through mid-October, an amphibious, boat-shape vehicle will drive you to the major landmarks in town, then plunge into the water for a cruise around Portland Harbor. The informative trolley tours of **Portland Discovery Land & Sea Tours** (⊠ *Long Wharf, 170 Commercial St.* ☎ *207/774–0808* ⊕ *www.portlanddiscovery.com*) detail Portland's historical and architectural highlights from Memorial Day through October. Options include combining a city tour with a bay cruise or a trip to four lighthouses.

WALKING TOURS

Learn about Portland's culinary history and sample local delights like lobster hors d'oeuvres, organic cheese, and the famous Maine whoopie pie, with **Maine Foodie Tours** (⊠ *Kiosk at 10 Moulton St.* ☎ *207/233–7485* ⊕ *www.mainefoodietours.com*). You also can sign up for a pub-crawl, a tour of microbreweries, or a "destination" trip to nearby farms and bakeries. Tours operate year-round; prices start at $29. **Greater Portland Landmarks** (⊠ *93 High St.* ☎ *207/774–5561* ⊕ *www.portlandlandmarks.org*) conducts 1½-hour walking tours of the Old Port from July through September; tours begin at the visitor's kiosk at **Tommy's Park** (⊠ *corner of Middle and Exchange St.*) and cost $10. The group also offers self-guided tours of the Old Port, Congress Street, historic churches, the West End, and other spots. Pick up maps and itineraries at their offices (a small fee is charged) or download them for free online.**Portland Freedom Trail** (☎ *207/591–9980* ⊕ *www.portlandfreedomtrail.org*) provides a self-guided tour, available for free download online, of sites associated with the Underground Railroad and the anti-slavery movement.

3

THE WEST END

A leisurely walk through Portland's West End, beginning at the top of the Arts District, offers a real treat to historic architecture buffs. Elaborate building began in the mid-1800s, encouraged by both a robust economy and Portland's devastating fire of 1866, which leveled nearly one-third of the city. The neighborhood, on the National Register of Historic Places, reveals an extraordinary display of architectural splendor, from High Victorian Gothic to lush Italianate, Queen Anne, and Colonial Revival.

A good place to start is at the head of the Western Promenade, which has parking, benches, and a nice view. From the Old Port, take Danforth Street all the way up to Vaughn Street; take a right and then an immediate left onto Western Promenade. You pass by the Western Cemetery, Portland's second official burial ground, laid out in 1829 (inside is the ancestral plot of famous poet Henry Wadsworth Longfellow); just beyond that is the parking area. Once on foot, you can happily get lost on side streets, each lined with statuesque homes.

You could easily spend an hour or two wandering the backstreets of the West End; longer if you bring a picnic to enjoy in the grassy park alongside the Promenade. If you're interested in the particular history of individual homes, download or pick up a brochure from **Greater Portland Landmarks.** A map is included, as well as the stories of some of the more prominent homes. The group also offers a guided house tour on Friday mornings, July through September. ⊠ *93 High St.* ☎ *207/774–5561* ☺ *Mon.–Fri., 9–5* ⊕ *www.portlandlandmarks.org.*

WHERE TO EAT

Despite its small size, Portland is blessed with a variety of exceptional restaurants and cuisines rivaling that of a far larger city. One reason for this is Maine's highly desirable quality of life, which attracts fine chefs who appreciate the intimacy and character of the downtown and the availability of fine local ingredients.

Fresh seafood, including the famous Maine lobster, is still understandably popular and prevalent, but there are plenty more cuisines to be enjoyed. More and more restaurants are using local meats, seafood, and produce as much as possible, buying outside the area only when necessary; changing menus reflect what is available in the region at the moment. As sophisticated as many of these establishments have become, the atmosphere is generally quite casual; with few exceptions, you can leave your jacket and tie at home.

Smoking is banned in all restaurants, taverns, and bars in Portland. As always, reservations are recommended and allowed unless we state otherwise.

WHAT IT COSTS					
	¢	$	$$	$$$	$$$$
At dinner	under $7	$7–$10	$11–$17	$18–$25	over $25

Restaurant prices are for a median main course at dinner, excluding 7% tax.

$ ✕ **Becky's.** You won't find a more local or unfussy place—or one that is
AMERICAN   more abuzz with conversation at 4 AM—than this waterfront institution, way down on the end of Commercial Street. Sitting next to you at the counter or in a neighboring booth could be rubber-booted fishermen back from sea, college students soothing a hangover, or suited business folks with Blackberries. The food is cheap, generous in proportion, and has that satisfying, old-time diner quality. Breakfast and lunch are served from 4 AM to 9 PM; dinner is available from 4 PM until closing. Nightly specials add to the large menu of fried seafood platters, salads, and sandwiches. Get a pie, cake, or pudding to go. ⊠ *390 Commercial St.* ☎ *207/773–7070* ⊕ *www.beckysdiner.com* ▭ *AE, D, MC, V.*

$–$$ ✕ **The Corner Room.** Eating at this comfy, unassuming place, you feel like
ITALIAN   you're in someone's (large, immaculate) kitchen. And in fact you are. Chef-owner Harding Lee Smith can often be glimpsed behind one of the exposed workstations with pots hanging overhead. The latest restaurant

in Smith's Portland oeuvre (grab a card when you come in and check out his two other ventures, as well), it encompasses the Italian triumvirate of pizza, pasta, and panini, plus classic *secondi* like chicken parmigiano. Order a smaller, "traditional size" pasta (the eggplant ravioli with goat cheese is divine) so you can load up on *antipasti* (clams in a buttery tomato broth; marinated mushrooms) and gelato. ⊠ *110 Exchange St.* ☎ *207/879–4747* ⊕ *www.hardingleesmith.com* ▭ *AE, D, MC, V* ⊙ *No lunch weekends* ⚇ *Reservations not accepted.*

$
MEXICAN
★
✕ **El Rayo Taqueria.** For the best Mexican food in town, head slightly out of your way to this hip joint housed in a former gas station on an industrial stretch above Commercial Street. The flavors here are as vibrant as the turquoise, yellow, and fuchsia decor. All of the salsas and guacamole are made fresh daily. Pull up a stool at the counter, sit at a table inside, or grab a bright, oilcloth-covered picnic table out front. Wash down achiote-seasoned fish tacos or a citrus-and-cumin-marinated chicken burrito with a virgin lemon-hibiscus *refresco* or house margarita and forget about feeding the meter—there's plenty of parking in the old filling-station lot. ⊠ *101 York St. (at High St.)* ☎ *207/780–8226* ⊕ *www.elrayotaqueria.com* ▭ *AE, D, MC, V* ⊙ *Closed Mon.*

$$$–$$$$
AMERICAN
Fodor's Choice
★
✕ **Five Fifty-Five.** Classic dishes are cleverly updated at this cozy Congress Street spot. The ubiquitous lobster roll, dubbed a "knuckle sandwich," consists of meat tossed with basil aioli and sandwiched between fried-green-tomato "bread"; the mac and cheese boasts artisanal cheeses and shaved black truffle. The menu changes seasonally (and sometimes daily) to reflect ingredients available within a 30-mi radius, but the seared local diver scallops, served in a buttery carrot-vanilla emulsion, are a mainstay—they are exquisite. The space, which features exposed brick and warm copper accents, is a former nineteenth-century firehouse. From a seat on the narrow balcony you can picture firefighters sliding down poles to the lower level—now an open kitchen and dining area. ⊠ *555 Congress St.* ☎ *207/761–0555* ⊕ *www.fivefifty-five.com* ▭ *AE, MC, V* ⊙ *No lunch Mon.–Sat.*

$–$$
PIZZA
☼
★
✕ **Flatbread Company.** Families, students, and bohemian types gather at this popular pizza place, known locally as "Flatbread's." A giant wood-fire oven, where the pies are cooked, is the heart of the soaring, warehouse-like space; in summer you can escape the heat by dining on the deck overlooking the harbor. The simple menu has eight signature pizzas plus weekly veggie and meat specials; everything is homemade, organic, and nitrate-free. Be sure to order the delicious house salad with toasted sesame seeds, seaweed, blue or goat cheese, and ginger-tamarind vinaigrette—you can try to re-create it at home, but trust us, it won't be the same. ⊠ *72 Commercial St.* ☎ *207/772–8777* ⊕ *www. flatbreadcompany.com* ▭ *AE, MC, V* ⚇ *Reservations not accepted for parties of fewer than 10.*

$$$–$$$$
AMERICAN
★
✕ **Fore Street.** One of Maine's best chefs, Sam Hayward, opened this restaurant in a renovated, airy warehouse on the edge of the Old Port. The menu changes daily to reflect the freshest local ingredients available. Every copper-top table in the main dining room has a view of the enormous brick oven and hearth and the open kitchen, where sous-chefs seem to dance as they create entrées such as three cuts of Maine island

lamb, Atlantic monkfish fillet, and breast of Moulad duckling. Desserts include artisanal cheeses. Reservations are strongly recommended—in fact, if you want to dine in July or August, book two months in advance, and a week or more at other times. Last-minute planners take heart: each night a third of the tables are reserved for walk-in diners. ⊠ *288 Fore St.* ☎ *207/775–2717* ⊕ *www.forestreet.biz* ⊟ *AE, MC, V* ⊗ *No lunch.*

$$-$$$
SEAFOOD
★

✕ **Gilbert's Chowder House.** This is the real deal, as quintessential as Maine dining can be. Clam rakes and nautical charts hang from the walls of this unpretentious waterfront diner. The flavors are from the depths of the North Atlantic, prepared and presented simply: fish, clam, corn and seafood chowders; fried shrimp; haddock; clam strips; and extraordinary clam cakes. A chalkboard of daily specials often features Alaskan king crab legs and various entrée and chowder combinations. Don't miss out on the lobster roll—a toasted hot-dog bun bursting with claw and tail meat lightly dressed with mayo but otherwise unadulterated. It sits on a leaf of lettuce, but who needs more? It's classic Maine, fuss-free and presented on a paper plate. ⊠ *92 Commercial St.* ☎ *207/871–5636* ⊕ *www.gilbertschowderhouse.com* ⊟ *D, MC, V.*

$$$$
ECLECTIC
★

✕ **Hugo's.** James Beard Award–winning chef-owner Rob Evans has turned Hugo's into one of the city's best restaurants. The warmly lighted dining room is small and open, yet you can hold a conversation without raising your voice. If you're adventurous, the six-course "blind-tasting" ($85 per person) is a lot of fun—you literally don't know what you're going to be served. You also can mix and match $10 to $20 items from the à la carte menu, such as roasted rib eye and crispy arctic char with seaweed slaw. Keep in mind that portions are small, as they're meant to be part of a four- to six-course meal. Serving the freshest local, organic foods is a high priority here, so the menu changes almost every day. ⊠ *88 Middle St.* ☎ *207/774–8538* ⊕ *www.hugos.net* ⊟ *AE, MC, V* ⊗ *Closed Sun. and Mon. No lunch.*

$$-$$$
SPANISH

✕ **Local 188.** As the name suggests, this funky Arts District eatery is a local favorite. Many diners don't bother with the menu, which is deliberately vague, and instead wait for their server to explain what just-caught seafood will decorate the paella and which fresh veggies are starring in the tortilla tapa. The vibe inside the 3,000-square-foot space, with its lofty tin ceilings and worn maple floors, is relaxed and slightly quirky—mismatched chandeliers dangle over the dining area

---

**WHAT'S ON TAP:
MICROBREWERIES**

Maine is home to more than 20 breweries, and several of the larger ones—Allagash Brewing, D.L. Geary Brewing, and Shipyard Brewing to name a few—are near or within Portland. These breweries are all open for tours and tastings. But beer lovers may prefer the intimate settings of the smaller brewpubs that make their own beer and serve it fresh from their own taps in neighborhood taverns. In the Old Port you'll find Gritty McDuff's and Sebago Brewing Company. In South Portland there's Sea Dog Brewing Company. If you're in town in November, check out the Maine Brewer's Festival (⊕ *www.mainebrew.com*).

and a pair of antlers crowns the open kitchen. This is also a popular spot to come for a drink. Sink into a comfy couch in the bar area and choose from 150 mostly European wines. ⊠ *685 Congress St.* ☎ *207/761–7909* ⊕ *www.local188.com* ☰ *AE, D, MC, V* ⊗ *No lunch weekdays.*

$$$–$$$$
SEAFOOD ✕ **Street and Co.** Mediterranean-style fish and seafood are the specialties at this Old Port establishment. Locals will ask to sit in either the "city"—the main dining room with a view of the open kitchen—or the "burbs," the quieter back room. You dine amid dried herbs and shelves of staples, at a copper-top table (so your waiter can place a skillet of sizzling seafood directly in front of you). The daily specials are usually a good bet, though pasta dishes are popular (garlic and olive-oil lovers rejoice; they're loaded with both). Listen to your server—chances are your plate is indeed very, very hot. ⊠ *33 Wharf St.* ☎ *207/775–0887* ⊕ *www.streetandcompany.net* ☰ *AE, MC, V* ⊗ *No lunch.*

$$–$$$$
AMERICAN ✕ **Walter's Cafe.** A fixture in the Old Port for more than 20 years, this casual, busy place is popular with suits and tourists alike. The menu manages a good balance of local seafood and meats with Asian and more eclectic flavors. Begin with calamari dressed with lemon–cherry pepper aioli; then move on to salmon marinated in miso sake or grilled duck breast with green-chili corn fritters. ⊠ *2 Portland Sq.* ☎ *207/871–9258* ⊕ *www.walterscafe.com* ☰ *AE, MC, V* ⊗ *No lunch Sun.*

WHERE TO STAY

As Portland's popularity as a vacation destination has increased, so have its options for overnight visitors. Though several large hotels—geared toward high-tech, amenity-obsessed guests—have been built in the Old Port, they have in no way diminished the success of smaller, more intimate lodgings, of which there are plenty. Inns and B&Bs have taken up residence throughout the city, often giving new life to the grand mansions of Portland's 19th-century wealthy businessmen. For the least-expensive accommodations, investigate the chain hotels near the interstate and the airport.

You can expect to pay from about $140 a night for a pleasant room (often with complimentary breakfast) within walking distance of the Old Port during high season, and up to more than $400 for the most luxurious of suites. In the height of the summer season many places are booked; make reservations well in advance, and ask about off-season specials.

WHAT IT COSTS					
	¢	$	$$	$$$	$$$$
For two people	under $60	$60–$99	$100–$149	$150–$200	over $200

Hotel prices are for two people in a standard double room, excluding service charges and 7% tax.

$$$$ ⚏ **Danforth Inn.** New ownership and extensive redecorating have transformed a once-shabby 1823 inn with grandmotherly decor into a stunning showpiece. It stands on a block known in the early 19th century as

"Social Corners" for the elaborate parties the owners hosted in what is now the downstairs lounge area. Updated with modern furnishings in coffee and cream shades, the space has a glamorous, Old Hollywood feel: you almost expect a young Elizabeth Taylor to come waltzing through the double doors. The guest rooms are individually decorated with vibrant patterns and original artwork; most have working fireplaces. Room 3, with its semi-circle design, bank of windows, and crystal chandelier over the bed, is exquisite. **Pros:** boutique hotel experience minutes from downtown. **Cons:** some third-floor rooms have very small windows. ⊠ *163 Danforth St.* ☎ *207/879–8755 or 800/991–6557* ⊕ *www.danforthmaine.com* ⊃ *9 rooms, 1 suite* ⚿ *In-room: no phone, DVD (some), Wi-Fi. In-hotel: Wi-Fi, parking (free), no kids under 16* ▭ *AE, MC, V* ⏀ *BP.*

$$–$$$ ⊞ **The Inn at Park Spring.** The husband and wife who own this small, comfortable town-house inn pride themselves on the fact that many of their guests have been returning for more than 30 years. They come for the reasonable rates, delicious, satisfying breakfast (think stuffed ham-and-cheese croissant or savory French toast with poached egg), and fabulous location: it's a less than five-minute walk to the Arts District and 10 minutes to Exchange Street. You can also spend a pleasant evening right here. Pick up a bottle of wine at the West End Deli downstairs and head a few doors down to Miyake (⊠ *129 Spring St.* ☎ *207/871–9170*), a tiny BYOB place, for inventive, phenomenally fresh sushi. **Pros:** fenced-in courtyard is lovely on a sunny day. **Cons:** no-frills decor; some rooms need to be updated. ⊠ *135 Spring St.* ☎ *207/774–1059 or 800/437–8511* ⊕ *www.innatparkspring.com* ⊃ *6 rooms* ⚿ *In-room: no TV, Wi-Fi. In-hotel: Internet terminal, Wi-Fi, parking (free)* ▭ *AE, D, DC, MC, V* ⏀ *BP.*

$$$–$$$$ ⊞ **Pomegranate Inn.** The classic facade of this handsome 1884 inn in
Fodor'sChoice the architecturally rich Western Promenade area gives no hint of the
★ surprises within. The common spaces have who-would-have-thunk-it combinations like bright faux-marble walls, a painted checkerboard floor, and leopard-print runner; most of the guest rooms are hand-painted with splashy florals or polka dots (look for the hidden signature of the artist). The inn feels a bit like a gallery, with almost every available surface covered with original contemporary art. (The paintings on the second floor are on loan from Portland's Cygnet Gallery and available for sale.) Somehow it all comes together, creating a whimsical, outrageous, and wonderful effect. **Pros:** heaven for art connoisseurs; close to Western Promenade. **Cons:** not within easy walking distance of Old Port. ⊠ *49 Neal St.* ☎ *207/772–1006 or 800/356–0408* ⊕ *www.pomegranateinn.com* ⊃ *8 rooms* ⚿ *In-room: no phone, Wi-Fi. In-hotel: Wi-Fi, parking (free), some pets allowed, no kids under 16* ▭ *AE, MC, V* ⏀ *BP.*

$$$$ ⊞ **Portland Harbor Hotel.** Making luxury its primary focus, the Harbor Hotel has become a favorite with business travelers seeking meetings on a more intimate scale and vacationing guests who want high-quality service and amenities. Book a massage or pedicure at the on-site Nine Stones spa. In season, eat on the enclosed garden patio. **Pros:** luxurious extras; amid the action of the Old Port and waterfront. **Cons:** not

for the quaint of heart. ⊠ *468 Fore St.* ☎ *207/775–9090 or 888/798–9090*⊕ *www.portlandharborhotel.com* ⤳ *88 rooms, 18 suites* ⚷ *In-room: Wi-Fi. In-hotel: restaurant, bar, gym, spa, bicycles, laundry service, Internet terminal, Wi-Fi, parking (paid), some pets allowed* ⊟ *AE, D, MC, V.*

$$$$ 🔲 **Portland Regency Hotel and Spa.** One of just a handful of major hotels in the center of the Old Port, the brick Regency building was Portland's armory in the late 19th century. Some of the traditionally furnished rooms have four-poster beds, and all have tall standing mirrors, desks, flat-screens, and terry robes. You can walk to shops, restaurants, and museums from the hotel. The full-service spa offers a variety of massage treatments, a sea-salt body polish, a seaweed wrap, an herb-and-fruit-infused facial, and even eyelash tinting! **Pros:** convenient to town; has all the amenities you'd want. **Cons:** some rooms on the third and fourth floors have low ceilings and no windows (there are skylights, however). ⊠ *20 Milk St.* ☎ *207/774–4200 or 800/727–3436* ⊕ *www.theregency.com* ⤳ *84 rooms, 11 suites* ⚷ *In-room: Wi-Fi. In-hotel: restaurant, bar, gym, spa, laundry service, Wi-Fi, parking (paid)* ⊟ *AE, D, DC, MC, V.*

$$$–$$$$ 🔲 **West End Inn.** Set among the glorious aged homes of the Western Promenade, this 1871 house displays much of the era's Victorian grandeur, with high tin ceilings, intricate moldings and ceiling medallions, and a dramatic ruby-red foyer. Spacious rooms are either brightly painted or papered with traditional Waverly prints, and all have private baths and alarm clocks with MP3 docks. For breakfast, innkeeper Beth Oliver often whips up a French toast casserole with blueberries and cream cheese; or sausage and herb quiche with a hash-brown crust. Oliver is also a fountain of Portland knowledge, and will cheerfully field questions, make reservations, and gently remind you to wear your walking shoes—it's a 20-minute stroll to the action downtown. **Pros:** elegant library with fireplace is a cozy place to relax. **Cons:** one room uses a bathroom across the hall. ⊠ *146 Pine St.* ☎ *207/772–1377 or 800/338–1377* ⊕ *www.westendbb.com* ⤳ *6 rooms* ⚷ *In-room: no phone, Wi-Fi. In-hotel: Wi-Fi, parking (free), no kids under 16* ⊟ *AE, MC, V* ⑩ *BP.*

NIGHTLIFE AND THE ARTS

NIGHTLIFE

Portland's nightlife scene is largely centered around the bustling Old Port and a few smaller, artsy spots on Congress Street. There's a great emphasis on local, live music and pubs serving award-winning local microbrews. Big, raucous dance clubs are few, but darkened taverns and lively bars (smoke-free by law) pulse with the sounds of rock, blues, alternative, and folk tunes. Several hip wine bars have cropped up, serving appetizers along with a full array of specialty wines and whimsical cocktails. It's a fairly youthful scene in Portland, in some spots even rowdy and rough around the edges, but there are plenty of places where you don't have to shout over the din to be heard.

Asylum (✉ *121 Center St.* ☎ *207/772–8274* ⊕ *www.portlandasylum. com*) oozes with live entertainment and dancing on two levels; it books local and regional rock, pop, and hip-hop groups. There's also a sports bar. To see live local and national acts any night of the week, try **The Big Easy** (✉ *55 Market St.* ☎ *207/775–2266* ⊕ *www.bigeasyportland. com*). For nightly themed brew specials, plenty of Guinness, and live entertainment, head to **Bull Feeney's** (✉ *375 Fore St.* ☎ *207/773–7210* ⊕ *www.bullfeeneys.com*), a lively two-story Irish pub and restaurant. **Gritty McDuff's** (✉ *396 Fore St.* ☎ *207/772–2739* ⊕ *www.grittys.com*) brews fine ales and serves British pub fare and seafood dishes. At **Novare Res Bier Café** (✉ *4 Canal Plaza, Exchange St. between Middle St. and Fore St.* ☎ *207/761–2437* ⊕ *www.novareresbiercafe.com*), choose from 25 rotating drafts and more than 300 bottled brews, relax on an expansive deck, and munch on antipasti. Happening Irish pub and restaurant **Ri Ra** (✉ *72 Commercial St.* ☎ *207/761–4446* ⊕ *www.rira.com*) has live music Thursday through Saturday nights; for a mellower experience, settle into a couch at the upstairs bar. **Space Gallery** (✉ *538 Congress St.* ☎ *207/828–5600* ⊕ *www.space538.org*) sparkles as a contemporary art gallery and alternative arts venue, opening its doors to everything from poetry readings to live music and documentary film showings.

THE ARTS

Art galleries and studios have spread throughout the city, infusing with new life many abandoned yet beautiful old buildings and shops. Many are concentrated along the Congress Street downtown corridor; others are hidden amid the boutiques and restaurants of the Old Port and the East End. A great way to get acquainted with the city's artists is to participate in the First Friday Art Walk, a self-guided, free tour of galleries, museums, and alternative art venues happening, you guessed it, on the first Friday of each month. Brochures and maps are available on the organization's Web site: *www.firstfridayartwalk.com.*

In summer, several organizations sponsor outdoor entertainment, including a concert series. Portland is also home to a handful of talented professional and community theater groups that hit the stage year-round.

Cumberland County Civic Center (✉ *1 Civic Center Sq.* ☎ *207/775–3458* ⊕ *www.theciviccenter.com*) hosts concerts, sporting events, and family shows. **Merrill Auditorium** (✉ *20 Myrtle St.* ☎ *207/842–0800* ⊕ *www. porttix.com*) has numerous theatrical and musical events, including performances by the Portland Symphony Orchestra, Portland Ovations (performing arts), and Portland Opera Repertory Theatre. On every other Tuesday from mid-June to the end of August, organ recitals (suggested $15 donation) are given on the auditorium's huge 1912 Kotzschmar Memorial Organ. **Portland Stage** (✉ *25-A Forest Ave.* ☎ *207/774–0465* ⊕ *www.portlandstage.com*) mounts theatrical productions from September to May on its two stages.

The Eastern Prom Trail

To experience the city's busy shoreline and grand views of Casco Bay, walkers, runners, and cyclists head out on the Eastern Prom Trail.

Beginning at the intersection of Commercial and India streets, this paved trail follows the old railroad tracks of the Maine Narrow Gauge Railroad Co. & Museum. There are plenty of places with benches and tables for a picnic break along the way. From the trailhead, it's about 1¼ mi to the small East End Beach.

You can continue along the trail, pass underneath busy I-295, and reemerge at Back Cove, a popular 3½-mi loop; or you can return to the Old Port by either backtracking along the trail or heading up a grassy hill to the Eastern

Promenade, a lovely picnic spot and playground.

Take a left back toward the Old Port. Starting down the hill, a gazebo and several old cannons to your left indicate the small Fort Allen Park. Use one of the coin-operated viewing scopes to view Ft. Gorges, a Civil War–era military garrison that was never used.

Where the Eastern Prom becomes Fore Street, either head straight back into the Old Port or take a left on India Street, which will bring you just about back to where you started.

Plan an hour to walk to East End Beach and back; add an hour or two if you continue along the Back Cove Trail.

SHOPPING

Trendy Exchange Street is great for arts-and-crafts and boutique browsing, while Commercial Street caters to the souvenir hound—gift shops are packed with nautical items, and lobster and moose emblems are emblazoned on everything from T-shirts to shot glasses.

Several art galleries bring many alternatives to the ubiquitous New England seaside painting. Modern art, photography, sculpture, and pottery now fill the shelves of many shops, revealing the sophisticated and avant-garde faces of the city's art scene.

ART AND ANTIQUES

Abacus (⊠ *44 Exchange St. Old Port* ☎ *207/772–4880* ⊕ *www.abacusgallery.com*), an appealing crafts gallery, has unusual gift items in glass, wood, and textiles, plus fine modern jewelry. **Foundry Lane Contemporary Crafts** (⊠ *221 Commercial St. Old Port* ☎ *207/773–2722* ⊕ *www.foundrylane.com*) sells beautiful, limited-edition jewelry, as well as glass and ceramic home accessories by 20 Maine artists. **Gleason Fine Art** (⊠ *545 Congress St. Arts District* ☎ *207/699–5599* ⊕ *www.gleasonfineart.com*) exhibits paintings by Maine artists from the 19th to 21st centuries. **Greenhut Galleries** (⊠ *146 Middle St. Old Port* ☎ *207/772–2693 or 888/772–2693* ⊕ *www.greenhutgalleries.com*) shows contemporary art and sculpture by Maine artists. The **Institute for Contemporary Art** (⊠ *522 Congress St. Old Port* ☎ *207/775–3052* ⊕ *www.meca.edu*), at the Maine College of Art, showcases contemporary artwork from around the world. An antiques junkie's dream, **Portland Architectural Salvage** (✉ *131 Preble St. north of Arts District* ☎ *207/780–0634* ⊕ *www. portlandsalvage.com*) has four floors of unusual reclaimed finds, including furniture, fixtures, hardware, and stained-glass windows.

BOOKS

Cunningham Books (✉ *188 State St. Arts District* ☎ *207/775–2246*) is a grand browsing (and buying) experience for book lovers. The owner knows in a moment whether your request is present amid the estimated 70,000 titles lining the walls. **Longfellow Books** (✉ *1 Monument Way Arts District* ☎ *207/772–4045* ⊕ *www.longfellowbooks.com*) is a great success story of the independent bookstore triumphing over the massive presence of large chains. The place is known for its good service and thoughtful literary collection. There's also a nice selection of greeting cards and magazines; author readings are scheduled regularly.

CLOTHING

Hip boutique **Bliss** (✉ *58 Exchange St. Old Port* ☎ *207/879–7125* ⊕ *www.blissboutiques.com*) stocks T-shirts, dresses, jewelry, and lingerie by cutting-edge designers, plus jeans by big names like 7 For All Mankind.

Photos of style icon Audrey Hepburn grace the walls of **Hélène M.** (✉ *425 Fore St. Old Port* ☎ *207/772–2564*), where you'll find classic, fashionable pieces by designers like Tory Burch, Diane von Furstenberg, and Rebecca Taylor.

For the style-conscious man, visit **Joseph's** (✉ *410 Fore St. Old Port* ☎ *207/773–1274* ⊕ *www.josephsofportland.com*), which sells garments by designers like Hugo Boss and Tommy Bahama. With a funky combination of good-quality consignment and new jewelry and clothing for both men and women, **Material Objects** (✉ *500 Congress St. Arts District* ☎ *207/774–1241*) makes for an affordable and unusual shopping spree. At **Sea Bags** (✉ *25 Custom House Wharf, Old Port* ☎ *888/210–4244* ⊕ *www.seabags.com*), totes made from recycled sailcloth and decorated with bright, graphic patterns are sewn right in the store.

HOUSEHOLD ITEMS/FURNITURE

Maine islander **Angela Adams** (✉ *273 Congress St., East End* ☎ *207/774–3523 or 800/255–9454* ⊕ *www.angelaadams.com*) specializes in simple but bold geometric motifs parlayed into dramatic rugs, handbags, trays, pillows, and paper goods. Her creations are sold in a handful of design and specialty stores throughout the country, but this little brick building on Portland's Congress Street is her only store and showroom.

For reproduction and antique furnishings with a Far East feel, head to one of the two locations of **Asia West** (✉ *219 Commercial St. Old Port* ☎ *888/775–0066* ✉ *125 Kennebec St. north of Arts District* ☎ *207/774–9300* ⊕ *www.asiawest.net.*) The former has mostly accessories; the latter is a furniture showroom. The handsome cherrywood pieces at **Green Design Furniture** (✉ *267 Commercial St. Old Port* ☎ *207/775–4234 or 800/853–4234* ⊕ *www.greendesigns.com*) are made locally with sustainable harvested wood and eco-friendly finishes. A unique system of joinery enables easy assembly after shipping.

SPORTS AND THE OUTDOORS

When the weather's good, everyone in Portland heads outside. Some drive out of the city to explore, but many take to the streets and trails with their bikes, their dogs, and/or their kids to enjoy the season. Portland has quite a bit of green space in its several parks, and in the heat of summer these places make for cool retreats with refreshing fountains and plenty of shade.

There are also many green spaces nearby Portland, including Fort Williams Park, home to Portland Head Light; Crescent Beach State Park; and Two Lights State Park. All offer biking and walking trails, picnic facilities, and water access. Bradbury Mountain State Park, in Pownal, has incredible vistas from its easily summited peak. In Freeport is Wolfe's Neck Woods State Park, where you can take a guided nature walk and see nesting ospreys. ⇨ *Side Trips from Portland for more on these.*

BICYCLING

For state bike trail maps, club and tour listings, or hints on safety, contact the **Bicycle Coalition of Maine** (✉ *341 Water St., No. 10, Augusta* ☎ *207/623–4511* ⊕ *www.bikemaine.org*). Rent bikes downtown at **Cycle Mania** (✉ *59 Federal St.* ☎ *207/774–2933* ⊕ *www.cyclemania1.com*) or **Gorham Bike and Ski** (✉ *693 Congress St.* ☎ *207/773–1700* ⊕ *www.gorhambike.com*).For local biking information, contact **Portland Trails** (✉ *305 Commercial St.* ☎ *207/775–2411* ⊕ *www.trails.org*), a group devoted to blazing (literally) new trails for cyclists and walkers. They can tell you about designated, paved routes that wind along the water, through parks, and beyond. For a map, call or get one online.

BOATING

Various Portland-based skippers offer whale-, dolphin-, and seal-watching cruises; excursions to lighthouses and islands; and fishing and lobstering trips. Board the ferry to see the nearby islands. Self-navigators can rent kayaks or canoes.

Casco Bay Lines (✉ *Maine State Pier, 56 Commercial St.* ☎ *207/774–7871* ⊕ *www.cascobaylines.com*) provides narrated cruises and transportation to Casco Bay Islands. **Lucky Catch Cruises** (✉ *Long Wharf, 170 Commercial St.* ☎ *207/761–0941* ⊕ *www.luckycatch.com*) sets out to sea in a real lobster boat so passengers can get the genuine experience, which includes hauling traps and the chance to purchase the catch. **Odyssey Whale Watch** (✉ *Long Wharf, 170 Commercial St.* ☎ *207/775–0727* ⊕ *www.odysseywhalewatch.com*) leads whale-watching and deep-sea fishing trips.For tours of the harbor and Casco Bay, including a trip to Eagle Island and an up-close look at several lighthouses, try **Portland Discovery Land & Sea Tours** (✉ *Long Wharf, 170 Commercial St.* ☎ *207/774–0808* ⊕ *www.portlanddiscovery.com*)

Portland Schooner Co. (✉ *Maine State Pier, 56 Commercial St.* ☎ *207/766–2500 or 877/246–6637* ⊕ *www.portlandschooner.com*) offers daily sails aboard a vintage 1912 or 1924 schooner. Bring your own food and beverage and help hoist the sails, take a turn at the wheel or just relax and enjoy the ride; overnight cruises also available.

HOT-AIR BALLOON RIDES

Hot Fun First Class Balloon Flights (☎ *207/799–0193* ⊕ *www.hotfunballoons. com*) offers mainly sunrise trips, and can accommodate up to three people. The price of $300 per person includes a post-flight champagne toast, snacks, and shuttle to the lift-off site.

SIDE TRIPS FROM PORTLAND

CASCO BAY ISLANDS

The islands of Casco Bay are also known as the Calendar Islands, because an early explorer mistakenly thought there was one for each day of the year (in reality there are only 140). These islands range from ledges visible only at low tide to populous Peaks Island, a suburb of Portland. Some islands are uninhabited; others support year-round communities as well as stores and restaurants. Fort Gorges commands Hog Island Ledge, and Eagle Island is the site of Arctic explorer Admiral Peary's home. The brightly painted ferries of Casco Bay Lines are the islands' lifeline. There is frequent service to the most-populated ones, including Peaks, Long, Little Diamond, and Great Diamond. A ride on the bay is a great way to experience the dramatic shape of the Maine Coast and catch a glimpse of some of its islands.

There is little in the way of brief overnight lodging on the islands; while the population swells during the warmer months, much of the increase is due to summer-long visitors and part-time residents. Tourism is passive—there are few restaurants or organized attractions other than the natural beauty of the islands themselves. Meandering about by bike or on foot is a good way to explore on a day trip; or you can spend the day viewing the areas from the ferry's bow.

GETTING HERE AND AROUND

Casco Bay Lines provides ferry service from Portland to the islands of Casco Bay. The CAT, a stunning, modern high-speed ferry, travels between Portland and Yarmouth, Nova Scotia.

Information Casco Bay Lines (☎ *207/774–7871* ⊕ *www.cascobaylines.com*). **The CAT** (☎ *877/359–3760* ⊕ *www.catferry.com*).

EXPLORING

Peaks Island. Nearest to Portland, this is the most developed of the Calendar Islands, but it still allows you to experience the relaxed pace of island life. Explore an art gallery or an old fort, and meander along the alternately rocky and sandy shore on foot, bike, or in a kayak, and break for an alfresco lunch. The trip here by boat is particularly enjoyable at sunset. A small museum with Civil War artifacts, open in summer, is maintained in the building of the **5th Maine Regiment** (⊠ *45 Seashore Ave., Peaks Island* ☎ *207/766–3330* ⊕ *www.fifthmainemuseum.org* ⊙ *Memorial Day–Columbus Day, weekends 11–4; July–Aug., weekdays 12–4* PM ⊠ *$5 suggested donation*). When the Civil War broke out in 1861, Maine was asked to raise only a single regiment to fight, but the state came up with several (the number eventually totaled 40), and sent the 5th Maine Regiment into the war's first battle, at Bull Run. Ask about a volunteer reenactment event, held in the summer. The museum also offers guidebooks for a two-hour self-guided tour of the World War II Peaks Island Reservation.

Eagle Island. Owned by the state and open to the public for day trips in summer, it was once the home of Admiral Robert E. Peary, the American explorer of the North Pole. Peary built a stone-and-wood house on the 17-acre island as a summer retreat in 1904, but ended up making it his permanent residence. Filled with Peary's stuffed Arctic birds, the quartz he brought home and set into the fieldstone fireplace, and antique furnishings, the house remains as it was when the admiral lived in it. A boat ride here offers a classic Maine experience, as you pass by a few of the hundreds of uninhabited, forested islands along the coast. The island is open to visitors from June 15 to Labor Day, daily 10 to 5; admission is $4.50. Once there, you can scout the house, rocky beach, and shoreline trails. **Portland Discovery Land & Sea Tours** offers a four-hour trip to Eagle Island, which includes a narrated boat ride and time to explore; combination trolley and boat tours and lighthouse cruises are also available. ⊠ *Long Wharf, 170 Commercial St.* ☎ *207/774–0808* ⊕ *www.portlanddiscovery.com* ⊠ *$30* ⊙ *Departures at 10* AM *Tues., Thurs., Fri., and weekends in late June–early-Sept., and weekends in mid to late-Sept.*

WHERE TO EAT AND STAY

$$ ✕ **Diamond's Edge Restaurant & Marina.** For an elegant meal in a quiet island setting, take the ferry to Great Diamond Island and get off at the Diamond Cove stop—this brick restaurant is a few yards from the dock. Feast on filet mignon or seared tuna, or, for lunch, try a crab cake or fried-scallop sandwich while sitting on the lawn or covered porch. Afterward, take a stroll up the hill to view the historic brick and Queen Anne-style homes of the former Fort McKinley (now residential and vacation-rental properties), where soldiers were stationed from the days of the Spanish-American War through the end of World War II. Time the ferry so you're not marooned here too long—by this point you will have seen pretty much everything there is to see. ⊠ *Diamond Cove, Great Diamond Island.* ☎ *207/766–5850* ⊕ *www.diamondsedge. com* ⊟ *AE, MC, V.*

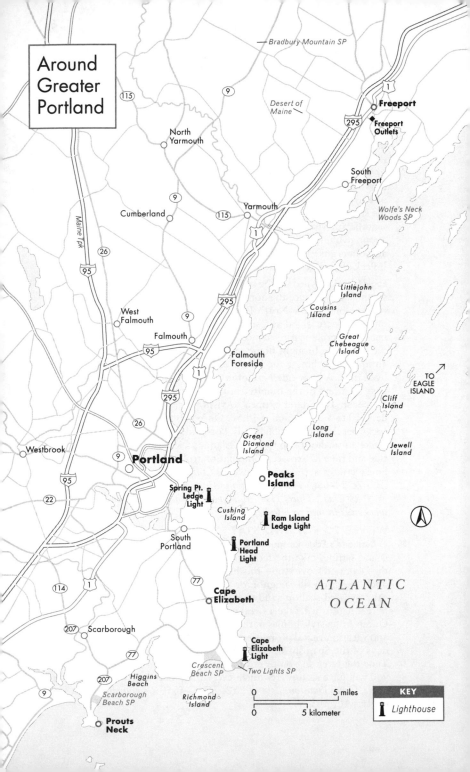

Around Greater Portland

Bradbury Mountain SP

115

9

North Yarmouth

Desert of Maine

1

● **Freeport**

295

◆ **Freeport Outlets**

South Freeport

Maine Tpk

9

Cumberland

115

Yarmouth

1

Wolfe's Neck Woods SP

26

95

295

Littlejohn Island

Cousins Island

West Falmouth

9

Falmouth

Great Chebeague Island

95

1

Falmouth Foreside

295

Cliff Island

TO EAGLE ISLAND

26

Great Diamond Island

Long Island

Jewell Island

Westbrook

9

Portland

95

22

Spring Pt. Ledge Light 🗼

Peaks Island ●

Cushing Island

Ram Island Ledge Light 🗼

South Portland

Portland Head Light 🗼

Cape Elizabeth

77

ATLANTIC OCEAN

114

1

207

Scarborough

77

Cape Elizabeth Light 🗼

Crescent Beach SP

Two Lights SP

207

Higgins Beach

9

Scarborough Beach SP

Richmond Island

● **Prouts Neck**

0   5 miles

0   5 kilometer

KEY

🗼 *Lighthouse*

$$ 🛏 **The Inn on Peaks Island.** The lovely, roomy suites at this waterfront inn invite you to spread out and relax. Decorated in cottage style with florals, stripes, and brightly painted furniture, they sleep four to six, with a combination of king or queen beds and pullout sofas. All rooms have Jacuzzi tubs, gas fireplaces, and private balconies, and most have harbor views; four of the six boast soaring cathedral ceilings. The on-site restaurant serves—what else?—delicious seafood, as well as pub fare, for lunch and dinner. **Pros:** luxurious cottage living. **Cons:** rooms are priced equally, without regard for the quality of the (or lack of) view. ⊠ *33 Island Ave.* ☎ *207/766–5100* ⊕ *www.innonpeaks.com* ⇥ *6 suites* ⚷ *In-room: refrigerator, DVD, Wi-Fi. In-hotel: restaurant, bar, Wi-Fi, parking (free)* ▭ *AE, MC, V.*

$$ 🛏 **Peaks Island House.** Simplicity by the sea is the motto here; the five rooms are simply decorated yet comfortable, and the views are stunning. There's also a two-bedroom cottage with a full kitchen and sun porch. The inn's restaurant serves lunch and dinner classics like shrimp scampi and lobster rolls. **Pros:** view of Mount Washington in clear weather; genuine island-life experience minutes from Portland. **Cons:** minimum two-night stay on Friday and Saturday nights. ⊠ *20 Island Ave.* ☎ *207/766–4400* ⊕ *www.thepeaksislandhouse.com* ⇥ *5 rooms, 1 cottage* ⊗ *Closed mid-Oct.–April* ⚷ *In-room: no a/c, refrigerator, Wi-Fi. In-hotel: restaurant, bar, Wi-Fi* ▭ *AE, D, MC, V.*

SPORTS AND THE OUTDOORS

Since the quieter, more independent element of ecotourism endures here, outdoor exploration is best done either by bike, on foot, or in a kayak.

KAYAKING **Maine Island Kayak Company** (⊠ *149 Island Ave., Peaks Island* ☎ *207/766–2373* ⊕ *www.maineislandkayak.com*) offers full-day ($110) and half-day ($65) guided trips for both seasoned paddlers and sporty beginners. Prices include all necessary gear and equipment; the full-day trip includes a picnic lunch. Reservations are recommended.

TOURS For guided tours of Peaks Island led by longtime residents the Mac-Isaac family, check out **Island Tours** (⊠ *Peaks Island* ☎ *207/766–5514* ⊕ *peaksislandtours.com*). Ramble about the island in style—in an open golf cart—for a very personalized and lively experience. Choose from sunset, history, or art and architecture themes. The season runs from May through October; prices are $15. Reservations are recommended.

CAPE ELIZABETH TO PROUTS NECK

EXPLORING

Fodor'sChoice **Portland Head Light.** Familiar to many from photographs and Edward
★ Hopper's painting *Portland Head-Light (1927),* this lighthouse was commissioned by George Washington in 1790. The towering white stone structure stands over the keeper's quarters, a white home with a blazing red roof, now the Museum at Portland Head Light. The lighthouse is in 90-acre Fort Williams Park, a sprawling green space with walking paths, picnic facilities, a beach and—you guessed it—a cool old fort *museum.* ⊠ *1000 Shore Rd., Cape Elizabeth* ☎ *207/799–2661*

⊕ *www.portlandheadlight.com* ✉ *$2* ⊗ *Memorial Day–mid-Oct., daily 10–4; Apr., May, Nov., and Dec., weekends 10–4.*

WHERE TO EAT

$–$$
ECLECTIC
✗ **Good Table.** Close to Two Lights State Park, this is a great place to get breakfast or brunch before visiting the beach. The omelets are big and fluffy, as is the French toast. The lunch and dinner menus include classic comfort food, like a hot turkey dinner with mashed potatoes and gravy. You'll also find fresh fried seafood, a very tasty lobster roll, and an array of Greek specialties such as spanakopita and a gyro sandwich. Sit under the colorful paper lanterns on the screened-in porch and enjoy the woodsy view. ✉ *527 Ocean House Rd. (Rt. 77), Cape Elizabeth* ☎ *207/799–4663* ⊕ *www.thegoodtablerestaurant.net* ▭ *D, MC, V* ⊗ *Closed Mon.*

$$$
SEAFOOD
✗ **Joe's Boathouse.** The two small dining rooms of this dockside establishment are simple, clean, and finished in sea-foam green, with large windows looking out to a marina. The ocean motif extends to a lobster boat on a mantle and a bar that houses an aquarium. Dinner specials include tuna steak and lobster fettuccine; for lunch try the grilled-crab and avocado club or Asian-inspired crispy salmon salad. In summer, enjoy the flavors and the scenery from the umbrella-dotted patio. Altogether, it is low-key, casual, and a hit with the locals. ✉ *1 Spring Point Dr., South Portland* ☎ *207/741–2780* ⊕ *www.joesboathouse.com* ▭ *AE, MC, V.*

$$
SEAFOOD
✗ **The Lobster Shack at Two Lights.** You can't beat the location—right on the water, below the lighthouse pair that give Two Lights State Park its name—and the food's not bad either. Just as the name implies, fresh lobster is the watchword here—enjoy it whole or piled into a hot-dog bun with a dollop of mayo. Other menu must-haves include chowder, fried clams, and fish-and-chips. It's been a classic spot since the 1920s. Eat inside or out. ✉ *225 Two Lights Rd., Cape Elizabeth* ☎ *207/799–1677* ⊕ *www.lobstershacktwolights.com* ▭ *MC, V* ⊗ *Closed Nov.–late Mar.*

WHERE TO STAY

$$$$
▦ **Black Point Inn.** Toward the tip of the peninsula that juts into the ocean at Prouts Neck stands this stylish, tastefully updated historic resort with spectacular views up and down the coast. Guests have access to beaches, trails, kayaking equipment, a country club with tennis courts and a golf course, and a yacht club. Finer touches abound, such as Frette linens and in-room terry-cloth robes. The Cliff Walk, a pebbled path that wanders past Winslow Homer's former studio, runs along the Atlantic headlands that Homer often painted. Rates include breakfast, dinner, and gratuities. The inn is 12 mi south of Portland and about 10 mi north of Old Orchard Beach. **Pros:** stunning water views; set amid scenery that inspired Winslow Homer. **Cons:** 18% "guest service charge" is tacked on to room rate to cover gratuities and access to nearby facilities. ✉ *510 Black Point Rd., Scarborough* ☎ *207/883–2500* ⊕ *www.blackpointinn.com* ⇆ *25 rooms* ⊗ *Closed late Oct.–early May* ⚒ *In-room: DVD (some), Wi-Fi. In-hotel: 2 restaurants, bar, pool, gym, bicycles, laundry service, Internet terminal, Wi-Fi, parking (free)* ▭ *AE, D, MC, V* ⦿ *MAP.*

$$$–$$$$ 🛏 **Inn by the Sea.** A multimillion-dollar renovation has transformed this sprawling, shingled inn overlooking the Atlantic. Every room, suite, and cottage has been updated with wood and rattan furnishings in natural shades, punctuated with bright pops of color; most guest quarters have ocean views. Equally appealing: it's a short walk down a private boardwalk to the white sands of Crescent Beach, a popular family spot. Dogs stay for free and are welcomed with a room-service pet menu, evening turndown treats, and giant beach towels. The Sea Glass Restaurant & Lounge ($$$–$$$$), open to nonguests, serves fine seafood and regional dishes. The sumptuous spa, a product of the renovation, was designed with eco-friendly materials and offers massage and aromatherapy treatments using chemical-free products. **Pros:** on Crescent Beach; a short drive to Two Lights, Portland Head, and Portland. **Cons:** minimum two-night stay during some weekends in high season; woofs and yaps can disturb the peace. ✉ *40 Bowery Beach Rd. (7 mi south of Portland), Cape Elizabeth* ☎ *207/799–3134 or 800/888–4287* ⊕ *www. innbythesea.com* ↗ *14 rooms, 25 suites, 18 cottages* ⚐ *In-room: kitchen (some), refrigerator, Wi-Fi. In-hotel: restaurant, bar, pool, gym, spa, children's programs (ages 2 to 10), laundry service, Internet terminal, Wi-Fi, parking (free), some pets allowed* ▤ *AE, D, MC, V.*

SPORTS AND THE OUTDOORS

This area is home to several state parks and long stretches of beachfront that are perfect for sunbathing, strolling, and exploring. Routes 77 and 207 are ideal for cyclists who like winding roads and pastoral scenery. Walkers can choose from miles of trails within the state parks, and there are plenty of spots for picnics and ocean-side barbecues. This is the region where Portland's city folk come to walk the beach and enjoy the open space.

The 243-acre **Crescent Beach State Park** (✉ *Rte. 77, Cape Elizabeth* ☎ *207/799–5871* 🎟 *$6.50* ⊗ *Memorial Day–Columbus Day, daily 9 AM–sunset*), about 8 mi south of Portland, has a sandy beach, picnic tables and grills, a seasonal snack bar, and a bathhouse. The nature trails that head into the woods beyond the beach are great for birdwatching and getting out of the sun. **Higgins Beach** (✉ *Off Rte. 77 [Spurwink Rd.], Scarborough*) is a good-size and very popular sandy expanse set amid a little beach-colony neighborhood. The spot is popular with surfers and sunbathers. Parking costs $10 in a public lot.

Scarborough Beach State Park (✉ *Rte. 207, Scarborough* ⊗ *Daily 9–7*) has a large beach area with ample parking, lifeguards, and lots of people-watching opportunities. There is a $4 parking fee.

CANOEING **Scarborough Marsh Audubon Center** (✉ *Rte. 9, Scarborough* ⊗ *mid-June–Labor Day, daily 9:30–5:30, and weekends Memorial Day–June* ☎ *207/883–5100 (in season), 207/781–2330 (headquarters)* ⊕ *www. maineaudubon.org*), part of the Maine Audubon Society, operates guided canoe trips and rents out canoes in the largest salt marsh in Maine. Programs at Maine Audubon's Falmouth headquarters (north of Portland) include nature walks and a discovery room for children.

★ **Two Lights State Park** (✉ *7 Tower Dr. (off Rte. 77), Cape Elizabeth* ☎ *207/799–5871* ⊗ *Daily 9 AM–sunset.* 🎟 *$4.50*) sits on just over 40 acres of Maine's quintessential rocky shoreline. Named for the two lighthouses atop the hill (one is now privately owned; the other has been in use since 1828), the park has picnic facilities, shoreline trails, and great views of the activities of Portland Harbor.

FREEPORT

17 mi northeast of Portland, 10 mi southwest of Brunswick.

Those who flock straight to L. L. Bean and see nothing else of Freeport are missing out on some real New England beauty. The city's charming backstreets are lined with historic buildings and old clapboard houses, and there's a pretty little harbor on the south side of the Harraseeket River. It's true, many who come to the area do so simply to shop—L. L. Bean is the store that put Freeport on the map, and plenty of outlets and some specialty stores have settled here. Still, if you choose, you can stay awhile and experience more than fabulous bargains; beyond the shops are bucolic nature preserves with miles of walking trails and plenty of places for leisurely ambling that don't require the overuse of your credit cards.

ESSENTIALS

Find restaurant menus, brochures, store coupons, and a shopping map at the **Freeport Merchants Association** (⊠ *23 Depot St.* ☎ *207/865–1212 or 800/865–1994* ⊕ *www.freeportusa.com* ☉ *Mon.– Fri. 9–5*). Pick up a village walking map, sign up for a tour, and check out historical exhibits at the **Freeport Historical Society** (⊠ *45 Main St.* ☎ *207/865–3170* ⊕ *www.freeporthistoricalsociety.com* ☉ *Mon., Thurs., and Fri. 10–5, Sat. 10–2*).

EXPLORING

Ⓒ **Desert of Maine.** Take a tram tour of sand dunes, walk nature trails, hunt for gemstones, and watch working sand artists at this 40-acre natural desert created by a glacier. ⊠ *95 Desert Rd., off I–295, Exit 20* ☎ *207/865–6962* ⊕ *www.desertofmaine.com* ⌦ *$8.75* ☉ *Early May– mid-Oct., 8:30–5:30 daily.*

OFF THE BEATEN PATH

Pettengill Farm. To escape Freeport's busy outlet scene, take a stroll back in time at this 19th-century farm. Operated by the Freeport Historical Society, the aged and beautiful farm is set on 140 acres of salt marsh, with open fields, exquisite gardens, and an original 1810 saltbox home. There are four walking trails; bring your camera and binoculars to see deer, fox, and a vast array of both migratory and native birds. Tours of the home are available on the first Sunday in October and by appointment any time of year. To reach the small parking area, head out of Freeport on Bow Street, pass over the Harraseeket River, and look for Pettengill Road on the right. It's a half-mile walk down a dirt road to the grounds. It's worth the trip for the sheer beauty and sense of historic solitude. ⊠ *Pettengill Farm Rd.* ☎ *207/865–3170* ⊕ *www. freeporthistoricalsociety.org.*

WHERE TO EAT

$$$
ITALIAN

✕**Azure Café.** This airy little café right on Main Street provides both an appealing atmosphere and an enticing menu. Local fruits, vegetables, meats, and seafood are highlighted, and many are treated to an Italian transformation. Dinner favorites include the orange Marsala-glazed pork tenderloin and Atlantic salmon with wild Maine blueberry barbecue sauce. For lunch you might try burgers made with meat from nearby Wolfe's Neck Farm, flatbread wraps, or Maine classics like clam chowder or a fried-haddock sandwich. During the summer, sit out on the street-side patio, listen to live jazz, savor the tiramisu, and forget about nearby outlet bargains for just a little while. ⊠ *123 Main St.* ☎ *207/865–1237* ⊕ *www.azurecafe.com* ▤ *AE, D, MC, V.*

$$$
AMERICAN
Fodor'sChoice
★

✕**Broad Arrow Tavern.** On the main floor of the Harraseeket Inn, this dark, wood-paneled tavern with mounted moose heads, decoys, snowshoes, and other outdoor sporty decor is known for both its casual nature and its sumptuous menu. The chefs use only organically grown food, with a nearly exclusive emphasis on Maine products, to create treats such as steaks, pizzas, seafood. About the only non-Maine ingredient is the wild salmon, which comes from Alaska and Oregon. ⊠ *162 Main St.* ☎ *207/865–9377* ⏃ *Reservations not accepted* ▤ *AE, D, DC, MC, V.*

$–$$
SEAFOOD

✕**Harraseeket Lunch & Lobster Co.** Seafood baskets and lobster dinners are the focus at this popular, bare-bones place beside the town landing in South Freeport. Order at the counter and bring your patience—long lines ensue in summer. Find a seat inside or out. ⊠ *On pier, end of Main St., South Freeport* ☎ *207/865–4888* ⊕ *www.harraseeketlunchandlobster. com* ⏃ *Reservations not accepted* ▤ *No credit cards* ⊙ *Closed mid-Oct.–Apr.*

WHERE TO STAY

$$$$
Fodor'sChoice
★

▥ **Harraseeket Inn.** Despite modern appointments such as elevators and whirlpool baths in some rooms, this 1850 Greek Revival home provides a pleasantly old-fashioned, country-inn experience just a few minutes' walk from L.L. Bean. Guest rooms have print fabrics and reproductions of Federal quarter-canopy beds. Ask for a second-floor, garden-facing room. The formal Maine Dining Room ($$$–$$$$) specializes in contemporary American regional (and organic) cuisine such as whole poached lobster and all-natural filet mignon. The casual yet excellent Broad Arrow Tavern ($$$) serves heartier fare and has a charming seasonal patio. Inn rates include a full buffet breakfast and afternoon tea. **Pros:** excellent on-site dining; walk to shopping district. **Cons:** building updates over the years have diminished some authenticity. ⊠ *162 Main St.* ☎ *207/865–9377 or 800/342–6423* ⊕ *www.harraseeketinn. com* ⇄ *82 rooms, 2 suites* ⏃ *In-room: refrigerator (some), Wi-Fi. In-hotel: 2 restaurants, bars, pool, gym, laundry service, parking (free), some pets allowed* ▤ *AE, D, DC, MC, V* ▯◎▯ *BP.*

$$$$

▥ **James Place Inn.** Set on a quiet side street yet within easy walking distance of shopping paradise, this peaceful inn is tastefully decorated with brightly painted walls, colorful floral bedspreads, hooked rugs, and four-poster beds. Maine-inspired artwork and fresh flowers add to the simple elegance of the place, which includes a full hot breakfast served in a light-dappled sunroom (or on a deck when the weather is nice). Some marbled bathrooms even provide two-person Jacuzzis. For winter visits, choose the room with a working fireplace. One room has a kitchenette. **Pros:** classic Maine Victorian-style cottage; close to shopping. **Cons:** proximity to buzzing shopping district detracts from country experience. ⊠ *11 Holbrook St.* ☎ *207/865–4486 or 800/964–9086* ⊕ *www.jamesplaceinn.com* ⇨ *7 rooms* ♿ *In-room: no phone, kitchen (some), refrigerator (some), DVD, Wi-Fi. In-hotel: Wi-Fi, parking (free)* ⊟ *AE, D, MC, V* �’⊙❘ *BP.*

$$$$ ⊡ **White Cedar Inn.** Travelers give Monica and Rock, the proprietors of this quaint B&B, a gold star for hospitality and memorable meals (like Rock's blueberry pancakes and spinach quiche). Ask, and the accommodating innkeepers will give you the recipes on printed notecards. Located on the less-bustling end of Main Street, just past the last of the shops, the Victorian abode was the boyhood home of Arctic explorer Donald B. MacMillian. The rooms have a homey, country feel, with floral wallpaper and patchwork quilts; two have gas fireplaces. Sit back on an Adirondack chair on the manicured grounds and enjoy afternoon cookies or brownies. **Pros:** warm and welcoming; two blocks from L.L. Bean. **Cons:** country decor may read as kitsch. ⊠ *178 Main St.* ☎ *207/865–9099 or 800/853–1269* ⊕ *www.whitecedarinn.com* ⇨ *7 rooms* ♿ *In-room: no phone, no TV (some), Wi-Fi. In-hotel: Wi-Fi, parking (free), some pets allowed* ⊟ *AE, D, MC, V* ❘⊙❘ *BP.*

NIGHTLIFE AND THE ARTS

Every Saturday from late June to early September, sit under the stars for the **L. L. Bean Summer Concert Series** (⊠ *Morse St.* ☎ *877/755-2326* ⊕ *www.llbean.com/events*). The free concerts start at 7:30 PM in downtown Freeport at L. L. Bean's Discovery Park. The entertainment ranges from folk, jazz, and country to rock and bluegrass, and includes some pretty big names. Bring a blanket and refreshments.

SHOPPING

The *Freeport Visitors Guide* (☎ *207/865–1212, 800/865–1994 or* ⊕ *www. freeportusa.com for a copy*) lists the more than 200 shops and factory outlet stores, including big names such as Coach, Brooks Brothers, Banana Republic, J.Crew, and Cole-Haan, that can be found on Main Street, Bow Street, and elsewhere. Don't overlook the specialty stores and crafts galleries.

Edgecomb Potters (⊠ *8 School St.* ☎ *207/865–1705* ⊕ *www.edgecombpotters.com*) showcases vibrant, hand-thrown porcelain tableware finished with an unusual crystalline glaze. **R.D. Allen Freeport Jewelers** specializes in brightly colored tourmaline and other locally mined gemstones. (⊠ *13 Middle St.* ☎ *207/865–1818 or 877/837–3835* ⊕ *www. rdallen.com*). Famed local furniture company **Thos. Moser Cabinetmakers** (⊠ *149 Main St.* ☎ *207/865–4519* ⊕ *www.thosmoser.com*) sells artful, handmade wood pieces with clean, classic lines.

Fodor's Choice   Founded in 1912 as a mail-order merchandiser of products for hunters,
★   guides, and anglers, **L. L. Bean** (⊠ *95 Main St. [U.S. 1]* ☎ *877/755–2326*) attracts more than 3 million shoppers a year to its giant store (open 24 hours a day) in the heart of Freeport's shopping district. You can still

find the original hunting boots, along with cotton and wool sweaters; outerwear; camping and ski equipment; comforters; and hundreds of other things for the home, car, boat, and campsitev For items related to specific activities and the home, as well as discounted merchandise (available at the L.L. Bean Outlet), head to the following nearby stores: **L.L. Bean Bike, Boat & Ski Store** (✉ *57 Main St.* ☏ *877/755–2326*), **L.L. Bean Home Store** (✉ *12 Nathan Nye St.* ☏ *877/755–2326*) **L.L. Bean Hunting & Fishing Store** (✉ *95 Main St.* ☏ *877/755–2326*), and **L.L. Bean Outlet** (✉ *One Freeport Village Station (Depot St.)* ☏ *207/552–7772*).

SPORTS AND THE OUTDOORS

CLASSES It shouldn't come as a surprise that one of the world's largest outdoor clothing and supply outfitters also provides its customers with instructional adventures to go with their products. L.L. Bean's year-round **Outdoor Discovery Schools** (☏ *888/552–3261* ⊕ *www.llbean.com/ods*) include half- and one-day classes, trips, and tours that encompass canoeing, shooting, biking, kayaking, fly-fishing, cross-country skiing, and other outdoor sports. Classes are for all skill levels; it's best to sign up several months in advance.

STATE PARKS **Bradbury Mountain State Park** (✉ *528 Hallowell Rd., Pownal* ☏ *207/688–4712* ⊕ *www.bradburymountain.com* ⊘ *9* AM–*sunset daily* ✉ *$4.50*) has moderate trails to the top of Bradbury Mountain. There are lovely views of the sea from the peak. A picnic area and shelter, a ball field, a playground, and 35 campsites are among the facilities. **Wolfe's Neck Woods State Park** (✉ *426 Wolfe's Neck Rd., follow Bow St. opposite L.L. Bean off U.S. 1* ☏ *207/865–4465* ✉ *$4.50* ⊘ *Apr.–Oct.*) has 5 mi of hiking trails along Casco Bay, the Harraseeket River, and a salt marsh. This is an excellent place to view nesting ospreys. Naturalists lead daily walks and activities in summer, and on weekends and holidays in spring and fall. The park has picnic tables and grills but no camping.

TOURS **Atlantic Seal Cruises** (✉ *South Freeport* ☏ *207/865–6112, 877/285–7325 late May to late Oct.*) operates day trips to Eagle Island and Seguin Island lighthouse, as well as evening seal and osprey watches. Admission is $30. Reservations are recommended.

The Mid-Coast Region

WORD OF MOUTH

"A little off the beaten path, near Bath, we love Georgetown cove. A lovely area with Reid State Park nearby. It's a lot less crowded than Camden or Rockland—and certainly Boothbay. Bath is a small, cute little town to explore—again not touristy or crowded at all."

—yestravel

Updated by
Michael de
Zayas

Lighthouses dot the headlands of Maine's Mid-Coast region, where thousands of miles of coastline wait to be explored. Defined by chiseled peninsulas stretching south from U.S. 1, this area has everything from the sandy beaches and sandbars of Popham Beach to the jutting cliffs of Monhegan Island. If you are intent on hooking a trophy-size fish or catching a glimpse of a whale, there are plenty of cruises available. If you want to explore deserted beaches and secluded coves, kayaks are your best bet. Put in at the Harpswells, or the Cushing and Saint George peninsulas, or simply paddle among the lobster boats and other vessels that ply these waters.

Tall ships often visit Maine, sometimes sailing up the Kennebec River for a stopover at Bath's Maine Maritime Museum, on the site of the old Percy and Small Shipyard. Next door to the museum, the Bath Iron Works still builds the U.S. Navy's Aegis-class destroyers. In Brunswick you can visit the home (now a museum) of General Joshua L. Chamberlain, hero at the pivotal Battle of Little Round Top at Gettysburg and once a professor at Bowdoin College.

Along U.S. 1, charming towns, each unique, have an array of attractions. Brunswick, while a bigger, commercial city, has rows of historic wood and clapboard homes, and is home to Bowdoin College. Bath is known for its maritime heritage. Wiscasset has arguably the best antiques shopping in the state. On its waterfront you can choose from a variety of seafood shacks competing for the best lobster rolls. Damariscotta, too, is worth a stop for its lively main street and good seafood restaurants where you can enjoy the fresh catch of the day.

South along the peninsulas the scenery opens to glorious vistas of working lobster harbors and marinas. It's here you find the authentic lobster pounds where you can watch your catch come in off the traps. Boothbay Harbor is the quaintest town in the Mid-Coast, and has lots of little stores that are perfect for window-shopping. It's one of three towns where you can take a ferry to Monhegan Island, which seems to be inhabited exclusively by painters at their easels, depicting the cliffs and weathered homes with colorful gardens.

TOP REASONS TO GO

- **Working fishing harbors:** Boats coming in and out of the harbor, lobster pounds, gorgeous coast: this is the region's defining scene.

- **Authentic lobster pounds:** The taste of real Maine Coast is at these humble coastline shacks serving the freshest lobster and clams.

- **Monhegan Island:** A veritable artists' colony on a remote island offers a quiet, forgotten slice of Maine life.

- **Lighthouse, river, whale, and bay cruises:** Get on one of many fantastic boat cruises to tour hundreds of Casco Bay islands, several rivers and inlets, and hidden lighthouses.

- **Bath shipbuilding:** Tour the Bath Iron Works, get on old ships and learn the history of shipbuilding at the Maine Maritime Museum.

4

ORIENTATION AND PLANNING

GETTING ORIENTED

Looking for Maine's famous rocky coast and seemingly endless drives among peninsulas and islands? Find it here in the Mid-Coast. The region's geography is such that U.S. 1 runs almost west-to-east along this stretch, rather than north-to-south. Thus, south of the towns along U.S. 1 are the famed peninsulas where the scenery is dramatically different, the towns smaller, less populated, and less trafficked; and the whole less commercialized. It takes approximately an hour and a half to circle from U.S. 1 down any given peninsula and back. If you're a fan of lobster, the farther south you go, the more likely you'll find working fishing harbors with authentic (and more inexpensive) lobster pounds.

VISITOR INFORMATION

Maine Tourism Association (⊠ *1100 U.S. 1 [I–95, Exit 17], Yarmouth* ☎ *207/846–0833 or 888/624–6345* ⊕ *www.mainetourism.com*). **Southern Midcoast Maine Chamber** (⊠ *Border Trust Business Center, 2 Main St., Topsham* ☎ *877/725–8797* ⊕ *www.midcoastmaine.com*).

PLANNING

WHEN TO GO

In summer, temperatures typically reach the 80s and occasionally the 90s, so visitors enjoy the long stretches of sun-splashed beaches and river cruises. In autumn the humidity is gone, the days are often sunny and warm, and the nights are crisp, dropping into the 40s and 50s. Fall foliage in the Mid-Coast region is spectacular, with brilliant reds and oranges bursting from maple trees and yellows illuminating the birch trees until late October. Fishing and hunting are popular activities, and kayaking and white-water rafting are invigorating under the brilliant blue skies.

In winter you don't have to reserve months ahead if you want a room in your favorite country inn or bed-and-breakfast—though some close for the off-season. You can enjoy skiing and snowmobiling, or just curl up by the fire with a good book. Sea storms can be dramatic in November and December; a visit to the coastline this time of year reveals how those boulders you find atop the cliffs got there. In spring the hotels and restaurants are not yet crowded either. Many businesses remain closed until early or mid-May, but you shouldn't have trouble finding at least a few antiques shops and art galleries that are open. April temperatures often don't reach above the 40s; the days gradually warm up in May.

GETTING HERE AND AROUND

A car is helpful if you want to get away from the towns, as the remoter areas are not served by public transportation. Buses from Boston's South Station and Logan Airport serve many coastal towns, including Portland, Brunswick, and Bath. The *Downeaster* Amtrak train carries passengers to and from Portland and Boston's North Station. Visitors to the area also can take a wonderful scenic train ride between Brunswick, Bath, and Wiscasset to Rockland and back from late May to mid-October (see *www.maineeasternrailroad.com* for details).

AIR TRAVEL

The Portland Jetport is convenient to the Mid-Coast region, only an hour from Brunswick via the Maine Turnpike or Interstate 295. Manchester International Airport, in New Hampshire, is two hours from the Mid-Coast region. Bangor International Airport is also about two hours away, but be aware that there are frequent cancellations at this small airport.

BIKE TRAVEL

There are two major bike routes in the Mid-Coast region. The Coastal Route tour goes all the way from Brunswick to Ellsworth, a distance of 187 mi along the rocky coastline. Some stretches are along heavily traveled roads. You can do a mostly level 5-mi round-trip ride along this route in Brunswick. You begin on Water Street at the west end of the Androscoggin River Bike Path. There are restrooms along the way and shady spots to rest along the river. The 60-mi Merrymeeting Tour, traversing small hills and one major climb, originates in Bath and travels round-trip to Wiscasset. Along the way you can see the Kennebec River and Merrymeeting Bay, famous for its variety of birds, including several types of ducks. For maps and info about the trail, visit www.krrt.org/.

BOAT TRAVEL

You can charter boats and go on scenic tours from almost any town in the Mid-Coast. Three towns have boats departing for Monhegan Island. The quickest is Port Clyde, the point of departure for the *Laura B.* The *Balmy Days II* sails daily to Monhegan from Boothbay Harbor, Memorial Day through Columbus Day at 9:30 AM. The ride from Boothbay is 90 minutes each way. Hardy Boat Cruises leave daily May through October at 9 AM; in summer there are departures at 9 AM and 2 PM. The boat from Shaw's Wharf in New Harbor is one hour each way.

Boat Lines Balmy Days (☎ *207/633–2284 or 800/298–2284*). **Hardy Boat Cruises** (☎ *207/677–2026 or 800/278–3346*). **Monhegan Boat Line** (☎ *207/372–8848*).

CAR TRAVEL

Travelers visiting the Mid-Coast region in summer and early fall may encounter fog, especially on the peninsulas and points of land. It's best to leave headlights on. Fog may stay around all day, or it may burn off by late morning. Winter driving in Maine can be challenging, when snow and ice coat the roads. "Black ice" is a special hazard along the coast, as the road may appear clear but is actually covered by a nearly invisible coating of ice. Four-wheel-drive vehicles are recommended for driving in winter.

TRAIN TRAVEL

Portland is the closest city with train service (⇨ *see Greater Portland, Getting Here and Around in Chapter 3 for train details*).

RESTAURANTS

Lobsters are the main draw—there are even lobster rolls on the menu at many McDonald's locations. Some of the freshest crustaceans are at the local lobster pounds. These are restaurants or small stands right on a pier, where the catch is hauled in and stored in saltwater pools, just waiting for you to pick which lobster you want for dinner. The area is also famous for its haddock sandwiches, homemade chowders, crab cakes, lobster bisque, and fried clams. Of course, steak and prime rib are here too. The amount of food may be daunting to light eaters, but many restaurants also offer smaller portions.

Casual dress is perfectly fine in all the restaurants covered in this chapter. Many restaurants accept reservations in summer when business is brisk, so call ahead to check.

HOTELS

The Mid-Coast offers accommodations ranging from oceanfront cabins to elegant bed-and-breakfasts and seaside resorts. Many of the most interesting lodgings are former sea captains' or shipbuilders' homes, beautifully restored and furnished with period pieces. From Memorial Day through Labor Day rates rise; many of the pricier places require a two-night minimum stay, and reservations are advised. Most accommodations have air-conditioning and cable TV, and many now have Internet access. At the lower end of the scale, you can still find clean, comfortable rooms with basic amenities. Stunning views can crop up in any of the price ranges. Most B&Bs in Maine do not allow smoking on the property.

Contacts Maine Office of Tourism (☎ *888/624–6345* ⊕ *www.usa.visitmaine. com*). **Maine Camping Guide** (☎ *207/782–5874* ⊕ *www.campmaine.com*).

GREAT ITINERARIES

IF YOU HAVE 3 DAYS

On the first day, visit **Bath,** setting aside a good half a day for the Maritime Museum. In addition to studying the ship models, paintings, and other artifacts on the 25-acre property, take a trolley ride at the neighboring Bath Iron Works and reserve a spot on one of the scenic river cruises that depart from here—it might just be the highlight of your trip. ■TIP→ **Boat and BIW tours almost always sell out, so book them well in advance through the museum.** Spend the rest of the day on one of the two peninsulas to the south. If you love rocky shoreline, head to Reid State Park, where you can climb up the ledges and watch the waves pound into the rocks below. If you prefer the beach, set your course for Popham Beach State Park, where the Kennebec and Morse rivers meet the sea. Arriving at or near low tide allows you to roam the miles of tidal flats and walk across to Fox Island. You also can make a 2-mi trek along the beach to Fort Popham, a Civil War–era fortification that is fun to explore.

On Day 2, drive along U.S. 1 to the cute town of **Wiscasset,** along the Sheepscot River. If you love antiques and books, budget a few hours for shopping here. Alternatively, sightseeing includes the Musical Wonder House, where tours begin on the hour. For lunch, have a lobster roll from one of the several shacks competing for your business across the street from Red's Eats—the hands-down visitor favorite—on Water Street and U.S. 1. In the afternoon, cross the river and head south to Boothbay Harbor, a touristy but scenic town, where you can shop, take a harbor cruise, or just enjoy an ice-cream cone as you walk about town.

On Day 3, drive about 18 mi north to Newcastle, cross the small bridge to Damariscotta, where you can have lunch on sprightly Main Street. In the afternoon, head south to the beautiful Pemaquid Point Light. Climb the lighthouse, stop in at its museum, and explore the dramatic rocky outcrops. For dinner, try an authentic lobster pound at either South Bristol, to the west; or New Harbor or Round Pond, to the north.

IF YOU HAVE 5 DAYS

If you have five days for the Mid-Coast, you have time for an overnight trip to Monhegan Island. Follow the itinerary for a three-day trip and sleep in New Harbor on the third night. On your fourth day, rise early and hop on the 9 AM ferry to **Monhegan Island,** where you can hike out to the bluffs and picnic with the circling seagulls. There are numerous hikes to explore on the island, a museum, and shops. Spend the night here, and take the ferry back on the afternoon of Day 5. You can spend the evening exploring the western side of the Pemaquid peninsula at **South Bristol,** crossing the span bridge onto **Rutherford Island,** and dining at a restaurant overlooking **Christmas Cove.**

WHAT IT COSTS					
	¢	$	$$	$$$	$$$$
Restaurants	under $7	$7–$10	$11–$17	$18–$25	over $25
Hotels	under $60	$60–$99	$100–$149	$150–$200	over $200

Restaurant prices are for a median main course at dinner, excluding sales tax of 7%. Hotel prices are for two people in a standard double room in high season, excluding service charges and 7% tax.

FROM BRUNSWICK TO WISCASSET

4

BRUNSWICK

10 mi north of Freeport, 30 mi northeast of Portland.

Lovely brick-and-clapboard buildings are the highlight of Brunswick's Federal Street Historic District, which includes Federal Street and Park Row and the stately campus of Bowdoin College. From the intersection of Pleasant and Maine streets, in the center of town, you can walk in any direction and discover an impressive array of restaurants. Seafood? German cuisine? A Chinese buffet that beats out all the competition? It's all here. So are bookstores, gift shops, boutiques, and jewelers. From pushcart vendors on the shady town green, known as the Mall, you can sample finger foods such as hamburgers, clam rolls, and that old Maine favorite, steamed hot dogs.

■TIP➔ The U.S. Naval Air Station in Brunswick is home to a squadron of P3 Orion aircraft, and when you're driving along the coast, you might see their trails crisscrossing the sky.

EXPLORING

The 110-acre campus of Bowdoin College, at Maine, Bath, and College streets, off the east end of Pleasant Street, is an enclave of distinguished buildings separated by pleasant gardens and grassy quadrangles. Famous Bowdoin graduates include Nathaniel Hawthorne, Henry Wadsworth Longfellow, and Civil War hero Joshua L. Chamberlain.

Bowdoin College Museum of Art. Set in a splendid Renaissance Revival–style building designed by Charles F. McKim in 1894 and impressively expanded and renovated, this is one of America's oldest college collections of art. The diverse collection encompasses Assyrian and classical art and works by Dutch, Italian, French, and Flemish Old Masters; a superb gathering of Colonial and Federal paintings, notably Gilbert Stuart portraits of Madison and Jefferson; and a Winslow Homer gallery of engravings, etchings, and memorabilia (open in summer only). The museum's collection also includes 19th- and 20th-century American painting and sculpture, with works by Mary Cassatt, Andrew Wyeth, Andy Warhol, and Robert Rauschenberg. ⊠ *Bath Rd. at Upper Maine St., Bowdoin College campus, Brunswick* ☎ *207/725–3275* ⊕ *www. bowdoin.edu/art-museum* ☒ *Free* ☉ *Tues., Wed., and Sat. 10–5; Thurs. 10–8; Sun. 1–5.*

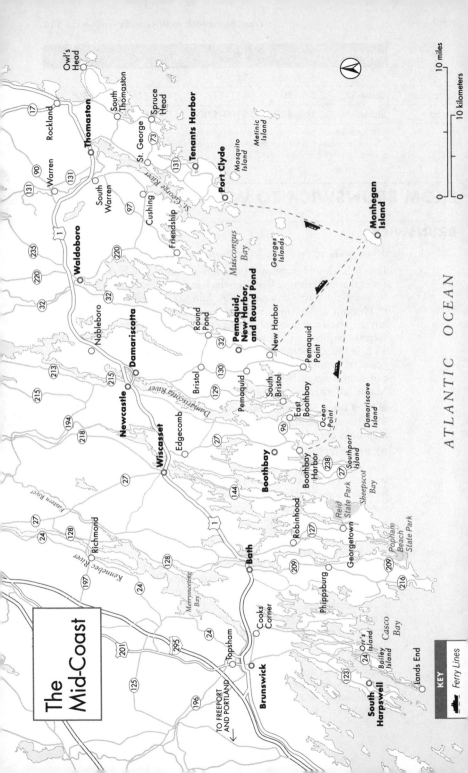

The Mid-Coast

KEY

Ferry Lines

10 miles

10 kilometers

ATLANTIC OCEAN

Owl's Head
South Thomaston
Spruce Head
Tenants Harbor
Rockland
Warren
Thomaston
Port Clyde
St. George
Mosquito Island
Metinic Island
Monhegan Island
Waldoboro
South Warren
Cushing
Friendship
Muscongus Bay
Georges Islands
Nobleboro
Pemaquid, New Harbor, and Round Pond
Round Pond
Bristol
Damariscotta
Newcastle
Pemaquid
New Harbor
South Bristol
Pemaquid Point
Edgecomb
Wiscasset
East Boothbay
Ocean Point
Damariscove Island
Boothbay
Boothbay Harbor
Southport Island
Sheepscot Bay
Robinhood
Reid State Park
Georgetown
Popham Beach State Park
Bath
Phippsburg
Richmond
Kennebec River
Eastern River
Merrymeeting Bay
Topsham
Cooks Corner
Casco Bay
Orr's Island
Bailey Island
Brunswick
South Harpswell
Lands End
TO FREEPORT AND PORTLAND

Damariscotta River
St. George River

General Joshua L. Chamberlain Museum. Through memorabilia, this museum documents the life of Maine's most celebrated Civil War hero, who was a governor of Maine in 1867 and, from 1871 to 1883, served as president of Bowdoin College. Across the street, on the edge of the Bowdoin College campus, a statue stands in memory of this general who played an instrumental role in the Union Army's victory at Gettysburg. ✉ *226 Maine St., Bowdoin College campus, Brunswick* ☎ *207/725–6958* 💳 *$5* ☉ *Late May–mid-Oct., Tues.–Sat. 10–4.*

Peary–MacMillan Arctic Museum. Think Maine is cold in the winter? Try the Arctic, where two of Bowdoin's most famous alumni, Admiral Robert E. Peary (class of 1877) and Donald B. MacMillan (class of 1898) seemed to feel right at home. If heroic exploration moves you, you'll get chills seeing the American flag that Peary unfurled on reaching the North Pole in 1909. Peary was quite possibly the first man to ever to reach the pole (controversy rages on whether it was he or Cook; or whether either of them ever made it to the true pole), and this museum has some of the principal artifacts from that expedition, including Peary's notebook page that reads "The pole at last!!!" You'll learn a lot about that expedition, including the almost clandestine fact that Peary's assistant, an African-American named Matthew Henson, was the only other man with Peary when he reached the pole, and he was actually in the lead. The schooner *Bowdoin,* now the flagship of the Maine Maritime Academy in Castine, was MacMillan's vessel for a later trip to the Arctic. Changing exhibits document conditions in the Arctic, as Bowdoin is home to an Arctic Studies program.The museum is in Bowdoin's imposing neo-Gothic Hubbard Hall, on the campus quadrangle. ✉ *Bath Rd. at Upper Maine St., Bowdoin College campus, Brunswick* ☎ *207/725–3416* 💳 *Free* ☉ *Tues.–Sat. 10–5, Sun. 2–5.*

WHERE TO EAT

$$–$$$

AMERICAN

Fodor'sChoice

★

✕ **Back Street Bistro.** Seafood paella and deep-sea scallops are signature dishes at this rustic American-style bistro open for dinner in downtown Brunswick. This two-floor establishment, next to the fire station, has two bars and an open deck upstairs. The wine list is extensive, and the service is exceptional. Try the soup of the day, especially if it's the sweet-potato bisque, which, with a dollop of cream and dash of ginger, goes down oh so smoothly. ✉ *11 Town Hall Pl., Brunswick* ☎ *207/725–4060* ⊕ *www.backstreetbistro.net* 🖃 *AE, MC, V* ☉ *No lunch.*

¢–$

CAFÉ

✕ **Barn Door Cafe.** Stop by this convenient café on the banks of the Androscoggin River, just over the bridge from downtown Brunswick, for coffee and a delicious homemade muffin or pastry, or come for lunch. Kids can order the PB&J, but there's soup and the favorite: an Italian sandwich. It's next to the Sea Dog Brew Pub. ✉ *4 Bowdoin Mill Island, Topsham* ☎ *207/721–3229* ⊕ *www.thebarndoorcafe.com* 🖃 *MC, V* ☉ *Closed Sun. No dinner Sat.*

¢–$

FAST FOOD

★

✕ **Fat Boy Drive-In.** Pull your car up under the green awning and turn on your vehicle's lights to catch the attention of the servers at this old-fashioned drive-in restaurant. The eatery is renowned for its BLTs made with Canadian bacon. Order one with onion rings and a frappé (try the blueberry). Baskets of fried clams and shrimp are also winners. It's as fun as it sounds! ⊠ *111 Bath Rd., Brunswick* ☎ *207/729–9431* ▭ *No credit cards* ⊘ *Closed mid-Oct.–mid-Mar.*

$$$
AMERICAN

✕**Henry and Marty's.** Candles on the table establish the atmosphere at this intimate dinner setting in downtown Brunswick. This is the place for a quiet evening, and guests appreciate being recognized by the staff when they come back for a return visit. Service is courteous, the wine list is extensive, and good food is the emphasis. "Organic" and "local" are key words here. Whether you order the popular beef brisket or paella valenciana, you won't be disappointed with your choice ⊠ *61 Maine St., Brunswick* ☎ *207/721–9141* ⊕ *www.henryandmarty.com* ▭ *AE, MC, V* ⊘ *No lunch.*

$$
AMERICAN

✕**Sea Dog Brew Pub.** Cross the Androscoggin River to reach the old Bowdoin Mill, a towering yellow brick building. Inside is the Sea Dog Brew Pub, where you can get hearty sandwiches, fresh seafood, and the specialty onion appetizer—don't miss the crispy calamari salad at the bar, and check the daily specials. Wash it down with a homemade root beer or microbrew. There's live evening entertainment Wednesday through Saturday. Eat inside or on the covered deck overlooking the river. ⊠ *1 Main St., Topsham* ☎ *207/725–0162* ⊕ *www.seadogbrewing. com* ▭ *AE, D, MC, V.*

¢–$
CAFE

✕**Wild Oats Bakery.** The scent of freshly baked scones and breads may draw you into this bakery inside the Tontine Mall, a downtown shopping center. Don't let the mall location scare you—this has been a local favorite since 1991. Try the hot soups and chowders or made-to-order sandwiches and salads. A variety of breads are baked daily, and many entrées are baked and frozen for your take-home convenience. ⊠ *149 Maine St., Brunswick* ☎ *207/725–6287* ⊕ *wildoatsbakery.com* ▭ *D, MC, V.*

WHERE TO STAY

$–$$

🛏**Black Lantern.** Comfortable and affordable lodging combines with sumptuous breakfasts in this quiet country setting—across the bridge from busy downtown Brunswick on the banks of the Androscoggin River. The inn features antique country furniture and homemade quilts. Black Lantern has a walkway to its own dock on the river. Rooms are decorated country-style, with quilts on the beds and wall hangings handmade by owners Judy and Tom Connelie. There are pictures throughout, some originals, and the floors are original pine. Ask for one of the rooms with a water view. Guests can participate in the paperback book exchange, where they leave a book and take a book. **Pros:** affordable rates; riverfront location. **Cons:** for those with allergies, two resident shih tzus could be troublesome. ⊠ *57 Elm St., Topsham* ☎ *207/725–4165 or 888/306–4165* ⊕ *www.blacklanternbandb.com* ⤶*3 rooms* ♿ *In-room: Wi-Fi. In-hotel: no kids under 10* ▭ *AE, D, MC, V* ⵔ*BP.*

$$–$$$

🛏**The Brunswick Inn.** If you're staying in Brunswick, this gracefully restored Greek Revival house on the green couldn't have a more central location: Bowdoin College is down the street. Crackling fires in the main room and breakfast area keep out the winter chill. Eight bedrooms grace the main house, while the carriage house has five bedrooms and two suites. Look for thoughtful touches such as terry robes in the baths. Distinctive features include a wine bar and a gallery of original art. Tuesday and Friday farmers' markets are across the street. Two first-floor units are handicapped accessible. **Pros:** beautiful porch overlooks town green. **Cons:** not near the water. ⊠ *165 Park Row, Brunswick* ☎ *207/729–4914 or 800/299–4914* ⊕ *www.thebrunswickinn.com* ⤵ *13 rooms, 2 suites* ⚲ *In-room: Wi-Fi, no TV (some). In-hotel: public Wi-Fi* ▤ *AE, MC, V* ⦿ *BP.*

NIGHTLIFE AND THE ARTS

☾ The **Maine State Music Theater** (⊠ *Bowdoin College, Brunswick* ☎ *207/725–8769* ⊕ *www.msmt.org*) stages Broadway-style shows from mid-June to September. A wonderful six-week summer concert series at Bowdoin College, the **Bowdoin International Music Festival** (⊠ *Bowdoin College, Brunswick* ☎ *207/373–1400* ⊕ *www.bowdoinfestival.org*) runs from late June to early August.

SHOPPING

Several good galleries in and around Brunswick sell everything from contemporary paintings to unusual pottery pieces. Each Tuesday and Friday, 8 AM–4 PM, from May through late November, a farmers' market fills the town green between Maine Street and Park Row next to the gazebo.

ART GALLERIES In Brunswick, **Wyler Craft Gallery** (⊠ *150 Maine St., Brunswick* ☎ *207/729–1321*) carries decorative crafts as well as jewelry, clothing, and toys. **Bayview Gallery** (⊠ *58 Maine St., Brunswick* ☎ *207/236–4534*) displays contemporary American impressionist and realist works.

☾ If you want a good Maine book, **Gulf of Maine Books** (⊠ *134 Maine St., Brunswick* ☎ *207/729–5083*) is worth a stop. Well known since 1979, it offers a superior selection of poetry, regional works, and environmental literature.

CLOTHING
AND JEWELRY Find unusual African imports, as well as jewelry and clothing, at **Indrani's of Brunswick** (⊠ *Tontine Mall, 149 Maine St., Brunswick* ☎ *207/729–6448*). Browse **What's Up** (⊠ *Tontine Mall, 149 Maine St., Brunswick* ☎ *207/725–4966*) for Pandora jewelry and fashionable women's clothing.

FOOD AND
WINE Need a bottle of vintage wine or a wedge of imported cheese? Check out **Provisions** (⊠ *148 Maine St., Brunswick* ☎ *207/729–9288*). **Tontine Fine Candies** (⊠ *Tontine Mall, 149 Maine St., Brunswick* ☎ *207/729–4462*) sells locally made chocolates, fudge, and other goodies.

SPORTS AND THE OUTDOORS

The 2½-mi marked and paved **Androscoggin River Bike Path** (⊠ *End of Water St., Brunswick04011*), running along U.S. 1 and the Androscoggin River, is open from dawn to dusk for joggers, walkers, bikers, and in-line skaters. Restrooms are available. Dogs on leashes are allowed.

THE HARPSWELLS

10 mi south of Brunswick.

From Brunswick, Routes 123 and 24 take you south to Harpswell Neck peninsula and the more than 40 islands that comprise the town of Harpswell, but which are known collectively as the **Harpswells.** Small coves along Harpswell Neck shelter lobster boats, and summer cottages are tucked away among birch and spruce trees. On your way down from Cook's Corner to Land's End at the end of Route 24, you cross Sebascodegan Island. Heading east here leads to East Harpswell and Cundy's Harbor. Continuing straight south down 24 leads to Orr's Island. Stop at Mackerel Cove to see a real fishing harbor; there are a few parking spaces where you can stop and picnic and look for beach glass, or put in your kayaks. Inhale the salt breeze as you cross the world's only cribstone bridge (designed so that water flows freely through gaps between the granite blocks) on your way to Bailey Island, home to a lobster pound made famous in part thanks to a Visa commercial.

WHERE TO EAT

$$$$
SEAFOOD
Fodor's Choice
★

✕ **Cook's Lobster House.** What began as a lobster shack on Bailey's Island in 1955 has grown into this huge, internationally famous family-style restaurant, complete with its own gift shop. They still catch their own fish and seafood, so you can count on the lobster casserole and the haddock sandwich to be delectable. But along with fame come prices; the shore dinner—the most expensive menu option—is $43, and includes a 1¼-lb lobster with steamed or fried clams or mussels, a choice of sides, and a bowl of chowder or lobster stew. Whether you choose inside or deck seating, you can watch the activity on the water: men checking lobster pots and kayakers fanning across the bay. ✉ *68 Garrison Cove Rd., Bailey Island* ☎ *207/833–2818* ⊕ *www.cookslobster. com* ♿ *Reservations not accepted* ▱ *D, MC, V* ☙ *Closed New Year's Day–mid-Feb.*

$$$
SEAFOOD

✕ **Dolphin Chowder House.** This clapboard-covered restaurant at the Dolphin Marina in Harpswell is famous for its fish chowder and lobster stew. Because it's right on the water, Dolphin is a haven for boaters. The simple but savory food makes the drive down Route 23 from Brunswick well worth it. Eat in the dining room or order takeout and eat on the dock so you can enjoy the view of Half Way Rock Lighthouse and several islands. ✉ *515 Basin Point Rd., South Harpswell* ☎ *207/833–6000* ⊕ *www.dolphinchowderhouse.com* ▱ *AE, D, MC, V* ☙ *Closed Nov.–May.*

WHERE TO STAY

$$–$$$

▦ **Captain's Watch Bed & Breakfast.** Built in 1862, the Captain's Watch is the oldest lodging on the Maine Coast. Although much smaller than when it was originally built as the Union Hotel, this property on the National Historic Register retains its distinctive octagonal cupola. A private dock is available to launch your kayaks, and you can arrange to go sailing with owner and Captain Ken Brigham aboard the inn's 38-foot sloop, *Symbion ll.* History buffs will enjoy the main hotel's array of intriguing photos from the days of schooners and steamers. Many of the rooms have pleasant water views. The owners also have added a second lodging at Card CoveEither home can be rented in full; no children under 12 are allowed except for when the entire home is rented. **Pros:** quiet, peaceful; ocean and sailing access. **Cons:** no air-conditioning. ✉ *926 Cundy's Harbor Rd., Harpswell* ☎ *207/725–0979* ⊕ *home.gwi.net/~cwatch* ⇖ *3 rooms, 1 suite* ♿ *In-room: no phone, no*

IF YOU LIKE

BICYCLING

The best in the state, the Androscoggin River Bike Path goes between U.S. 1 and the Androscoggin River. Great blue herons prowl in the shallows, and hawks patrol above—you might even see a bald eagle surveying the landscape (the national bird, which was seldom seen in these parts a few years ago, has made a comeback, with more than 477 nesting pairs now in the state as of 2008). There are also two longer bike paths in this region: the Coastal Route, a 187-mi journey, goes along the rocky coastline. The 60-mi Merrymeeting Tour travels between Bath and Wiscasset.

BEACHES

Maine has some of the country's most dramatic beaches. As you drive north, they are apt to be rocky rather than sandy. In the southern Mid-Coast region there are two awesome ones, both unique in their ways: Popham Beach, part of Popham Beach State Park near Phippsburg, and Mile Beach at Reid State Park. Popham stretches for miles, and when the tide is low you can explore the sandbars and tide pools, which teem with sea creatures. On one end of the beach is Fort Popham, a fortress dating from the Civil War. At Reid State Park's Mile Beach, climb the rocky ledges and watch the surf smash into the rocks—this is the best place to watch the waves during a storm. If you are here in mid-July or later, bring insect spray for the notorious "green heads," a hardy fly that defies killing. Slap at them and they'll just go for your feet and ankles.

LIGHTHOUSES

Of the 16 lighthouses in the Mid-Coast region, about half are accessible by car. The Doubling Point Light and Kennebec River Light on the Kennebec River are accessible from Route 209 in Bath. Squirrel Point Light, south of Bath, is accessible via a three-road journey and short hike: Route 127, Steen Road, and Bald Head Road, where you leave your car and hike for about a mile. Farther north, Pemaquid Point Light stands watch over long rocky ledges. The former lighthouse keeper's cottage is now the Fishermen's Museum, featuring artifacts on the area's commercial fishing history. Marshall Point Lighthouse at Port Clyde also has been turned into a museum and small shop, with picnic tables on the grounds. On Owl's Head just south of Rockland is Owl Head Light, one of the few that still has its original Fresnel lens in place. Lighthouse cruises from Bath take in almost a dozen lights, including Seguin Light, the tallest lighthouse in Maine, while cruises from Boothbay Harbor provide a view of Ram Island Light. A Boothbay Cruise to Burnt Island Light includes two hours on the island. Visit the Rockland Lighthouse Museum on Rockland Harbor to see a dozen Fresnel lenses.

4

cable TV (some). In-hotel: Internet terminal, public Wi-Fi ▭ MC, V for deposit only (remainder must be paid by cash or check) 🍴 BP.

$$–$$$$ ★ **Harpswell Inn Bed & Breakfast.** The smell of the salt air greets you at this charming B&B on Lookout Point. The inn was originally the old cookhouse at Curtis Shipyard, where schooners and brigs were built around the time of the Civil War. Rooms are furnished with antiques, and many have fireplaces and balconies with a view of the sunset over Middle Bay. You can enjoy acres of oak-shaded lawns on the knoll overlooking the ocean, making it popular for weddings. Ask the owners about their list of walking and hiking suggestions. The facility also rents out four cottages for $975–$1,450 a week. Pets are allowed in cottages; kids are best accommodated in suites or cottages. Kayaks are free to guests. **Pros:** spectacular view; a large property to explore; water access. **Cons:** not many shops or restaurants are within walking distance. ✉ *108 Lookout Point Rd., Harpswell* ☎ *207/833–5509 or 800/843–5509* 🌐 *www.harpswellinn.com* *9 rooms, 3 suites, 4 cottages* *In-room: Wi-Fi, no a/c (some), no phone. In-hotel: public computer, public Wi-Fi* ▭ *D, MC, V* 🍴 *BP.*

$$$–$$$$ **Log Cabin Inn.** These cheery contemporary rooms and apartments on Bailey Island have full kitchens and private decks that look out over Mackerel Cove, making them great for families or for long stays for exploring the Harpswells. An eccentric doctor once lived in a log cabin that now serves as the dining room. Get a room on the upper floor, these have the sunniest decks. Four rooms have wonderful outdoor hot tubs. Maine art is featured in each room, and colorful comforters drape the beds. If you like space, one option is a fully equipped two-story house. **Pros:** relaxing and expansive water views; private decks. **Cons:** rooms are furnished in a contemporary style, so those craving a quaint B&B should look elsewhere. ✉ *5 Log Cabin La., Bailey Island* ☎ *207/833–5546* 🌐 *www.logcabin-maine.com* *9 rooms* *In-room: Wi-Fi, DVD, refrigerator, no a/c. In-hotel: bar, pool* ▭ *AE, D, MC, V* *Closed Nov.–Mar.* 🍴 *BP.*

SHOPPING

ART GALLERIES In Harpswell, **Sebascodegan Artists Cooperative** (✉ *4 Old Orr's Island Rd., Harpswell* ☎ *207/833–5717*) displays work by Maine artists.

CLOTHING AND JEWELRY At the tip of Bailey Island, **Land's End Gifts** (✉ *Land's End, Bailey Island* ☎ *207/833–2313* *Apr.–Nov.*) is a spacious two-story shop overlooking the water. From April through October it sells cards, calendars, and collectibles as well as T-shirts, sweatshirts, and hats.

FOOD AND WINE Look for tiny **Hawke's Lobster and Gifts** (✉ *992 Cundy's Harbor Rd., Cundy's Harbor* ☎ *207/721–0472* 🌐 *www.hawkeslobster.com*), with its lights sparkling in the sunlight or out of the fog next to Holbrook's Wharf. It has Maine-made home-and-garden items as well as lobsters for sale. It is open Memorial Day to Columbus Day, though it sells lobsters year-round. Turtles, brittle, and English toffee are highlights of **Island Candy Company** (✉ *1795 Harpswell Islands Rd., Orr's Island* ☎ *207/833–6639*) —watch them make it in the back of the store. They also sell Shain's ice cream made in nearby Sanford.

POTTERY See how pottery is fired at **Ash Cove Pottery** (✉ *75 Ash Cove Rd., Harpswell* ☎ *207/833–6004*). The cooperative gallery and its two retail shops are open all year.

SPORTS AND THE OUTDOORS

The coast near Brunswick is full of hidden nooks and crannies waiting to be explored. By kayak you can seek out secluded beaches and ★ coves along the shore, and watch gulls and cormorants diving for fish. **H2Outfitters** (✉ *Rte. 24, Orr's Island* ☎ *207/833–5257 or 800/205–2925* ⊕ *www.h2outfitters.com*) is the place in Harpswells to get on the water. They are at the end of Orr's Island just before the cribstone bridge. They provide top-notch kayaking instruction and gear for people of all skill levels.

4

BATH

11 mi northeast of Brunswick, 38 mi northeast of Portland.

Bath has been a shipbuilding center since 1607. The result of its prosperity can be seen in its handsome mix of Federal, Greek Revival, and Italianate homes along Front, Centre, and Washington streets. In the heart of Bath's historic district are some charming 19th-century homes, including the 1820 Federal-style home at 360 Front St., the 1810 Greek Revival–style mansion at 969 Washington St., covered with gleaming white clapboards, and the Victorian gem at 1009 Washington St., painted a distinctive shade of raspberry. All three operate as inns. An easily overlooked site is the town's City Hall. The bell in its tower was cast by Paul Revere in 1805. Step inside to see the day's front page from the Bath Daily Times 100 years ago.

The venerable Bath Iron Works completed its first passenger ship in 1890. During World War II BIW—as it's locally known—launched a new ship every 17 days. It is still building today, turning out destroyers for the U.S. Navy. BIW is one of the state's largest employers, with about 5,600 workers. It's a good idea to avoid U.S. 1 on weekdays from 3:15 PM to 4:30 PM, when a major shift change takes place. You can tour BIW through the Maine Maritime Museum.

EXPLORING

Fort Popham. Follow Route 209 south 15 mi from Bath to reach the site of the short-lived Popham Colony, established in 1607. This granite-walled museum was built in 1861 for use during the Civil War. It also was employed in the Spanish-American War and World War I. Outside the walls are picnic tables. ✉ *Rte. 209, Phippsburg* ☎ *207/389–1335*).

Fodor's Choice **Maine Maritime Museum.** No trip to Bath is complete without a visit to ★ this cluster of buildings that once made up the historic Percy & Small Shipyard. Plan on half a day at the museum, which examines the world of shipbuilding and is the only way to tour the Bath Iron Works. In summer, boat tours cruise the scenic Kennebec River, the very best way to get to know the area. A particular favorite is the lighthouse tour that covers the area of the Kennebec from Bath down to Fort Popham at the mouth of the river. A number of impressive ships, including the 142-foot Grand Banks fishing schooner *Sherman Zwicker,* are on display in summer. Inside the main museum building, exhibits use ship models, paintings, photographs, and historical artifacts to tell the maritime history of the region. From May to November, hour-long tours of the shipyard show how these massive wooden ships were built. You can watch boatbuilders wield their tools in the boat shop. A separate historic building houses a fascinating lobstering exhibit. It's worth coming here just to watch an 18-minute video on lobstering written and narrated by E.B. White. A gift shop and bookstore are on the premises, and you can grab a bite to eat in the cafe or bring a picnic to eat on the grounds. Kids ages four and younger get in free. ✉ *243 Washington St.* ☎ *207/442–0961* ⊕ *www.mainemaritimemuseum.org* 🖃 *$12* ⊙ *Daily 9:30–5.*

OFF THE BEATEN PATH

☻ **Popham Beach State Park** (✉ *Rte. 209, Phippsburg* ☎ *207/389–1335*) has bathhouses and picnic tables. There are no restaurants at this end of the beach, so pack a picnic or get takeout from Spinney's Restaurant near the Civil War–era Fort Popham or Percy's Store (✉ *6 Sea St.* ☎ *207/389–2010*) behind Spinney's. At low tide you can walk miles of tidal flats and also out to a nearby island, where you can explore tide pools or fish off the ledges. Drive past the entrance to the park, and on the right you can see a vista often described as "Million Dollar View." The confluence of the Kennebec and Morse rivers creates an ever-shifting pattern of sandbars.

WHERE TO EAT

$$$
SEAFOOD

✕ **Anna's Water's Edge Restaurant.** You'll find seafood as fresh as it gets at this humble place on Sebasco Wharf. Specialties include fresh traditional pan-fried fish, cooked by dipping fish fillets in a mixture of flour and egg, and then sizzling them in a skillet. Other favorites include baked local scallops stuffed with crabmeat and topped with Parmesan cheese sauce. Soups and chowders are all made on the premises. ✉ *75 Black's Landing Rd., Sebasco Estates* ☎ *207/389–1803* ⊕ *www.thewatersedgerestaurant.com/* 🖃 *MC, V* ⊙ *Closed Sept.–May.*

$$
AMERICAN

✕ **Beale Street Barbecue.** Ribs are the thing at this barbecue joint. Hearty eaters should ask for one of the platters piled high with pulled pork, pulled chicken, or shredded beef. If you can't decide, there's always the massive barbecue sampler. Jalapeño popovers and chili served with corn bread are terrific appetizers. Enjoy a beer at the bar while waiting for your table. ✉ *215 Water St.* ☎ *207/442–9514* ⊕ *www.mainebbq.com* 🖃 *MC, V.*

¢–$
CAFÉ

✕ **Café Crème.** This café is the social hub of town. Changing exhibits by local artists hang on the walls of this downtown coffee shop. Its prime location, on a corner facing Front Street, lets you take a break from window-shopping. Come in for a cup of espresso, a blueberry muffin, or one of the delicious house-made scones. Light lunches include freshly prepared salads, stuffed croissants, and quiche. There's also Maine-made ice cream. ■ **TIP→ If you are in the area in fall or winter, you can catch Tuesday-evening readings by local poets and try your hand at the open mike session.** ✉ *56 Front St.* ☎ *207/443–6454* 🖃 *MC, V.*

$–$$
SEAFOOD
★

✕ **Five Islands Lobster Company.** Drive to the end of Route 127 to relax in the ocean breezes at this lobster shack on the dock at Five Islands Marina, not too far from Reid State Park. On this working wharf you can watch lobstermen baiting their traps or repairing their boats while you feast on fresh lobster rolls and sample Maine-made ice cream. The "secret" of the infamous tartar sauce is dill. ⊠ *1447 Five Islands Rd., Georgetown* ☎ *207/371–2990* ⊕ *www.fiveislandslobster.com/* ▤ *AE, MC, V* ☾ *Closed Columbus Day–early May.*

$$–$$$ ⨯ **J.R. Maxwell and Company.** Famous for its prime rib and seafood
AMERICAN entrées, this longtime local favorite serves great seafood chowder and steamed clams. The dining room displays half-hull models of several ships built in Bath and an assortment of handsome stained-glass lamp shades. You can enjoy a glass of wine at either of two bars, including the downstairs Boat Builders Pub. ⊠ *122 Front St.* ☎ *207/443–2014* ▤ *D, MC, V.*

$$–$$$ ⨯ **Kennebec Tavern & Marina.** Standing alongside the Kennebec River,
AMERICAN Bath's only waterfront restaurant has its own marina, where you can tie up your boat and come in for a delicious lunch or dinner. Eat inside or out on the canopied deck. Specialties include smoked cream of tomato soup and the fried calamari. Try the fried parsnip appetizer—it's hard to beat this crisp chip anywhere. For your entrée there's no better choice than the pan-blackened catch-of-the-day. The dining room has wonderful views, and the walls are hung with old photos of Bath. If you prefer, you can eat in the bar, which also has a view of the boats. ⊠ *119 Commercial St.* ☎ *207/442–9636* ⊕ *www.kennebectavern.com* ▤ *AE, D, DC, MC, V.*

$ ⨯ **North Creek Farm.** This delightful local favorite, part hippie paradise,
AMERICAN part foodie beacon, is just off the side road to Sebasco Estates. Walk through the door, and you'd think you were in a boutique grocery and garden store, with hard-to-find spices, sauces, Spanish anchovies, wines, locally made gifts, seeds, and gardening tools. Walk out the back door and you'll end up meandering under arches along pergolas and through delightful gardens of fresh herbs and bright flowers, some of which are for sale. But back inside is the best find of all, within the almost hidden kitchen where owner Suzy Verrier cooks up delicious inexpensive sandwiches, soups, and pastries each day, largely using produce grown outside. There are a few tables here, but you'll likely find yourself eating outside in the gardens. ⊠ *24 Sebasco Rd., Phippsburg* ☎ *207/389–1342* ⊕ *northcreekfarm.org* ⬧ *Reservations not accepted* ▤ *AE, MC, V* ☾ *Open daily.*

$$–$$$ ⨯ **The Osprey.** Traditional Maine fare draws folks to this Robinhood
SEAFOOD Marina restaurant overlooking the harbor. Open only in summer, the
★ Osprey has wonderful views of the boats as well as an osprey nest. Choice dishes include the sweet potato–encrusted haddock and grilled strawberry spinach salad. For something a little different, try the lobster corn chowder. ⊠ *358 Robinhood Rd., Georgetown* ☎ *207/371–2530* ▤ *AE, D, MC, V* ☾ *Closed Columbus Day–Memorial Day.*

$$$–$$$$ ⨯ **Robinhood Free Meetinghouse.** This 1855 church and meetinghouse is
AMERICAN a remarkable setting for a meal. On occasion you can even eat upstairs among the pews. Though owned by acclaimed chef and owner Michael Gagné—whose multilayer cream-cheese biscuits are shipped all over the country—this meetinghouse serves meals that are primarily made by chef de cuisine Troy Mains. The menu changes daily, but always has

a variety of seafood, vegetables, and dairy products purchased locally. You might begin with the lobster and crab cakes, then move on to grilled fillet of beef stuffed with crab or the confit of duck. Finish up with the signature Obsession in Three Chocolates. The wine list offers an array of choices to accompany Mains's creations. The service is excellent. The dining room evokes its meetinghouse past with cream-color walls, pine floorboards, and cherry Shaker-style chairs. Crisp linens add an elegant touch. ⊠ *210 Robinhood Rd., Georgetown* ☎ *207/371–2188* ⊕ *www.robinhood-meetinghouse.com* ▤ *AE, D, MC, V* ◎ *No lunch.*

$–$$$
SEAFOOD

✕ **Spinney's.** Looking for a really inexpensive but hearty breakfast with a great view? Omelets, pancakes, home fries, and eggs cooked to order are on the menu for early risers at this waterfront restaurant with a view of Fort Popham. For lunch or dinner there are tasty lobster rolls or rolls with clams, scallops, crab, or shrimp. Locals describe two dishes as "wicked good": the Popham Platter (every type of seafood you can imagine) and the Wood Island Wreck Platter (shrimp, scallops, and steak hot off the grill). ⊠ *987 Popham Rd., Phippsburg* ☎ *207/389–1122* ▤ *MC, V* ◎ *Closed late Oct.–Mother's Day.*

¢
CAFÉ
★

✕ **Starlight Café.** Just downhill from the corner of Lambard and Front streets, this bright, delightful little eatery is so easy to pass right by it's a locals' secret. Omelets and pancakes make for premier breakfast choices, while sandwiches and pizzas are top lunch-menu picks. Breads are baked daily. Arrive before 2 PM, because the café isn't open for dinner. ⊠ *15 Lambard St.* ☎ *207/443–3005* ▤ *No credit cards* ◎ *Closed weekends. No dinner.*

WHERE TO STAY

$$–$$$
★

▥ **1774 Inn.** On a little hill overlooking a wide bend of the Kennebec River, this Georgian-style pre-Revolutionary mansion offers the very best of Phippsburg. Expect handsome interior detailing and magnificent antiques. The Ships Carpenter's quarters was an addition built in 1870; it features the Woodshed Room, which has a private veranda with steps leading down to 250 private feet of Kennebec frontage. New owners John Atkinson and Jacqueline Hogg (via England and Ireland), provide energy and attention to detail. **Pros:** private river frontage; Colonial-era features. **Cons:** may be too quiet for some; no TV. ⊠ *44 Parker Head Rd., Phippsburg* ☎ *207/389–1774* ⊕ *www.1774inn.com* ⇌ *8 rooms* ⚘ *In-room: Wi-Fi, no TV. In-hotel: public computer, public Wi-Fi, no kids under 12* ▤ *no credit cards* ⦿ *BP.*

$$–$$$
★

▥ **Coveside Bed & Breakfast.** If you're looking for a quiet waterside retreat on Georgetown peninsula, look no further. Near the village of Five Islands on secluded and quiet-as-can-be Georgetown Island, this traditional shingled cottage sits on five secluded acres that run along Gott's Cove. Every room has a water view and features local art. Bring your kayak, or alternatively, use the canoe or one of the several bicycles available for outings. The inn's dock is perfect for sunbathing or watching the water. Stroll along nearby nature preserves or visit Reid State Park. Gulls, herons, and osprey are frequently sighted here, and you may catch a glimpse of the occasional seal or even a moose. Amenities include complimentary beer, coffee, soda, and cookies. **Pros:** waterfront relaxation; great boating; clean and cheery rooms. **Cons:**

13 mi from town. ⊠ *6 Gott's Cove La., Georgetown* ☎ *207/371–2807 or 800/232–5490* ⊕ *www.covesidebandb.com* ⮐ *7 rooms* ⚴ *In-room: Wi-Fi, no a/c. In-hotel: bicycles, no kids under 12* ⊟ *AE, D, MC, V* ⊘ *Closed mid-Oct.–late May* ⦿| *BP.*

$$–$$$ 🏨 **Kennebec Inn.** There are three rooms in the old Captain Perkins house that combines Greek Revival, Italianate, and Early American architecture. Though it's up some very steep steps, the English Country Room is cheery, with windows on three sides. You'll definitely want to stay here if you're a swimmer—there's an outdoor lap pool measuring 40 feet by 60 feet in landscaped grounds. There is also a piano available for guests who like to play. **Pros:** pool; piano. **Cons:** on other side of U.S. 1; a few blocks from Front Street. ⊠ *696 High St.* ☎ *207/443–5324 or 888/595–1564* ⊕ *www.kennebecinn.com* ⮐ *3 rooms* ⚴ *In-room: Wi-Fi. In-hotel: public Wi-Fi* ⊟ *D, MC, V* ⦿| *BP.*

$$$$
Fodor's Choice
★
🏨 **Kismet.** You're not likely to encounter another B&B in New England like this. Let's get some basics out of the way: it has the best location of any inn in Bath; the furnishings are minimalist and impeccable; the food is refined and delicious; it's much cleaner than any place you've ever stayed in (in fact, the innkeeper insists on waiting a full day between guest rentals for every room). With that said, it's not for everybody—but if you're the kind to appreciate being required to take off your shoes at the door; the kind who believes in an organic lifestyle; the kind who thinks that decor should reflect the spirit; well then, welcome to paradise. Shadi Towfighi is the meticulous Irani innkeeper who has created this unlikely haven across the street from City Park and its famous statue *Spirit of the Sea.* She is responsible for preparing organic, natural foods, and has decorated the rooms with custom-designed beds, family heirlooms, and select artifacts from her international travels. The inn also has a spa that features massages and body exfoliation, as well as a spacious and airy third-floor yoga studio. For the right guest, a stay here is a complete rejuvenation. **Pros:** luxurious simplicity; yoga and treatments; steam showers or Japanese soaking tubs in rooms; top location; great organic breakfast. **Cons:** some travelers will be turned off by having to take off their shoes. ⊠ *44 Summer St.* ☎ *207/443–3399* ⊕ *www.kismetinnmaine.com* ⮐ *5 rooms* ⚴ *In-room: no TV, no phone. In-hotel: public Wi-Fi, no kids allowed* ⊟ *No credit cards* ⦿| *BP.*

$$–$$$ 🏨 **Mooring Bed & Breakfast.** Originally the home of Walter Reid, who donated the land for Reid State Park, this inn has stayed in the same family for generations. It is now owned by Reid's great-granddaughter and her family. The five guest rooms all have air-conditioning and great ocean views, and some have wood floors. Rooms with themes played out in their colors and decor include the Lighthouse, Violet, and Rose rooms; art compliments each theme. Retreat to the Spanish Room with a good book for a quiet place, or catch the ocean breeze on a screened porch, a relaxing place to have breakfast. Well-tended gardens grace the grounds, and its location on the bank of the Kennebec River has made it a favorite for weddings, conferences, and reunions. **Pros:** on the water; impressive views. **Cons:** 11 mi from town. ⊠ *132 Seguinland Rd., Georgetown* ☎ *207/371–2790 or 866/828–7343* ⊕ *www.themooringb-b.*

4

com ⌚ *5 rooms* ♿ *In-room: Wi-Fi. In-hotel: public Wi-Fi* ⊟ *MC, V* ⊗ *Closed mid-Oct.–mid-May* ⏚ *BP.*

$$$–$$$$
★

⌂ **Popham Beach Bed & Breakfast.** The sound of the waves is the sound-track to your stay here, in a wonderful sunlight-filled 1863 lifesaving station, originally constructed for stranded seamen. Talk about loca-tion—this casual bed-and-breakfast sits right on Popham Beach! The owner provides beach chairs and umbrellas, good for your explora-tions of what amounts to your front yard—the juncture of Kennebec River with the Atlantic, and views of a fishing village, two lighthouses, sea islands, and historic Fort Popham. Sun-filled rooms are comfort-ably furnished. The nicest quarters include the one aptly named the Library, where two walls are lined with books. Guests can stroll up to the cupola for more amazing views before enjoying a two-or three-course breakfast in the former mess hall. A casual seafood restaurant is close by, and you can order lunch at North Creek Farm. **Pros:** right on Popham Beach. **Cons:** no air-conditioning. ⊠ *4 Riverview Ave., Phipps-burg* ☎ *207/389–2409* ⊕ *www.pophambeachbandb.com* ⌚ *3 rooms, 1 suite* ♿ *In-room: no phone, no TV, Wi-Fi. In-hotel: public Wi-Fi, no kids under 15, beachfront.* ⊟ *MC, V* ⏚ *BP.*

$$

⌂ **Pryor House Bed & Breakfast.** An elegant double staircase in the foyer welcomes you to this 1820s Federal-style home gazing down on the Kennebec River. It's in the historic district of Bath, so shops and res-taurants are nearby. The Tall Chimney Room, with its own private outdoor deck, has a railroad theme, with a working model train that runs around the chimney. There's also an indoor hot tub big enough for two. Nautical themes are reflected in the Captain's Room suite, with its wide pine floorboards and windows overlooking the river, and the Elizabeth Room, decorated in Victorian style in pinks and whites. The owner is an enthusiastic cook, and serves many creative dishes for breakfast, never the same thing two days in a row. **Pros:** in-town location; multi-course breakfasts. **Cons:** steep driveway. ⊠ *360 Front St.* ☎ *207/443–1146* ⊕ *www.pryorhouse.com* ⌚ *3 rooms* ♿ *In-room: no TV (some), Wi-Fi (some). In-hotel: no kids under 12, public Wi-Fi* ⊟ *AE, D, DC, MC, V* ⏚ *BP.*

$$$–$$$$
Fodor's Choice
★

⌂ **Sebasco Harbor Resort.** This destination family resort spread across 575 acres at the foot of the Phippsburg Peninsula has an exceptional range of accommodations and services. Comfortable guest rooms in the clapboard-covered main building have antique furnishings and new bathrooms, while rooms in a building designed to resemble a lighthouse have wicker furniture, paintings by local artists, and rooftop access. The Fairwinds Spa Suites are corporate luxury units next to the resort's spa; prices for combo room and treatment packages range from $369 to $399. The recently added Harbor Village Suites are set in exquisitely landscaped grounds and include 18 spacious and air-conditioned rooms. These units rent for $319–$459. The resort's Pilot House restaurant ($$–$$$) is known for its innovative take on classic dishes, and is a wonderful spot for watching sunsets. In summer there are wonderful outdoor lobster and clambakes. Kids club activities include sessions with a staff naturalist. **Pros:** ocean location; excellent food and service; kids activities. **Cons:** some rooms do not have a/c; pricey ⊠ *29 Kenyon*

Rd,, off Rte. 217, Sebasco Estates ☎ *207/389–1161 or 800/225–3819* ⊕ *www.sebasco.com* ⌑ *115 rooms, 23 cottages* ⌕ *In-room: Wi-Fi (some). In-hotel: 3 restaurants, bar, golf course, tennis courts, pool, gym, bicycles, public Wi-Fi, airport shuttle* ▤ *AE, D, MC, V* ⊗ *Closed Nov.–mid-May* ⑩ *MAP.*

$$$$ ⚏ **Stonehouse Manor at Popham Beach.** If you're looking for beach-side
↺ peace and tranquillity, this is your place. The 11-acre property includes the wonderful 1897 stone-and-shingle Arts and Crafts manor and a long lawn leading to Silver Lake, where you can use one of the paddleboats. You might want to do the 3-mi beach loop that starts just a few minutes' walk away at Popham Beach. At low tide you can walk to coastal islands, and fishing can be really good where the Kennebec River meets the sea at the beach. Owners Jane and Tim Dennis are great hosts. **Pros:** extensive grounds and gardens; easy access to all beaches, but you can retreat to this tranquil estate. **Cons:** far from town. ⊠ *907 Popham Rd., Phippsburg* ☎ *207/389–1141 or 877/389–1141* ⌑ *1 room, 4 suites* ⌕ *In-room: Wi-Fi. In-hotel: public Wi-Fi* ▤ *No credit cards* ⑩ *BP.*

NIGHTLIFE AND THE ARTS

The **Chocolate Church Arts Center** (⊠ *804 Washington St.* ☎ *207/442–8455 http://chocolatechurcharts.org*) hosts folk, jazz, and classical concerts, as well as theatrical performances for adults and children. Shows are held inside the spectacular 1843 Gothic Revival church. The adjacent gallery space exhibits works in various mediums by local artists. Classes in watercolors and pastels are available.

SHOPPING

ANTIQUES
AND COL-
LECTIBLES

Open year-round, **Brick Store Antiques** (⊠ *143 Front St.* ☎ *207/443–2790*) displays genuine antiques—no reproductions. You'll spot an authentic tepee as you approach **Native Arts** (⊠ *183 U.S. 1, Woolwich* ☎ *207/442–8399*), which carries fine crafts, from carvings made by Inuits in Alaska to beadwork produced in South America. Native drums are on display. There are classes held every couple weeks on drum- and flute-making. The **Montsweag Flea Market** (⊠ *Mountain Rd. and U.S. 1, Woolwich* ☎ *207/443–2809*) is a roadside attraction with treasure, trash, and everything in between. If you're looking for "Maine stuff" to take home, this might be your best bet. It's open Wednesday, Saturday, and Sunday from May through mid-October.

CLOTHING

At **Magnolia** (⊠ *129 Front St.* ☎ *207/442–8989* ⊕ *www.magnoliagiftstore.com* ⊗ *Mon.–Sat.*) hard-to-find items, including "elegant indulgences" and cute kids' clothing, are a speciality.

HOME
ACCESSORIES

Backroads by the Sea (⊠ *459 Main Rd., Phippsburg* ☎ *207/443–9604*) is a neat little gift shop on the way to Popham Beach. The owner is known for her colorful restored furniture, even pieces like a lavender table! She also carries jewelry, quilts, handbags, and pottery, all made by Maine crafters. Maine art and a small selection of Maine books and kids' books are also available.

BOOKS

Open Door Books (⊠ *178 Front St.* ☎ *207/443–8689* ⊗ *Mon.–Sat.*) is great for used books, with a specialty in old and rare.

SPORTS AND THE OUTDOORS

Fodor'sChoice   **Reid State Park.** On Georgetown Island, this park has 1½ mi of sand split
★   between two beaches. Families love the white sand and dunes here, and
the views from the park's rocky Griffith Head are great, too. In summer,
parking lots fill by 11 AM on weekends and holidays. If swimming, be
aware of the possibility of an undertow. During a storm this is a great
place to observe the ferocity of the waves crashing onto the shore.
⊠ *R375 Seguinland Rd, off Rte. 127* ☎ *207/371–2303.*

GOLF   A par 70, 18-hole championship golf course distinguishes the **Bath Country Club** (⊠ *387 Whiskeag Rd.* ☎ *207/442–8411*), where you can find
a tavern and the biggest pro shop in Maine. The 9-hole **Sebasco Estates
Golf Course** (⊠ *Rte. 217, Phippsburg* ☎ *207/389–1161*) sits right on the
water, so you can enjoy the salt breeze while you play.

HIKING   The tranquil **Josephine Newman Sanctuary** (⊠ *Bay Point Rd., Georgetown* ⊗ *Daily*) is a 119-acre nature preserve on the Georgetown Peninsula. The walking trails are operated by the Maine Audubon Society.
Protect yourself from deer ticks by wearing long pants and sleeves.
Morse Mountain Preserve (⊠ *Rte. 216, Phippsburg* ☎ *No phone*), a 600-
acre preserve owned by Bates College, has trails through the woods that
lead to Sewall Beach. There is a small parking area off the side of the
road just after the junction with Route 209.

WATER   To cruise the Kennebec or other coastal rivers in the area, arrange a
SPORTS   tour through the Maine Maritime Museum (reserve ahead). Otherwise
contact **Long Reach Cruises** (⊠ *75 Commercial St.* ☎ *888/538–6786*),
which operates excursion and sightseeing tours out of Bath's Waterfront
Park; rates begin at $20. Cruises past some of the region's distinctive
sights are the company's specialty; you learn all the local history from
the knowledgeable captain and crew. This outfit also heads to Merrymeeting Bay, Harpswell Sound, and Damariscotta Bay. If you want
to explore on your own, **Bay Point Sports** (⊠ *Rte. 127, Georgetown*
☎ *888/349–7772*) rents kayaks from April to Labor Day.

EN   Coastal Route 1, which runs between Bath and Wiscasset, takes you
ROUTE   over a bridge that crosses the Kennebec River. Along the way you pass
Bath Iron Works and its busy yard, where U.S. Navy destroyers are
built. Between the two towns is an eclectic collection of shops. Take
home a small statue for your flower garden or a model ship for your
mantel. Traffic on the highway is heavy on weekends and between 3
and 4 PM ON WEEKDAYS, when the shift changes at Bath Iron Works, so
plan to take your time and stop along the way.

WISCASSET

10 mi north of Bath, 46 mi northeast of Portland.

Settled in 1663, Wiscasset sits on the banks of the Sheepscot River.
It bills itself "Maine's Prettiest Village," and it's easy to see why: it
has graceful churches, old cemeteries, and elegant sea captains' homes
(many converted into antiques shops or galleries).

Pack a picnic and take it down to the dock, where you can watch the
fishing boats or grab a lobster roll from Red's Eats or the lobster shack

on the dock. Wiscasset has expanded its wharf, and this is a great place to catch a breeze on a hot day. U.S. 1 becomes Main Street, and traffic often slows to a crawl. If you park in town, you can walk to most galleries, shops, restaurants, and other attractions. ■ TIP➜ **Try to arrive early in the morning to find a parking space—you'll likely have success if you try to park on Water Street rather than Main.**

EXPLORING

Castle Tucker. Learn the history of Wiscasset through the story of the Tucker family, who lived in this Regency-style mansion from 1858 to 2003. Now run as a house museum by Historic New England, the circa-1807 house has extravagant architecture, Victorian appointments, and a freestanding elliptical staircase. Standing on top of a hill overlooking the Sheepscot River, the structure was built by Judge Silas Lee when Wiscasset was the busiest port east of Boston ⊠ *2 Lee St.* ☎ *207/882–7169* ✉ *$5* ⊙ *June 1–Oct. 15, Wed.–Sun. 11–5; tours on the hr 11–4.*

★ **Musical Wonder House.** This grand 1852 former sea captain's home, is now a museum with 5,000 antique music boxes from around the world, including musical porcelains, furniture, and paintings. Also see player pianos and other musical rarities. Your entry will set one of the music boxes to start playing. Tours of the main floor or the entire house are available on the hour beginning at 10 AM. Kids 11 and younger are admitted free. ⊠ *18 High St.* ☎ *207/882–7163 or 800/336–3725* ⊕ *www.musicalwonderhouse.com* ✉ *$10 for 45-min tour; $20 for whole-house tour* ⊙ *Memorial Day–Halloween., Mon.–Sat. 10–5, Sun. noon–5.*

.**Nickels-Sortwell House.** This manse, now owned by Historic New England, is an outstanding example of the high Federal style. Built in 1807 by Captain William Nickels, a shipowner and trader, the house recalls the prosperity of the time. After Nickels's death the house was run as an inn from 1814 to 1899, when the mayor of Cambridge, Massachusetts, Alvin Sortwell, purchased it for a family summer retreat. The home was then lovingly restored in the Colonial Revival style, with fine antiques from the 17th through the 19th centuries. ⊠ *121 Main St.* ☎ *207/882–7169* ✉ *$5* ⊙ *June–mid-Oct., Fri.–Sun. 11–5, tours on the hr 11–4.*

Wiscasset Waterville & Farmington Railway. Here you can celebrate Maine's railroad heritage with train rides and the best selection of railroad books in the state. It's run entirely by volunteers. Trains runs weekends June through November, but call ahead for a full schedule. ⊠ *Rte. 218, 5 mi north of U.S. 1, Alna* ☎ *207/882–4193* ⊕ *www.wwfry.org* ✉ *Museum free; train $6* ⊙ *Weekends 9–5 Memorial Day weekend–Columbus Day weekend; Saturday only remainder of year.*

WHERE TO EAT

¢ ✕ **Red's Eats.** You've probably driven right past this little red shack on FAST FOOD the Wiscasset side of the bridge if you've visited this area and seen the long line of hungry customers. Red's is a local landmark famous for its hot dogs, burgers, crisp onion rings, lobster and crab rolls, and even its ice cream—if you spot a kid with an ice-cream cone, it probably came from Red's. Try the black raspberry or the pistachio. There are a few picnic tables, but you can get your food to go and walk down to the dock to enjoy the view. Watch out for the seagulls; they like lobster rolls, too. ✉ *41 Water St.* ☎ *207/882–6128* ▭ *No credit cards* ⊘ *Closed mid-Oct.–mid-Apr.*

¢–$
AMERICAN

✕**Sarah's Café.** This family-friendly restaurant is at the harbor directly across U.S. 1 from Red's Eats, and has lovely views from indoors or outside on the deck, which overlooks the water. The menu covers a lot of ground, with entrées ranging from Mexican to Italian. There is also the catch of the day and the usual seafood items at market prices. Lunch and dinner are served all week and breakfast on weekends. The soups are excellent, as are the breads. ☎ *04578207/882–7504* ⊕ *www. sarahscafe.com* ▭ *AE, D, MC, V.*

NEED A BREAK?

Treats (✉ *80 Main St.* ☎ *207/882–6192*) stocks wonderful cheeses, wines, and fresh-baked breads, as well as decadent sandwiches that are perfect for an impromptu picnic at Waterfront Park.

WHERE TO STAY

$$

🛏**Marston House.** Rooms are $100 all year at this two-bedroom inn and antiques store on U.S. 1, a block from Red's Eats and a stone's throw away from Wiscasset's galleries and shops. Both rooms have private entrances and fireplaces, and are furnished simply with Shaker- and Colonial-style pieces. The rooms can be joined to make a suite perfect for families. A hearty continental breakfast is delivered to your room, or to the garden upon request, as there are no common rooms. **Pros:** located in the heart of town. **Cons:** no common rooms besides garden ✉ *101 Main St.* ☎ *207/882–6010 or 800/852–4137* 🛏 *2 rooms* △ *In-room: Wi-Fi, no TV, no a/c. In-hotel: public Wi-Fi* ▭ *AE, MC, V* ⊘ *Closed Nov.–Apr.* ❍ *CP.*

$$–$$$

🛏**Snow Squall Bed & Breakfast.** Built in the early 1850s, this carefully renovated inn is just a few blocks from Wiscasset's shops and harbor. Each of the four guest rooms is named for a clipper ship built in Maine: the White Falcon, the Golden Horn, the Flying Eagle, and the Red Jacket. Two rooms have fireplaces. There are also three two-bedroom suites, two of which are in the carriage house, with private entrances. The public area offers wireless Internet access and a TV. A yoga studio and meditation area are in a renovated barn, along with two massage treatment rooms. Owner Melanie Harris specializes in yoga and massage; her husband Paul, a professional chef, will make you a great breakfast. **Pros:** children welcome. **Cons:** off of busy Route 1. ✉ *5 Bradford Rd.* ☎ *207/882–6892* ⊕ *www.snowsquallinn.com* 🛏 *4 rooms, 2 suites* △ *In-room: Wi-Fi, no TV (some). In-hotel: public Wi-Fi* ▭ *MC, V* ⊘ *Closed Nov.–May, except by reservation* ❍ *BP.*

$$–$$$

🛏**Squire Tarbox Inn.** Built around 1763, this small country inn is listed on the National Register of Historic Places. The eponymous squire is buried next door in the family plot. Some of the charming guest rooms have fireplaces. Mountain bikes let you explore the surrounding woods, while a rowboat allows you to get a look at the coast. Breakfast includes European specialties like home-baked croissants, yogurt, and fresh fruit, along with traditional American pancakes or bacon and eggs. Freshly brewed coffee and a variety of teas are available. At the restaurant ($$$$), dine indoors or on the screened-in deck overlooking beautiful landscaped grounds and the organic garden that provides all of the inn's vegetables in season. Look for entrées such as rosemary-roasted rack of lamb and sea scallops in a garlic-butter sauce. Dinner is available daily in season for you as well as for the public. The hosts speak English, German, Italian, and French. The hotel accepts some credit cards, but checks are preferred. **Pros:** organic produce; dinners available; expansive grounds; great breakfasts. **Cons:** small showers; bar closes at night, owner can come across as gruff. ⊠ *1181 Main Rd. (Rte. 144)* ☎ *207/882–7693 or 800/818–0626* ⊕ *www.squiretarboxinn. com* ⮎ *11 rooms* ⅏ *In-room: no TV. In-hotel: public Wi-Fi, bicycles, no kids under 12* ▤ *MC, V* ⊗ *Closed Jan.–Mar.* ⦿ *BP.*

SHOPPING

ANTIQUES AND HOME FURNISHINGS The Wiscasset area rivals Searsport as a destination for antiquing. Shops line Wiscasset's main streets and extend over the bridge into Edgecomb. The **Butterstamp Workshop** (⊠ *55 Middle St.* ☎ *207/882– 7825*) manufactures and sells handcrafted folk art made from antique butter and chocolate molds. **Ingram Art and Antiques** (⊠ *85 Main St.* ☎ *207/882–7790* ⊗ *June–Oct,*) carries antiques as well as Oriental rugs and contemporary art. **Marston House American Antiques** (⊠ *101 Main St.* ☎ *207/882–6010*) specializes in 18th- and 19th-century painted furniture, homespun textiles, and antique garden accessories and tools. If you have a garden, don't miss the roadside spread at **North of the Border** (⊠ *605 Bath Rd.* ☎ *207/882–5432* ⊗ *Mid-Apr.–late Nov.*), which includes an array of stone and terra-cotta lawn and garden ornaments imported from Mexico.

★ **Elliott Healy Books** (⊠ *53 Middle St.* ☎ *207/882–5446*) is a spectacular antiquarian bookstore with a specialty in photography and illustrated books. It's worth a visit to meet Elliott, a local expert, and see the Japanese gardens in back. It is open daily from Memorial Day through Columbus Day.

ART AND CRAFTS **Blooms of Wiscasset** (⊠ *65 Main St.* ☎ *207/882–9901* ⊕ *www.blooms-ofwiscasset.com*) displays lots of metalware for sale, in addition to plants, flowers, and homemade chocolates. Not to be missed is **Edge-comb Potters** (⊠ *727 Boothbay Rd., Edgecomb* ☎ *207/882–9493* ⊕ *www. edgecombpotters.com*), which specializes in pricey, exquisitely-glazed porcelain and has one of the best selections in the area. It also carries jewelry. There are plenty of studios and galleries with eclectic collections in this part of Maine, and the **Maine Art Gallery** (⊠ *315 Warren St.* ☎ *207/882–7511*) is no exception. Presenting works by local artists, the bright and colorful gallery is filled with a variety of new and exciting pieces. **Rock, Paper, Scissors** (⊠ *78 Main St.* ☎ *207/882–9930*) is a stationery store with lots of items for children's activities. **Sheepscot River Pottery** (⊠ *34 U.S. 1, Edgecomb* ☎ *207/882–9410* ⊕ *www.sheepscot.com*) boasts beautifully glazed kitchen tiles as well as kitchenware and home accessories. The **Wiscasset Bay Gallery** (⊠ *67 Main St.* ☎ *207/882–7682* ⊕ *www.wiscassetbaygallery.com*) displays a fine collection of works by 19th- and 20th-century artists.

BOOTHBAY AND PEMAQUID PENINSULAS

If you head north from Wiscasset on U.S. 1, you'll reach Route 27 just after crossing the Wiscasset Bridge into Edgecomb. Route 27 brings you into the heart of Boothbay Harbor, a seaside community with myriad shops and restaurants. Whale-watching, lighthouse trips, puffin-spotting, and sightseeing cruises are popular pastimes. Farther south along Route 27 is Southport Island, where you can enjoy the ocean scenery and peek into a gallery or two. Route 96 takes you from Boothbay Harbor to East Boothbay, where you can see Ocean Point's rocky ledges and a handful of lobster shacks.

If you bypass Route 27 and continue north on U.S. 1 from Wiscasset, you'll come to Route 130, which leads to the Pemaquid Peninsula. Art galleries, antiques shops, and lobster shacks are found here and there along the country roads that meander through the countryside. At the tip of the point you can find a much-photographed lighthouse perched on an unforgiving rock ledge. Exploring here reaps many rewards, including views of salt ponds and boat-filled harbors. The twin towns of Damariscotta and Newcastle anchor the region, but small fishing villages such as Pemaquid, New Harbor, and Round Pond give the peninsula its pure Maine flavor.

BOOTHBAY HARBOR

13 mi southeast of Wiscasset via U.S. 1 to ME–27.

When Portlanders want a break from city life, many come north to the Boothbay region, which is made up of Boothbay proper, East Boothbay, and Boothbay Harbor. This part of the shoreline is a craggy stretch of inlets where pleasure craft anchor alongside trawlers and lobster boats. Boothbay Harbor is like a smaller version of Bar Harbor—touristy but friendly and fun—with pretty winding streets and lots to explore. Commercial Street, Wharf Street, Townsend Avenue, and the By-Way are lined with shops and ice-cream parlors. You can browse for hours in the trinket shops, crafts galleries, clothing stores, and boutiques around the harbor. And don't miss the old-fashioned candlepin bowling alley.

Excursion boats and ferries to Monhegan Island leave from the piers off Commercial Street. Drive out to Ocean Point in East Boothbay for some incredible scenery. Or head south to the endearing town of South Bristol, which has one of the busiest (and smallest) swing drawbridges in the world. Just over the bridge is Rutherford Island circling around Christmas Cove. The cove was named when explorer Captain John Smith anchored here one Christmas Eve in the early 1600s. Since that time the cove has been a snug harbor for watercraft of all kinds.

ESSENTIALS

Visitor Information Boothbay Harbor Region Chamber of Commerce (⌂ *P.O. Box 356, Boothbay Harbor 04538* ☎ *207/633–2353* ⊕ *www.boothbayharbor.com*).

EXPLORING

Boothbay Railway Village. About 1 mi north of Boothbay you'll find more than 50 antique automobiles and a gift shop, and you can ride 1½ mi on a coal-fired, narrow-gauge steam train that goes through a model of a century-old New England village. ⊠ *586 Wiscasset Rd. [Rte. 27]* ☎ *207/633–4727* ⊕ *www.railwayvillage.org* ⊠ *$9* ⊙ *Memorial Day– Columbus Day, daily 9:30–5.*

Burnt Island Light. Built in 1821, this lighthouse near Boothbay Harbor can be toured weekdays at 10 AM and 12:45 PM during the summer. Balmy Day Cruises gets you here from Pier 8 in Boothbay Harbor. **Cuck- olds Light,** which lies less than a mile off the southern tip of Southport Island, can also be seen here, unless it is fogged in. The fog signal was built in 1892, and the light was added in 1907 to prevent heavy ship- ping traffic entering the harbor from running aground.

★ **Coastal Maine Botanical Garden.** About a mile from Boothbay Center, this is the biggest botanical garden in New England, and one of its newest. Its 248 acres feature magnificent ornamental gardens, sculp- tures, a mile of tidal frontage, and wooded areas. ⊠ *Barters Island Rd., 1¼ mi from Boothbay Center, before coming into Boothbay Harbor* ☎ *207/633–4333* ⊕ *www.mainegardens.org.*

Maine State Aquarium. Here you can pet a baby shark at the petting pool, see marine creatures up close in the tide pools, and view tanks with rare blue lobsters. Bring a picnic lunch and enjoy the views of Boothbay Harbor. ⊠ *194 McKown Point Rd., West Boothbay Harbor* ☎ *207/633–9559* ⊕ *www.maine.gov/dmr* ⊠ *$5* ⊙ *Memorial Day–Sept. 30, daily 10–5.*

Rowmar Bowling. Boothbay is the kind of place that lends itself to whole-
★ some fun. This eight-lane candlepin bowling place has been here since 1946, and it oozes good times. Its nonagenarian owner, Charlie Row, still performs daily maintenance on the old-time lanes. You pay $3.25 per 10-frame "string" and each frame gives you three grapefruit-sized balls to roll. A diner-style counter offers hot dogs and burgers, and there are pinball and video games, too. ⊠ *19 Bridge St. 04538* ☎ *207/633– 5721* ⊠ *$8* ⊙ *June–Sept., daily noon–10.*

WHERE TO EAT

$–$$ ✕ **Boothbay Lobster Wharf.** Crustacean lovers will find something to sat-
SEAFOOD isfy their craving at this dockside working lobster pound. It's nothing fancy, but needless to say, you won't find fresher lobster anywhere else, and the steamed mussels and clams are mouthwatering. Eat in the din- ing room or outside, where you can watch the lobstermen at work. Pick up fresh fish from the fish market. The restaurant is on the pier near the Fisherman's Memorial across the harbor. ⊠ *97 Atlantic Ave., Booth- bay Harbor* ☎ *207/633–4900* ⊕ *www.boothbaylobsterwharf.com* ▭ *D, MC, V* ⊙ *Closed mid-Oct.–mid-May.*

¢–$$ ✕ **Ebb Tide.** Open all year for breakfast, lunch, and dinner, this friendly sea-
AMERICAN side restaurant is easy to spot because of its red-and-white awnings. Many original wooden booths in the dining room have views of the harbor. The establishment is known for its fish sandwiches, shrimp baskets, and lob- ster dinners. It also serves a good grilled-cheese sandwich. Everything on

the menu can be packed for takeout. Many people stop by in the afternoon for a cup of coffee and a piece of downright delicious homemade pie; the walnut is especially scrumptious. If you're here off-season, this is a great place to meet friends for a cup of coffee. ⊠ *46 Commercial St., Boothbay Harbor* ☎ *207/633–5692* ▭ *No credit cards.*

> **GOTTA LOTTA MOXIE?**
>
> It's difficult to get very far in Maine without running into Moxie—the nation's oldest soft drink, invented by Dr. Augustin Thompson of Union, Maine, in 1884. You'll recognize it by its bright orange label. It comes in bottles and cans and is sold in just about every supermarket and convenience store in Maine. A word of warning, however: you gotta get past that first taste!

$$ ✕ **Lobster Dock.** Dine inside or out
SEAFOOD at this waterfront restaurant on the far side of the footbridge, built on the site of the Reed Shipyard, which operated here from the late 1800s to the early 1900s. There's nothing like twin lobsters and a pitcher of cold beer out on the deck. Specialties of the house include the area's only hot lobster roll. Daily specials might feature lobster spring rolls, seafood risotto, or lobster gnocchi. If you want a landlubber meal, order a rack of lamb or the filet mignon. No meal is complete without a slice of the homemade pie. Rover can come, too, if you eat on the outside deck. ⊠ *49 Atlantic Ave., Boothbay Harbor* ☎ *207/633–7120* ⊕ *www.thelobsterdock.com* ▭ *MC, V* ✪ *Closed Oct.–May.*

$$ ✕ **McSeagull's.** This casual eatery on Pier 1 overlooking the harbor is
AMERICAN Boothbay's nighttime hot spot. It serves a mouthwatering, rich lobster
★ bisque and a fresh fish of the day, which you can eat inside or out on the deck. The service is great. If you are hankering for a lobster roll, this one is overflowing with lobster meat and is accompanied by the salad of the day or fries. There's also a wide selection of soups, chowders, salads, and sandwiches. Reservations are recommended for dinner, but they're not accepted for the outdoor deck perched right above the water. ☎ *207/633–5900* ⊕ *www.mcseagullsonline.com* ▭ *MC, V* ✪ *Closed Columbus Day–Memorial Day.*

WHERE TO STAY

$$$ ▦ **Anchor Watch Bed & Breakfast.** The two bright and spacious rooms at this hillside and waterfront B&B are named for the boats that delivered mail to Monhegan Island in the early 20th century (the owners also run Balmy Days Cruises). Comfortable beds are piled high with colorful quilts, and each room has a balcony with a view of the ocean. Guests can use the private pier here to moor kayaks or just sit out and enjoy the harbor scenery. The inn is only a few minutes from the activities of town, yet it feels completely out of the way and residential. **Pros:** central location, private pier. **Cons:** continental breakfast only. ⊠ *9 Eames Rd., Boothbay Harbor* ☎ *207/633–7565* ⊕ *www.anchorwatch.com* ➥ *2 rooms* ♨ *In-room: Wi-Fi, no a/c (some). In-hotel: public Wi-Fi, no kids under 8* ▭ *MC, V* ✪ *Closed Dec.–Feb.* ⏽*CP.*

$$$–$$$$ ▦ **Blue Heron Seaside Inn.** This wonderful inn on Boothbay Harbor offers large, clean rooms with private decks overlooking the water, as well as kayaks and a paddleboat for guests to use at no charge. Phil and Laura

Chapman do a great job at tending to the gardens and home, which is as cute as a Maine postcard. Elegant air-conditioned rooms have four-poster beds throughout, sitting areas, and high-definition flat-panel TVs. Each floor has a different theme: Victorian, Colonial, and nautical. **Pros:** at one end of town's main streets; waterfront; free paddleboat use. **Cons:** no elevator means a climb for third-floor guests. ⊠ *65 Townsend Ave.* ☎ *207/633–7020 or 866/216–2300* ⊕ *www.blueheronseasideinn. com* ➯ *5 rooms, 1 suite* ⚭ *In-room: Wi-Fi, refrigerator. In-hotel: public Wi-Fi, no kids 12 and under* ➡ *V, MC* ☺ *Closed Jan.–Feb.* ⦿*BP.*

$$$–$$$$
★
🏨 **Five Gables Inn.** You can see this beautifully restored Victorian inn from the water. It is the last of the turn-of-the-20th-century hotels that once welcomed guests in the Boothbays. The gabled roof and beautiful gardens give this hillside lodging a distinctive look. The guest rooms tucked underneath the eves have the most charm, though not ideal for tall people. All rooms have period furnishings, including four-poster beds. Some have fireplaces, and all but one have views of the islands scattered around Linekin Bay, so bring your kayaks and access the water directly off this property. The broad veranda overlooking the bay has plenty of comfy chairs from which you can enjoy the view along with your breakfast or afternoon tea and cookies. **Pros:** water access; quiet. **Cons:** low ceilings. ⊠ *107 Murray Hill Rd., East Boothbay* ☎ *207/633–4551 or 800/451–5048* ⊕ *www.fivegablesinn.com* ➯ *16 rooms* ⚭ *In-room: Wi-Fi, no TV, no a/c. In-hotel: no kids under 12* ➡ *MC, V* ☺ *Closed mid-Oct.–Memorial Day* ⦿*BP.*

$–$$$
🏨 **Harbor House Inn.** Built in the 1880's by Captain Mitchell Reed, this inn sits atop McKown Hill above Boothbay Harbor, and offers a full breakfast in the dining room or on the veranda. Enjoy the perennial breeze and the water views, all within a two-minute walk of shops and restaurants and the waterfront. Two rooms have Jacuzzi baths and two have wireless access; one has air-conditioning, but you don't really need it up here on the hill. Kids are welcome here, but not pets. Guests have the use of a refrigerator, and each day there are complimentary snacks and bottled water. **Pros:** an Old World feel; convenient to everything. **Cons:** those with pet allergies beware—a shih tzu calls this place home. ⊠ *80 McKown St.* ☎ *207/633–2941 or 800/856–1164* ⊕ *www.harborhouse-me.com* ➯ *7 rooms* ⚭ *In-room: Wi-Fi (some). In-hotel: public Wi-Fi* ➡ *MC, V* ☺ *Closed Columbus Day–Memorial Day weekend* ⦿*BP.*

$$$–$$$$
Fodor'sChoice
★
🏨 **Inns at Greenleaf Lane.** It's hard to top these two wonderful side-by-side inns right across from the waterfront in the heart of Boothbay Harbor's bustling harbor. They are perfectly situated for exploring the town. One of the properties is an 1830 sea captain's house; the other is another charmer, built in 1849. Guests can use the facilities at either property—both have inviting parlors filled with games, books, and maps. All rooms have fireplaces, and some have private decks overlooking the water. On rainy days you can relax by the cozy woodstove in the sunroom, a remarkable all-glass perch overlooking the harbor from its hill vantage. Service and amenities are excellent, with attentive staff, full breakfasts, and quality linens and very clean rooms. **Pros:** open all year; unbeatable town and harbor setting; great service. **Cons:** rooms lack

coziness. ✉ *71 Commercial St., Boothbay Harbor* ☎ *207/633–2474 or 800/644–1878* ⊕ *www.admiralsquartersinn.com* ⇱ *9 rooms, 5 suites* ⚒ *In-room: Wi-Fi. In-hotel: Internet terminal, public Wi-Fi, no kids under 12* ▤ *AE, D, MC, V* ⦿ *BP.*

$$–$$$ 🏨 **Linekin Bay Bed & Breakfast.** If you are looking for a quiet retreat, consider this charming B&B. The bright sunroom and outdoor patio are ringed by lovely gardens, where guests tend to gather after their daily adventures to enjoy the view of the bay and boats moored below from chairs on the lawn. Enjoy a full breakfast in the morning in the sunroom; return for delicious desserts in the afternoon. The sunroom has guest refrigerators and a microwave, as well as an area for preparing snacks. All rooms have hardwood floors, handsome fireplaces, and water views. Bathrooms are stocked with such products as Tom's of Maine toothpastes. **Pros:** immaculate rooms, peaceful. **Cons:** may be too removed for some who want to be in the thick of it. ✉ *531 Ocean Point Rd., East Boothbay* ☎ *207/633–9900 or 800/596–7420* ⊕ *www.linekinbaybb.com* ⇱ *4 rooms* ⚒ *In-room: Wi-Fi. In-hotel: no kids under 12* ▤ *MC, V* ⦿ *BP.*

$$ 🏨 **Linekin Bay Resort.** All your meals are included when you stay at this
♻   all-inclusive summer camp-style family resort, with 37 cabins and 5 lodges that will accommodate 150 guests. The only thing you have to worry about is whether you'll spend the day hiking in the 15 acres of wooded land or fishing at the edge of the harbor, or learning to sail one of the resort's 20 Rhodes sailboats. You can fish from the dock, swim in the outdoor heated saltwater pool, or challenge a friend to a game of tennis, basketball, or Ping-Pong. Kayaks, canoes, and rowboats are available for guests. Open only to guests, the dining room has lobster bakes twice a week. **Pros:** informal camp atmosphere; lots to do; kids under 3 stay for free. **Cons:** no-frills, older cabin-style rooms. ✉ *92 Wall Point Rd., Boothbay Harbor* ☎ *207/633–2494 or 866/847–2103* ⊕ *www.linekinbayresort.com* ⇱ *37 cabins* ⚒ *In-room: Wi-Fi, no phone, no TV. In-hotel: restaurant, tennis court, pool. In-hotel: public Wi-Fi.* ▤ *MC, V* ⊙ *Closed late Sept.–mid-June* ⦿ *AI.*

$$–$$$$ 🏨 **Ocean Point Inn.** Less than 7 mi from Boothbay Harbor, this lodging at the end of Ocean Point lets you enjoy some spectacular scenery. Choose a rustic cottage or a room in the main building or in the old farmstead. Some are warmed by gas fireplaces. The inn has one of the area's largest outdoor heated pools and a hot tub, and direct access to the bay, making it perfect for rowing and kayaking. You can stroll along the shore and watch lobstermen bringing in their catch. **Pros:** location right on the point. **Cons:** away from town. ✉ *191 Shore Rd., East Boothbay* ☎ *207/633–4200 or 800/552–5554* ⊕ *www.oceanpointinn.com* ⇱ *61 rooms, 7 cottages* ⚒ *In-room: refrigerator. In-hotel: restaurant, pool, public Wi-Fi* ▤ *AE, D, MC, V* ⊙ *Closed mid-Oct.–Memorial Day.*

$$–$$$ 🏨 **Topside.** If you want a glimpse of the harbor, this 19th-century sea captain's house perched on a hillside has views from every room. The front lawn is a great place to watch the activities on the harbor below. From here you can walk to dozens of antiques shops, art galleries, and restaurants. Rooms are divided between the main house and two annexes called the Windward House and the Leeward House. The rooms in the main house are decorated in a comfortable beach-house style. The guesthouses are styled a bit more simply. **Pros:** always a breeze; great views. **Cons:** not on the water. ✉ *60 McKown St., Boothbay Harbor* ☎ *207/633–5404 or 877/486–7466* ⊕ *www.topsideinn. com* ⤴ *21 rooms* ⚭ *In-room: Wi-Fi (some). In-hotel: public Wi-Fi, no kids under 6, some pets allowed (summer only)* ⊟ *D, MC* ⊘ *Closed late Oct.–mid-Apr.* ⑩ *BP.*

$$–$$$$ ⊡ **Welch House.** This 1889 shipbuilder's house sits high on a hill near Boothbay Harbor. Antiques, artworks, and bric-a-brac from the owner's travels around the world adorn the rooms. From the shared third-floor deck you can take in the 180-degree views of the water. Breakfast on the lower deck usually includes one of the chef's specialties, which might mean caramel-apple and pecan-crusted French toast. The location puts you a few minutes' walk from the center of town. **Pros:** hilltop views of the harbor; convenient to town. **Cons:** no elevator. ✉ *36 McKown St., Boothbay Harbor* ☎ *207/633–3431 or 800/279–7313* ⊕ *www. welchhouseinn.com* ⤴ *14 rooms* ⚭ *In-room: Wi-Fi. In-hotel: public Wi-Fi, some pets allowed* ⊟ *AE, MC, V* ⊘ *Closed Dec.–Mar.* ⑩ *BP.*

SHOPPING

Find Maine- and other American-made pottery and wood carvings, jewelry, collectibles, and fruit preserves at **Mung Bean** (✉ *37 Townsend Ave., Boothbay Harbor* ☎ *207/633–5512*) ; it's open until 9:30 PM in summer, so it's perfect for after-dinner browsing. For antiques and crafts, visit the **Palabra Shop** (✉ *53 Commercial St., Boothbay Harbor* ☎ *207/633–4225* ⊕ *www.palabrashop.com* ⊘ *Daily, Mar.–Dec.; weekends in Feb by appt.*). **Sadie Green's Curiosity Shop** (✉ *23-25 Townsend Av.* ☎ *207/633– 0573* ⊕ *www.sadiegreens.com* ⊘ *Closed weekdays Jan.–April.*) is one of six Sadie Green's shops in New England. This one carries an array of gifts, jewelry, clothing, nautical items, and art.

CLOTHING AND   **The Cannery** (✉ *3 By-Way* ☎ *207/633–6503 or 888/633–6503* ⊘ *May–*
ACCESSORIES   *mid-Dec.*) is a bright, colorful shop on the water, offering pretty jewelry, colorful and fashionable summer clothing, and cute things for kids. The upscale **House of Logan** (✉ *20 Townsend Ave., Boothbay Harbor* ☎ *207/633–2293* ⊕ *www.houseoflogan.com*) stocks casual and formal attire for men and women. **A Silver Lining** (✉ *17 Townsend Ave.* ☎ *207/633–4103* ⊕ *www.asilverlining.com*) has a large selection of original jewelry. It's open all year. Beautiful housewares and attractive clothing for the kids can be found inside a beautiful old house at the **Village Store & Children's Shop** (✉ *20 Townsend Ave., Boothbay Harbor* ☎ *207/633–2293*).

FOOD   No trip to Boothbay Harbor is complete without a stop at **Orne's Candy Store** (✉ *11 Commercial St., Boothbay Harbor* ☎ *207/633–2695* ⊕ *www.ornescandystore.com*), which has been here since 1885, and is a must for anyone with a sweet tooth. All the candy is made in Maine. Try the turtles and fudge.

SPORTS AND THE OUTDOORS

When you are ready to escape the hustle and bustle of Boothbay Harbor, rent a kayak and explore the harbor to your heart's content. To get a bit farther away, sign up for one of the sightseeing or whale-watching

4

cruises from the piers on Commercial Street. You can also catch a ride on a lobster boat and help haul the traps. Don't miss the new Coastal Maine Botanical Gardens, the largest in the United States.

BOATING   On Pier 8, **Balmy Day Cruises** (✉ *62 Commercial St., Boothbay Harbor* ☎ *207/633–2284 or 800/298–2284* ⊕ *www.balmydaycruises.com*) offers day trips to Monhegan Island, cruising or sailing tours of the harbor, and mackerel fishing. A guided tour of the Burnt Island Lighthouse is available, with two hours on the island. Cruises run from mid-April to mid-October. Setting sail from Pier 6, **Boothbay Whale Watch** (✉ *Pier 6, Boothbay Harbor* ☎ *207/633–3500 or 800/942–5363* ⊕ *www.whaleme.com*) conducts whale-watching tours and sunset cruises on the *Harbor Princess* from June to mid-October.

On Pier 1, **Cap'n Fish's Boat Trips** (✉ *Pier 1, Boothbay Harbor* ☎ *207/633–3244 or 800/636–3244* ⊕ *www.capnfishsboats.com*) runs regional sightseeing cruises, including puffin-watching adventures, lobster-hauling and whale-watching rides, trips to Damariscove Harbor and Pemaquid Point, and Kennebec River to Bath excursions. Cruises run from late May to late October.

HIKING   Explore more than 30 mi of groomed trails crisscrossing more than 1,700 acres of natural habitat at the **Boothbay Region Land Trust** (✉ *1 Oak St.* ☎ *207/633–4818* ⊕ *bbrlt.org*) ; hikes range from easy to difficult.

KAYAKING   **Tidal Transit Ocean Kayak Co.** (✉ *18 Granary Way, Boothbay Harbor* ☎ *207/633–7140* ⊕ *www.kayakboothbay.com*) has equipment to rent and offers guided tours of the coastline. The company also rents bicycles. It's open from Memorial Day to late September.

DAMARISCOTTA

18 mi north of Boothbay Harbor via Rte. 27 and U.S. 1.

The Damariscotta region comprises several communities along the rocky coast. The town itself sits on the water, and is a lively place filled with attractive shops and several good restaurants.

A few minutes' walk across the bridge over the Damariscotta River is the town of Newcastle, between the Sheepscot and the Damariscotta rivers. Newcastle was settled in the early 1600s. The earliest inhabitants planted apple trees, but the town later became an industrial center, home to several shipyards and a couple of mills. The oldest Catholic church in New England, St. Patrick's, is here, and the church still rings its original Paul Revere bell to call parishioners to worship.

Bremen, which encompasses more than a dozen islands and countless rocky outcrops, offers numerous sporting activities. Nobleboro was settled in the 1720s by Colonel David Dunbar, sent by the British to build the fort at Pemaquid. Neighboring Waldoboro is situated on the Medomak River and was settled largely by Germans in the early 1770s. You can still visit the old German Meeting House, built in 1772. The peninsula stretches south to include Bristol, Round Pond, South Bristol, New Harbor, and Pemaquid.

ESSENTIALS

Visitor Information **Damariscotta Region Chamber of Commerce** (⌂ *Box 13, Damariscotta 04543* ☎ *207/563–8340* ⊕ *www.damariscottaregion.com*).

EXPLORING

Chapman-Hall House. One of the oldest houses in Damariscotta, this home was completed in 1754 by Nathaniel Chapman. Unlike nearby houses that have been remodeled, it closely resembles the original design. Tours are given in July and August. ⊠ *Main St. at Church St.* ☎ *No phone* ✉ *Free* ⊙ *Mid-June–mid-Sept., Tues.–Sun. 1–5.*

WHERE TO EAT

$$–$$$ ✕ **Damariscotta River Grill.** It's easy to be drawn to the dock scene for
AMERICAN dinner, but don't overlook this very popular and delicious Main Street eatery. The menu provides a twist on most of the old reliables on the Maine coast. Thai fish stew and the Italian seafood stew, for example, are popular entrées. Pemaquid oysters, scallops, and lobster risotto are other winners. You can also get a good steak here anytime, and Friday is prime rib night. Sunday brunch is delicious year-round. ⊠ *155 Main St.* ☎ *207/563–2992* ▤ *MC, V.*

$$–$$$ ✕ **King Eider's Pub & Restaurant.** The classic pub bills itself as having the
AMERICAN finest crab cakes in New England. Other specialties of the house include
★ lobster Courvoisier and house-made ravioli that vary day to day. A crabmeat-stuffed ravioli was out of this world, as was the penne pasta in a creamy dill sauce with a mound of sea scallops. With exposed brick walls and low wooden beams, it's a cozy place to enjoy your favorite ale. There is also seating on the deck. Stop by in the evening for live entertainment. ⊠ *2 Elm St.* ☎ *207/563–6008* ⊕ *www.kingeiderspub. com* ⚖ *Reservations essential* ▤ *D, MC, V.*

$$–$$$ ✕ **Salt Bay Café.** Seafood devotees as well as those who hanker for meat
AMERICAN or vegetarian fare will all like this downtown restaurant. On the menu you can find sandwiches and burgers or delicious dishes such as fettuccine Florentine, seafood Alfredo, and filet mignon cooked to perfection. Not to be missed are the scallops Mediterranean, fresh scallops sautéed in olive oil with peppers, mushrooms, fresh garlic, kalamata olives, artichoke hearts, tomato, basil, and white wine topped with feta cheese served over linguine. Want meat? Roasted rack of lamb is available. Everything on the menu is made from scratch, from the soups to the desserts. A fireplace keeps the place toasty on winter nights. ⊠ *88 Main St.* ☎ *207/563–3302* ⚖ *Reservations essential* ▤ *MC, V.*

WHERE TO STAY

$$–$$$ ▦ **Flying Cloud.** Each room here is named for a legendary port of call made by the *Flying Cloud,* a clipper ship that was christened in 1851. The main house elegantly combines the original 1790 Cape Cod–style house with an 1840 Greek Revival–style addition. There are water views of the Damariscotta River from every room and from the outdoor deck. The sumptuous full breakfast is a great way to start the day. You can enjoy it indoors or on a screen porch looking out on the owners' lovely gardens. **Pros:** closest Newcastle B&B to Damariscotta shops. **Cons:** no water access. ⊠ *45 River Rd. Newcastle* ☎ *207/563–2484* ⊕ *www.*

theflyingcloud.com 📠 *4 rooms, 1 suite* ♿ *In-room: Wi-Fi, no TV, no a/c. In-hotel: public Wi-Fi, no kids under 10* 🍴 *AE, MC, V* 🍽️ *BP.*

$$$–$$$$ 🏨 **Newcastle Inn.** A riverside location and an excellent dining room make this country inn a classic. All the guest rooms are filled with antiques and decorated with sumptuous fabrics; some rooms have fireplaces and whirlpool baths. There are two rooms designated pet friendly—and they have private entrances. On pleasant mornings breakfast is served on the back deck overlooking the river. The dining room ($$$$), which is open to the public by reservation, serves six-course meals and is open Tuesday through Saturday in season. The emphasis is on local seafood. **Pros:** innkeepers' reception evenings with cocktails and hors d'oeuvres. **Cons:** away from town. ✉️ *60 River Rd. Newcastle* ☎️ *207/563–5685 or 800/832–8669* ⊕ *www.newcastleinn.com* 📠 *14 rooms, 3 suites* ♿ *In-room: no phone, no TV (some). In-hotel: no kids under 12* 🍴 *AE, MC, V* 🍽️ *BP.*

$$–$$$ 🏨 **Oak Gables.** If you're looking for tranquillity and can stay put a while,
  ★   there is no better lodging choice in the area. Nestled on 11 pristine acres alongside the Damariscotta River, this facility is a little bit of heaven, but requires a minimum two-night stay in summer. There are four rooms in the main house, as well as two immaculate apartments and a separate cottage with a full kitchen, all available for weekly rentals only. The in-ground pool is heated, and you can sit on the serene boathouse right above the water to watch gulls and ducks winging in over the bay. **Pros:** walking distance to town; boat access to river; peaceful boathouse haven. **Cons:** 2-nights minimum in summer. ✉️ *36 Pleasant St.* ☎️ *207/563–1476 or 800/335–7748* ⊕ *www.oakgablesbb.com* 📠 *3 rooms, 2 apartments, 1 cottage* ♿ *In-room: kitchen (some). In-hotel: pool* 🍴 *MC, V* 🍽️ *BP for rooms, not for cottage and apartments.*

NIGHTLIFE AND THE ARTS

Musicals and plays are staged regularly at the downtown **Lincoln County Community Theater** (✉️ *2 Theater St.* ☎️ *207/563–3424* ⊕ *www.lcct.org*). It also hosts concerts and screens movies throughout the year.

SHOPPING

Create your own necklace or bracelet from a large selection of new and vintage beads at **Aboca Beads** (✉️ *157 Main St.* ☎️ *207/563–1766*), in the Damariscotta Center. If plants are your passion, **Bramble's** (✉️ *157 Main St.* ☎️ *207/563–2800*) carries gardening tools, topiaries, and pots. **Delphiniums Glassworks** (✉️ *112 Main St.* ☎️ *207/563–6333*) carries gifts and more; it specializes in glass engraving. You can browse to your heart's content through the shelves at **Maine Coast Book Shop & Café** (✉️ *158 Main St.* ☎️ *207/563–3207*). Enjoy a cup of coffee and a blueberry muffin at the adjoining café. If you're looking for a fine wine or special beer, you'll find them at **Quacks** (✉️ *50 Main St.* ☎️ *207/563–8259*). It also carries cheeses from Artisanal shops in New York and Salumeria Biellese deli meats. You never know what you'll find at **Reny's** (✉️ *121 Main St.* ☎️ *207/563–5757*). Sometimes there's merchandise from L. L. Bean or a coat from a famous designer. This bargain chain has outlets in many Maine towns, but this is its flagship store. **River Gallery, L.L.C.** (✉️ *79 Main St.* ☎️ *207/563–6330 or 207/529–5558* ⊕ *www.rivergalleryfineart.com*) carries fine European and American paintings for the discriminating buyer. The barnlike **Stable Gallery** (✉ *26 Water St.* ☎ *207/563–1991*) stocks paintings and prints by the more than 100 Water Street artists in a big open space that sets off each item at its best. Jewelry, metals, textiles, ceramics, and furniture make this a must-see for art aficionados. Color everywhere, fun stuff, and unique clothing is what customers keep coming back for at **Two Fish Boutique** (✉ *133 Main St.* ☎ *207/563–2220*), which carries special gifts and children's items.

SPORTS AND THE OUTDOORS

GOLF In the Sheepscot River valley, **Sheepscot Links** (✉ *824 Townhouse Rd., Whitefield* ☎ *207/549–7060*) is a 9-hole course with greens fees of $15 for 9 holes and $22 for 18 holes. It's in Whitefield, about 16 mi northwest of Damariscotta. From U.S. 1, take Route 215 west to Route 194 north to Townhouse Road. In Walpole, **Wawenock Country Club** (✉ *685 Rte. 129, Walpole* ☎ *207/563–3938*) is just minutes from Damariscotta. Take Route 129 south from U.S. 1 at Damariscotta. Open in late May to November, the country club includes a public-access course, driving range, and pro shop. Greens fees are $15 for 9 holes, $20 for the 18-hole par 70 course.

KAYAKING To rent a sea kayak or to sign up for lessons, visit **Midcoast Kayak** (✉ *47 Main St.* ☎ *207/563–5732* ⊕ *www.midcoastkayak.com*). Great local excursions include Muscongus Bay and the Damariscotta River.

PEMAQUID, NEW HARBOR, AND ROUND POND

17 mi south of Damariscotta via U.S. 1 to Rte. 129 to Rte. 130.

Route 130 brings you to Pemaquid Point, home of the famous lighthouse and its attendant fog bell and tiny museum. If you are going to New Harbor or Round Pond, take a left onto Route 32 where it intersects Route 130 just before Pemaquid Point. New Harbor is about 4 mi away, and Round Pond about 6 mi beyond that. Just north of New Harbor on Route 32 is the Rachel Carson Salt Pond Preserve.

EXPLORING

Colonial Pemaquid Restoration. In the early 17th century, English mariners established this fishing and trading settlement on a small peninsula jutting into the Pemaquid River. The excavations at Fort William Henry, begun in the mid-1960s, have turned up thousands of artifacts from the settlement, including the remains of an old customs house, a tavern, a jail, a forge, and several homes. Some older items are from earlier American Indian settlements. The state operates a museum that displays many of these artifacts. The Colonial Pemaquid Tavern is on-site, as are a picnic area and restrooms. ✉ *Rte. 130, New Harbor* ☎ *207/677–2423* 🖾 *$2* ☉ *Memorial Day–Labor Day, daily 9:30–7.*

☾ **Pemaquid Point Light.** At the terminus of Route 130, this lighthouse ★ looks as though it sprouted from the ragged, tilted chunk of granite that it commands. The former keeper's cottage is now the Fishermen's Museum, which displays historic photographs, scale models, and artifacts that explore commercial fishing in Maine. Also here is the original fog bell and bell house built in 1897 for the two original Shipman engines. Pemaquid Art Gallery, on-site, mounts exhibitions by area artists in July and August, and admission to the gallery, once you have paid your fee to be on the lighthouse property, is free. Restrooms, picnic tables, and barbecue grills are all available on this site. Next door to this property is the Sea Gull Shop, with a dining room, gift shop, and ice-cream parlor. The museum on-site is adjacent to the lighthouse. ✉ *Rte. 130 (Bristol Rd.), Pemaquid* ☎ *207/677–2494* 🖼 *$1* ☯ *Memorial Day–Columbus Day, Mon.–Sat. 10–5, Sun. 11–5* 🖼 *$5.*

WHERE TO EAT

$$
AMERICAN
✗ **Anchor Inn Restaurant.** Round Pond is one of the best dining spots in Maine. You can eat on the water at one of the two pounds, or indoors at this warm restaurant overlooking the harbor. Jean and Rick Hirsch (Rick is the chef and Jean runs the front of house) have run this place popular with locals since 1988, and there's an undeniably convivial atmosphere. Scallop Peepers—broiled barbecue-marinated sea scallops wrapped in bacon—are a popular appetizer. Sample their lobster stew, and accompany it with a small house salad. Fresh fish, pasta specials, lobster—it's all here, and the atmosphere is casual and comfortable; the scenery peaceful. Desserts always feature home-baked pies, as well as cheesecakes and cakes. ✉ *Anchor Inn Rd. off Rte. 32, Round Pond* ☎ *207/529–5584* ⊕ *anchorinnrestaurant.com* ▭ *D, MC, V* ☯ *Closed mid-Oct.—May.*

$–$$
SEAFOOD
★
✗ **Muscongus Bay Lobster Company.** When you reach the docks at Round Pond you'll find two gems: this place and the Fisherman's Coop. You'll have to try both to figure out which one is your favorite. Both are authentic to the hilt: dockside pounds overlooking the working harbor. It sounds facetious to say that this is the fancier of the two, but it's true: Moscungus Bay serves refreshments—as well as exceptional oysters from Dodge Cove Marine Farms. Its dock is also a bit larger, with a perhaps better views than those at the Coop. ✉ *Town Landing Rd., Round Pond* ☎ *207/529–2600* ▭ *MC, V* ☯ *Closed Labor Day–Memorial Day.*

$–$$
SEAFOOD
Fodor's Choice
★
✗ **Round Pond Fisherman's Coop.** At this humble but adored shack on the Round Pond pier you point to your favorite specimen from the lobster tank, it's dropped into the steamer, and after a few minutes you're called to collect your dinner, which you eat at one of the many picnic tables. You can't find lobster any fresher or any cheaper. The best deal in town is the nightly dinner special: a 1-pound lobster, steamers, corn-on-the-cob, and a bag of chips. (In 2009, the price was $14.) Regulars often bring their own beer, wine, bread, and salads, none of which are offered here. If you're into frills, there's a soda vending machine around the side of the shack. For many, this is the essence of the best of the Maine good life. Settle in and take in the view over dreamy Round Pond Harbor. ✉ *Town Landing Rd., Round Pond* ☎ *207/529–5725* ▭ *MC, V* ☯ *Closed Labor Day–Memorial Day.*

WHERE TO STAY

$$$–$$$$
🏠 **Bradley Inn.** The Bradley Inn is the most elegant of the Mid-Coast's places to stay. The gray shingled inn is a short walk from the Pemaquid Point and the lighthouse, but it feels removed from the crowds of visitors. This former rooming house was originally built as a private residence for sea captain John Bradley. It has guest rooms that are

comfortable and uncluttered; some have fireplaces, and those on the third floor have ocean views. Nautical knickknacks and works by local artists decorate the rooms in the main inn, the carriage house, and the garden cottage. The Bradley Inn has one of the region's best dining rooms ($$$–$$$$). The menu changes nightly but always emphasizes fresh, local foods. You can eat in the dining room or outside on the deck. The pub has piano music on weekends in summer. **Pros:** spa, with yoga, massage, and Pilates. **Cons:** far from town ⊠ *3063 Bristol Rd., New Harbor* ☎ *207/677–2105 or 800/942–5560* ⊕ *www.bradleyinn. com* ⤸ *12 rooms, 4 suites* ⚘ *In-room: no TV (some), no a/c. In-hotel: restaurant, bar, bicycles, spa, public Wi-Fi* ⊟ *AE, MC, V* ⊧ *BP.*

$$–$$$$ ⊡ **Hotel Pemaquid.** As they say, location is everything. Step back in time at
⟳   this beautifully restored 1888 inn less than 500 feet from the lighthouse at Pemaquid Point. The main building is Victorian in style; cottages and bungalow units have a more contemporary feel. The carriage-house suite is ideal for honeymooners or others seeking a romantic retreat. Relax on the big wraparound porch or enjoy sitting in front of the stone fireplace. Antiques decorate the comfortable rooms. The grounds are good for kids because they are open and large, and it is a short walk to the Pemaquid Point lighthouse. **Pros:** quiet; reasonably priced. **Cons:** no frills; no food. ⊠ *3098 Bristol Rd., New Harbor* ☎ *207/677–2312* ⊕ *www.hotelpemaquid.com* ⤸ *28 rooms, 6 suites, 2 cottages, 1 apartment* ⚘ *In-room: no phone, no a/c. In-hotel: no breakfast* ⊟ *No credit cards* ⊙ *Closed mid-Oct.–mid-May.*

$$–$$$ ⊡ **Inn at Round Pond.** Once a stagecoach stop, this 1830s mansard-roofed Colonial sits on the eastern shore of Pemaquid Peninsula and has a picture-postcard view straight from the front lawn, where you can sit in the colorful Adirondack chairs all lined up and waiting. At this restful retreat you won't be bothered by ringing telephones or blaring televisions. Instead, enjoy the gardens and private pond. Kayaking, golf, fishing, and boat cruises are all nearby. The trio of tastefully appointed suites—the Foster Suite, the Prentice Suite, and the Monhegan Suite— have separate sitting areas decorated with original artwork. All have harbor views. A full country breakfast is served each morning. **Pros:** scenic; tranquil. **Cons:** no Internet access. ⊠ *1442 Rte. 32, Round Pond* ☎ *207/529–2004* ⊕ *www.theinnatroundpond.com* ⤸ *3 suites* ⚘ *In-room: no phone, no TV. In-hotel: no kids under 12* ⊟ *AE, D, MC, V* ⊙ *Closed Columbus Day–Memorial Day* ⊧ *BP.*

$$ ⊡ **Mill Pond Inn.** A quiet residential street brings you to this circa-1780 inn, which sits on a lake that is home to loons, otters, and bald eagles. You can see them up close on an excursion in the owner's 17-foot antique lapstrake boat. Or just drop a kayak into the water: the inn is on a gorgeous stretch of lake. The rooms are warm and inviting, though you may find it hard to tear yourself away from the hammocks-for-two overlooking the water. The owner provides complimentary canoes and bicycles. Swimming is big here, and afternoon gatherings on the deck make the most of this location right on the water. **Pros:** peaceful waterfront setting, relaxing getaway spot. **Cons:** no wireless access. ⊠ *50 Main St., off Rte. 215 N, Nobleboro* ☎ *207/563–8014* ⊕ *www.millpondinn.com* ⤸ *6*

rooms, 1 suite ⌂ In-room: no phone, no TV, no a/c (some). In-hotel: bar, bicycles, no kids under 10 ☐ No credit cards ⎪⚪⎪ *BP.*

$–$$ ⌂ **Sunset Bed & Breakfast.** This cottage dating from the 1850s is right on the bay, and kayakers are especially welcome here. There's a view of the bay from the front porch. The guest rooms are upstairs under the eaves and have skylights that let in lots of sun. The homespun decor includes colorful quilts piled on the beds. You can walk to nearby Christmas Cove and watch the swing bridge open to allow boats to pass. The full breakfast includes breads and muffins, granola and cereals, and fresh fruit in season. It's a simple affair, but this is one of the most beautiful parts of the Mid-Coast. **Pros:** on the water. **Cons:** shared bath unless you want to pay for both rooms. ⊠ *16 Sunset Loop, South Bristol* ☏ *207/644–8849* ⊕ *www.sunsetbnb.com* ⌐ *2 rooms without bath* ⌂ *In-room: no TV, no a/c. In-hotel: Internet* ☐ *No credit cards* ⊘ *Closed Oct.–Apr.* ⎪⚪⎪ *BP.*

$$ ⌂ **Unique Yankee Bed & Breakfast.** If you are traveling with a dog, you'll find few more accommodating spots in Maine than this out-of-the way place on Rutherford Island. One room even has its own fenced-in dog play yard. Though it's a 6-minute drive to the water, the inn has a tower where, if you have a clear day, you might see all the way to Monhegan Island. The 2.3-acre property is surrounded by a 2-acre greenbelt, so it's quite private. The main house has rooms with four-season electric fireplace, microwave, coffee pot, and two-person jetted bath (plus separate shower). A newer annex has very large rooms with modern amenities. **Pros:** great if you're traveling with dogs; long views of Pemaquid on clear days from lookout. **Cons:** dogs on premises. ⊠ *53 Coveside Rd., South Bristol* ☏ *207/644–1502 or 866/644–1502* ⊕ *www. uniqueyankeeofmaine.com* ⌐ *6 rooms* ⌂ *In-room: Wi-Fi, refrigerator, DVD. In-hotel: some pets allowed* ☐ *MC, V* ⎪⚪⎪ *BP.*

SHOPPING

Of the villages on Pemaquid Peninsula, Damariscotta has the most boutiques and galleries. New Harbor and Round Pond have crafts stores and antiques shops as well as artisans' studios. Antiques shops also dot the main thoroughfares through the region. The **Granite Hall Store** (⊠ *9 Back Shore Rd., Round Pond* ☏ *207/529–5864*) has penny candy, wicker baskets, and cards on the first floor and antiques and books on the second. Order ice-cream cones through a window on the side. It's open May to mid-October.

ART GALLERIES   Sculpture and art can be found at **Kathleen Mack Studio** (⊠ *1360 Rte. 32, Walpole* ☏ *207/529–5633* ⊕ *www.kathleenmack.com* ⊘ *Daily, but call first in winter*) in the village of Round Pond. The work of more than 50 Maine artisans is displayed in the 15 rooms of the **Pemaquid Craft Co-op** (⊠ *2545 Bristol Rd., New Harbor* ☏ *207/677–2077* ⊘ *May–Sept., daily; Oct.–Dec. 24, Tues.–Sat.*). **Susan Bartlett Rice Studio** (⊠ *36 Split Rock Rd., Walpole* ☏ *207/563–6023* ⊕ *www.susanbartlettrice.com*), open year-round off Route 129 on the way south toward Pemaquid, is worth a stop if you like oil paintings that show real life in Maine.

SPORTS AND THE OUTDOORS

BEACHES
AND PARKS

Pemaquid Beach Park (⊠ *Rte. 130, New Harbor* ☎ *207/677–2754*) has a sandy beach that's popular with families. There's a snack bar, changing facilities, and picnic tables overlooking John's Bay.

CRUISES

You can take a cruise to Monhegan with **Hardy Boat Cruises** (⊠ *Shaw's Wharf, New Harbor* ☎ *207/677–6026*). On the sightseeing cruises you can spot seals and puffins. At **Salt Water Charters** (⊠ *Round Pond Harbor, Round Pond* ☎ *207/677–6229* ⊕ *www.saltwater-charters.com*) the fishing vessel *Paige Elizabeth* takes passengers on sightseeing cruises.

CUSHING AND ST. GEORGE PENINSULAS

4

These two peninsulas bring to life the state's seafaring traditions. The town of Waldoboro has a beautiful downtown filled with houses that combine several architectural styles. Sea captains were intrigued by what they saw during their travels and came back with ideas for their own homes. Thomaston, another seaside town, is known for the clapboard houses lining its streets.

On a rocky part of the coast, Tenants Harbor has a lobstering tradition that is still strong today. The harbor is full of boats that go out once or twice daily to retrieve crustaceans from the ocean floor. You can grow familiar with their distinctive chug-chug as they enter and leave the harbor. Artists favor this area, and you can browse in many of their studios. Port Clyde is the jumping-off point to Monhegan Island, but has some sights of its own. Marshall Point Lighthouse is within walking distance of the town landing, and there is a small museum, shop, and picnic area on the site.

WALDOBORO

10 mi northeast of Damariscotta.

Veer off U.S. 1 onto Main Street or down Route 220 or 32 and you can discover a seafaring town with a proud shipbuilding past. Waldoboro's Main Street is lined with houses representing numerous architectural styles: Cape Cod, Queen Anne, Stick, Greek Revival, and Italianate.

EXPLORING

Fawcett's Toy Museum. This kid-drawing attraction comes up fast on Route 1, but the flags and banners are flying, so look for them on your left as you head north. Adults and children alike will be delighted with collectible toys, from Betty Boop and Popeye to Charlie Brown and Mickey Mouse. There's also original comic art. ⊠ *3506 U.S. 1* ☎ *207/832–7398* 🖭 *$5* ☉ *Memorial Day–Columbus Day, Thurs.–Mon. 10–4; Columbus Day–Christmas Eve, weekends noon–4.*

Friendship Museum. Friendship is the birthplace of the distinctive Friendship sloop, and you can go inside the museum to see exhibits on this popular sailboat, as well as local historical artifacts. The little brick museum was built in 1857 as a one-room schoolhouse. ⊠ *1 Martin Point Rd., at Rte. 220, Friendship* ☎ *207/832–4826* ⊕ *www.friendshipmuseum.org*

🖼 *Free* ⊗ *July–Labor Day, Mon.–Sat. 1–4; Labor Day–Columbus Day 1–4, Sat. 1–4, Sun. 2–4.*

Olson House. Between 1893 and 1968 Andrew Wyeth painted his famous Christina pictures from within these walls. Reproductions of many of these enigmatic portraits are hung throughout this historic house, now part of the Farnsworth Museum. ⊠ *384 Hathorn Point Rd., Cushing* 🖼 *207/354–0102* ⊕ *www.farnsworthmuseum.org* 🖼 *$4* ⊗ *Memorial Day–Columbus Day, daily 11–4.*

Waldoborough Historical Society Museum. Several buildings make up this museum, including the one-room Boggs Schoolhouse, built in 1857; the Town Pound, built in 1819; and a barn filled with artifacts, from hooked rugs, housewares, and tools to clothing and antique toys. ⊠ *1164 Main St. and Rte. 22004572* 🖼 *No phone* 🖼 *Free* ⊗ *June–Sept., Tues.–Sun., daily 1–4.*

WHERE TO EAT AND STAY

¢–$ ✕ **Moody's Diner.** Settle into one of the well-worn wooden booths or snag
AMERICAN a counter stool at this old-style diner known for its home cooking. It's right on U.S. 1, so you can't miss it. Breakfast is served all day (except no oatmeal or omelets after 11 AM) at this local landmark where coffee is only 85¢. ■**TIP→ Don't miss the legendary walnut pie and the home-made whoopie pies.** ⊠ *1885 U.S. 1* 🖼 *207/832–7785* ▤ *D, MC, V.*

$$ 🖼 **Blue Skye Farm.** Guests often choose this historic 18th-century country house for superior bird-watching opportunities. Waterfowl, eagles, and ospreys can be seen regularly, and the light over the marshes is ideal for the many watercolor painters who stay here. There are lots of interesting nooks and crannies, old beams, and wide views of the marshes. Hundreds of acres await your visit outside the back door. Guests have use of the kitchen in the evening. The rooms are furnished in period antiques and vary in size; one has bunks and is good for kids. **Pros:** peaceful; lots of land to explore; all rooms have a view. **Cons:** no TVs. ⊠ *1708 Friendship Rd.* 🖼 *207/832–0030* ⊲ *4 rooms* ⚲ *In-room: Wi-Fi, no a/c. In-hotel: Wi-Fi hot spot* ▤ *MC, V* |⊚| *BP.*

$ 🖼 **Outsiders' Inn Bed & Breakfast.** If you are looking for a quiet retreat convenient to the sights, consider this inn at the corner of Routes 97 and 220. The original homestead was built by Zenas Cook in 1830, and the current owners have preserved much of the charm with period furnishings and decorations. Rooms, some with private baths, are comfortably furnished. A full breakfast with home-baked specialties is served every morning. The owners also operate Wild Bill's Outfitting and Guide Service, and will rent you kayaks and equipment to paddle to your heart's content or take you on a guided tour. At the end of your day, take a stroll to the harbor. **Pros:** water access; one of lowest prices in state; prices include full breakfast. **Cons:** no air-conditioning; no TVs. ⊠ *4 Main St., Friendship* 🖼 *207/832–5197* ⊲ *3 rooms, 2 share a bath, 1 cottage with private bath* ⚲ *In-room: no TV, Wi-Fi.* ▤ *MC, V* |⊚| *BP.*

NIGHTLIFE AND THE ARTS

The **Waldo Theatre** (✉ *916 Main St.* ☎ *207/832–6060* ⊕ *www.thewaldo. org*), a Greek Revival–style movie house with an Art Deco interior, stages concerts, plays, bluegrass concerts, Celtic singers, and other live performances.

SHOPPING

The **Waldoboro 5 & 10** (✉ *17 Friendship St.* ☎ *207/832–4624*) is the oldest continually operated five-and-dime store in the country. It offers deli-type sandwiches, soups, and ice cream, plus it sells a nice selection of toys. There's also a penny-candy counter popular with kids.

THOMASTON

4

10 mi northeast of Waldoboro, 72 mi northeast of Portland.

Thomaston is a delightful town, full of beautiful sea captains' homes and dotted with antiques and specialty shops. A National Historic District encompasses parts of High, Main, and Knox streets. The town is the gateway to the two peninsulas, so you will be looking at water on both sides as you arrive.

EXPLORING

Montpelier. Built in 1930, the home is a replica of the late-18th-century mansion of Major General Henry Knox, a commander in the Revolutionary War and secretary of war in George Washington's cabinet. Antiques, including many Knox family possessions, fill the interior. Architectural appointments include an oval room and a double staircase. Groups should call ahead to reserve space on the half-hourly tours. ✉ *U.S. 1 at Rte. 131* ☎ *207/354–8062* ⊕ *www.generalknoxmuseum.org* 🎫 *$6* ⊙ *Memorial Day–Columbus Day, Tues.–Sat. 10–4.*

WHERE TO EAT AND STAY

$$–$$$$ ✕ **Harbor View Restaurant.** If you're dining in Thomaston, you won't find
AMERICAN   a better location than this harborside seafood place. The menu features everything from steak to scallops au gratin, and, of course, delicious crab and lobster rolls, steamed clams, and boiled or baked stuffed lobsters. This is the kind of place where you can order everything from escargots to fish-and-chips. Like lobster but don't want the mess? Try the "lazy" variety, with the lobster meat already pulled out for you! Eat in the dining room or outside on the porch overlooking the water. ✉ *Public Landing* ☎ *207/354–8173* ⊕ *www.harborviewrestaurant.com* 🍴 *Reservations essential* ▤ *MC, V.*

$$–$$$ ✕ **Thomaston Café & Bakery.** A changing selection of works by local art-
AMERICAN   ists adorns the walls of this small café, and it is situated next door to an independent bookstore. You might actually run into a writer or an artist or two here, since this is a popular meeting place for locals. Entrées, prepared with locally grown ingredients, include seared fresh tuna on soba noodles, lobster ravioli with lobster sauce, and filet mignon with béarnaise sauce. Soups and sandwiches are delicious. ✉ *154 Main St.* ☎ *207/354–8589* ⊕ *www.thomastoncafe.com* ▤ *MC, V* ⊙ *No dinner Sun.–Thurs.*

$$ ⊞ **Weskeag Inn.** Built in the 1830s, this charming B&B is near the reversing falls in the village of South Thomaston. Anglers line the banks in search of stripers in spring, and sun worshippers swim or float on inner tubes in summer. Bring your kayaks, because you can launch right here. Watch herons, egrets, and ospreys; sometimes even eagles come here to catch their dinner. Guest rooms are bright and tastefully decorated with period antiques; make sure to ask for one with a view of the water. **Pros:** a staircase leads to the water. **Cons:** no Internet. ⊠ *14 Elm St. (Rte. 73), South Thomaston* ☎ *207/596–6676* ⊕ *www.weskeag.com* ⤴ *7 rooms, 1 suite, all with private baths* ♿ *In-room: no TV (some). In-hotel: public Internet* ⊟ *MC, V* ⑩ *BP.*

SHOPPING

The **Maine State Prison Showroom Outlet** (*Main St.* ☎ *207/354–2535*), on the right as you come into the village, carries an impressive collection of wooden model boats at very good prices. Other wooden items including furniture, bowls, cutting boards, decorative boxes, and children's toys—yes, all fashioned by prisoners—are for sale. Browse the comprehensive selection of books and original art and cards at the **Personal Book Shop** (⊠ *144 Main St.* ☎ *207/354–8058* ⊟ *AE, D, MC, V*). The proprietress, Marti Reed, is a Scrabble afficionado—challenge her to a game!

TENANTS HARBOR

10 mi south of Thomaston.

Tenants Harbor is a quintessential coastal harbor—dominated by lobster boats, its shores are rocky and slippery, and its downtown streets are lined with clapboard houses, a church, and a general store. It's a favorite with artists, and galleries and studios welcome browsers.

EXPLORING

Owls Head Light. At Owls Head Light State Park, the beautifully maintained lighthouse has shown the way since 1825. On West Penobscot Bay, the local landmark indicates the entrance to Rockland Harbor. The grounds are open to the public, but the lighthouse and keeper's house are not. This lighthouse still has its original Fresnel lens in place, in use since it was installed in 1856. ⊠ *Rte. 73, Owls Head.*

WHERE TO EAT AND STAY

$$
SEAFOOD
Fodor's Choice
★

✕ **Waterman's Beach Lobster.** This is one of a handful of unbeatable lobster shacks on the Maine coast—authentic, inexpensive, and scenic. Eat lunch or dinner right on a pier overlooking the Atlantic. Steamed clams and lobster and clam rolls are the stars, of course, but there are also freshly baked pies from old family recipes, as well as locally made ice cream. There's a private beach where you can stroll while you wait for your dinner, so make sure to bring your binoculars to get a closer look at the lobster boats. ⊠ *359 Waterman Beach Rd., off Rte. 73, South Thomaston* ☎ *207/596–7819 or 207/594–7518* ⊕ *www.watermansbeachlobster.com* ⊟ *No credit cards* ☉ *Closed Labor Day–Father's Day. Closed Mon. and Tues.*

$$$
Fodor's Choice
★
Craignair Inn. It's tough to find a better waterfront location than Craignair, which overlooks Wheeler's Bay and Clark Island on four waterfront acres. It was originally built to house granite workers from nearby quarries. The annex house was the chapel where the stonecutters and their families worshipped. Rooms aren't as wonderful as the views, but are clean and functional. What's also great about the inn is that you can easily explore Clark Island by walking over a narrow isthmus. Another perk is the excellent food. Chef Seiler, most recently from the Samoset Resort, wins awards for his creative cuisine served in the inn's dining room ($$$). You might want to start with the Caribbean jerk grilled shrimp brochettes, or steamed great eastern mussels, and move on to pecan-crusted salmon, bacon-wrapped tenderloin, or baked stuffed haddock. The dessert menu might feature lemon pudding cake, Key lime square, or a mini créme bruleé. **Pros:** stellar food; waterfront location. **Cons:** pets allowed in some rooms can be troublesome to those with allergies. ⊠ *5 3rd St., Spruce Head* ☎ *207/594–7644 or 800/320–9997* ⊕ *www.craignair.com* ⟲ *21 rooms, 13 with bath* ⟳ *In-room: Wi-Fi, no a/c. In-hotel: public Wi-Fi, some pets allowed* ⊟ *D, MC, V* ⏛*BP.*

$$–$$$
★
East Wind Inn & Meeting House. Built as a sail loft in 1830, this comfortably old-fashioned inn on the water has a wraparound porch with a wide view of the island-studded harbor. Some of the guest rooms in the Meeting House, a converted sea captain's house, are warmed by fireplaces. A grand piano graces the great room. Suites here run slightly higher at $201 a night, and the apartment rents for $221. The inn's ocean-view restaurant ($$$) emphasizes local seafood and is open to the public, while a take-out restaurant on the wharf serves lighter fare. The suites are equipped with TVs, and so are the common rooms in the main building. **Pros:** great view; good food. **Cons:** pets allowed in some rooms can be troublesome to those with allergies. ⊠ *21 Mechanic St.* ☎ *207/372–6366 or 800/241–8439* ⊕ *www.eastwindinn.com* ⟲ *23 rooms, 16 with bath; 3 suites; 4 apartments* ⟳ *In-room: no TV (some), no a/c. In-hotel: 2 restaurants, some pets allowed* ⊟ *AE, D, MC, V* ⊘ *Closed Nov.–Easter* ⏛*BP.*

PORT CLYDE

2 mi south of Tenants Harbor via Rte. 131.

The fishing village of Port Clyde sits at the end of the St. George Peninsula. The road leading to Port Clyde meanders along the St. George River, passing meadows and farmhouses. Shipbuilding was the first commercial enterprise here, and later the catching and canning of seafood. You can still buy Port Clyde sardines. Port Clyde's boat landing is home to the *Elizabeth Ann* and the *Laura B,* the mail boats that serve nearby Monhegan Island. Several artists make their homes in Port Clyde, so check to see if their studios are open while you are visiting.

EXPLORING

Marshall Point Lighthouse. An 1895 keeper's house has been turned into a museum containing memorabilia from the town of St. George (a few miles north of Tenants Harbor) with a small shop in the facility.

The setting has inspired Jamie Wyeth and other noted artists. You can stroll the grounds, have a picnic, and watch boats sail in and out of Port Clyde. The lighthouse is about 1 mi from the Port Clyde boat landing, and the original 1898 fog bell is also here. Grounds are open all year. ⊠ *Marshall Point Rd.* ☎ *207/372–6450* ⊠ *Free* ☉ *Memorial Day–Columbus Day., weekdays 1–5, Sat. 10–5; May and Oct., weekends 1–5.*

Ocean House Gallery. This new gallery above the apartment adjacent to the Ocean House hotel in Port Clyde displays the work of many artists, including Jamie Wyeth, Jerry Cable, Susan Cooney, and Susan Murdock. ⊠ *870 Port Clyde Rd.,* ☎ *207/372–6930* ⊕ *www.oceanhousehotel. com.*

WHERE TO EAT AND STAY

¢–$
AMERICAN

✕ **The Dip Net.** On a summer day you can grab a crab or lobster roll or a slice of pizza or sandwich here before taking a boat to Monhegan Island or hiking to Marshall Point Lighthouse. Lobster doesn't get any fresher than those cooked right beside the sea where they are caught. Dine inside or eat out on the deck at tables with umbrellas for your comfort. You can also order takeout. Beer and wine are available here. ⊠ *1 Cold Storage Rd.* ☎ *207/372–6307* ⊟ *No credit cards* ☉ *Closed Labor Day–Memorial Day.*

$–$$$
SEAFOOD

✕ **Miller's Lobster Company.** Enjoy a lobster at this family-owned restaurant overlooking beautiful Wheeler's Bay. People come here for its friendly vibe and great food. Lobster rolls, crabmeat rolls, and shrimp are on the menu, as are steamed clams and mussels, and lobsters fresh from the fishermen who bring them in daily. If you've got room, order a twin lobster special and top it off with a slice of homemade pie. Miller's also serves a good steamed hot dog. Eat in the dining room or outside on the deck. ⊠ *38 Fuller Rd., Spruce Head* ☎ *207/594–7406* ⊕ *www. millerslobster.com* ⊟ *No credit cards* ☉ *Closed Labor Day–late June.*

$–$$

🏨 **Ocean House.** Little has changed at the Ocean Hotel since it first opened for business in the 1820s, but it now has wireless access in the common room and an apartment next door with the Ocean House Gallery upstairs. The cottage has two bedrooms and two baths. Most of the furniture in the main building is original, including some of the wrought-iron beds. From the rooms and the apartment there are excellent views of the harbor. On the walls hang several Jamie Wyeth paintings, and the hotel often hosts the artist himself. Breakfast is available for guests of the inn and their visitors, and a specialty of the house is blueberry pancakes. The hotel is within walking distance of the boat dock, The Dip Net, the general store, the post office, and the lighthouse. **Pros:** center of town location, authentic old inn; original art adds to the artsy vibe. **Cons:** some rooms must share a bathroom. ⊠ *At Monhegan Island boat landing, Box 66* ☎ *207/372–6691 or 800/269–6691* ⊕ *www.oceanhousehotel.com* 🛏 *10 rooms, 8 with bath* ♿ *In-room: no TV, no a/c. In-hotel: public Wi-Fi* ⊟ *No credit cards* ☉ *Closed Nov.–Apr.* ⦿ *BP.*

EN
ROUTE

On the way to Rockland, stop at the **Owls Head Transportation Museum** (⊠ *73 Rte. 73, Owls Head* ☎ *207/594–4418* ⊕ *www.owlshead.org*) to see a collection of antique aircraft, automobiles, motorcycles, carriages, bicycles, and engines. It is open throughout the year except certain

CLOSE UP

Lighting the Way

Ever wonder what makes Maine's more than five-dozen lighthouses so bright? It has to do with the lens; you need the right kind of lens to magnify the light. Resembling giant beehives, the original Fresnel lenses used in these lighthouses were made of prisms that redirected light from a lamp into a concentrated beam.

The first Fresnel lens was made in France in 1822 by French physicist Augustine Fresnel. Most lenses that were placed in lighthouses along the coasts of Europe and North America were handmade and shipped unassembled from France. The largest of these lenses, called a first-order lens, could be as much as 12 feet tall. Rings of glass prisms arranged above and below the center drum were intended to bend the light beam. Later designs incorporated a bull's eye into the center of the lens, which acted like a magnifying glass to make the beam even more powerful. A Fresnel lens captured all but 17% of the available light, whereas an open flame, even with reflectors behind it, lost 83% of its light.

You can see some of the smaller original lenses in museums in Maine, but you can also see a first-order lens in the Mid-Coast area in the lighthouse on Seguin Island, 10 mi from shore. You can go by boat from the Maine Maritime Museum. The Seguin Light is the only first-order lens in Maine, and one of only two remaining lenses still in use north of Virginia. The lens shines with 282 prisms.

The Seguin Island Light was commissioned by George Washington in 1795, and is one of the oldest lighthouses in the United States. Most of the original lenses used in lighthouses in this part of the country were mounted on mercury bases that were designed to rotate; these lenses were later replaced because of the danger of mercury poisoning. Seguin is a fixed light, meaning that it does not rotate. It used no mercury, so it could be kept in place. Ships can see this beacon 20 mi out to sea. Today the lens reflects the light of a 1,000-watt bulb. Before electricity, incandescent oil vapor was used.

Early Fresnel lenses were fairly standard in size and shape, but that posed problems as more lighthouses were built along the coasts. The captain of a ship could not tell one light from another in the dark and stormy night, so he didn't know what headland or ledge he was approaching. The lenses were eventually designed to have different personalities that made them easily identifiable. Many lights became known for their distinctive flash patterns. Seguin Island Light is a fixed white light, whereas the Pemaquid Point Light flashes every 6 seconds. Monhegan Island Light, visible from Port Clyde, has a white light that flashes for 2.8 seconds every 30 seconds. In Phippsburg, Pond Island Light shines a white beam with 6-second intervals of white and dark. And don't miss the Rockland Lighthouse Museum to see a dozen Fresnels on display.

More of Maine's historic lighthouses are being opened to the public each year. Only recently, for example, has it become possible to enter and tour the lighthouses at Owl's Head and Pemaquid. Much of that success can be credited to volunteers and organizations. For more information, visit www.americanlighthousefoundation. org.

4

holidays. During the museum airplane show each year (timing varies), see a full-size replica of the Wright Brothers' Kitty Hawk Flyer. The museum is adjacent to the Knox County Airport if you are flying in, and the fee is $8.

SHOPPING

If you need to stock up on anything before heading out to Monhegan Island, drive to the end of Route 131 to the dock-side **Port Clyde General Store** (⊠ *Cold Storage Rd.,* ⒹＰ.O. *Box 276 04855* ☎ *207/372–6543*), under new ownership. Open throughout the year, it now has a full service deli, expanded meat counter and produce section, 20 boat moorings and marine fuel, as well as gas for cars. There are daily lunch specials that people literally line up for, and coffee is always available.

MONHEGAN ISLAND

Fodor's Choice   *East of Pemaquid Peninsula, 10 mi south of Port Clyde.*

★   Simple and artful living is the order of the day on remote Mongehan Island. To get here you'll need to take a ferry. A tiny hamlet greets you at the harbor. There are no paved roads. Everywhere you look artists stand before their canvases, rendering the landscape of serene gardened cottages and rugged coast. It doesn't take long to grasp that Monhegan is a throwback from another era.

The island was known to Basque, Portuguese, and Breton fishermen well before Columbus discovered America. About a century ago, Monhegan was discovered again by some of America's finest painters, including Rockwell Kent, Robert Henri, A. J. Hammond, and Edward Hopper, who sailed out to paint its open meadows, savage cliffs, wild ocean views, and fishermen's shacks. Tourists followed, and now three excursion boats dock here *(⇨ Boat Travel in Mid-Coast Getting Here and Around section at the beginning of this chapter)* for a few hours each day in the warm months when harbor shops and artist studios bustle with activity.

You can escape the crowds on the island's 17 mi of hiking trails, which lead to the lighthouse and to the cliffs. Or spend a night and feel some of the privacy that the island can afford. Note that if you're the kind of traveler who likes a lot of activity, skip Monhegan. A day trip is typified by a little shopping and a hike across the island to view the bluffs. If the weather's bad, there's little to do. But if you enjoy a good hike, nature, or the concept of an island that's home to just artists and fishermen, the silence and serenity the high cliffs at White Head, Black Head, and Burnt Head, and the serendipitous pleasures that the island creates will be unforgettable.

EXPLORING

Monhegan Museum. Housed in an 1824 lighthouse and the adjacent assistant keeper's house, this museum has wonderful views of Manana Island, and you can see the original doriess used by the first Monhegan fishermen. Inside, informative displays depict island life and local flora and fauna. ⊠ *White Head Rd.* ☎ *No phone* 🖾 *Donations accepted* ☉ *July–mid-Sept., daily 11:30–3:30.*

WHERE TO EAT AND STAY

$$
SEAFOOD
Fodor's Choice
★

✕ **Fish House.** If it's your first time on the island, it's easy to overlook Monhegan's best dining experience. That's because this little place right on the water doesn't trumpet itself. It doesn't build its menu around the local seafood because it's chic; it does it because it's the way that the few locals here love to eat. You order inside the little hut by the water, and when your meal is ready, eat it at an outdoor table inches from the shoreline, lapping up the view of the bay and the lobster boats moored here. Bring your own wine or beer and savor outstanding fish chowder or a steamed lobster. If you're lucky, the owner, Shermie Stanley—who is also the harbormaster, a lobsterman, and one of the island's favored sons—will have just finished smoking salmon. If so, buy one or two thick pieces of one of the coast's most delicious delicacies. Devouring the salty, wonderfully flavorful fish while staring out at the foggy coast is a supreme pleasure. ⊠ *1 Fish Beach Rd., Monhegan Island* ☎ *no phone* ⊟ *No credit cards.*

$$–$$$$
★

⊞ **Island Inn.** This wonderful three-story inn, which dates from 1907, lords it over the Monhegan Island harbor. It's the first sight when you get off the ferry and the last when you leave. Design has remained authentic to its original construction, and there is original art everywhere, reflecting the presence of many studios and galleries on this island. It also nicely conveys a spirit of informal relaxation that prevails here. The waterfront rooms are the nicest, of course, with views of the sunset over stark Manana Island. But everyone can breathe in the same scene from the wide porch and the numerous Adirondack chairs set out on the lawn (many guests end up doing a lot of reading here). Facilities now include the adjacent Pierce Cottage, with two suites with private baths. The inn also runs a café on the pier—and their dining room serves breakfast, lunch, and dinner. **Pros:** great food; great view. **Cons:** pricey. ⊠ *1 Ocean Ave.* ☎ *207/596–0371* ⊕ *www.islandinnmonhegan. com* ⟿ *28 rooms, 20 with bath; 4 suites* ⟡ *In-room: no phone, no TV, no a/c. In-hotel: restaurant, Internet terminal* ⊟ *MC, V* ☼ *Closed Columbus Day–Memorial Day* ⟊ *BP.*

$$–$$$$

⊞ **Shining Sails Bed & Breakfast.** Thinking of staying a while? This is your source for cottage rentals. Additionally, Shining Sails is a very relaxed B&B. It's the best choice if you like an intimate lodging experience, with friendly owners, and airy rooms kept cheery with fresh flowers. Most have private decks with ocean views. A common room in the B&B facility with a wood-burning stove is filled with games. This facility has nine efficiency apartments. They rent out 27 cottages (the majority of structures on the island) with a one-week minimum stay. **Pros:** friendly, carefree environment. **Cons:** only continental breakfast served. ⊠ *Monhegan Island,* ☎ *207/596–0041* ⊕ *www.shiningsails.com* ⟿ *2 rooms, 9 efficiency apartments, 30 cottages* ⟡ *In-room: Wi-Fi, no phone, kitchen (some), no TV, no a/c. In-hotel: public Wi-Fi* ⊟ *D, MC, V* ⟊ *CP.*

4

Penobscot Bay

WORD OF MOUTH

"Camden and Rockport in the Mid-Coast area are beautiful settings—go for a windjammer cruise, and have chowder overlooking the bay. Check out the performance schedule at the Rockport Opera House or enjoy a lobster roll as you take in the beautiful scenery."

—dowzerw

By Stephen
and Neva
Allen

Few could deny that Penobscot Bay is one of Maine's most dramatically beautiful regions. Its 1,000-mi-long coastline is made up of rocky granite boulders, wild and often undeveloped shore, a sprinkling of colorful towns, and views of the sea and shore that are a photographer's dream.

The second-largest estuary in New England, Penobscot Bay stretches 37 mi from Port Clyde in the south to Stonington, the little fishing village at the tip of Deer Isle, in the north. The bay begins where the Penobscot River ends, near Stockton Springs, and terminates in the Gulf of Maine, where it is 47 mi wide. It covers an estimated 1,070 square mi and is home to hundreds of islands.

Initially, shipbuilding was the primary moneymaker here. In the 1800s, during the days of the great tall ships, or Down Easters as they were often called, more wooden ships were built along Penobscot Bay than in any other place in America. This golden age of billowing sails and wooden sailing ships did not last long, however. It came to an end with the development of the steam engine. Ships propelled by steam-driven pistons were faster, safer, more reliable, and could hold more cargo. By 1900, sailing ships were no longer a viable commercial venture in Maine. However, as you will see when traveling the coast, the tall ships have not disappeared—they have simply been revived as recreational boats, known as windjammers. Today, once again, there are more tall ships along Penobscot Bay than anywhere else in the country.

PLANNING AND ORIENTATION

GETTING ORIENTED

The only route for exploring this region is the historic two-lane U.S. 1, which winds all the way along Penobscot Bay, from Rockland to Bucksport and farther. Although the distance from Rockland to Bucksport is only 45 mi, the going is slow; U.S. 1 is an old highway, and the summer months bring heavily congested traffic. There are some impressive coastal views along the drive, but don't expect to see the ocean continuously. The water is blocked for a good part of the way by woods, which are beautiful in their own right. Driving the entire distance without stopping should take about two hours, but you'll probably want to stop along the way and spend a day or two in some of the more colorful towns. If you're driving at night, be wary of moose crossing the road.

TOP REASONS TO GO

■ **Setting Sail.** Take a trip on a windjammer from Rockland or Camden.

■ **Bridge to Adventure.** Ascend Bucksport's 420-foot Penobscot Narrows Bridge Observatory, the highest bridge observatory in the world.

■ **Historic Sites.** Visit the mysterious Fort Knox (not the one with all the gold) at Bucksport. It was built in 1844 to protect the Penobscot River from a British invasion (which never came).

■ **Palate Pleasers.** Dig into an authentic Maine "Shore Dinner" at an area lobster pound.

■ **Museum Musts.** Learn about Maine's maritime history at Searsport's Penobscot Marine Museum, or visit the famous Farnsworth Art Museum, which features work by the noted Wyeth family.

5

PLANNING

WHEN TO GO

High season starts in the middle of May and runs until mid-October. Crowds are a little thinner just after the public schools open in early September and just before they close in mid-June. Though many residents enjoy the long cold winters, most visitors avoid them. The Camden Snow Bowl, with its 11 downhill ski trails, is one of the few attractions to entice visitors in the winter months. Many of the motels, bed-and-breakfasts, restaurants, and other businesses along U.S. 1 close for the winter.

GETTING HERE AND AROUND

There is no train service or public transportation in the Penobscot Bay area, but there is a luxury bus service, Concord Coach Lines, which runs from Bangor to Logan Airport in Boston. Exploring the Penobscot Bay coast by water is also a possibility. Ferries travel back and forth from Lincolnville and Rockland to islands such as Islesboro and Vinalhaven, and romantic windjammer cruises sail from Camden and Rockland along the coast to various islands or town destinations.

AIR TRAVEL

Bangor International, off I–95, is the major airport in the Penobscot Bay area. Delta, Northwest, and US Airways service Bangor International to and from the key cities of Boston, New York, Newark, Philadelphia, Cincinnati, Atlanta, Detroit, and Minneapolis–St. Paul. From the airport you can access local and regional bus service, taxis, and rental cars.

Airport Bangor International Airport (✉ *287 Godfrey Blvd., Bangor* ☎ *207/992–4600* ⊕ *www.flybangor.com*).

BIKE TRAVEL

The most popular bike route on Maine's Penobscot Bay is historic U.S. 1. But note that for most of it, this is a two-lane highway, and tourists naturally are gawking at the sights. Most of the highway does have a designated bike lane—but you still need to be very careful.

BOAT TRAVEL

Ferry service runs from Rockland and Lincolnville to the islands of Islesboro and Vinalhaven.

Contact Maine State Ferry Service at Rockland Harbor. (⌂ *P.O. Box 645, Rockland 04841* ☎ *207/596–2202 or 800/491–4883*).

BUS TRAVEL

Concord Coach Lines (⊠ *1039 Union St., Bangor* ☎ *800/639–3317* ⊕ *www. concordcoachlines.com*), a luxury bus service, with snacks, drinks, and movies, runs two buses a day from the University of Maine, at Orono, through Bangor and then down the coast all the way to Boston's Logan International Airport. It stops at all major towns along the way.

CAR TRAVEL

Major roads going near or through the Penobscot Bay region are U.S. 1 and, for faster travel, I–95. Historic U.S. 1 is a two-lane highway. Despite being narrow, it is a fairly good road. If you are coming up I–95 and want to get off to begin your coastal tour in the Penobscot Bay area, take the Augusta exit and follow the signs to Route 3 and U.S. 1. ■ TIP➡ **U.S. 1 is old and only two lanes. Look at the scenery if you wish, but also keep your eyes on the road. At night, watch out for the possibility of a moose running out on the road. Moose can weigh up to 800 pounds, so hitting one will not be good for you, or the moose.**

In winter the Maine Department of Transportation keeps most major roads plowed and graveled. However, you should always drive with caution in snowy conditions.

TRAIN TRAVEL

Amtrak (⊕ *www.amtrak.com*) runs from Boston to Portland and back (⇨ *see Greater Portland in Chapter 3*).

RESTAURANTS

Seafood is the name of the game along Penobscot Bay. "Lobstah" is, of course, a staple on most menus, and it comes cooked in myriad ways: whole lobster dinners (boiled or steamed in the shell), broiled lobster tails, fried lobster, lobster stew, and lobster rolls, which are sold even at McDonald's.

Dining establishments are generally informal, and casual dress is almost always acceptable. Most restaurants are open for lunch and dinner, and some are open for breakfast. From June through August, reservations are always a good idea, particularly at the more popular or smaller restaurants.

For a truly authentic Maine experience, try one of the lobster pounds in Lincolnville or Belfast.

HOTELS

Large luxury hotels are few and far between in this region; motels, B&Bs, and campgrounds are more the norm. Accommodations are generally modest, but many of them sit right on the edge of the ocean. A good share of the B&Bs are in historic Federal or Colonial-style homes that date back to the 1850s and are filled with period antiques. Please note that while many of the smaller accommodations and B&Bs—as well as some of the restaurants and many of the museums—are not air-conditioned, ocean breezes usually keep things amply cool. If you're planning to come between mid-May and mid-October, reservations are recommended at least a month in advance. ■ TIP→ **If you are handicapped, call ahead to see if a property can accommodate you. Many B&Bs along the Maine Coast do not have ramps.**

WHAT IT COSTS					
	¢	$	$$	$$$	$$$$
Restaurants	under $7	$7–$10	$11–$17	$18–$25	over $25
Hotels	under $60	$60–$99	$100–$149	$150–$200	over $200

Restaurant prices are for a median main course at dinner, excluding sales tax of 7%. Hotel prices are for two people in a standard double room in high season, excluding service charges and 7% tax.

ROCKLAND AREA

The name "Rockland" defines this area's history. If you set fishing aside, rock cutting—specifically granite and limestone—was once the area's principal occupation. In fact, numerous government buildings across the United States were built using granite blocks from Rockland and other nearby quarries. Just outside the town of Rockland a large cement factory on U.S. 1 serves as a reminder of this rocky past.

ROCKLAND

4 mi northeast of Thomaston, 14 mi northeast of Tenants Harbor.

In September 2007 *National Geographic Adventure* magazine named Rockland "one of the top 50 adventure towns in the United States." The town is considered the gateway to Penobscot Bay, and is the first stop on U.S. 1 offering a glimpse of the often sparkling and island-dotted blue bay. Though once merely a place to pass through on the way to tonier ports like Camden, Rockland now attracts attention on its own, thanks to a trio of attractions: the renowned Farnsworth Museum, the increasingly popular summer Lobster Festival, and the lively North Atlantic Blues Festival. Rockland's Main Street Historic District, with its Italianate, Mansard, Greek Revival, and Colonial Revival buildings, is on the National Register of Historic Places. Specialty shops and galleries line the main street, and at least one of the restaurants, Primo (which is on the borderline between Camden and the little village of Owls Head), has become nationally famous. The town has a growing popularity as a summer destination, but it is still a large fishing port and the commercial hub of this coastal area. You can find plenty of working boats moored alongside the yachts.

Rockland Harbor is the berth of more windjammer ships than any other port in the United States. The best place in Rockland to view these beautiful vessels as they sail in and out of the harbor is the mile-long granite breakwater, which bisects the outer portion of Rockland Harbor. To get there, go north on U.S. 1, turn right on Waldo Avenue, and right again on Samoset Road; go to the end of this short road.

ESSENTIALS

Visitor Information Penobscot Regional Chamber of Commerce (⊠ *1 Park Dr., Rockland* ☎ *207/596–0376 or 800/562–2529* ⊕ *www.therealmaine.com*).

EXPLORING

Fodor'sChoice
★
Farnsworth Art Museum. This is one of the most important small museums in the country. The **Wyeth Center** is devoted to Maine-related works of the famous Wyeth family: N.C. Wyeth, an accomplished illustrator whose works were featured in many turn-of-the-20th-century books; his son Andrew, one of America's best-known painters; and Andrew's son James, also an accomplished painter who lives on nearby Monhegan Island. Some works from the personal collection of Andrew and Betsy Wyeth include *The Patriot, Adrift, Maiden Hair, Dr. Syn, The Clearing,* and *Watch Cap.* Also on display are works by Fitz Henry Lane, George Bellows, Frank W. Benson, Edward Hopper (his paintings of old Rockland are a highlight), Louise Nevelson, and Fairfield Porter. Works by living Maine artists are shown in the **Jamien Morehouse Wing.** The **Farnsworth Homestead,** a handsome circa-1852 Greek Revival dwelling that is part of the museum, retains its original lavish Victorian furnishings. There is a museum store next to the Morehouse Wing. In Cushing, a tiny town a few miles south of Thomaston, on the St. George River, the museum also operates the **Olsen House** (⊠ *Hathorn Point Rd., Cushing*), which is depicted in Andrew Wyeth's famous painting *Christina's World.* ⊠ *16 Museum St., Rockland* ☎ *207/596–6457* ⊕ *www.farnsworthmuseum.org* ⊠ *museum and Olsen House, $12; Olsen House only, $4* ⊙ *Daily 10–5.*

OFF THE
BEATEN
PATH
Maine Eastern Railroad. You can't really say this attraction is "off the beaten track" since it operates *on* tracks. If your kids have never been on a train, this might be their opportunity. Composed of restored vintage railroad cars, this train will take you from Rockland to Wiscasset ("the most beautiful village in Maine") to Bath (home of the great shipyard) to the end of the line in Brunswick. But you can board at any one of those towns and get off at any one. The train runs Wednesday through Sunday, four times a day. ⊠ *4 Union St.* ☎ *207/596–6725 or 866/637–2457* ⊕ *www.maineeasternrailroad.com* ⊠ *$40 round-trip adults from Rockland to Brunswick, $20 children.* ⊙ *Closed Nov.–Apr. except for some holiday trains in Dec.*

Ⓒ
Fodor'sChoice
★

★
The Strand Theatre. The Strand is a very special place. It could even be called "the performing arts center of Mid-Coast Maine." Originally built in 1923, it was once just a movie theatre, but since 1999 has evolved into an arts center hosting movies, live music, and other

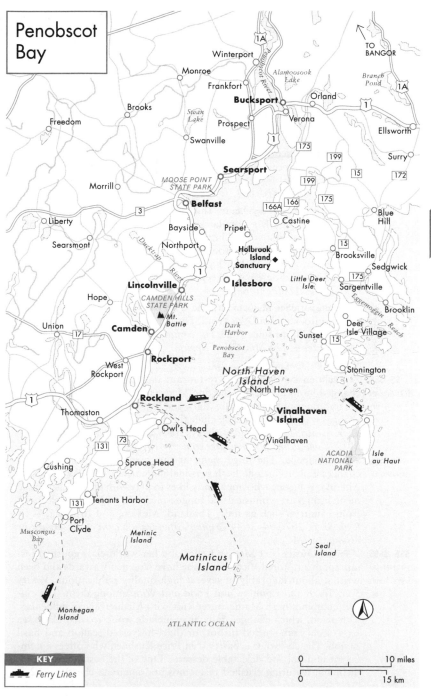

Penobscot Bay

To BANGOR

1A

Winterport

Monroe

Frankfort

Alamoosook Lake

Brooks

Orland

Verona

Ellsworth

Branch Pond

1A

Bucksport

Prospect

Swanville

1

175

Surry

199

15

172

Freedom

Swan Lake

Searsport

Morrill

MOOSE POINT STATE PARK

199

166

175

Liberty

3

Belfast

166A

Castine

Blue Hill

Bayside

Pripet

Searsmont

Northport

Holbrook Island Sanctuary

15

Brooksville

Sedgwick

Ducktrap River

1

Islesboro

Little Deer Isle

175

Sargentville

Hope

CAMDEN HILLS STATE PARK

Brooklin

Eggemoggin Reach

Union

17

Camden

Mt. Battie

Dark Harbor

Sunset

Deer Isle Village

15

West Rockport

Rockport

Penobscot Bay

Stonington

Rockland

North Haven Island

North Haven

Thomaston

1

Vinalhaven Island

Owl's Head

131

73

Vinalhaven

ACADIA NATIONAL PARK

Isle au Haut

Cushing

Spruce Head

131

Tenants Harbor

Metinic Island

Seal Island

Port Clyde

Muscongus Bay

Matinicus Island

Monhegan Island

ATLANTIC OCEAN

KEY

Ferry Lines

0   10 miles

0   15 km

attractions. If you're looking for first-class entertainment during your visit, this is the place. The theatre is centrally located on Main Street. You can pick up a schedule of events at the theatre or by mail. ✉ *345 Main St. Downtown* ☎ *207/594–0070* ⊕ *www.rocklandstrand.com* ✆ *Admission varies* ⊙ *Hrs vary.*

☾★ **Maine Lighthouse Museum/Maine Discovery Museum.** The lighthouse museum displays the largest collection of the famed Fresnel lighthouse lenses to be found anywhere in the world. It also displays a collection of lighthouse artifacts and Coast Guard memorabilia. Sharing the same building are the Maine Discovery Museum, which is great for kids, and the Penobscot Bay Regional Chamber of Commerce, where tourists and visitors can pick up maps and area information. ✉ *1 Park Dr.* ☎ *207/594–3301* ⊕ *www.mainelighthousemuseum.com* ✆ *$5* ⊙ *Weekdays 9–5, weekends 10–4.*

Rockland Breakwater Lighthouse. This 19th-century light located at the end of the breakwater is a popular subject for photographers. A wooden lighthouse was first erected here in 1888, but it was moved four times before 1895. The current stone light tower, which is at the end of the breakwater, is only 18 feet high and was erected between 1900 and 1902. The lighthouse had a keeper until 1963, but is now automated. ⊕ *www.rocklandlighthouse.com.*

☾★ The **Transportation Museum** and the **Owls Head Lighthouse** are only 3 mi south of Rockland in Owls Head. This landmark has shown the way to Rockland Harbor since 1825. *For complete information on these sights see Chapter 4, The Mid-Coast Region.*

WHERE TO EAT

$$–$$$
MEDITERRANEAN
★ ✕ **Amalfi on the Water.** This restaurant has expanded its name and changed its location, but the fine Mediterranean fare, influenced by the traditions of France, Spain, Italy, and Greece, is the same. The menu changes seasonally, but may include the house paella with chorizo or the duck risotto. The seafood is always fresh. ✉ *12 Water St.* ☎ *207/596–0012* ⊕ *www.amalfionthewater.com* ▭ *AE, MC, V.*

$$–$$$
AMERICAN
✕ **Café Miranda.** The huge menu at this friendly, casual restaurant changes daily to include fresh seasonal ingredients. Chef-owner Kerry Alterio is someone who apparently likes to play with his food, since the menu listings are whimsical and tongue-in-cheek, with ethnic selections from countries such as Italy, Thailand, Mexico, and Armenia. ✉ *15 Oak St.* ☎ *207/594–2034* ⊕ *www.cafemiranda.com* ⚑ *Reservations essential* ▭ *MC, V.*

$$$–$$$$
CONTINENTAL
Fodor's Choice
★ ✕ **Primo.** Owner-chef Melissa Kelley and her world-class gourmet restaurant in a restored Victorian home have won many awards and been written about favorably in several high-quality publications, *Vanity Fair, Town and Country,* and *Food and Wine* among them. The cuisine combines fresh Maine ingredients with Mediterranean influences. The menu, which changes daily, may include wood-roasted black sea bass, local crab-stuffed turbot, or diver-harvested scallop and basil ravioli. The co-owner is pastry chef Price Kushner, who offers a number of unusual and delectable desserts. One of the best is his cannoli Siciliana, featuring crushed pistachios and amarena cherries. ✉ *2 S.*

GREAT ITINERARIES

IF YOU HAVE 3 DAYS

On the morning of your first day, visit the Farnsworth Museum in **Rockland** with its wonderful collection of paintings by the Wyeth family. Then drive up to **Camden,** one of the most charming towns along the coast, and take a two-hour excursion on a windjammer high-masted sailing ship. Consider staying at the Lord Camden Inn, in the heart of the downtown, or at one of the many delightful B&Bs.

On Day 2 drive up to **Belfast,** where you can wander around the downtown area, walk down to the harbor, and have a seafood lunch at the Weathervane restaurant at the harbor. In the afternoon, drive north on U.S. 1 to **Searsport** to browse its antiques shops and flea markets. Plan on spending the night at a B&B. A good choice for dinner would be Anglers, a favorite of the locals.

On Day 3 continue north on U.S. 1 to **Bucksport** to explore historic Fort Knox and go from there to the highest bridge observatory tower in America, atop the Penobscot Narrows Bridge. Spend the night in Bucksport, and have dinner at McLeod's restaurant.

IF YOU HAVE 5 DAYS

Begin your itinerary in **Rockland.** Start with a morning visit to the Farnsworth Museum. Then head to Rockland's Maine State Ferry Terminal. Take the ferry (with your car) to **Vinalhaven Island** and spend the day exploring and watching the lobster boats and fishermen down by the harbor. Stay overnight at the Tidewater Motel (make advance reservations).

On Day 2 take the ferry back to Rockland and drive north to **Camden,** where you can explore the shops and galleries, try the excellent restaurants, and stay the night in a charming B&B. Spend your third day and night aboard a windjammer (arrange this ahead of time).

On your fourth day, drive to **Belfast,** where you can walk down the colorful main street, shop, and explore the harbor. For an authentic Maine dinner, take U.S. 1 across the bridge on the way to Searsport and turn right on Mitchell Avenue to reach Young's Lobster Pound. Stay overnight at the Belfast Harbor Inn nearby. On your last day, drive to **Searsport** and spend the morning exploring the Penobscot Marine Museum with its wonderful exhibits on the history of Penobscot Bay.

5

Main St., Rockland (on the border between Rockland and the little village of Owls Head; if you see the sign that reads "Welcome to Owls Head," you've passed Primo by 100 feet.) ☎ *207/596–0770* ⊕ *www. primorestaurant.com* ▤ *AE, D, MC, V* ⊙ *Open Wed.–Sun. No lunch. Closed mid-Jan.–mid-Apr.*

$$
SEAFOOD
★

✕**Rockland Café.** It may not look like much from the outside, but the Rockland Café is probably the most popular eating establishment in town, especially among locals. It's famous for the size of its breakfasts and is also open for lunch and dinner. The restaurant is a real bargain if you go for the all-you-can-eat seafood special. At dinner, the seafood combo of shrimp, scallops, clams, and fish is excellent, or there's the classic liver and onions. ⊠ *441 S. Main St., Rockland* ☎ *207/596–7556* ⊕ *www.rocklandcafe.com* ⊟ *AE, D, MC, V.*

$–$$ ✕ **Rustica.** Chef and owner John Stowe's Italian restaurant opened in
ITALIAN 2005 and has been popular from the start. The food is traditional Italian, and the entire menu is available for takeout. An unusual special is the salmon fettuccine with proscuitto. ⊠ *315 Main St.* ☎ *207/594–0015* ⊟ *MC, V.*

WHERE TO STAY

$$$–$$$$ 🏨 **Berry Manor Inn.** Originally the residence of prominent Rockland mer-
★   chant Charles H. Berry, this 1898 inn is in a historic residential neighborhood. Staying in this B&B will make you feel like you are back in the beginning of the last century. The large guest rooms are elegantly furnished with antiques and reproduction pieces. All rooms have fireplaces; TVs are available upon request, and some rooms have whirlpools. A guest pantry is stocked with sweets. **Pros:** in a nice, quiet neighborhood, within walking distance of downtown and the harbor. **Cons:** not much of a view. ⊠ *81 Talbot Ave.* ☎ *207/596–7696 or 800/774–5692* ⊕ *www. berrymanorinn.com* ⌨ *12 rooms* ⚐ *In-room: a/c, DVD In-hotel: room service, parking* ⊟ *AE, MC, V* ⏐○⏐ *BP.*

$$–$$$$ 🏨 **Captain Lindsey House.** Originally owned by a sea captain, this charming inn is filled with artifacts and treasures from all over the world, much as a sea captain's home would have been in the early 1800s. It is now owned by co–sea captains Ken and Ellen Barnes, who for many years captained the historic windjammer *Stephen Tabor.* The spacious rooms are furnished with antiques. All the beds have European-style down comforters. **Pros:** common rooms are a veritable treasure of seafaring memorabilia and antiques. **Cons:** if you're expecting a typical B&B, this is not as quaint as you may like; the walls are a trifle thin. ⊠ *5 Lindsey St.* ☎ *207/596–7950 or 800/523–2145* ⊕ *www.lindseyhouse. com* ⌨ *9 rooms* ⚐ *In-room: a/c, Wi-Fi. In-hotel: some pets allowed* ⊟ *AE, D, MC, V* ⏐○⏐ *BP.*

$$–$$$$ 🏨 **LimeRock Inn.** This inn is in the center of town, so you can easily walk
★   to the Farnsworth Museum or any of the other downtown attractions and restaurants. The house is built in the Queen Anne–Victorian style, and among the meticulously decorated rooms is one called Island Cottage, which features a whirlpool tub and doors that open onto a private deck overlooking a garden. The Grand Manan room has a fireplace, a whirlpool tub, and a four-poster king-size bed. Room TVs are available upon request. **Pros:** this is like living in an old New England house; free Wi-Fi. **Cons:** no pets allowed; not much of a view. ⊠ *96 Limerock St.* ☎ *207/594–2257 or 800/546–3762* ⊕ *www.limerockinn.com* ⌨ *8 rooms* ⚐ *In-room: no TV, Wi-Fi. In-hotel: Internet terminal.* ⊟ *AE, D, MC, V* ⏐○⏐ *BP.*

$–$$$ 🏨 **Navigator Motor Inn.** Across the street from the Maine State Ferry terminal, the Navigator is extremely convenient if you'll be heading out on an island ferry to Vinalhaven, North Vinalhaven, or Mantinicus. All rooms have bay views. Smokers will feel welcome in a number of rooms; 14 are pet-friendly. The inn's Oceanside Seafood & Steakhouse ($–$$$) is open for breakfast, lunch, and dinner. **Pros:** convenient to ferry; wonderful views from the balcony rooms in the front. **Cons:** location on U.S.

1 means lots of traffic in summer; can be a little noisy in front rooms. ⊠ *520 Main St. (U.S. 1)* ☎ *207/594–2131 or 800/545–8026* ⊕ *www. navigatorinn.com* ⇨ *80 rooms, 5 suites* ⚒ *In-room: refrigerator. In-hotel: restaurant, bar* ⊟ *AE, D, MC, V* ☉ *CP.*

$–$$ ⚏ **Trade Winds Motor Inn.** Rockland's largest accommodation by far, Trade Winds sits on the edge of the harbor and across from the Lighthouse Museum. Many rooms have balconies overlooking the harbor and marina. The restaurant ($–$$$) seats up to 150 and features dishes such as steamed mussels, pecan-encrusted halibut, and Maine shrimp in a garlic cream sauce over pasta. Some smoking rooms are available. **Pros:** great location; convenient to nearly everything. **Cons:** can be noisy and a little boisterous in summer. ⊠ *2 Park Dr.* ☎ *207/596–6661 or 800/834–3130* ⊕ *www.tradewindsmaine.com* ⇨ *138 rooms, 4 suites* ⚒ *In-room: Wi-Fi (free). In-hotel: restaurant, pool, gym, some pets allowed* ⊟ *AE, D, MC, V* ☉ *CP.*

NIGHTLIFE AND THE ARTS

Although there is not much in the way of nightlife in Rockland, the **Black Bull Tavern** (⊠ *420 Main St. 04841* ☎ *207/593–9060*), in the center of town, offers live entertainment throughout the summer. The tavern has large picture windows offering a view of downtown Rockland; weather permitting, patrons can drink and dine alfresco. Tin ceilings and pleasant mustard and mahogany furnishings give the Bull an authentic pub feel. The **Time Out Pub** (⊠ *275 Main St.* ☎ *207/593–9336*) has live music on Monday nights and karaoke on Saturday nights.

FESTIVALS More than a dozen well-known artists gather for the **North Atlantic Blues** ☪ **Festival** (☎ *207/593–1189* ⊕ *www.northatlanticbluesfestival.com*), a ★ two-day weekend affair held every July. The show officially takes place at Harbor Park, but it also includes a Blues Club Crawl Saturday night through downtown Rockland, which gives this staid old Maine town the atmosphere of New Orleans. Admission is $25 in advance, $30 at the gate. Rockland's annual **Maine Lobster Festival** (☎ *207/596–0376 or 800/562–2529* ⊕ *www.mainelobsterfestival.com*), in early August, is more than 60 years old and has become the biggest local event of the year. People come from all over the country to sample lobster in every possible form. During the few days of the festival tons of lobsters (about 10 tons, to be exact) are steamed in the world's largest lobster cooker—you have to see it to believe it. The festival, held in Harbor Park, includes a parade, entertainment, craft and marine exhibits, food booths—and, of course, the crowning of the Maine Sea Goddess. In mid-September the **Rockland Harborfest Jazz and Art Festival** (☎ *207/596–3076*), a traditional end-of-summer one-night musical event, takes place at Buoy Park, which is at the Public Landing, off South Main Street. There are tours of windjammer ships, kids' activities, arts and crafts, food, and entertainment, including the event's highlight: the annual Bay Chamber Concert Jazz Gala.

SHOPPING

The **Farnsworth Art Museum Store** (⊠ *356 Main St.* ☎ *207/596–5789*) sells jewelry, books, and prints of the museum's paintings. The motto at **Planet Inc.** (⊠ *318 Main St.* ☎ *207/596–5976*), Maine's largest toy store, is "You're never too old to play." Planet Inc. also has a store in Camden. **Rock City Books & Coffee** (⊠ *328 Main St.* ☎ *207/594–4123* ⊕ *www.rockcitybooksandcoffee.com*) is a wonderful place for book lovers. The staff is friendly, and you can enjoy coffee and a homemade pastry. The **Wine Seller** (⊠ *15 Tillison Ave.* ☎ *207/594–2621* ⊕ *www. fruitothevine.com*) sells domestic and imported wines.

ART GALLERIES There are more art galleries in this little town than you would expect. Most are on Main Street—note that Main Street was originally called Elm Street, and some of the older businesses still use Elm Street in their address. The **Caldbeck Gallery** (⊠ *12 Elm St.* ☎ *207/594–5935* ⊕ *www.caldbeck.com*) displays contemporary Maine works. **Dowling Walsh Gallery** (⊠ *357 Main St., across from the Farnsworth Museum* ☎ *207/596–0084* ⊕ *www.dowlingwalsh.com*) is a big and beautiful place, which represents more than 200 New England artists, including some from Monhegan Island. **Harbor Square Gallery** (⊠ *374 Main St.* ☎ *207/594–8700*) is another big gallery with rooms full of Maine-related arts and crafts. They also have a lovely roof deck where you can enjoy some refreshments.

SPORTS AND THE OUTDOORS

AERIAL TOURS **Downeast Air** (☎ *207/596–5557 or 888/594–2171* ⊕ *www.downeastair.*
Ⓒ *com*) offers lighthouse or island tours—or name your own destination— by plane, helicopter, or glider.

Ⓒ **Maine Windjammer Association** (⌂ *P.O. Box 1144, Blue Hill 04614*
Fodor'sChoice ☎ *800/807–9463* ⊕ *www.sailmainecoast.com*) can set you up with a
★ sailing excursion that very well may end being up the highlight of your vacation. Windjammer ships docked in Rockland include *Wendameen* (one-night cruises), *American Eagle, Heritage, Isaac Evans, J&E Riggin, Nathaniel Bowditch,* and *Simplicity.* Other windjammers can be found in the nearby towns of Rockport and Camden. Prices are about $180 for an overnighter and $395 to $875 for a three- to six-day cruise, with all meals included.

VINALHAVEN

★ *East of Rockland via Maine State Ferry.*

The largest inhabited island in Maine, Vinalhaven has 1,200 residents. It's nearly 8 mi long by 5 mi wide, and is mostly wooded. At one time the granite industry was booming here, but the quarries are now mostly used for swimming and picnicking. Many islanders work in the lobster-harvesting business. They even have a special season when they can gather lobsters while those on the mainland cannot (to compensate them for living on an island).

Most of Penobscot Bay's islands have infrequent ferry service, or are totally uninhabited. Vinalhaven, however, is relatively accessible—*relatively* being the key word here. There are six ferry trips per day to and from Vinalhaven in summer. The Maine State Ferry Terminal is right in the center of Rockland, on U.S. 1, across from the Navigator Motor Inn. The ferry runs throughout the year (except on major holidays), but the times change somewhat from the end of October through December, so

Windjammer Excursions

Nothing defines the Maine coastal experience more than a sailing trip on a windjammer. Windjammers were built all along the East Coast in the 19th and early 20th centuries. Designed to carry cargo primarily, these iron- or steel-hulled beauties have a rich past—the *Nathaniel Bowditch* served in World War II, for example, while others plied the waters in the lumbering and oystering trades. They vary in size, but could be as small as 40 feet and hold 6 passengers (plus a couple of crew members) or more than 130 feet and hold 40 passengers and 10 crew members. During a windjammer excursion passengers not only have the opportunity to ride on a historic vessel, but in most cases they are able to participate in the navigation, be it hoisting a sail or playing captain at the wheel.

The majority of windjammers are berthed in Rockland, Rockport, or Camden. You can get information on the fleets by contacting one of two windjammer organizations: **The Maine Windjammer**

Association (☎ *800/807–9463* ⊕ *www.sailmainecoast.com*) or **Maine Windjammer Cruises** (☎ *207/236–2938* or *800/736–7981* ⊕ *www.mainewindjammercruises.com*). Cruises can be anywhere from one day or one overnight to up to eight days. The price, ranging from nearly $200 to $900, depending on length of trip, includes all meals. Trips leave from Camden, Rockland, and Rockport.

Here is a selection of some of the best windjammer cruises in the area.

CAMDEN-ROCKPORT: *Angelique* (☎ *207/785-6036*). *Appledore*, which can take you out for just a day sail (☎ *207/236-8353*). *Mary Day*, Coastal Cruises (☎ *207/785-5670*). *Olad*, Downeast Windjammer Packet Co. (☎ *207/236-2323*). *Schooner Heron* (☎ *207/236-8605* or *800/599-8605*).

★ **ROCKLAND:** *American Eagle* and *Schooner Heritage*, North End Shipyard (☎ *207/594-8007* ⊕ *www.schoonerheritage.com*). *Nathanial Bowditch* (☎ *800/288-4098*). *Summertime* (☎ *207/563-1605* or *800/562-8290*).

it's best to call first. Ferry service to North Haven and to Mantinicus, a small island 23 mi from Rockland, is also available.

■ **TIP→** These old ferries are very minimal in their amenities. You won't find a restaurant, snack bar, lounge, or even a vending machine.

The village of Vinalhaven is small and easy to explore. There is a designated walking path on the north side of Main Street that runs from the ferry terminal to the center of town. Within a 1-mi radius of the ferry dock you will find two town parks and a nature conservancy area. There is only one road on the island, so it's pretty easy to find your way around. Biking the island can be fun, though there are no designated bike paths and the road can be a little rough outside the village. There is no public transportation on the island.

OFF THE BEATEN PATH

Matinicus Island is one of Maine's most-remote inhabited islands. It's 23 mi from the mainland, more than two hours by ferry (from the Maine State Ferry Terminal in Rockland). During the off-season the ferry runs only once a month; in June, July, and August it runs once a week. **Tuckanuck Lodge** (☎ *207/366–3830*) is the only place to stay on the island (*$–$$*).

North Haven Island is, appropriately, just north of Vinalhaven across a small stretch of sea, 12 mi from the mainland. This is the smaller of the two islands, but it's home to some large summer residences of the rich if not famous. There is one general store, a small restaurant, and a small B&B on the island. The year-round population is only about 330. The Maine State Ferry runs between North Haven and Rockland three times a day throughout the year (except for major holidays).

> ### CATCH THE FERRY
>
> Be aware of the ferry schedule. If you miss the last ferry back, or if there simply is not enough room for your car on the last ferry, you will have to spend the night on the island, and chances are you'll be sleeping in your car, since there is not a lot in the way of accommodations on Vinalhaven.
>
> ■TIP➔ Be sure to reserve well in advance if you'd like to spend the night on the island.

WHERE TO EAT AND STAY

$$–$$$
SEAFOOD
✕**Harbor Gawker.** Decorated with old wooden lobster traps and fishing gear, this mariner-theme restaurant has been in business for 30 years. The fare, seafood of course, is abundant and tasty. Try a lobster dinner or the ever-popular lobster roll. Insider tip: They don't have a liquor license, but if you like to have wine with your dinner, you can stop at the nearby Tidewater Motel and buy it at their Island Spirits shop. The Gawker will let you bring it in. ⊠ *Main St., Vinalhaven* ☎ *207/863–9365* ▭ *MC, V* ☾ *Mon.–Sat. 11–8. Closed Sun. and mid-Nov.–mid-Apr.*

$–$$
★
▦**Our Place Inn & Cottages.** On North Haven Island, this is a classic 19th-century farmhouse with five rooms in the main house and three separate but self-contained cottages. The inn is 2 mi from town, but only a short walk from Pulpit Harbor. Three of the rooms in the main house have private baths. The cottages are small, but all have a private bath and kitchenette. For something *really* different, you can ask to stay in the self-contained lighthouse. **Pros:** taking one of the inn's free bicycles for a ride on the island can be a lot of fun. **Cons:** it's a bit of a walk to town. ⊠ *Crabtree Point Rd., North Haven* ☎ *207/867–4998* ⊕ *www.ourplaceinn.com* ↵ *5 rooms, 3 with bath; 3 cottages* ♨ *In-room: no a/c, kitchen (some). In-hotel: bicycles* ▭ *MC, V* ꙳ *CP.*

$$–$$$$
▦**Tidewater Motel.** This little motel is the only place to stay that's on the waterfront and near the ferry dock. It was built on a bridge overlooking the harbor, and all rooms have wonderful views. If you want a real treat, get up early enough to watch the lobster boats leave around 5 AM. They usually come back sometime between 3 and 5 PM the same day. The property has several cars available for rent by guests. They also offer an excellent variety of wines at their Island Spirits shop. **Pros:** location on the harbor and in the center of town. **Cons:** difficult to get a room here during high season. ⌂ *P.O. Box 546* ⊠ *Carver's Harbor, Vinalhaven 04863* ☎ *207/863–4618* ⊕ *www.tidewatermotel. com* ↵ *19 rooms* ♨ *In-room: kitchen (some), no a/c. In-hotel: bicycles, water sports* ▭ *AE, D, MC, V* ꙳ *CP.*

ROCKPORT, CAMDEN, AND LINCOLNVILLE

ESSENTIALS

Visitor Information Camden-Rockport-Lincolnville Chamber of Commerce
(⊠ *2 Public Landing, Camden* ☎ *207/236–4404* ⊕ *www.visitcamden.com*).

ROCKPORT

4 mi north of Rockland on U.S. 1.

Heading north on U.S. 1, you come to Rockport before you reach the tourist mecca of Camden. The most interesting part of Rockport—the harbor—is not right on U.S. 1, so many people drive by without realizing it's here. You can get here by following the first ROCKPORT sign you see off U.S. 1 at Pascal Road.

Rockport, originally called Goose River, was part of Camden until 1891. The cutting and burning of limestone was once a major industry in this area. The stone was cut in nearby quarries and then burned in hot kilns. The resulting lime powder was used to create mortar. Some of the massive kilns are still here.

One of the most famous sights in Rockport is the **Rockport Arch,** which crosses Union Street at the town line. It was first constructed of wood and mortar in 1926, demolished in 1984, then rebuilt by popular demand in 1985. The arch has been displayed in a number of movies, including *Peyton Place* and *In the Bedroom.*

EXPLORING

Center for Maine Contemporary Art. Here you can view the work of some of Maine's best—and newest—artists. The exhibits, in four galleries, range from traditional art and photography to various forms of artistic expression. Exhibits change on a rotating basis. ⊠ *162 Russell Ave., Rockport* ☎ *207/236–2875* ⊕ *www.cmcanow.org* ⊠ *$5 adults, children free.* ☾ *Tues.–Sat. 10–5, Sun. 1–5.*

WHERE TO EAT

$$–$$$
FRENCH

✕ **Helm Restaurant.** In addition to the expected seafood, the Helm offers French and American cuisine, accompanied by excellent views. Specialties include the bouillabaisse and the coq au vin. There's also charbroiled steaks, and homemade soups and chowders. Locals rave about the huge salad bar. Specials include baked stuffed haddock and the complete Maine Shore Dinner, which comes with lobster, stew or chowder, steamed or fried clams, corn on the cob, and dessert. ⊠ *141 Commercial St. (U.S. 1)* ☎ *207/236–4337* ▭ *D, MC, V* ☾ *Closed Tues.*

$$$–$$$$
FRENCH
Fodor'sChoice
★

✕ **Marcel's.** If you're a serious gourmet and only have time to sample one dining experience in the Rockport-Rockland-Camden area, this lavish restaurant in the big Samoset Resort ought to be the one. Marcel's offers a fine array of continental cuisine. Enjoy table-side preparation of a classic rack of lamb, chateaubriand, or steak Diane while admiring the bay view. The menu includes a variety of Maine seafood and a fine wine list. The Sunday brunch buffet, with some of the finest seafood along the coast, is notable and draws a crowd. ⊠ *220 Warrenton St., off U.S.*

5

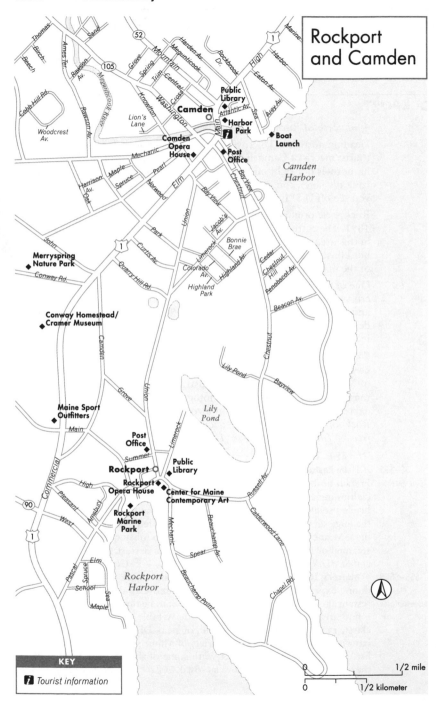

Rockport
and Camden

KEY

ℹ️ *Tourist information*

0 _____ 1/2 mile

0 _____ 1/2 kilometer

THE PRETTIEST WALK IN THE WORLD

A few years ago *Yankee*, the quintessential magazine of New England, did a cover story on what it called "The Prettiest Walk in the World." The two-lane paved road, which winds up and down, with occasional views of the ocean, connects Rockport to Camden. To judge the merits of this approximately 2-mi journey for yourself, you can travel on foot or by car. Begin at the intersection of U.S. 1 and Pascal Road. Take a right off U.S. 1 toward Rockport harbor, then cross the bridge and go up the hill. On your left is Russell Avenue. Take that all the way to Camden. Lining the way are some of the most beautiful homes in Maine,

surrounded by an abundance of flora and fauna. Keep an eye out for Aldermere Farm and its Belted Galloway cows, as well as views of the sparkling ocean. For those who may not know, these rare cows get their name from the foot-wide white "belt" around their middles; the rest of them is black. The walk or drive is beautiful at any time of the year, but in fall it's breathtaking. Like the rest of New England, the coast of Maine gets a large number of fall-foliage "leaf peepers." The reds and golds of the chestnut, birch, and elm trees along this winding route are especially beautiful.

1 ☎ 207/5593–1529 ⊕ *www.samoset.com* ⚓ *Reservations essential, jacket required* ⊟ *AE, D, MC, V* ⊗ *No lunch.*

$–$$ ✕ **The Offshore Restaurant.** Seafood is the specialty here, but the large
SEAFOOD menu also includes steak, prime rib, liver, and chicken. The restaurant is bright and airy, and there is a lovely view of the bay from the large windows. ✉ *770 Commercial St. (U.S. 1)* ☎ *207/596–6804* ⊟ *AE, D, MC, V* ⊗ *Closed Mon.*

$–$$$ ✕ **Prism Glass Gallery & Cafe.** This is a most unusual place in that it com-
AMERICAN bines a fine-art glass gallery with a fine restaurant. The basic decor of the restaurant is quite simple, but the unique glass works from more than 80 artists displays glass art in all sizes, shapes and colors. Steak is a specialty here, but for something unusual, try the lobster macaroni and cheese. *297 Commercial St. (U.S. 1)* ☎ *207/230–0061* ⊕ *www. prismglassgallery-café.com* ⊟ *AE, D, MC, V* ⊗ *Closed Mon.–Tues.*

WHERE TO STAY

$–$$ ⊞ **Claddagh Motel & Suites.** You may be in Maine, but you'll get "Irish hospitality" from hosts Alex and Sioban Gilmore. The main building resembles a New England–style clapboard house, with white paint and green awnings. Rooms are in a small wing in the back. Potted flowers and plants add extra charm to this small motel. All rooms are handicapped accessible (but have no special fixtures in the bathrooms). **Pros:** rooms are more spacious than you would expect; rates are lower than you would expect. **Cons:** U.S. 1 can get a little noisy at night. ✉ *1038 Commercial St. (U.S. 1), Box 988* ☎ *207/594–8479 or 800/871–5454* ⊕ *www.claddaghmotel.com* ⇱ *13 rooms, 6 suites* ⚬ *In-room: Wi-Fi. In-hotel: pool* ⊟ *AE, D, MC, V* ⊗ *Closed mid-Nov.–mid-Apr.* ⦿ *CP.*

$$$–$$$$ ⊞ **The Country Inn.** This inn has 36 country-style rooms in the main building and 11 private cottage suites. All rooms have private decks;

some also include fireplaces and Jacuzzis. Five of the rooms are pet-friendly, and two are handicapped accessible, including the bathroom. **Pros:** well situated between Rockport and Camden. **Cons:** a drive to dinner. ⊠ *8 Country Inn Ln.* ⌂ *P.O. Box 277 04856* ☎ *207/236–2725 or 888/707–3945* ⊕ *www.countryinnmaine.com* ⇨ *36 rooms, 11 cottage suites* ⚿ *In room: refrigerator. In-hotel: public Internet, Wi-Fi, pool, sauna, gym, laundry service* ☰ *AE, D, MC, V* ¶ *CP.*

¢–$ ⚠ **Megunticook Campground by the Sea.** You can't have a better location for an RV park and campground than this: it is easy to find, since the entrance is right on U.S. 1 just north of Rockland, and many of the sites in the campground face the sea. In addition to RV spots and tent-camping sites, cabin rentals are available. Rates during the high season are $35 a night for basic campsites, $45 a night for full-hookup sites, and $72 a night for cabins. **Pro:** a great location for easy access to Rockland or Camden; you may be able to get a site with a sea view. **Con:** can get crowded and noisy with children during the peak season. ⊠ *620 Commercial St. (U.S. 1)* ☎ *207/594–2428 or 800/884–2428* ⊕ *www.campgroundbythesea.com* ⇨ *87 tent/RV sites, 10 cabins* ⚿ *Full hookup, basic hookup* ☰ *MC, V* ☯ *Closed mid-Oct.–mid-May.*

$$–$$$$ ⛱ **Samoset Resort.** This 230-acre, all-encompassing oceanside resort on
Fodor's Choice   the Rockland-Rockport town line offers luxurious rooms and suites,
★   all with a private balcony or patio and an ocean or garden view. The spacious rooms are decorated in deep green and burgundy tones. The resort has three dining options: Marcel's, the Breakwater Cafe, and the Clubhouse Grille. The flagship restaurant Marcel's ($$$–$$$$) features French and American cuisine, as well as seafood specials. Reservations are essential here, and men must wear a jacket. For a less-formal affair, try the Breakwater Cafe, featuring basic New England fare such as homemade chowder and lobster rolls; there's outdoor seating when the weather is nice. The Clubhouse Grille, catering to the golf crowd, serves casual food, which you can enjoy inside or on the porch. *Golf Digest* called the resort's 18-hole championship golf course the "Top Ranked Resort Course in New England," and the "Seventh Most Beautiful Course in America." **Pros:** a resort property that seems to meet every need. **Cons:** not within walking distance of Rockland or Camden shops. ⊠ *220 Warrenton St., Rockport* ☎ *207/594–2511 or 800/341–1650* ⊕ *www.samoset.com* ⇨ *156 rooms, 22 suites* ⚿ *In-room: Internet, Wi-Fi. In-hotel: 3 restaurants, bar, golf course, tennis courts, pools, gym, concierge, children's programs (ages 3–12), laundry service, public Internet, airport shuttle* ☰ *AE, D, MC, V* ¶ *CP.*

$–$$ ⛱ **White Gates Inn.** This family-run inn is nestled in a quiet rural setting, surrounded by huge oak trees and spacious lawns and gardens. The rooms, many of which are rustic in nature with knotty-pine paneling, are all on the ground level. Adorning each room is an old-fashioned Maine quilt. (A big cottage industry in the state, Maine quilts are all hand-stitched.) The proprietors, Charlie and Ann Emerson, live on the property. **Pros:** all rooms are on the ground floor, so there are no stairs to climb; parking is available right in front of your room. **Cons:** restaurants and stores are a drive away. ⊠ *700 Commercial St. (U.S. 1)*

☎ *207/594–4625* ⊕ *www.whitegatesinn.com* ↙ *15 rooms* ↻ *In-room: a/c, Wi-Fi. In-hotel: Wi-Fi, some pets allowed* ⊟ *AE, MC, V* ⦿ *CP.*

NIGHTLIFE AND THE ARTS

★ The **Bay Chamber Concerts** (⌖ *58 Bay View St., Camden 04843* ☎ *207/236–2823 or 888/707–2770* ⊕ *www.baychamberconcerts.org*) feature major artists performing classical, jazz, dance, and more. Past performers have included the St. Lawrence String Quartet, Joseph Silverstein, Regina Carter, and Dave Brubeck and his sons. Concerts are held Wednesday and Thursday nights in July and August; Wednesday at the Strand Theater (⊠ *345 Main St., Rockland*) and Thursday at the historic Rockport Opera House (⊠ *6 Central St., Rockport*). Additional concerts take place at other times during the year.

SPORTS AND THE OUTDOORS

OUTFITTER **Maine Sport Outfitters** (⊠ *115 Commercial St. [U.S. 1]* ☎ *207/236–7120 or 888/236–8797* ⊕ *www.mainesport.com*) offers a big selection of sports clothing and gear in its huge, two-story building. It also rents bikes, camping equipment, canoes, kayaks, cross-country skis (for skiing at popular Camden Snow Bowl), ice skates, and snowshoes.

5

CAMDEN

★ *8 mi north of Rockland, 5 mi south of Lincolnville.*

More than any other town along Penobscot Bay, Camden is the perfect picture-postcard of a Maine coastal village. It is one of the most popular destinations on the Maine Coast, so June through September the town is crowded with visitors—but don't let that scare you away; Camden is worth it. Just come prepared for busy traffic on the town's Main Street (U.S. 1), and make lodging reservations well in advance. You'll also want to make restaurant reservations whenever possible.

Camden is famous not only for its geography but also for its large fleet of windjammers—relics and replicas from the age of sailing—with their romantic histories and great billowing sails. At just about any hour during the warm months you're likely to see at least one windjammer tied up in the harbor. The excursions, whether for an afternoon or a week, are best from June through September.

The town's compact size makes it perfect for exploring on foot: shops, restaurants, and galleries line Main Street (U.S. 1), as well as side streets and alleys around the harbor. Especially worth inclusion on your walking tour is Camden's residential area. It is quite charming and filled with many fascinating old period houses from the time when Federal, Greek Revival, and Victorian architecture were the rage among the wealthy. Many of them now are B&Bs. The chamber of commerce, at the Public Landing, can provide you with a walking map.

NEED A BREAK? Down by the harbor, a number of independent fast-food stands offer clam chowder, fried fish, and lobster rolls. For something sweet, try **Boynton-McKay** (⊠ *30 Main St.* ☎ *207/236–2465*), an 1890s ice-cream parlor serving ice cream made the old-fashioned way, as well as modern-day smoothies.

WHERE TO EAT

$$$–$$$$
SEAFOOD

✕ **Atlantica.** Right on the water's edge, the Atlantica is in a historic clapboard building. Its lower deck is cantilevered over the water, offering a romantic setting with great views. The interior decor is a mix of red walls and contemporary paintings. Fresh seafood with French and Asian accents is the specialty here. Favorites include pan-roasted split lobster tails with lemon butter, lobster stuffed with scallops, and pan-roasted king salmon. ⊠ *Bayview Landing* ☎ *207/236–6011 or 888/507–8514* ⊕ *www.atlanticarestaurant.com* ⌂ *Reservations essential* ▭ *AE, MC, V* ⊗ *No lunch.*

¢–$
AMERICAN
★

✕ **Camden Deli.** If you're looking for a quick and easy place for lunch, the Camden Deli may be it. The deli seems to be the most popular place in Camden for lunch among the locals, and it's centrally located. For a spectacular view, ask to sit on the rooftop deck. ⊠ *37 Main St., Downtown* ☎ *207/236–8343* ⊕ *www.camdendeli.com* ▭ *AE, D, MC, V.*

$–$$
SEAFOOD
★

✕ **Cappy's Chowder House.** Cappy's has been around for so long (more than two decades) it's become somewhat of a Camden institution. As you would expect from the name, Cappy's "chowdah" is the thing to order here—it's been written up in the *New York Times* and in *Bon Appétit* magazine—but there are plenty of other seafood specials on the menu, too. Don't be afraid to bring the kids—this place has many bargain meals. ⊠ *1 Main St.* ☎ *207/236–2254* ⊕ *www.cappyschowder. com* ⌂ *Reservations not accepted* ▭ *MC, V.*

$$–$$$
CONTINENTAL

✕ **Ephemere Cafe.** If you want to be a success in the difficult restaurant business, here's what you do: start small but build a BIG reputation. That's what Patrick and Heidi Cazemajou have done with Ephemere. This small restaurant is done in a minimalist design with simple tables and bare walls. Menu items include coconut shrimp, mussels marinière, and, of course, lobster. ⊠ *51 Bayview St., a little south of downtown* ☎ *207/236–4451* ▭ *AE, D, MC, V* ⊗ *Closed Sun. No lunch.*

$$–$$$
FRENCH
★

✕ **Francine Bistro.** A small place in a little old house, Francine's doesn't look like much from the outside—or the inside—but what a following it has! The restaurant is the brainchild of chef/owner Brian Hill, who uses the freshest and most organic local produce, meats, poultry, and seafood. The menu changes daily depending on Brian's whims, but recent dishes included sautéed calamari and seared scallops. ⊠ *55 Chestnut St., in south end of town* ☎ *207/230–0083* ⊕ *www.francinebistro. com* ⌂ *Reservations essential* ▭ *MC, V* ⊗ *Closed Sun. and Mon. No lunch.*

$$$$
SEAFOOD
★

✕ **Hartstone Inn.** At this elegant restaurant in a historic inn, the specialty is a five-course prix-fixe menu that changes daily. Items prepared by acclaimed chef Michael Salmon may include grilled salmon Niçoise with rosemary-roasted potatoes; haddock "Oscar," with Maine crabmeat; and, of course, Maine lobster. A specialty is the Mosaic of Maine Seafood dish, which includes a little of everything. Chef Michael also offers cooking classes every Saturday and Sunday (2 hr. a day) from November through May. Weekend packages ($305–$485) include two nights' lodging, breakfast, a gourmet dinner for two, and enrollment for one person in a cooking class. ⊠ *41 Elm St. (U.S. 1)* ☎ *207/236–4259 or 800/788–4823* ⊕ *www.hartstoneinn.net* ▭ *MC, V* ⊗ *No lunch.*

$$–$$$ ✕ **Natalie's.** This restaurant seems to have become the most sought-after
FRENCH- and respected dining spot in Camden. It's the creation of Dutch owners
AMERICAN Raymond Brunyanszki and Oscar Verest, and is located in the Camden
Fodor'sChoice Harbour Inn—if you're staying there, you're in for a real treat. The res-
★ taurant is fine dining with a French-American flair, and offers a variety
of prix-fixe menus, such as the "Menu Saisonnier," which showcases
fresh, seasonal ingredients, and the "Homard Grand Cru," which is
only for the *real* lobster lover. It is a cascade of lobster dishes— lobster
gazpacho, followed by lobster with squid ink, followed by lobster with
fiddleheads, only to be followed by lobster with beef cheek and foie-
gras ravoli. The lounge is a perfect place for a pre-dinner cocktail in
front of the big fireplace. ⊠ *83 Bay View St.* ☎ *207/236–7008* ⊕ *www.*
camdenharbourinn.com ⊟ *AE, D, MC, V.*

$$$ ✕ **Paolina's Way.** Although Paolina's serves a variety of Italian dishes,
ITALIAN it has what many describe as "the best pizza in Maine," so why order
anything else? The Prosciutto Crudo pizza is especially popular, as is
and the Paolina's Way Special, which has a little of everything. The
restaurant is right at the harbor, so great views are guaranteed. ⊠ *10*
Bayview Landing, Harbor ☎ *207/230–0555* ⊕ *www.paolinasway.com*
⚑ *Reservations essential* ⊟ *MC, V.*

$$–$$$ ✕ **Peter Ott's Steakhouse & Tavern.** This place has a perfect location—
AMERICAN right in the heart of the downtown and right next to the harbor. Steak,
seafood, and pasta are the specialties here, and they also have a tavern
menu, which is less expensive, for those with a lighter appetite. ⊠ *16*
Bayview St., Downtown ☎ *207/236-4032* ⊕ *www.peterottscamden.*
com ⊟ *D, MC, V.*

$$ ✕ **Waterfront Restaurant.** Come here for a ringside seat on Camden Har-
AMERICAN bor. The best view, when the weather cooperates, is from the deck. The
fare is primarily seafood, but also on the menu are beef and chicken
entrées and salads. Lobster and crabmeat rolls are highlights at lunch.
⊠ *40 Bay View St.* ☎ *207/236–3747* ⊕ *www.waterfrontcamden.com*
⚑ *Reservations not accepted* ⊟ *AE, MC, V.*

$$–$$$ ✕ **The White Lion.** This relatively new restaurant advertises itself as
SEAFOOD a "Raw Bar and Bistro." (If you like your seafood uncooked—raw
oysters, for example—this is the place to come.) But they also serve
European bistro fare, such as foie gras, venison, and charcuterie; the
salmon tartare is a favorite. ⊠ *20 Bayview St.* ☎ *207/230–7097* ⊟ *MC,*
V ☉ *Closed Tue. No lunch.*

WHERE TO STAY

$$–$$$$ ⌂ **Beloin's on the Maine Coast.** Beloin's sits on a natural sea ledge on the
edge of the ocean, so it offers spectacular views and easy shore access.
There are nine rooms in the motel, five one-bedroom shore cottages,
and two two-bedroom shore cottages. The property includes a private
beach, and there are picnic tables and grills. Camden Hills State Park
is nearby. Smoking is allowed throughout. **Pros:** wonderful views of
the sea from the shore cottages; the rooms on the non-shore side are
relatively inexpensive. **Cons:** this is not the place to go if the smell of
smoke bothers you, since smoking is allowed in any room. ⊠ *254 Bel-*
fast Rd. (U.S. 1) ☎ *207/236–3262* ⊕ *www.beloins.com* ⚑ *9 rooms, 7*

5

A CHILD OF PENOBSCOT BAY

It was a warm August night in 1912 when the young Rockland poet Edna St. Vincent Millay appeared at the Whitehall Inn. She was there to read her poem "Renascence," to an audience of inn guests and employees.

All I could see from where I stood

Was three long mountains and a wood;

I turned and looked another way,

And saw three islands in a bay.

(Edna St. Vincent Millay, "Renascence")

The woman who was to become one of America's most famous poets was born in 1892 in the unlikely city of Rockland, a working town of seamen and stonecutters. Like many artists before her, she became famous almost by accident. At the age of 20 she entered a poem, "Renascence,"

in a poetry contest. The poem only took fourth place, but it was enough to bring her attention from academics, and she was awarded a scholarship to prestigious Vassar College.

She continued writing and winning awards, and eventually she was awarded a Pulitzer Prize for her poetry. She was renowned for her beauty, and spent most of her adult life leading a rather wild existence in Greenwich Village, in New York City.

Eventually, she married a man much older than herself, Eugen Boissevain, who became her manager and supporter. A heavy smoker, she died in 1950 at the age of 58. She had written in one of her most famous poems that she was a person who had burned her candle at both ends, and she lamented that it "would not last the night."

cottages ⟨In-room: kitchen (some), no a/c, some pets allowed. In-hotel: beachfront ⊟ MC, V.*

$$$$ **Camden Harbour Inn.** This inn, which has been in existence since 1874,
★   is well named, since it has a panoramic view of Camden's colorful harbor. All the rooms include hand-picked flowers or a basket of fruit. While retaining some of its 19th-century characteristics, the inn also blends in the modern. Its new owners from the Netherlands renovated it in 2007 with new furnishings, a gourmet restaurant, and a cozy bar. Some rooms have decks or balconies, some have fireplaces, and many have claw-foot bathtubs. King-size feather beds and flat-screen TVs (with DVD player) are in all rooms. **Pros:** the inn's Natalie's restaurant is one of the best in the Camden area. **Cons:** a bit pricey. ⊠ *83 Bay View St.* ☎ *207/236–4200 or 800/236–4266* ⊕ *www.camdenharbourinn.com* ⟋ *17 rooms, 1 suite* ⟨In-room: Wi-Fi, DVD. In-hotel: restaurant, spa* ⊟ *AE, D, MC, V* ⊗ *Closed Nov.–Apr.* ⎮◎⎮ *BP.*

$$–$$$$ **Camden Hartstone Inn.** This downtown 1835 mansard-roofed Victo-
★   rian home has been turned into an elegant and sophisticated retreat and a fine culinary destination. No detail has been overlooked, from soft robes, down comforters, and chocolate truffles in the guest rooms to china, crystal, and silver in the elegantly decorated dining room. The inn hosts seasonal food festivals. **Pros:** on-site restaurant is excellent. **Cons:** no water views, but the harbor and the downtown are not far away. ⊠ *41 Elm St. (U.S. 1)* ☎ *207/236–4259 or 800/788–4823* ⊕ *www.*

hartstoneinn.com ⌐ *6 rooms, 6 suites* ⌂ *In-room: Internet. In-hotel: restaurant, spa* ▭ *MC, V* ⦿ *BP.*

CAMPING ⛺ **Camden Hills State Park Camping.** The 106-site camping area, open
$–$$ from mid-May to mid-October, operates on a first-come, first-served basis. Some of the sites offer electricity, water, and Wi-Fi. Thirty-five of them are for RVs; the rest are for people with tents. There is also a picnic area and playground. The entrance is 2 mi north of Camden off U.S. 1. **Pros:** RVs allowed. **Cons:** seasonal, closed from November through April. ⊠ *280 Belfast Rd. (U.S. 1)* ☎ *207/236–3109* ⌂ *Flush toilets, water, electric, sewer, cable, dumping, recreation hall, store, laundry, Internet access, swimming, pets allowed.*

$–$$$ ⊞ **High Tide Inn on the Ocean.** This is an unusual arrangement of accommodations. They have an inn, cottages, and two motor inns, most with wonderful ocean views. They also have their own private beach, and there is plenty of room for walking along the beach. **Pros:** a home-baked breakfast in a room overlooking the sea. **Cons:** you will need to drive to dinner. ⊠ *505 Belfast Rd (U.S. 1)* ☎ *207/236–3724 or 800/778–7068* ⊕ *www.hightideinn.com* ⌐ *30 rooms, 1 deckhouse* ⌂ *In-room: refrigerator (some). In hotel: beachfront, some pets allowed* ▭ *AE, D, MC, V* ⊗ *Closed mid-Oct.–mid-May* ⦿ *CP.*

$$$$ ⊞ **Inn at Sunrise Point.** This is seaside luxury at its finest. Guests are
★ offered a spectacular setting in this luxury inn. The main house and cottages are right on the ocean, with beautiful ocean views from nearly all rooms. Amenities such as plush robes and oversize tubs and showers are standard; some rooms include romantic wood-burning fireplaces and Jacuzzis. **Pros:** spectacular views. **Cons:** pricey; no restaurants nearby. ⊠ *Fire Rd. 9, off U.S. 1* ⌁ *Fire Rd. 9, Lincolnville, ME 04849* ☎ *207/236–7716* ⊕ *www.sunrisepoint.com* ⌐ *3 rooms, 4 cottages, 2 suites* ⌂ *In-room: Wi-Fi, DVD* ▭ *AE, MC, V* ⦿ *BP.*

$$$–$$$$ ⊞ **Lord Camden Inn.** If you want to be right in the center of Camden
★ and near the harbor, this is the place. The exterior of the building is red brick with bright blue-and-white awnings. The colorful interior is furnished with restored antiques and paintings by local artists. Despite being downtown, the inn offers plenty of ocean views from the upstairs rooms, and some rooms have lovely old-fashioned four-poster beds. There's no on-site restaurant, but you can find plenty of dining options within walking distance. **Pros:** the most centrally located accommodation in Camden. **Cons:** in the front rooms the U.S. 1 traffic may keep you awake. ⊠ *24 Main St. (U.S. 1)* ☎ *207/236–4325 or 800/336–4325* ⊕ *www.lordcamdeninn.com* ⌐ *37 rooms* ⌂ *In-room: refrigerator (some), Wi-Fi (free), DVD player. In-hotel: gym, some pets allowed.* ▭ *AE, MC, V* ⦿ *BP.*

$$$–$$$$ ⊞ **Norumbega Inn.** This is the most photographed piece of real estate in
Fodor'sChoice the state of Maine, and once you take a look at it, you'll understand
★ why. This castle B&B looks as if it was created by Stephen King (a Maine resident) or Count Dracula. It's easy to find, since it's right on U.S. 1, just a little north of downtown Camden. The outside is gray stone walls covered with ivy, but inside it's cheerier and elegant, with many of the antiques-filled rooms offering fireplaces and private balconies overlooking the bay. The inn was built in 1886 by local businessman

and inventor (of duplex telegraphy) Joseph Stearns. Before erecting his home, he spent a year visiting the castles of Europe and adapted the best ideas he found. He named the castle after the original 17th-century name for what is now Maine, "Norumbega." The home was converted into a B&B in 1984. Pets are not allowed. The Penthouse Suite, with grand views, is the very best. **Pros:** beautiful views; close to town. **Cons:** guests who have difficulty in climbing stairs will not find it comfortable. ⊠ *63 High St. (U.S. 1* ☎ *207/236–4646 or 877/363–4646* ⊕ *www. norumbegainn.com* ⊅ *12 rooms* ⚷ *In-room: Wi-Fi (free) DVD (some), no a/c* ⊟ *AE, MC, V* ⊚| *BP.*

$$–$$$ ⊞ **Whitehall Inn.** One of Camden's best-known inns, the Whitehall is
★   an 1834 white-clapboard sea captain's home just north of town. The Millay Room, off the lobby, preserves memorabilia of the poet Edna St. Vincent Millay, who grew up in the area and read her poetry here. The inn is a delightful blend of the old and the new. The telephones are antiques, but the electronics are brand new. The rooms, remodeled in 2007, have dark-wood bedsteads, white bedspreads, and claw-foot tubs. The dining room serves traditional and creative American cuisine as well as many seafood specialties, and the popular prix-fixe dinner is $36 a person. **Pros:** Edna St. Vincent Millay—wow! **Cons:** only some of the rooms have water views. ⊠ *52 High St.* ☎ *207/236–3391 or 800/789–6565* ⊕ *www.whitehall-inn.com* ⊅ *50 rooms, 45 with bath* ⚷ *In-room: Wi-Fi (free), no a/c. In-hotel: restaurant, tennis court, public Internet* ⊟ *AE, D, MC, V* ⊗ *Closed mid-Oct.–mid-May* ⊚| *BP.*

NIGHTLIFE

Offering live music, dancing, pub food, and local brews, **Gilbert's Public House** (⊠ *12 Bay View St. (underneath Peter Ott's pub)* ☎ *207/236–4320*) is the favorite drinking place of the windjammer crowd.

SHOPPING

Camden has some of the best shopping in the region. The downtown area is a shopper's paradise with lots of interesting places to spend money. Most of the shops and galleries are along Camden's main drag, U.S. 1, so you can easily complete a shopping tour on foot. Start at the Camden Harbor, turn right on Bay View, and walk to Main/High Street. ■TIP➔ **U.S. 1 has three different names within the town limits—it starts as Elm Street, changes to Main Street, then becomes High Street. So don't let the addresses listed below throw you off.**

ABCD Books (⊠ *23 Bay View St.* ☎ *207/236–3903 or 888/236–3903* ⊗ *Mon–Sat 10–5*) has a discriminating selection of quality antiquarian and rare books. **Maine Gathering** (⊠ *21 Main St.* ☎ *207/236–9004*) is a premier showplace for Maine crafts and American Indian arts and crafts. **Planet Toys** (⊠ *10 Main St.* ☎ *207/236–4410*) has unusual gifts—including books, toys, and clothing—from Maine and other parts of the world. **Lili, Lupine & Fern** (⊠ *44 Bayview St.* ☎ *207/236–9600*) offers a wonderful array of gourmet foods, wines, and cheeses.

GALLERIES   **Bayview Gallery** (⊠ *33 Bay View St.* ☎ *207/236–4534* ⊕ *www.bayview-gallery.com*) specializes in original art, prints, and posters, most with Maine themes. **Small Wonder Gallery** (⊠ *Public Landing* ☎ *207/236–6005*

⊕ *www.smallwondergallery.com*) has watercolors, wood engravings, metal sculptures, tiles, porcelain, and prints.

SPORTS AND THE OUTDOORS

Although their height may not be much more than 1,000 feet, the hills in **Camden Hills State Park** (⊠ *U.S. 1 just north of Camden* ☎ *207/236–3109*) are lovely landmarks for miles along the low, rolling reaches of the Maine Coast. The 5,500-acre park contains 25 mi of hiking trails, including the easy nature trail up Mt. Battie. Hike or drive to the top for a magnificent view over Camden and island-studded Penobscot Bay. There also is a campground here with 106 campsites. **Merryspring Nature Park** (⊠ *Conway Rd. off U.S. 1* ☎ *207/236–2239* ⊕ *www.merryspring.org* ⊠ *Free* ☉ *Daily dawn–dusk*) is a 66-acre retreat with herb, rose, rhododendron, hosta, and children's gardens as well as 4 mi of walking trails. Also, if you're traveling with a doggie, there's a leash-free dog meadow here.

FESTIVAL One of the biggest and most colorful events of the year in Camden is **Windjammer Weekend,** which usually takes place at the beginning of September and includes the single largest gathering of windjammer ships in the world, plus lots of good eats. ☎ *207/374–2993 or 800/807–9463* ⊕ *www.sailmainecoast.com*.

SAILING For the voyage of a lifetime, you and your family should think seriously about a **windjammer trip**—which can be as short as a couple of hours or as Fodor's Choice long as a week. Prices range from $30 for a day sail to $1,000 for a week ★ or more. All meals are included—and often that means a lobster bake on a deserted island beach. The following windjammers leave from Camden Harbor; most are of the schooner type. You can find out about all of them by contacting the Maine Windjammer Association (⊕ *P.O. Box 1144, Blue Hill, 04614* ☎ *800/807–9463 (WIND)* ⊕ *www.sailmainecoast.com*). **Lazy Jack** (☎ *207/230–0602* ⊕ *www.schoonerlazyjack.com*). **Olad** (☎ *207/236–2323* ⊕ *www.maineschooners.com*). **Windjammer Surprise** (☎ *207/236–4687* ⊕ *www.camdenmainesailing.com*).

SKI AREAS The Maine Coast isn't known for skiing, but the **Camden Snow Bowl** (⊠ *Hosmer Pond Rd.* ☎ *207/236–3438, 207/236–4418 snow phone* ⊕ *www.camdensnowbowl.com*) has a 950-foot-vertical mountain with 11 trails accessed by one double chair and two T-bars. The complex also includes a small lodge with a cafeteria, and ski and toboggan rentals. Activities include skiing, night skiing, snowboarding, tubing, tobogganing, and ice-skating—plus magnificent views over Penobscot Bay. The North American Tobogganing Championships, a tongue-in-cheek event open to anyone, is held annually in early February. At **Camden Hills State Park** (⊠ *U.S. 1 just north of downtown Camden* ⊕ *P.O. Box 1207 04843* ☎ *207/236–0849*), there are 10 mi of cross-country skiing trails.

LINCOLNVILLE

6 mi north of Camden via U.S. 1.

Looking at a map, you may notice there are two parts to Lincolnville: Lincolnville Beach on U.S. 1 and the town of Lincolnville Center a little inland on Route 73. The area of most interest—where you can find the restaurants and the ferry to Islesboro—is Lincolnville Beach. This is a tiny area; you could be through it in less than a minute. Still, it has a history going back to the Revolution, and you can see a few small cannons on the beach that were intended to repel the British in the War of 1812 (they were never used). Lincolnville is close to Camden, so it's a great place to stay if rooms in Camden are full—or if you just want someplace a little quieter.

NEED A BREAK?

☾ The beach at Lincolnville is open to the public at no cost and is popular with families. Children can enjoy wading in the shallow water. While you're there, look for the old canon that was put on the beach to repel the British (if needed) in the war of 1812.

WHERE TO EAT

$$–$$$
FRENCH

✕ **Chez Michel.** This little restaurant on U.S. 1 offers nice views of the bay. The menu consists of French and American cuisine, with an emphasis on steak and seafood. Owner-chef Michel Hetuin's bouillabaisse is the specialty. The potpourri of ingredients is all local and fresh. A bargain for the traveler is the less-expensive early-bird menu, served 4 PM–5:30 PM. ⊠ *2532 Atlantic Hwy. (U.S. 1), Lincolnville Beach* ☏ *207/789–5600* ▭ *AE, D, MC, V* ☉ *No lunch Mon.–Fri.*

$$$–$$$$
SEAFOOD
Fodor's Choice
★

✕ **The Edge.** This restaurant in the Inn at Ocean's Edge is one of the best restaurants on the coast of Maine. The setting, overlooking the sea, is beautiful and elegant. The menu can change on a nightly basis, but two of the regular specials are fire-roasted Maine lobster and butter-roasted salmon. Technically, the restaurant is in Lincolnville, but it is also considered a dining destination for nearby Camden. Caution: If you park in the lot designated for restaurant patrons and follow the sign, it will take you for a long downhill walk through the forest to get there. The walk is lovely and lighted at night, but is definitely not for those who have trouble walking, especially since it's uphill on the way back. There is an easier alternate route by car; just ask when you make your reservation. ⊠ *24 Stonecoast Rd., off U.S. 1* ☏ *207/236–4430* ⊕ *www.diningattheedge.com* ⌁ *Reservations essential* ▭ *AE, D, MC, V.*

$$–$$$
SEAFOOD
★

✕ **Lobster Pound Restaurant.** If you're looking for an authentic place to have your Maine lobster dinner, this is it. This simple restaurant looks more like a cannery than a restaurant, with rustic wooden picnic tables and hundreds of live lobsters swimming in tanks—you can pick out your own lobster. It'll be served to you with clam chowder and corn. Forget about ordering a pre-dinner cocktail or wine with dinner; have an iced tea instead. On U.S. 1, right on the edge of the sea, the Lobster Pound provides beautiful views from both its indoor and outdoor seating. On the menu here you will see the classic "Shore Dinner," which consists of lobster stew or fish chowder, steamed or fried clams, 1½-pound lobster, potato, and dessert. Lobster and seafood are, of course, the reason to come here, though turkey and steak are also available. This restaurant has seating for nearly 300, so even if it's a busy time, you won't have to wait long. There's also a 70-seat picnic area if you want to take your food to go. ⊠ *2521 Atlantic Hwy. (U.S. 1)* ☏ *207/789–5550* ⊕ *www.lobsterpoundmaine.com* ▭ *AE,D, MC, V* ☉ *Closed Nov.–Apr.*

$$–$$$ ✕**Whale's Tooth Pub & Restaurant.** The Revolutionary patriots could have
SEAFOOD met in a pub that looked like this. It's in a historic old brick building
★ with an interior that is reminiscent of an Old English pub: dark heavy
woods, dark atmosphere, a wood-burning fireplace, copper kettles. The
restaurant and the pub are basically one, and among the things on the
menu you will find steamed lobsters and mussels, fried calamari, broiled
scallops, and other seafood, as well as prime rib, charbroiled steaks,
and pasta dishes—the most popular dish is the British style fish-and-
chips. There is a deck for nice-weather days. ⊠ *2531 Atlantic Hwy.*
(U.S. 1) ☎ *207/789–5200* ⊕ *www.whalestoothpub.com* ▭ *AE, MC,*
D, V ⊘ *Closed Tues.*

WHERE TO STAY

$$$$ ⌂ **Inn at Ocean's Edge.** This beautiful white inn on 22 acres has one of
★ the loveliest settings in the area, with heavy forest on one side and the
ocean on the other. The inn looks as if it has been here for decades, but
the original building was only built in 1999, with the upper building
following in 2001. The rooms are styled simply but with old-fashioned
New England elegance: a lot of quilts and throws and Colonial-style
furniture. Every room has a king-size bed, an ocean view, a fireplace,
and a whirlpool for two. The inn also includes a fine award-winning
restaurant, The Edge, with oceanfront dining. You don't have to be a
guest of the inn to dine here. **Pros:** it would be tough to find an accommodation in a more beautiful setting. **Cons:** a little on the pricey side;
you will have to drive to go shopping, in Camden, several miles away.
⊠ *24 Stonecoast Rd. (U.S. 1), Lincolnville* ☎ *207/236–0945* ⊕ *www.*
innatoceansedge.com ⊅ *29 rooms, 3 suites* ⌂ *In-room: DVD, Wi-Fi*
(free). In-hotel: bar, gym, pool, restaurant ▭ *AE, D, MC, V* ⊺⊙⊦ *BP.*

$$–$$$ ⌂ **The Spouter Inn.** Before air-conditioning, the rich owned luxurious
summer mansions in Maine as a way of staying cool. The Spouter
will make you think you are living in the early part of the 1900s. The
rooms are beautifully furnished with antiques, and you can watch the
moon going down over the sea from the front porch. **Pros:** every room
has a view of the sea. **Cons:** restaurants are in walking distance, but if
you want to go shopping, you will have to drive; walls are somewhat
thin, so you may hear your neighbors. ⊠ *2506 Atlantic Hwy. (U.S. 1)*
☎ *207/789–5171 or 800/387–5171* ⊕ *www.spouterinn.com* ⊅ *7 rooms*
⌂ *In-room: no TV (some). In-hotel: Internet terminal, Wi-Fi (free), free*
parking ▭ *AE, D, MC, V* ⊺⊙⊦ *BP.*

$$$–$$$$ ⌂ **Victorian by the Sea.** With a quiet waterside location well off U.S. 1,
★ the Victorian feels as if it's a world away from all the hustle and bustle of
town. Most rooms and the wraparound porch have magnificent views
over island-studded Penobscot Bay. Romantic touches include canopied
brass beds, braided rugs, white wicker furniture, and floral wallpapers.
Six guest rooms have fireplaces; four more fireplaces are in common
rooms, including the glass-enclosed breakfast room. **Pros:** ocean views
from nearly every room; some rooms have fireplaces. **Cons:** you have
to drive to dinner. ⊠ *33 Sea View Dr., Lincolnville* ☎ *207/236–3785*
or 800/382–9817 ⊕ *www.victorianbythesea.com* ⊅ *5 rooms, 2 suites*
⌂ *In-room: Wi-Fi, no TV.* ▭ *AE, D, MC, V* ⊺⊙⊦ *BP.*

5

$$$ ☷ **Youngtown Inn and Restaurant.** Inside this white Federal-style farm-
Fodor's Choice   house you'll find a French-inspired country retreat. The inn's bucolic
★   location, only five minutes by car from busy Camden, guarantees quiet,
and it is a short walk from beautiful Lake Megunticook. Simple, airy
rooms open to decks with views of the rolling countryside. Four have
fireplaces. The restaurant ($$–$$$), open to the public for dinner, serves
entrées such as rack of lamb and breast of pheasant with foie gras
mousse. **Pros:** a nationally renowned establishment, with one of the
best French-cuisine restaurants in Maine. **Cons:** if you want to do some
shopping in Camden, you'll have to drive. ⊠ *581 Youngtown Rd., Rte.
52 off U.S. 1 to Youngtown Rd.,* ⌂ *P.O. Box 4246, Lincolnville 04849*
☏ *207/763–4290 or 800/291–8438* ⊕ *www.youngtowninn.com* ⇆ 6
rooms ⌂ In room: Wi-Fi. In-hotel: restaurant ⊟ AE, MC, V ⏏ BP.*

SHOPPING

Maine Artisans Collective (⊠ *2528 Atlantic Hwy. [U.S. 1]* ☏ *207/789–
5376* ⊗ *May–Oct.*) is a large craft gallery right across from Lincolnville
Beach. **Windsor Chairmakers** (⊠ *2526 Atlantic Hwy. (U.S. 1)* ☏ *207/789–
5188 or 800/789–5188* ⊕ *www.windsorchair.com*) sells custom-made
handcrafted beds, chests, china cabinets, dining tables, highboys, Shaker
furniture, and chairs. You can even go to the back of the shop and watch
the furniture being made.

ISLESBORO

★   *3 mi east of Lincolnville via Islesboro Ferry (terminal on U.S. 1).*

If you would like to visit one of Maine's islands but don't have much
time, Islesboro is the best choice. The island is only a 20-minute ferry
ride off the mainland. You can take your car with you. The drive from
one end of the island to the other (on the island's only road) is lovely. It
takes you through Warren State Park, a nice place to stop for a picnic
and the only public camping area on the island. There are two stores
on the island where you can buy supplies for your picnic: the Island
Market is a short distance from the ferry terminal on the main road,
and Durkee's General Store is 5 mi farther north at 863 Main Road.
Next to the island's ferry terminal are the Sailor's Memorial Museum
and the Grindle Point Lighthouse, both worth a brief look.

The permanent year-round population of Islesboro is about 625, but it
swells to around 3,000 in summer. Most of the people who live on the
island full time earn their living in one way or another from the sea.
Some of them work at the three boat yards on the island, others are
fishermen, and most others run small businesses. Seasonal residents may
include some familiar faces: John Travolta and his wife, Kelly Preston,
have a home here, as does Kirstie Alley.

The **Islesboro Ferry,** operated by the Maine State Ferry Service, departs
from Lincolnville Harbor, a few hundred feet from the Lobster Pound
Restaurant. Try to head out on one of the early ferries so you have
enough time to drive around and get back. If you miss the last ferry,
you'll have to stay on the island overnight. The ferry runs back and
forth nine times a day from April through October and seven times a

day from November through March. There are fewer trips on Sunday. The round-trip cost for a vehicle and one passenger is $22.25, slightly more with additional passengers, less if you leave the vehicle behind. Call for schedules at *207/789–5611*.

⚠ **If you are just visiting the island and don't have friends there to stay with, make sure that you don't miss the last ferry. There are NO public accommodations on the island. You would have to sleep in your car.**

**EN
ROUTE**

A brief detour off U.S. 1, a few miles south of Belfast on your way up from Lincolnville, will take you through **Bayside**, a delightful little Victorian resort village by the sea. In the past, it was a summer Methodist community. Small old houses are clustered in a truly beautiful setting.

BELFAST TO BANGOR

The farther you get up the coast and away from Camden, the less touristy the area becomes and the more you see of the real Maine. Traffic jams and crowded restaurants give way to a more relaxed and casual atmosphere, and locals start to treat you like a potential neighbor.

As you drive north on U.S. 1, you pass through the charming coastal towns of Belfast, Searsport, and Bucksport. Bangor is 20 mi inland. If you're driving up U.S. 1 on a "coastal trip," you can probably leave Bangor off your itinerary. If you want to fly in, however, Bangor International Airport is the quickest point of access to northern Penobscot Bay, Bar Harbor, Mount Desert Island, and Acadia National Park.

BELFAST

10 mi north of Lincolnville, 46 mi northeast of Augusta.

A number of Maine coastal towns, such as Wiscasset and Damariscotta, like to think of themselves as the prettiest little town in Maine, but Belfast (which was originally to be named Londonderry) may be the true winner of this title. It has a full variety of charms: a beautiful waterfront; an old and interesting main street climbing up from the harbor; a delightful array of B&Bs, restaurants, and shops; and a friendly population. The downtown even has old-fashioned street lamps, which set the streets aglow at night. If you like looking at old houses, many of which go all the way back to the Revolution and are in the Federal and Colonial style, just drive up and down some of the side streets. The only thing Belfast does not have is traffic jams. In 2007 Belfast was called "one of the top-10 culturally cool towns in the country" by *USA Today*. It also has been named "one of the best places you never heard of" by *Budget Travel* magazine.

Belfast's economy has seen many changes over the years. In the 1800s the town was a shipbuilding center and home to many ship captains. Starting in the early 1900s a shoe factory, a chicken-processing plant, and a sardine-packing factory were the primary employers. The first two disappeared about 30 years ago, and the sardine-packing plant packed up in 2002. The biggest employer in Belfast now is Bank of America (which took over the facilities formerly owned by MBNA), the credit card giant, although tourism is also becoming an important industry.

■ TIP→ As you walk around Belfast, you will see a number of cream-color signs labeled THE MUSEUM IN THE STREETS. Be sure to read them. They will tell you in easy-to-access fashion everything that you'd want to know about the history of Belfast. They are written in both English and French, for the benefit of Maine's neighbors to the north.

VISITOR INFORMATION

In the mid-1800s Belfast was home to a number of wealthy business magnates. Their mansions still stand along High Street, offering some excellent examples of Greek Revival and Federal architecture. The **Belfast Chamber of Commerce Visitor Center** (✉ *14 Main St. [a block from the harbor]* ☎ *207/338–5900* ⊕ *www.belfastmaine.org*) has a large array of magazines, guidebooks, maps, and brochures that cover the entire Mid-Coast. They also can provide you with a free walking-tour brochure that describes the various historic homes and buildings, as well as the old business section in the harbor area. Ask them to tell you about the Museum in the Streets signage.

EXPLORING

Belfast Historical Society & Museum. This historical society and museum is housed in an Federal-style brick building dating back to 1835. The museum contains many paintings, photographs, and artifacts relating to the town's maritime history. ✉ *10 Market St., near courthouse* ☎ *207/338–9229* ⊘ *Thurs. and Sun. 1–4.*

WHERE TO EAT

¢–$
AMERICAN
★

✕ **Belfast Co-op.** The Co-op is a very special place in Belfast, and it's not unusual to hear the expression, "I'll meet you at the Co-op." As the name would imply, this is a members' cooperative store that sells organic, locally grown vegetables and other provisions. But you don't have to be a member to buy things. They also have one of the best selections of wines in town. The popular Co-op Cafe offers coffees, teas, sandwiches, and homemade pastries. This is an excellent and inexpensive place for breakfast or lunch. There is no waiter service; you just order at the counter and pick up your food when it's ready. ✉ *123 High St., 1 block from town center* ☎ *207/338–3522* ⊕ *www.belfast.coop.com* ⊟ *AE, D, MC, V.*

$–$$
CONTINENTAL
★

✕ **Darby's Restaurant and Pub.** Darby's, a charming old-fashioned restaurant and bar, is probably the most popular restaurant in town with the locals. The building, with pressed-tin ceilings, was constructed in 1865 and has been a bar or a restaurant ever since. The antique bar is an original and has been there since 1865. The first Darby is long gone, but his name remains. Artwork on the walls is by local artists and may be purchased. A lot of the regular items on the menu, such as the pad thai and the Seafood à la Greque, are quite unusual for a small-town restaurant. It also has hearty homemade soups and sandwiches, as well as dishes with an international flavor. ✉ *155 High St.* ☎ *207/338–2339* ⊕ *www.darbysrestaurant.com* ⊟ *AE, D, MC, V.*

$–$$
SEAFOOD
☺

✕ **Dockside Family Restaurant.** On Main Street, less than a block from the harbor, Dockside has convenience strongly in its favor. It also has really good seafood—it's famous for its clam chowder and lobster stew. The decor is plain and simple, and the emphasis is on family dining, meaning that kids are always welcome, and the menu has special portions for them. When the weather is nice, you can sit out on the back deck and watch the boats in the harbor. ⊠ *30 Main St.* ☎ *207/338–6889* ⊟ *AE, D, MC, V* ☺ *Closed Mon.*

¢–$ ✕**Three Tides.** Owners and managers David and Sarah Carlson have cre-
AMERICAN ated a labor of love here, and if you like the idea of dinner on a deck
★ overlooking the bay, this is the place. Some of the popular-with-locals favorites are the varied tapas, the crab quesadilla, and the steamed mussels and oysters. They also offer 13 original beers and ales, which they make in their next-door Marshall Wharf Brewing Co. Try the Pemaquid Oyster Stout, or, if you want something unusual, absinthe is on the menu. ⊠ *26 Marshall Wharf, near Belfast Landing* ☎ *207/338–1707* ⊟ *D, MC, V* ☺ *Closed Mon.*

$$–$$$ ✕**Weathervane Seafood Restaurant.** Part of a New England seafood
SEAFOOD chain, this restaurant is large—so you shouldn't have to wait long for a table—and has usually good food and service, although things can get a little rushed in summer. The restaurant sits right on the edge of Belfast Harbor, overlooking the bay, and tugboats are parked outside. In summer you can sit on the outside deck. The large menu features seafood, pasta, and steaks. A popular special is the Maine Lobster Clambake, which is boiled lobster, steamed clams, and corn on the cob. Fresh seafood is also available to go. ⊠ *1 Main St., Public Landing, at foot of Main St.* ☎ *207/338–1774* ⊕ *www.weathervaneseafoods.com* ⊟ *AE, D, MC, V.*

$$–$$$ ✕**Young's Lobster Pound.** The place looks more like a corrugated-steel
SEAFOOD fish cannery than a restaurant, but it is one of the places to have an
★ authentic Maine lobster dinner. Young's sits right on the edge of the water, across the river from Belfast Harbor (cross Veterans Bridge to get here and turn right on Mitchell Avenue). When you first walk in, you'll see tanks and tanks of live lobsters of varying size. The traditional meal here is the Shore Dinner: fish or clam chowder, steamed clams or mussels, a 1½-pound boiled lobster, corn on the cob, and rolls and butter. Order your dinner at the counter, then find a table inside or on the deck.
■ TIP➜ **If you are enjoying your lobster at one of the outside tables, don't leave the table with no one to watch it. Seagulls are notorious thieves—and they LOVE lobster.** ⊠ *2 Fairview St.* ☎ *207/338–1160* ⊕ *www.youngslobsterpound.com* ⊟ *AE, D, MC, V* ☺ *Closed Labor Day–Easter.*

WHERE TO STAY

$$–$$$ ☷ **Belfast Bay Inn & Luxury Suites.** One of the unusual things about Belfast has been that until recently, there were NO hotels or motels in the downtown central area or even on the outskirts. But that changed with the opening of the small but lavish and award-winning Belfast Bay Inn in 2008. The inn is on Main Street, right in the heart of the downtown, and it has ample free parking nearby. Owners Ed and Judy Hemmingsen transformed a historic 1800s building into eight suites. Some suites include gas fireplaces, balconies, and water views. **Pros:** this is luxury lodging at its best; several good restaurants within walking distance. **Cons:** pricey. ⊠ *72 Main St., Downtown* ☎ *207/338–5600*

⊕ *www.belfastbayinn.com* ⇴ *8 suites* ⚸ *In-room: DVD, Internet, Wi-Fi* ⊟ *AE, MC, V.*

$–$$ ⊡ **Belfast Harbor Inn.** Facing U.S. 1 in one direction and Penobscot Bay in the other, the Harbor Inn is the second-largest accommodation in the area. Half of the rooms have beautiful views of the sea across the spacious lawn; the other half overlook the pool. The upstairs rooms have private balconies; the lower ones have patios. There is also a nice bridal suite with a king-size bed. The rooms have been remodeled, and the complimentary continental breakfast is more generous than most, with a lot of fresh fruit and homemade pastries. **Pros:** abundant complimentary breakfast; Fox Landing Steakhouse & Pub is right next door, so you can walk to dinner. **Cons:** it's a drive to downtown shopping. ⊠ *91 Searsport Ave. (U.S. 1)* ☏ *207/338–2740 or 800/545–8576* ⊕ *www. belfastharborinn.com* ⇴ *61 rooms* ⚸ *In-room: a/c, Wi-Fi. In-hotel: pool, laundry facility, some pets allowed* ⊟ *AE, D, MC, V* ⌾ *CP.*

$$–$$$ ⊡ **The Jeweled Turret Inn.** Turrets, columns, gables, and magnificent wood-
★ work embellish this inn, originally built in 1898 as the home of a local attorney. The inn is named for the jewel-like stained-glass windows in the stairway turret. The gem theme continues in the den, where the ornate rock fireplace is said to include rocks from every one of the contiguous 48 states. Elegant Victorian pieces furnish the rooms: the Opal Room has a marble bath with whirlpool tub, in addition to a French armoire and a four-poster bed. **Pros:** a truly beautiful place; within easy walking distance of the downtown with its shops and restaurants. **Cons:** not handicapped accessible. ⊠ *40 Pearl St.* ☏ *207/338–2304 or 800/696–2304* ⊕ *www.jeweledturret.com* ⇴ *7 rooms* ⚸ *In-room: no TV* ⊟ *AE, D, MC, V* ⌾ *BP.*

$–$$$ ⊡ **Penobscot Bay Inn & Restaurant.** This lovely accommodation is on five
Fodor's Choice meadowed acres overlooking Penobscot Bay and is owned and man-
★ aged by Kristina and Valentinas Kurapka. The rooms are bright and airy and decorated in pastel shades, with old-fashioned New England quilts on the beds. Some rooms even have their own fireplaces. The inn's continental gourmet restaurant ($$–$$$$) is one of the best in the area. **Pros:** you don't have to go out for dinner. **Cons:** no special views from the restaurant; if you want to explore Belfast's colorful downtown, you will have to drive. ⊠ *192 Northport Ave.* ☏ *207/338–5715 or 800/335–2370* ⊕ *www.penobscotbayinn.com* ⇴ *19 rooms* ⚸ *In-room: refrigerator (some) In-hotel: restaurant, bar* ⊟ *AE, D, MC, V* ⌾ *BP.*

$–$$ ⊡ **Point Lookout Resort.** This is a special place right on U.S. 1 between
Fodor's Choice Lincolnville and Belfast. In the past, it was a retreat and training center
★ for the credit-card giant MBNA. But now it is open for public accommodation—and it is a real treasure. It consists of 106 rustic cabins in a lovely forested setting. Hiking and walking trails, a fitness center, a bowling alley, and a small restaurant are all on-site. **Pros:** wonderful woodland setting with inviting hiking trails; great place to stay if you have kids in tow. **Cons:** If you don't want to eat at the little restaurant here, you will need to drive for dinner. ⊠ *67 Atlantic Hwy. (U.S. 1) North-port* ☏ *207/789–5013 or 800/515–3611* ⊕ *www.visitpointlookout.com* ⇴ *106 cabins* ⚸ *In-room: kitchen (some), refrigerator (some), Internet, Wi-Fi. In-hotel: parking (free), some pets allowed* ⊟ *AE, D, MC, V.*

$$–$$$ White House. This 1840 landmark by Maine architect Calvin Ryder
★ is considered to be one of the most sophisticated examples of Greek
Revival architecture in New England. An eight-sided cupola tops the
house; inside are ornate plaster ceiling medallions, Italian marble fireplaces, a flying staircase, and intricate moldings. Crystal chandeliers,
Oriental rugs, antiques, and reproduction pieces elegantly decorate the
spacious rooms. You can relax in the English garden, in the gazebo, or
under the enormous copper beech tree. **Pros:** if you like staying in a place
with a lot of early American history, this would be it. **Cons:** you may
wish to drive for dining and shopping. ⊠ *1 Church St.* ☎ *207/338–1901
or 888/290–1901* ⊕ *www.mainebb.com* ⇨ *4 rooms, 2 suites* ⌂ *In-room:
a/c, Wi-Fi (free), DVD. In-hotel: bicycles* ⊟ *AE, D, MC, V* ⧖⧗ *BP.*

NIGHTLIFE AND THE ARTS

NIGHTLIFE **Lookout Bar & Grill** (⊠ *37 Front St.* ☎ *207/338–8900*) has a great location
just a few feet from the harbor. It offers a huge variety of menu items
like pizzas, burgers, wings, chili, and sandwiches. They also have 17
beers on tap and live music on the weekends.

★ **Rollie's Bar & Grill** (⊠ *37 Main St.* ☎ *207/338–4502* ⊕ *www.rollies.
me.com* ⊟ *MC, V*) looks like it's been here 100 years, but actually it's
been here only since 1972. The tavern is right in the heart of Main
Street, and at first glance it might look like a bikers' bar. It is that—
and a lot more. If you recognize the interior, it's because it was used as
a setting in the Stephen King film *Thinner*. The vintage bar is from an
1800s sailing ship. Rollie's is the most popular watering spot in town
with the locals, and it just may serve the best hamburgers in the state
of Maine. They also have opened a sister site in nearby Searsport with
the same name, same fare, and located on U.S. 1.

THE ARTS The **Colonial Theater** (⊠ *163 High St.* ☎ *207/338–1930*) is a wonderful
old-fashioned movie palace with an elephant on the roof. If you ask,
"Why is there a statue of an elephant on the roof?" owner and former
Belfast Mayor Mike Hurley would simply respond, "Why not?" **Belfast
Maskers** (⊠ *43 Front St.* ☎ *207/338–9668* ⊕ *www.belfastmaskers.org*)
is a small award-winning theater company with its own theater down
by the waterfront. They present a number of plays during year, and
in the summer they offer outdoor musicals on the Belfast Commons
by the harbor. **Northport Music Theater** (⊠ *851 Atlantic Hwy. [U.S. 1].*
☎ *207/338–8383* ⊕ *www.northportmusictheater.com*) is a relatively
new addition to the theater scene here. It is just a little way south of
Belfast on U.S. 1 and presents three productions every summer.

FESTIVALS **Arts in the Park** (⊕ *www.belfastmaine.org/artsinthepark* ⧖ *Free*) takes
& EVENTS place in mid-July down by the harbor, and features the works of more
than 70 Maine-area artists. **Belfast Summer Nights** (☎ *207/338–8448*) features a variety of interesting live music events every Thursday evening,
from 5:30 to 7:30, for 11 weeks in summer. It takes place at the Belfast
Commons near the harbor and is free of charge. **Maine Celtic Celebration**
(⊕ *www.maineceltccelebration.com*) is a fairly recent annual event,
but it's a big hit both with locals and visitors. There's food, music, and
live entertainment, representing Ireland, Scotland, Wales, Isle of Man,
Cornwall, and Brittany.

SHOPPING

Belfast is an easy town in which to shop: nearly all of the interesting little stores are centered around the intersection of Main and High streets. **All About Games** (⊠ 78 Main St. ☎ 207/338–9984) sells any kind of game you could want, including a "Maine" version of Monopoly. The name and the storefront window of the **Chocolate Drop Candy Shop** (⊠ 60 Main St.) are a little deceiving, since they imply simple old-fashioned candies, but the reality is that on the inside, it's a gourmet candy shop with handmade luxury chocolates. Try the white Russian Kahlua truffle. **Colburn Shoe Store** (⊠ 79 Main St. ☎ 207/338–1934 or 877/338–1934) is worth a visit simply because it's the oldest shoe store in America. At one time, the making of shoes was a major industry in Belfast. Another interesting bookshop just a few doors from Fertile Mind, and on the same side of the street is the **Old Professor's Bookshop** (⊠ 99 Main St. ☎ 207/338–2006), which is actually owned by a retired old professor, George Siscoe, and has a fascinating collection of books, many from his own library. The **Green Store** (⊠ 71 Main St. ☎ 207/338–4045) sells environmentally friendly products from lightbulbs to clothing. The **Purple Baboon** (⊠ 31 Front St., just off Main near the harbor ☎ 207/338–6505) is an unusual shop that sells gifts, collectibles, and souvenirs. If you like browsing through old vinyl records and 8-track tapes or new CDs, you will have a great time at **Wild Rufus Records** (⊠ 135 High St. ☎ 207/338–1909 ⊕ www.wildrufus.com). **Beyond the Sea** (⊠ 74 Main St. ☎ 207/338–2100 ⊕ www.beyondtheseamaine.com)is the kind of shop where you not only can browse for that perfect gift but also relax with a coffee and pastry. Books, gifts, art—and espresso.

GALLERIES At the **Parent Gallery** (⊠ 92 Main St. ☎ 207/338–1553 ⊕ www.nealparent.com), a talented father and daughter have their paintings and photographs displayed. The **Phoenix Gallery** (⊠ 157 High St. ☎ 207/338–0087 ⊕ www.phoenixloftgallery.com) has an interesting collection of regional and local artists. **Galerie Dufour** (⊠ Main St. ☎ 207/338–6448 ⊕ www.du4photo.com) is another photography gallery right next to the Parent Gallery. While Charlie Dufour's landscapes of Maine are beautiful, the real specialty here is nudes, many of them floating, in beautiful and interesting settings.

SHOP EN ROUTE

One of the first places you come to after you cross the U.S. 1 bridge heading north toward Searsport is the legendary **Perry's Nuthouse** (⊠ 17 Searsport Ave. [U.S. 1] ☎ 207/338–1630). Perry's has been here since 1927, and the building dates back to 1850. The delicious treats for sale include nuts from around the world, homemade fudge, local honeys, and Maine maple syrup. American Indian handicrafts are also available. **Mainely Pottery** (⊠ 181 Searsport Ave. [U.S. 1] ☎ 207/338–1108 ⊕ www.mainelypottery.com) offers outstanding pottery from 30 Maine potters.

SPORTS AND THE OUTDOORS

AERIAL TOURS **Coastal Helicopters.** Now here's what we call a fun trip. Take the kids up for a spectacular view of the Maine Coast from a helicopter. See lighthouses, schooners, islands, and maybe even wildlife. Prices start at $225 for ½-hour rides. ⊠ 26 Airport Rd., Belfast Airport ☎ 207/338–3755

⊕ *www.coastalhelos.com* ⊙ *Tours are not on any schedule, they are offered year-round on an as-called basis* ⊟ MC, V.

BOATING **Belfast Bay Cruises** (⊠ *Thompson Wharf, near Belfast Landing* ☎ *207/* ℭ *322–5530* ⊕ *www.belfastbaycruises.com* ☜ *$15–$30* ⊙ *Mid-June–* ★ *Oct.*) sets passengers asea on the *Good Return,* which seats about 45 people and takes trips to the beautiful little town of Castine and back. During the layover in Castine you might want to have lunch at Dennett's, which sits right over the water. The *Good Return* also offers harbor cruises and lobstering cruises. Owner Melissa Terry is your captain. If you just wanted to go on a short and inexpensive sailing trip on Penobscot Bay, the **Friendship Sloop Amity** (⊠ *Belfast Landing, 1 Main St.* ☎ *207/469–0849 or 207/323–1443* ⊕ *www.friendshipsloopamity. com* ☜ *Morning and afternoon sail $20 a person.* ⊙ *Late May–early Oct.*) may be the one for you. The sloop was built in 1901 but is still in fine shape. You can even help to raise the sails or take a turn at the helm if you want. Morning sails are 1½ hours, afternoon sails are 2½ hours, and there are also two-hour sunset sails. **Wanderbird Expedition Cruises** (⊠ *Belfast Landing* ⊡ *P.O. Box 272 04915* ☎ *207/338–3088 or 866/732–2473* ⊕ *www.wanderbirdcruises.com* ⊙ *May–Oct.*) offers cruises on a big former fishing trawler. Given its size, it can take trips to distant points, as far away as northern Labrador and Greenland.

CURLING **Belfast Curling Club** (⊠ *211 Belmont Ave., [Rte. 3], 3 mi west of Belfast* ☎ *207/338–9851*) is just about the only place in this area of Maine where you can see the strange sport of curling. Activities take place throughout the week, November through March. Call for times.

HIKING **Little River Trail.** We're going to tell you about a great hiking trail that hardly anyone knows about—not even many of the people who live in the area—and here's how you find it. Go south on U.S. 1 from Belfast a short distance. You will see the Little River Church on your right. Just past that—look closely—you will see a sign for the Belfast Water District. Pull in there and park at the sign that says HIKERS. The beautiful woodland trail, which winds along the Little River, is 4 mi long and takes about 3 hours. You might want to just hike half of it and then back—or have someone meet you with a car at the other end, which is Walsh Park on Rt. 52 in Belfast.

KAYAKING **Water Walker Sea Kayak** (⊠ *152 Lincolnville Ave.04915* ☎ *207/338–6424* ⊕ *www.touringkayaks.com* ⊟ *AE, DS, MC, V*) provides guided sea-kayak trips among the islands of Penobscot Bay. Paddlers of all levels are welcome. Instructions, rentals, and sales also are available.

NEED A BREAK?

ℭ What could be better for you and the kids than an ice-cream break? You will find a wonderful array of all things ice cream at **Scoops & Crepes** (⊠ *35 Main St.* ☎ *207/338–3350*), right in the heart of downtown.

ℭ Just a block away from Scoops is the **Little Red Lunch Wagon** (⊠ *31 Main St. 04915* ☎ *207/338–9296*), which offers delicious and inexpensive lobster rolls and crab rolls.

SEARSPORT

6 mi northeast of Belfast, 57 mi northeast of Augusta.

Searsport is well known as the antiques and flea-market capital of Maine, and with good reason: the Antique Mall alone, on U.S. 1 just north of town, contains the offerings of 70 dealers, and flea markets during the visitor season line both sides of U.S. 1.

But antiques are not the town's only point of interest; Searsport also has a rich history of shipbuilding and seafaring. In the early to mid-1800s there were 10 shipbuilding facilities in Searsport. The population of the town was about 1,000 people more than it is today because of the ready availability of jobs. By the mid-1800s Searsport was home to more than 200 sailing-ship captains, more than any other town in America, according to the Penobscot Marine Museum. It was commonly said then that when a captain took a cargo to Hong Kong, if he walked down the main street he was more likely to meet someone from Searsport than from China.

Except for a few rotting pilings down at the waterfront, signs of the shipbuilding industry are gone now. It all disappeared after the invention of the steam engine and the growth of the steamship business. Steamships were larger, could carry more cargo, and were more efficient and safer. But thanks to those old shipyards, Searsport still has the second-deepest port on the coast of Maine, after Portland. If you read the Tom Clancy novel *The Hunt for Red October,* or saw the movie, you may recall that the men on the stolen submarine were looking on a sea chart for a little-used deepwater port on the Atlantic Coast where they could hide out submerged and undetected. They found it at Searsport. For further info, check the Searsport Web site: ⊕ *www.searsportme.net.*

■ TIP→ Searsport's seafaring history can best be studied at Maine's largest maritime museum, the Penobscot Marine Museum. It's also evident in the many former sea captains' homes along U.S. 1, many of which have been converted to bed-and-breakfasts.

GETTING HERE AND AROUND
Searsport's downtown area is only a block long, and can easily be explored in less than an hour.

ESSENTIALS
Visitor Information **Searsport Chamber of Commerce** (⊠ *1 Union St., Searsport* ☎ *207/548–0173* ⊕ *www.searsportme.com*).

EXPLORING
ⓒ **Penobscot Marine Museum.** This museum is dedicated to the history of
Fodor'sChoice Penobscot Bay and Maine's maritime history. The exhibits, artifacts,
★ souvenirs, and paintings are displayed in a unique setting of seven historic buildings, including two sea captains' houses and five other buildings in an original seaside village. The museum's outstanding collection of marine art includes the largest gathering in the country of works by Thomas and James Buttersworth. Also of note are photos of local sea captains; a collection of China-trade merchandise; artifacts of life at sea (including lots of scrimshaw); navigational instruments; tools

from the area's history of logging, granite cutting, fishing, and ice cutting; treasures collected by seafarers from around the globe; and models of famous ships. The museum also has a rotating exhibit every year on a different theme. Two recent themes have been "Pirates!" and "Lobstahs!" Next to the museum you can find the Penobscot Marine Museum Store, where you can buy anything nautical. ⊠ *5 E. Main St. (US. 1)* ☎ *207/548–2529* ⊕ *www. penobscotmarinemuseum.org* ✉ *$8* ⊗ *Memorial Day–mid-Oct., Mon.– Sat. 10–5, Sun. noon–5.*

> **DID YOU KNOW?**
>
> The word "penobscot" is believed to be a derivative of the original Algonquin Indian word meaning "waters of descending ledges." Descending rock ledges can, in fact, be seen along the Penobscot River.

OFF THE BEATEN PATH

Sears Island. This is the largest uninhabited island off the coast of Maine, measuring some 940 acres. The forested island is about a mile long and a half-mile wide, and is home to a variety of wildlife, plants, and birds. Although you cannot drive on the island—you have to walk across a causeway to get here—a paved road bisects the island, making it an excellent place for a bike ride, hike, or picnic. The 9-mi shoreline perimeter also makes an excellent hike at low tide (check the daily paper). You might even see seals sunning themselves on the rocks. Camping is not allowed. ⊠ *Take U.S. 1 north from Searsport and turn right on Sears Island Rd.* ✉ *Free.*

WHERE TO EAT

$–$$
SEAFOOD

✕ **Anglers.** This little restaurant has been around for a long time and has a large local following. It can be a little hard to get into on a busy night, but it's worth the wait. The seafood is good, the prices are reasonable, and the service is friendly—this is the kind of place where the waitresses call you "Hon." ⊠ *215 U.S. 1* ☎ *207/548–2405* ⊕ *www. anglersseafoodrestaurant.com* ▤ *D, MC, V.*

$–$$
AMERICAN

✕ **The Mariner.** This cozy spot in the heart of downtown has a simple, pub-like atmosphere, with good drinks and good, inexpensive food. In summer, lobster and crabmeat rolls are on the menu, along with the year-round selections of burgers, sandwiches, and, of course, lobster stew. Dinner entrées include fried jumbo shrimp and fried haddock. ⊠ *23 E. Main St. (U.S. 1)* ☎ *207/548–6600* ▤ *MC, V.*

NEED A BREAK?

If you would like to stop for a coffee or tea and a delicious pastry or light lunch, just pop in to the **Coastal Coffee House** (⊠ *25 Main St.* ☎ *207/548– 6243*) right in the middle of town. They also offer "lobstah" and crab rolls.

$$$–$$$$
Fodor's Choice
★
FRENCH

✕ **Rhumb Line.** Yes, there is such a word as "rhumb." For those who are not sailors, a rhumb line is one of the points of a mariner's compass. But more important than that, this is a dining experience that draws people from long distances. The restaurant, in an 18th-century sea captain's home, delivers fine dining, and is operated by owners/chefs Charles and Diana Evans. Specials include pan-seared peppered swordfish with Vidalia onion piccalilli, horseradish-crusted salmon with rémoulade sauce, and grilled rack of lamb with fig-infused balsamic mint sauce. ⊠ *200*

CLOSE UP

Maine's Ice Age

In the mid-1800s there was a major industry in Maine that gave work to thousands of men each winter. The product was so valuable that it was shipped around the world in the great tall-masted schooners. The industry no longer exists, although the product does. Can you guess what this profitable product and industry was? Believe it or not, it was ice.

During Maine's freezing cold winter months, loggers and farmers who couldn't do their normal work would go out to Maine's freshwater rivers and lakes and cut ice from the frozen waters. Using string lines, the men would section the ice off into 2-by-4-

foot rectangles. Then they would use one-handled saws to cut the ice into blocks weighing about 200 pounds each. The blocks of ice would be loaded onto horse-drawn sleds and taken to an icehouse. Finally, the ice would be loaded aboard a schooner for transport. They packed the ice in straw and sawdust to help insulate it, but they still lost about 20% to melt. The other 80% could be sold for a generous profit all over the world. On the way back they could even sell the dried-out straw. There are pictures and examples of tools left from the ice industry on display at the Penobscot Marine Museum in Searsport.

E. Main St. (U.S. 1) ☎ *207/548–2600* ⊕ *www.therhumblinerestaurant. com* ═ *MC, V* ☉ *Closed Mon. and Tues. No lunch.*

$–$$
AMERICAN
✕ **Rollie's.** This is the new sister version of the very famous Rollie's in Belfast. The food and the atmosphere are the same, but this restaurant is much bigger, with a large parking lot. This is important, because one of the things Rollie's in Belfast has been famous for is attracting the motorcycle crowd. The motto of the tavern/restaurant ought to be "Rollie's is Rollicking," since it gets very noisy during major sporting events. They also are known for serving the best hamburger in Maine. Other standard dishes include chowder, homemade chili, and smoked baby back ribs. During the warmer months you can enjoy your food and drink out on the deck, which overlooks what was once a millstream. ⊠ *1 E. Main St. (U.S. 1)* ☎ *207/548–2901* ⊕ *www.rollies.me* ═ *D, MC, V.*

WHERE TO STAY

$$–$$$
★
🏨 **1794 Watchtide . . . by the Sea.** This inn, on the National Register of Historic Places, was built, as the name implies, in 1794. It has been a favorite of many visitors, among them Eleanor Roosevelt, who stayed here many times on her way up to Campobello Island. The first owner of the property was Henry Knox, George Washington's Secretary of War. Today's owners are Patricia and Frank Kulla, former publishing mavens who created Lyceum Books. All of the rooms are furnished in New England style, and two of them have great views of Penobscot Bay. Breakfast out on the glassed-in porch overlooking the sea is a three-course affair. **Pros:** you can sleep in the room where Eleanor Roosevelt slept! **Cons:** you need to drive to dinner or shopping; since it's right on U.S. 1, some of the rooms can be a little noisy. ⊠ *190 W. Main St. (U.S. 1)* ☎ *207/548–6575 or 800/698–6575* ⊕ *www.watchtide.com*

🛏 *4 rooms, 1 suite* ♿ *In-room: refrigerator, no TV.* 🖃 *AE, D, MC, V* ⊘ *Closed Nov.–Apr.* ¶◎¶ *BP.*

$–$$ 🏚 **Carriage House Inn.** Ernest Hemingway liked this place. How's that
★ for an endorsement? This stately Victorian mansion is one of the most-photographed homes in Maine, and is listed on the National Register of Historic Places. The home was built in 1874 by one of Searsport's many clipper-ship captains, John McGilvery. Later, it became the home of the impressionist painter Waldo Pierce. Pierce was a close friend of Ernest Hemingway, whom he met in the ambulance corps, and Hemingway came here a number of times. The house is filled with heirlooms from the 19th-century era of the great clipper ships, and there is a solid stone fireplace in the downstairs den. When you walk into one of the old-fashioned guest rooms you'll feel you have entered the early part of the last century. **Pros:** you could stay in the room where Hemingway slept! **Cons:** not near any restaurants. ⊠ *120 E. Main St. (U.S. 1)* ☎ *207/548–2167 or 800/578–2167* ⊕ *www.carriagehouseinmaine.com* 🛏 *3 rooms* ♿ *In-room: no TV, Wi-Fi. In-hotel: Wi-Fi* 🖃 *AE, D, MC, V* ¶◎¶ *BP.*

CAMPING   ⚠ **Searsport Shores Ocean Camping.** This campsite sits right on the edge
¢–$ of the ocean, and offers spectacular views from most of its sites. It has
★   120 sites on 40 acres for RVs and tents. Also offered are attractive gardens, nature trails, art classes, and activities for the kids. **Pros:** has spectacular view of the bay. **Cons:** campground is nationally famous, so it fills up quickly during peak season; there are no sit-down restaurants within walking distance. ⊠ *216 W. Main St. (U.S. 1)* ☎ *207/548–6059* ⊕ *www.campocean.com* ♿ *beachfront, flush toilets, partial hookup, drinking water, guest laundry, showers, fire pits, picnic tables, public telephone, Wi-Fi* 🖃 *D, MC, V* ⊘ *Closed Nov.–Apr.*

NEED A BREAK?

If you're looking for a quick, easy, and inexpensive place to stop on U.S. 1 for breakfast or lunch, the most popular spot in the Stockton Springs area is **Just Barb's**, just a few miles north of Searsport on U.S. 1 (⊠ **24 W. Main St. (U.S. 1)** ☎ **207/567–3886**), which has simple food and friendly waitresses.

NIGHTLIFE AND THE ARTS

FESTIVALS   **Fourth of July Fireworks.** People come from miles around to watch Sears-
AND EVENTS   port's free annual Fourth of July fireworks display, which is set off from
☺   Mosman Park at the edge of the sea. The fireworks start at 9 PM, and
★   the best place to view them is from the nearby public pier at the end of Steamboat Avenue. The **Lobster Boat Races** are an annual series of events that take place in the major fishing communities (eight of them) up and down Penobscot Bay. The original intention of the races was to give lobstermen a way to blow off a little steam and to show off their boats and abilities. Thanks to the American spirit of obsessive competition, however, some boatmen in recent years have had high-powered lobster boats constructed specifically for these races. They'll burn up an expensive engine and swamp other nearby boats just to win the competition and a $50 trophy. "Bragging rights," it's called. But hey, it's all in the spirit of fun, and for observers and participants, it *is* a lot of fun. The Searsport race takes place in the middle of July at the town pier at the end of Steamboat Avenue. Call the town office at

207/548–6372 for the exact date. There's no charge to watch the race, and the crowds—especially the boatmen—turn it into a big party.

SHOPPING

ANTIQUES In Searsport, shopping usually implies antiques or flea markets. Both stretch along both sides of U.S. 1 a mile or so north of downtown. **All Small Antiques** (⊠ *357 W. Main St.* ☎ *207/338–1613*) has just what the name implies. In the very heart of town, **Captain Tinkham's Emporium** (⊠ *34 E. Main St.* ☎ *207/548–6465*) offers antiques, collectibles, old books, magazines, records, paintings, and prints. **Pumpkin Patch Antiques** (⊠ *15 W. Main St.* ☎ *207/548–6047*) displays such items as quilts, nautical memorabilia, and painted and wood furniture from about 20 dealers. It's open April through Thanksgiving or by appointment. The biggest collection of antiques is in the **Searsport Antique Mall** (⊠ *149 E. Main St., [U.S. 1]* ☎ *207/548–2640*), which has more than 70 dealers.

BOOKS **Left Bank Books** (⊠ *21 E. Main St.* ☎ *207/548–6400*) is a labor of love
AND ART by three book-loving ladies. The shop is in a historic brick building that was the home of Searsport's first bank in 1840. It displays 6,000 books in the categories of fiction, nonfiction, biography, history, travel, and children's. **Penobscot Books** (⊠ *164 W. Main St.* ☎ *207/548–6490* ⊙ *Closed Mon.*) carries nearly 40,000 books, specializing in books about fine art and architecture. From U.S. 1 you can't miss this place— it's huge and yellow.

GIFTS AND The **Grasshopper Shop** (⊠ *37 E. Main St.* ☎ *207/548–2244*) is devoted
MORE to clothing, jewelry, and Maine-made gifts. More than 70 craft dealers show their wares at **Silkweeds Country and Victorian Gifts** (⊠ *191 E. Main St., U.S. 1* ☎ *207/548–6501*), which is part of a chain. The store is large, and specializes in Christmas goodies, among other things, including many varieties of homemade fudge. If you're looking for live lobsters to cook on your own and a nice wine to go with them, you can't go wrong at Searsport's large and varied market, **Tozier's** (⊠ *220 E. Main St.* ☎ *207/548–6220*). It has lobsters in the tank, sandwiches made to order, excellent pizza, and a fine variety of wines.

MARINE- **Bluejacket Shipcrafters** (⊠ *160 E. Main St.,* ☎ *207/548–9970* ⊕ *www.*
RELATED *bluejacketinc.com*) is the largest model-ship company in the United States. The **Penobscot Marine Museum Store** (⊠ *40 E. Main St.* ☎ *207/548– 0334* ⊕ *www.penobscotmarinemuseum.org* ⊙ *Closed Nov.–Apr.*) is right next to the museum and has a large collection of pottery, paintings, books, and ship paraphernalia.

SPORTS AND THE OUTDOORS

The Searsport Town Landing, at the end of Steamboat Avenue, provides several floats where you can fish for mackerel or, occasionally, stripers. Kids like to do a little crabbing with bait at the end of a line here as well. Shore fishing is possible at the Sears Island Causeway, at the end of Sears Island Road, off U.S. 1.

GOLF The **Searsport Pines Golf Course** (⊠ *240 Mt. Ephraim Rd.* ☎ *207/548– 2854*) is a 9-hole, 36-par public course just west of town. It also has a pro for golf lessons. Greens fees are $20 ($30 with cart). Mt. Ephraim Road starts in the very heart of the two-block downtown.

**EN
ROUTE**

As you head north on U.S. 1 from Searsport, a detour at the little town of Stockton Springs will take you to the **Fort Point State Park & Lighthouse** (✉ *100 Cape Jellison Rd.* ☏ *207/567–3356*). This lovely park sits on a peaceful peninsula jutting into the bay. This is a delightful place for a picnic, and there are many nice walks through the woods.

Maine is famous for its blueberries, one of the most important crops in the state. In August and September you can pick your own blueberries at **Staples Homestead** (✉ *1194 Cape Jellison Rd., Stockton Springs* ☏ *207/567–3393*). This farm has been in the same family since 1838. Call first for directions.

A little north of Stockton Springs U.S. 1 separates into U.S. 1 and U.S. 1A. U.S. 1 goes to Bucksport and Bar Harbor, while U.S. 1A goes to Bangor. If you take 1, you will go through Bucksport and Ellsworth before you get to Mount Desert Island. If you take 1A, you will go through Frankfort, Winterport, and Hampden before you get to Bangor. **The Old Winterport Commercial House** (✉ *114 Main St. U.S. 1, Winterport* ☏ *207/223–5854* ⊕ *www.antiquesandreusables.com*), on the road from Searsport to Bucksport, is worth a stop. It has 3,200 square feet of American and European furniture, antiques, and curios. If you're heading up U.S. 1A to Bangor, an interesting and inexpensive place you can stop for lunch is **Rosie's Diner** (✉ *136 Main St. [U.S. 1A], Winterport* ☏ *207/223–5003*). If you have a hankering for good old-fashioned home-style diner food, this is the place. Rosie's hasn't been there that long, but it looks like it's been there since the fifties.

BUCKSPORT

9 mi north of Searsport via U.S. 1.

The new Penobscot Narrows Bridge, spanning the Penobscot River, welcomes visitors to Bucksport, a town founded in 1763 by Jonathan Buck. A Puritan, Buck hated witchcraft and sentenced to death a local woman thought to be a witch. Legend has it that before she was hanged she cast a curse upon him, saying that he would never escape her presence, even in his grave.

Buck died in 1795 and was buried in a cemetery east of Bucksport. A monument to honor the founder of the town was erected at the gravesite in 1852. As the monument weathered, an image in the shape of a woman's leg began to form under his name. You can see her leg on his stone to this day.

But a more important part of Bucksport history is that it was the site of the second worst naval defeat in American history (the first was Pearl Harbor). This defeat was back in 1779, when a British Armada defeated the fledgling American Navy. It became known as "the disaster on the Penobscot." You can learn more about it at the museum in Bucksport or at the Penobscot Marine Museum in Searsport.

EXPLORING

Penobscot Narrows Bridge & Observatory Tower/Fort Knox Historic Site. These two attractions, which previously were considered separate, have been combined into one—with one admission—since they are situated right

Fodor's Choice
★

next to each other. The 2,120-ft.-long Penobscot Narrows Bridge, opened at the end of 2006, has been declared an engineering marvel. It is certainly beautiful to look at or to drive over (no toll). Spanning the Penobscot River at Bucksport, the bridge replaced the old Waldo-Hancock bridge, built in 1931. The best part of it is the observation tower at the top of the western pylon. This was the first bridge observation tower built in America and, at 420 ft. above the river it's the highest bridge observation tower in the world. An elevator

> ### BIG FOOT IN MAINE?
>
> Guess what they found when they blasted the rocks in the huge cliff near the Penobscot Narrows Bridge? A nearly 20-foot-high footprint, complete with five toes, imprinted on the rock. You can see it if you stop at the observation area on U.S. 1 just before the bridge; walk up toward the bridge and look up to your left. What's the explanation for it? Nobody knows, but it's fun trying to guess.

shoots you to the top. The cost is $5, which includes a visit to the nearby Fort Knox Historic Site. Don't miss it—the view, which encompasses the river, the bay, and the sea beyond, is breathtaking.

Fort Knox is the largest fort in Maine, The fort was built between 1844 and 1869, when the British were disputing the borderline between Maine and New Brunswick. It was intended to protect the Penobscot River valley from a British naval attack. The fort never saw any actual fighting, but it was used for troop training and a garrison during the Civil War and the Spanish-American War. Visitors are welcome to explore the fort's passageways and many rooms. Guided tours are available during the summer season. ⊠ *711 Ft. Knox Rd., at U.S. 1, Prospect* ☎ *207/469–6553* ⊕ *www.maine.gov.observatory* ☉ *Open 8:30* AM *to dusk, May–Apr.*

Bucksport Harbor Tours. This narrated tour on the lower Penobscot River will take you past Fort Knox and under the Penobscot Narrows Bridge. Call for hours and rates. ⊠ *96 Main St (Bucksport town dock),* ☎ *207/469–7498* ⊕ *www.bucksportharbortours.com.*

WHERE TO EAT AND STAY

$$
AMERICAN
✕ **MacLeod's Seafood & Steak House.** There are not many places to eat in Bucksport, so MacLeod's, right across the street from the Best Western motel, is your best option. The menu is impressive for a small-town place, and includes dishes such as raspberry roasted duck, steak, ribs, and a dinner called the Seafood Boat, with scallops, haddock and shrimp. ⊠ *51 Main St.* ☎ *207/469–3963* ▭ *D, MC, V* ☉ *Closed Mon.*

$$–$$$
★
▥ **Williams Pond Lodge.** If peaceful seclusion in a forested setting with a large pond is what you're looking for, this is the place. This B&B is the loving creation of David Weeda and Dominick Rizzo. An interesting aspect is that it is "off the grid" in the sense that it is solar-powered. Activities, if you wish to take part, can include kayaking, canoeing, swimming, hiking, and picnicking. Don't be surprised if you hear the cry of a loon at night or a bagpipe during the day. This place is definitely off the beaten track, so check their Web site or call for directions. **Pros:** quiet and secluded; a chance to observe solar power in action.

Cons: it's a little hard to get to, so you will need to pay attention to the directions. ✉ *327 Williams Pond Rd.* ☎ *207/460–6064* ⊕ *www. williamspondlodge.com* ⇆ *3 rooms* ♿ *In-room: Wi-Fi, no phone, no TV, no a/c.* ▤ *MC, V.* ⑩ *CP.*

EN ROUTE ★ Halfway between Bucksport and Ellsworth on U.S. 1 an abandoned chicken-processing facility has been converted into the **Big Chicken Barn Books & Antiques** (✉ *1768 Bucksport Rd.* ☎ *207/667–7308* ⊕ *www. bigchickenbarn.com*). Have a love for books? Especially old books? Here's the place for you. Antiques, collectibles, and thousands of books cover 21,000 square feet of retail space. It's worth a stop.

BANGOR

133 mi northeast of Portland, 20 mi northwest of Bucksport, 46 mi west of Bar Harbor.

The second-largest city in the state (Portland being the first), Bangor is about 20 mi from the coast and is the unofficial capital of northern Maine. Back in the 19th century the "Queen City's" most important product and export was lumber from the state's vast North Woods. Bangor's location on the Penobscot River helped make it the world's largest lumber port. A 31-foot-tall statue of legendary lumberman Paul Bunyan stands in front of the Bangor Auditorium.

Lumber is no longer at the heart of its economy, but Bangor has thrived in other ways. Because of its airport, Bangor has become a gateway to Mount Desert Island, Bar Harbor, and Acadia National Park.

Bangor International is also the first American airport where troops returning from Iraq touch down. There is always a welcoming party of locals waiting for them, no matter what hour of the day or night.

The city is also home to author Stephen King, who lives in an old Victorian house on West Broadway notable for its bat-winged iron gate. King and his wife, Tabitha, are active members of the community and contribute to local charities, the arts, and education.

GETTING HERE AND AROUND

Bangor has a very good bus system. The **BAT Community Connector** (☎ 207/992–4670 ⊕ *www.bgrme.org*) goes in a number of directions and as far away as Hampden to the south.

ESSENTIALS

Visitor Information Bangor Region Chamber of Commerce (✉ *519 Main St., Bangor* ☎ *207/947–0307* ⊕ *www.bangorregion.com*). **Greater Bangor Convention & Visitors Bureau** (✉ *40 Harlow St., Bangor* ☎ *207/947–5205 or 800/91–MOOSE [916–6673]* ⊕ *www.bangorcvb.org*).

EXPLORING

★ **Cole Land Transportation Museum.** This museum chronicles the history of transportation in Maine through historical photographs and 200 vehicles. It is also the home of a World War II Memorial, the Korean War Memorial, a Vietnam Veterans Memorial, and a Purple Heart Memorial. ✉ *405 Perry Rd.* ☎ *207/990–3600* ⊕ *www.colemuseum.org* ⌨ *$6 adults, free to children under 19.* ☉ *May–mid-Nov., daily 9–5.*

○ **Maine Discovery Museum.** The largest children's museum north of Boston, it has three floors with more than 60 interactive exhibits. Kids can explore Maine's ecosystem in Nature Trails, travel to foreign countries in Passport to the World, and walk through Maine's literary classics in Booktown. ⊠ *74 Main St.* ☎ *207/262–7200* ⊕ *www.maine-discoverymuseum.org* ✉ *$7.50* ☾ *Tues.–Sat. 9:30–5, Sun. 11–5.*

> **BANGOR'S CHAINS**
>
> Large chain hotels with standard rooms and amenities in Bangor are the **Holiday Inn** (☎ *207/947–0101* ⊕ *www.holiday-inn.com*), **Motel 6** (☎ *207/947–6921* ⊕ *www.atmotel6.com*), and **Ramada Inn** 207 (☎ *207/947–6961* ⊕ *www.bangorramada. com*). Chain hotels near Bangor's airport include the **Sheraton Four Points** (☎ *207/947–6721* ⊕ *www.fourpoints.com*), which is connected to Bangor International Airport via a skywalk; the **Fairfield Inn Marriott** (☎ *207/990–0001* ⊕ *www.fairfieldinn.com*) ; the **Days Inn** (☎ *207/942–8272* ⊕ *www.daysinn.com*) ; and the Hampton Inn (☎ *800/426–7833*).

WHERE TO EAT

$–$$
AMERICAN
★

✕ **Nicky's Cruisin' Diner.** If you just want something that is fast, easy, inexpensive, and most of all, *fun,* drive up to Nicky's. And we do mean drive up, because you can eat in your car or go inside. Just like a scene out of the movie *Grease,* on weekends you'll usually find a bunch of cars from the 1950s in the parking lot. Fare includes burgers, fries, and shakes. ⊠ *957 Union St.* ☎ *207/942–3430* ▭ *AE, D, MC, V.*

$$–$$$
AMERICAN

✕ **Thistle's.** Paintings by local artists adorn the walls in this bright storefront restaurant. The diverse menu includes entrées such as Argentinian steak with chimichurri sauce, pickled ginger salmon piccata, and roast duckling. Musicians often perform during dinner. ⊠ *175 Exchange St.* ☎ *207/945–5480* ⊕ *www.thistlesrestaurant.com* ▭ *MC, V* ☾ *Closed Mon.*

WHERE TO STAY

$–$$

⊞ **Bangor Motor Inn.** This is one of the largest—103 rooms—accommodations in Bangor, and it's easy to find since it's near I–95 at the Bangor Mall exit. The rooms are simply decorated but clean, and 10 of them are two-room suites. **Pros:** centrally located near Bangor's only mall and many restaurants. **Cons:** can be very busy at times, as it caters to large conferences. ⊠ *701 Hogan Rd.* ☎ *207/947–0355 or 800/244–0355* ⊕ *bangormotorinn.com* ➥ *103 rooms* ⌂ *In-room: Wi-Fi (free). In-hotel: parking (free)* ▭ *AE, D, MC, V* ⏃❙ *CP.*

$–$$

⊞ **Best Western Black Bear Inn.** This hotel is close to Bangor Mall and the University of Maine at Orono. The rooms are large and airy, with king-size beds. Some have balconies and some pets are allowed. **Pros:** a good choice if you're planning to visit the nearby University of Maine. **Cons:** breakfast buffet seems a little skimpy. ⊠ *4 Godfrey Dr., Exit 51 off I–95 going north* ☎ *207/866–7120* ⊕ *www.blackbearinnorono.com* ➥ *68 rooms* ⌂ *In-room: Wi-Fi. In-hotel: gym, executive floor, some pets allowed* ▭ *AE, D, MC, V* ⏃❙ *CP.*

$–$$

⊞ **The Charles Inn.** One of just a few accommodations in downtown Bangor, the inn boasts that it is "Bangor's first art gallery hotel." The hotel displays many modern paintings, as well as works of Maine artists. If you want to be close to downtown businesses and restaurants, this is the place. The Charles offers both a great location and the charm of New England B&B. **Pros:** great location near the downtown area; free parking. **Cons:** getting in and out of this area can be quite a nuisance; far from the Interstate. ✉ *20 Broad St., Downtown* ☎ *207/992–2820* ⊕ *www.thecharlesinn.com* ⤺ *33 rooms* ⚮ *In-room: Wi-Fi. In-hotel: parking (free)* ⊟ *AE, D, MC, V* ⦿⟮ *CP.*

$$–$$$ ⊡ **Lucerne Inn.** This is one of the most famous and respected inns in New
Fodor's Choice   England. Nestled in the mountains, the Lucerne overlooks beautiful
★   Phillips Lake. The inn was established in 1814, and in keeping with that history every room is furnished with antiques. Most rooms have a view of the lake, gas-burning fireplaces, and a whirlpool tub; some have wet bars, refrigerators, and balconies as well. There's a golf course directly across the street. The inn's restaurant ($$–$$$$) is nearly as famous as the inn itself, and draws many of the local people for its lavish Sunday brunch buffet. The traditional dinner is the boiled Maine lobster. The inn is about 15 mi from Bangor. **Pros:** some rooms have lovely views of Phillips Lake (you can request one); Sunday brunch is famous—but be sure to make a reservation. **Cons:** some rooms are a little on the shabby side. ✉ *2517 Main St. (Rte. 1A), Dedham* ☎ *207/843–5123 or 800/325–5123* ⊕ *www.lucerneinn.com* ⤺ *31 rooms, 4 suites* ⚮ *In-room: Wi-Fi. In-hotel: restaurant, bar, pool* ⊟ *AE, D, MC, V* ⦿⟮ *CP.*

NIGHTLIFE AND THE ARTS

The **Bangor Symphony Orchestra** (✉ *51A Main St., Maine Center for the Arts, Orono* ☎ *207/942–5555 or 800/639–3221*) performs in nearby Orono (home of the University of Maine) at the Maine Center for the Arts. The **Penobscot Theatre Company** (✉ *131 Main St.* ☎ *207/942–3333* ⊕ *www.penobscottheatre.org*) stages classic and contemporary plays from October to May. During the summer they offer an outdoor musical in a park right across from their office. **Hollywood Slots** (✉ *500 Main St.* ☎ *877/779–7771* ⊕ *www.hollywoodslots.com* is a relatively new addition, with a casino (slots only) and a seven-story hotel. You can also bet on harness racing. The hotel has 148 rooms and four suites. It also has a large parking garage.

Fodor's Choice   The **American Folk Festival** (✉ *40 Harlow St., Bangor* ☎ *207/992–2630*
★   *or 800/916–6673* ⊕ *www.americanfolkfestival.com*) is the biggest event of summer, attracting thousands of people. The three-day, multistage event takes place on the waterfront and includes traditional folk performers from around the country and around the world. Events include a rich array of music and dance performances, workshops, storytelling, parades, craft exhibits, and tons of food. Music may include blues, gospel, jazz, bluegrass, country-western, Cajun, mariachi, honky-tonk, and zydeco. Some of the craft exhibits include pottery, blacksmithing, quilting, musical instrument making, boatbuilding, and woodcarving, as well as a variety of crafts from the American Indian groups in Maine. The festival is held at the end of August, and admission is free.

5

SHOPPING

The **Bangor Mall** (✉ *Hogan Rd., Exits 48A and 49 off I–95* ☎ *207/947–7333* ⊕ *www.bangormall.com*) has the best shopping in the area. Anchor stores include Macy's, JC Penney, Sears, and Dick's Sporting Equipment.

SPORTS AND THE OUTDOORS

GOLFING   The **Bangor Municipal Golf Course** (✉ *278 Webster Ave.* ☎ *207/941–0232*), a public club, has both an 18-hole course and a 9-hole course. Both courses are fairly flat and easy to walk. Greens fees are $35 for 18 holes, $15 for 9. Golf carts are available for an additional fee. The **Penobscot Valley Country Club** (✉ *366 Main St., take I–95 north from Bangor and then follow signs to Orono, Orono* ☎ *207/866–2060* ⊕ *www.penobscotvalleycc.com* ☉ *Mid-Apr.–mid-Oct.*) used to be a private club, but now is semiprivate, and guests are welcome. The greens are set beside the Penobscot River. The golf course was designed in 1924 by Donald Ross. A new clubhouse was built in 2001, and a comprehensive restoration of the original design was completed in 2008. The 18-hole course is 6,442 yards with a par of 72. Facilities include a pro shop and a grill serving lunch and dinner.

CRUISES   **Bangor Harbor Cruises** (✉ *1 Bar Harbor Pier, Bangor* ☎ *207/941–0952 or 207/546–2927* ⊕ *www.bangorharborcruises.com*) takes passengers on scenic cruises of the Penobscot River aboard a 72-foot replica of a 19th-century steam ferry, *The Patience.* You can choose a one-hour harbor cruise, a 1½-hour sunset cruise, or a two-hour dinner cruise; boats depart from Bangor Landing thrice daily, Friday, Saturday, and Sunday mid-June through mid-October. Prices begin at $20. The company also operates the *Margaret Todd* windjammer trips in Bar Harbor.

The Blue Hill Peninsula

WORD OF MOUTH

"We enjoyed the Maine Coast north of Portland all the way to Campobello Island. The coast is dotted with one picturesque town after another. Just do a search on Maine and you will come up with lots of interesting stops."

—Barblab

Updated
by George
Semler

If you want to see unspoiled Down East Maine land- and seascapes, explore art galleries, savor exquisite meals, or simply enjoy life at a relaxed pace, you should be content on the Blue Hill Peninsula. The area is not at all like its coastal neighbors, as very little of it has been developed. There aren't many must-see attractions, so you are left to investigate the area on your own terms, seeking out the villages, hikes, restaurants, or views that interest you most. Blue Hill and Castine are the area's main business hubs.

The peninsula, approximately 16 mi wide and 20 mi long, juts south into Penobscot Bay. Not far from the mainland are the islands of Deer Isle, Little Deer Isle, and the picturesque fishing town of Stonington. It lacks the mountains, lakes, ponds, and vast network of trails of neighboring Mount Desert Island. Instead, a twisting labyrinth of roads winds through blueberry barrens and around picturesque coves, linking the towns of Blue Hill, Brooksville, Sedgwick, and Brooklin. This is a place to meander for views of open fields reaching to the water's edge or, around the next bend, a tree-shaded farmhouse with apple trees and stone walls marking property lines.

Painters, photographers, sculptors, and other artists are drawn to the area. You can find more than 20 galleries on Deer Isle and in Stonington, and at least half as many on the mainland. And with its small inns, charming bed-and-breakfasts, and outstanding restaurants scattered across the area, the Blue Hill Peninsula may just persuade you to leave the rest of the coastline to the tourists.

ORIENTATION AND PLANNING

GETTING ORIENTED

To explore the Blue Hill Peninsula thoroughly, you should have a car, a good map, and a relaxed schedule. Be prepared to get lost, and don't worry if you do. The roads can be confusing to those unfamiliar with the area, as they crisscross, overlap, branch off in odd directions, and sometimes seem to run parallel to themselves. If you are traveling north through the state on U.S. 1 and Route 3, you can reach the peninsula on Route 15 off Route 175 just east of Bucksport. If you're traveling south, your best bet is to follow Route 172 where it branches off near Ellsworth. Acadia National Park (⇨ see Chapter 7) is an easy day trip.

Deer Isle, Little Deer Isle, and Stonington are accessible by bridge. Route 15 leads you onto Little Deer Isle and Deer Isle. When you reach the village of Deer Isle the road splits, with Route 15 following a more or less direct route to Stonington while Route 15A reaches the same destination but meanders along the island's western edge. Neither route has great views. For those wishing to travel on to Isle au Haut in Acadia National Park, ferry service is the only way to get there.

Exploring the area on bicycle or boat will give you a more complete picture than if you stick to the car. In fact, an ideal (if strenuous) way to explore is by kayak. Because the mainland is so undeveloped and there are so many islands to explore, traveling by kayak allows you to take in spectacular scenery at every turn, observe coastal wildlife, and escape civilization for a while. Beyond the peninsula, an archipelago of uninhabited islands known as Merchant's Row is a favorite with kayakers.

TOP REASONS TO GO

Water Music. Sleep to the sounds of the sea at oceanfront inns and B&B's.

String Quartets. Listen to chamber music at Blue Hill's Kneisel Hall.

Seascapes. Admire Penobscot Bay from atop Sedgwick Ridge or Caterpillar Hill.

Birding Bounty. Count blue herons and bald eagles at the Holbrook Island Sanctuary.

Learn a Craft. Try your hand at blacksmithing at Haystack Mountain School of Crafts.

6

PLANNING

WHEN TO GO

Because it is relatively undiscovered, the Blue Hill Peninsula does not have what you would call a high season. The best time to visit is from late May or early June to the end of daylight savings time in late October. There are few lodging options, so it's a good idea to reserve rooms well in advance. Outside of these months you will find that many restaurants and hotels have closed for the season. During the summer months, galleries open their doors, concerts enliven the evenings, and a handful of festivals draw locals and visitors alike. Check with the local chambers of commerce for schedules of events.

GETTING HERE AND AROUND
AIR TRAVEL

Trenton's Hancock County–Bar Harbor Airport is near the Blue Hill Peninsula, but only one commuter airline—Colgan Air, a subsidiary of US Airways, flies here to and from Boston. The Boston–Bar Harbor flight offers, on a clear day, bird's-eye views of the Maine Coast, but bad weather often makes arrivals and departures uncertain. Most travelers to the peninsula prefer Bangor International Airport, an hour's drive from Blue Hill, into which American, Continental, Delta, Midwest Express, Northwest, and US Airways fly.

Airports Bangor International Airport (✉ *287 Godfrey Blvd., Bangor* ☎ *207–992–4600* ⊕ *www.flybangor.com*). **Hancock County–Bar Harbor Airport** (✉ *Rte. 3, Trenton* ☎ *207–667–7329* ⊕ *www.bhbairport.com*).

GREAT ITINERARIES

IF YOU HAVE 1 DAY

For a comprehensive one-day tour of the Blue Hill Peninsula, without spending all of it in an automobile, start with a stroll around **Blue Hill** and hike up Blue Hill Mountain for 360-degree views. Then drive 45 minutes to **Stonington** via panoramic Caterpillar Hill and the Deer Isle bridge for lunch in one of the restaurants over the harbor, followed by a walk around town. In the afternoon, drive back to the mainland, taking scenic Route 175 through **Sargentville**, **Sedgwick**, and **Brooklin** before crossing the Blue Hill Falls bridge and driving west on Route 172 to Route 177 and South Penobscot. Continue on to **Castine** for an exploratory tour through town.

IF YOU HAVE 3 DAYS

If you have three days on the peninsula, stay in **Blue Hill.** Visit the town's shops and galleries your first morning, then take the afternoon tour to neighboring **Brooklin,** home to the world-famous Wooden Boat School, and **Brooksville,** where you can find the Sow's Ear Winery. On Day 2, climb Blue Hill Mountain for 360-degree views of the peninsula, then head to **Castine** and take the town walking tour—be sure to see historic homes like the Ives House and landmarks like the Abbott School and the Unitarian Church. On Day 3, explore **Deer Isle** and **Stonington** to learn about the region's rocky past at the Deer Isle Granite Museum and Settlement Quarry.

BIKE TRAVEL

The Blue Hill Peninsula's winding roads rarely have adequate bike lanes, so be on your guard when exploring the region. Although there are a few bike-rental shops in the area, your best bet is to take your own bike if you're going to Isle au Haut or Acadia National Park.

RESTAURANTS

Dining options on the Blue Hill Peninsula tend to fall into one of two categories: expensive restaurants where you can expect gourmet cuisine, or more casual places where you can grab a burger, or crab roll. You can always count on finding fresh seafood, but many restaurants on the peninsula proudly promote their locally raised produce and meats. This emphasis is not just about eating healthier foods; it's also a deliberate effort to support local farmers and fishermen.

HOTELS

You won't find grand hotels on the Blue Hill Peninsula. Instead, the countryside is dotted with inns, bed-and-breakfasts, and small but distinguished hotels. Be prepared to find that your room lacks a TV or even a phone. Many accommodations also do without air-conditioning. Although summer days in August can still get quite warm, ocean breezes will cool your room at night.

WHAT IT COSTS					
	¢	$	$$	$$$	$$$$
Restaurants	under $8	$8–$12	$13–$20	$21–$30	over $30
Hotels	under $70	$70–$99	$100–$149	$150–$200	over $200

Restaurant prices are for a median main course at dinner, excluding sales tax of 7%. Hotel prices are for two people in a standard double room in high season, excluding service charges and 7% tax.

VISITOR INFORMATION

Contacts **Blue Hill Peninsula Chamber of Commerce** (✉ *107 Main St., Blue Hill* ☎ *207/374–3242* ⊕ *www.bluehillpeninsula.org*). **Deer Isle–Stonington Chamber of Commerce** (✉ *Rte. 15, Deer Isle* ☎ *207/348–6124* ⊕ *www. deerisle.com*).

BLUE HILL AND ENVIRONS

Blue Hill, Castine, and Stonington are the most-visited towns on the peninsula, though they have managed to retain an off-the-beaten-path charm. For villages with an even more secluded feel, visit Brooklin, Brooksville, Sedgwick, or Deer Isle.

CASTINE

30 mi southeast of Searsport.

A summer destination for more than 100 years, Castine is a well-preserved village rich in history. Although American Indian tribes inhabited the area before the 1600s, French explorer Samuel de Champlain was the first European to record its location on a map. The French established a trading post here in 1613, naming the area Pentagoet. A year later Captain John Smith claimed the area for the British. The French regained control of the peninsula with the 1667 Breda Treaty, and Jean Vincent d'Abbadie de St. Castin obtained a land grant in the Pentagoet area, which would later bear his name. Castine's strategic position on Penobscot Bay and its importance as a trading post led to many battles for control until 1815. The Dutch claimed the area in 1674 and 1676, and England made it a stronghold during the Revolutionary War. In the 19th century Castine was an important port for trading ships and fishing vessels. The Civil War and the advent of train travel brought its prominence as a port to an end, but by the late 1800s some of the nation's wealthier citizens had discovered Castine as a pleasant summer retreat.

Federal- and Greek Revival–style architecture, spectacular views of Penobscot Bay, and a peaceful setting make Castine an ideal spot to spend a day or two. Well worth exploring are its lively harbor, two small museums, and the ruins of a British fort. For a nice stroll, park your car at the landing and walk up Main Street toward the white Trinitarian Federated Church. Among the white-clapboard buildings ringing the town common are the Ives House (once the summer home of poet Robert Lowell), the Abbott School, and the Unitarian Church, capped

IF YOU LIKE

FLOWER FESTIVAL

In June the fields and roadsides of the Blue Hill Peninsula are decorated with the blues, pinks, and purples of one of Maine's most popular flowers, the lupine. Although the flower thrives throughout coastal Maine, nowhere is it more celebrated than here. The Deer Isle–Stonington Lupine Festival, the third Saturday in June, showcases everything you can do with the buds. Festival events include a bean cook-off, a rummage sale and bazaar, and an art show. There's also food and live music. A map indicating prime viewing spots is available from area businesses.

FOLIAGE FOOD AND WINE FESTIVAL

The Annual Foliage Food and Wine Festival (⊕ www.bluehillpeninsula. org/foodandwine) in mid-October brings the area's restaurants, chefs, and food producers together for a wine dinner, a champagne luncheon, and tasting events, all at the height of the autumnal riot of hardwood reds, yellows, and ochers (not to mention the magentas of the blueberry barrens). The fourth edition of the festival held from the 15th to the 18th of October 2009 was a major success, starring local chefs Rich Hanson of Cleonice and Table, Jonathan Chase of Buck's, and Arborvine's John Hikade, along with an ample supporting cast of cheese makers, chocolatiers, vegetable growers, and cider brewers.

GALLERY HOPPING

If you're visiting the Blue Hill Peninsula area to collect antiques or find new artwork, you might want to pick up a copy of the annual *Arts Guide*, which showcases shops and galleries on Deer Isle–Stonington and the Blue Hill Peninsula. Make sure to see the Haystack Mountain School of Crafts, which has tours every Wednesday at 1 PM as well as interesting evening lectures. You can find galleries in and around downtown Deer Isle that exhibit oil and watercolor paintings, photography, and sculpture. Stonington has a few galleries, as does the village of Blue Hill. As you drive along the peninsula's winding roads, you can find studios selling everything from pottery to handmade paper.

by a whimsical belfry. Historical markers are posted throughout town, making it ideal for a self-guided walking tour.

EXPLORING

Wilson Museum. This attraction is made up of four historic structures. The main building houses anthropologist-geologist John Howard Wilson's collection of prehistoric artifacts from around the world. The **John Perkins House** is a restored Colonial-era house originally built on what is now Court Street, in 1763, and enlarged in 1774 and 1783. The house fell into disrepair until the 1960s, when the Castine Scientific Society had it taken down piece by piece and reassembled on the grounds of the Wilson Museum. Inside, you can find Perkins family heirlooms and 18th- and early-19th-century furnishings. The kitchen and four front rooms appear as they did in 1783. The **Blacksmith Shop** holds demonstrations showing all the tricks of this old-time trade. Inside the **Hearse House** you can see the summer and winter hearses that serviced Castine more than a century ago. ⊠ *107 Perkins St.* ☎ *207/326–9247*

⊕ *www.wilsonmuseum.org* ✉ *Museum, Blacksmith Shop, and Hearse House, free; John Perkins House, $5* ⊙ *Museum late May–late Sept., daily 2–5; John Perkins House, Blacksmith Shop, Hearse House July and Aug., Sun. and Wed. 2–5.*

WHERE TO EAT AND STAY

$$
AMERICAN

✕ **Dennett's Wharf.** Originally built as a sail-rigging loft in the early 1800s, this longtime favorite is a good place for oysters and fresh seafood of all kinds. The waterfront restaurant also serves burgers, sandwiches, and other light fare. There are several microbrews on tap, including the tasty Dennett's Wharf Rat Ale. Eat in the dining room or outside on the deck. ✉ *15 Sea St.* ☎ *207/326–9045* ⊕ *www.dennettswharf.net* ▤ *MC, V* ⊙ *Closed Columbus Day–May.*

$$–$$$$

▦ **Castine Inn.** Built in 1898, the Castine Inn is a delightful place to stay. Most of the guest rooms are simple, but they are bright and airy and have ocean views. A seascape mural covers the walls of the dining room, now used just for breakfast. After dinner in town you can relax in the garden or unwind in the English-style pub. **Pros:** at the hub of Castine's buzzing day and nightlife. **Cons:** occasionally noisy. ✉ *33 Main St.* ☎ *207/326–4365* ⊕ *www.castineinn.com* ⟳ *15 rooms, 4 suites* ⚡ *In-room: no phone, no TV, no a/c. In-hotel: restaurant, bar, no kids under 8* ▤ *MC, V* ⊙ *Closed Nov.–late Apr.* ¶◎¶ *BP.*

$$–$$$$

▦ **Manor Inn.** Bordering a 95-acre forest with trails that lead all the way to the bay, this 1895 inn resembles an English manor house. Rooms are individually decorated—four have fireplaces and one has a private porch. Some bathrooms have marble tubs and walk-in showers. The dining room ($$–$$$), overlooking the lawn and gardens as well as sweeping seascapes, offers eclectic international cuisine emphasizing local ingredients and accommodates up to 200 people. The pub serves lighter fare. Yoga classes are held in a fully equipped studio three times a week. **Pros:** great breakfast buffet. **Cons:** somewhat removed from the waterfront; some rooms do not have a/c. ✉ *15 Manor Dr., off Battle Ave.* ☎ *207/326–4861* ⊕ *www.manor-inn.com* ⟳ *14 rooms* ⚡ *In-room: no TV (some), Wi-Fi. In-hotel: restaurant, bar, Wi-Fi, some pets allowed* ▤ *AE, DC, MC, V* ¶◎¶ *BP.*

$$–$$$$

▦ **Pentagoet Inn.** With period lithographs in the common rooms, claw-foot tubs in the bathrooms, and a cozy pub, the owners of this inn strive to create an air of romance. Guest rooms are in the Queen Anne-style main building with a three-story turret and numerous gables or in a nearby 18th-century sea captain's home. The most memorable is Room 3, which has a balcony covered with flowers and views of town. The restaurant ($$$) offers fresh seafood. Enjoy a full breakfast in a room adjacent to the garden, and freshly baked cookies each afternoon. **Pros:** at the center of Castine's bustling town life; superb breakfast buffet. **Cons:** rooms somewhat cluttered and creaky. ✉ *26 Main St.* ☎ *207/326–8616 or 800/845–1701* ⊕ *www.pentagoet.com* ⟳ *16 rooms* ⚡ *In-room: no phone, no TV, no a/c. In-hotel: restaurant, bar* ▤ *MC, V* ⊙ *Closed late Oct.–May* ¶◎¶ *BP.*

NIGHTLIFE AND THE ARTS

Stella's (✉ *26 Water St.* ☎ *207/326–9710*) offers live jazz from 8 to 11 every evening as well as eclectic cuisine from 5:30 to 10.

6

SHOPPING

Compass Rose Bookstore & Café (⌧ *3 Main St.* ☎ *207/326–9366*) carries books, music, and games. The coffee shop has cookies and a self-serve lunch. **Four Flags** (⌧ *19 Water St.* ☎ *207/326–8526*) has nautical charts, prints of old maps, and other souvenirs. **Leila Day Antiques** (⌧ *53 Main St.* ☎ *207/326–8786*) specializes in interesting antiques, colorful quilts, and nautical accessories. **Sara Sara's** (⌧ *1 Main St.* ☎ *207/326–4442*) stocks light summer styles, silks based on Indian saris, and accessories for women. **Dolphin Books & Prints** (⌧ *314 Castine Rd.* ☎ *207/326–0888*) has more than 10,000 used and out-of-print volumes specializing in Maine, Americana, maritime, and travel themes.

SPORTS AND THE OUTDOORS

At Eaton's Wharf, **Castine Kayak Adventures** (⌧ *17 Sea St.* ☎ *207/866–3506* ⊕ *www.castinekayak.com*) operates tours run by owner Karen Francoeur (aka Kayak Karen), a master Maine Seakayak Instructor and Registered Maine Guide. You can sign up for a half-day of kayaking along the shore, a full day of kayaking by shipwrecks, reversing falls, and islands in Penobscot Bay, or an extended five- to seven-day kayaking trip to the Outer Islands with the mothership *Wanderbird* (⊕ *www.wanderbirdcruises.com*), a refurbished 90-foot fishing boat, as base camp. **Belfast Bay Cruises** (⌂ *P.O. Box 14, Belfast 04915* ☎ *207/322–5530* ⊕ *www.belfastbaycruises.com*) ferries visitors between Belfast and Castine and cruises Penobscot Bay under the command of Maine Maritime Academy graduate Melissa Terry. The day sailer *Guildive* charters out of Dennett's Wharf (⌧ *Dennett's Wharf 04421* ☎ *207/326–9045*) for full-day or half-day excursions.

BLUE HILL

19 mi east of Castine.

Snuggled between 943-foot Blue Hill Mountain and Blue Hill Bay, the village of Blue Hill sits cozily beside its harbor. Originally known for its granite quarries, copper mines, and shipbuilding, today the town is known for its pottery, and the plethora of galleries, shops, and studios that line its streets. Blue Hill is also a good spot for shopping, as there are numerous bookstores and antiques shops. The Blue Hill Fair (⊕ *www.bluehillfair.com*), held Labor Day weekend, is a tradition in these parts, with agricultural exhibits, food, rides, and entertainment.

EXPLORING

☾ **Marine Environmental Research Institute.** Focusing on how pollution affects marine mammals, this institute has programs for all ages, including guided walks along the beach. A weekly story hour for kids includes crafts projects, usually directed by a local artist. Children can hold small sea creatures from a "touch tank," including green crabs, sea stars, whelks, and periwinkles. Two viewing tanks house lobsters, rock crabs, anemones, and other small sea creatures. ⌧ *55 Main St.* ☎ *207/374–2135* ⊕ *www.meriresearch.org* ⌺ *Free* ☾ *Mon.–Fri. 9–5.*

Parson Fisher House. Jonathan Fisher, the first permanent minister of Blue Hill, built this home from 1814 to 1820. It provides a fascinating

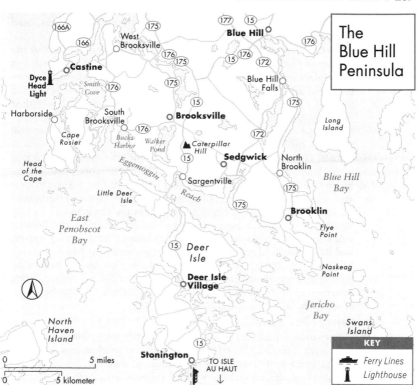

The
Blue Hill
Peninsula

166A
175
177 15
166
West Brooksville
Blue Hill
176
176
175
Castine
15 176
172
Dyce Head Light
Smith Cove
176
Blue Hill Falls
175
Harborside
South Brooksville
Brooksville
Long Island
Cape Rosier
Bucks Harbor
Walker Pond
Caterpillar Hill
Blue Hill Bay
Head of the Cape
Eggemoggin
15
Sedgwick
North Brooklin
Little Deer Isle
Sargentville
Reach
175
East Penobscot Bay
15 *Deer Isle*
175
Brooklin
Flye Point
Naskeag Point
Deer Isle Village
Jericho Bay
North Haven Island
Swans Island
15
0 5 miles
Stonington
TO ISLE AU HAUT

KEY
Ferry Lines
Lighthouse

0 5 kilometer

6

look at his many accomplishments and talents, which included writing and illustrating books, painting, farming, and building furniture. Also on view is a wooden clock he crafted while a student at Harvard; the face holds messages about time written in English, Greek, Latin, Hebrew, and French. The site is on the National Register of Historic Places. ⊠ *44 Mines Rd. (Rte. 15/176, west of intersection with Rte. 172)* ☎ *207/374–2459* ⊕ *www.jonathanfisherhouse.com* ⊠ *$5* donation suggested ☺ *July–mid-Sept., Thurs.–Sat. 1–4.*

WHERE TO EAT

$$$ ✕**Arborvine.** Glowing (albeit ersatz) fireplaces, period antiques, and
CONTINENTAL hardwood floors covered with Oriental rugs create an elegant and cozy
Fodor's Choice atmosphere in each of the four candlelit dining rooms in this renovated
★ Cape Cod–style house. You might begin with a salad of mixed greens, sliced beets, and pears with blue cheese crumbled on top. For your entrée, choose from dishes such as medallions of beef and goat cheese with shoelace potatoes, or pork tenderloin with sweet cherries in a port-wine reduction. The specials and fresh fish dishes are superb, as are the crab cakes. Be sure to save room for a dessert; the lemon mousse and the creamy cheesecake are especially delicious. A take-out lunch menu is available at the adjacent Moveable Feasts deli, where the Vinery piano bar offers drinks, tapas, and live music in the evening. ⊠ *33 Tenney Hill*

☎ *207/374–2119* ⊕ *www.arborvine.com* ⊟ *AE, DC, MC, V* ⊘ *Closed Mon. and Tues. Sept.–June. No lunch.*

¢–$
AMERICAN
★

✕ **The Café.** The Blue Hill Co-Op Community market and Café at the bottom of Green's Hill at the beginning of Rte. 172 to Ellsworth is a prime place for coffee, soups, salads, sandwiches, and organic gourmet food products from local farmers. The bread selection alone is worth a stop, as is the magazine rack carrying every food periodical published in North America. Fresh organic chickens are roasted daily for either takeout or on-premises consumption. ⊠ *4 Ellsworth Rd., Blue Hill* ☎ *207/374–2165* ⊕ *www.bluehill.coop* ⊟ *MC, V.*

$$$
AMERICAN
Fodor's Choice
★

✕ **Table.** The creative force behind Cleonice, the Ellsworth tapas bar that won a James Beard nomination in 2008, Rich Hanson opened this farmhouse bistro in the center of Blue Hill in June 2009. Specializing in local and organic products and a contemporary interpretation of traditional Maine cooking, Table offers classics such as the Ploughman's Lunch, which includes Maine Buggywhip cheddar, brie from nearby Brooksville's Sunset Acres Farm, chewy country bread with a chunky terrine, and Raye's mustard and pickles from just down east at Eastport. Fresh fish from the adjacent Blue Hill Bay and lobster pot-au-feu help make the dinner menu one of Blue Hill's most creative and innovative dining offerings. ⊠ *66 Main St.* ☎ *207/374–5677* ⊕ *www.farmkitchentable. com* ⊟ *AE, DC, MC, V* ⊘ *Closed Oct.–May.*

WHERE TO STAY

$$–$$$
🏨 **Barncastle.** Opened in June 2007 as a hotel, restaurant, and wood-oven pizza specialist, this establishment has had solid success, especially as a restaurant. Its location is in an unusual building, resembling, as its name suggests, an architectural hybrid between a barn and a castle. Designed in 1890 by George Clough, Boston's first city architect, the wooden towers and turrets around the drive-through carport create a whimsical Loire-meets-Down East effect. The pizzas ($–$$$) are excellent, as is the selection of salads and sandwiches. Rooms are quirky and rambling but charming. The turret suite is the most spectacular. **Pros:** views over woodlands to Mount Desert. **Cons:** landlocked; facing Blue Hill's fastest and least-appealing thoroughfare. ⊠ *125 South St. (Rte. 175)* ☎ *207/374–2300* ⊕ *www.barncastlehotel.com* ➥ *3 suites, 2 rooms* ♿ *In-room: Wi-Fi, no phone, no TV, no a/c. In-hotel: restaurant, bar, Wi-Fi* ⊟ *AE, DC, MC, V* ⫶○⫶ *BP.*

$–$$
🏨 **Blue Hill Farm Country Inn.** Just under two miles west of the town of Blue Hill, this rambling farm centered around a restored barn offers a restful and bucolic interlude at a comfortable remove from the madding crowds of summer. Managers Joan Brewer and John Danico run an efficient and helpful operation devoted to providing their guests with pleasant stays. Rooms are homey and decorated in country fabrics. **Pros:** well outside of the town of Blue Hill, wilder, and more rural. **Cons:** truck traffic steaming up nearby Rte. 15 can be noisy for streetside rooms; a drive back and forth to restaurants in town is inevitable. ⊠ *Rte. 15, P.O. Box 437* ☎ *207/374–5126* ⊕ *www.bluehillfarminn.com* ➥ *14 rooms, 7 with shared baths* ♿ *In-room: no phone, no TV, no a/c. In-hotel: Wi-Fi* ⊟ *AE, D, MC, V* ⫶○⫶ *BP.*

$$$–$$$$ 🏠 **Blue Hill Inn.** This inn dating from 1830 is a comfortable place to
★ relax after climbing Blue Hill Mountain or exploring the town. Original
pumpkin pine and painted floors set the tone for the mix of Empire and
early-Victorian pieces that fill the two parlors and guest rooms, several
of which have working fireplaces. One of the nicest rooms is No. 8,
which has exposures on three sides and views of the flower gardens
and apple trees. Two rooms have antique claw-foot tubs perfect for
soaking. The spacious Cape House Suite (available after the rest of the
inn has closed for the season) has a bed as well as two pullout sofas,
a full kitchen, and a private deck. The inn has a bar offering an ample
selection of wines and whiskies. Here you can enjoy appetizers before
dinner or try specialty coffees and liqueurs when you return. **Pros:** the
bedroom fireplaces and the antique floorboards make you want to stay
here forever. **Cons:** some rooms are on the small side; walls are thin.
✉ *40 Union St.* ☎ *207/374–2844 or 800/826–7415* ⊕ *www.bluehillinn.
com* 🛏 *11 rooms, 2 suites* ♿ *In-room: no phone, no TV. In-hotel: bar,
Wi-Fi, public Internet* ▤ *AE, MC, V* 🍴 *BP.*

NIGHTLIFE AND THE ARTS
The **Kneisel Hall Chamber Music Festival** (✉ *137 Pleasant St.* ☎ *207/374–
2203*) has concerts on Sunday afternoons and Friday evenings in sum-
mer. The first Saturday of each month a **Contra Dance** is held at the
Blue Hill Town Hall (✉ *18 Union St.*). Similar to square dancing, contra
dancing involves two couples dancing specific patterns.

SHOPPING
ANTIQUES **Blue Hill Antiques** (✉ *33 Water St.* ☎ *207/374–8825* ⊕ *www.bluehillan-
tiques.com*) displays and sells furniture and a careful selection of objects
and curios collected on the owners' annual buying trips to Europe. The
adjoining Red Gap Books is a good spot for a browse through rare and
used books and for a taste of the best espresso in Hancock County.

HANDCRAFTED **Andean Downeast** (✉ *27 Water St.* ☎ *207/374–2313*) has a surprising col-
ITEMS lection of alpaca wool products, jewelry, and textiles from the Andes of
Bolivia and Peru. **Bella Colore** (✉ *27 Water St.* ☎ *207/374–5343*) stocks
handcrafted gifts and jewelry, much of it by gifted store owner Ginger
Manna. **Handworks Gallery** (✉ *48 Main St.* ☎ *207/374–5613*) carries
unusual crafts made by local artists, such as bookshelves fashioned from
bark-peeled tree branches, wooden boxes, jewelry, dishes, and other
items. **North Country Textiles** (✉ *38 Main St.* ☎ *207/374–2715* ⊕ *www.
northcountrytextiles.com*) specializes in fine woven shawls, throws,
baby blankets, place mats, and pillows in subtle patterns and color
schemes. **String Theory** (✉ *132 Beech Hill Rd.* ☎ *207/374–9990*) makes
and markets hand-dyed yarn and fine arts from local artists.

ART GALLERIES **Blue Hill Bay Gallery** (✉ *11 Tenny Hill* ☎ *207/374–5773* ⊕ *www.bluehill-
★ baygallery.com* ☉ *Memorial Day–Labor Day, daily; mid-May–Memorial
Day and Labor Day–mid-October, weekends*) sells oil and watercolor
paintings of the local landscape. Bird carvings and other items are
also available. **Jud Hartmann Gallery** (✉ *79 Main St.* ☎ *207/374–9917*
⊕ *www.judhartmanngallery.com*) displays bronze sculptures of Iriquois
and Abenaki American Indians. Some sculptures are busts, while others
depict a scene. Oil and watercolor paintings by other artists are also

on display. **Leighton Gallery** (⊠ *24 Parker Point Rd.* ☎ *207/374–5001* ⊕ *www.leightongallery.com*) shows oil paintings, lithographs, watercolors, and other contemporary art. Outside, granite, bronze, and wood sculptures are displayed in a gardenlike setting under apple trees and white pines. **Liros Gallery** (⊠ *14 Parker Point Rd.* ☎ *207/374–5370* ⊕ *www.lirosgallery.com*) exhibits oil and watercolor paintings, hand-colored engravings, and woodcuts of birds and flowers.

HOUSEHOLD
GOODS

New Cargoes (⊠ *49 Main St.* ☎ *207/374–3733*) sells cookware, glassware, tea towels, clothing, quilts, and other products, many of them made in Maine. **Rackliffe Pottery** (⊠ *126 Ellsworth Rd.* ☎ *207/374–2297*) sells colorful pottery made with lead-free glazes. You can choose between water pitchers, tea-and-coffee sets, and sets of canisters. **Rowantrees Pottery** (⊠ *9 Union St.* ☎ *207/374–5535*) has an extensive selection of dinnerware, tea sets, vases, and decorative items. The shop makes many of the same pieces it did 60 years ago, so if you break a favorite item, you can find a replacement.

SPORTS AND THE OUTDOORS

Maps of hiking trails are available at **Blue Hill Heritage Trust** (⊠ *101 Union St.* ☎ *207/374–5118* ⊕ *www.bluehillheritagetrust.org*). The Osgood Trail provides hikers with breathtaking 360-degree views of the Blue Hill Peninsula from **Blue Hill Mountain** (⊠ *Mountain Rd.*). The dirt path meanders through the woods, over rocky ledges, and up stone steps. A second trail is accessible to hikers as well as all-terrain vehicles.

You can rent kayaks, canoes, and bicycles at the **Activity Shop** (⊠ *61 Ellsworth Rd.* ☎ *207/374–3600* ⊕ *www.theactivityshop.com*). Pick them up at the shop or have them delivered. **Rocky Coast Outfitters** (⊠ *5 Webster Rd.* ☎ *207/374–8866* ⊕ *www.rockycoastoutfitters.com*) has kayaks, canoes, and bicycles by the day or by the week. Delivery is available.

EN
ROUTE

Offering kayakers surfable currents when the tide is running full force, **Blue Hill Falls** (⊠ *Rte. 175 south of Blue Hill*) is a reversing falls on Route 175 between Blue Hill and Brooklin. Water flowing in and out of the salt pond from Blue Hill Bay roars under the Stevens Bridge. See it on foot or by kayak, but use caution, especially with children, on the bridge itself, as the noise drowns out the sound of oncoming cars.

SEDGWICK, BROOKLIN, AND BROOKSVILLE

Winding through the hills, the roads leading to the villages of Sedgwick, Brooklin, and Brooksville take you past rambling farmhouses, beautiful coves, and blueberry barrens studded with occasional masses of granite. From the causeway at Sedgwick to the Deer Isle bridge along Route 175 an anthology of typical Maine farmhouses lines the road, while the view from Caterpillar Hill merits a special detour.

Incorporated in 1798, **Sedgwick** runs along much of Eggemoggin Reach, the body of water that separates the mainland from Deer Isle, Little Deer Isle, and Stonington. The village of **Brooklin,** originally part of Sedgwick, established itself as an independent town in 1849. Today it is home to the world-famous Wooden Boat School, a 64-acre oceanfront campus offering courses in woodworking, boatbuilding, and seamanship. The town of **Brooksville,** incorporated in 1817, is almost completely surrounded by water, with Eggemoggin Reach, Walker Pond, and the Bagaduce River marking its boundaries.

EXPLORING

Naskeag Point. A few miles south of Brooklin, Naskeag Point Road leads to a broken-shell beach at the end of Naskeag Point. From here you can take in views of the small islands in Jericho Bay as you picnic under the apple trees. A bench remembers "all the fishermen who brave the sea." This area, famous for being the site of the 1778 Battle of Naskeag, has a long history. An ancient Nordic coin was discovered on the beach. To reach Naskeag Point Road, turn east at the Brooklin General Store.

Sow's Ear Winery. Head here if you'd like to taste locally produced fruit wines. Owner Tom Hoey grows apples and rhubarb for his cider and rhubarb wine, and he uses local blueberries and cranberries for his berry wines (⊠ *303 Coastal Rd., Brooksville* ☎ *207/326–4649* ☉ *Daily*).

WHERE TO EAT

¢–$ ✕ **Bagaduce Lunch.** Winner of a 2008 James Beard Award, this little fried-
AMERICAN fish specialist next to the reversing falls on the Bagaduce River on Rte.
Fodor's Choice 176, seven miles west of Blue Hill, is the perfect place for a lunch of
★ clams, scallops, halibut, and onion rings. Seals, bald eagles, and ospreys provide natural entertainment in this rich estuary that fills and empties with the tides. ⊠ *145 Franks Flat Rd., Brooksville* ☎ *207/326–4197* ▤ *No credit cards* ☉ *Closed Sept. 15–June 15*.

$$–$$$ ✕ **Buck's.** Popular among cruisers mooring in Buck's Harbor, this fine-
AMERICAN dining gem is behind **Buck's Harbor Market,** itself a key food destina-
Fodor's Choice tion for its wines, cheeses, olive oils, and sandwiches. Jonathan Chase,
★ a chef and restaurateur with more than 30 years of success on the Blue Hill Peninsula, has put together a superlative and constantly changing market-based menu strong in local ingredients, starring fresh fish, scallops, duck, and lamb. The seared duck breast with cranberries, beer, and maple barbecue sauce is a favorite, as are the sautéed sea scallops. The restaurant has a reasonably priced, carefully selected wine list and a deck for outdoor dining in summer. ⊠ *6 Cornfield Hill Rd., at Rte. 176, South Brooksville* ☎ *207/326–8683* ▤ *MC, V* ☉ *Closed Jan.–May*.

$–$$ ✕ **El El Frijoles.** You can find burritos, nachos, crab-meat empanadas,
MEXICAN tacos, and the full range of fiery south-of-the-border morsels right here
★ in the land of L.L. Bean. Flank steak and fresh Maine lobster are also available, albeit improved by Mexican spices. ⊠ *41 Caterpillar Rd., Sargentville* ☎ *207/359–2486* ▤ *MC, V* ☉ *Closed Mon.–Tues*.

WHERE TO STAY

$–$$ ▥ **Brooklin Inn.** A comfortable yet elegant atmosphere distinguishes this
★ B&B. There are plenty of homey touches like hardwood floors and beds piled with cozy quilts. The restaurant ($$–$$$$) specializes in fresh fish and locally raised beef, poultry, and lamb. It also has fine soups, salads, and desserts worth saving room for. In summer you can dine on the enclosed porch. An Irish pub downstairs showcases local musicians most Saturday nights. **Pros:** relaxing; on-site dining. **Cons:** rooms are small; walls are paper-thin. ⊠ *Rte. 175, Brooklin* ☎ *207/359–2777* ⊕ *www.*

6

brooklininn.com 🛏 *5 rooms, 3 with bath* ⚓ *In-room: no phone, no TV, no a/c. In-hotel: restaurant, Wi-Fi* 🖃 *AE, D, DC, MC, V* 🍴 *BP.*

$–$$ 🛏 **Eggemoggin Oceanfront Lodge.** Open year-round, this graceful inn over-
★ looking Eggemoggin Reach 2.5 mi west of Brooklin offers comfortable rooms, moorings for yachters, kayaking, beachcombing, and fine
dining. The main lodge is a handsome post-and-beam structure with
a roaring fireplace. The kitchen staff packs prizewinning picnics for
boaters and hikers, and the owners are dedicated to making every visit
memorable. **Pros:** great views; cozy fireside. **Cons:** eastern exposure
cold and bitter during northesterly storms. ✉ *482 Reach Rd. Brooklin*
☎ *207/359–5057* ⊕ *www.eggemogginlodge.com* 🛏 *21 rooms* ⚓ *In-
room: no phone, no TV, no a/c. In-hotel: restaurant, Wi-Fi* 🖃 *AE, D,
DC, MC, V* 🍴 *BP.*

$$–$$$$ 🛏 **Oakland House Seaside Resort.** Set between Eggemoggin Reach and a
★ private pond, this relaxing retreat sits on more than 50 acres of shore-
front property. Open since 1889, the resort has accommodations rang-
ing from comfortable guest rooms furnished in Arts and Crafts style
to more rustic cottages with fireplaces. Ask for Room 7, which has a
sitting area and ocean views on three sides. The resort's well-known
restaurant ($$$–$$$$) offers a five-course menu that changes daily.
Dinner might begin with seared tuna with wasabi vinaigrette followed
by lobster bisque and prime rib. Every Thursday you can join a lobster
picnic. The resort has hiking trails leading through the woods, including
one that ends at a peak overlooking Pumpkin Island Lighthouse and
beyond. A dock is available for boaters. Weeklong artist workshops
are held throughout the season, including painting and photography.
Pros: panoramic seascapes; cozy fireplaces for northeasterly storms.
Cons: weddings are frequently held here. ✉ *435 Herrick Rd., Brooks-
ville* ☎ *207/359–8521 or 800/359–7352* ⊕ *www.oaklandhouse.com*
🛏 *10 rooms, 7 with bath; 15 cottages* ⚓ *In-room: no phone, kitchen,
Wi-Fi, no TV, no a/c. In-hotel: restaurant, Wi-Fi, beachfront* 🖃 *MC, V*
🌙 *Closed mid-Oct.–late May* 🍴 *BP, MAP.*

NIGHTLIFE AND THE ARTS

A popular way to spend Monday evenings is to attend a street dance with
music performed by the steel-drum band **Flash! In the Pans** (☎ *207/374–
5247* ⊕ *www.peninsulapan.org*). This dynamic group performs regu-
larly around the Blue Hill Peninsula from late June to early September.
There are regular performances in Blue Hill, Castine, East Blue Hill, and
Sedgwick. Proceeds from the dances benefit area schools, fire depart-
ments, and ambulance crews.

SHOPPING

The **Gallery at Caterpillar Hill** (✉ *328 Caterpillar Hill Rd.* ☎ *207/359–
4600*) is a spectacular refuge for looking at landscape paintings and
other artifacts competing, sometimes successfully, with the Penobscot
Bay panorama out the window. On Route 15 just north of Caterpillar
hill, **Old Cove Antiques** (✉ *106 Caterpillar Hill Rd.* ☎ *207/359–8585*)
specializes in antique furniture, quilts, wood carvings, and more.

SPORTS AND THE OUTDOORS

The 1,230-acre **Holbrook Island Sanctuary** (✉ *172 Indian Bar Rd., Brooksville* ☎ *207/326–4012*) protects the region's fragile ecosystem. You have a good chance of spotting a blue heron, osprey, or bald eagle. Open from 9 AM to sunset, the park has nine hiking trails, a gravel beach with splendid views, and a picnic area. You can get a trail map at the parking areas. At Buck's Harbor Marina the 44-foot cruising ketch *Perelandra* (✉ *Coastal Rd., South Brooksville* ☎ *207/326–4279*) sails from Buck's Harbor Marina daily. A maximum of six people can cruise around Penobscot Bay and the nearby islands. Prices start at $40 for two hours.

EN ROUTE

As you travel south toward Deer Isle, scenic Route 15 passes through Sedgwick before taking you over the graceful green suspension bridge that crosses Eggemoggin Reach. The picnic area at **Caterpillar Hill,** on the mainland about 1 mi south of the junction of Routes 15 and 175, has a fabulous view of Penobscot Bay. You can even see across the bay to the Camden Hills, southwest of the Blue Hill Peninsula. With good reason, this spot is known as Million Dollar View.

DEER ISLE AND STONINGTON

6

Separated from the Blue Hill Peninsula by Eggemoggin Reach, Deer Isle and Stonington are significantly off the beaten path. The area was settled by farmers in 1755, but today is primarily devoted to fishing. That's why the annual Fishermen's Day, in late July, is so popular. Coast Guard demonstrations, rowboat races, and a codfish relay race mark the celebration. A Stonington Independence Day festival includes a "fish and fritter fry" and fireworks.

DEER ISLE VILLAGE

16 mi south of Blue Hill.

Around Deer Isle Village, thick woods give way to tidal coves. Stacks of lobster traps populate the backyards of shingled houses, and dirt roads lead to secluded summer cottages. This region is prized by artists, and studios and galleries are plentiful.

EXPLORING

Haystack Mountain School of Crafts. Want to learn a new craft? This school offers two- and three-week-long courses for people of all skill levels in such skills as blacksmithing, basketry, printmaking, and weaving. Artisans from around the world present evening lectures throughout summer. You can take a free tour of the facility at 1 PM on Wednesday, June through September. In autumn, shorter courses are available to New England residents. The school is 6 mi from Deer Isle Village, off Route 15. ✉ *89 Haystack School Dr.* ☎ *207/348–2306* ⊕ *www.haystack-mtn. org* ▣ *Free (tours)* ☉ *Daily, June–Sept.*

WHERE TO STAY

$$$–$$$$ ⊞ **Goose Cove Resort.** A country lane leads to this spectacular oceanfront property, where cottages and suites are scattered through the woods and along a sandy beach. Most of the guest rooms have fireplaces to keep out the chill. At low tide you can walk across a sandbar to the beautiful Barred Island Preserve. Reservations are essential at the Cockatoo ($$–$$$), specializing in Portuguese fare. On Monday nights in July and August you can join a lobster feast on the beach. **Pros:** lovely sea views; sense of isolation and escape. **Cons:** the waterfront location can be cold and dreary in bad weather. ⊠ *300 Goose Cove Rd., Sunset* ☎ *207/348–2600; restaurant 207/348-2300* ⊕ *www.goosecovelodge. com* ⊃ *2 rooms, 7 suites, 13 cottages* ⚮ *In-room: no phone, no TV, no a/c. In-hotel: 2 restaurants, beachfront* ⊟ *D, MC, V* ⊗ *All but 3 units closed mid-Oct.–mid-May* ⦿*BP.*

$$–$$$$ ⊞ **Pilgrim's Inn.** A four-story gambrel-roof house, this inn dates from
★   about 1793. Wing chairs and Oriental rugs fill the library; a downstairs taproom has a huge brick fireplace and pine furniture. Guest rooms, some with exposed beams and supports, others with canopy frames overhead, overlook a millpond and harbor. Three cottages—Rugosa Rose, Ginny's One, and Ginny's Two—are perfect for families. The excellent hotel restaurant, the Whale's Rib Tavern ($$$–$$$$), is rustic yet elegant with exposed beams, hardwood floors, and French oil lamps. **Pros:** memorable architecture and early-American interior; an oasis of fine cuisine. **Cons:** creaky floors; thin walls. ⊠ *20 Main St.* ☎ *207/348–6615 for restaurant reservations 207/348–5222* ⊕ *www. pilgrimsinn.com* ⊃ *12 rooms, 3 cottages* ⚮ *In-room: no phone, no TV, no a/c. In-hotel: restaurant, Wi-Fi, bicycles, some pets allowed* ⊟ *AE, D, MC, V* ⊗ *Closed mid-Oct.–mid-May* ⦿*BP.*

SHOPPING

Blue Heron Gallery (⊠ *22 Morey Farm Drive (off Sunshine Rd. on the way to Haystack Mountain School of Crafts)* ☎ *207/348-6051* ⊕ *www. blueherondeerisle.com*) sells work by the artists from the Haystack Mountain School of Crafts. Meet the artists at receptions from 3 to 5 PM every other Sunday in June and August. Purchase a handmade quilt from **Dockside Quilt Gallery** (⊠ *928 Sunshine Rd.* ☎ *207/348–2849* ⊕ *www. docksidequiltgallery.com*). Call for an appointment to see quilts or commission a custom-designed quilt. **Harbor Farm** (⊠ *29 Little Deer Isle Rd. (Rte. 15), Little Deer Isle* ☎ *207/348–7737* ⊕ *www.harborfarm.com*) carries wonderful products for the home, such as pottery, linens, and folk art. **Nervous Nellie's Jams and Jellies** (⊠ *598 Sunshine Rd.* ☎ *207/348–6182 or 800/777–6845* ⊕ *www.nervousnellies.com*) sells jams and jellies, operates the Mountainville café, and has a woods and meadow sculpture park with over 75 works by sculptor Peter Beerits. **Turtle Gallery** (⊠ *61 N. Deer Isle Rd.* ☎ *207/348–9977* ⊕ *www.turtlegallery.com*) exhibits contemporary painting, sculpture, and crafts.

SPORTS AND THE OUTDOORS

BOAT TOURS   Registered guide Captain Walt Reed takes a maximum of five passengers on boat tours around Deer Isle with **Guided Island Tours** (⊠ *27 Seabreeze Ave., Stonington* ☎ *207/348–6789* ⊕ *www.guidedislandtours. com*). For cruising the outer islands around Isle au Haut and Acadia

National Park, check with the **Isle Au Haut Company** (✉ *27 Seabreeze Ave., Stonington* ☎ *207/367–5193* ⊕ *www.isleauhaut.com*).

One- and two-person canoes and kayaks are available at **Finest Kind Canoe & Kayak Rentals** (✉ *70 Center District Crossroad, near Rtes. 15 and 15A* ☎ *207/348–7714* ⊕ *www.finestkindenterprises.com*). The company offers free delivery and pick-up.

Deer Isle has numerous nature preserves and parks grouped under the stewardship of the **Island Heritage Trust** (✉ *420 Sunset Road Deer Isle* ☎ *207/348–2455* ⊕ *www.islandheritagetrust.org*). For brochures and more information about the nature preserves listed below (as well as others), contact Island Heritage President Mike Little.

Famous landscape architect Frederick Law Olmsted once owned **Barred Island Preserve** (✉ *Goose Cove Rd.* ☎ *No phone* ✉ *Free* ☉ *Daily dawn–dusk*). His grandniece, Carolyn Olmsted, donated it to the Nature Conservancy in 1969. The island is accessible only at low tide. The mile-long trail leading to the island offers great views of Penobscot Bay. Pick up a brochure at the Deer Isle–Stonington Chamber of Commerce for a map of the islands you can see from the area. The parking area fills quickly, so arrive early. While enjoying miles of woodland and shore trails at the **Edgar M. Tennis Preserve** (✉ *Tennis Rd. off Sunshine Rd.* ☎ *No phone* ✉ *Free* ☉ *Daily dawn–dusk*), you can look for hawks, eagles, and ospreys, and wander among old apple trees, fields of wildflowers, and ocean-polished rocks. For picnics, bird-watching, or launching kayaks and canoes, visit **Mariners Memorial Park** (✉ *Fire Rd. 501 off Sunshine Rd., Deer Isle* ☎ *No phone* ✉ *Free* ☉ *Daily dawn–dusk*), overlooking secluded Long Cove. There is a half-mile walking loop and a small garden maintained by the Evergreen Garden Club. A mixture of hard- and softwood trees makes an excellent habitat for songbirds at **Shore Acres Preserve** (✉ *Greenlaw District Rd., off Sunshine Rd.* ☎ *No phone* ✉ *Free* ☉ *Daily dawn–dusk*) on the eastern edge of Deer Isle. On a 1½-mi walking trail you can see native plants like juniper, blueberry, and cranberry, as well as mushrooms, mosses, and ferns. You might even spot a fox, a red squirrel, or a hawk.

STONINGTON

7 mi south of Deer Isle.

Stonington is at the southern end of Rte. 15, which has helped retain its unspoiled small-town flavor. The boutiques and galleries lining Main Street cater mostly to out-of-towners, but the town remains a fishing community at heart. The principal activity is at the waterfront, where boats arrive overflowing with the day's catch. The sloped island that rises to the south is Isle au Haut, which contains a remote section of Acadia National Park; it's accessible by mail boat from Stonington.

EXPLORING

Deer Isle Granite Museum. This tiny museum documents Stonington's quarrying tradition. The museum's centerpiece is an 8- by 15-foot working model of quarrying operations on Crotch Island and the town of Ston-

Stonington Granite

CLOSE UP

Although you can see almost no sign of it today, the granite industry used to be a vital part of Stonington's economy. The first quarry was established in the 1860s, when the area known as Green's Landing had a population of approximately 300 people. From 1869 to 1969, area granite was used to build the Brooklyn Bridge, the Boston Museum of Fine Arts, the Smithsonian Institution, and other well-known sites. Demand was so high during the late 1800s that the town welcomed a wave of immigrants from Italy and Sweden, swelling the population to more than 5,000 people.

In 1897 Green's Landing split from Deer Isle and became known as Stonington. Since no bridge connected the area to the mainland until 1939, the community had to be completely self-sufficient. The boom was short-lived, however. With the rediscovery of concrete in the early 20th century, the granite industry ground to a sudden halt. Although one quarry reopened in the 1960s to fashion the granite blocks used in the Kennedy Memorial, it was unable to remain profitable. Today, Stonington's year-round population totals less than 1,200. The only remaining active quarry is on Crotch Island, just off the coast of Stonington. Its granite is shipped to Rhode Island, where it is cut for countertops and building facades.

—Lelah Cole

ington at the turn of the last century. ☒ *51 Main St.* ☎ *207/367–6331* ☜ *Free* ☼ *Memorial Day–Labor Day, Mon.–Sat. 10–5, Sun. 1–5.*

Settlement Quarry. Once a busy mine employing hundreds of men, the quarry closed in the 1980s. Visit the grounds for the panoramic views and easy walking trails. ☒ *Off Oceanville Rd.* ☜ *Free* ☼ *Daily.*

WHERE TO EAT

$–$$
AMERICAN
★

✕ **Lily's.** Homemade baked goods, delicious sandwiches, and fresh salads are on the menu at this friendly café. Try the Italian turkey sandwich, which has slices of oven-roasted turkey and jack cheese on homemade sourdough bread. The dining room's glass-top tables display seashells and various treasures inside. ☒ *450 Airport Rd. (Corner of Rte. 15 and Airport Rd.)* 04681 ☎ *207/367–5936* ☐ *MC, V.*

$$
AMERICAN
★

✕ **Maritime Café.** This harborside terrace restaurant is an ideal, if slightly pricey, perch for watching the Stonington fishing port in action while also enjoying some of its freshest produce. Guests can enjoy crepes and espresso while they take in the view, and not necessarily stay for a full dinner—although they might be tempted by the restaurant's excellent crab cakes. Seafood is the specialty here. ☒ *27 Main St.* ☎ *207/367–2600* ⊕ *www.maritimecafe.com* ☐ *MC, V.*

WHERE TO STAY

$$–$$$

⌂ **Inn on the Harbor.** From the street side, this inn made up of four century-old Victorian buildings looks as quaint and traditional as the town in which it is located. But on the waterfront side is an expansive deck over the harbor—a pleasant spot for morning coffee or afternoon cocktails. Rooms on the harbor side have lovely views, and some have fireplaces and private decks. One room is wheelchair accessible. **Pros:** lovely harbor views; a sense of partaking in the life at the fishing port. **Cons:** lobster-boat traffic jams at 5 AM can be disruptive; street-side rooms are noisy at night. ⊠ *45 Main St.* ☎ *207/367–2420 or 800/942–2420* ⊕ *www.innontheharbor.com* ⬧ *12 rooms, 2 suites* ⬧ *In-room: Wi-Fi, no a/c. In-hotel: no kids under 12* ⊟ *AE, D, MC, V* ⦿ *CP.*

SHOPPING

Art and miscellaneous gifts are for sale at **The Seasons of Stonington** (⊠ *6 Thurlow's Hill* ☎ *207/367–6348* ⊕ *www.theseasonsofstonington.com*), as well as food items and wine. Facing the harbor, **Dockside Books & Gifts** (⊠ *62 W. Main St.* ☎ *207/367–2652*) stocks an eclectic selection of books. **The Dry Dock** (⊠ *24 Main St.* ☎ *207/348–5528*) offers clothing, gifts, and accessories (many made of Deer Isle granite) and is described by owner Janet Chaytor as "a creative department store." **gWatson Gallery** (⊠ *68 Main St.* ☎ *207/367–2900* ⊕ *www.stoningtongalleries.com/gwatson.gallery*) shows contemporary art and landscape paintings. **Hoy Gallery** (⊠ *80 E. Main St.* ☎ *207/367–2777* ⊕ *www.jillhoy.com*) exhibits contemporary landsapes by painter Jill Hoy.

OFF THE BEATEN PATH

Off-Shore Islands. Many of the uninhabited islands near Deer Isle and Stonington are open for public use. One of the most popular is Green Island, which has an old quarry that is perfect for swimming. Some are for day-use only, while others allow overnight camping. All of these islands operate on a "leave no trace" basis, meaning that you must stay on marked trails and carry out what you carry in.

Island Heritage Trust (⊠ *3 Main St., Deer Isle* ☎ *207/348–2455*). **Maine Island Trail Association** (⊠ *328 Main St., Rockland* ☎ *207/596–6456* ⊕ *www.mita.org*).

SPORTS AND THE OUTDOORS

Old Quarry Ocean Adventures (⊠ *130 Settlement Rd.* ☎ *207/367–8977* ⊕ *www.oldquarry.com*) rents bicycles, canoes, and kayaks, and offers guided tours of the bay. Captain Bill Baker's three-hour boat tours leave from Webb Cove and take you past Stonington Harbor on the way to the outer islands. You can see Crotch Island, which has one of the area's two active stone quarries, and Green Island, where you can swim in a water-filled quarry. Sunset cruises are also available.

ISLE AU HAUT

14 mi south of Stonington.

Isle au Haut thrusts its steeply ridged back out of the sea south of Stonington. French explorer Samuel D. Champlain discovered Isle au Haut—or "High Island"—in 1604, but heaps of shells suggest that native populations lived on or visited the island prior to his arrival. The island is accessible only by mail boat, but the 45-minute journey is well worth the effort. As you pass between the tiny islands of Merchants Row, you might see terns, guillemots, and harbor seals. The ferry makes two trips a day between Stonington and the Town Landing from Monday to Saturday, and adds a Sunday trip from mid-May to mid-September. From mid-June to mid-September the ferry also stops at

Duck Harbor, located within Acadia National Park. The ferry will not unload bicycles, kayaks, or canoes at Duck Harbor, however.

Except for a grocery store, a chocolatier, the Sea Urchin gift shop, and a natural-foods store, Isle au Haut offers few opportunities for shopping. The island is ideal for day-trippers intent on exploring its miles of trails, or those seeking a night or two of low-key accommodations and delicious homemade meals at the Inn at Isle au Haut.

EXPLORING

★ **Acadia National Park.** Half of Isle au Haut is part of Maine's beautiful national park. More than 18 mi of trails wind through quiet spruce woods, along beaches and seaside cliffs, and over the spine of the central mountain ridge. The park's small campground, with five lean-tos, is open from mid-May to mid-October and fills up quickly. Reservations are essential. You can access Acadia from the Town Landing. If you turn right when you arrive at the dock, the ranger station is a short walk or bike ride away. Public rest rooms are here, as is the trailhead for the Duck Harbor Trail. ⊠ *Isle au Haut* ☎ *207/288–3338* ⊕ *www. us-parks.com/acadia-national-park/isle-au-haut.*

NEED A BREAK? For goods ranging from seafaring hero Linda Greenlaw books to homemade quilts, drop by the **Sea Urchin** (⊠ *1 Main Street* ⊹ *From boat landing, turn right on town road and walk ½ mi* ☎ *207/335–2021*).

WHERE TO STAY

$$$$

Fodor's Choice

★

🛏 **Inn at Isle au Haut.** This sea captain's home from 1897 retains its architectural charm. On the eastern side of the island, the seaside inn has views of sheep roaming around distant York Island and Cadillac Mountain. Comfortable wicker furniture is scattered around the porch, where appetizers are served when the weather is good. Downstairs, the dining room has original oil lamps and a model of the sea captain's boat (which sank just offshore). Breakfast includes granola and a hot dish like a spinach, tomato, and cheese frittata. Dinner is an elaborate five-course meal, usually incorporating local seafood. The first-floor Captain's Quarters, the only room with a private bath, has an ocean view, as do two of the three upstairs rooms. **Pros:** nonpareil views; first-class dining. **Cons:** shared baths. ⊠ *78 Atlantic Ave.* ☎ *207/335–5141* ⊕ *www.innatisleauhaut.com* 🛏 *4 rooms, 1 with bath* ⚭ *In-room: no phone, no TV, no a/c. In-hotel: bicycles* ⊟ *No credit cards* ⊗ *Closed Oct.–May* ⍟ *MAP.*

SPORTS AND THE OUTDOORS

There's no place to rent bicycles on Isle au Haut. If you want to bike around the island, head to **Old Quarry Ocean Adventures** (⊠ *130 Settlement Rd., Stonington* ☎ *207/367–8977* ⊕ *www.oldquarry.com*), which specializes in everything from puffin and whale-watch outings to kayaking adventures, and can carry you and your bikes to Isle au Haut.

Acadia National Park and Mount Desert Island

WORD OF MOUTH

"Get up at 3 AM and watch the sunrise from the top of Cadillac Mountain, the first place in the U.S. to see the sun rise."

—tbelgian

Updated
by George
Semler

With some of the most dramatic and varied scenery on the Maine Coast, and home to Maine's one and only national park, Mount Desert Island (pronounced "Mount Dessert" Island by locals), it's no wonder this is Maine's most popular tourist destination, attracting more than 2 million visitors a year. Much of the approximately 12-mi-long by 9-mi-wide island belongs to Acadia National Park. The rocky coastline rises starkly from the ocean, appreciable along the scenic drives. Trails for hikers of all skill levels lead to the rounded tops of the mountains, providing views of Frenchman and Blue Hill bays and beyond. Ponds and lakes beckon you to swim, fish, or boat. Ferries and charter boats provide a different perspective on the island and a chance to explore the outer islands, all of which are a part of Maine but not a part of Mount Desert. A network of old carriage roads lets you explore Acadia's wooded interior, filled with birds and other wildlife.

Mount Desert Island has four different townships, each with its own personality. The town of Bar Harbor is on the northeastern corner of the island, and includes Bar Harbor and the little villages of Hulls Cove, Salisbury Cove, and Town Hill. The town of Mount Desert comprises the southeastern corner of the island and parts of the western edge, and includes Mount Desert and the little villages of Somesville, Hall Quarry, Beech Hill, Pretty Marsh, Northeast Harbor, Seal Harbor, and Otter Creek. As its name suggests, the town of Southwest Harbor is on the southwestern corner of the island, although the town of Tremont is at the southernmost tip of the west side. This area includes the villages of Southwest Harbor, Manset, Bass Harbor, Bernard, and Seal Cove. The island's major tourist destination is Bar Harbor, which has plenty of accommodations, restaurants, and shops. Less congested are the smaller communities of Northeast Harbor, Southwest Harbor, and Bass Harbor. Mount Desert Island is a place with three personalities: the hustling, bustling tourist mecca of Bar Harbor, the "quiet side" of the island composed of the little villages, and the vast natural expanse that is Acadia National Park.

TOP REASONS TO GO

Looping the Park. Take the circle drive through Acadia National Park.

Cadillac of Views. Hike—or drive—to the 1,532-foot top of Cadillac Mountain for a spectacular view.

Snaps of Light. Climb down the rocks to the edge of the ocean to shoot the most photographed light-house in Maine, Bass Harbor Head Light.

International Excursions. Hop a ride on the CAT (high-speed catamaran) from Bar Harbor to Nova Scotia, Canada.

Powerful Popovers. The gigantic Jordan Pond House popovers filled with strawberry jam have been delighting visitors for more than 100 years.

ORIENTATION AND PLANNING

GETTING ORIENTED

Shaped like an upside-down "U"(some have likened it to the look of a lobster claw), Mount Desert Island is relatively easy to navigate. It may, however, take longer than you expect to reach some of the more distant points around the island. Somes Sound, the only fjord on the East Coast, runs up the middle of the island, requiring drivers at the ends of the "U" to drive quite a long distance to reach a town that is actually quite close as the crow flies. Beyond the geographical barriers, summer traffic can slow your progress and make finding a parking space, especially in Bar Harbor, nearly impossible. To combat this problem, Acadia National Park has created a free bus system called the Island Explorer. The system, which operates during the high season (Memorial Day through Labor Day), links the island's villages and campgrounds. These propane-propelled buses, which are air-conditioned and outfitted with bike racks, are kinder to the environment than most cars.

Acadia's Park Loop Road provides an excellent overview of the island, but to get a feel for the island's natural beauty you must leave your car behind. Instead, seek as many opportunities as you can for hiking, biking, and boating.

PLANNING

WHEN TO GO

Memorial Day and Labor Day mark the official beginning and end of high season on Mount Desert Island. The reality, however, is that there is no reason you have to visit during this narrow window. Temperatures often begin to rise in April or May. You may have to contend with minor irritants such as ice and snow on the trails through Acadia National Park, but the crowds are smaller during these months.

GREAT ITINERARIES

IF YOU HAVE 1 DAY

If you only have one day to explore Mount Desert Island, spend as much of it as you can driving and hiking the carriage roads in **Acadia National Park**, saving **Bar Harbor** for dinner at McKay's or This Way Café. Start at Hulls Cove Visitor Center to pick up maps and information and then drive **Park Loop Road** with stops at scenic points such as **Cadillac Mountain, Jordan Pond House**, and **Thunder Hole**.

IF YOU HAVE 3 DAYS

If you have three days on Mount Desert Island, stay in **Bar Harbor.** There are plenty of things in this popular resort town to keep you occupied on your first day—from bustling boutiques to interesting museums. On Day 2, stop at the Hulls Cove Visitor Center to pick up information about special events, then head to Acadia National Park. A drive around **Park Loop Road** is a great way to learn the lay of the land. Stop along the way—a lot of the scenic overlooks have informational signs you may find interesting. Finish up the Park Loop Road

journey by driving to the top of **Cadillac Mountain** to enjoy the sunset. On Day 3, rent a bike and explore the network of carriage roads that crisscross the island. Take in the spectacular view of **Jordan Pond** from the observation deck of the Jordan Pond House, a restaurant known for its massive popovers with lots of strawberry jam. For the afternoon's entertainment, hike South Bubble Mountain (easier) or Penobscot Mountain (more challenging). As an alternative to the above, you may want to consider a one-day excursion to Nova Scotia via the CAT, if it's running that day (⇨ *See listing in Bar Harbor section).*

IF YOU HAVE 5 DAYS

Follow the three-day itinerary above. On Day 4, drive to **Northeast Harbor,** the summer home of many of the country's wealthiest families. Take in the Asticou Azalea Garden and Thuya Gardens. On your last day, take a sightseeing cruise in the morning. In the afternoon, head to Bass Harbor Head Lighthouse, taking in **Somesville** and **Southwest Harbor** along the way.

By September the heat and humidity of summer begin to taper off, making it one of the most enjoyable months to visit. Autumn foliage peaks between the end of September and the middle of October, enhancing the already spectacular views. Although many seasonal businesses close their doors after Columbus Day, the island does not shut down entirely. You can still find some good restaurants and a small number of lodging options throughout the winter months.

Regardless of when you decide to go, you will enjoy your visit to the island more if you book your accommodations in advance, especially if you have a particular type of lodging in mind or if you'll be visiting on a holiday weekend. Although it's possible to find last-minute lodging during the summer months, it may take several phone calls. From November to April your challenge shifts from finding an open room to finding an open hotel, motel, or bed-and-breakfast. Call ahead.

GETTING HERE AND AROUND
AIR TRAVEL
Although Trenton's Hancock County–Bar Harbor Airport offers the closest airport to the Mount Desert Island region, only one commuter airline, Colgan Air (operated by US Airways Express), services the airport. It flies to Boston and Rockland. With weather and visibility always uncertain at Trenton, most people prefer Bangor International Airport, an hour's drive from the island. Direct flights are available to and from Boston, New York LaGuardia, Philadelphia, Cincinnati, Detroit, and Albany.

Concord Trailways operates shuttle service from Bangor International Airport to Bar Harbor, with stops along the way in Bangor and Ellsworth. From there, Downeast Transportation operates buses from Ellsworth to various locations on Mount Desert Island.

Airports Bangor International Airport (☎ 207/992–4600 ⊕ www. flybangor.com). **Hancock County–Bar Harbor Airport** (☎ 207/667–7329 ⊕ www.bhbairport.com).

Buses/Shuttles Bar Harbor-Bangor Shuttle Bus (☎ 207/479–5911 ⊕ www. barharborshuttle.com). **Downeast Transportation** (☎ 207/667–5796 ⊕ www. exploreacadia.com).

BUS TRAVEL
The free Island Explorer shuttle service circles the entire island from the end of May to September, with limited service continuing through mid-October. Buses, which are equipped with racks for bicycles, service the major campgrounds, Acadia National Park, and Trenton's Hancock County–Bar Harbor Airport. They also run from Bar Harbor to Ellsworth.

Bus Contact Island Explorer (☎ 207/667–5796 ⊕ www.exploreacadia.com).

CAR TRAVEL
From the gateway towns of Ellsworth and Trenton, Route 3 leads to Mount Desert Island. When you reach the island, Route 3 continues to Bar Harbor. Route 102 heads toward Somesville and Southwest Harbor. In summer, traffic can slow considerably, especially in the afternoon. If Northeast Harbor is your first destination when arriving on the island, take Route 102 to Somesville, then turn onto Route 198.

In Acadia National Park, the 27-mi Park Loop Road is accessible from Hulls Cove (visitor center entrance), Otter Creek (Sieur de Monts Spring entrance), and Seal Harbor (Jordan Pond House entrance). You can also access the Park Loop Road from Bar Harbor (Cadillac Mountain entrance).

RESTAURANTS
With some of the nation's wealthiest families making Mount Desert Island their summer residence, a handful of restaurants cater to those seeking an upscale dining experience. These restaurants offer carefully prepared dishes, extensive wine lists, and impressive service. Like most of the coast, the area is also home to many restaurants specializing in hamburgers and other typical American fare. You won't see fast-food chains, but you will find good food at reasonable prices. Many

area restaurants carry locally produced microbrews on draft or by the bottle. If you like pale ales, brown ales, or stouts, you should be able to find something to tempt the palate. **Note:** In accordance with Maine state law, smoking is not allowed in any place that serves food, be it a restaurant or a bar.

HOTELS

Mount Desert Island offers a range of accommodations to suit every budget. Whether you are looking for campgrounds, bed-and-breakfasts, or resort hotels, there are lodging options to meet your needs. Bar Harbor is the island's best-known community, and it's a good choice for being close to shopping and nightlife, but the other villages offer accommodations that are equally—or even more—enticing, especially if you want a quieter lodging experience. If you drive along Route 3, you can spot a number of roadside motels and cabin-style accommodations that fall into lower price categories. Some bed-and-breakfasts can also be quite reasonable. Those looking to stay in a sprawling resort hotel or a beautifully appointed seaside inn should be prepared for prices in the top categories. Acadia National Park offers two wooded campgrounds but no cabins or lodges.

The high-season rates go into effect during the second half of June and don't drop again until after Labor Day. Rates often dip significantly in spring and autumn. Winter rates are the lowest.

WHAT IT COSTS					
	¢	$	$$	$$$	$$$$
Restaurants	under $8	$8–$12	$13–$20	$21–$30	over $30
Hotels	under $70	$70–$99	$100–$149	$150–$200	over $200

Restaurant prices are for a median main course at dinner, excluding sales tax of 7%. Hotel prices are for two people in a standard double room in high season, excluding service charges and 7% tax.

VISITOR INFORMATION

Contacts Bar Harbor Chamber of Commerce (✉ *1201 Bar Harbor Rd., Bar Harbor* ☎ *207/288–5103* ⊕ *www.barharbormaine.com*). **Mount Desert Chamber of Commerce** (✉ *18 Harbor Rd., Northeast Harbor* ☎ *207/276–5040* ⊕ *www.mountdesertchamber.org*). **Mount Desert Island Chambers and Acadia National Park Information Center** (✉ *Rte. 3, Thompson Island* ☎ *207/288–3411* ⊕ *www.acadiachamber.com*).

GATEWAYS TO MOUNT DESERT ISLAND

Ellsworth and Trenton are unlikely to be focal points during your vacation, but you can't avoid them if you're traveling to Mount Desert Island. Ellsworth is a good place to pick up supplies for your journey, while Trenton's best offering is the view you see when crossing the bridge to the island. On clear days the sunlight sparkles off the ocean, and the bald peaks of Acadia's mountains stand out starkly against the rich forests of conifers and evergreens. The beauty of it is overwhelming.

ELLSWORTH

140 mi northeast of Portland, 28 mi south of Bangor.

Ellsworth is the eye of the storm through which all vehicles traveling to Mount Desert Island must pass. As such, the few short miles of U.S. 1 that pass through the city can be fraught with frustration in summer. Traffic can back up for miles as cars wait to pass through the four traffic lights along High Street. Despite the congestion, Ellsworth is a good spot for refueling—literally and figuratively. With two supermarkets, several good restaurants, and a range of shops, the city has nearly anything you need. The main shopping roads are High Street, where you find two malls; and Main Street, home to distinctive shops set in attractive brick buildings.

Ellsworth is about a half-hour drive from most of the island's attractions. Despite its relatively close proximity to such natural beauty, Ellsworth doesn't have a great deal of charm, and accommodations aren't likely to be much cheaper than those on the island.

ESSENTIALS

Visitor Information Ellsworth Area Chamber of Commerce (⊠ *163 High St., Ellsworth* ☎ *207/667–5584* ⊕ *www.ellsworthchamber.org*).

EXPLORING

Woodlawn Museum. Between 1824 and 1828 Colonel John Black built an elegant Federal-style house on a 180-acre estate of fields and woods. Inside are an especially fine elliptical flying staircase and period artifacts from the three generations of the family that lived here. Outside, Woodlawn has 2 mi of walking trails that Colonel Black used as a bridle path. As a visitor, you can wander through several different gardens. The formal garden, enclosed by a lilac hedge, features flowers popular in the 19th century, including iris, daylilies, and phlox. The Woodlawn Museum is also the home of the increasingly popular Ellsworth Antiques Show, which takes place in mid-August. ⊠ *19 Black House Rd.* ☎ *207/667–8671* ⊕ *www.woodlawnmuseum.org* ⊠ *$10, free access to gardens and grounds* ۞ *May–Oct., Tues.–Sat. 10–5, Sun 1–4.*

WHERE TO EAT

$$$

MEDITERRANEAN

★

✕**Cleonice Mediterranean Bistro.** Locals rave about this place—and with good reason. Chef and owner Rich Hanson is a lover of tapas, and he will most likely make you love them as well. The cuisine is Mediterranean, and the menu offers authentic Catalan, Spanish, Italian, and Greek tapas ranging from *escalivada* (roasted vegetable salad) to *sepia calabrese* (stewed cuttlefish) to *spanikopita* (Green spinach pie) pastries. Small plates include selections such as lamb osso bucco, and autumn-leaves pasta (with pumpkin, apple, and Fontal cheese sauce), while entrées are strong on fresh fish dishes such as the grilled albacore tuna *putanesca* (with tomato, capers, hot peppers, anchovies, olives, and herbs). Try the Paella Cleonice (which, like the restaurant, is named after the chef's mother), a medley of surf 'n turf ingredients from littleneck clams, mussels, and scallops to organic chicken and Spanish chorizo sausage with saffron-scented Spanish Montasia rice. ⊠ *112 Main St.* ☎ *207/664–7554* ⊕ *www.cleonice.com* ⊟ *AE, MC, V.*

7

IF YOU LIKE

FISHING

Fishing is not a principal reason to visit Acadia National Park. Brook trout, landlocked salmon, lake trout, brown trout, large- and small-mouth bass, and white perch reside in Eagle Lake, Echo Lake, Jordan Pond, Lower Hadlock Pond, Bubble Pond, and Witch Hole Pond, but in the summer only deep trolling is effective. In June and September surface fly-fishing is more productive. Mackerel, bluefish, and striped bass run in July and August, but striped bass fishing has been on the wane in recent years. If you're an angler, stop by the **Hulls Cove Visitor Center** (✉ Rte. 3, Bar Harbor ☎ 207/288–3338) to find out which species thrive in the dozens of ponds and lakes scattered around the island. Some are popular in the warmer months, while others are better for ice fishing.

Maine residents 16 and older and non-Maine residents 12 and older must have a license to fish in freshwaters. Fishing licenses are not required for ocean fishing. Fishing licenses may be purchased online through MOSES (Maine Online Sportsman Electronic System) or at town halls and at some stores. In Bar Harbor you can pick up a fishing license at the **Bar Harbor Municipal Office** (✉ 93 Cottage St., Bar Harbor ☎ 207/288–4098). Non-Resident fishing licenses cost $11 (1 day), $23 (3 days), $36 (7 days), $40 (15 days), and $52 (season). A resident fishing license costs $20. In Northeast Harbor you can pick up a fishing license at the **Mount Desert Municipal Office** (✉ 21 Sea St., Northeast Harbor ☎ 207/276–5531). In Southwest Harbor you can pick up a fishing license at the **Southwest Harbor Town Office** (✉ 26 Village Green Way, Southwest Harbor ☎ 207/244–5404). In Tremont you can pick up a fishing license at the **Tremont Town Office** (✉ 119 Tremont Rd., Tremont ☎ 207/244–7204).

BOATING

You can rent canoes in Bar Harbor and other towns. Most of the lakes and ponds have well-marked public access points, making boating even easier. If you are planning on using motorized watercraft anywhere besides the ocean, check with the park rangers first—many lakes and ponds don't allow motorboats or may restrict the size of the engine.

With its dramatic coastline, Mount Desert Island is a great spot for sea kayaking. There are shops all over the island that are happy to provide you with gear, offer expert instruction, and give tips on possible routes. Along the way you'll see cormorants and other birds, and you might catch a glimpse of harbor seals.

$-$$ ✕ **Riverside Café.** The only thing better than the food at this popular
AMERICAN eatery is the staff's camaraderie. The employees are fast, friendly, and frequently banter back and forth across the restaurant. Open early for breakfast, the café offers everything from French toast and blueberry pancakes to omelets and breakfast burritos. On Sunday the menu expands to include raspberry-stuffed French toast and pumpkin pancakes with maple cream. For lunch you can choose between sandwiches, quiches, and salads. The baked goods, including muffins and biscuits, are baked on the premises. Works by a different area artist are displayed

each month. ⊠ *151 Main St.* ☎ *207/667–7220* ▤ *AE, MC, V* ⊘ *No dinner Sun.–Thurs.*

$–$$

AMERICAN

✕ **Union River Lobster Pot.** Ellsworth's only waterfront restaurant occupies an historic location used in earlier times as a lumber wharf and a seafood market. Sit in the screened-in porch or on the outdoor terrace and have your choice of everything from lobster, seafood, and fish and clam chowders to stews, meat, and chicken; the blueberry pie is the de rigueur dessert. ⊠ *8 South St.* ☎ *207/667–5007* ⊕ *www.lobsterpot.com* ▤ *AE, MC, V* ⊘ *Closed Oct.–May. No lunch.*

WHERE TO STAY

$$–$$$

🛏 **Comfort Inn.** Open throughout the year, this chain hotel has simply decorated rooms with some nice touches like hair dryers and irons. It sits adjacent to the L.L. Bean factory outlet and several eateries. **Pros:** breakfast included; there's a nice restaurant, Jasper's, within walking distance. **Cons:** High Street can get noisy at night. ⊠ *130 High St.* ☎ *207/667–1345* ⊕ *www.comfortinn.com* ⇋ *63 rooms* ♿ *In-room: refrigerator (some), Wi-Fi. In-hotel: gym* ▤ *AE, DC, MC, V* ▯⧠ *CP.*

CAMPING

¢–$$$

⛺ **Patten Pond Camping Resort.** This is a huge and attractive RV campground with a lot of amenities, including full hookups, wireless access, and areas for swimming, boating, and fishing on a 740-acre lake. Boats—canoes, motorboats, paddleboats, and kayaks—and bikes are available for rent. In addition to the RV and tent sites, there are rental cabins (with fire ring and bathroom outside) and one cottage (with kitchen and bath inside). Tent sites run $25–$28 per night, while RV site rates are $40–$49. Cabins are $45–$50 per night, and the cottage is a weekly rate of $1,295. Weekends bring live entertainment and blueberry-pancake breakfasts on Saturday morning. **Pros:** full-service and fun activities like ice-cream socials and hayrides. **Cons:** if you like to dine out for dinner, you will need to drive. ⊠ *1470 Bucksport Rd. (U.S. 1)* ☎ *207/667–7600* ⊕ *www.pattenpond.com* ⇋ *90 RV sites, 30 tent sites* ♿ *flush toilets, portable toilets, full hookups, partial hookups, dump station, drinking water, guest laundry, showers, fire grates, picnic tables, electricity, public telephone, general store, play area, swimming, Wi-Fi* ▤ *DC, MC, V* ⊘ *Closed mid-Oct.–mid-May.*

NIGHTLIFE AND THE ARTS

A local landmark, the **Grand Auditorium** (⊠ *165 Main St.* ☎ *207/667–9500* ⊕ *www.grandonline.org*) opened as a movie theater in 1938. It fell into disrepair, sitting vacant from the '50s to the '70s. The theater reopened in 1975 and since then has staged plays and concerts and shown films.

SHOPPING

GIFTS

The **Grasshopper Shop** (⊠ *124 Main St.* ☎ *207/667–5816* ⊕ *www.grasshoppershop.com* ⊘ *Daily*) sells fun and unique gifts. You can find books, candles, linens, jewelry, women's clothing and shoes. Most of the lower level is dedicated to items for children. With a selection of organic and natural foods, **John Edwards Market** (⊠ *158 Main St.* ☎ *207/667–9377* ⊕ *www.johnedwardsmarket.com* ⊘ *Daily*) is a pleasant alternative to the supermarket when you're stocking up on supplies. Downstairs are a wine cellar and an art gallery that showcases works by area artists.

7

You can find everything for your kitchen at **Rooster Brothers** (✉ *29 Main St.* ☎ *207/667–8675* ⊕ *www.roosterbrothers.com* ☉ *Mon.–Sat.*), including nonstick cookware and bamboo steamers, as well as wines, cheese, and freshly ground coffee. The second floor sells everything from coffee grinders to assorted licorices to molasses ginger cookies.

SPORTING GOODS   One of the best sporting goods stores in the state, **Cadillac Mountain Sports** (✉ *34 High St.* ☎ *207/667–7819* ⊕ *www.cadillacmountainsports.com* ☉ *Daily*) has developed a following among locals and visitors alike. A branch of the original store in Bar Harbor, this location carries top-quality bicycles, canoes, kayaks, cross-country skis, and a selection of hiking and camping equipment. If you need a pair of hiking boots, some running shoes, a bike helmet, or a warmer jacket, this is where you should stop (they do not rent equipment).

SPORTS AND THE OUTDOORS

Bar Harbor Bicycle Shop (✉ *193 Main St.* ☎ *207/667–6886* ⊕ *www.barharborbike.com* ☉ *Daily*) rents road bikes plus recreational and high-performance bikes.

TRENTON

5 mi south of Ellsworth via Rte. 3.

Like Ellsworth, Trenton is a town that everyone traveling to Mount Desert Island must pass through. The town offers little in the way of dining or lodging options, but it does have the closest airport to the island, which is filled with private jets in summer. Sightseeing flights by plane or glider are popular. Carroll's Supermarket usually has the cheapest gas around—and often the longest lines at the pumps.

ESSENTIALS

Visitor Information Southwest Harbor/Tremont Chamber of Commerce (✉ *Main St.* ✍ *Box 1143, Southwest Harbor 04679* ☎ *207/244–9264 or 800/423–9264* ⊕ *www.acadiachamber.com*).

EXPLORING

Ⅽ **Kisma Preserve.** In its fields and woods this attraction shelters about 45 species of wild and domestic animals, including reindeer, alligators, wolves, and a moose. A converted barn serves as a rain-forest habitat for monkeys, birds, reptiles, and other Amazon creatures. Having a one-on-one encounter with a moose or a wolf in this exotic animal rescue facility is mostly on an advance-notice basis. ✉ *446 Bar Harbor Rd.* ☎ *207/667–3244* ⊕ *www.kismapreserve.org* ✉ *$12.50* ☉ *May–Dec., daily 9:30–dusk.*

SPORTS AND THE OUTDOORS

About 8 mi from Route 3, the seaside **Lamoine State Park** (✉ *23 State Park Rd., Lamoine* ☎ *207/667–4778 or 207/941–4014* ⊕ *www.campwithme.com* ✉ *Park $3, camping sites $15–$20* ☉ *Apr.–Oct., except cross-country skiing in season*) offers a quiet respite from the crowds on Mount Desert Island. During the day you can stroll along the pebble beach, eat lunch at one of the picnic tables, or even camp in the park. There is also a fishing area.

The **Bar Harbor Golf Course** (⊠ *51 Jordan River Rd., intersection of Rtes. 3 and 204, Trenton* ☎ *207/667–7505* ⊕ *www.barharborgolfcourse. com*) is an 18-hole par 71 course open to the public. Greens fees are $40 for 18 holes, $25 for nine holes. If you want to practice your swing, try **Vokes Driving Range** (⊠ *10 Bar Harbor Rd.* ☎ *207/667–9519* ⊗ *Open daily, 8–7, weather permitting*). There's also a miniature golf course.

☺ **Seacoast Fun Park** (⊠ *50 Bar Harbor Rd.* ☎ *207/667–3573* ⊕ *www. seacoastfunpark.com* ⊗ *May–Sept., daily 10–9*) has go-karts, two waterslides, a 32-foot climbing wall, bungee trampolines, and a miniature golf course.

BAR HARBOR

160 mi northeast of Portland, 22 mi southeast of Ellsworth.

A resort town since the 19th century, Bar Harbor is the artistic, culinary, and social center of Mount Desert Island. It also serves visitors to Acadia National Park with inns, motels, and restaurants. The island's unique topography was shaped by the glaciers of the most recent Ice Age. Around the turn of the last century—before the days of airconditioning—the island was known as the summer haven of the very rich because of its cool breezes; lavish mansions were built throughout the island. Many of them were destroyed in a great fire that devastated the island in 1947, but many of those that survived have been converted into businesses. Shops are clustered along Main, Mount Desert, and Cottage streets. Take a stroll down West Street, a National Historic District, where you can see some fine old houses.

The island and its surrounding Gulf of Maine are home to a great variety of wildlife: whales, seals, eagles, falcons, ospreys, puffins (probably the most unusual-looking birds in the world), and denizens of the forest such as moose, deer, foxes, coyotes, and black bears.

GETTING HERE AND AROUND

BY BIKE   Although Acadia National Park is a bicycle-friendly area, traveling along the island's major thoroughfares can be challenging. Bike lanes are narrow or nonexistent on many stretches of road, leaving bikers the choice of biking in roadside gravel, which can be soft when wet, or sharing the road with vehicle traffic. In summer, when traffic is heavy and many drivers are distracted by the scenery, it's a good idea to avoid the main roads. (⇨ *Sports and the Outdoors for bicycling outfitters.*)

BY BOAT   The **Bar Harbor Ferry** (⊠ *Bar Harbor Inn Pier* ☎ *207/288–2984* ⊕ *www.*
AND FERRY   *barharborferry.com*) travels six times daily between Bar Harbor and Winter Harbor, home to Acadia National Park's Schoodic Peninsula. Along the way passengers are treated to great views of the mountains and a few lighthouses. A free bus shuttle from the ferry terminal goes to Winter Harbor, Schoodic Point, Birch Harbor, and Prospect Harbor. You can bring a bike along.

For tour information, ⇨ *see Boat Tours under Sports and the Outdoors.*

7

Abbe
Museum **2**

Atlantic Brewing
Co. **6**

Bar Harbor
Historical Society
Museum **1**

Bar Harbor Whale
Museum **3**

George B. Dorr
Museum of Natural
History **4**

Mount Desert
Oceanarium
& Lobster
Hatchery **5**

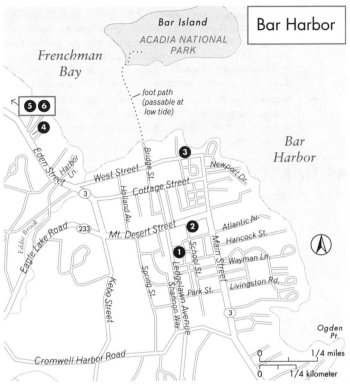

ESSENTIALS

Visitor Information Bar Harbor Chamber of Commerce (✉ *1201 Bar Harbor Rd.* ☎ *207/288–5103, or 800/345–4617* ⊕ *www.barharborinfo.com*). **Bar Harbor Merchant's Association** (✉ *Box 431, Bar Harbor 04609* ⊕ *www. barharbormerchants.com*) is a good place to contact if you're planning to come during any of the off-seasons—spring, fall, and winter.

EXPLORING

② **Abbe Museum.** This is the only museum devoted solely to Maine's American Indian heritage, with a collection of artifacts spanning thousands of years. Open since 2001, the museum has permanent and changing exhibits. A good time to visit this museum would be during the annual Native American Festival at the nearby College of the Atlantic (Route 3) the first week in July. (Note: Don't confuse this museum with the one in Acadia National Park.) ✉ *26 Mount Desert St.* ☎ *207/288–3519* ⊕ *www.abbemuseum.org* ✉ *$6.50* ☉ *Mid-May–mid-Oct., daily 9–5.*

⑥ **Atlantic Brewing Company & Bar Harbor Cellars Farm Winery.** Near Bar Harbor in the village of Town Hill, this microbrewery has free tastings. It's also the home of America's first blueberry ale. Tours at 2, 3, and 4 PM last approximately 45 minutes. A barbecue restaurant, Mainely Meat (☎ *207/288–9200),* is also on the premises. ✉ *15 Knox*

Rd., off Rte. 3, Town Hill ☎ *207/ 288–2337* ⊕ *www.atlanticbrewing. com* ⊠ *Free* ⊙ *May–late Oct., daily 10–5.*

❶ **Bar Harbor Historical Society Museum.** The museum displays photographs of Bar Harbor from the "Gilded Age" of 1880 to 1930. Other exhibits document the great fire that devastated the town and its surrounding areas in 1947. ⊠ *33 Ledgelawn Ave.* ☎ *207/288–3807 or 207/288– 0000* ⊕ *www.barharborhistorical. org* ⊠ *Free* ⊙ *Mid-June–mid-Oct., Mon.–Sat. 1–4.*

FARMERS MARKETS

Farmers' markets, in which a portion of a street is blocked off once a week so that farmers may set up stands and carts selling their fresh-from-the-farm wares, are becoming increasingly popular in Maine. On Sunday there is one in Bar Harbor next to the YMCA; on Thursday in Northeast Harbor across from the Kimball Terrace Inn; and on Friday in Southwest Harbor near the elementary school.

❸ **Bar Harbor Whale Museum.** Learn
Ⓒ about the history of whaling, the anatomy of whales, and how biologists are working to gain more information about these massive creatures at this interesting museum. All proceeds from the gift shop benefit Allied Whale, a nonprofit organization that conducts marine mammal research. ⊠ *52 West St.* ☎ *207/288– 0288* ⊕ *www.barharborwhalemuseum.org* ⊠ *Free* ⊙ *June, daily 9–10; July and Aug., daily 9–9.*

❹ **George B. Dorr Museum of Natural History.** This small museum at the Col-
Ⓒ lege of the Atlantic displays the natural history of Maine through a human perspective. It has wildlife exhibits, a hands-on discovery room, interpretive programs, and summer field studies for children. ⊠ *105 Eden St.* ☎ *207/288–5395 or 207/288–5015* ⊕ *www.coa.edu/nhm* ⊠ *Donation* ⊙ *Mid-June–Labor Day, Mon.–Sat. 10–5; Labor Day– mid-Nov. and mid-Jan.–mid-June, Fri. and Sun. 1–4, Sat. 10–4.*

❺ **Mount Desert Oceanarium & Lobster Hatchery.** The oceanarium will tell
Ⓒ you everything you ever wanted to know about lobsters. There also are exhibits on the fishing and sea life of the Gulf of Maine. ⊠ *Rte. 3, Salisbury Cove* ☎ *207/288–5005* ⊕ *www.theoceanarium.com* ⊠ *$9* ⊙ *Mid-May–late Oct., Mon.–Sat. 9–5.*

WHERE TO EAT

$$$–$$$$ ✕ **Burning Tree.** One of the top restaurants in Maine, this lovingly run
SEAFOOD specialist in organic produce (much of it from the owners' garden)
Fodor'sChoice combines a love of raw materials with culinary originality. Local art
★ adorns the walls in the two dining rooms and on the porch at this easy-to-miss gem on Route 3 between Bar Harbor and Otter Creek. The ever-changing menu emphasizes freshly caught seafood, and seven species of fish are offered every day, all from the Gulf of Maine. Entrées include pan-sautéed monkfish, oven-poached cod, and gray sole. There are always two or three vegetarian options. ⊠ *69 Otter Creek Drive (Rte.3) Otter Creek* ☎ *207/288–9331* ▤ *DC, MC, V* ⊙ *Closed Tues. and mid-Oct.–mid-June.*

FIDDLING WITH FIDDLEHEADS

As you head toward Mount Desert Island, it's common to see vendors on the side of the roadways selling produce from the back of a pickup truck. In spring you're likely to see signs offering CLEAN FIDDLEHEADS. Unknown to many Americans, the fiddlehead fern is one of nature's true delicacies. Fiddleheads are the tightly coiled tips of newly emerging fronds, and are about the size of two or three quarters stacked on top of each other.

Fiddleheads come from different varieties of ferns. The best fiddleheads come from ostrich ferns, which, unlike most ferns, have hairless casings. You can also eat the fiddleheads from cinnamon ferns, but they have a fuzzier casing. You shouldn't fiddle with some ferns, however. The bracken fern is similar to the ostrich fern, but it's hairy and can give you quite a stomachache.

It can be difficult to identify ferns, but if you are determined to forage, you can identify the type of fern by examining the dead stalks from the previous year. Often these stalks will hold firmly to the plant even after a winter of heavy snow and ice.

Even the best fiddleheads require a good cleaning, and should be thoroughly cooked. If you pick some fiddleheads, be sure to boil them for 10 to 15 minutes. The best method is to boil them for about 7 minutes in one pot, then discard the water and boil them in fresh water until they are tender. Fiddleheads have a distinct flavor that aficionados say is somewhere between asparagus and spinach. Many area restaurants will offer them as a side dish, toss them with pasta, or add them to other dishes. Be sure to give them a try if you are visiting in springtime.

$$$
ECLECTIC
Fodor's Choice
★

✕ **Café This Way.** Named for a street sign aiming customers in the right direction, this hip and savvy restaurant has gained deserved fame as one of Bar Harbor's off-the-beaten-path gems. Paintings by local artists and bookshelves surround the relaxed dining room, while the sun porch is ideal for breakfast and lunch alfresco. Breakfasts include the wickedly delicious eggs Benedict with smoked trout, and dinners offer grilled lamb sirloin with a fennel and mint chimichurri, or pecan-crusted halibut with garlicky spinach and a Cajun tartar sauce (in honor of Acadia's earliest settlers). The wine list runs the gamut from over-the-top terrific to affordable and good, such as the La Linda Malbec or the Matua Sauvignon Blanc. Service staff is smart and saucy. ✉ *14 Mount Desert St.* ☎ *207/288–4483* ⊕ *www.cafethisway.com* ⌚ *Reservations essential* ▭ *DC, MC, V* ☺ *Closed mid-Oct.–early May (opens Mother's Day).*

$$
CONTINENTAL

✕ **Carmen Verandah.** Who would name this restaurant/nightspot "Carmen Verandah?" The answer is easy: The same people who would name the next door restaurant "Rupununi." (Both were, as a matter of fact, founded by the same people but now operate under separate management.) Carmen has a loyal following for its wacky dishes that range from "Bless the Pig" (pork loin, bacon, and ham with caramelized onions) and "Not Your Momma's Tuna" (sushi-grade ahi tuna with cole slaw) sandwiches to Lobster Verandah, shrimp-stuffed lobster. It also has a huge beer and wine selection, and houses Bar Harbor's largest dance floor with live music, dancing, and karaoke. ✉ *119 Main St. (upstairs)* ☎ *207/288–2766* ⊕ *www.carmenverandah.com* ☐ *DC, MC, V* ☺ *Closed Nov.–mid-to-late May.*

$–$$
AMERICAN
✗ **Galyn's.** Open most of the year, this casual restaurant serves lighter fare such as a Cajun pork sandwich and a chicken focaccia sandwich for lunch. For dinner, the emphasis switches to lobster dishes, steak, and seafood, with options such as garlic shrimp tossed with linguine. The delicious Indian pudding, a traditional molasses dessert dating back to the Pilgrims and generally served at Thanksgiving, is available here year-round. ✉ *17 Main St.* ☎ *207/288–9706* ⊕ *www.galynsbarharbor. com* ⚅ *Reservations essential* ☐ *AE, DC, MC, V* ☺ *Closed Dec.–Feb.*

¢–$
AMERICAN
✗ **Geddy's.** Geddy's is a legendary Bar Harbor pub/restaurant open every day of the year except Thanksgiving and Christmas, offering fun food and fine nightly entertainers, from Grammy-winning jazz musician Wynton Marsalis to folk singer Arlo Guthrie. If you're looking for an easy-to-find place with inexpensive food and a refreshing atmosphere, this is it. A warning, however, about the menu: the owner apparently has a sense of humor. Among the choices on the menu are "Ba Haba Gull Wings," "Deep-fried Guppies," and "Spam on the Half Shell." ✉ *19 Main St.* ☎ *207/288–5077* ⊕ *www.geddys.com* ☐ *MC, V.*

$$$
ITALIAN
★
✗ **Guinness & Porcelli's.** This well-respected dinner-only restaurant used to be in the Queen City of Bangor before moving to Bar Harbor. An explanation of the name: "Italian food with Irish hospitality." The menu changes frequently, but current recommendations include the pan-roasted duck breast with blood orange and a reduction of Modena balsamic vinegar, or the grilled Portobello mushrooms. The lobster stuffed with risotto is another winner. ✉ *191 Main St.* ☎ *207/288–0030* ⊕ *www.guinnessporcellis.com* ☐ *AE, DC, MC, V* ☺ *No lunch.*

$$$
LATIN AMERICAN
★
✗ **Havana.** As you would expect from the name, this is dining with a Latin flair. Soft jazz playing in the background sets the tone at this storefront restaurant on the edge of downtown Bar Harbor. The pumpkin-color walls and wood floors lend an air of sophistication. The Latin-influenced menu emphasizes local ingredients and changes weekly. Lobster? Of course, but it's prepared south of the border-style, poached in butter and served with sweet-corn drizzle, saffron potato, and grilled asparagus. The menu may also include selections like manchego-crusted Halibut, Argentinian hanger steak, and Havana's Tuna (pan-seared, chile-dusted tuna served over charred carrots, goat cheese, and arugula). On the huge wine list there are more than 500 choices. ✉ *318 Main St.* ☎ *207/288–2822* ⊕ *www.havanamaine.com* ⚅ *Reservations essential* ☐ *MC, V* ☺ *Closed Jan.–mid-April. No lunch.*

$$–$$$
ECLECTIC
✗ **Mache Bistro.** Painted with muted earth tones and decorated with flickering candles, this restaurant's low-key ambience allows for the rustic French-accented food to take center stage. The menu changes weekly but always begins with freshly baked bread. Choose from appetizers such as seared scallops and fiddlehead ferns tossed with penne and Alfredo sauce. Entrées include a seared salmon fillet with ginger and basil, and panfried tofu with apricots. The seafood stew is highly recommended. There's also a cheese course featuring local blue cheese and chèvre. Choose from a short but thoughtfully selected wine list and

7

be sure to save room for one of the homemade desserts—the lemon tart is excellent. ⊠ *135 Cottage St.* ☎ *207/288–0447* ⊕ *www.machebistro. com* ☴ *MC, V* ☽ *Closed Mon. No lunch.*

$–$$
AMERICAN

✕ **McKay's Public House.** If the name sounds like this could be a fun place, you're right: it is. Low lighting and glowing candles set the right mood for relaxed but elegant dining. The pub menu includes familiar favorites such as fish-and-chips, but also more unusual options such as lamb burgers and shepherd's pie. The restaurant also emphasizes fresh seafood, with crab cakes, porcini halibut, and seared scallops among the offerings. The Moroccan lamb kebabs are highly recommended. Key lime pie, crème brûlée, cheesecake, and other desserts will tempt your palate. ⊠ *231 Main St.* ☎ *207/288–2002* ⊕ *www.mckayspublichouse. com* ☴ *AE, MC, V.*

$$$–$$$$
CONTINENTAL
Fodor's Choice
★

✕ **Reading Room at the Bar Harbor Inn & Spa.** This elegant restaurant serves continental fare along with Maine specialties such as lobster pie and Indian pudding. There's live music nightly. When the weather is nice, what could be more romantic than dining out under the stars at the inn's Terrace Grille with the ships of beautiful Bar Harbor right at your feet? The natural thing to order here would be the Maine lobster bake with all the fixings. For something different, you might try the lobster stew, which is served in a bread bowl. The restaurant is also famous for its Sunday brunch, 11:30 AM–2:30 PM. ⊠ *7 Newport Dr.* ☎ *207/288–3351 or 800/248–3351* ⊕ *www.barharborinn.com* ⌕ *Reservations essential* ☴ *AE, DC, MC, V* ☽ *Closed late Nov.–late Mar.*

$$–$$$
AMERICAN

✕ **Rupununi.** Named after a river in Brazil, the Rup also calls itself "an American Bar & Grill." It's hugely popular with the collegiate crowd and the young people of Bar Harbor. They come for the drinks and the good, inexpensive, slightly exotic food such as the Moqueca stew (lobster meat, shrimp, and mussels simmered in a Brazilian stew of onions, peppers, tomatoes and coconut milk). The decor is made up of signs, pictures, and "things" from all over the world. When it comes to wines, beers, and microbrews, the choices are many, and the price is reasonable. ⊠ *119 Main St.* ☎ *207/288–2886* ⊕ *www.rupununi.com* ☴ *AE, DC, MC, V* ☽ *Closed Nov.–mid-Apr.*

WHERE TO STAY

$$$$
★

▦ **Balance Rock Inn.** This grand summer cottage built in 1903 commands a prime waterfront location. An expansive lawn and gardens full of annuals lead down to the ocean. The Carriage House, 50 yards from the main building, offers four more rooms. Even if your room doesn't have an ocean view, you can enjoy it from a wicker chair on the porch. Rooms are spacious and meticulously furnished with reproduction pieces—four-poster and canopy beds in guest rooms, crystal chandeliers and a grand piano in common rooms. All rooms have whirlpool tubs, and some have fireplaces. A buffet-style breakfast is served each morning. **Pros:** a lovely, old-fashioned place with a good breakfast. **Cons:** a little on the pricey side. ⊠ *21 Albert Meadow* ☎ *207/288–2610 or 800/753–0494* ⊕ *www.balancerockinn.com* ⇥ *27 rooms, 3 suites* ⌕ *In-room: DVD, Wi-Fi. In-hotel: bar, pool, gym, concierge, Wi-Fi* ☴ *AE, D, MC, V* ☽ *Closed late Oct.–early May* ⊗ *BP.*

$$–$$$$ ⊞**Bar Harbor Grand Hotel.** The look and the feeling of this hotel is that of turn-of-the-20th-century—and yet it was recently built, in 1994. In the heart of Bar Harbor, it is a short walk from the waterfront and downtown. Comfortable guest rooms have thoughtful additions such as coffeemakers and refrigerators. Meal plans at another hotel, the Bar Harbor Inn, can be arranged. Nearby, a shuttle service takes you to Acadia National Park. **Pros:** good location for easy walking to restaurants. **Cons:** not right on the water (but close to it). ⊠ *269 Main St.* ☎ *207/288–5226 or 888/766–2529* ⊕ *www.barharborgrand.com* ⮑ *70 rooms* ⌂ *In-room: refrigerator, DVD, Wi-Fi. In-hotel: pool, gym, laundry facilities, public Wi-Fi* ⊟ *AE, DC, MC, V* ⊙ *Closed mid-Nov.– mid-Apr.* �CP.

$$$–$$$$
Fodor's Choice
★
⊞**Bar Harbor Inn & Spa.** Originally established in the late 1800s as a men's social club, this waterfront inn has rooms spread out over three buildings on well-landscaped grounds. Most rooms have gas fireplaces and balconies with great views. Rooms in the Oceanfront Lodge have private decks overlooking the ocean. Many rooms in the main inn have balconies overlooking the harbor. Should you need more room, there are also some two-level suites. A relatively new addition to the inn is a luxury spa, which offers everything from massages and mud wraps to aromatherapy and facials. The inn is a short walk from town, so you're close to all the sights, and a terrific restaurant, the Reading Room, is on-site. **Pros:** one of those resort hotels that truly seems to meet every need, plus it's right at the harbor. **Cons:** not as close to Acadia National Park as some other Bar Harbor properties. ⊠ *Newport Dr.* ☎ *207/288–3351 or 800/248–3351* ⊕ *www.barharborinn.com* ⮑ *138 rooms, 15 suites* ⌂ *In-room: safe, refrigerator, DVD, Wi-Fi. In-hotel: 2 restaurants, pool, gym, Wi-Fi* ⊟ *AE, DC, MC, V* ⊙ *Closed late Nov.–late Mar.* ⟡CP.

$$$–$$$$
★
⊞**Bass Cottage Inn.** This elegant and refreshing inn, dating from 1885 but renovated in 2004, respects its Victorian history—without the stuffy Victorian decor. All rooms have their own character—each was designed by the owner with a family member or friend in mind. Light-color walls, hardwood floors, and gas fireplaces give them a comfortable, contemporary feel. Although the inn has ocean views from only four rooms, it is a short walk from most Bar Harbor attractions. Wine and hors d'oeuvres are served each evening, and a full gourmet breakfast is available in the atrium each morning. You can relax on the sun porch, in the parlor, or in the reading room by the fireplace. The club-style lounge is filled with puzzles and games. Appointments with a licensed massage therapist are available. **Pros:** a full breakfast is served in the morning; wine and hors d'oeuvres in the evening. **Cons:** no restaurant; you will need to drive to dinner. ⊠ *14 The Field* ☎ *207/288–1234 or 866/782–9224* ⊕ *www. basscottage.com* ⮑ *10 rooms* ⌂ *In-room: DVD, Wi-Fi. In-hotel: public Internet, Wi-Fi* ⊟ *AE, MC, V* ⊙ *Closed Nov.–mid-May* ⟡BP.

$$–$$$$ ⊞**Bluenose Inn–Bar Harbor Hotel.** This resort is perched on the top of a hill overlooking Frenchman Bay. Most of the guest rooms have excellent views, and all have gas fireplaces. After touring Acadia National Park you can relax in the hotel's hot tub or steam room, or swim a few laps in the indoor or outdoor pool. Fine dining is provided at the Rose Garden restaurant ($$$$), which features seafood and beef entrées as

part of the three-course prix-fixe and five-course tasting menus. **Pros:** spectacular views of the bay and outer islands; wonderful on-site dining. **Cons:** a bit of a hike to town (you'll probably want to drive). ⊠ *90 Eden St.* ☎ *207/288–3348 or 800/445–4077* ⊕ *www.bluenoseinn.com* ➦ *97 rooms, 1 suite* ⟁ *In-room: safe, refrigerator, DVD, Wi-Fi. In-hotel: 2 restaurants, bar, pools, gym, public Internet, Wi-Fi.* ☐ *AE, D, DC, MC, V* ⊘ *Closed Nov.–late Apr.*

$–$$ ⊡ **Cromwell Harbor Motel.** If you like flowers, you will love this blossom-bedecked motel. Less than a mile from downtown Bar Harbor, this clean and pleasant motel is set amid pretty gardens. From here you can walk to a quiet section of Acadia National Park. **Pros:** clean and modestly priced; a choice of one, two, or three-person bedrooms. **Cons:** most Bar Harbor restaurants will require a drive for dinner. ⊠ *359 Main St.* ☎ *207/288–3201 or 800/544–3201* ⊕ *www.cromwellharbor.com* ➦ *26 rooms* ⟁ *In-room: Wi-Fi, refrigerator (some). In-hotel: pool, public Internet, Wi-Fi* ☐ *AE, D, MC, V.*

$–$$ ⊡ **Eden Village Motel & Cottages.** Children can learn to fish at the pond on
☽ this 25-acre property, 5 mi from downtown Bar Harbor. Although the furnishings are not new, the rooms certainly are comfortable, and most have views of the top of Cadillac Mountain. A back porch that extends the length of the building has picnic tables and grills. Cottages vary in size, but all have working fireplaces, barbecue grills, and screened porches. A mile-long nature trail passes by blueberry bushes and cherry and apple trees. It's a good place for outdoorsy types. One small dog per cabin is allowed; no cats. **Pros:** inexpensive; friendly setting. **Cons:** somewhat rustic and remote; some rooms do not have a/c. ⊠ *986 Rte. 3* ☎ *207/288–4670* ⊕ *www.edenvillage.com* ➦ *10 rooms, 11 cottages* ⟁ *In-room: kitchen (some). In-hotel: Wi-Fi, some pets allowed* ☐ *DC, MC, V* ⊘ *Closed Nov.–Apr.*

$$$$ ⊡ **Harborside Hotel & Marina.** One of Bar Harbor's newest lodgings, this Tudor-style hotel has a prime location next to the harbor. The guest rooms are elegantly decorated in soft yellows and greens; the baths are tiled in marble. Most rooms have balconies, and many have water views. Suites have high-definition televisions and surround-sound stereo; penthouse suites have a full kitchen, dining room, hot tub, and fireplace. A spa is on the premises. The inn's restaurant, the Pier ($$–$$$), is open to the public for lunch and dinner and specializes in fresh seafood, including lobster and jumbo scallops. **Pros:** great views of the harbor and surrounding islands. **Cons:** not every room has great views, somewhat erratic service and cleaning; a sense that the establishment is resting on its laurels (location). ⊠ *55 West St.* ☎ *207/288–5033 or 800/328–5033* ⊕ *www.theharborsidehotel.com* ➦ *168 rooms, 9 suites, 10 studios* ⟁ *In-room: kitchen (some), Wi-Fi. In-hotel: 3 restaurants, tennis court, pools, gym, spa, laundry service* ☐ *AE, DC, MC, V* ℗ *CP.*

¢–$$ ⊡ **Seacroft Inn.** It's an easy walk to Bar Harbor or the shore path from this rambling, gracious inn. The property has seven efficiency units, including one two-bedroom unit that is a good choice for families. A breakfast basket containing homemade muffins, fresh fruit, juice, cereals, yogurt, and coffee is delivered to your room each morning for an extra $5 per person. **Pros:** pretty views of the garden and pool; nice walk to town. **Cons:** no on-site restaurant for dinner. ✉ *18 Albert Meadow* ☎ *207/288–4669 or 800/824–9694* ⊕ *www.seacroftinn.com* ⇆ *6 rooms, 1 2-bedroom unit* ♿ *In-room: refrigerator, Wi-Fi. In-hotel: Wi-Fi* ▭ *MC, V* ⊘ *Closed mid.-Nov.–May* ¶❚ *CP.*

$$$–$$$$

Fodor's Choice

★

▦ **Ullikana.** Inside the stucco-and-timber walls of this traditional Tudor cottage antiques are juxtaposed with contemporary country pieces, vibrant color with French country wallpapers, and abstract art with folk creations. The combination not only works—it shines. Though the property is small, rooms are large with ample windows; many have fireplaces, and some have decks. Breakfast is an elaborate multicourse affair. The popular "A Yellow House" across the drive has six additional rooms decorated in traditional Bar Harbor style. **Pros:** lovely setting; lots of character and charm. **Cons:** only three rooms have water views; some rooms do not have a/c. ✉ *16 The Field* ☎ *207/288–9552* ⊕ *www.ullikana.com* ⇆ *16 rooms* ♿ *In-room: Wi-Fi, no phone, no TV. In-hotel: Wi-Fi* ▭ *MC, V* ⊘ *Closed Nov.–mid-May* ¶❚ *BP.*

$$–$$$

▦ **Wonder View Inn & Suites.** They've got the right name for this place. A lot of vacationers come to Bar Harbor looking for a view, and they've got it here, since the inn is high on a hill overlooking Frenchman Bay. The Wonder View is spread out over 14 acres, so if you like to walk, this is the place. **Pros:** an excellent restaurant, the Rinehart Dining Pavilion, is right on the premises, so you don't have to drive to dinner. **Cons:** for shopping you probably will want to drive to downtown. ✉ *50 Eden St. (Rte. 3)* ☎ *207/288–3358 or 888/439–8439* ⊕ *www.wonderviewinn. com* ⇆ *69 rooms, 3 suites* ♿ *In room: Wi-Fi, refrigerator. In-hotel: restaurant, bar, pool, Wi-Fi, some pets allowed* ▭ *AE, DC, MC, V* ⊘ *Closed Nov.–mid-May.* ¶❚ *CP.*

NIGHTLIFE AND THE ARTS

Although Bar Harbor is known for its beautiful scenery, its wonderful harbor, and its first-class accommodations and restaurants, it is not especially known for its nightlife. Perhaps people are just too tired from their day's activities and boating by then. However, there are some goings-on in town if you look.

The **Bar Harbor Music Festival** (✉ *59 Cottage St.* ☎ *207/288–5744* ⊕ *www. barharbormusicfestival.org*) hosts jazz, classical, opera, and pop concerts by young professionals from July to early August at the Criterion Theater. Recent operas have included *La Bohème, La Traviata,* Bizet's *Carmen,* and Donizetti's L'Elisir d'Amore. The Art Deco–style **Criterion Theater** (✉ *35 Cottage St.* ☎ *207/288–3441* ⊕ *www.criteriontheater. com*) offers movies and stages concerts, plays, and other live performances. **ImprovAcadia** (✉ *15 Cottage St., 2nd fl.* ☎ *207/288–2503* ⊕ *www.improvacadia.com*) is one of the most interesting and entertaining places in town. As the name would imply, it's an improv comedy theater. The **Reel Pizza Cinerama** (✉ *33-B Kennebec Pl.* ☎ *207/288–3811* ⊕ *www.reelpizza.net*) shows first-run movies.

7

If you want to shoot some pool or throw some darts, try the **Carmen Verandah** (✉ *119 Main St.* ☎ *207/288–2766* ⊕ *www.carmenverandah. com*). The upstairs bar has live music and dancing.

For good food, 15 kinds of beer, live entertainment ranging from Manhattan jazz great Bill McHenry to local Hancock County stars Phelan and Ross Gallagher, the **Lompoc Café** (✉ *36 Rodick St.* ☎ *207/288–9392* ⊕ *www.lompoccafe.com*) is the hottest place in town.

SHOPPING

Bar Harbor is a shopper's paradise, but it is not for people who are looking for Wal-Mart–type bargains. Tourism shoppers not only come from the land, they also come from the sea, since some very large steamships, including the *Queen Elizabeth,* have made Mount Desert Island a destination.

GALLERIES

Fodor'sChoice
★

Paint your own pottery or piece together a mosaic at **All Fired Up** (✉ *101 Cottage St.* ☎ *207/288–3130* ⊕ *www.acadiaallfiredup.com*). The gallery also sells glass sculptures, pendants, paintings, and decorative pottery. The **Alone Moose Fine Crafts** (✉ *78 West St.* ☎ *207/288–4229 www.mainefinecrafts.com*) is the oldest made-in-Maine gallery on the island. It offers bronze wildlife sculpture, jewelry, pottery, and watercolors. To take some of the Maine Coast home with you, check out the land- and seascapes at the midtown **Argosy Gallery** (✉ *110 Main St.* ☎ *207/288–9226* ⊕ *www.argosygallery.com*). The **Eclipse Gallery** (✉ *12 Mount Desert St.* ☎ *207/288–9048* ⊕ *www.eclipsegallery.us*) carries handblown glass, ceramics, and wood furniture. **Island Artisans** (✉ *99 Main St.* ☎ *207/288–4214* ⊕ *www.islandartisans.com*) sells basketry, pottery, fiber work, and jewelry created by more than 100 of Maine's artisans. The gallery is co-op owned and operated by the artists. **Native Arts Gallery** (✉ *99 Main St.* ☎ *207/288–4474* ⊕ *www.nativeartsgallery. com*) sells American Indian silver and gold jewelry.

GENERAL

One of the best sporting-goods stores in the state, **Cadillac Mountain Sports** (✉ *28 Cottage St.* ☎ *207/288–4532* ⊕ *www.cadillacmountainsports. com*) has developed a following of locals and visitors alike. You can find top-quality climbing, hiking, and camping equipment. In winter you can rent cross-country skis, ice skates, and snowshoes. For one-hour photo developing, visit **First Exposure** (✉ *156 Main St.* ☎ *207/288–5868*). The shop also stocks camera equipment. **Michael H. Graves Antiques** (✉ *10 Albert Meadow* ☎ *207/288–3830*) specializes in maps and books focusing on Mount Desert Island. **Songs of the Sea** (✉ *47 West St.* ☎ *207/288– 5653* ⊕ *www.songsea.com*) specializes in folk music. It sells handcrafted Irish and Scottish musical instruments.

TREATS

Ben and Bill's Chocolate Emporium (✉ *66 Main St. 04609* ☎ *207/288–3281* ⊕ *www.benandbills.com*) is a chocolate lover's nirvana. It also has more than 20 flavors of ice cream, including lobster and the popular KGB (Kahlua, Grand Marnier, and Bailey's).

SPORTS AND THE OUTDOORS

AIR TOURS

★ There are few places in America as beautiful to see from the air as the Mount Desert Island and Acadia National Park areas. **Scenic Biplane & Glider Rides Over Bar Harbor** (✉ *968 Bar Harbor Rd. [Rte. 3], Trenton* ☎ *207/667–7627* ⊕ *www.acadiaairtours.com*) is a part of Acadia Air Tours and provides exactly what the name suggests: biplane and glider rides over Bar Harbor and Acadia National Park. Tours run from 25 minutes to an hour in length and range in price from $225 to $425 for two people. The sunset tour is $50 extra. Helicopter tours are also available on occasion.

BICYCLING

Acadia Bike Rentals & Coastal Kayaking Tours (✉ *48 Cottage St.* ☎ *207/288– 9605 or 800/526–8615* ⊕ *www.acadianfun.com*) rents mountain bikes good for negotiating the trails in Acadia National Park. The **Bar Harbor Bicycle Shop** (✉ *141 Cottage St.* ☎ *207/288–3886 or 800/824–2453* ⊕ *www.barharborbike.com*) rents bikes by the half or full day. **Caution:** Riding a bike around Bar Harbor is fun, but be careful; the town is full of motorized sightseers and many of the streets are narrow.

BIRDING

Down East Nature Tours (⌂ *150 Knox Rd., Box 521, Bar Harbor 04609* ☎ *207/288–8128* ⊕ *www.downeastnaturetours.com*) leads excursions for individuals and small groups. You can learn the basics of birding, including how to identify species by plumage, calls, and habitat.

BOAT TOURS

ℭ **The CAT.** Surely the best boat excursions out of Bar Harbor must be the rides on "The CAT," North America's fastest international ferry. This is a high-speed (55 mph) catamaran that, in season, jets from Bar Harbor across the Gulf of Maine to Yarmouth, Nova Scotia, and back. You can do it all in one day, or you can take one of the one- or two-night package trips that include tours. The CAT can whisk you to Nova Scotia in a mere 2¾ hours. You can have lunch at a waterside restaurant, do a little shopping, and come back the same day. On board you will find a café for food, a bar for drinks, and a duty-free gift shop. Morning departures are at either 8 or 9, and returns from Yarmouth are at 4 or 5 PM. ✉ *12 Eden St.* ☎ *888/249–7245* ⊕ *www.catferry.com.*

Fodor's Choice ★

ℭ The big 151-foot four-masted schooner **Margaret Todd** (✉ *Bar Harbor Inn Pier* ☎ *207/288–4585* ⊕ *www.downeastwindjammer.com*) operates 1½- to two-hour trips three times a day among the islands of Frenchman's Bay from mid-May to October. The sunset sail is the most popular. The schooner **Rachel B. Jackson** (✉ *848 Eagle Lake Rd., Harborside Hotel & Marina* ☎ *207/288–2216* ⊕ *www.downeastsail.com*) offers two-hour sails and sunset cruises for $30.

★

ℭ If you are curious about what's lurking in the deep, ship out at Starfish Enterprise with Diver Ed and his **Dive-In Theater** (✉ *105 Eden St., College of the Atlantic Pier* ☎ *207/288–3483* ⊕ *www.divered.com*). While Diver Ed is exploring the bottom of the sea with his underwater video

7

FODOR'S FIRST PERSON

Mike Nalepa
Fodor's Writer

When my wife, Sharon, and I visited Acadia National Park, we joined the throngs at most of the typical views—the scenic overlooks along the Park Loop Road, Eagle Lake, and the Cadillac Mountain summit. But none of these vistas was as phenomenal as seeing the park *from* the water. We ventured out with National Park Sea Kayak Tours, and it was one of our trip highlights.

We'd gone kayaking back home in New Jersey a few times, but paddling on the ocean (OK, technically a bay) was a completely different experience. Our little canal back home doesn't have currents, waves, and wind—thus it doesn't provide such an exciting ride. We had the wind at our back for most of the trip, so it always felt like we were moving at a nice clip. At certain points when we caught a wave, it felt like we were surfing.

Despite the rocky conditions on the water, our kayak never felt unstable (they rarely flip—our guide said that he hadn't had a customer go in for a drink all year). The boat's skirts kept us warm and dry as we paddled, and there were ample opportunities for snapping photos along the way (they even provide a waterproof gear bag for your camera during the trip).

The best part of the tour, though, was the scenery. During our four-hour paddle we saw a soaring bald eagle and a swimming seal, and visited two gorgeous islands (one uninhabited, the other inhabited by the Rockefellers). We covered about 6 nautical miles of shimmering, deep-blue water surrounded by craggy coastlines, towering forests, and picture-perfect bays and inlets. And we got a nice workout to boot (full disclosure: we are *not* in very good shape; anyone with a moderate fitness level would be able to handle a trip like this).

camera, you can see what he finds by watching an LCD screen on the boat; also get an up-close look at the creatures he brings back.

CANOEING AND KAYAKING

Coastal Kayaking Tours (✉ *48 Cottage St.* ☎ *207/288–9605 or 800/526–8615* ⊕ *www.acadianfun.com*) conducts tours of the rocky coastline led by registered guides. **National Park Sea Kayak Tours** (✉ *39 Cottage St.* ☎ *207/288–0342 or 800/347–0940* ⊕ *www.acadiakayak.com*) leads guided two-man kayak tours (a half-day costs $48) in search of wildlife on the western side of Mount Desert Island.

GOLF

☙ One of Maine's best courses, the **Kebo Valley Golf Club** (✉ *Eagle Lake Rd.* ☎ *207/288–3000* ⊕ *www.kebovalleyclub.com*) is a classic links-style 18-hole course. Peak-season greens fees are $85. You can play 18 holes of miniature golf for $7.95 at **Pirates Cove Adventure Golf** (✉ *368 Rte. 3* ☎ *207/288–2133* ⊕ *www.piratescove.net*).

ROCK CLIMBING

On an island with steep rock faces, rock climbing is—not surprisingly—a popular outdoor activity. The **Acadia Mountain Guides Climbing School** (⊠ *198 Main St.* ☎ *207/288–8186 or 888/232–9559* ⊕ *www.acadiamountainguides.com*) has private and group instruction for rock and ice climbing. In summer the school sponsors weeklong camps for teens. The **Atlantic Climbing School** (⊠ *24 Cottage St.* ☎ *207/288–2521* ⊕ *www.climbacadia.com*), rated Maine's top climbing school, offers instruction for climbers of all skill levels, and can tailor climbs for families or groups with rock-bottom climber-to-guide ratios.

WHALE-WATCHING

There are two truly unique experiences you can have at Bar Harbor, and both of them are ideal for family outings. One is a trip on the fast CAT boat to Nova Scotia. The other, also at sea, is whale-watching. **Bar Harbor Whale Watch Co.** (⊠ *1 West St.* ☎ *207/288–2386 or 800/942–5374*) ⊕ *www.whalesrus.com*) merged with the Acadian Whale Watcher to make one big company with four boats, one of them a 138-foot jet-propelled catamaran with spacious decks. In season the outfit also offers lobsters and seals cruises, a nature cruise, and puffins cruises. How likely are you to actually see a whale? Very. In fact, the company can practically guarantee it—they apparently have some sort of arrangement with the whales.

ACADIA NATIONAL PARK

4 mi northwest of Bar Harbor.

With more than 30,000 acres of protected forests, beaches, mountains, and rocky coastline, Acadia National Park is the second-most-visited national park in America (the first is Great Smoky Mountains National Park). According to the National Park Service, more than 2.2 million people visit Acadia each year. The park holds some of the most spectacular scenery on the Eastern seaboard: a rugged coastline of surf-pounded granite, and an interior graced by sculpted mountains, quiet ponds, and lush deciduous forests. Cadillac Mountain (named after a Native American, not the car), the highest point of land on the East Coast, dominates the park. Although it's rugged, Acadia National Park also has graceful stone bridges, horse-drawn carriages, and the elegant Jordan Pond House restaurant.

The 27-mi Park Loop Road provides an excellent introduction, but to truly appreciate the park you must get off the main road and experience it by walking, biking, sea kayaking, or taking a carriage ride. If you get off the beaten path, you can find places you can have practically to yourself. Mount Desert Island was once a preserve of summer homes for the very rich (and still is for some), and, because of this, Acadia is the only national park in America that was largely created by donations of private land. A small part of the park is on Isle au Haut, which is out in the ocean and more than 10 mi away.

7

PARK ESSENTIALS

ADMISSION FEE

A user fee is required if you are anywhere in the park. The fee is $20 per vehicle for a seven-consecutive-day pass. Or use your National Park America the Beautiful Pass, which allows entrance to any national park in the United States. See ⊕ *www.nps.gov* for details.

ADMISSION HOURS

The park is open 24 hours a day, year-round, though the roads often are closed in winter because of snow. Operating hours are 8 AM–4:30 PM April 15–October, and until 6 PM in July and August

PARK CONTACT INFORMATION

Acadia National Park (🖂 *Acadia National Park, Box 177, Bar Harbor 04609* ☎ *207/288–3338* ⊕ *www.nps.gov/acad*).

EXPLORING

HISTORIC SITES AND MUSEUMS

Abbe Museum at Sieur de Monts Spring. The original Abbe Museum (a larger one is in Bar Harbor) has exhibits on the history of the Abbe people who once inhabited this area. The museum is on the National Register of Historic Places. 🖂 *26 Mt. Desert St., Sieur de Monts Spring exit from Rte. 3 or Park Loop Rd.* ☎ *207/288–3519* ⊕ *www.abbemuseum. org* 🖾 *$3* ☉ *Memorial Day–mid-Oct., daily 10–4.*

★ **Bass Harbor Head Light.** Built in 1858, this lighthouse is one of the most photographed lights in Maine. Now automated, it marks the entrance to Blue Hill Bay. The grounds and residence are Coast Guard property, but two trails around the facility provide excellent views. ■ TIP➔ **The best place to take a picture of this small but beautiful lighthouse is from the rocks below—but watch your step, they can be slippery.** 🖂 *Rte. 102, halfway between Tremont and Manset Bass Harbor* 🖾 *Free* ☉ *Daily 9–sunset.*

SCENIC DRIVES AND STOPS

★ **Cadillac Mountain.** At 1,532 feet, this is the first place in America to see the sun's rays at break of day. It is the highest mountain on the Eastern seaboard north of Brazil. Dozens of visitors make the trek to see the sunrise or, for those less inclined to get up so early, sunset. From the smooth summit you have an awesome 360-degree view of the jagged coastline that runs around the island. Decades ago a train took visitors to a hotel at the summit. Today a small gift shop and some restrooms are the only structures at the top. The road up the mountain is generally closed from the end of October through March because of snow.

Jordan Pond. The water source for the village of Seal Harbor, Jordan Pond is best seen from the observation deck next to the Jordan Pond House restaurant. Rising above the water are the Bubbles, two mountains of similar size and shape. Maps and other items are available at the information booth beside the restaurant. Many people leave their cars in the overflow parking lots north of the restaurant's parking lot when setting off on biking or hiking trips along the carriage roads that converge here.

☺ ★ **Park Loop Road.** This 27-mi road provides a perfect introduction to the park. You can do it in an hour, but allow at least half a day or more for the drive so that you can explore the many sites along the way. Traveling south on Park Loop Road toward Sand Beach, you'll reach a small ticket booth, where, if you haven't already, you will need to pay the park's good-for-seven-consecutive-days $20 entrance fee (the fee is not charged from November through April). Traffic is one-way from the Route 233 entrance to the Stanley Brook Road entrance south of the Jordan Pond House. The section known as Ocean Drive is open year-round.

TAKE A TOUR

Acadia National Park Tours operates a 2½-hour bus tour of Acadia National Park, narrated by a naturalist, from May to October, and 2½-hour narrated trolley tours. Columbia Air Services, at Hancock County Airport between Ellsworth and Bar Harbor, rents aircraft and flies seven aerial sightseeing routes from spring to fall.

Tour Information Acadia National Park Tours (☎ 207/ 288–3327 ⊕ www.acadiatours. com). **Columbia Air Services** (☎ 207/667–5534 ⊕ www. columbiaairservices.com).

Sand Beach. This small stretch of pink sand is one of the few sandy beaches on the island. A lifeguard is on duty from Memorial Day through Labor Day. Although people do swim here, the water temperature rarely exceeds 55°F. Restrooms and changing facilities are available. You may recognize this beach from the movie *The Cider House Rules*. **Caution:** the water here is *cold*.

Thunder Hole. The ocean "thunders" into this natural seaside cave, spraying water all the way up to the viewing area. This is a popular stop along Park Loop Road, especially on stormy or windy days, though extreme caution is advised here. Although the closest view of this attraction is reached by a stairway, a wheelchair-accessible path provides fairly good views. A parking area and gift shop are across the road. This is best seen at high tide; at low tide, it's not all that impressive. Check the *Bangor Daily News* for tide times.

Valley Cove. A parking area near Fernald Point Road leads to a carriage road accessing scenic Valley Cove. Along Somes Sound, Valley Cove offers hiking trails that lead to Acadia and Flying mountains. ⊠ *Southeastern end of Fernald Point Rd.*

Wild Gardens of Acadia. Adjacent to Sieur de Monts Springs, several gardens display well-labeled plants that are representative of the island's many habitats. ⊠ *Off Rte. 3 or Park Loop Rd. (Sieur de Monts Spring exit), about 1 mi from Bar Harbor* ☎ *207/288–3400* 🖾 *Free.*

VISITOR CENTER

☺ At the Hulls Cove entrance to Acadia National Park, northwest of Bar Harbor on Route 3, the **Hulls Cove Visitor Center,** operated by the National Park Service, is a great spot to get your bearings. A large relief map of Mount Desert Island gives you the lay of the land, and you can watch a free 15-minute video about everything the park has to offer.

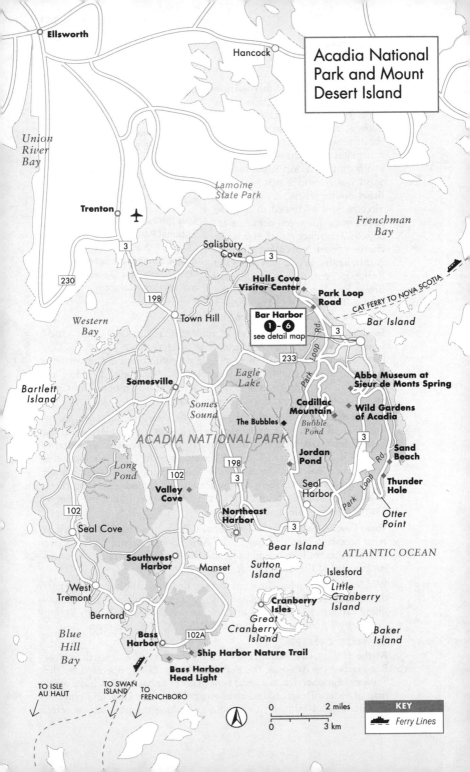

Acadia National Park and Mount Desert Island

Ellsworth

Hancock

Union River Bay

Lamoine State Park

Trenton

230

3

198

Salisbury Cove

3

Frenchman Bay

Hulls Cove Visitor Center

Park Loop Road

CAT FERRY TO NOVA SCOTIA

Bar Island

Western Bay

Town Hill

Bar Harbor
1 - 6
see detail map

233

3

Park Loop Rd.

Bartlett Island

Somesville

Eagle Lake

Abbe Museum at Sieur de Monts Spring

Somes Sound

The Bubbles

Cadillac Mountain

Bubble Pond

Wild Gardens of Acadia

ACADIA NATIONAL PARK

Jordan Pond

3

Long Pond

102

Valley Cove

198

3

Seal Harbor

Sand Beach

Park Loop Rd.

Thunder Hole

102

Seal Cove

Northeast Harbor

3

Otter Point

Bear Island

ATLANTIC OCEAN

Southwest Harbor

Manset

Sutton Island

Islesford

Little Cranberry Island

West Tremont

Cranberry Isles

Great Cranberry Island

Baker Island

Bernard

Blue Hill Bay

Bass Harbor

102A

Ship Harbor Nature Trail

Bass Harbor Head Light

TO ISLE AU HAUT

TO SWAN ISLAND

TO FRENCHBORO

0   2 miles
0   3 km

Carriage Roads

Roads and cars often go hand in hand, but this is not always true in Acadia National Park. Between 1913 and 1940 John D. Rockefeller Jr. designed and funded the construction of more than 40 mi of carriage roads. Rockefeller, a summer resident of Mount Desert Island, wanted to maintain a way for horse-drawn carriages to safely travel the island after the arrival of automobiles.

Today the carriage roads provide hours of enjoyment to walkers, joggers, and bikers. The roads wind through fields and forests, past lakes, ponds, and swamps, and around hills and mountains. You can admire the Canadian mayflowers and young, curled ferns in spring; nibble at blueberries that grow among the granite boulders in summer; collect the fallen crimson leaves of sugar maples in autumn; or enjoy the solitude of the winter landscape on snowshoes or cross-country skis. The network of roads offers excursions of varying length and difficulty, so be sure to pick up a map to plan your best routes.

Pick up guidebooks, maps of hiking trails and carriage roads, schedules for naturalist-led tours, and recordings for drive-it-yourself tours. Don't forget the *Acadia Beaver Log*, the park's free newspaper detailing guided hikes and other ranger-led events. Junior-ranger programs for kids, nature hikes, photography walks, tide-pool explorations, and evening talks are all popular. The visitor center is off Route 3 at Park Loop Road. ⊠ *Park Loop Rd., Hulls Cove* ☎ *207/288–3338* ⊕ *www. nps.gov/acad* ☉ *Mid-June–Aug., daily 8–6; mid-Apr.–mid-June, Sept., and Oct., daily 8–4:30.* The **Acadia National Park Headquarters** is on Route 233 in the park not far from the north end of Eagle Lake. It serves as the park's visitor center during the off-season.

DID YOU KNOW? Fido doesn't have to stay home! Pets are allowed throughout Acadia National Park, but they must be on leashes no longer than six feet.

SPORTS AND THE OUTDOORS

The best way to see Acadia National Park is to get out of your vehicle and explore on foot or by bicycle or boat. There are more than 40 mi of carriage roads that are perfect for walking and biking in the warmer months and cross-country skiing and snowshoeing in winter. There are more than 115 mi for hiking, numerous ponds and lakes for canoeing or kayaking, two beaches for swimming, and steep cliffs for rock climbing.

BICYCLING

The more than 40 mi of carriage roads that crisscross the island are open to bicycles. Originally designed and funded by John D. Rockefeller to facilitate carriage travel after automobiles were introduced, these well-maintained gravel roads provide a range of terrains for bikers of all levels. Even during the busiest months you can find quiet stretches where you can get close-up looks at the native ferns, mosses, and trees.

You may also spot chipmunks, birds, or even deer.

The two most popular places to start your ride are Eagle Lake and Jordan Pond. Eagle Lake has a small parking lot that fills up quickly, so don't be surprised if you have to park on the roadside. The 6-mi carriage road around Eagle Lake is popular with families. It meets up with other carriage roads along the way. Jordan Pond has a larger parking lot and a number of different trails. You may want to bike from Eagle Lake to Jordan Pond, where you can stop for tea and popovers at Jordan Pond House restaurant. Perhaps the most challenging route is the Around the Mountain Trail, an 11-mi loop with an extended climb up the northwest side of Parkman Mountain. Other places to start your ride—with less parking—are the Gate House and Parkman Mountain in Northeast Harbor.

> **BOOK A CARRIAGE RIDE**
>
> If you would like to take a horse-drawn carriage ride down one of these roads, you can do so from mid-June to mid-October by making a reservation with Wildwood Stables (☎ 207/276–3622). Two of their carriages can accommodate two wheelchairs each.

Remember that horses and carriages still use these roads—in fact, you can ride a horse along this road, too (though you must bring your own horse). It is best to yield to horses when they approach and to warn the rider when approaching from behind. Although it is not nearly as peaceful, you can bike along Park Loop Road. You must follow the traffic on the one-way section between the Route 233 entrance and the Stanley Brook Road entrance. If you want to bike the entire loop, ride clockwise. Biking is not allowed on any of the hiking trails.

Although the carriage roads are marked at most intersections, it's a good idea to carry a map. With so many side roads and loops, it is easy to extend or shorten your trip. You can pick up trail maps at the Hulls Cove Visitor Center.

BOATING

Mount Desert Island has numerous lakes and ponds that attract canoers and kayakers. Motorboats are permissible, but Eagle Lake, Jordan Pond, Lower Hadlock Pond, and Upper Hadlock Pond have a 10-horsepower limit. Motorboats are most often seen on the ocean, which gives you a great view of this and neighboring islands. Public launching areas are available at each town pier.

CROSS-COUNTRY SKIING

When the snow falls on Mount Desert Island, the more than 40 mi of carriage roads used for biking and hiking during the rest of the year are transformed into a cross-country skiing paradise. With so few visitors on the island at this time of year, you can ski or snowshoe for miles without seeing anyone else. Be sure to bring a carriage road map with you. Snowshoe tracks are usually to the right of or between the ski trails.

FISHING

Several lakes and ponds throughout Acadia National Park attract anglers. Maine residents 16 and older and non-Maine residents 12 and older must have a license to fish in freshwaters. Fishing licenses can be purchased at town halls and at some stores. Fishing licenses are not required for ocean fishing.

HIKING

Acadia National Park maintains more than 120 mi of hiking paths,

> ### CAUTION
>
> A couple of people a year fall off one of the park's trails or cliffs and are swept out to sea. There is a lot of loose, rocky gravel along the shoreline, and sea rocks can often be slippery—so watch your step. Don't bring a sudden end to your visit by trying to get that "impossible" photo op.

from easy strolls around lakes and ponds to rigorous treks with climbs up rock faces and scrambles along cliffs. Although most hiking trails are on the east side of the island, the west side also has some scenic trails. For those wishing for a long climb, try the trails leading up Cadillac Mountain or Dorr Mountain. Another option is to climb Parkman, Sargeant, and Penobscot mountains. Most of the hiking is done from mid-May to mid-October. Snow falls early in Maine, so from late October to the end of March, cross-country skiing and snowshoeing replace hiking.

■ TIP→ The Hulls Cove Visitor Center and area bookstores have trail guides and maps and will help you match a trail with your interests and abilities. You can park at one end of any trail and use the free shuttle bus to get back to your starting point.

Distances for trails are given for the round-trip hike.

EASY **Cadillac Summit.** The ½–mi trail around the summit is mostly level and offers panoramic views of Bar Harbor, Frenchman Bay, and the outer islands. ⊠ *Cadillac Summit parking lot.*

Carriage Roads. A treasure because of their historical significance and scenic vistas, the park's carriage roads make for an easy walk. There are several to choose from; distances vary. ⊠ *Throughout the park.*

Jordan Pond Nature Trail. This 1-mi trail loops through a forest setting. ⊠ *Jordan Pond parking lot.*

★ **Ocean Patch Trail.** This 3.6-mi, easily accessible trail runs parallel to the Loop Road from Sand Beach to Otter Point. It has some of the best scenery in Maine: the cliffs and boulders of pink granite at the ocean's edge, the twisted branches of the dwarf jack pines, and ocean views that stretch to the horizon. ⊠ *Sand Beach or Otter Point parking area.*

Ship Harbor Nature Trail. Located on the southwestern side of the island, just beyond Seawall, this mostly flat 1.3-mi trail winds through the woods and along the seashore. The nearby Wonderland Trail offers a similar walk. ⊠ *Ship Harbor parking area.*

MODERATE **Bowl Trail.** Beginning 100 feet north of Sand Beach, this 1.4-mi trail goes through forest and includes granite ledges and a pond. ⊠ *Sand Beach parking area.*

Bubble Rock Trail. The 1-mi trail through the forest includes views of Jordan Pond. ⊠ *Bubble Rock parking area.*

Jordan Pond Shore Trail. This 3.3-mi loop follows the water's edge; there are some rocky sections. ⊠ *Jordan Pond parking area.*

DIFFICULT
★ **Acadia Mountain Trail.** This is the king of the trails. The 2½-mi round-trip climb up Acadia Mountain is steep and strenuous—but the payoff is grand: views of Somes Sound and Southwest Harbor. If you want a guided trip, look into the ranger-led hikes for this trail. ⊠ *Acadia Mountain parking area, on Rte. 102.*

Beehive Trail. This 0.8-mi hike is a steep climb from woods to exposed cliffs. ⊠ *100 ft north of Sand Beach parking area.*

> ### ACADIA LEAF PEEPING
>
> The fall foliage in Maine can be spectacular. Because of the moisture, the fall foliage comes later along the coast than it does in the interior of the state. In the interior it's usually the last week of September, whereas along the coast it's usually around the middle of October. The best way to catch the colors along the coast is travel on the Acadia National Park Loop Road. In fall 2007 the National Park Service placed Acadia National Park on its fall foliage list of "The 10 Best Places in the U.S. to Take Photographs." For up-to-date information, go online to *www.mainefoliage.com.*

Cadillac Mountain South Ridge Trail. Only for the experienced hiker, this 7.4-mi trail ascends gradually from a beautiful forest setting to granite. ⊠ *100 ft south of Blackwoods Campground.*

Pemetic Mountain Trail. This 2.2-mi trail packs a punch with its array of terrain: forest, ocean, and lake views. ⊠ *Bubble Pond parking area.*

Precipice Trail. This 1.6-mi, nearly 1,000-foot vertical climb is the most challenging trail and is only for the most experienced and the most physically fit. Watch for peregrine falcons along the way. ⊠ *Schooner Head parking area of the Park Loop Rd.*

HORSEBACK RIDING

Acadia National Park does not have its own horseback riding program, but you can arrange for carriage rides or board your own horse at **Wildwood Stables** (⊠ *Park Loop Rd., Seal Harbor* ☎ *207/276–3622 or 859/356–7139* ⊕ *www.acadia.net/wildwood*). With more than 40 mi of carriage roads, the park is an excellent place to ride your horse at a slow, comfortable pace. The stables, which do not rent horses, are ½ mi south of the Jordan Pond House restaurant.

ROCK CLIMBING

Acadia National Park has plenty of rock faces to challenge both novice and advanced climbers. Otter Cliffs and Champlain Mountain are popular for face climbing, and Gorham Mountain offers good boulder climbing.

SNOWMOBILING

Once the snow falls, most of Park Loop Road closes to cars, and snowmobiles take over. Except for a few well-marked places, snowmobiles are not allowed on the carriage roads. The speed limit for snowmobiles is 35 mph.

SWIMMING

The park has two beaches that are perfect for swimming, Sand Beach and Echo Lake Beach. Sand Beach, along Park Loop Road, has changing rooms, restrooms, and a lifeguard on duty from Memorial Day to Labor Day. The water temperature here rarely reaches above 55°F. Echo Lake Beach, on the western side of the island just north of Southwest Harbor, has much warmer water. There are changing rooms, restrooms, and a lifeguard on duty throughout summer.

WHERE TO EAT AND STAY

Jordan Pond House is the only restaurant in the park, but there are many excellent places around the

> ### THE EARLY BIRD GETS THE SUN
>
> During your visit to Mount Desert, pick a day when you are willing to get up very early, such as 4:30 or 5 AM. Drive with a friend to the top of Cadillac Mountain in Acadia National Park. Stand on the highest rock you can find there and wait for the sun to come up. When it does, have your friend take a photo of you looking at it from behind. Then you can label the photo something like: "The first person in America to see the sun come up on June 1, 2010."

Loop Road to have a picnic, and bathrooms are available (including handicapped accessible) at the Fabbri, Thompson Island, and Seawall picnic areas.

Acadia National Park does not have its own hotel, and there are no cabins or lodges. There are more than 500 campsites within the park. There are no hookups, though some sites can fit RVs. Blackwoods Campground has 16 wheelchair-accessible sites. There are also five primitive sites in the part of the park on Isle au Haut, out to sea 10 mi away. Visitors with RVs do need to be warned, however, that facilities at both of the Acadia National Park campgrounds are deliberately kept minimal. So if you are used to and like a lot of facilities, you may wish to opt for campgrounds outside the park. Both campgrounds within the park are wooded, and both are within a 10-minute walk of the ocean, but neither is located right on the water.

$–$$
AMERICAN
✕**Jordan Pond House.** Oversize popovers with strawberry jam or homemade ice cream are a century-old tradition at this restaurant overlooking Jordan Pond. Dine outside on the tea lawn or the brick patio, or inside an enclosed porch or dining room. The lunch menu emphasizes sandwiches and salads, while the dinner menu includes seafood as well as beef and chicken. With two satellite parking lots, the restaurant makes an ideal base for hiking or biking along the nearby carriage roads. You can also use the adjacent boat launch for canoeing or kayaking on Jordan Pond. The gift shop sells bottled water, juices, and sodas daily from 9 to 9. ✉ *Park Loop Rd. at Jordan Pond* ☎ *207/276-3316* ⊕ *www.jordanpond.com* ▭ *AE, D, MC, V* ☉ *Closed late Oct.–Apr.*

CAMPING
¢
⌂**Blackwoods Campground.** One of only two campgrounds located inside inland Acadia National Park, Blackwoods is open throughout the year (though restrictions apply for winter camping; call ahead for details). Reservations are handled by the National Recreation Reservation Service (☎ *877/444-6777*), not by the park. Reservations for high season (May–Oct.) can be made up to six months in advance. During

the off-season a limited number of campsites are available for primitive camping, and a camping permit must be obtained from the park head-quarters. Rates drop by 50% for the shoulder season (April and November). ⊠ *Rte. 3, 5 mi south of Bar Harbor, Otter Creek* ☎ *207/288–3274 or 800/365–2267* ⊕ *www.nps.gov* ⮐ *35 RV sites; 198 tent sites* ⛺ *no hookups or utilities; bathrooms, water, showers, picnic tables, fire pits, shuttle bus* ▭ *DC, MC, V.*

¢ ⛺ **Seawall Campground.** On the "quiet side" of the island, this camp-ground does not accept reservations but offers space on a first-come, first-served basis, starting at 8 AM. Seawall is open from late May to late September. Walk-in tent sites are $14 per night, while drive-in sites for tents and RVs are $20. ⊠ *Rte. 102A, 4 mi south of Southwest Harbor, Manset* ☎ *207/244–3600* ⮐ *www.nps.gov* ⮐ *42 RV sites; 163 tent sites* ⛺ *no hookups or utilities; bathrooms, showers, fire pits, picnic tables* ▭ *MC, V* ⊘ *Closed late Sept.–late May.*

AROUND MOUNT DESERT ISLAND

While Bar Harbor is the best-known town on Mount Desert Island, there's plenty to see and do around the entire island. Take a scenic drive along Sargent Drive for spectacular views of Somes Sound—the only fjord on the East Coast. Visit the villages of Northeast Harbor, Somesville, and Southwest Harbor, each with its own unique charac-ter. The west side of the island—also known as the "back side" or the "quiet side"—has its own restaurants and accommodations. To get a unique perspective of the island, take a cruise. Away from the crowds and traffic, you'll have plenty of time to discover some of the island's less-obvious charms.

NORTHEAST HARBOR

12 mi south of Bar Harbor via Rtes. 3 and 198 or Rtes. 233 and 198.

The summer community for some of the nation's wealthiest families, Northeast Harbor is a quiet place to stay. The village has one of the best harbors on the coast, and fills with yachts and powerboats during peak season. It's a great place to sign up for a cruise around Somes Sound or to the Cranberry Islands. Other than that, there isn't much to hold your attention for long. There are a handful of restaurants, boutiques, and art galleries on the downtown streets.

EXPLORING

Asticou Azalea Garden. With many varieties of rhododendrons and aza-leas, this Japanese-style garden is spectacular from the end of May to the middle of June. Even when the pink, white, and blue flowers are not in full bloom, you can find plenty to admire. Originally designed by Charles Savage, the gardens contain many plants from landscape gardener Beatrix Farrand's Bar Harbor garden. Both Asticou and Thuya Gardens are now part of the Mount Desert Land and Garden Preserve. ⊠ *15 Peabody Dr. (Rtes. 198 and 3)* ☎ *207/276–3699* ⊕ *www.asticou. com/gardens.html* 🎫 *$2* ⊘ *Daily 7–7.*

A Green Thumb's Legacy

When Beatrix Farrand, one of the country's first well-known female landscape gardeners, was preparing to retire in the 1950s, she offered her own estate to Bar Harbor as a public park. Since she had designed plant-filled retreats for estates everywhere from the College of the Atlantic to the White House, she assumed the town would jump at the chance.

Instead, the town politely declined Farrand's offer, saying that the property taxes for the site would be too high. She decided to dismantle the garden and gave her friends a year to come and collect any plants they desired. Her friend Charles Savage, also a landscape designer, retrieved several of Farrand's rhododendrons and azaleas and used them when he created the Asticou Azalea Garden and Thuya Gardens in Northeast Harbor. Some of her beloved blooms remain in the gardens today.

Thuya Gardens. Hidden atop a hill on Peabody Drive, these gardens are part of what was once the summer home of Boston architect Joseph Henry Curtis. Today the site is a peaceful and elegant spot to take in formal perennial gardens. Designed by Charles Savage and named for the property's majestic white cedars, *Thuja occidentalis,* the garden is filled with colorful blooms throughout summer. Walk the immaculately groomed grass paths or enjoy the view from a well-placed bench. You'll find delphiniums, daylilies, dahlias, heliotrope, snapdragons, and other types of vegetation. If you have time, take a look inside the Curtis home, which has a large collection of books compiled by Savage. To get to the gardens, park in the small lot near the Asticou Inn and climb the foot path across the road. Alternatively, continue down Peabody Drive and make a left on Thuya Drive. ⊠ *Peabody Dr.* ☎ *207/276–5130* ⊕ *www. gardenpreserve.org* ✑ *$2* ☼ *Daily.*

WHERE TO EAT

$$$–$$$$ ✕ **Abel's Lobster Pound.** You can watch the sun set and the cooks steam
SEAFOOD your lobster from the panoramic windows of this restaurant, situated a stone's throw from Somes Sound. If you want a slight variation on the famed crustacean, try the Lobster Newburg. ⊠ *Rte. 198 south of junction with Rte. 233* ☎ *207/276–5827* ⊕ *www.merchantcircle.com* ▱ *MC, V* ☼ *Closed Labor Day–mid-June.*

$–$$ ✕ **Bassa Cocina de Tapeo.** If you like Mediterranean food, particularly
SPANISH those little morsels from Spain known as tapas (appetizers or hors d'oeuvres), this is the place for you. But in fact, the food of 17 countries is offered. Italian, Spanish, and French sausage, *paella marinera* (seafood paella), and lamb tenderloin in a green peppercorn glaze are among the house favorites. ⊠ *3 Old Firehouse La.* ☎ *207/276–0555* ⊕ *www.bassacocina.com* ▱ *MC, V.*

¢–$$ ✕ **Colonel's Delicatessen.** Known around town simply as "The Colonel's,"
AMERICAN this restaurant serves up simple fare for breakfast, lunch, and dinner. In front, the bakery turns out delicious breads, rolls, croissants, turnovers, and muffins, as well as cookies, cakes, Maine's famous whoopie pies, and other sumptuous desserts. Try one of the glazed doughnut twists,

with or without chocolate drizzled over the top. The adjacent deli offers a range of premium meats. At the restaurant in the rear you can eat in the dining room or take your food outside to the deck. The kitchen serves seafood specials as well as burgers and pizza. ✉ *143 Main St.* ☎ *207/276–5147* ▭ *D, MC, V* ⊙ *Closed mid-Oct.–mid-May.*

$–$$$ SEAFOOD ✕ **The Docksider.** As its name suggests, this roll-up-your-sleeves restaurant sits just above the Northeast Harbor Marina. If you're looking for a lobster dinner with a minimum amount of fuss, this is the place. There are also superb hamburgers and other quick bites. Finish off with an ice-cream cone or a milk shake. Eat inside or on the deck, or take it with you. ✉ *14 Sea St.* ☎ *207/276–3965* ▭ *MC, V* ⊙ *Closed mid-Oct.–May.*

WHERE TO STAY

$$–$$$$ **Asticou Inn.** Established in 1883, this grand inn overlooking Northeast Harbor has some of the best views you'll find. The attractively furnished guest rooms have hardwood floors, hand-braided rugs, and brass beds. The restaurant ($$–$$$$) is open to the public for breakfast and dinner, as well as lunch in July and August. You can eat in the dining room or outside on the deck overlooking the harbor. The inn is close to Acadia National Park's hiking trails and carriage roads. **Pros:** stunning views; sense of the turn-of-the-20th-century grace and elegance that brought tycoons here from Manhattan on the overnight Bar Harbor Express until the late 1950s. **Cons:** exterior elegance not always consistent with in-room comfort; sloping floors; threadbare in places; some rooms do not have a/c. ✉ *15 Peabody Dr.* ☎ *207/276–3344 or 800/258–3373* 🌐 *www.asticou.com* *24 rooms, 24 suites* *In-room: no TV (some). In-hotel: restaurant, tennis court, pool, public Internet, Wi-Fi* ▭ *MC, V* ⊙ *Closed mid-Oct.–mid-May* *CP.*

$$–$$$$ **Harbourside Inn.** Built in 1888 by noted architect Fred Savage, this hillside inn sits at the edge of the woods. It's easy to get to Acadia National Park, as trails begin in the backyard. A unique collection of maps hangs in the public rooms, including one of the United States dating back to 1860. Rooms have hardwood floors, Oriental rugs, and flowers plucked from the surrounding gardens. Some 19th-century furnishings add to the period feel. Most bathrooms have marble sinks and wonderful tubs for soaking. Some rooms have real wood-burning fireplaces, and some have small kitchenettes. **Pros:** Old World elegance and furnishings; unpretentious. **Cons:** no credit cards are accepted—just checks, debit cards, or cash. ✉ *Harborside Rd.* ☎ *207/276–3272* 🌐 *www.harboursideinn.com* *11 rooms, 3 suites* *In-room: kitchen (some), no TV, Wi-Fi, no a/c. In-hotel: Wi-Fi* ▭ *No credit cards* ⊙ *Closed mid-Sept.–mid-June* *CP.*

$–$$$ **Kimball Terrace Inn.** Overlooking Northeast Harbor, this lodging offers clean, comfortable accommodations. Many of the guest rooms have views of the marina or the surrounding mountains. A short distance from the center of the village, the inn is close enough to walk to shops and galleries but far enough away to feel a bit secluded. Adjacent to the inn, the Main Sail restaurant serves breakfast, lunch, and dinner. Dine inside or out on the deck. **Pros:** nicely kept; good views of the harbor. **Cons:** not near downtown shopping. ✉ *10 Huntington Rd.*

☎ *207/276–3383 or 800/454–6225* ⊕ *www.kimballterraceinn.com* ⌨ *70 rooms* ♿ *In-room: Wi-Fi. In-hotel: restaurant, bar, pool, public internet, Wi-Fi* ▭ *AE, DC, MC, V.*

$$–$$$$ 🔲 **Northeast Harbor Bed & Breakfast Inn.** (Includes Maison Suisse Inn and the Peregrine Lodge.) A bit removed from the hustle and bustle of Main Street, this inn—at least the Maison Suisse section of it—dates back to the late 1800s. Surrounded by gardens, the main building has sunny common areas where guests congregate. The guest rooms, each individually decorated, are filled with antiques, and some have beautiful silk-screened wallpaper. Many of the rooms have terraces and private porches. Peregrine Lodge has five additional rooms, each with a fireplace. **Pros:** a truly lovely place that will make you feel like you are in a private home in Europe. **Cons:** somewhat remote from local restaurants, requiring a drive to dinner; some rooms do not have a/c. ✉ *144 Main St.* ☎ *207/276–5223 or 800/624–7668* ⊕ *www.maisonsuisse.com* ⌨ *11 rooms, 5 suites* ♿ *In-room: Wi-Fi. In-hotel: public Internet, Wi-Fi* ▭ *AE, MC, V* ☺ *Closed late Nov.–Apr.* ⦿ *BP.*

SHOPPING

You won't find Northeast Harbor's main street lined with T-shirt and souvenir shops. Instead, the town has many upscale stores selling jewelry, clothing, and fine art. A smaller version of the Bar Harbor shop **Island Artisans** (✉ *119 Main St.* ☎ *207/276–4045* ⊕ *www.islandartisans. com*) sells work by area artists, including pottery, tiles, jewelry, and clothing. The **Kimball Shop** (✉ *135 Main St.* ☎ *207/276–3300* ⊕ *www. kimballshop.com*) carries fine china, glassware, and cookware. There are also soaps and candles that make nice gifts. **Pine Bough Antiques and Wikhegan Rare Books** (✉ *117 Main St.* ☎ *207/276–5079*) collects and sells antiques, art, porcelain, and pottery, as well as out-of-print books, postcards, and prints. You can find unique ornaments at **Shaw Jewelry** (✉ *100 Main St.* ☎ *207/276–5000* ⊕ *www.shawjewelry.com*). These pieces are designed by more than 100 nationally recognized artists. **Smart Studio** (✉ *137 Main St.* ☎ *207/276–5152* ⊕ *www.smart-studio. com* ☺ *June–Oct.*) was the first gallery in Northeast Harbor, but soon other galleries followed. Wini Smart and her daughter Gail Cleveland have two floors of showroom space with works by Maine artists.

SPORTS AND THE OUTDOORS

BEACH Only a few miles from Northeast Harbor, **Seal Harbor Beach** (✉ *Rte. 3, Seal Harbor*) gives those daring enough to brave the cold water a chance to swim in the ocean. There's ample parking across the street, where you can also find public restrooms.

BOATING A number of different boat charter companies operate tours out of Northeast Harbor. The desk near the harbormaster's office has information about the different companies. Boat charters and tours usually begin on Memorial Day weekend and run through Columbus Day, but schedules vary depending on the weather. Call ahead if you're visiting at the beginning or the end of the season. **Beal & Bunker Mail Boat Ferry Service (Cranberry Isles)** (✉ *Northeast Harbor 04662* ☎ *207/244–3575* ⊕ *www.cranberryisles.com*) is the easiest way to travel to Little or Great Cranberry Island. The boat departs from the Northeast Harbor marina every two hours during the day, seven days a week, and stops at both islands. The company also has boats available for excursions around the area. Departing from Northeast Harbor or Southwest Harbor, the **Delight** (☞ *Available in summer only* ☎ *207/244–5724*) takes you on tours or transports you to other ports. Specializing in photography charters and picnic charters, **MDI Water Taxi** (☎ *207/244–7312*) can transport you to an outer island or provide private charter services for sightseeing tours. The boat departs from Northeast Harbor or Southwest Harbor. The same company also operates **Downeast Sloop Charters** (☎ *207/266– 5210* ⊕ *www.sailacadia.com*). **The Sea Princess** (✉ *Northeast Harbor* ☎ *207/276–5352*) offers two different nature cruises, a sunset dinner cruise, and a trip around Somes Sound. These naturalist-narrated tours will introduce you to the wildlife you may encounter in the inland waters. The nature cruises include a stop at Little Cranberry Island, where you will have time to visit the Islesford Historical Museum. The sunset cruise stops here for dinner at the Islesford Dock Restaurant.

GOLFING The **Northeast Harbor Golf Club** (✉ *15 Sargeant Dr.* ☎ *207/276–5335* ☉ *Mid-May–mid-Nov.*) has an 18-hole course built in 1895. Peak-season greens fees are $85 to walk and $109 to ride. The club may close to the public during holiday weekends.

EN ROUTE The best way to see Somes Sound—the only fjord on the East Coast of North America—is to take the scenic **Sargeant Drive,** which branches off Route 198. A long stretch of the roadway is edged by granite cliffs on one side and the shore on the other. Along the way you can take in views of Valley Cove and Hall Quarry. In summer you can watch sailboats and large yachts cruising the fjord. In winter the ice masses that form on the cliffs create a spectacular show. The road is a bit narrow and is closed to large vehicles.

SOMESVILLE

7 mi northwest of Northeast Harbor via Rtes. 198 and 102.

Most visitors pass through Somesville on their way to Southwest Harbor, but this well-preserved village, the oldest on the island, is more than a stop along the way. Originally settled by Abraham Somes in 1763, this was once a bustling commercial center with shingle, lumber, and wool mills; a tannery; a varnish factory; and a dye shop. Today Route 102, which passes through the center of town, takes you past a row of white-clapboard houses with black shutters and well-manicured lawns. Designated a historic district in 1975, Somesville has one of the most-photographed spots on the island: a small house with a footbridge that crosses an old millpond. Get out your camera. In spring, summer, or fall, this scene will remind you of a Thomas Kinkade painting. Maybe even in winter, too.

EXPLORING

★ **Seal Cove Auto Museum**. View around 100 immaculately maintained vehicles from the "Brass Era," which ran from the beginning of auto production until about 1915. See gasoline, steam, and electric vehicles and some interesting rarities. Each car has a sign detailing its history. The museum also displays 35 antique motorcycles. ✉ *1414 Tremont*

Rd. Seal Cove ☎ 207/244–9242 ⊕ www.sealcoveautomuseum.org ☞ $5 ⊙ June 1–Oct., daily 10–5.

Somesville Museum. Come here to purchase a booklet detailing a self-guided walking tour of the village. If the island's long history interests you, take a look at the changing exhibits; an activity for children corresponds to the topic. The museum is operated by the Mount Desert Island Historical Society. Outside are two gardens with flowers and herbs. ⊠ *Old School House & Museum, 2 Oak Hill Rd., the intersection of Routes 3 and 198 ☎ 207/276–9323. ⊕ www.mdihistory.org ☞ Donations accepted ⊙ Mid-June–Sept., Tues.–Sat. 1–4.*

NEED A BREAK?

Maintained by Acadia National Park, the **Pretty Marsh Picnic Area** (⊠ *4 mi southwest of Somesville, Rte. 102A, Pretty Marsh ☞ Free ⊙ Daily May–Oct.*) is a secluded spot well suited for a picnic lunch, an afternoon barbecue, or a lobster bake. There are fire pits, picnic tables, and restrooms.

WHERE TO STAY

¢ 🏕 **Mount Desert Campground.** Near the village of Somesville, this campground has one of the best locations imaginable. It lies at the head of Somes Sound, the only fjord on the East Coast of North America. The campground prefers tents, so vehicles longer than 20 feet are not allowed. Many sites are along the waterfront, and all are tucked into the woods for a sense of privacy. Restrooms and showers are placed sensibly throughout the campground and are kept meticulously clean. Canoes and kayaks are available for rent, and there's a dock with access to the ocean. The Gathering Place has baked goods in the morning and ice cream and coffee in the evening. **Pros:** a lovely location for sightseeing. **Cons:** fills up quickly during peak season. ⊠ *516 Sound Dr. ☎ 207/244–3710 ⊕ www.mountdesertcampground.com ⇋ 150 sites ♿ flush toilets, drinking water, showers, fire pits, food service, swimming (ocean) ▭ MC, V ⊙ Closed mid-Sept.–mid-June.*

NIGHTLIFE AND THE ARTS

Across the road from the Somesville Fire Station, the **Acadia Repertory Theatre** (⊠ *Rte. 102 ☎ 207/244–7260 ⊕ www.acadiarep.com*) produces plays for both adults and children throughout summer. This small, informal theater is an excellent place to spend a summer evening.

SPORTS AND THE OUTDOORS

WATER SPORTS At the south end of Echo Lake, **Echo Lake Beach** (⊠ *Rte. 102*) has a sandy beach where many people brave the icy waters. Lifeguards are on duty in summer. Look for the sign just before you reach Southwest Harbor. **Long Pond** (⊠ *Pretty Marsh Rd.*) is the largest body of freshwater on the island. It's a great spot for canoeing, kayaking, and swimming. Several feet from Long Pond, the largest pond on Mount Desert Island, is **National Park Canoe & Kayak Rentals** (⊠ *Pretty Marsh Rd. ☎ 207/244–5854 or 877/378–6907*). You can be in the water in minutes.

SOUTHWEST HARBOR

5 mi south of Somesville via Rte. 102S.

On what is known as the "quiet side" of the island, Southwest Harbor has fewer attractions than other towns. It can still be quite busy in summer, however. This working port is home to well-known boatbuilding companies, a major source of employment in the area. To reach the harbor from Route 102, make a left onto Clark Point Road.

EXPLORING

Mount Desert Oceanarium. Learn about the fishing and sea life of the Gulf of Maine, watch a live-seal program, and feel a creature from the touch tank. ■TIP➔ **The museum closes at 5, but you should get there no later than 4 if you want to see everything.** ⊠ *Clark Point Rd.* ☎ *207/244–7330* ⊕ *www.theoceanarium.com* ✉ *$10* ⊗ *Mid-May–late Oct., Mon.–Sat. 9–5.*

Wendell Gilley Museum. View wildlife art plus bird carvings by Gilley, who gives carving demonstrations and workshops. The carvings are to scale and include the ruffed grouse, upland sandpiper, American goldfinch, Atlantic puffin, and loon. ⊠ *4 Herrick Rd.* ☎ *207/244–7555* ⊕ *www.wendellgilleymuseum.org* ✉ *$5* ⊗ *July and Aug., Tues.–Sun. 10–5; June, Sept., and Oct., Tues.–Sun. 10–4; May, Nov., and Dec., Fri.–Sun. 10–4.*

WHERE TO EAT

$–$$$
SEAFOOD
✕**Beal's Lobster Pier.** You can watch lobstermen hauling in their catch at this working lobster pound. Lobster, clams, and other seafood make up most of the menu. You can eat your meal outside at the picnic tables. If you want to organize your own lobster bake, order the critters to go. ⊠ *182 Clark Point Rd.* ☎ *207/244–7178* ⊕ *www.bealslobster.com* ▭ *AE, MC, V* ⊗ *Closed mid-Oct.–mid-May.*

¢–$$
AMERICAN
✕**Café 2/Eat-A-Pita.** Fresh vegetables are the focus of the menu at this downtown eatery. Offering two kinds of pita bread, a hefty list of crisp veggies, and other fillings, this restaurant is a good bet for lunch. Try a whole-wheat pita stuffed with chickpeas, tomatoes, leaf lettuce, cucumbers, shredded carrots, alfalfa sprouts, green onions, bell peppers, and marinated chicken drizzled with honey-mustard dressing. At night the restaurant turns into Café 2, which features salmon, lamb, and other heartier fare. ⊠ *326 Main St.* ☎ *207/244–4344* ▭ *MC, V* ⊗ *Closed mid-Oct.–May.*

$$$
CONTINENTAL
Fodor's Choice
★
✕**Fiddler's Green.** Perhaps the most difficult part of dining at this harborside restaurant is selecting just one entrée. Chef Derek Wilbur's truly heavenly seafood sampler "Elysian," with smoked salmon, lobster, scallops, roe, seaweed, smoked mussels, and oysters, almost (but not entirely) takes your mind off the pan-seared yellowfin tuna with wasabi-and-tamarind sauce. But the scallops with asparagus, spinach, tomato, pancetta, and grilled polenta are still hard to ignore. Everything here is fresh, including the locally grown organic produce. The desserts—vanilla-bean crème brûlée and Grand Marnier bundt cake—make for hard decisions. Choose a bottle from a wine list that regularly includes 130 selections and has as many as 180 at the height of summer. ⊠ *411 Main St.* ☎ *207/244–9416* ⊕ *www.fiddlersgreenrestaurant.com* ▭ *AE,*

DC, MC, V ⊘ Closed mid-Oct.–late-May, Mon. in July and Aug., and Mon.–Wed. late May–June and Sept.–mid-Oct.

$$$
CONTINENTAL
★
✕**Red Sky.** Whether you're dressed for a night on the town or have just tied your boat up at the pier, you feel comfortable at this downtown restaurant. Start with a salad of locally grown greens topped with chunks of blue cheese, caramelized pears, and balsamic vinaigrette, or the baby lamb chops with a bittersweet-chocolate-and-cider-mint reduction. For an entrée, choose from among delicious dishes like lobster risotto with asparagus and porcini mushrooms, and maple-glazed baby back ribs. The restaurant has more than 110 wines by the bottle and 10 wines by the glass. Save room for the cheese course. ✉ *14 Clark Point Rd.* ☎ *207/244–0476* ⊕ *www.redskyrestaurant.com* ▤ *AE, DC, MC, V ⊘ Closed Mar.*

$$$–$$$$
CONTINENTAL
★
✕**Sips.** What began as a wine bar (hence, sips) has turned into a perfect spot in downtown Southwest Harbor Village for a glass of wine at the bar or a full dinner. Wine tasting by two-ounce sips, five-ounce glasses, or by the bottle is also available in three-wine samplers for comparative purposes. Beef, pasta, risottos, and seafood fill out the menu, with a variety of daily specials chalked up on the specials board. Live entertainment features folk singers and jazz musicians. ✉ *4 Clark Point Rd.* ☎ *207/244–4550* ▤ *DC, MC, V ⊘ Closed Mar.*

$$$
CONTINENTAL
★
✕**XYZ Restaurant.** This hideaway, popular with other area chefs and restaurateurs (always a good sign), is named for the three Mexican towns of Xalapa, Yucatán, and Zacatecas, and serves well-respected Mexican fare. Try the seven-chili chili or the *mole poblano* (chicken thighs with four types of chilies and a hint of Ibarra chocolate), with a margarita or a house wine. All entrées are $24 and come with a salad. Reservations are absolutely essential. ✉ *80 Seawall Rd. (at the end of Bennett Lane)* ☎ *207/244–5221* ⊕ *www.xyzrestaurant.com* ▤ *DC, MC, V ⊘ Closed Columbus Day–Memorial Day. No lunch.*

7

WHERE TO STAY

$$–$$$
🛏**Harbour Cottage Inn.** This elegant yet casual lodging is close to the harbor. Built in 1870 as part of the island's first summer hotel, the inn has tastefully decorated rooms that are named after different kinds of boats. All have private bathrooms, most with steam showers or whirlpool tubs. A carriage house is also available. The nearby oceanfront property, Pier One, has four suites and one cottage rented by the week. **Pros:** good location; easy walk to the harbor. **Cons:** breakfast is early (between 8 and 9 AM); some rooms do not have a/c. ✉ *9 Dirigo Rd.* ☎ *207/244–5738 or 888/843–3022* ⊕ *www.harbourcottageinn.com* ⤶ *8 rooms, 3 suites* ♿ *In-room: Wi-Fi. In-hotel: bar, Wi-Fi* ▤ *MC, V ⊘ Closed Nov.–mid-Apr.* ⫮〇 *BP.*

$$–$$$
🛏**Island House.** This B&B in a peaceful spot on the "quiet side" of the island has two simple and bright rooms in the main house and one suite in the carriage house. The carriage-house suite has a living area and a kitchenette and is perfect for families. Owners Charlie and Ann have exquisite taste and make staying here like a private visit to old friends. Breakfast accompanied by recorded classical music is a perfect start to the day. **Pros:** nice, quiet setting; friendly and helpful owners. **Cons:** no sea views. ✉ *36 Freedman Ridge Rd.* ☎ *207/244–5180*

⊕ *www.islandhousebb.com* ⊋*2 rooms, 1 suite* ⚷ *In-room: Wi-Fi, no phone, kitchen, no TV, no a/c. In-hotel: Wi-Fi, no kids under 5* ⊟ *MC, V* ⎮◎⎮ *BP.*

$$–$$$ ⊡ **Kingsleigh Inn.** It's the details that make the difference at this inn in Southwest Harbor. In your guest room you'll find fresh flowers, a bottle of port, and divine homemade chocolate truffles, and in the bath there are fluffy robes and slippers. Built in 1904, the inn is decorated with period furnishings. Guest rooms have atmospheric additions like ceiling fans. Several rooms have balconies with harbor views. The third-floor suite has hardwood floors, a wood-burning fireplace, and a telescope for stargazing or watching boats travel in and out of the harbor. You can relax by the fireplace in the living room or take in the fresh sea air from the wraparound porch. **Pros:** bend-over-backwards customer service; an excellent four-course gourmet breakfast. **Cons:** most breakfasts don't include meat. ✉ *373 Main St.* ☎ *207/244–5302* ⊕ *www.kingsleighinn. com* ⊋*8 rooms, 1 suite* ⚷ *In-room: Wi-Fi, no phone, no TV, no a/c (some). In-hotel: Wi-Fi* ⊟ *AE, MC, V* ⊘ *Closed Nov.–Apr.* ⎮◎⎮ *BP.*

$$–$$$$ ⊡ **Lindenwood Inn.** If you're looking for something other than Victoriana, try the accommodations at this harborside inn. The sunny rooms are decorated with art from around the world. The penthouse has a deck with an outdoor hot tub. A separate bungalow has a downstairs bedroom, a sleeping loft, and a kitchen. **Pros:** a variety of accommodations. **Cons:** you will probably need to drive to dinner. ✉ *118 Clark Point Rd.* ☎ *207/244–5335 or 800/307–5335* ⊕ *www.lindenwoodinn. com* ⊋*5 rooms, 3 suites, 1 bungalow* ⚷ *In-room: Wi-Fi. In-hotel: pool* ⊟ *MC, V* ⊘ *Closed Jan.–Mar.* ⎮◎⎮ *BP.*

CAMPING   ⚠ **Smuggler's Den Campground.** Whether you're camping in a tent or
    ¢   sleeping in a recreational vehicle, Smuggler's has everything you need. Located in a wooded area, the campground has amenities such as basketball and volleyball courts and a heated pool. There are hot showers, a coin laundry, and a camp store for any last-minute needs. The simple cabins can accommodate up to five people. Campsites are available for any length of time, while cabins are rented by the week. They have 100 sites for RVs and tents. **Pros:** a good array of amenities. **Cons:** sites fill up quickly during peak season. ✉ *Rte. 102* ☎ *207/244–3944 or 877/244–9033* ⊕ *www.smugglersdencampground.com* ⊋*4 cabins, 100 RV and tent sites* ⚷ *Flush toilets, full hookups, drinking water, showers, fire pits, picnic tables, public telephone, general store, play area, swimming (heated pool)* ⊟ *MC, V.*

NIGHTLIFE AND THE ARTS

Sponsored by the Southwest Harbor/Tremont Chamber of Commerce, **Oktoberfest** (☎ *207/244–9264 or 800/423–9264* ⊕ *www.acadiachamber. com/oktoberfest.html*) has become a rite of autumn. Visit with the 23 Maine brewmasters, sample new foods, and enjoy music and entertainment.

SHOPPING

Aylen & Son (✉ *320 Main St.* ☎ *207/244 7369* ⊘ *Mon.–Sat. 9–6*) sells fine jewelry using stones from local, national, and international sources. All pieces are in sterling silver or 18-karat gold. The **Moody Mermaid** (✉ *366 Main St.* ☎ *207/244–3121* ⊘ *Mon.–Sat. 10–6*) sells clothing, sandals, and athletic footwear. You can find a superb selection of wines, olives, and cheeses at **Sawyer's Specialties** (⊠ *353 Main St.* ☎ *207/244–3317* ☽ *Mon.–Sat. 9–6*).

SPORTS AND THE OUTDOORS

Southwest Cycle (⊠ *370 Main St.* ☎ *207/244–5856* ⊕ *www.southwest-cycle.com*) rents bicycles by the day or week.

If you want to hit the links, there's a challenging 9-hole golf course ($35) at the **Causeway Club** (⊠ *10 Fernald Point Rd., Southwest Harbor* ☎ *207/244–7220* ⊕ *www.thecausewayclub.org*).

The **Maine State Sea Kayak Guide Service** (⊠ *254 Main St., Southwest Harbor* ☎ *207/244–9500 or 877/481–9500* ⊕ *www.mainestatekayak.com*) offers half-day sea kayak tours for up to six people. Tours are tailored to suit both beginning and experienced paddlers. If you want to explore on your own, **Mansell Boat & Marine** (⊠ *Rte. 102A, Manset* ☎ *207/244–5625*) rents small powerboats and sailboats. **Manset Yacht Service** (⊠ *113 Shore Rd., Manset* ☎ *207/244–4040*) charters power-boats and sailboats. Specializing in photography tours, **MDI Water Taxi** (⊠ *41 Harbor Dr.* ☎ *207/244–7312*) can transport you to the outer islands. The boat departs from the docks at Southwest Harbor or Northeast Harbor.

Next to the Coast Guard Station, **Vagabond Fishing** (⊠ *72 East Ridge Rd.* ☎ *207/244–5385*), formerly called the Masako Queen Fishing Company, has half-day fishing trips and full-day deep-sea fishing excursions. Each passenger is assigned a lobster trap and can keep any legal lobsters caught in that trap. These trips fill up fast, so reservations are recommended.

BASS HARBOR

4 mi south of Southwest Harbor via Rte. 102 or Rte. 102A.

Bass Harbor is a tiny lobstering village with a relaxed atmosphere and a few accommodations and restaurants. If you're looking to get away from the crowds, consider using this hardworking community as your base. Although Bass Harbor does not draw as many tourists as other villages, the Bass Harbor Head Light in Acadia National Park is one of the region's most popular attractions and is undoubtedly the most-photographed lighthouse in Maine. (The best picture is taken from the rocks below, but be careful: they can be slippery.) From Bass Harbor you can hike on the Ship Harbor Nature Trail or take a ferry to Frenchboro.

GETTING HERE AND AROUND

The **Maine State Ferry Service** (⊠ *114 Grandville Rd.* ☎ *207/244–3254*) operates a ferry, the Captain Henry Lee, carrying both passengers and a maximum of 19 vehicles per voyage, to Swans Island (30 min., $17.50) and Frenchboro (50 min., $11.25).

WHERE TO EAT AND STAY

$–$$$

SEAFOOD

✕ **Seafood Ketch.** You can watch lobster boats in the harbor while you enjoy fresh seafood on the deck or in the dining room at this family-owned restaurant. If you're looking for fried clams or steamed lobster dinners with all the fixings, you can find them here. ⊠ *1 McMullin Ave.* ☎ *207/244–7463* ▤ *DC, MC, V* ☉ *Closed Nov.–Apr.*

¢–$$ ✕ **Thurston's Lobster Pound.** On the peninsula across from Bass Harbor, SEAFOOD Thurston's is easy to spot because of its bright yellow awning. You can buy fresh lobsters to go or sit at outdoor tables. Order everything from a grilled-cheese sandwich to a boiled lobster served with clams or mussels. ⊠ *1 Thurston Rd., at Steamboat Wharf, Bernard* ☎ *207/244–7600* ▤ *MC, V* ☉ *Closed Columbus Day–Memorial Day.*

$$$ ☷ **Bass Harbor Gables.** For all the comforts of home, step into one of the two-level apartments or the cottage at this lodging near the water. The upstairs rooms of both apartments have ocean views. North Gables, the smaller of the two, has a cozy living room, a full kitchen, and two bedrooms. Grand Gables has hardwood floors and a spiral staircase leading to a master bedroom with cathedral ceilings and two other bedrooms. The cottage has a separate living room with a pull-out sofa, a full kitchen, and sliding-glass doors opening out to two decks with views of the water. **Pros:** several different kinds of accommodations can be found here. **Cons:** no credit cards. ⊠ *10 Earl's Way* ☎ *207/244–3699* ⊕ *www.bhgables.com* ➣ *2 apartments, 1 cottage* ₺ *In-room: no phone, DVD, no a/c. In-hotel: some pets allowed* ▤ *No credit cards* ☉ *Closed Nov.–Apr.*

$–$$ ☷ **Bass Harbor Inn.** If you're looking for someplace away from the crowds, consider this lodging near the harbor. Built in 1870, the inn has a relaxed atmosphere. Two of the ground-floor rooms lead out to sunny decks. The third-floor studio has cathedral ceilings, a kitchenette, and views of the ocean. **Pros:** great location; reasonable rates. **Cons:** away from the action. ⊠ *28 Shore Rd.* ☎ *207/244–5157* ⊕ *www.bassharborinn.com* ➣ *6 rooms, 1 studio* ₺ *In-room: no phone, no TV, kitchen (some), no a/c.* ▤ *AE, MC, V* ☉ *Closed Nov.–Apr.* ❢◎❢ *CP.*

SHOPPING

E. L. Higgins (⊠ *270 Main St., Bernard* ☎ *207/244–3983* ⊕ *www.antiquewicker.com*) carries antique wicker, furniture, and glassware.

SPORTS AND THE OUTDOORS

At Little Island Marina, **Island Cruises** (⊠ *Shore Rd.* ☎ *207/244–5785*) offers a lunch cruise to Frenchboro and an afternoon nature cruise through Blue Hill Bay. These popular cruises are scheduled from mid-June to late September.

THE OUTER ISLANDS

If your schedule permits, take the time to visit one or more of the islands off Mount Desert Island. You're likely to see seals and other wildlife, as well as unobstructed views of Mount Desert Island's mountains. Each island has its own unique character, and some offer more amenities than others. Explore on foot or by bicycle.

CRANBERRY ISLES

1–5 mi south of Mount Desert Island via boat.

Off the southeast shore of Mount Desert Island lie the five Cranberry Isles—Great Cranberry, Islesford (also frequently called Little Cranberry), Baker Island, Sutton Island, and Bear Island. Ferry trips to Great Cranberry, Islesford, and Baker Island are a great way to escape the crowds on Mount Desert Island. Consider bringing a bike to Great Cranberry and Islesford. Be sure to look for the beautiful lighthouse on Bear Island, located just before the entrance to Northeast Harbor.

Of the Cranberry Islands, Islesford has the closest thing to a village. You can find a cluster of houses, a church, a market, and a fishermen's co-op near the ferry dock.

EXPLORING

Baker Island. The remotest of the Cranberry Isles, Baker Island looks almost black from a distance because it is covered by a thick spruce forest. The Islesford Ferry from Northeast Harbor conducts a 4½-hour narrated tour, during which you are likely to see ospreys, cormorants, and harbor seals. Because Baker Island has no natural harbor, you ride in a fishing dory to get to shore.

Islesford Historical Museum. Run by Acadia National Park, this museum displays the William Otis Sawtelle Collection, consisting of a fascinating potpourri of ship models, dolls, cradles, grandfather clocks, barrel stays, ship logs, tools, and other artifacts that document the island's history. The museum also exhibits paintings by local artists such as Charles Edward Kinkead, Harold B. Warren, and C. Scott White. ⊠ *Islesford* ☎ *207/244–9224* ⊠ *Free* ☉ *Mid-June–late Sept., daily 10–noon and 12:30–3.*

WHERE TO EAT

$$ ✕**Islesford Dock Restaurant.** You can't ask for a better seaside atmosphere SEAFOOD than at this restaurant. Overlooking the harbor, this ramshackle but comfortable town hub and nerve center has great views of the ocean and Mount Desert Island. You can dine on traditional chowders, shellfish, and seafood fare or opt for the surprisingly ample selection of steaks. An added plus is that most of the vegetables and herbs are grown on the premises. ⊠ *Islesford* ☎ *207/244–7494* ⊟ *DC, MC, V* ☉ *Closed Labor Day–mid-June. No lunch Sun. and Mon.*

SPORTS AND THE OUTDOORS

BOATING Sailing from Northeast Harbor, the **Beal & Bunker Mail Boat Ferry Service** (☎ *207/244–3575*) serves Great Cranberry, Islesford, and Sutton Island. The **Cranberry Cove Boating Company** (☎ *207/244–5882* ⊕ *www. barharborferry.com*) runs from Southwest Harbor to Great Cranberry, Islesford, and Sutton Island. There are six trips daily in peak season.

Explore the Cranberry Isles in two-person kayaks from **Joy of Kayaking** (⊠ *Islesford* ☎ *207/244–4309*). Life jackets, laminated maps, and compasses are provided. Make sure to reserve a day or two ahead.

7

FRENCHBORO

8 mi south of Bass Harbor via boat.

The popular catchphrase "You can't get there from here" applies to the island of Frenchboro. You *can* get to Frenchboro, but only on certain days of the week. The ferry service runs two round-trip voyages to Frenchboro on Friday, and one-way voyages on Wednesday, Thursday, and Sunday. Some charter services also will take you to Frenchboro. A bed-and-breakfast has opened on the island, but Frenchboro is really better for just a day trip. You won't find streets lined with galleries and boutiques here, but if you want to see an authentic fishing community, this is the place.

GETTING HERE AND AROUND

The **Maine State Ferry Service** (✉ *114 Grandville Rd. Bass Harbor* ☎ *207/ 244–3254 or 800/491–4883* ⊕ *www.state.me.us/mdot/opt/ferry/ferry. htm*) operates round-trip passenger ferry service between Frenchboro and Bass Harbor from April to October.

EXPLORING

Frenchboro Historical Society Museum. The best thing here is the gift shop, which sells locally made crafts and a cookbook compiling recipes from island residents. You also can stop here to pick up a map detailing the island's walking trails. ✉ *Frenchboro* ☎ *207/334–2932* ▣ *Free* ⊙ *Memorial Day–Labor Day, daily noon–5.*

Frenchboro Lobster Festival. If you're traveling in the region around the beginning of August, check out this annual festival. A tradition for half a century, the festival is always held the second Saturday of August. Round-trip ferry service is available. ☎ *207/334–2974 or 207/334– 2923* ⊕ *www.frenchboroonline.com*)

WHERE TO EAT

$–$$$ ✕ **Lunt's Dockside Deli.** Popular among visitors to the island, this dockside
SEAFOOD   restaurant serves up lobster rolls, crab rolls, seafood chowder, sandwiches, and salads, along with full lobster dinners and other options including burgers for visitors who have redlined their lobsterometers. ✉ *2 Westside, Frenchboro Dock* ☎ *207/334–2922* ⊙ *Closed Sun. and Oct.–June* ▭ *DC, MC, V.*

Way Down East

WORD OF MOUTH

"Last summer my husband and I visited Campobello [Island] en route to our vacation on Prince Edward Island. We stopped for the night in Lubec, ME, just across the border from Campobello. It really was planned as just an overnight stop, but if I'd known how nice the area was, I might have planned an extra day there."

—Sara

By Mary Ruoff   Slogans such as "The Real Maine" ring truer Way Down East. The raw, mostly undeveloped coast in this remote region is more accessible than it is farther south. Pleasure craft don't crowd out lobster boats and draggers in small harbor towns the way they do in other coastal towns. Even in summer here you're likely to have rocky beaches and shady hiking trails to yourself. The slower pace is as calming as a sea breeze.

One innkeeper relates that visitors who plan to stay a few days often opt for a week after learning more about the region's offerings, which include historic sites, museums on local history, culture, and art, national wildlife refuges, state parks and preserves, and increasingly, conservancy-owned public land. Cutler's Bold Coast, with its dramatic granite headlands, is protected from development. Waters near Eastport have some of the world's highest tides. Lakes perfect for canoeing and kayaking are sprinkled inland. Rivers snake through marshland as they near the many bays. Boulders are strewn on blueberry barrens. Rare plants thrive in coastal bogs and heaths. Dark-purple and pink lupines line the roads in late June.

Despite its beauty, the region remains one of the poorest in the state. Residents often work a series of seasonal jobs, and with their signs beckon you to stop at homestead galleries, roadside stands, and quiet inns.

ORIENTATION AND PLANNING

GETTING ORIENTED

Way Down East covers roughly a fourth of the state's coast, at least as the crow flies. A car is essential for exploring this vast swath of land. You can take a bus from Bangor that stops in towns along U.S. 1 and rent a car in Calais and Machias or just south of the region in Ellsworth. U.S. 1, usually following the coast slightly inland, is the main transportation spine. Towns highlighted are along this highway or nearby on the area's many bays and peninsulas, where cell-phone reception may be spotty at best (Canadian cell towers pick up calls in Lubec, Eastport, and Calais). The inland countryside is sprinkled with lakes and rolling with hills, so consider returning via an inland route.

TOP REASONS TO GO

Hike Cutler's bold coast: The open ocean views are stupendous, but what also makes hiking here so memorable is peering down at coves below the cliffs, or at wild cranberries between the rocks at your feet.

Meet the innkeepers: Some offer rooms with shared baths without apology, others pride themselves on private baths with spa tubs, but all share a passion for the area and will give you pamphlets galore.

Savor chocolate at the end of the road: Way up the Maine Coast in Lubec there are not one but two scrumptious chocolatiers. You pass another on the way to Calais, where it's a short walk across the bridge downtown to the Chocolate Museum in St. Stephen, New Brunswick.

Explore Campobello Island: Roosevelt Campobello International Park is a must-see, but there are other gems on this Canadian island, like the wide sand beach at Herring Cove and the village of Wilson's Beach, where the water views are like unfurling ribbons en route to East Quoddy Head Lighthouse.

Mingle with artisans: Artists selling fine paintings and crafters offering less pricey wares all have stories to tell, about themselves and the region and why they are here.

PLANNING

WHEN TO GO

Reservations are recommended in July and August, although it's usually possible to find last-minute rooms. The exception is during one of the popular summer festivals, when you may find that hotels are booked solid, even in neighboring towns. Temperatures in summer average about 70°F during the day. Nights are cool, so be sure to bring a light jacket. Fog is likely this time of year—and more common than in the south—so come prepared to appreciate its haunting beauty. Many establishments and businesses that rely heavily on tourism are open from Memorial Day weekend through Columbus Day, but lots of the restaurants and some inns and motels are open year-round. Folks trickle in for winter getaways—the scenery never disappoints. Winter-sports outfitters are rare, but may increase with the 2009 opening of the multiuse Down East Sunrise Trail, which is groomed for snowmobiling and cross-country skiing when the snow flies.

GETTING HERE AND AROUND

AIR TRAVEL

Hancock County–Bar Harbor Airport, 13 mi from the town of Hancock, is served by US Airways Express. However, most visitors traveling by air to this region use Maine's two major commercial airports in Bangor and Portland. Bangor International Airport is 99 mi from Calais. Portland International Jetport is 226 mi from Calais. (⇨ *See Transportation in the Travel Smart Maine Coast section at the end of the book.)*

BOAT TRAVEL

East Coast Ferries provides ferry service between Eastport and Deer Island and Deer Island and Campobello from late June to mid-September. Ferries run on Atlantic time, which is one hour ahead of Eastern time. Bar Harbor Ferry provides passenger service between Bar Harbor and Winter Harbor from mid-May to early October.

Ferry Lines Bar Harbor Ferry (☎ 207/288–2984 ⊕ www.barharborferry.com). **East Coast Ferries** (☎ 506/747–2159 ⊕ www.eastcoastferries.nb.ca).

Water Taxis Winter Harbor Water Taxi and Tours. A 22-ft boat taxis up to six passengers across Frenchman Bay between Winter Harbor and Bar Harbor. The taxi departs from Winter Harbor MarineThe service runs from April 15 to November 15. ⊠ 88 Sargent St., Winter Harbor ☎ 207/963–7007 ☎ round-trip, $75.

Marina at the Wharf. From mid-June through September, this marina on Lubec's working waterfront operates a water taxi between here and Eastport. The 12-passenger, 27-foot To & Fro makes up to four scheduled trips daily during the summer. Trips are $8 one-way per person; you can bring your bike or rent one here. The marina also rents kayaks and powerboats and runs lighthouse and whale-watching tours. It is part of a complex that includes a sardine factory-turned-inn-and-seafood shop. ⊠ 69 Johnson St., Lubec ☎ 207/733–4400 ⊕ www.theinnatthewharf.com.

BUS TRAVEL

West's Coastal Connection provides bus service between Calais and Bangor via Ellsworth, stopping at towns en route on U.S. 1.

Information West's Coastal Connection (☎ 207/546–2823 or 800/596–2823 ⊕ www.westbusservice.com).

CAR TRAVEL

U.S. 1 is the primary coastal route in this region, with smaller roads leading to towns along the coast. Route 182 between Franklin and Cherryfield, a pleasant inland route, is a Maine Scenic Byway. The Schoodic National Scenic Byway follows U.S. 1 through Sullivan, then turns south on Route 186 on its way to the Schoodic Peninsula. Route 1A shaves several miles off a coastal trip north of Milbridge but bypasses historic Cherryfield. The most direct route to Lubec is Route 189, but Route 191 between East Machias and West Lubec is a scenic coastal drive through Cutler. Coastal U.S. 1 winds its way to Calais, but the quickest route from Bangor is Route 9 (known as "the Airline" because it's so direct). Route 191 is a scenic route from the Calais area back Down East. From Machias, take Route 192 to Route 9.

NEW DOWN EAST TRAIL

Following an old rail bed inland through the region, the state's 87-mi **Down East Sunrise Trail** (⊕ www.parksandlands.com) is to be fully open by September 2010. About a third of this multi-use trail opened for walkers, runners, cross-country skiers, and riders (bikes, ATVs, equestrians, snowmobiles) in 2009. When completed, the trail will run from near the Hancock border in Ellsworth to Ayers Junction south of Calais in Pembroke. There will be a number of parking areas along the way, including several in Machias and East Machias.

RESTAURANTS

You won't find fast-food chains Way Down East except for a few in Calais and Machias. If you don't have time to stop at a restaurant, you can grab a sandwich or slice of pizza at most convenience stores. Your only choice for a sit-down meal is often one of the many family establishments serving breakfast, lunch, and dinner. All of these places have massive menus heavy on the seafood (it's not all fried), and many have added items like wraps and Cobb salads. Save room for the desserts, often made right on the premises. Upscale dining establishments serving more creative cuisine are scattered throughout the region; Machias has a nice cluster. Don't be surprised if you find that the best restaurant is in the inn where you're staying.

HOTELS

In the villages and along the back roads you can find wonderful bed-and-breakfasts run by innkeepers eager to share Way Down East's laid-back charms. Some are cozy places where you might feel you're staying in a friend's country house, while others are grand homes where the rooms are filled with antiques. Hardly any have air conditioning—with cooling sea breezes you don't need it. Don't write off anything called a cottage; many in this region are lovely. Inns often charge less than you might think; upscale establishments that would command $150 a night or more in Bar Harbor often have rooms for about $100 here. What you won't find Way Down East are chain hotels, though there are some inexpensive roadside motels, most of them in larger towns.

WHAT IT COSTS					
	¢	$	$$	$$$	$$$$
Restaurants	under $7	$7–$10	$11–$17	$18–$25	over $25
Hotels	under $60	$60–$99	$100–$149	$150–$200	over $200

Restaurant prices are for a median main course at dinner, excluding sales tax of 7%. Hotel prices are for two people in a standard double room in high season, excluding service charges and 7% tax.

VISITOR INFORMATION

Many chambers of commerce in the region distribute free copies of the pamphlet *Maine's Washington County: Just Off the Beaten Path*. It is several cuts above the usual tourist promotion booklet.

Contacts DownEast & Acadia Regional Tourism (✉ *Box 4, Cherryfield* ☎ *207/546–3600 or 800/665–3278* ⊕ *www.downeastacadia.com*).

EASTERN HANCOCK COUNTY

As you drive east from Ellsworth, Mount Desert Island rises across Frenchman Bay. Eastern Hancock County attracts people who come to visit Acadia National Park and busy Bar Harbor but want a respite from the crowds. With dramatic seaside scenery, out-of-the-way fishing villages, and artists in droves, lots of folks come just to stay put.

HANCOCK

9 mi north of Ellsworth via U.S. 1.

A small triangular green with a Civil War monument marks the center of Hancock. Not far away are the summer cottages at Hancock Point, where stunning views await, especially at sunset, across Frenchman Bay. You can pick up items for an impromptu picnic in Hancock or across the bridge in Sullivan, where you'll find another town green and more mountain-framed views.

EXPLORING

Willowbrook Garden. Beside their homestead gallery, Paul and Ann Breeden painstakingly created this whimsical, nationally profiled half-acre shade garden. Below tall trees, paths wend past water-lily pools, perennial beds, wild plants, sculptures—even a teahouse and a toy-stocked playhouse. ☒ *19 Willowbrook La., Sullivan* ☎ *207/422–3007* ⊕ *www.willowbrookgarden.com* ☒ *Free* ☉ *May–Oct., daily 9–5.*

Donnell Pond Public Reserved Land. Just a short drive from U.S. 1 in Eastern Hancock County, this 15,384-acre state preserve, which has three large lakes and three good-sized mountains (1,000-plus ft. elevation), is a great spot to hike, canoe, fish, and camp. Schoodic Beach on lake-size Donnell Pond is a popular swimming spot that is dotted with picnic tables. Several trailheads lead from the beach, including the mile trail up Schoodic Mountain, where the coastal views sweep out to Mount Desert Island. ☒ *From U.S. 1 turn off onto Rte. 182 in Hancock or Rte. 183 in Sullivan* ☎ *207/827–1818* ⊕ *www.parksandlands.com* ☒ *Free* ☉ *Daily.*

Frenchman Bay Conservancy Tidal Falls Preserve. One of New England's best-known reversing falls, a phenomenon created when the current "reverses" from the bay to the harbor, is also a great picnic spot (covered pavilion, picnic tables). White water roils from an hour before to an hour after low or high tide, but the falls always put on a good show. Look for educational displays on the exterior of a building that once housed a restaurant (now the conservancy's office). Music concerts are held on Monday evenings, usually starting at 6:30 PM, from mid-July through mid-August. ☒ *71 Tidal Falls Rd.* ✛ *turn on East Side Rd. from U.S. 1* ☎ *207/422–2328* ⊕ *www.frenchmanbay.org* ☒ *Free* ☉ *Daily, dawn to dusk.*

WHERE TO EAT

$$$$ ✕ **Le Domaine Inn & Restaurant.** In the French country–style dining room,
FRENCH opened in 1946, you can order the five-course prix-fixe dinner ($35) or select from a changing menu with dishes like filet mignon with bordelaise sauce, and veal sweetbreads and truffle sauce on microgreens. The poultry is almost always duck or quail. An extensive wine list (French and California vintages) complements the French cuisine, and has earned *Wine Spectator* magazine awards for several years running. The popular Sunday brunch always includes crab cakes. Le Domaine is known primarily for its food, but the deck-fronted guest rooms and suites, with furnishings from Provence, sitting areas, and Egyptian cotton towels and robes, deliver for the price ($$$–$$$$). ☒ *1513 U.S.*

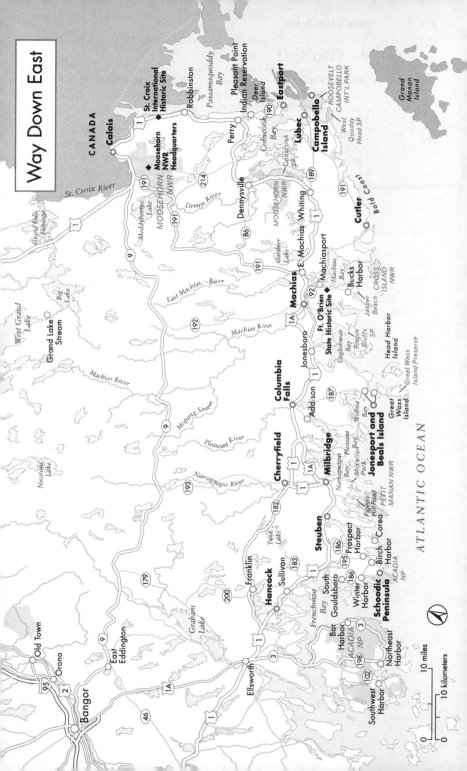

Way Down East

CANADA

St. Croix River

Grand Falls Flowage

Meddybemps Lake

MOOSEHORN NWR

Mooshorn NWR Headquarters

Dennys River

St. Croix International Historic Site

Calais

Robbinston

Passamaquoddy Bay

Pleasant Point Indian Reservation

Perry

Deer Island

Eastport

ROOSEVELT CAMPOBELLO INT'L PARK

Campobello Island

Lubec

West Quoddy Head SP

Cobscook Bay

Cobscook SP

190

189

Denysville

214

86

Whiting

E. Machias

191

Gardner Lake

Machias

1

1A

92

Machiasport

Machias Bay

Bucks Harbor

CROSS ISLAND NWR

Jasper Beach

Cutler

Bold Coast

Grand Manan Island

West Grand Lake

Big Lake

Grand Lake Stream

East Machias River

192

Machias River

Ft. O'Brien State Historic Site

Jonesboro

Englishman Bay

Roque Bluffs SP

Head Harbor Island

Great Wass Island

Great Wass Island Preserve

Nicatous Lake

Machias River

9

Columbia Falls

Addison

187

Jonesport and Beals Island

Wohoa Bay

Pleasant Bay

ATLANTIC OCEAN

Mopang Stream

Pleasant River

Cherryfield

1

1A

Milbridge

Narraguagus Bay

Mistchelle Bay

Pigeon Hill Road

PETIT MANAN NWR

193

Narraguagus River

182

Tunk Lake

Steuben

186

Prospect Harbor

195

Corea

186

Birch Harbor

Schoodic Peninsula

ACADIA NP

Franklin

183

Sullivan

Hancock

1

South Gouldsboro

Winter Harbor

Frenchman Bay

179

200

Graham Lake

Ellsworth

1

3

Bar Harbor

ACADIA NP

Northeast Harbor

198

102

3

Southwest Harbor

Old Town

Orono

95

2

Bangor

9

East Eddington

46

1A

1

0 10 miles

0 10 kilometers

IF YOU LIKE

PUFFIN CRUISES

Set sail from Cutler or Jonesport on a cruise to Machias Seal Island, the state's largest puffin colony. Many people come Way Down East just to visit this treeless, rocky isle 10 mi off the coast, a summer home puffins share with scores of other seabirds, including razorbills, common terns, arctic terns, common murres, black guillemots, and common eiders. With clownish ways and a "stuffed toy" look—white breasts beneath jet-black coats, goggle-like eyes, and blue bands on red-orange beaks—thousands of puffins steal the show. Canada and the United States dispute ownership of the migratory bird sanctuary, but tour operators cooperate with the Canadian Wildlife Service to control access. Weather can prevent boat landings, as there is no pier, but if you go ashore you can walk on boardwalks and grassy paths to closetlike blinds where four people can stand comfortably as puffins court, clatter, and nuzzle.

Bring layers: temperatures in July and August can drop to 50°F.

SEA KAYAKING

Since much of the coastline of Way Down East remains undeveloped, it's no surprise that paddlers—novice and experienced—love it here. The glacier-carved topography makes this a top kayaking destination. Many fjordlike bays offer stunning scenery on both sides of the boat. Islands near the mainland entice paddlers to explore. Pink granite ledges are common in the southern half of the region. North of Jonesport the coast changes, and these smooth rocks are replaced with jagged shorelines. Here in Machias Bay you can see where American Indians left their mark on the landscape: this region is home to what some consider the most significant petroglyph sites on the East Coast. Two are easy to reach by sea kayak. Paddle out to see carvings of a caribou, a walrus, and humans adorned with antlered headdresses.

1 ☎ 207/422–3395 or 800/554–8498 ⊕ www.ledomaine.com ☱ AE, D, MC, V ☉ Closed late Oct.–May. Restaurant closed Mon. No lunch Tues.–Sat. ⧖ CP.

$$ ✗ **Ruth & Wimpy's.** Identifiable by the giant statue of "Wilbur the Lob-
SEAFOOD ster" and a red 1947 Pontiac, this is a popular stop for families. Eat
⧖ in the large dining room or outside beside a wood-fired cooker where lobsters, clams, and mussels are steamed. The menu includes more than 25 lobster dishes, including fried lobster, lobster Newburg, and lobster with haddock. You can order sandwiches and fish or chicken baskets at dinner. ✉ 792 U.S. 1 ☎ 207/422–3723 ⊕ www.ruthandwimpys.com ☱ D, MC, V ☉ Closed Sun. and mid-Dec.–Mar.

WHERE TO STAY

$$–$$$ ⬚ **Crocker House Inn.** Set amid towering fir trees, this shingle-style lodg-
★ ing was built in 1884. The inn holds comfortable rooms decorated with authentic antiques and country-style furnishings. The accommodations in the carriage house, where there is a den for all inn guests, are perfect for families. The inn's restaurant ($$$–$$$$) draws diners from Bangor and beyond with dressed-up versions of traditional New England

fare, like scallops sautéed in white wine and topped with garlic, lemon, mushrooms, scallions, and tomatoes. **Pros:** only lodging on exclusive Hancock Point; hot tub off den. **Cons:** no water views; no elevator to third-floor rooms; some rooms do not have a/c. ✉ *967 Point Rd.* ☎ *207/422–6806 or 877/715–6017* ⊕ *www.crockerhouse.com* ➟ *11 rooms* ♿ *In-room: no TV, Wi-Fi. In-hotel: restaurant, bicycles, public Wi-Fi, some pets allowed* ▤ *AE, D, MC, V* ☽ *Closed Jan.–Mar., early–mid-Nov., and Mon.–Thurs. Apr. and late Nov.–Dec. No lunch.* ⏽ *BP.*

$$–$$$ ⊡ **Island View Inn.** Built in the late 1880s as a summer "cottage" for wealthy owners, this spacious shingled house is filled with original furnishings. Steps lead from the manicured lawn to a private beach, where the views extend directly across Frenchman Bay to Mount Desert Island. Padded rocking chairs line the wraparound porch. All rooms have water views and open onto shared porches. The massive living room has an antique game table and built-in seats beside a fieldstone fireplace with an exposed chimney rising through an atrium-like space. **Pros:** large rooms; wide lawn. **Cons:** one porch looks up at U.S. 1; no Wi-Fi. ✉ *12 Miramar Ave., Sullivan* ☎ *207/422–3031* ⊕ *www.maineus.com/ islandview* ➟ *4 rooms* ♿ *In-room: no phone, no TV, no a/c. In-hotel: beachfront, water sports, some pets allowed,* ▤ *D, MC, V* ☽ *Closed mid-Oct.–May* ⏽ *BP.*

$$ ⊡ **Three Pines Bed & Breakfast.** The owners' impeccable saltbox on Sul-
☾ livan Harbor is connected to a two-story guesthouse by a covered walkway. You can enjoy the lacto-ovo vegetarian (eggs and dairy, but no meat) breakfast on the screened porch, in the dining room, or in your room. The meal often includes eggs, maple syrup, and fruit taken from the small organic farm. A path along the shore looks toward Cadillac Mountain, while trails traverse the mostly wooded 40 acres. **Pros:** kids love the farm animals; certified "green" lodging. **Cons:** no Wi-Fi; Pay-Pal must be used when paying with a credit card (guests can use inn's computer and also its PayPal account to do so). ✉ *274 East Side Rd.* ☎ *207/460–7595* ⊕ *www.threepinesbandb.com* ➟ *2 rooms* ♿ *In-room: no phone, DVD (some), no TV, no a/c. In-hotel: water sports, bicycles, some pets allowed* ▤ *AE, D, MC, V* ⏽ *BP.*

NIGHTLIFE AND THE ARTS

At Ray Murphy's **Chainsaw Sawyer Art Stage Show** (✉ *734 U.S. 1* ☎ *207/ 565–3377* ⊕ *www.chainsawentertainer.com* ✉ *$10* ☽ *Mid-June–early Oct., daily at 7* PM), the nationally profiled sawyer creates 15 works in five minutes and saws numbers on a toothpick. Shows are in a large building with bleachers next to his "Wild Mountain Man" Art Gallery (⇨ *see Shopping*).

SHOPPING

FOOD The **Sullivan Harbor Farm Smokehouse** (✉ *1545 U.S. 1* ☎ *207/422–2209 or 800/422–4014* ⊕ *www.sullivanharborfarm.com*) cold-smokes salmon and other seafood in the traditional Scottish manner. Watch workers through the inside window in the shop, where you can buy wood tips and pans for smoke-flavored grilling, as well as purchase bagels, crackers, and sauces to complement the seafood.

GALLERIES   Acclaimed regional artist Philip Barter's boldly hued paintings of Down East scenes dominate at **Barter Family Gallery** (⊠ *318 S. Bay Rd., off U.S. 1 in Sullivan, Franklin* ☎ *207/422–3190* ⊕ *www.barterfamilygallery* ⊙ *June 15–Oct. 15*). This playful gallery near Sullivan also showcases sculpture, woolen rugs, and other art by talented family members. It's worth the trip down the long dirt drive to **Gull Rock Pottery** (⊠ *103 Gull Rock Rd., off East Side Rd.* ☎ *207/422–3990* ⊕ *www.gullrockpottery.com*), which sells pretty hand-painted dishware depicting local wildlife, flowers, and water scenes.

Heron-patterned dinnerware is one of the specialties at **Hog Bay Pottery** (⊠ *245 Hog Bay Rd., Franklin* ☎ *207/565–2282* ⊕ *www.hogbay.com* ⊙ *May–Oct.*), which also sells handwoven wool rugs with geometric designs. The potter fires his wood-burning kiln three times a year; his wife makes the rugs. Walkways connect Japanese-style pavilions at **Lunaform** (⊠ *66 Cedar La., Sullivan* ☎ *207/422–0923* ⊕ *www.lunaform.com*), which makes large, hand-turned concrete urns and planters for gardens and homes. Human figures fuse with animals and the natural world in Russell Wray's sculpture, etchings, and engravings, sold at **Raven Tree Gallery** (⊠ *536 Point Rd.* ☎ *207/422–8273* ⊕ *www.raventreegallery.com* ⊙ *June–Oct.*), which also carries the artist's jewelry and his wife's pottery. Some of the sculpture (bronze, wood, terracotta) is displayed in the welcoming gardens.

★   Ann and Paul Breeden's **Spring Woods Gallery** (⊠ *19 Willowbrook La., Sullivan* ☎ *207/422–3007* ⊕ *www.springwoodsgallery.com* ⊙ *May–Oct.*), nestled between their home and a large shade garden for visitors, is illuminated by a tall arched window. Local farm animals appear often in her colorful, playful oil paintings. His strikingly realistic acrylic paintings capture the intensity of the Maine Coast. Eagles and bears sawed from pine-tree trunks tower along the roadside at **"Wild Mountain Man" Art Gallery** (⊠ *742 U.S. 1* ☎ *207/565–3377* ⊕ *www.thewildmountainman.com*), where "chainsaw sawyer artist" Ray Murphy's folk art also includes smaller figures and wall plaques.

SPORTS AND THE OUTDOORS

You can paddle on open water in Frenchman Bay or follow the shores of Taunton Bay on kayak excursions with **Hancock Point Kayak Tours** (⊠ *58 Point Rd.* ☎ *207/422–6854* ⊕ *www.hancockpointkayak.com*). The company also arranges overnight kayaking and backpacking, cross-country skiing, and snowshoeing trips.

EN ROUTE   Heading north on U.S. 1, the **Schoodic National Scenic Byway** starts at the Hancock-Sullivan bridge. Panel displays located at a rest area here and at spots along the way, detail the region's history, culture, and natural resources. The byway turns south on Route 186 en route to the Schoodic section of Acadia National Park, but you don't have to wait until then for awesome views of Cadillac Mountain across Frenchman Bay. One of the best is 1½ mi north of the bridge. On the **Blackwoods Byway** along State Route 182, overhanging trees create a tunnel of color come fall. From U.S. 1, take Route 182 to Franklin, a quaint town where the 13-mi scenic drive begins. If there's time, stop along the way to enjoy a dip at Tunk Lake or Donnell Pond (easy mile walk to beach), or hike Schoodic Mountain and neighboring peaks, all part of the 15,384-acre Donnell Pond Public Reserved Land. Tunk Lake is about 6 mi from Franklin. The state byway ends in Cherryfield, where you can return to U.S. 1.

SCHOODIC PENINSULA

16 mi southeast of Hancock via U.S. 1 and Rte. 186, 25 mi east of Ellsworth.

The landscape of Schoodic Peninsula makes it easy to understand why the overflow from Bar Harbor's wealthy summer population settled in Winter Harbor. The craggy coastline, the towering evergreens, and views over Frenchman Bay are breathtaking year-round. A drive through the well-to-do summer community of Grindstone Neck shows what Bar Harbor might have been like before so many mansions there were destroyed in the Great Fire of 1947. Artists and artisans have opened galleries in and around Winter Harbor. Anchored at the foot of the peninsula, Winter Harbor was once part of Gouldsboro, which wraps around it.

ESSENTIALS

Visitor Information Schoodic Area Chamber of Commerce (🖂 *Box 381, Winter Harbor 04693* ⊕ *www.acadia-schoodic.org*).

EXPLORING

Coastal Villages. Within Gouldsboro on the Schoodic Peninsula are several small coastal villages. You drive through **Wonsqueak** and **Birch Harbor** after leaving the Schoodic section of Acadia National Park. Near Birch Harbor you can find **Prospect Harbor,** a small fishing village nearly untouched by tourism. There's also **Corea,** where there's little to do besides watch the fishermen at work, wander along stone beaches, or gaze out to sea—and that's what makes it so special.

Fodor's Choice **Acadia National Park.** The only section of Maine's national park that sits
★ on the mainland is at the southern side of the Schoodic Peninsula in the town of Winter Harbor. The park has a scenic 6-mi one-way loop that edges along the coast and yields views of Grindstone Neck, Winter Harbor, Winter Harbor Lighthouse, and, across the water, the park's Cadillac Mountain. At the tip of the point, huge slabs of pink granite lie jumbled along the shore, thrashed unmercifully by the crashing surf (stay away from water's edge), and jack pines cling to life amid the rocks. Fraser Point at the beginning of the loop is an ideal place for a picnic. Work off lunch with a hike up Schoodic Head for the panoramic views up and down the coast. A free bus called the Island Explorer (☎ *207/288–4573* ⊕ *www.exploreacadia.com*) takes passengers from Prospect Harbor, Birch Harbor, and Winter Harbor and drops them off anywhere in the park. In Winter Harbor you can get off at the ferry to Bar Harbor. The $20 per car park admission fee is generally not charged when you're just visiting Schoodic. *For more on Acadia National Park, ⇨ see Chapter 7. 🖂 Moore Road, turn off Rte. 186, Winter Harbor* ☎ *207/288–3338* ⊕ *www.nps.gov/acad* 🎫 *$20 per car* ☉ *Year-round, 24/7.*

WHERE TO EAT

$–$$$ ✕ **Chase's Restaurant.** The orange booths may remind you of a fast-food
SEAFOOD joint, but this family restaurant has a reputation for serving good, basic
fare. In this region that means a lot of fish. There are large and small
fried seafood dinners and several more expensive seafood platters. Try
the sweet-potato fries as a side. Lunch fare, sold all day, includes wraps
and burgers. It's also open for breakfast. ⊠ *193 Main St. (Rte. 186),
Winter Harbor* ☎ *207/963–7171* ⊟ *AE, D, MC, V.*

$–$$ ✕ **J. M. Gerrish Provisions.** The store that opened here in the early 1900s
CAFÉ was the place where locals and visitors alike went for ice cream. The
name remains, as well as part of the old marble counter, but today it is
a deli and café where folks bustle in for light meals or linger over coffee at tables inside and on the porch. A simple menu has soups, salads,
and savory sandwiches, such as turkey and cheddar topped with cranberry relish. The deli case offers salads, from potato to Mediterranean
octopus, and dishes such as baby back ribs. Baked goods crowd the
counter, ice cream is still sold, and you can buy wine and beer to go.
⊠ *352 Main St., Winter Harbor* ☎ *207/963-6100* ⊟ *MC, V* ☻ *Closed
mid-Oct.–mid-May.*

WHERE TO STAY

$$–$$$ ⬚ **Black Duck Inn.** The comfortable common areas and guest rooms at
this B&B are tastefully furnished with antiques, including the owner's
toy collection. The walls are decorated with works by nationally known
artists and artists who've stayed here. A beach-stone fireplace is the
focal point of the cozy den. The first-floor guest room has a separate
entrance and a private deck. Two tiny cottages are perched on the harbor. Salt marshes and a small bay are accessed by trails on the inn's 12
acres. **Pros:** spacious common areas; rent two rooms at special rate.
Cons: B&B sits back from the water. ⊠ *36 Crowley Island Rd., off
Rte. 195, Corea* ☎ *207/963–2689* ⊕ *www.blackduck.com* ⇗ *2 rooms,
1 suite, 2 cottages* ⬙ *In-room: no phone, no TV (some), Wi-Fi (some),
no a/c. In-hotel: Wi-Fi, no kids between 2 and 7* ⊟ *D, MC, V* ☻ *Closed
mid-Oct.–mid-May* ⦿ *BP.*

$–$$ ⬚ **Bluff House Inn.** Combining the service of a hotel with the ambience
☻ of a cozy lodge, this modern two-story inn on a secluded hillside has
★ expansive views of Frenchman Bay. You can see the bay's granite shores
from the inn's partially screened wraparound porches. There's a picnic
area with grill (a lobster pot is available for those who want to boil their
own dinner). A stone fireplace warms one of the knotty-pine lounge
areas. The individually decorated guest rooms have furnishings from
around the state. **Pros:** close to things but secluded; apartment has two
bedrooms; Cranberry room has sleeper sofa. **Cons:** path to water a bit
steep. ⊠ *57 Bluff House Rd., off Rte. 186, Gouldsboro* ☎ *207/963–
7805* ⊕ *www.bluffinn.com* ⇗ *8 rooms, 1 apartment* ⬙ *In-room: no TV
(some), kitchen (some), DVD (some), Wi-Fi, no a/c. In-hotel: Wi-Fi,
some pets allowed* ⊟ *MC, V* ⦿ *CP.*

$$–$$$ ⬚ **Oceanside Meadows Inn.** This place is a must for nature lovers. Trail
☻ maps guide you through a 200-acre preserve dotted with woods,
Fodor'sChoice streams, salt marshes, and ponds. Inspired by the moose, eagles, and
★ other wildlife that thrive here, the innkeepers created the Oceanside

GREAT ITINERARIES

IF YOU HAVE 3 DAYS

Head to the **Schoodic Peninsula,** where you can explore the tide pools on the surf-beaten ledges of Acadia National Park. Then amble about the downtown area of tranquil Winter Harbor—bustling Bar Harbor across the bay seems a world away. There are more shops to discover all around Schoodic Peninsula, where many artists have galleries beside their homes. Spend the night at a small inn in Gouldsboro, Corea, or Prospect Harbor. On Day 2, travel north to **Milbridge,** where you can enjoy the Milbridge Histori-cal Museum, with displays on weir fishing and the town's shipbuilding heyday. In **Cherryfield,** follow the Narraguagus River while checking out the impressive Victorian homes. Next, tour historic Ruggles House in **Columbia Falls.** Continuing north, take the road to **Jonesport.** When you arrive, cross the bridge to **Beals Island** for a late-afternoon hike at the Great Wass Island Preserve. Spend the night in Jonesport or nearby in **Machias.** The next day, take a morning puffin cruise from Jonesport, then, in the afternoon visit the historic Burnham Tavern

Museum in downtown Machias and Ft. O'Brien State Historic Site in Machiasport. Before dining in Machias or East Machias, relax or stretch your legs—each town has a small riverside park.

IF YOU HAVE 5 DAYS

Follow the three-day itinerary and on Day 4, drive to **Lubec** and cross the bridge to New Brunswick's **Campo-bello Island.** (Bring your passport or passport card.) Tour the Roosevelt Cottage at Roosevelt Campobello International Park and, if tides allow, walk out to East Quoddy Head Light-house. Then head to West Quoddy Head Light in Lubec to hike along the shore. Stay overnight in Lubec or on Campobello Island. On Day 5, visit downtown Lubec, checking out galleries and chocolate shops and taking a tour of the Historic McCurdy Smokehouse. Then head to Eastport for more galleries and water views and a visit to the Tides Institute & Museum of Art. Or, if returning south on U.S. 1, visit the handful of gal-leries in and near Machias or travel down to Roque Bluffs State Park for a hike or swim.

8

Meadows *Inn*stitute for the Arts & Sciences, which holds lectures, musical performances, art exhibits, and other events in the restored barn. Furnished with antiques, country pieces, and family treasures, and scented with flowers from the extensive gardens, the inn has sunny, inviting living rooms with fireplaces and a separate guest kitchen. Guest rooms are spread between two white clapboard buildings fronting a private beach flanked by granite ledges. Breakfast is an extravagant mul-ticourse affair that includes chilled fruit soup. **Pros:** one of the region's few sand beaches; many spacious rooms; packages include lobster din-ner, boat tour, etc. **Cons:** need to cross road to beach. ⊠ *202 Corea Rd. (Rte. 195), Prospect Harbor* ☎ *207/963–5557* ⊕ *www.oceaninn. com* ⇱ *13 rooms, 2 suites* ⬧ *In-room: no TV, Wi-Fi, no a/c. In-hotel: beachfront, laundry services, public Wi-Fi, some pets allowed* ⊟ *AE, D, DC, MC, V* ☉ *Closed Nov.–Apr.* ⊖| *BP.*

NIGHTLIFE AND THE ARTS

CONCERTS   Schoodic Arts for All presents local musicians at the 1904 **Hammond Hall** (✉ *427 Main St.* ☎ *207/963–2569* ⊕ *www.schoodicartsforall.org*). Classical and jazz music is featured during the Hammond Hall Renaissance Concert Series, held the second Friday of the month from May to October. Local musicians take the stage for Last Friday Coffee House on the last Friday of the month throughout the year.

FESTIVALS   Afternoon and evening musical, poetry, puppet, magic, dance, and the-
AND EVENTS   ater performances, and talks by authors and artists, are part of the **Schoodic Arts Festival** (☎ *207/963–2569* ⊕ *www.schoodicartsforall.org*), which takes place at venues throughout the peninsula for two weeks in late July and early August. Sculptors from around the world bring their drills and blades to the biennial **Schoodic International Sculpture Symposium** (⊕ *www.schoodicsculpture.org*). This free event is held from late July through early September outdoors at the Schoodic Education and Research Center in the Schoodic section of Acadia National Park off Route 186 in Winter Harbor. Watch and listen—it's noisy!—as large public sculptures are made from Maine granite for area communities. A driving tour (available online, or pick up a pamphlet at Maine Visitor Information Centers and area businesses and lodgings) leads to area towns with public sculptures created at previous symposiums, including Cleat, which rises from the water in Winter Harbor. Free concerts and lectures on topics such as Maine's lobster fishery and the Ice Age's impact on the region are held at **Oceanside Meadows Innstitute for the Arts & Sciences** (✉ *202 Corea Rd. [Rte. 195], Prospect Harbor* ☎ *207/963–5557*) from late June through September. Lobster boats from up and down the Maine Coast race in the **Winter Harbor Lobster Festival** (⊕ *www.acadia-schoodic.org*) on the second Saturday of August. The free event also includes a parade, an arts-and-crafts fair, a pancake breakfast, and a lobster dinner that draws hundreds.

SHOPPING

ANTIQUES   Hand-cast bronze doorbells and wind bells are among the items sold
& MORE   at **U.S. Bells** (✉ *56 W. Bay Rd. [Rte. 186], Prospect Harbor* ☎ *207/963–7184* ⊕ *www.usbells.com* ☉ *June–Dec.*). You can also buy finely crafted quilts, wood-fired pottery, and wood and bronze outdoor furniture, all made by family members of the foundry owner. Tours of the foundry are given frequently. Children appear in many of the watercolor, pastel, and Asian ink paintings of Down East landscapes by Wendilee Heath O'Brien, the friendly artist-owner of **whopaints** (✉ *316 Main St., Winter Harbor* ☎ *207/963–2076* ⊕ *www.whopaints.com*); the artist's studio-gallery is beside her home. You're welcome to listen in if she's teaching a class. In three buildings fronted by gardens, **Winter Harbor Antiques & Works of Hand** (✉ *424–426 Main St., Winter Harbor* ☎ *207/963–7900 or 207/963–2547* ☉ *June–Columbus Day*) stocks antiques and local arts and crafts, from wool scarves to paintings to stained glass. Author-signed Maine books and antique linens are a specialty. Step back in time at **Winter Harbor 5 & 10** (✉ *349 Main St., Winter Harbor* ☎ *207/963–7927* ⊕ *www.winterharbor5and10.com*), a tried-and-true dime store with a big selection of local T-shirts and sweatshirts.

ART GALLERIES The owner's colorful hooked rugs with animal and nature themes and handcrafted jewelry by area artisans are sold in an old school at **Chapter Two** (✉ *611 Corea Rd. [Rte. 195], Corea* ☎ *207/963–7269*) ⊕ *www. chaptertwocorea.com*). You can enjoy a cup of tea, and you might catch a hooking group or class in action. Art of the Schoodic Peninsula is sold in the Spurling House Gallery next door as well as the old school, which also carries books by area authors. The garage is stocked with used books. Window glass is fused in a kiln at **Lee Fusion Art Glass Studio** (✉ *679 S. Gouldsboro Rd. [Rte. 186], Gouldsboro* ☎ *207/963–7280* ⊕ *www. leefusionartglass.com* ☾ *June–Oct.*) to create unusual glass dishware. Colorful enamel accents depict birds, lighthouses, flowers, and designs made from doilies. Stoneware and porcelain sinks and dishware are the mainstay at **Maine Kiln Works and Water Stone Sink** (✉ *115 S. Gouldsboro Rd. [Rte. 186], Gouldsboro* ☎ *207/963–5819* ⊕ *www.waterstonesink. com* ☾ *Apr.–mid-Oct.*), but you can also buy botanical lamp shades. Watch the potter hard at work in this former general store.

FOOD The wines and spirits sold at **Bartlett Maine Estate Winery and Spirits of Maine Distillery** (✉ *175 Chicken Mill Rd., off U.S. 1, Gouldsboro* ☎ *207/ 546–2408* ⊕ *www.bartlettwinery.com* ☾ *May–mid-Oct.*) are produced from locally grown apples, pears, blueberries, and other fruit. A pioneering organic grower on West Bay, **Darthia Farm** (✉ *51 Darthia Farm Rd., off Rte. 186, Gouldsboro* ☎ *207/963–7771 or 800/285–6234* ⊕ *www.darthiafarm.com*) operates a store, from June through September, where you can buy produce and herbs, along with preserves, hand-spun yarn, knitted items, and other handcrafts. The farm is open late May through mid-October and offers sleigh rides in winter, weather-allowing. Salmon pâté and smoked salmon, mussels, and cheese are among specialty foods sold at **Grindstone Neck of Maine** (✉ *311 Newman St. [Rte. 186], Winter Harbor* ☎ *207/963–7347 or 866/831–8734* ⊕ *www.grindstoneneckofmaine.com*), which gives tours of its smokehouse. You can also watch workers through the inside picture window. Load up for a picnic—coolers are sold and loaned out for a deposit. Along with mostly organic local produce, **Winter Harbor Farmers' Market** (✉ *10 Newman St. [Rte. 186], Winter Harbor* ☎ *207537-5673* ☾ *June–early Sept., Tues. 9–noon*) sells goat cheese, baked goods, beef and chicken, hand-spun yarn, knitted items, Indian food, and maple syrup, chutney, and preserves.

SPORTS AND THE OUTDOORS

GOLFING You can see the ocean from every green at the 9-hole **Grindstone Neck Golf Course** (✉ *106 Grindstone Ave., Winter Harbor* ☎ *207/963–7760* ⊕ *www.grindstonegolf.com*), one of Maine's oldest courses. Greens fees are $24 to $45.

KAYAKING **SeaScape Kayaking.** Led by a Registered Maine guide, SeaScape's morning and afternoon kayak tours include an island stop and a blueberry snack. The company also rents canoes, kayaks, and bikes from its location in Birch Harbor. ✉ *18 E. Schoodic Dr., Birch Harbor* ☎ *207/963–5806 or 207/479–9912* ⊕ *www.seascapekayaking.com.*

8

STEUBEN TO CHERRYFIELD

Towns in the southwestern corner of Washington County seem more like one community than those off at the ends of necks and peninsulas farther Down East. Though it's less well known as a destination, the area's wildlife refuge, charming architecture, wild salmon river, and historical museums make this a path to beat.

STEUBEN

17 mi north of Hancock via U.S. 1.

Steuben is the first town in Washington County if you're heading north on U.S. 1. The village is east of the highway, largely hidden by trees. At the least, drive through (there's a second turnoff if you miss the first one). Settled in the 1760s, Steuben was named for a Revolutionary War general at the suggestion of Jacob Townsley, an aide-de-camp to General George Washington. Townsley's 1785 Federal-style manse still stands on a hill across from the town center. Steuben has a lost-in-time feel. The 1850s Greek Revival Steuben Union Church beside the village green is a classic. The handsome Henry D. Moore Parish House next door, built in 1910, is a public library.

SPORTS AND THE OUTDOORS

Visitors are welcome at **Petit Manan National Wildlife Refuge,** a 2,166-acre sanctuary of fields, forests, and rocky shorefront at the tip of a peninsula. The wildlife viewing and bird-watching are renowned. In August the park is a popular spot for hand-picking wild blueberries. You can explore the refuge on two walking trails; towering granite and a large cove are along the shore trail, which looks out on sand-color Petit Manan Lighthouse, Maine's second-tallest light. ⊠ *End of Pigeon Hill Rd.* ☎ *207/546–2124* ⊕ *www.fws.gov/northeast/mainecoastal* ⊠ *Free* ⊗ *Daily, sunrise–sunset.*

MILBRIDGE

22 mi north of Hancock via U.S. 1.

Lumbering spurred the shipbuilding that thrived here in the 1800s, and Milbridge is still a commercial center. As you enter town, you pass a Christmas wreath wholesaler and blueberry packager's headquarters.

ESSENTIALS

Visitor Information Milbridge Area Merchants Association (🖃 *Box 536, Milbridge 04658* ⊕ *www.milbridge.org*).

EXPLORING

Milbridge Historical Museum. The facade of this museum may lack period charm, but the interior more than makes up for it. Permanent exhibits document maritime industries past and present: shipbuilding, sardine canning, weir fishing, and lobstering. There are also displays about blueberry production and a lighthouse in nearby Addison. Changing exhibits occupy about a third of the display space, and the meeting room doubles as an art gallery—local artists are on a waiting list.

✉ *83 Main St.* ☎ *207/546–4471* ⊕ *www.milbridgehistoricalsociety.org* 🎫 *Free* ⊗ *June–early Sept., weekends 1–4; July and Aug., Tues. and weekends 1–4.*

WHERE TO EAT

$$ ✕ **44 Degrees North Restaurant & Pub.** With dishes like grilled sword-
AMERICAN fish and seafood lasagna, it's clear that the menu here isn't heavy on fried seafood. Lobster is boiled or baked with seafood stuffing. On Friday and Saturday nights locals come for the prime-rib special. Order wraps and sandwiches at lunch. Works by local artists (for sale) hang above the booths in the dining room. Old black-and-white photos of Milbridge adorn the pub, where there's a big-screen TV. ✉ *17 Main St.* ☎ *207/546–4440* ⊕ *www.44-degrees-north.com* ▭ *AE, MC, D, V* ⊗ *Closed Sun.*

NIGHTLIFE AND THE ARTS

The town's largest annual event is the **Milbridge Days Celebration** (☎ *207/546–2422* ⊕ *www.townofmilbridge.webs.com*), held each year on the last weekend of July. There's a blueberry-pancake breakfast, clam-and-lobster bake, parade, crafts show, and most famously, a codfish relay race. There's only one screen at **Milbridge Theatre** (✉ *26 Main St.* ☎ *207/546–2038* ⊗ *Memorial Day–Oct.; weekends Nov. and Dec.*), but it's a large one and the price is right—$4.50. The owner of the only movie theater between Ellsworth and Calais is likely to greet you in the little lobby—he hasn't missed a show since opening the place in 1978. If you're lucky, you'll catch one of his occasional performances on the 1920 player piano down in front.

SPORTS AND THE OUTDOORS

The town may be small, but it has 75 mi of coastline spread about several peninsulas and bays that are waiting to be explored. You can hike along the shore and enjoy views of the islands dotting Narraguagus Bay at the 10-acre **McClellan Park.** Rounded boulders swathe the shore, and smaller stones form a gray- and black-hue beach near the waterfront picnic area. A dozen campsites accommodate tents and small to medium recreational vehicles. For more information on camping, contact the town office (☎ *207/546–2422*). There are no electrical hookups. ✉ *356 Tom Leighton Pt. Rd., from U.S. 1 turn on Wyman Rd.* ⊕ *www. townofmilbridge.webs.com* ⊗ *May–Oct., daily,*

WHALE-
WATCHING Departing from Milbridge Marina in a six-passenger lobster boat,
AND OTHER **Robertson Sea Tours & Adventures** (☎ *207/483–6110 or 207/461–7439*
CRUISES ⊕ *www.robertsonseatours.com*) runs sightseeing excursions and whale-watching tours, and puffin-watching trips to Petit Manan Island. Passengers can haul a few of the captain's lobster traps. Prices start at $60 per person. You can also charter the boat for a lobster lunch or dinner cruise or island lobster bake. The company operates from mid-May through October.

8

CHERRYFIELD

6 mi north of Milbridge via U.S. 1.

Up the Narraguagus River from Milbridge, Cherryfield was a lumbering center in the 1800s. The river was once lined with lumber mills. Now this stretch is a lovely waterway (with native salmon) overlooked by a gazebo in a small town park. The industry's legacy remains in the surprising number of ornate Victorian homes, unusual for a small New England village. The town has 52 buildings on the National Historic Register in such styles as Colonial Revival, Greek Revival, Italianate, and Queen Anne. The historic district runs along U.S. 1 and the handful of side streets. You can pick up a guide to the district at the town office (⊠ *12 Municipal Way, off U.S. 1) and the Cherryfield Free Public Library* (⊠ *35 Main St.).* Today Cherryfield is known as the "Blueberry Capital of the World." Maine's two largest blueberry plants sit side by side on Route 193. To see the area's wild blueberry barrens, head north past the factories and take a right onto Ridge Road. The best way to explore this hilly landscape is by bicycle.

EXPLORING

Cherryfield-Narraguagus Historical Society Museum. Overlooking the Narraguagus River, this museum has exhibits on logging and local history in an 1840s homestead. A pine blanket chest from the 1750s belonged to the area's first settler. The society sponsors a historic-home tour in July. ⊠ *88 River Rd.* ☎ *No phone* ✉ *Free* ☉ *July and Aug., Sat. 1–4 or by appointment.*

A highlight of the historic-home tour is the **William M. Nash House** on River Road. This lavishly embellished Second Empire mansion perched high on a hill was considered as a location for one of the *Addams Family* movies.

WHERE TO STAY

$ 🏠 **Englishman's Bed & Breakfast.** Built in 1793 by a prominent early settler, this large, historic Federal home has matching front and back "scissors" stairs in the central hall and decorative moldings in the parlor. Breakfast is served beside the original cooking hearth with baking oven. Enjoy a cup of tea (the innkeepers sell fine teas as a sideline) on the L-shape deck, as you are lulled by the rush of the tidal Narraguagus River. A charming guesthouse beside the deck sleeps four. **Pros:** see artifacts found in restoration; afternoon tea. **Cons:** the main house's two guest rooms share a hall bath with shower (one also has a private half bath). ⊠ *122 Main St.* ☎ *207/546–2337* ⊕ *www.englishmansbandb.com* ➪ *2 rooms, 1 suite* ⚭ *In room: no phone, kitchen (some), Wi-Fi, no a/c. In hotel: public Wi-Fi* ☰ *MC, V* ⊙ *BP.*

COLUMBIA FALLS TO CUTLER

It's hard to tell where one bay ends and another begins among the points and peninsulas of this section of Way Down East. Above Jonesport the granite shores become more jagged. Fishing villages here retain their centuries-old culture even as more tourists trickle in.

COLUMBIA FALLS

48 mi north of Ellsworth via U.S. 1, 74 mi west of Calais.

Founded in the late 18th century, Columbia Falls is a pretty village along the Pleasant River. True to its name, a waterfall tumbles into the river in the center of town. Once a prosperous shipbuilding center, Columbia Falls still has a number of stately homes dating from that era. U.S. 1 used to pass through the center of town, but now it passes to the west. It's worth driving through even if you don't have time to stop.

EXPLORING

Downeast Salmon Federation. Check out the salmon in the fish tanks, then head for the deck out back, where a staff person will explain the depletion of native river salmon on the area's rivers and the federation's efforts to restore them. The deck overlooks a defunct fish ladder just below Columbia Falls' namesake falls on the Pleasant River. With views of the marshlands beyond, it's the perfect spot to hear this intriguing fish tale. See the hatchery in action from January through March. ⊠ *187 Main St.* ☎ *207/483–4336* ⊕ *www.mainesalmonrivers. org* ⊠ *Free* ⊗ *Weekdays 9–5.*

★ **Ruggles House.** Judge Thomas Ruggles, a wealthy lumber dealer, store owner, postmaster, and justice of the Court of Sessions, built this home around 1820. The house's distinctive Federal architecture, flying staircase, Palladian window, and intricate woodwork were crafted over three years by Massachusetts wood-carver Alvah Peterson. On guided tours you'll also learn about the outstanding collection of period furnishings, much of it original to the home. ⊠ *146 Main St.* ☎ *207/483–4637* ⊕ *www.ruggleshouse.org* ⊠ *$5* ⊗ *June–mid-Oct., Mon.–Sat. 9:30–4:30, Sun. 11–4:30.*

WHERE TO STAY

¢–$ ⌂ **Blueberry Patch Motel.** Midway up the coast from Bar Harbor and convenient to Machias and Jonesport, this tidy lodging has rooms with doubles and queens in a building near the road. Tiny but classic roadside cabins from the 1930s and a few larger, newer units are set back where the highway used to be. **Pros:** motel pool is quite nice, and a rarity in these parts; free coffee and muffins in the morning. **Cons:** older baths in vintage cabins. ⊠ *550 U.S. 1, Jonesboro* ☎ *207/434–5411* ⌂*10 rooms, 9 cabins* ⌂ *In room: refrigerator (some), kitchen (some), Wi-Fi. In hotel: pool, some pets allowed, public Wi-Fi* ▤ *AE, D, MC, V* ⊗ *Closed mid-Oct.–May.*

¢–$ ⌂ **Pleasant Bay Bed & Breakfast.** This Cape Cod–style inn takes advantage
⟳ of its riverfront location. Stroll the nature paths on the 110-acre prop-
★ erty, which winds around a peninsula and out to Pleasant Bay—you can even take one of the inn's llamas along for company. A screened porch and deck overlook the Pleasant River, and the suite has a private deck and kitchenette. The country-style rooms, all with water views, are decorated with antiques, as are the roomy common areas. A library with a fireplace is tucked away from the family room. **Pros:** fireplace at one of three waterfront picnic areas; river mooring; extra bed or pullout couch in most quarters. **Cons:** some may find it too far off the beaten path ⊠ *386 West Side Rd., Addison* ☎ *207/483–4490* ⊕ *www.*

8

pleasantbay.com ⇄ *3 rooms, 1 with bath; 1 suite* ⚇ *In-room: no phone (some), refrigerator (some) Wi-Fi, no a/c. In-hotel: public Wi-Fi* ▭ *MC, V* ⦿ *BP.*

SHOPPING

Yes, the deep-blue geodesic dome housing **Wild Blueberry Land** (✉ *1067 U.S. 1* ☎ *207/483–2583* ◷ *mid-June–Columbus Day*) is supposed to resemble a giant blueberry. In addition to foods filled with blueberries and all sorts of blueberry-themed gifts, you can watch a video about the local cash crop.

SPORTS AND THE OUTDOORS

GOLF   Blueberry barrens border the 9-hole **Barren View Golf Course** (✉ *1354 U.S. 1, Jonesboro* ☎ *207/434–6531* ⊕ *www.barrenview.com*), which also has a driving range and clubhouse. Greens fees are $15 to $25.

JONESPORT AND BEALS ISLAND

12 mi northeast of Columbia Falls via U.S. 1 and Rte. 187, 20 mi southwest of Machias.

The birding is superb around Jonesport and Beals Island, a pair of fishing communities joined by a bridge over the harbor. A handful of stately homes ring Jonesport's Sawyer Square, where Sawyer Memorial Congregational Church's exquisite stained-glass windows are illuminated at night. But the towns are less geared to travelers than those on the Schoodic Peninsula. Lobster traps are still piled in the yards, and lobster-boat races near Moosabec Reach are the highlight of the community's annual Independence Day celebration.

EXPLORING

Great Wass Island Preserve. At the tip of Beals Island is the Nature Conservancy's 1,540-acre preserve, where you can find stunted pines and raised peat bogs. Rugged trails lead through the woods and emerge onto the undeveloped coast, where you may spot gray seals as you make your way among the rocks and boulders. Parking is limited. No pets are allowed. If it's been raining, it may be too wet for hiking here. (✉ *Beals Island,* ⟴ *take Bay View Drive to Black Duck Cove Road, turn right and watch for a sign on left* ☎ *207/729–5181* ⊕ *www.nature.org/ maine* ⌨ *Free, dawn to dusk* ◷ *Daily*).

Maine Coast Sardine History Museum. Hundreds of sardine packing plants have operated along the Maine Coast since 1875, with the biggest concentration in harbor towns Way Down East. Only one remains, but the industry's story lives on at this intriguing small museum. Displays include old photos, unopened sardine cans with colorful, artful labels, and sealing and labeling machines. A wall is hung with scissors (each is different) that packers used to cut off herring heads and tails. On most days the museum founders, who live next door and spent many years salvaging items to exhibit, are on hand. ✉ *34 Mason Bay Rd. (Rte. 187)* ☎ *207/497–2961* ⊕ *www.mainesardinemuseum.org* ⌨ *$4* ◷ *Late June–Sept., Tues.–Fri. and Sun., noon–4, Memorial Day, July 4th, and Labor Day, noon–4, or by appointment.*

Wild for Blueberries

CLOSE UP

There's no need to inquire about the cheesecake topping if you dine out in August when the wild blueberry crop comes in. Anything but blueberries would be unthinkable.

Way Down East, wild blueberries have long been a favorite food—and a key ingredient in cultural and economic life. Maine produces about a third of the commercial harvest, which totals about 70 million pounds annually, Canada supplying virtually all the rest. Washington County yields 65% of Maine's total crop, which is why the state's largest blueberry processors are here: Jasper Wyman & Son and the predecessor of what is now Cherryfield Foods were founded shortly after the Civil War.

Wild blueberries, which bear fruit every other year, thrive in the region's cold climate and sandy, acidic soil. Undulating blueberry barrens stretch for miles in Deblois and Cherryfield—"the Blueberry Capital of the World"—and are scattered throughout Washington County. Look for tufts among low-lying plants along the roadways. In spring the fields shimmer as the small-leaf plants turn myriad shades of mauve, honey-orange, and lemon-yellow. White flowers appear in June. Fall transforms the barrens into a sea of red.

Amid Cherryfield's barrens, a plaque on a boulder lauds the late J. Burleigh Crane for helping advance an industry that's not as wild as it used to be. Honeybees have been brought in to supplement native pollinators. Fields are irrigated. Barrens are burned and mowed to rid plants of disease and insects, reducing the need for pesticides. Most of the barrens in and around Cherryfield are owned by the large blueberry processors.

About 80% of Maine's crop is now harvested with machinery. That requires moving boulders, so the rest continues to be harvested by hand with blueberry rakes, which resemble large forks and pull the berries off their stems. Years ago, year-round residents did the work. Today migrant workers make up 90% of this seasonal labor force.

Blueberries get their dark color from anthocyanins, believed to provide their antioxidant power. Wild blueberries have more of these antiaging, anticancer compounds than their cultivated cousins. Smaller and more flavorful than cultivated blueberries, wild ones are mostly used in packaged foods. Less than 1% of the state's crop—about 500,000 pints—is consumed fresh, mostly in Maine. Look for fresh berries (sometimes starting in late July and lasting until early September) at roadside stands, farmers' markets, and supermarkets.

Wild Blueberry Land in Columbia Falls sells everything blueberry, from muffins and candy to socks and books. Find farm stores, stands, and markets statewide, many selling blueberries and blueberry jams and syrups, at www.getrealgetmaine.com, a Maine Department of Agriculture site that promotes Maine foods.

—Mary Ruoff

8

WHERE TO EAT AND STAY

$$
SEAFOOD

✕**Tall Barney's.** Salty accents add plenty of flavor at this down-home restaurant, which serves a late-morning breakfast (10 to 11 weekdays, 8 to 11 on Saturday), lunch, and dinner. A pamphlet tells the story of Tall Barney, a brawny fisherman who left truly tall tales in his wake. Your server may be among his multitudinous descendants. The menu includes five types of seafood stew, grilled, baked, and fried seafood, vegetarian dishes, and oversize desserts including seasonal pies. Call the night before to order a boxed lunch. ⊠ *52 Main St.* ☎ *207/497–2403* ⊕ *www. tallbarneys.com* ⊟ *MC, V* ⊘ *Closed Mon.; generally closed Mon. and Tues. late Sept.–mid.-Nov., Sun.–Wed. late Nov.–mid-May.*

$$
★

⊞**Harbor House on Sawyer Cove.** The two spacious rooms on the third floor of this harborfront building have big windows overlooking the water. Both have separate sitting areas and are tastefully furnished with Victorian flourishes such as cabbage-rose wallpaper and handwoven rugs. Breakfast is served on the enclosed porch. You can relax on the lawn, which is flanked by beach roses. Don't miss the telegraph office in an original storefront, now the inn's antiques and gift shop. **Pros:** nice yard with picnic table; private entrance to rooms. **Cons:** no common parlor. ⊠ *27 Sawyer Sq., Jonesport* ☎ *207/497–5417* ⊕ *www.harborhs. com* ⇘ *2 rooms* ᓚ *In-room: no phone, Wi-Fi, no a/c. In-hotel: public Wi-Fi, no kids under 12* ⊟ *D, MC, V* ⦿ *BP.*

NIGHTLIFE AND THE ARTS

A Grammy award–winning pianist is among the past performers at the **Music in the Library** (⊠ *162 Main St.* ☎ *207/497–3003* ⊕ *www. peabodymemorial.com* ✉ *Free)* concert series, held in the main room of the town's Peabody Memorial Library from late spring through early fall. The music varies, from Celtic to jazz.

SHOPPING

Years ago, many Down East fishermen hunted sea ducks to help feed their families, and the area's decoy-carving tradition lives on at **Nelson Decoys** (⊠ *13 Cranberry La.* ☎ *207/497–3488* ⊘ *Open May–mid-Dec. or by appointment)*, whose owner carves and paints black ducks, puffins, and other waterfowl, as do her daughter and son-in-law. The store, in an old elementary school, also carries works by other Maine artists, including watercolor paintings and sea-glass sculptures.

You often catch the artist at work at **Pierce-Kettering Gallery** (⊠ *344 Main St.* ☎ *207/497–2874* ⊘ *June–Oct.)*, where there's a salon feel to parlors hung with oil and acrylic paintings of animals and local landscapes. Relax on the sofa with a cup of tea or enjoy the gardens and porch, which show the artist's touch.

SPORTS AND THE OUTDOORS

In business since circa 1940, **Norton of Jonesport** (☎ *207/497–5933* ⊕ *www.machiassealisland.com)* takes passengers on day trips to Machias Seal Island, where thousands of puffins nest. Arctic terns, razorbill auks, common murres, and many other seabirds also nest on the rocky island. Trips, which cost $100 per person, are offered from late May through August. Mistake Island, home to 72-foot Moose Peak Light, is a highlight of scenic cruises offered by **Coastal Cruises &**

Dive Downeast (☎ *207/598–6362* ⊕ *www.cruisedowneast.com*). A six-passenger boat traverses island-strewn waters, spotting seabirds, eagles, and seals. Prices start at $50 per person.

MACHIAS

20 mi northeast of Jonesport.

The Machias area—Machiasport, East Machias, and Machias, the Washington County seat—lays claim to being the site of the first naval battle of the Revolutionary War, which took place in what is now Machiasport. Despite being outnumbered and outarmed, a small group of Machias men under the leadership of Jeremiah O'Brien captured the armed British schooner *Margaretta*. That battle, fought on June 12, 1775, is now known as the "Lexington of the Sea." The Margaretta Days Festival on the second weekend in June commemorates the event with period reenactors and a parade. The town's other claim to fame is wild blueberries. On the third weekend in August the annual Machias Wild Blueberry Festival is a community celebration complete with parade, crafts fair, concerts, and plenty of blueberry dishes.

ESSENTIALS

Visitor Information **Machias Bay Area Chamber of Commerce** (⊠ *85 Main St. Suite 2, Machias* ☎ *207/255–4402* ⊕ *www.machiaschamber.org*).

EXPLORING

★ **Burnham Tavern Museum.** It was in this gambrel-roofed tavern home that the men of Machias laid the plans that culminated in the capture of the *Margaretta* in 1775. After the Revolutionary War's first naval battle, wounded British sailors were brought here. Tour guides dressed in period garb highlight exhibits and tell colorful stories of early settlers. Period furnishings and household items show what life was like in Colonial times. On the National Register of Historic Places, the dwelling is among 21 in the country deemed most important to the Revolution. ⊠ *14 Colonial Way (Rte. 192)* ☎ *207/255–6930* ⊕ *www.burnhamtavern.com* ⊠ *$5* ⊗ *Mid-June–Sept., weekdays 9:30–4 (last tour at 3:30), or by appointment.*

Fort O'Brien State Historic Site. An active fort during the Revolutionary War, the War of 1812, and the Civil War, this site sits at the head of Machias Bay, where a naval battle was waged in 1775. Climb atop the grass-covered earthworks to take in the expansive water views. A panel display details the successive forts built here and relates the dramatic story of patriots, armed mostly with farm implements, who captured a British tender two miles offshore. A stone marker honors the site as a "birthplace" of the U.S. Navy. ⊠ *Rte. 92, just south of village center, Machiasport* ☎ *207/941–4014* ⊗ *Memorial Day–Labor Day, 9–sunset.*

Nathan Gates House. The 1810 home-turned-museum contains an extensive collection of old photographs, period furniture, housewares, and other memorabilia, and is the headquarters of the Machiasport Historical Society. The Marine Room highlights the area's seafaring and shipbuilding past. A model schoolroom and post office and a large collection of carpentry tools occupy the adjacent Cooper House, a utilitarian building constructed in 1850. There's also a genealogical library. ⊠ *344 Port Road (Rte. 92), Machiasport* ☎ *207/255–8461* 🖾 *Free* ⊙ *Early July–Fri. before Labor Day, Tues.–Fri. 12:30–4:30, or by appointment.*

NEED A BREAK?

Bad Little Falls Park (⊠ *Intersection of Rte. 92 and U.S. 1*) is a great picnic stop in downtown Machias, with a bridge over the falls on the Machias River. A trail leads to O'Brien Cemetery, the final resting place for many of Machias' early settlers.

WHERE TO EAT

$$

AMERICAN

✕ **Blue Bird Ranch.** Family restaurants dominate Way Down East, and this is a favorite of people throughout the region. The Blue Bird Ranch is known for its home-style cooking and reasonable prices. The dining rooms are large and the staff is chipper. The menu includes everything from spinach salad with Maine blueberries and blue cheese to fried, boiled, or sautéed fish dinners. ⊠ *3 E. Main St.* ☎ *207/255–3351* ⊕ *www.bluebirdranchrestaurant.com* 🖃 *AE, D, DC, MC, V.*

$$$$

AMERICAN

✕ **Chandler River Lodge.** Housed in a 1797 homestead, this restaurant is perched above the Chandler River on 20 acres that are well set back from U.S. 1. The menu changes monthly, but you'll always find dishes featuring Maine seafood and veal from a Maine farm. Entrées, which come with a salad, may include veal cutlet roulade with crabmeat, and lamb chops with peanut sauce. There are water-view tables and fireplaces in both dining rooms. Come summer, you can eat on the veranda and watch the river flow. Four B&B rooms, three with queen beds and one with a king bed and spa tub, are upstairs. ⊠ *654 U.S. 1 Jonesboro* ☎ *207/434–2540* ⊕ *www.chandlerriverlodge.com* 🖃 *AE, D, MC, V* ⊙ *Closed Sun.–Wed., Dec.–May. No lunch, late Sept.–mid-June and Sat.–Wed. late June–mid-Sept.*

$$$–$$$$

AMERICAN

★

✕ **Riverside Inn & Restaurant.** A bright yellow exterior invites a stop at this delightful restaurant in a former sea captain's home perched on the bank of the Machias River. Ask for a table in the intimate sunroom, which has water views and opens to the other dining room. The chef owner brings a special flair to traditional dishes, such as pork served with a pistachio crust. His signature dish is salmon stuffed with crabmeat and shrimp. In summer months the menu includes dressed-up dinner salads—try pairing one with standout appetizers like hake cakes and red-tuna wontons. Also a charming inn (open daily except in early winter) with Victorian touches, Riverside has two guest rooms in the main house and two suites in the coach house. ⊠ *608 Main St. (U.S. 1), East Machias* ☎ *207/255–4134 or 888/255–4344* ⊕ *www.riversideinn-maine.com* 🖃 *MC, V* ⊙ *Closed Jan.–early Feb., Mon.–Wed. mid-Feb.–mid-June and Nov. and Dec., Mon. late June–Oct. No lunch.*

WHERE TO STAY

$ **Captain Cates Bed & Breakfast.** The main portion of this Victorian home was built in the 1840s. On a bright morning or afternoon you can relax in the two parlors or on the swing on the front lawn, overlooking a wide stretch of the Machias River. Rooms are furnished with antiques and have water views, some better than others. Second-floor rooms are elegant; cottage-style third-floor rooms make a nice family suite. **Pros:** lower rate with three nights' stay; $75 one-person room. **Cons:** three rooms share a bath on each floor. ⊠ *309 Port Rd., (Rte. 92) Machiasport* ☏ *207/255–8812* ⊕ *www.captaincates.com* ↴ *6 rooms without bath* & *In-room: no phone, no TV, Wi-Fi, no a/c. In-hotel: public Wi-Fi* ⊟ *MC, V* ⍩ *BP.*

$ **Micmac Farm.** Grouped along the Machias River at this wonderfully secluded 50-acre property are three spacious cabins with pine interiors, kitchenettes, and decks. Also fronting the waterway is the historic cape house B&B, which has an antiques-filled parlor that looks much as it did when the home was built in 1776. The single guest room here is off the parlor in a modern addition with river-view deck and a whirlpool bath. **Pros:** hiking trail; sweeping river views; whirlpool bath in B&B. **Cons:** cabins close together. ⊠ *47 Micmac La., Machiasport* ☏ *207/255–3008* ⊕ *www.micmacfarm.com* ↴ *1 room, 3 cabins* & *In-room: no phone, kitchen (some), no TV (some), DVD (some), no a/c. In-hotel: some pets allowed* ⊟ *MC, V* ⊘ *Closed late Oct.–mid May* ⍩ *CP (B&B only).*

NIGHTLIFE AND THE ARTS

Although small, the **Art Galleries at the University of Maine** (⊠ *9 O'Brien Ave.* ☏ *207/255–1200*) have a strong selection of paintings by John Marin and other regional artists. Two galleries showcase rotating exhibits of works from the permanent collection. Don't miss the William Zorach sculpture just outside the front door. In July and early August the **Machias Bay Chamber Concert Series** (⊠ *7 Centre St.* ☏ *207/255–4259* ⊕ *www.machiasbaychamberconcerts.com* ⍉ *$15*) is held on Tuesday at 7:30 PM at Centre Street Congregational Church. Head to the vestry afterwards for punch and to see work by local artists.

SHOPPING

ARTS AND CRAFTS   High-fire porcelain dinnerware and housewares in abstract designs, decorative raku pieces, yoga-inspired porcelain jewelry, and colorful tile backsplashes and tables are for sale at **Connie's Clay of Fundy Pottery** (⊠ *Main St. [U.S. 1], 1 mi north of village center, East Machias* ☏ *207/255–4574 or 888/255–8131* ⊕ *www.clayoffundy.com*). The potter and owner gives demonstrations in the attached studio, and invites visitors to relax on the deck. Art of all kinds can be found at the congenial **Woodwind Gallery** (⊠ *104 Dublin St. [U.S. 1]* ☏ *207/255–3727*). Exhibitors range from a self-taught watercolor painter to a leading pastel artist.

FOOD   Stock up on fresh fruits and vegetables, or flowers early in the season, at **Machias Valley Farmers' Market** (⊹ *South end of U.S. 1 causeway* ☏ *207/255–8556*), held early May through October from 9 AM to 1 PM. Friday and Saturday are the busiest days, but you may find vendors here any day. Get organic produce and other picnic picks at **Whole Life Natural Market** (⊠ *4 Colonial Way [Rte. 192 section]* ☎ *207/255–8855* ⊕ *www.wholelifemarket.com*), or call ahead for a box lunch. Fresh, organic food to go, from Indonesian rice salad to spanakopita, can also be enjoyed at the window-side tables. There's free Wi-Fi and a nice selection of Maine-made gifts, from jewelry to soap.

SPORTS AND THE OUTDOORS

KAYAKING **Sunrise Canoe & Kayak** (⊠ *Hoyttown Rd., off U.S. 1, Machias* ☎ *207/255–3375 or 877/980–2300* ⊕ *www.sunrisecanoeandkayak.com*) offers sea-kayaking day trips to petroglyphs (many 1,500 to 3,000 years old) carved on slate ledges in Machias Bay. The company also outfits canoes and leads overnight sea-kayaking and canoe trips, including trips on the Machias River. If you prefer to go solo, there are bike, kayak, and canoe rentals; drop-off service is available.

STATE PARK Down East's rock- and fir-bound shores give way to a crescent-shape pebble beach at **Roque Bluffs State Park** (⊠ *145 Schoppee Point Rd., follow signs from U.S. 1 in Jonesboro or Machias, Roque Bluffs* ☎ *207/255–3475 or 207/941–4014* ⊕ *www.parksandlands.com* ✉ *$3 Maine residents, $4.50 nonresidents* ⊘ *Staffed May 15–Oct. 15, daily 9–half hour before sunset*). Just beyond the beach you can find a freshwater pond that's ideal for swimming and kayaking—rent flatwater kayaks here. The park has changing areas, restrooms, a picnic area with grills, and a playground. Miles of trails traverse woods, apple orchards, and blueberry fields. The trailhead is just before the park entrance at Roque Bluffs Community Church.

CUTLER

13 mi southeast of East Machias via Rte. 191.

Cutler's natural beauty is what makes it worth exploring. Puffin cruises depart from the protected harbor, which opens like a keyhole onto the ocean and is known as Little River because of its shape. The Bold Coast, as the towering headlands flanking the harbor entrance are called, has some of Maine's best shoreline trails.

EXPLORING

Little River Lighthouse. Hike in the state preserve in Cutler (⇨ *see Sports and the Outdoors)* for views of this lighthouse facing the ocean on a tiny, wooded island at the harbor's mouth. You can also kayak to its rocky, cliff-clad shores. The island is always open (there's a grill and pavilion), and Friends of Little River Lighthouse give free tours by appointment. It also hosts two open houses each summer, ferrying visitors over from the boat ramp in town, and offers overnight stays in the charming keeper's house. Available by reservation from early July through mid-September, rooms cost between $125 to $150 (shared bath and kitchen; linens and towels not provided; no children under 12; caretaker on-site). (☎ *207/259–3833* ⊕ *www.littleriverlight.org*)

SHOPPING

Picturesque labels, including one of Cutler's harbor, adorn the canned mussels, clams, lobster meat, chowders, and bisques packed in small batches at **Look's Gourmet Seafood** (⊠ *1112 Cutler Rd. [Rte. 191] Whiting* ☎ *207/259–3341* ⊕ *www.barharborfoods.com*). Buy them at the small shop at the plant, which also carries baked beans and Indian pudding, both New England favorites, and sauces and dips. It is open weekdays year-round.

SPORTS AND THE OUTDOORS

It's about a 45-minute trip to Machias Seal Island, a favored nesting place for puffins and many other seabirds. **Bold Coast Charter Co.** (☎ *207/259–4484* ⊕ *www.boldcoast.com*) takes visitors to the island from May to August. The knowledgeable and amiable Captain Andrew Patterson also gives scenic tours of the Bold Coast and Down East islands, with lots of opportunities to spot marine life. Trips are $60 to $100 per person.

★ The beautiful coastal trails at **Cutler Coast Public Reserved Land** (⊠ *Rte. 191, 17 mi from East Machias* ☎ *207/827–1818* ⊕ *www.parksandlands. com* ⊠ *Free* ☉ *Daily*) are likely to take your breath away. The 12,000-acre state preserve northeast of Cutler Harbor includes 4½ mi of the undeveloped Bold Coast between Cutler and Lubec. Although much of Maine's coast is chiseled with large bays and coves, here a wall of steep cliffs—some 150 feet tall—juts below ledges partially forested with spruce and fir. Look for whales, seals, and porpoises while taking in views of cliff-ringed Grand Manan Island and the Bay of Fundy. Climb down the log ladders to reach the pebble beaches. Revealing the area's unusual terrain, the two hiking trails loop inland, passing peat bogs, salt marshes, blueberry barrens, swamps, and meadows. The trail from the parking area to the coast is 1½ mi; the longer hiking trails are 6 and 10 mi long. There are three primitive campsites here.

Maine Coast Heritage Trust's **Western Head Preserve** (⊠ *End of Destiny Bay Rd.* ☎ *207/729–7366* ⊕ *www.mcht.org* ⊠ *Free* ☉ *Daily, dawn to dusk*) flanks the coast southeast of Cutler Harbor. This pristine 247-acre preserve is known for its awesome views. Along the steep cliffs, wind and salt spray have sculpted spruce and fir trees into odd, stunted shapes. Cranberries, iris, and juniper grow from rock ledges. There are beaches here.

EN ROUTE After dipping to Cutler from East Machias, Route 191 loops toward Lubec. Mounded, treeless terrain is found along this lonely stretch. Heaths and bogs form a subarctic ecosystem where rare plants thrive in the acidic soil.

COBSCOOK AND PASSAMAQUODDY BAYS

Distances can be confusing in this part of the region. It's only a mile or so by boat from Lubec, on Cobscook Bay, to Eastport, facing Passamaquoddy Bay, while the circuitous land route is nearly 40 mi. The area's huge tides are as high as 28 feet, and the largest whirlpool in the Northern Hemisphere, called "Old Sow," swirls off Eastport. Canadian islands, including Campobello, can be seen directly across the water. In summer you can take the ferry from Campobello to Canada's Deer Island and on to Eastport. Or take the "Quoddy Loop," ferrying to the Canadian mainland from Deer Island and returning by land. Calais, upriver from where the St. Croix River widens into Passamaquoddy Bay, is across from St. Stephen, Canada.

LUBEC

28 mi northeast of Machias via U.S. 1 and Rte. 189.

Lubec is the first town in the United States to see the sunrise. A popular destination for outdoor enthusiasts, it offers plenty of opportunities for hiking and biking, and the birding is renowned. It's a good base for day trips to New Brunswick's Campobello Island, reached by a bridge—the only one to the island—from downtown Lubec. The village is perched at the end of a narrow strip of land, so you often can see water in three directions.

ESSENTIALS
Visitor Information Cobscook Bay Area Chamber of Commerce (⌦ *Box 42, Whiting 04691* ☎ *207/733–2201* ⊕ *www.cobscookbay.com*).

EXPLORING
Historic McCurdy Smokehouse. Small buildings clustered on piers on the downtown waterfront are what remain of the nation's last herring smokehouse, which operated here from the 1890s until 1991. Restoration is ongoing, but you can take a guided tour of the skinning and packing sheds, which have exhibits about the smoking operation and the local fisheries industry. The property, fronted by an informal garden, is on the National Register of Historic Places. ⌦ *Water St. next to Lubec Landmarks, 50 Water St.* ☎ *207/733–2197* ⌦ *Free* ☼ *Memorial Day weekend–Labor Day, Mon. and Tues. and Thurs.–Sun. 10–4, Mon. after Labor Day–Columbus Day, weekends 10–4, or by appointment.*

★ **Quoddy Head State Park.** The easternmost point of land in the United States is marked by candy-striped West Quoddy Head Light. In 1806 President Thomas Jefferson signed an order authorizing construction of a lighthouse on this site. You can't climb the tower, but the former light keeper's house has a museum with a video showing the interior. The museum also has displays on Lubec's maritime past and the region's marine life. A gallery displays lighthouse art by locals. A mystical 2-mi path along the cliffs here, one of four trails, yields magnificent views of Canada's cliff-clad Grand Manan Island. Whales can often be sighted offshore. The 540-acre park has a picnic area. ⌦ *973 S. Lubec Rd., off Rte. 189* ☎ *207/733–0911 or 207/941–4014* ⊕ *www.parksandlands. com* ⌦ *$3* ☼ *May 15–Oct. 15, 9–sunset.*

▮ **TAKE A TOUR** On educational tours by **Tours of Lubec and Cobscook** (⌦ *135 Main St. (Route 189).* ☎ *207/733–2997 or 888/347–9302* ⊕ *www. toursoflubecandcobscook.com*) you can visit historic locales, view lighthouses by boat, walk the shoreline to learn about the area's high tides and tide pools, tour a ninth-generation farm on Cobscook Bay, and explore a bog. Tours run from May through October, and start at $10 per person. The tour office is at the tourism Info Stop, which shares a building with the Lubec Historical Society Museum.

WHERE TO EAT AND STAY

$–$$
AMERICAN
✕ **Atlantic House Deli and Sweetery.** From this restaurant's two small decks you can gaze past the old smokehouses at the Lubec Narrows. Enjoy favorites such as chowder in a bread bowl, or opt for pizza, a sandwich, hotdog, or lobster roll. For a sweet treat, there are ice cream, doughnuts, and yummy pastries, all made on the premises, as is the bread. Also try the breakfast sandwiches. The owner's affordable Betsy Ross Lodging ($95) is across the street. A replica of its Philadelphia namesake, it has four gleaming pine-walled guest rooms on two floors (two rooms sleep four, one has flag comforters). Rates include breakfast at the Atlantic House. ⊠ *52 Water St.* ☎ *207/733–0906* ⊕ *www.atlantichouse.net* ▤ *No credit cards* ⊗ *Closed late Oct.–mid-May.*

$$$
SEAFOOD
✕ **Home Port Inn.** The elegant restaurant in a rear addition to this 1880 hilltop Colonial house is one of the region's best. Before dinner, enjoy a glass of wine and savor the sea breeze on the deck. The menu emphasizes seafood, but the steak au poivre is a favorite with locals. Lobster is served in a casserole with drawn butter, sherry, and bread crumbs, pan-seared over linguine, or in a salad with artichoke hearts and a creamy tarragon dressing. The seven guest rooms in the grand lodging are generously sized and furnished with family antiques; one has outstanding water views. ⊠ *45 Main St.* ☎ *207/733–2077 or 800/457–2077* ⊕ *www.homeportinn.com* ▤ *AE, D, MC, V* ⊗ *Closed mid-Oct.–mid-May. No lunch.*

$$
SEAFOOD
✕ **Uncle Kippy's Restaurant.** There isn't much of a view from the picture windows, but locals don't mind—they come here for the satisfying seafood. There's one large dining room with a bar beside the main entrance. The menu includes seafood dinners and combo platters, and the fresh-dough pizza is popular. A take-out window and ice-cream bar are open June through September. ⊠ *170 Main St.* ☎ *207/733–2400* ⊕ *www.unclekippys.com* ▤ *MC, V, D* ⊗ *Generally closed Mon. and Tues. Dec.–June.*

$–$$
★
⊡ **Peacock House.** Five generations of the Peacock family lived in this white-clapboard house before it was converted into an inn. With a large foyer, library, and living room, the 1860 sea captain's home has plenty of places where you can relax. Minglers are drawn to the sunroom, which opens to the deck and has a handsome bar with glasses for your wine or spirits. The best of the rooms has a separate sitting area and a wet bar and gas fireplace. **Pros:** piano in living room; lovely garden off deck. **Cons:** only one off-street parking space. ⊠ *27 Summer St.* ☎ *207/733–2403 or 888/305–0036* ⊕ *www.peacockhouse.com* ⇨ *5 rooms, 2 suites* ⚲ *In-room: no phone, refrigerator (some), DVD (some), no TV (some), Wi-Fi, no a/c. In hotel: public Wi-Fi* ▤ *MC, V* ⊗ *Closed Nov.–Apr.* ⧀ *BP.*

8

NIGHTLIFE AND THE ARTS

Offering free classical and jazz performances, the **Mary Potterton Memorial Concert Series** has performances on Wednesday evenings from June to August or early September at the Congregational Christian Church (✉ *3 Church St., at Main St. 04652*). The series is sponsored by **SummerKeys** (☎ *207/733–2316* ⊕ *www.summerkeys.com*), which offers summer "music vacation" workshops.

SHOPPING

ARTS AND CRAFTS Two cozy rooms are outfitted with a nice variety of Maine-made gifts and art at **Northern Tides Art and Gift Gallery** (✉ *24 Water St.,* ☎ *207/733–2500* ◷ *Open Memorial Day–Christmas Eve*), from $6 felted soap to pricey paintings. Changing exhibits of local art are shown at **Lubec Landmarks** (✉ *50 Water St.* ☎ *207/733–2197* ◷ *Open Memorial Day–Columbus Day. Closed Weds., only open weekends after Labor Day*), in the old Mulholland Bros. Market building. There is a small gift shop where you buy local crafts and T-shirts of the historic smokehouse next door.

FOOD Sampling is encouraged at **Bayside Chocolates** (✉ *37 Water St.* ☎ *207/733–8880* ⊕ *www.baysidechocolates.com*), where quality chocolate is made in small batches. You can order an espresso after admiring shelves of wrapped and boxed delights like dipped blueberries and chocolates with lemon zest nougat centers. Come early (it opens at 8) for homemade donuts, bagels, and muffins. Pick up a six-pack—of smoked salmon kebabs—at **Bold Coast Smokehouse** (✉ *224 County Rd. [Rte. 189]* ☎ *207/733–8912 or 888/733–0807* ⊕ *www.boldcoastsmokehouse. com*). Other offerings include smoked lobster pâté and gravlax, a sugar-and-salt-cured salmon. Scrumptious boxed and wrapped chocolates are artfully arranged at **Monica's Chocolates** (✉ *100 County Rd. [Rte. 189]* ☎ *866/952–4500* ⊕ *www.monicaschocolates.com*), where many of the delights use a filling from the owner's native Peru. The large selection also includes blueberry clusters and needhams, a Maine tradition, with a coconut and potato filling.

GIFTS Loaded with local souvenirs such as moose T-shirts, and of course puffin stuff galore, **Puffin Pines Country Gift Store** (✉ *240 U.S. 1, Whiting* ☎ *207/733–9782* ⊕ *www.puffinpines.com* ◷ *Apr.–Dec.*) also carries Passamaquoddy Indian dream catchers and has a well-stocked information booth.

SPORTS AND THE OUTDOORS

GUIDED TOURS The registered Maine guides who own **Cobscook Hikes and Paddles** (✉ *13 Woodcock Way, Robbinston* ☎ *207/454–2130 or 207/726–4776* ⊕ *www.cobscookhikesandpaddles.com*) lead lake and sea kayaking, canoeing, hiking, birding, and snowshoeing day trips.

CAMPOBELLO ISLAND, CANADA

28 mi east of Machias.

A popular excursion from Lubec, New Brunswick's Campobello Island has two fishing villages, Welshpool and Wilson's Beach. The only bridge is from Lubec, but in summer a car ferry shuttles passengers from

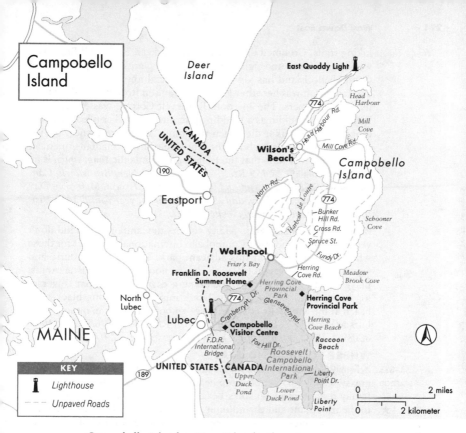

Campobello Island

Deer Island

East Quoddy Light

774

Head Harbour

Head Harbour Rd.

Mill Cove

Wilson's Beach

Mill Cove Rd.

Campobello Island

CANADA

UNITED STATES

190

North Rd.

774

Harbour de Loutre

Bunker Hill Rd.
Cross Rd.
Spruce St.

Schooner Cove

Eastport

Welshpool

Friar's Bay

Franklin D. Roosevelt Summer Home

Fundy Dr.

Herring Cove Rd.

Meadow Brook Cove

North Lubec

774

Herring Cove Provincial Park

Glensevern Rd.

Herring Cove Provincial Park

Lubec

Cranberry Pt. Dr.

Campobello Visitor Centre

Herring Cove Beach

Fox Hill Dr.

Raccoon Beach

F.D.R. International Bridge

Roosevelt Campobello International Park

UNITED STATES CANADA

189

Upper Duck Pond

Lower Duck Pond

Liberty Point Dr.

Liberty Point

MAINE

KEY

🗼 Lighthouse

--- Unpaved Roads

0   2 miles

0   2 kilometer

Campobello Island to Deer Island, where you can continue on to the Canadian mainland. (⇨ *See the Travel Smart Maine Coast section at the back of the book for information on passports or other documents U.S. citizens need when traveling between the United States and Canada.*)

ESSENTIALS

Visitor Information Campobello Island Tourism Association (✉ *1977 Rte. 774, Wilson's Beach, New Brunswick, Canada* ☎ *506/752–2419* ⊕ *www. campobelloislandtourism.com*).

EXPLORING

East Quoddy Head Lighthouse. Stop in at the information center (open mid-May to mid-October) after passing customs for an update on tides—specifically, when you will be able to walk to this lighthouse. You can tour the tower and keeper's house for an additional fee. On a tiny island off the eastern end of Campobello, this distinctive lighthouse is marked with a large red cross and is accessible only at and around low tide, but it's worth a look no matter the sea level. You may spot whales in the island-dotted waters off the small park on the rock-clad headland across from the light. ✉ *East end of Rte. 774, Wilson's Beach* 🗓 *$5 CAN.*

★ **Roosevelt Campobello International Park.** A joint project of the American and the Canadian governments, this park is crisscrossed with interesting hiking trails. Groomed dirt roads attract bikers. Eagle Hill Bog has a wooden walkway and signs identifying rare plants. Neatly manicured Campobello Island has always had a special appeal for the wealthy and famous. It was here that President Franklin Roosevelt and his family spent summers. The 34-room Roosevelt Cottage was presented to Eleanor and Franklin as a wedding gift, and the wicker-filled structure looks essentially as it did when the family was in residence. A visitor center has displays about the Roosevelts and Canadian-American relations. ■TIP➜ Note that the Islands are on Atlantic Time, which is an hour later than EST. ⊠ *459 Rte. 774, Welshpool, New Brunswick, Canada* ☎ *506/752–2922* ⊕ *www.fdr.net* ✉ *Free* ☉ *House, Memorial Day weekend–Columbus Day, daily 10–6; Grounds, year-round 24/7; Visitor Center, Memorial Day weekend–Oct.*

Herring Cove Provincial Park. Many visitors to Campobello Island don't venture beyond Roosevelt Campobello International Park, but for those who do, much awaits at this adjacent park. There's a golf course and restaurant, 88 campsites (40 with electric hookups), four rustic cabins, playgrounds, and six trails, including a carriage road that traverses log bridges and spruce forests. Don't miss the mile-long black-sand beach at the namesake cove, with sea-smoothed stones in mesmerizing hues at low tide. ⊠ *Herring Cove Rd. off Rte. 774* ☎ *506/752–7010 or 800/561–0123* ⊕ *www.nbparks.ca* ✉ *Free* ☉ *Daily, 24/7.*

WHERE TO EAT AND STAY

$$–$$$
SEAFOOD
☾
★

✕ **Family Fisheries.** Seafood lovers know that fried fish doesn't have to be greasy. That's why people keep heading across the bridge to eat at this family restaurant in Wilson's Beach. The freshest seafood is delivered to the restaurant and the adjoining fish market. Order fried haddock, scallops, shrimps, or clams alone or as part of a seafood platter. Lobsters are cooked outside. Eat in the large dining room or near the playground at picnic tables or in a screened room. You can buy ice cream at the take-out window; the restaurant also serves breakfast. ⊠ *1977 Rte. 774, Wilson's Beach* ☎ *506/752–2470* ⊟ *MC, V* ☉ *Closed late Dec.–Mar. No dinner Sun.*

$$–$$$

▦ **Lupine Lodge.** Next to Roosevelt Campobello International Park, this inn overlooking Friar's Bay was originally a Roosevelt cousin's summer compound. Rooms are the same cedar-walled sleeping quarters used years ago. Some have the original huge baths with claw-foot tubs. Decks connect the three log buildings: two with lodging rooms, and the other housing a den for guests and a water-view restaurant warmed by a soaring two-sided fieldstone fireplace. **Pros:** park trails border property; spacious suite has fireplace. **Cons:** a few rooms are a bit dark; only a few have full water views. ⊠ *610 Rte. 774, Welshpool, New Brunswick, Canada* ☎ *506/752–2555 or 888/912–8880* ⊕ *www.lupinelodge.com* ➟ *10 rooms, 1 suite* ⚲ *In-room: no phone, no TV, no a/c. In-hotel: restaurant, public Wi-Fi* ⊟ *MC, V* ☉ *Closed mid-Oct.–mid-May.*

$$–$$$
★

▦ **Owen House.** Built in 1835 by an admiral, this large, handsome seaside home has an unusual two-sided staircase. A spinning wheel and horsehair couch are among the many furnishings dating back to the 19th century. Quilts add a homey touch to the historic property. Relax in the two sitting rooms and wainscoted sunporch, admire the owner's art in the gallery, or stroll about the expansive lawn. Breakfast is shared around the dining room table. **Pros:** path to secluded point with benches; wall map of island-hopping ferry route to points north; near ferry landing. **Cons:** no Wi-Fi. ✉ *11 Welshpool St., Welshpool, New Brunswick, Canada* ☎ *506/752–2977* ⊕ *www.owenhouse.ca* ⇆ *8 rooms, 6 with bath; 1 suite* ⚲ *In-room: no phone, no TV, no a/c. In-hotel: no kids under 6 (Aug. only)* ▤ *MC, V* ⊘ *Closed late Oct.–mid-May* ⼁◎⼁ *BP.*

SPORTS AND THE OUTDOORS

Spot whales and other creatures from a 20-passenger lobster boat operated by **Island Cruises** (✉ *1 Head Harbour Wharf Rd., Wilson's Beach* ☎ *506/752–1107 or 888/249–4400* ⊕ *www.bayoffundywhales. com* ⊘ *Open daily July–Sept.*). Cruises cost $49 CAN and depart from Head Harbour Wharf.

EN ROUTE Fingers of land extend into Whiting Bay and Broad and Burnt coves at the 888-acre **Cobscook Bay State Park** (✉ *40 S. Edmunds Rd., off U.S. 1, Edmunds Township* ☎ *207/726–4412* ⊕ *www.parksandlands. com* ⼂ *$3* ⊘ *Daily 9–sunset*), a great place to spend the afternoon between Lubec and Eastport. You won't be disappointed if you arrive at low tide—the islands rising from the mud flats after the water has receded have an ethereal beauty. A short hiking trail to a rock crest with views of Whiting Bay links with a longer trail. There are 106 primitive campsites.

EASTPORT

39 mi northeast of Lubec via Rte. 189, U.S. 1, and Rte. 190; 109 mi north of Ellsworth via U.S. 1 and Rte. 190.

Connected by a granite causeway to the mainland at Pleasant Point Reservation, Eastport has wonderful views of the nearby islands, and you can sometimes spot whales from the waterfront because the harbor is so deep. Known for its diverse architecture, the island city was one of the nation's busiest seaports in the early 1800s. In the late 19th century 14 sardine canneries operated here. The industry's decline in the 20th century left the city economically depressed, but now the town has set its sights on salmon, shipping, tourism, and the arts—performing and visual arts are thriving here. The weekend after Labor Day the Maine Salmon Festival attracts large crowds with boat tours of salmon pens, arts and crafts show, a historic-home walking tour, wine tasting, and dinner featuring the local delicacy and live music. On the same weekend the Eastport Pirate Festival brings folks out in pirate attire for a ship race, parade, and other events, including a children's breakfast and schooner ride, with pirates of course.

Get downtown early to secure a viewing spot for Maine's largest July 4th parade. Canadian bagpipe bands make this an event not to be missed. The day culminates with fireworks over the bay. On the weekend of the second Sunday in August, locals celebrate Sipayik Indian Days at the Pleasant Point Reservation. This festival of Passamaquoddy culture includes canoe races, dancing, drumming, children's games, fireworks, and traditional dancing.

8

ESSENTIALS

Visitor Information Eastport Area Chamber of Commerce (⌂ *Box 254, Eastport 04631* ☎ *207/853–4644* ⊕ *www.eastport.net*).

EXPLORING

National Historic Waterfront District. Anchoring downtown Eastport is this waterfront district that extends from the Customs House down Water Street to Bank Square and the Peavey Memorial Library. Spanning such architectural styles as Federal, Victorian, Queen Anne, and Greek Revival, the district was largely built in the 19th century. A cannon sits on the lawn at the Romanesque Revival library, one of the many interesting structures. Benches are beside an iron drinking trough-turned-fountain downtown. Take the waterfront walkway to watch the fishing boats and freighters. The tides, among the highest in the world, fluctuate as much as 28 feet. That explains the ladders and steep gangways necessary to access boats.

Raye's Mustard Mill. As you enter town, the yellow trim of the mill makes it hard to miss. This is the only remaining mill in the United States producing stone-ground mustard. This historic property once served the sardine-packing industry. You can tour the mill and purchase mustards made on the premises at its Pantry Store. Try award-winners like Fall Harvest, with native cranberries, or Winter Garden, with dill, garlic and celery. The store also stocks Maine-theme gifts. A small café serves light fare at lunch and sweet treats throughout the day. ⊠ *83 Washington St.* ☎ *207/853–4451 or 800/853–1903* ⊕ *www.rayesmustard.com* ⊠ *Free* ⊘ *Jan.–late May, weekdays 9–4, Sat. 10–4; Memorial Day weekend– Dec., weekdays 8:30–5, weekends 10–5.*

Tides Institute & Museum of Art. This museum, housed in a former bank, largely exhibits works depicting the Passamaquoddy Bay area from the 1800s through the present, but coastal and maritime art from elsewhere is also displayed. With tall windows letting in lots of light, the main room is ideal for viewing photos of fishermen or a dreamy painting of Grand Manan Island's towering cliffs. Changing exhibits show photography, paintings, and prints. ⊠ *43 Water St.* ☎ *207/853–4047* ⊕ *www. tidesinstitute.org* ⊠ *Free* ⊘ *Mid-June–mid-Sept., Tues.–Sun. 10–4; mid-Sept.–mid-June, Wed.–Sat., 10–4.*

WHERE TO EAT

$$–$$$
SEAFOOD

✕ **Eastport Chowder House.** Just north of downtown Eastport, this expansive waterfront eatery sits on the pier next to where the ferry docks. Built atop an old cannery foundation, it has original details such as wood beams and a stone wall. Eat in the downstairs pub, upstairs in the dining room, or on the large deck. The house specialties include a smoked fish appetizer and seafood pasta in a wine-and-cheese sauce. Lunch, served until 4, includes fried seafood plates, burgers, wraps, and sandwiches. ⊠ *169 Water St.* ☎ *207/853–4700* ▭ *D, MC, V* ⊘ *Closed mid-Oct.–mid-May.*

$$–$$$
AMERICAN
★

✕ **Pickled Herring.** Linger near the open kitchen and you may hear diners pay homage to the chef at the wood-fired grill as he prepares dishes like duck with a maple-peppercorn glaze; salmon with house pesto; and the popular strip sirloin (12, 14, or 16 ounces). Thin soft-crust pizza with toppings like caramelized onions, lobster, and blue cheese offer a lighter choice. Housed in landmark downtown storefront with soaring windows and ceilings, the wonderful food and atmosphere have made this a "destination" restaurant. Pictures of Eastport's former sardine plants hang on a brick wall, and gas-burning lanterns and street lamp-like lights throw a soft glow. Urbanites will feel at home, but locals do, too. A fun bar is hidden behind an interior wall. Specialty cocktails like the "Foghorn" (Tanqueray, fresh-squeezed lime juice, and ginger ale) have a Down East twist. ⊠ *32 Water St.* ☎ *207/853–2323* ⊕ *www. thepickledherring.com* ⊟ *AE, D, MC, V* ☺ *Closed Jan. and Feb., and Mon.–Wed. late Sept.–Dec. and March–early June. No lunch.*

$–$$ ╳ **Quoddy Bay Lobster.** Locals and innkeepers love sending visitors to
SEAFOOD this waterfront eatery at the end of a dirt lane. The fishermen owners unload their catch at the pier next to a utilitarian building where one of the fisherman's wife oversees a cheery storefront. Order food to eat under the pavilion outside or for takeout (fresh fish is also sold). The simple menu includes steamed lobster, hand-picked lobster and crab rolls, seafood-loaded chowders, and salmon wraps and pâtés. ⊠ *7 Sea St.* ☎ *207/853–6640* ⊟ *MC, V* ☺ *No dinner. Closed Mon., mid-May–mid-Oct. Closed late Oct.–early May.*

WHERE TO STAY

$$–$$$ ⌂ **Chadbourne House Bed and Breakfast.** With two fireplaces and comfortable armchairs and couches, the large double parlor is inviting in this 1821 Federal-style home. There are antiques and paintings of local landscapes; the feel is elegant and uncluttered. The large third-floor room has a sitting area, TV, skylights, a king bed, and a twin bed. **Pros:** gas fireplaces in two rooms; large yard with gardens. **Cons:** two-night minimum on weekends June through October; no shoes inside (shoe covers and slip-proof socks provided, slippers are OK). ⊠ *19 Shackford St.* ☎ *207/853–2727 or 888/853–2728* ⊕ *www.chadbournehouse.com* ⇨ *4 rooms* ♤ *In room: no phone, DVD (some), no TV (some), Wi-Fi, no a/c. In hotel: public Wi-Fi, no kids under 16* ⊟ *AE, MC, V* ☺ *Closed Nov.–March.* ¶⊙ *BP.*

$$ ⌂ **Motel East.** These rooms with a view also happen to be a good value. All the spacious accommodations at this three-level waterfront motel on the edge of downtown look across Passamaquoddy Bay to Campobello Island. Furnishings such as wing chairs are a step above those found at most motels. Rooms have balconies or terraces, and some have kitchenettes. The adjacent cottage has a deck and its own yard. **Pros:** easy walk to sites; helpful staff. **Cons:** stone steps to waterfront a challenge for some. ⊠ *23A Water St.* ☎ *207/853–4747* ⊕ *www.eastportme. info/moteleast.html* ⇨ *14 rooms, 1 cottage* ♤ *In-room: kitchen (some), refrigerator, Wi-Fi, no a/c. In-hotel: public Wi-Fi, some pets allowed* ⊟ *AE, D, MC, V.*

$ ⌂ **Todd House.** This pre–Revolutionary War home has changed little over the years. Latched plank doors, wood floors, a large cooking hearth, and a two-sided "good morning" staircase are all original. Antiques and artifacts add to the feeling of having stepped back in time. Two parlors downstairs have been converted into guest rooms. Two upstairs rooms share a bath, while a pair of large, modern rooms in an addition have private baths. **Pros:** grill on outside deck; water views from most rooms. **Cons:** some baths are dated; common areas aren't set up for relaxing. ✉ *1 Capen Ave.* ☎ *207/853–2328* ⇌ *6 rooms, 4 with bath* ⟁ *In-room: no phone, kitchen (some), refrigerator (some), no a/c. In-hotel: some pets allowed* ═ *No credit cards* ⟊⟊*BP July–Oct. only.*

NIGHTLIFE AND THE ARTS

A summer concert series, Sunday movies, and plays by community theater company Stage East are performed at **Eastport Arts Center** (✉ *36 Washington St.* ☎ *207/853–4650* ⊕ *www.eastportartscenter.com*).

Feel the pulse of Eastport's arts scene at the **Rose Garden Cafe** (✉ *9 Dana St.* ☎ *207/853–9585*) housed in the old Maybe Lumber building just up from Water Street. Open year-round, it hosts bands and holds poetry readings. The eclectic decor includes a mask collection, and even at night you can browse in the art gallery and antiques store in what was the covered lumber yard.

SHOPPING

Bird lovers flock to **Crow Tracks** (✉ *11 Water St.* ☎ *207/853–2336* ⊕ *www.crowtracks.com* ⊘ *Apr.–Sept. and by appointment*), a gallery that sells the owner's vividly painted carvings of all sorts of fowl, including some on driftwood. Giant bowls, vases, and garden sculptures catch your eye at **Earth Forms** (✉ *5 Dana St.* ☎ *207/853–2430* ⊕ *www. earthforms.biz* ⊘ *March–Dec. and by appointment*), but there are many more manageable sizes as well.

Adirondack-style chairs (they're for relaxing) and seasonal displays on the veranda draw people to the **45th Parallel** (✉ *1362 U.S. 1, Perry* ☎ *207/853–9500* ⊘ *May–Dec.*). This large store stocks a fun mix of antiques, gifts, jewelry, nautical decorations, and home furnishings. Bowls made from gourds and tree burls, silk jackets, Passamaquoddy baskets, and glass-bead jewelry are some of the items found at the **The Commons** (✉ *51 Water St.* ☎ *207/853–4123* ⊕ *www.thecommonseastport.com*), which represents more than 92 area artists and artisans.

Selling nautical supplies since 1818, the nation's oldest ship chandlery, **S. L. Wadsworth & Son** (✉ *42 Water St.* ☎ *207/853–4343*) is still run by the same family. An interesting pamphlet details its history. Check out the nautical maps and old photos of Eastport's waterfront. A souvenir-loaded gift shop is in a connecting storefront. Pick up farm-fresh eggs, locally grown produce, naturally raised meats, and fresh flowers and crafts at **Sunrise County Farmers' Market** (✉ *36 Washington St.* ☎ *287/454–3896* ⊘ *June–early Oct., Sat. 10–1.*), held in the Eastport Arts Center parking lot.

SPORTS AND THE OUTDOORS

From the short trail that begins in the parking area, **Shackford Head State Park** (✉ *18 Deep Cove Rd.* ☎ *207/941–4014* ⊕ *www.parksandlands. com* ⊡ *Free* ⊘ *Daily, 9–sunset*) has wonderful views of Cobscook Bay and over Passamaquoddy Bay to Campobello Island. From here you can see the pens for Eastport's salmon-farming industry. Side trails lead to a pebble beach and a rock promontory with caves and arches at its base. Retrace your steps or return on a loop trail around the undeveloped peninsula that's home to this 90-acre park.

WHALE-
WATCHING
AND FISHING

Operated by a family that's plied local waters for five generations, **Eastport Windjammers** (✉ 104 Water St. ☎ 207/853-2500 ⊕ www.east-portwindjammers.com) offers whale-watching and sunset cruises on the 49-passenger Sylvina W. Beal, a schooner built in 1911. You can help hoist the red sails on the windjammer, which docks downtown. Eastport Windjammers generally operates from June to mid-October. Sunset cruises are $28, and whale-watching trips are $38. Reservations are recommended. The ticket office shares space with the company's ice-cream shop opposite the city's main pier.

EN
ROUTE

Much of U.S. 1 to Calais is a **scenic drive** that cruises along the St. Croix River, which enters Passamaquoddy Bay in Robbinston. The river often resembles the elongated bays along the coast Way Down East, and can be just as breathtaking. Don't miss the overlook in Robbinston across from a Greek Revival mansion. Keep an eye out for the 12 granite milestones between Robbinston and Calais, erected in the late 1800s by a wealthy Calais lumberman, abolitionist, author, and diplomat who liked to pace his horses between the river city and his summer estate.

CALAIS

28 mi north of Eastport via Rte. 190 and U.S. 1.

The St. Croix River is tidal from Passamaquoddy Bay to Calais. Tides here can surge more than 30 feet, the highest in the continental United States. France's settlement of North America started on St. Croix Island; its 400th anniversary was the cause of much celebrating in 2004. A shipbuilding and lumbering center in the 1800s, Calais struggled economically in the late 20th century, but tourism is beginning to change the tide. There is a riverfront park with a walkway; one of the nation's oldest wildlife refuges is nearby.

St. Stephen, in New Brunswick, shares a border crossing with Calais. During the first two weeks of August the cities team up for the International Homecoming Festival, which concludes with a street fair, fireworks, and parade on the last weekend. Traffic delays at the downtown bridge can last an hour or longer in summer, but walking from downtown to downtown takes only a few minutes. A bridge north of downtown is less busy; a third bridge was to open by the end of 2009. (⇨ See the Travel Smart Maine Coast section at the back of the book for information on passports or other documents U.S. citizens need when traveling between the United States and Canada.)

ESSENTIALS

Visitor Information St. Croix Valley Chamber of Commerce (✉ 39 Union St., Calais ☎ 207/454-2308 or 888/422-3112 ⊕ www.visitstcroixvalley.com).

EXPLORING

♻ **Chocolate Museum.** Treat yourself to free samples at this sweet spot in downtown St. Stephen, New Brunswick. The museum tells the story of one of Canada's leading candy companies, Ganong Bros., the first in North America to sell chocolates in heart-shape boxes. Housed in Ganong's original factory, the museum has interactive exhibits and a delightful collection of candy boxes, some depicting Acadian heroine

Evangeline, Ganong's marketing symbol for years. You can buy hand-dipped chocolates at the store next door. ⊠ *73 Milltown Blvd., St. Stephen, New Brunswick* ☎ *506/466–7848* ⊕ *www.chocolatemuseum.ca* ⊠ *$7 (CAN)* ☉ *Early Mar.–late June, weekdays 10–5; late June–early Sept., Mon.–Sat. 9:30–6:30, Sun. 11–3; early Sept.–late Sept., Mon.–Sat. 10–4; late Sept.–mid-Dec., weekdays 10–4.*

St. Croix Island International Historic Site. Statues of French settlers and Passamaquoddy Indians grace the path at the mainland section of this historic site, 8 mi south of downtown Calais. It looks out at the small island in the St. Croix River where France's settlement of the New World began. An accompanying illustrated text tells the story of the American Indians who came to the aid of French settlers after ice floes trapped them on the now uninhabited island, which they abandoned for the mainland at what became Port Royal, Canada, after a harsh winter. A pavilion shelters a model of the 1604 settlement based on a drawing by Samuel Champlain, who was part of the expedition. Rangers offer programs in July and August. ⊠ *76 St. Croix Dr.* ✛ *off U.S. 1* ☎ *207/454–3871 in season, 207/288–3338* ⊕ *www.nps.gov/sacr* ⊠ *Free* ☉ *May–Veteran's Day, daily 8–dusk.*

WHERE TO EAT AND STAY

$$–$$$

MEXICAN

✕ **Julianna's World Café.** The "Best Food on Earth" says the sign outside this fun downtown restaurant, and it might not be too much of an overstatement. Mexican food is the specialty here. Chicken with a creamy tequila lime sauce is the signature dish, and the corn tortillas and enchilada sauce are homemade. Locals love the chicken sandwich on sourdough with bacon, provolone, and house Caesar dressing. To-die-for soups, like spiced red lentil with coconut, and West African peanut, change regularly. Tables have fresh flowers or plants. Sip margaritas—or all-natural sodas, New England ales, or Maine-roasted coffee—at bar seats in front of the picture window. ⊠ *28 North St.* ☎ *207/454–2299* ⊕ *www.juliannasworldcafe* ☐ *D MC V AE* ☉ *Closed Sun.*

$$–$$$

SEAFOOD

✕ **Solos.** The front parlor in this modest old homestead is a cozy coffee bar. Walls were removed to make the dining area beyond more open, a nice change from the restaurant (Chandler House) that had operated here for many years. Solo musicians—hence the name—play at dinner on Friday and Saturday. The popular Korean hanger, a super-tender steak with a soy marinade, is one of the many appetizers and also served as an entrée. Dishes like tuna with wasabi ginger sauce and catfish with chipotle tartar sauce spice up the menu. Honey wheat bread with cinnamon butter sweetens every dinner. Lunch includes lobster rolls and smaller fish and steak entrées. ⊠ *9 Chandler St.* ☎ *207/454–0400* ⊕ *www.solosmaine.come* ☐ *MC, V* ☉ *Closed Mon. No lunch Sun.*

$

Redclyffe Shore Motor Inn. Overlooking the St. Croix River and Passamaquoddy Bay, this tidy lodging 12 mi from Calais has good-sized rooms, all with water views. Beside the motel is a landmark 1863 Victorian Gothic with ornate gingerbread trim. An addition to the building houses the motel office and a dinner-only restaurant that serves steak-and-seafood combos as well as veal, chicken, and duck dishes. **Pros:**

some rooms have private decks; next to scenic rest area. **Cons:** close to road ⊠ *553 U.S. 1, in village center, Robbinston* ☎ *207/454–3270* ⊕ *www.redclyffeshoremotorinn.com* ⇄ *16 rooms* ⚲ *In-room: refrigerator, Wi-F, no a/c. In-hotel: restaurant* ▭ *D, MC, V* ☺ *Motel closed Nov.–Apr.; restaurant closed mid-Jan.–Apr. No lunch.*

SHOPPING

Maine books are displayed at the front of the comfortably crowded **Calais Bookshop** (⊠ *405 Main St.* ☎ *207/454–1110* ☺ *Open Mon.–Sat. Sunday by chance*), where the inviting selection of used, rare, and new books includes many on American Indians, open year-round. Fill your basket with local produce, baked goods, maple syrup, and naturally raised meat at **Sunrise County Farmers' Market** (⊠ *15 Union St.* ☎ *207/454–3896* ☺ *open June–Oct., Tues. 10–2.*), where you'll also find crafts. Housed in an 1880s bank building downtown, the **Urban Moose** (⊠ *345 Main St.* ☎ *207/454–8277*) stocks a stylish mix of gifts, household decor, and jewelry (sea glass, sterling silver, beaded), plus Maine T-shirts. Don't miss the store's namesake—a 1957 BMW Isetta with antlers and a faux hide—or the old walk-in savings vault, where items are half off.

SPORTS AND THE OUTDOORS

EXPEDITIONS The registered Maine guides who own **Cobscook Hikes and Paddles** (⊠ *13 Woodcock Way, Robbinston* ☎ *207/454–2130 or 207/726–4776* ⊕ *www.cobscookhikesandpaddles.com*) lead lake and sea kayaking, canoeing, hiking, birding, and snowshoeing day trips.

REFUGES AND PARKS One of Down East's best birding spots is the **Moosehorn National Wildlife Refuge** (⊠ *103 Headquarters Rd., turn off U.S. 1 on Charlotte Rd., Baring* ☎ *207/454–7161* ⊕ *www.fws.gov/northeast/moosehorn* ⊠ *Free* ☺ *Daily sunrise–sunset*). Spread across 29,000 acres, the refuge is home to game birds, songbirds, shorebirds, wading birds, and waterfowl. An observation deck overlooks platforms where bald eagles and osprey nest. Look for moose and other wildlife along 60 mi of roads and trails used for biking, hiking, and cross-country skiing. Several lakes and streams are open to fishing.

EN ROUTE The Grand Lake Stream region 50 mi west of Calais is a remote watershed of cove-lined lakes and flowages world-famous for fishing, especially for landlocked salmon and smallmouth bass. Classic fishing camps and lodges here also attract families who come to swim, canoe, hike, and kayak. The village of Grand Lake Stream, off U.S. 1 on West Grand Lake, was one of the world's largest tannery centers in the late 1800s. Today the tiny town is known for the Grand Laker, a square-end wood canoe built specifically for use on the often windy lakes in this region. On the last full weekend of July the Grand Lake Stream Folk Arts Festival (☎ *207/796–8199* ⊕ *www.thecclc.org/glsfaf*) attracts thousands of visitors with art, canoe, and antique quilt exhibits, and bluegrass, jazz, and folk music performances.

8

Travel Smart Maine Coast

WORD OF MOUTH

"Rent bikes in Bar Harbor and plan your route to include popovers at [Acadia National Park's] Jordan Pond. It's a beautiful ride and Jordan Pond House doesn't blink an eye at sweaty riders and hikers. They have a wonderful outdoor eating area on the lawn, too."

—cindyj

"We finally got to Monhegan [Island] on our last visit to Maine. There's only enough time [on a day-trip] to do one hike but we're not hikers. We just enjoyed taking a picnic lunch and binoculars and finding a place to sit on the rocks and just look."

—dfrostnh

GETTING HERE AND AROUND

If you plan to travel along the coast of Maine a car is a *must*. The only rail connections are along Amtrak's *Downeaster* line from Portland to Boston, and regional travel by air is expensive. Concord Coach Lines (☎ 800/639–3317 ⊕ *www.concordcoachlines.com*) runs a luxury bus several times a day from Orono, near Bangor, to Logan International Airport, in Boston, and makes stops at major towns along the way, but schedules are often inconvenient. An inland route stops in Bangor and Portland, and the company has express bus service between Portland and Logan.

The two main hubs to access the Maine coast are the cities of Portland and Bangor, approximately 133 mi from one another. Both can be reached by the Maine Turnpike, and each one is served by an airport. Once in the state, travel along the coast is best enjoyed by car, enabling you to take as relaxed a pace as you wish while reserving the right to follow whatever country road you choose. Unless you visit in the dead of winter, there are no particular impediments to driving, though local traffic can be heavy during rush hour.

■ TIP→ **The Maine Turnpike is rather boring, but the various routes that follow the coast, especially Route 1, pass through one picturesque town after another.**

TRAVEL TIMES FROM PORTLAND TO . . .	BY AIR	BY CAR
Acadia National Park/ Bar Harbor	½ hour	3 hours
Boston	½ hour	1½ hours
Montreal	4 hours	5½ hours
New York City	1½ hours	6 hours
Quebec City	4¾ hours	5 hours

■ AIR TRAVEL

Flying time from New York City is about 1¼ hours to Portland and 1¾ hours to Bangor. Flying time from Boston to Portland is less than an hour, as is the time from Boston to Bangor.

AIRPORTS

The two primary airports serving the Maine Coast area are Portland International and Bangor International. Manchester-Boston Regional Airport, in New Hampshire, is only 45 mi from the beginning of the Maine Coast, and is becoming an increasingly popular airport because of the number of discount airlines, such as Southwest, that fly there. Boston is about 65 mi (a roughly 90-minute drive) from the southern end of the Maine Coast; Boston's Logan International is the closest major international airport.

Airport Information Bangor International (BGR) (☎ 207/992–4600 ⊕ www.flybangor. com). **Logan International (BOS)** (☎ 800/235–6426 ⊕ www.massport.com/logan). **Manchester-Boston Regional Airport (MHT)** (☎ 603/624–6556 ⊕ www.flymanchester.com). **Portland International (PWM)** (☎ 207/874–8877 ⊕ www.portlandjetport.org).

Air Travel Resources in Maine Office of the Maine Attorney General (⊕ www.maine. gov/ag).

Air Travel Security Issues Transportation Security Administration (⊕ www.tsa.gov).

GROUND TRANSPORTATION

Portland is small enough that getting to and from Portland International is simple and quick. Downtown is less than 15 minutes away in traffic, and the Maine Turnpike is right next to one of the airport's entrances. It's a short drive from the turnpike to Bangor International, which is about 10 minutes from downtown. Taxi fare between downtown Portland or Bangor and their respective airports is about $15 one-way.

FLIGHTS

Portland International is served by a half-dozen airlines and Bangor International by three, with no one carrier dominating at either airport. Southwest is the major carrier serving Manchester, New Hampshire.

Airline Contacts AirTran Airways (☎ 800/247–8726 ⊕ www.airtran.com). **Allegiant Air** (☎ 702/505–8888 ⊕ www. allegiantair.com). **American Airlines** (☎ 800/433–7300 ⊕ www.aa.com). **Continental Airlines** (☎ 800/523–3273 for U.S. and Mexico reservations, 800/231–0856 for international ⊕ www.continental.com). **Delta Airlines** (☎ 800/221–1212 for U.S. reservations, 800/241–4141 for international ⊕ www.delta.com). **jetBlue** (☎ 800/538–2583 ⊕ www.jetblue.com). **Southwest Airlines** (☎ 800/435–9792 ⊕ www.southwest.com). **United Airlines** (☎ 800/864–8331 ⊕ www. united.com). **US Airways** (☎ 800/428–4322 for U.S. and Canada reservations, 800/622–1015 for international ⊕ www.usairways.com).

■ BOAT TRAVEL

Maine State Ferry Service provides ferry service to the islands of Mantinicus, Vinalhaven, North Haven, Islesboro, Swans Island, and Frenchboro. The CAT is a swift catamaran seasonal car ferry that travels between Yarmouth, Nova Scotia, and Maine, generally from late May through mid-October. Depending on the day, it runs between Portland and Yarmouth or Bar Harbor and Yarmouth. You can bring your car on the ferries to Islesboro, Vinalhaven, North Haven, and Mantinicus.

Casco Bay Lines connects the city of Portland with the islands of Casco Bay. The best way to experience island life is on foot or by bike, but if you must bring your car, make sure to reserve a spot on one of the car ferries.

A number of ferries, most seasonal and some passenger-only, operate along the coast. Passenger-only ferries to popular Monhegan Island depart from New Harbor, Port Clyde, and Boothbay Harbor.

For detailed information about private and public ferries serving Maine, visit the state Department of Transportation's helpful Web site, ⊕ www.exploremaine. org/ferry/index.html.

Information Casco Bay Lines (☎ 207/774–7871 ⊕ www.cascobaylines.com). **The CAT** (☎ 888/249–7245 ⊕ www.catferry.com). **Maine State Ferry Service** (☎ 207/596–2202 or 800/491–4883).

■ CAR TRAVEL

The Maine Coast is best explored by car. You can drive at your own pace, and you can check out any country road or fishing village on a whim. Just be sure to watch for deer and even moose crossing the road, especially at night.

GASOLINE

There are numerous gas stations along the Maine Coast, but in smaller locales many close at 6 or 7 PM. Irving stations are among those open 24 hours; they have a convenience store, and pride themselves on the cleanliness of their restrooms. Nearly all gas stations are self-service, and allow you to pay with a credit card at the pump.

PARKING

Outside major cities, parking along the Maine Coast is neither difficult nor expensive, with the exception of larger beach towns in Southern Maine during high season. Many of the more picturesque towns don't even bother with parking meters. In Portland metered on-street parking is available at 25¢ per quarter-hour, usually with a two-hour maximum. Parking lots and garages can be found downtown, in the Old Port, and on the waterfront; most charge $1 per hour or $8–$12 per day. If you're shopping or dining, remember to ask local vendors if they participate in the Park & Shop program, which provides an hour of free parking for each participating vendor visited.

ROAD CONDITIONS

Most principal roads in Maine are well maintained, and plowed and treated in winter before things get too messy. Secondary roads are another matter; beware of potholes and frost heaves. Watch out for deer and moose on the road; the number of accidents caused by moose is astonishingly high.

U.S. 1 is a well-paved and maintained highway, but it's only two lanes wide for much of its length and can be quite slow in southern Maine and when passing through popular destinations like Camden. You may get more quickly to a destination like Bar Harbor by taking I-95.

ROADSIDE EMERGENCIES

Emergency Services AAA Northern New England (☎ 800/222-4357 ⊕ www.aaanne.com). **Paragon Motor Club** (☎ 866/247-3728 ⊕ www.paragonmotorclub.com).

RULES OF THE ROAD

The speed limit on the Maine Turnpike, or interstate, is 65 mph except where posted otherwise (55 mph in urban areas of Bangor and Portland). The speed limit on secondary roads is 35 to 55 mph.

Maine has zero tolerance for driving under the influence of alcohol—the legal limit is .08—and penalties are severe. Car radars are legal, as are right turns on a red light. Although you are not required by law to stop and get off the road when using a cell phone, Maine state police suggest that it is a good practice to do so. Pedestrians have the right of way at all marked crossings; you have to stop for them. Always strap children under 40 pounds into approved child-safety seats; children under eight years of age, weighing between 40 and 80 pounds need to be strapped into an approved child-restraint system.

CAR RENTAL

A car is essential in most parts of the Maine Coast. All the major car-rental agencies have counters at the two major airports, with the exception of Enterprise's Bangor facility, which is nearby and has an airport shuttle and phone kiosk. You can also rent a car at the small commercial airports near Rockland and Bar Harbor and in larger coastal towns. Rental rates average about $45 per day, or $300 per week for a compact car. To rent a car at most agencies, you must be at least 21 years of age and have a major credit card.

When you reserve a car, ask about cancellation penalties, taxes, drop-off charges (for one-way rentals), and surcharges (for being under or over a certain age, for additional drivers, or for driving across state or country borders or beyond a certain mileage). If you want car seats and extras such as GPS, request them when you book.

Rates are virtually always better if you book in advance through a rental agency's Web site. There are other reasons to book ahead, though: for popular destinations, during busy times of the year, or to ensure that you get a certain type of vehicle.

■TIP➔ **Make sure that a confirmed reservation guarantees you a car. Agencies sometimes overbook, particularly for busy weekends and holiday periods.**

Major Rental Agencies Alamo (☎ 800/462-5266 ⊕ www.alamo.com). **Avis** (☎ 800/331-1212 ⊕ www.avis.com). **Budget** (☎ 800/527-0700 ⊕ www.budget.com). **Enterprise** (☎ 800/261-7331 ⊕ www.enterprise.com). **Hertz** (☎ 800/654-3131 ⊕ www.hertz.com). **National Car Rental** (☎ 877/222-9058 ⊕ www.nationalcar.com).

▮ TRAIN TRAVEL

Amtrak's *Downeaster* connects Portland with Boston. The train makes five daily runs to and from Boston, with six stops along the way (seven when Old Orchard is added, generally May through October). The fare is $24 each way.

Contact Amtrak *Downeaster* (☎ 207/780-1000 ⊕ www.thedowneaster.com).

ESSENTIALS

■ ACCOMMODATIONS

Beachfront and roadside motels and historic-home B&Bs make up the majority of accommodation options along the Maine Coast. There are a few large luxury resorts, such as the Samoset Resort in Rockport or the Bar Harbor Inn in Bar Harbor, but most accommodations are simple and relatively inexpensive. Many properties close during the off-season—mid-October until mid-May; some that stay open drop their rates dramatically. There is a 7% state hospitality tax on all room rates.

The lodgings we list are the best in each price category. We always list the facilities that are available, but we don't specify whether they cost extra; when pricing accommodations, you may want to ask what's included and what's extra. Properties are assigned price categories based on the range between their least and most expensive standard double rooms at high season. Lodgings are indicated in the text by a house icon, ⬚. ➪ *See hotel Price Charts in each individual chapter.*

■TIP➔ **Assume that hotels operate on the European Plan (EP, no meals) unless we specify that they use the Breakfast Plan (BP, with full breakfast), Continental Plan (CP, continental breakfast), Full American Plan (FAP, all meals), or Modified American Plan (MAP, breakfast and dinner), or are all-inclusive (AI, all meals and most activities).**

APARTMENT AND HOUSE RENTALS

Seasonal apartments and houses for rent are common along the Maine Coast, but they are also popular and expensive. Firms that market seasonal rentals rely heavily on their Web sites and are often, but not always, affiliated with a local real-estate firm. The following are some of the best property-rental agencies along the coast.

Local Agents Entire Coast: **A1 Vacations** (⊕ www.A1vacations.com). **Cottage Connection of Maine** (☎ 800/823–9501 ⊕ www.cottageconnection.com). **Find Vacation Rentals** (⊕ www.findvacationrentals. com). **Great Rentals** (⊕ www.greatrentals. com). **Vacation Rentals by Owner** (⊕ www. vrbo.com). Southern Coast: **Garnsey Bros. Rentals** (☎ 207/646–8301 ⊕ www.garnsey. com). **Port Properties** (☎ 207/967–4400 or 800/443–7678 ⊕ www.portproperties.com). **Seaside Vacation Rentals** (☎ 207/363–1825 or 866/681–8081 ⊕ www.seasiderentals.com). Mid-Coast and Penobscot Bay areas: **Camden Accommodations** (☎ 207/236–6090 or 800/334–4830 ⊕ www.camdenac.com). **Jaret and Cohn** (☎ 207/236–9626 ⊕ www. jaretcohn.com). **On the Water in Maine** (☎ 800/930–2561 ⊕ www.onthewaterinmaine. com). Blue Hill Peninsula: **Peninsula Property Rentals** (☎ 207/374–2428 ⊕ www. peninsulapropertyrentals.com). Mount Desert Island: **Mt. Dessert Island Real Estate** (☎ 207/ 244–7117 ⊕ www.mountdesertislandrealestate. com). Way Down East: **Hearts of Maine Seaside Rental Properties** (☎ 207/483–4396 ⊕ www.heartsofmaine.com).

BED & BREAKFASTS

The B&Bs of Maine offer some of the region's most distinctive lodging experiences. Many are in historic homes, have beautiful views of the ocean, and provide full American-style breakfasts.

Reservation Services **Bed & Breakfast.com** (☎ 512/322–2710 or 800/462–2632 ⊕ www. bedandbreakfast.com). **Bed & Breakfast Inns Online** (☎ 310/280–4363 or 800/215–7365 ⊕ www.bbonline.com). **BnBFinder.com** (☎ 888/547–8226 ⊕ www.bnbfinder.com).

HOME EXCHANGES

With a home exchange you stay in someone else's home while they stay in yours.

Exchange Clubs **HomeExchange.com** (☎ 800/877–8723 ⊕ www.homeexchange. com) ; $99.95 for a one-year online listing. **HomeLink International** (☎ 800/638–3841 ⊕ www.homelink.org) ; $115 for one year; $175 includes printed directories. **Intervac**

Home Exchange (☎ 800/756–4663 ⊕ *www. intervacus.com*) ; $99.99 for Web-only membership; $199 also includes phone consults to help with listing and exchanging your home.

HOTELS

The Maine Coast is liberally supplied with small, independent motels, which run the gamut from the tired to the tidy. Don't overlook these mom-and-pop operations; they frequently offer cheerful, convenient accommodations at lower rates than the chains, which are only in the larger destinations. If you stay at a motel located directly on U.S. 1, request a room in the back to avoid noise caused by traffic. Keep in mind that many motels shut down from mid-October until mid-May.

Reservations are always a good idea, and they are particularly recommended in summer and winter resort areas; in college towns in September and at graduation time in spring; and at areas renowned for autumn foliage.

When booking reservations, carefully check the lodging's cancellation policy. Many hotels and motels, because they are independently owned and not in major cities, require at least two days' notice to cancel a reservation. It's best to call ahead if you plan to arrive late. Most lodgings will hold a late reservation for you if you guarantee your reservation with a credit-card number.

Information Maine Innkeepers Association (☎ *207/865–6100* ⊕ *www.maineinns.com*). **The Unofficial Maine State Lodging Directory** (⊕ *www.visitmaine.net*).

■ CHILDREN IN MAINE

Perhaps the most extensive guide for what to do with your children when visiting Maine, *Maine-ly Fun!: Great Things to Do with Kids in Maine*, published by Down East, features almost 800 things to do and places to visit. The book's 20 chapters are arranged by topics, such as "Beaches," "Things to Cook," and "Great Ideas from Famous Maine Folks."

For a host of activities and exhibits all in one location, visit the Children's Museum of Maine, situated next to the Portland Museum of Art, or the Maine Discovery Museum in downtown Bangor. Want a quick and easy idea to occupy the kids? Head to any of Maine's beaches for a few hours of beachcombing and tidal-pool exploring.

■TIP➔ **If you are renting a car, don't forget to arrange for a car seat when you reserve.**

LODGING

Most hotels in Maine allow children under a certain age to stay in their parents' room at no extra charge, but others charge for them as extra adults; be sure to find out the cutoff age for children's discounts. Bed-and-breakfasts usually have tighter age restrictions; under state law, those with five rooms or less can bar children or set age limits if the owners live on the premises.

SIGHTS AND ATTRACTIONS

Places that are especially appealing to children are indicated by a rubber-duckie icon (🐤) in the margin.

■ EATING OUT

The one signature dinner on the Maine Coast is, of course, the lobster dinner, or as some restaurants in the more-visited destinations call it, the Shore Dinner. It generally includes boiled lobster, a clam or seafood chowder, corn on the cob, and coleslaw or perhaps a salad. Lobster prices vary from day to day; most restaurants list "market price" next to the lobster dinners on their menus. Generally, a full lobster dinner should cost around $25; without all the add-ons, about $18.

FOR INTERNATIONAL TRAVELERS

CURRENCY

The dollar is the basic unit of U.S. currency. It has 100 cents. Coins are the penny (1¢); the nickel (5¢), dime (10¢), quarter (25¢), half-dollar (50¢), and the very rare golden $1 coin and even rarer silver $1. Bills are denominated $1, $5, $10, $20, $50, and $100, all mostly green and identical in size; designs and background tints vary. You may come across a $2 bill, but the chances are slim.

CUSTOMS

Information U.S. Customs and Border Protection (⊕ www.cbp.gov).

DRIVING

Driving in the United States is on the right. Speed limits are posted in miles per hour (usually between 55 mph and 70 mph). Watch for lower limits in small towns and on back roads (usually 30 mph to 40 mph). Most states require front-seat passengers to wear seat belts; many states require children to sit in the backseat and to wear seat belts. In major cities rush hour is between 7 and 10 AM; afternoon rush hour is between 4 and 7 PM. To encourage carpooling, some freeways have special lanes, ordinarily marked with a diamond, for high-occupancy vehicles (HOV)—cars carrying two people or more.

Interstates—limited-access, multilane highways designated with an "I–" before the number—are fastest. Interstates with three-digit numbers circle urban areas, which may also have other limited-access expressways, freeways, and parkways. Tolls may be levied on limited-access highways. U.S. and state highways aren't necessarily limited-access but may have several lanes.

Gas stations are plentiful. Most stay open late (24 hours along major highways and in big cities) except in rural areas, where Sunday hours are limited and where you may drive for long stretches without a refueling opportunity. Along larger highways, roadside stops with restrooms, fast-food restaurants, and sundries stores are well spaced. State police and tow trucks patrol major highways. If your car breaks down on an interstate, pull onto the shoulder and wait for help. If you carry a cell phone, dial *55, noting your location on the small green roadside mileage marker.

ELECTRICITY

The U.S. standard is AC, 110 volts/60 cycles. Plugs have two flat pins set parallel to each other.

EMBASSIES

Contacts Australia (☎ 202/797–3000 ⊕ www.usa.embassy.gov.au). **Canada** (☎ 202/682–1740 ⊕ www.canadianembassy. org). **United Kingdom** (☎ 202/588–7800 ⊕ www.britainusa.com).

EMERGENCIES

For police, fire, or ambulance, dial 911 (0 in rural areas).

HOLIDAYS

New Year's Day (January 1); Martin Luther King Day (third Monday in January); Presidents' Day (third Monday in February); Memorial Day (last Monday in May); Independence Day (July 4); Labor Day (first Monday in September); Columbus Day (second Monday in October); Thanksgiving Day (fourth Thursday in November); Christmas Eve and Christmas Day (December 24 and 25); and New Year's Eve (December 31).

MAIL

You can buy stamps and aerograms and send letters and parcels in post offices. Stamp-dispensing machines can occasionally be found in airports, bus and train stations, office buildings, drugstores, and convenience stores. U.S. mailboxes are stout, dark-blue steel bins; pickup schedules are posted inside the bin (pull down the handle to see them). Parcels weighing more than a pound must be mailed at a post office or at a private mailing center.

Within the United States a first-class letter weighing 1 ounce or less costs 44¢; each additional ounce costs 17¢. Postcards cost 28¢. A 1-ounce airmail letter or postcard to most countries costs 98¢; a 1-ounce letter or postcard to Canada costs 75¢, and to Mexico 79¢.

Contacts DHL (☎ *800/225–5345* ⊕ *www. dhl.com*). **Federal Express** (☎ *800/463–3339* ⊕ *www.fedex.com*). **The UPS Store/ Mail Boxes Etc.** (☎ *800/789–4623* ⊕ *www. theupsstore.com*). **United States Postal Service** (⊕ *www.usps.com*).

PASSPORTS AND VISAS

Visitor visas aren't necessary for citizens of Australia, Canada, the United Kingdom, or most citizens of European Union countries coming for tourism and staying for fewer than 90 days. If you require a visa, the cost is $100, and waiting time can be substantial, depending on where you live. Apply for a visa at the U.S. consulate in your place of residence; check the U.S. State Department's Destination USA Web site for further information. *If you plan to visit Canada on a trip to Maine (you can get there by bridge or ferry from several places along the coast), make sure you have the proper documents in hand.* U.S. citizens over age 15 need a passport, passport card, or other federal government–approved travel document to re-enter the country after traveling to Canada, even for day trips. Children under 16 need a birth certificate or other proof of citizenship, such as a naturalization certificate (copies of either are OK). Permanent legal residents need their permanent resident card.

PHONES

Numbers consist of a three-digit area code and a seven-digit local number. Within many local calling areas you dial only the seven digits; in others you dial "1" first and all 10 digits—just as you would for calls between area-code regions. The same is true for calls to numbers prefixed by "800," "888," "866,"

and "877"—all toll-free. For calls to numbers prefixed by "900" you must pay—usually dearly. Maine's single area code is 207.

For international calls, dial "011" followed by the country code and the local number. For help, dial "0" and ask for an overseas operator. Most phone books list country codes and U.S. area codes. The country code for Australia is 61, for New Zealand 64, for the United Kingdom 44. Calling Canada is the same as calling within the United States, whose country code, by the way, is 1.

For operator assistance, dial "0." For directory assistance, call 555–1212 or occasionally 411 (free at many public phones). You can reverse long-distance charges by calling "collect"; dial "0" instead of "1" before the 10-digit number.

Cell Phones

The United States has several GSM (Global System for Mobile Communications) networks, so multiband mobiles from most countries (except for Japan) work here. In remote places in Maine, of which there are many, cell coverage may be spotty or nonexistent. Phones may pick up signals from Canadian towers in Way Down East towns that are across the water from Canada (you'll know if your phone is an hour ahead on Atlantic time; calling then can be costly.) Unfortunately, it's almost impossible to buy a pay-as-you-go mobile SIM card in the United States—which allows you to avoid roaming charges—without also buying a phone. That said, cell phones with pay-as-you-go plans are available for well under $100.

Contacts AT&T (☎ *888/333–6651* ⊕ *www.wireless.att.com*). **Virgin Mobile** (☎ *888/322–1122* ⊕ *www.virginmobileusa. com*).

For guidelines on tipping see Tipping.

MEALS AND MEALTIMES

Many breakfast spots along the coast open as early as 6 AM to serve the going-to-work crowd. Lunch generally runs 11–2:30; dinner is usually served 5–9. Only in the larger cities will you find full dinners being offered much later than 9, although you can usually find a bar or bistro serving a limited menu late into the evening in all but the smallest towns.

Many restaurants in Maine are closed Monday, though this isn't true in resort areas in high season. However, resort-town eateries often shut down completely in the off-season. Unless otherwise noted, restaurants in this guide are open daily for lunch and dinner.

Credit cards are accepted for meals throughout Maine, even in some of the most modest establishments.

RESERVATIONS AND DRESS

It's a good idea to make a reservation if you can. In our listings we mention them specifically only when reservations are essential (there's no other way you'll ever get a table) or when they are not accepted. For popular restaurants, book as far ahead as you can (often 30 days), and reconfirm as soon as you arrive. (Large parties should always call ahead to check the reservations policy.) We mention dress only when men are required to wear a jacket or a jacket and tie.

WINES, BEER, AND SPIRITS

The drinking age in Maine is 21, and a photo ID must be presented to purchase alcoholic beverages. Most bars and taverns are open until 2 AM. Beer and wine are sold at convenience stores, and hard alcohol is available at the large supermarkets (no Sunday sales before 9 AM). There are a number of good local microbreweries along the Maine Coast, a couple of them in the Camden area, where you also find a handful of wineries.

No matter what you might see in the local parks, drinking alcohol in public parks or on the beaches is illegal. It is also illegal to have open containers of alcohol in motor vehicles.

∎ HEALTH AND SAFETY

HEALTH

Maine seems to have more doctors than most states, but if you have an emergency, there are a dozen hospitals along the Maine Coast in addition to two in both Portland and Bangor.

Maine is famous in late spring and early summer for its black flies, and the farther inland you go, the worse they seem to get. Packing a good insect repellent is recommended if you are going to be outside. For some reason, they are not as bothersome along the coast as they are inland. An old salt told us: "The flies don't like the salt air." Maybe he's right.

Maine's other greatest insect pest is the mosquito. Mosquitoes can be a nuisance just about everywhere in summer—they're at their worst following snowy winters and wet springs. The best protection against both pests is repellent containing DEET. A particular pest of coastal areas, especially salt marshes, is the greenhead fly. Their bite is nasty; repel them with a liberal application of Avon Skin So Soft.

Coastal waters attract seafood lovers who enjoy harvesting their own clams and mussels; permits are required, and casual harvesting of lobsters is strictly forbidden. Amateur clammers should be aware that Maine shellfish beds are periodically visited by red tides, during which microorganisms can render shellfish poisonous. To keep abreast of the situation, inquire when you apply for a license (usually at town halls or police stations) and watch for red-tide postings.

SAFETY

Maine is for the most part a safe place to travel, even when walking about at night, but standard precautions are still applicable. Always lock your car and room doors, for example, and be discreet when using cash machines and credit cards.

You're probably safe wearing jewelry, though ostentatious displays will stand out in this down-to-earth state. People will rarely approach you on the street asking for money.

Safety Transportation Security Administration (*TSA*; ⊕ *www.tsa.gov*).

■ HOURS OF OPERATION

In general, banks are open from 9 to 4, but hours are often later in larger towns; post offices from 8 to 5. Most large grocery stores or supermarkets are open from 7 AM to at least 9 PM; in larger towns chain stores many stay open until 10 PM or, come summer, 11 PM. Some convenience stores, such as the Irving chain, where you also can get gas, are open 24/7.

Most museums in Maine are open from 9 to 5, some close on Sunday, and many of them, such as the Penobscot Marine Museum in Searsport, close during the off-season, mid-October to mid-May. Restaurants that serve dinner are often open until 9 or 10 PM.

Many shops are open from 9 to 5, seven days a week. Even during the tourist season, some galleries and gift stores close on Sunday, though many also extend hours until 6 or longer. Those that cater to the tourism business, in Camden for example, are often open until 9 PM in the high season. Throughout Maine you'll find stores that close off-season, though whether that's post-Labor Day, mid-October, or even after Christmas varies.

■ MONEY

Prices throughout this guide are given for adults. Substantially reduced fees are almost always available for children, students, and senior citizens.

CREDIT CARDS

Most major credit cards are accepted everywhere along the coast; some restaurants and accommodations do not accept American Express or Diners Club. Throughout this guide, the following abbreviations are used: **AE**, American Express; **D**, Discover; **DC**, Diners Club; **MC**, MasterCard; and **V**, Visa.

■ PACKING

The rule on weather in Maine is that there are no rules. A cold foggy morning in spring can, and often does, become a bright, 60°F afternoon. A summer breeze can suddenly turn chilly, and rain often appears with little warning. It can go from comfortably warm to sweat-inducing humid in a matter of hours. Accordingly, the best advice on how to dress is to layer your clothing. Rain showers are frequent, so pack a raincoat and umbrella. Even in summer, bring long pants, a sweater or sweatshirt (or two), and a waterproof windbreaker; evenings can be chilly.

Casual sportswear, including walking shoes and jeans or khakis, will take you almost everywhere, but swimsuits and bare feet will not: shirts and shoes are required attire at even the most casual beachside venues. Dress in restaurants is generally casual. Jeans are often frowned upon at the few upscale resorts, and these resorts will, at the very least, require men to wear collared shirts at dinner.

In summer, bring a hat and sunscreen. Remember also to pack insect repellent to protect you from black flies, mosquitoes, and the tiny biting flies called no-see-ums (you'll-feel-um for sure, trust us). To prevent Lyme disease, you need to guard against ticks from early spring through summer.

PACKING FOR AIR TRAVEL

Security has been exceptionally tight at Portland International Jetport ever since some of the 9/11 bombers made it through the gates there. Be absolutely sure to follow the latest rules for what items can be carried on and checked in your baggage. (Check your airline's Web site for specifics.)

■ SHOPPING

There's a lot to shop for in Maine. Opportunities run the gamut from large regional malls to small boutiques; from name-brand outlet stores to the tackiest of tourist traps that peddle cheap T-shirts and lobsters emblazoned on everything you could think of. Some of the best finds are located off the beaten path; stores that sell artisan wares such as local pottery, paintings, and one-of-a-kind jewelry. Many small-town Main streets have been revitalized with such stores.

KEY DESTINATIONS

Maine shopping is best known for the numerous outlet stores in Freeport, which include the world headquarters of L.L. Bean. Though Main Street is chockablock with stores (and hundreds of shoppers), the city has the kind of strict zoning in place that required McDonald's to locate within a white Victorian building and forego a drive-through and its prominent golden arches. Farther south along the coast in Kittery are additional outlets, though the experience is nothing near that of Freeport.

The Maine Mall in South Portland is the state's largest, with almost 120 stores, restaurants, and kiosks.

SMART SOUVENIRS

Candy made from Maine maple sugar is a delicious and uncommon treat outside Maine. Buy it at some of the nicer shops that target tourists in downtown Portland. Cool as a Moose has stores in Portland, Freeport, and Bar Harbor; it sells funky, fun shirts, hats, pants, and more that feature the likeness of the large animal that symbolizes Maine.

■ SPORTS AND THE OUTDOORS

No visit to the Maine Coast is complete without some outdoor activity–be it generated by two wheels, two feet, two paddles, or by pulling a bag full of clubs.

BICYCLING

Bicycling is an ideal (and healthy) way to explore the coast of Maine, with Acadia National Park a special favorite among road bikers. The Bicycle Coalition of Maine and Explore Maine by Bike are both excellent sources for trail maps and other riding information, including where to rent bikes.

Information Bicycle Coalition of Maine (☎ 207/623–4511 ⊕ www.bikemaine.org). **Explore Maine by Bike** (☎ 207/624–3300 ⊕ www.exploremaine.org/bike).

GOLF

A round or two of golf is more enjoyable with the ocean as your backdrop and sea breezes to energize you. The Maine State Golf Association is a center of information for amateur golfers, courses, and schedules of events. Check out the Golf Maine Association to find courses and locate golf schools.

Information Maine State Golf Association (☎ 207/829–3549 ⊕ www.mesga.org). **The Golf Maine Association** (☎ 877/553–4653 ⊕ www.golfme.com).

HIKING

Exploring the Maine coast on foot is a quick way to acclimate to the relaxed pace of life here. Healthy Maine Walks has comprehensive listings for quick jaunts as well as more involved hikes.

Information Healthy Maine Walks (⊕ www. healthymainewalks.com).

KAYAKING

Nothing gets you literally off the beaten path like plying the salt waters in a graceful sea kayak. Members of the Maine Association of Sea Kayaking Guides and Instructors offer instructional classes and guided tours, plan trips, and rent equipment. More seasoned paddlers can get maps of Maine's famous sea trails system at the Maine Island Trails Association.

Information Maine Association of Sea Kayaking Guides and Instructors (⊕ www. maineseakayakguides.com). **Maine Island**

Trails Association (☎ 207/761–8225 ⊕ www.mita.org).

STUDENTS IN MAINE

Most major attractions in the region offer discount admissions to students.

IDs & Services STA Travel (☎ 800/781–4040 24-hr service center ⊕ www.statravel.com). **Travel Cuts** (☎ 800/592–2887 in the U.S. ⊕ www.travelcuts.com).

TAXES

Maine state sales tax is 5% and applies to all purchases except prepackaged food. Maine's hospitality tax is 7%, and applies to all lodging and restaurant prices.

TIME

Maine is in the Eastern Standard Time zone; it observes daylight saving time. If crossing into New Brunswick, Canada, you will be in the Atlantic Time zone (one hour ahead; daylight saving time is also observed).

TIPPING

At restaurants, a 15% tip is standard for waiters; up to 20% is expected at more expensive establishments. The same goes for taxi drivers and hairdressers. Tip bartenders $1 to $5 per round of drinks. Coat-check operators usually expect $1 to $2; bellhops and porters should get $1 to $5 per bag; hotel maids should get about $1 to $3 per day of your stay. Hotel concierges should be tipped if you utilize their services; the amount varies widely depending on the nature of service. On package tours, conductors and drivers usually get $10 per day from the group as a whole; check whether this has already been figured into your cost. For local sightseeing tours, you may tip the driver-guide 10%, depending on the length of the tour, the number of people in your party, and whether he or she has been helpful or informative.

TOURS

GUIDED TOURS

In Maine, Boundless Journeys offers custom walking tours in the Penobscot Bay and Acadia National Park regions, complete with fine dining and inn lodging.

Contact Boundless Journeys (☎ 800/941–8010 ⊕ www.boundlessjourneys.com).

SPECIAL-INTEREST TOURS

ART

Contact Smithsonian Journeys (☎ 877/338–8687 ⊕ www.smithsonianjourneys.org).

BIKING

Contact Summerfeet Maine Coast Cycling Adventures (☎ 866/857–9544 ⊕ www.summerfeet.net).

SAILING

Contacts Maine Adventure Sails (⊕ www.maineadventuresails.com). **Maine Windjammer Association** (☎ 800/807–9463 ⊕ www.mainewindjammers.com).

SEA KAYAKING

Contact Carpe Diem Kayaking Company (☎ 207/669–2338 ⊕ www.carpediemkayaking.com).

INDEX

A

Abbe Museum, *230*
Abbe Museum at Sieur de Monts Spring, *242*
Academy Street Inn ⌧ , *38–39*
Acadia Mountain Trail, *248*
Acadia National Park and Mount Desert Island, 8, 14, 19, 221–262, 273
around Mount Desert Island, 250–260
Bar Harbor, 229–241
dining, 223–224, 225–227, 231–234, 251–252, 256–257, 259–260, 261, 262
gateways to Mount Desert Island, 225–228
itineraries, 222
lodging, 224, 227, 234–237, 252–253, 255, 257–258, 260
nightlife and the arts, 227, 237–238, 255, 258
Outer Islands, 260–262
shopping, 227–228, 238, 253, 258–259, 260
sports and the outdoors, 228–229, 239–241, 245–250, 253–254, 255, 259, 260, 261
transportation, 223, 229, 245, 25, 262
when to tour, 221–222
Acadia National Park, *218*
Aerial tours, *164, 186–187, 239, 243*
Air travel, *10, 303–304*
Acadia National Park and Mount Desert Island, 223
Blue Hill Peninsula, 201
Mid-Coast region, 108
Penobscot Bay, 155
Portland area, 77
Southern Coast, 30
Way Down East, 265
All Fired Up (art gallery), *238*
Amalfi on the Water ✕ , *160*
American Folk Festival, *197*
Amore Breakfast ✕ , *51–52*
Amusement parks, *45, 70, 229*
Apartment and house rentals, *306*
Aquariums, *131, 206, 231, 256*
Arborvine ✕ , *207–208*
Arrows ✕ , *52*
Arts District (Portland), *79–83*
Asticou Azalea Garden, *250*

B

Back Street Bistro ✕ , *113*
Bad Little Falls Park, *286*
Bagaduce Lunch ✕ , *211*
Baker Island, *261*
Balance Rock Inn ⌧ , *234*
Balloon rides, *94*
Bangor, *181, 195–198*
Bar Harbor, *229–241*
Bar Harbor Historical Society Museum, *231*
Bar Harbor Inn & Spa ⌧ , *235*
Bar Harbor Whale Museum, *231*
Bar Harbor Whale Watching Co., *241*
Barred Island Preserve, *215*
Bass Cottage Inn ⌧ , *235*
Bass Harbor, *259–260*
Bass Harbor Head Light, *242*
Bath, *119–126*
Bay Chamber Concerts, *171*
Bayside, *181*
Beach Plum Farm, *55*
Beaches, *14, 18–19*
Acadia National Park and Mount Desert Island, 243, 249, 254, 255
Blue Hill Peninsula, 211
Mid-Coast region, 117, 126, 143
Penobscot Bay, 178
Portland area, 99–100
Southern Coast, 45, 55, 59, 65, 72
Way Down East, 268, 278, 288, 289, 294
Beachcoming, *18–19*
Beals Island, *282, 284–285*
Bed & breakfasts, *306*
Belfast, *181–187*
Belfast Bay Cruises, *187*
Belfast Co-op ✕ , *182*
Belfast Historical Society and Museum, *182*
Berry Manor Inn ⌧ , *162*
Berwicks, The, *35, 37–39*
Bicycling and bike travel, *10, 19, 313*
Acadia National Park and Mount Desert Island, 228, 229, 239, 245–246, 259
Blue Hill Peninsula, 202
Mid-Coast region, 108, 117
Penobscot Bay, 157

Portland area, *77, 93*
Southern Coast, 30, 44, 68
Big Chicken Barn Books & Antiques, *195*
Bike tours, *313*
Bintliff's Restaurant ✕ , *52*
Bird watching
Acadia National Park and Mount Desert Island, 239
Blue Hill Peninsula, 214–215
Way Down East, 270, 278, 284-285, 301
Blue Hill, *206–210*
Blue Bay Gallery (shop), *209*
Blue Hill Falls, *210*
Blue Hill Inn ⌧ , *209*
Blue Hill Peninsula, 8, 200–218
Blue Hill and environs, 203–213
Deer Isle and Stonington, 213–218
dining, 202, 205, 207–208, 211, 216
itineraries, 202
lodging, 202, 205, 208–209, 211–212, 214, 216–217, 218
nightlife and the arts, 205, 209, 212
shopping, 206, 209–210, 212, 214, 217
sports and the outdoors, 206, 213, 214–215, 217, 218
transportation, 201–202
visitor information, 203
when to tour, 201
Blue Sky on York Beach ✕ , *46*
Blueberries, *16, 193, 283*
Bluff House Inn ⌧ , *274*
Boat and ferry travel, *165, 166, 313*
Acadia National Park and Mount Desert Island, 229, 261, 262
Mid-Coast region, 108–109
Penobscot Bay, 164–165, 180–181
Way Down East, 267
Boating and boat tours, *313*
Acadia National Park and Mount Desert Island, 226, 239–240, 246, 253–254, 259, 260, 261
Blue Hill Peninsula, 206, 214–215
Mid-Coast region, 126, 136, 143
Penobscot Bay, 164–165, 187, 194, 198
Portland area, 93–94, 103
Southern Coast, 35, 55, 68

Way Down East, *272, 279, 284–285, 289, 292, 301*
Boothbay, *130–136*
Boothbay Railway Village, *131*
Bowdoin College Museum of Art, *111*
Bowling, *131*
Bradbury Mountain State Park, *103*
Brick Store Museum, *61*
Broad Arrow Tavern ✕ , *101*
Brooklin, *210–213*
Brooklin Inn ⚑ , *211–212*
Brooksville, *210–213*
Brunswick, *111, 113–115 101*
Buck's ✕ , *211*
Bucksport, *193–195*
Burnham Tavern Museum, *280*
Burning Tree ✕ , *231*
Burnt Island Light, *131*
Bus tours and travel
  Acadia National Park and Mount Desert Island, 223
  Penobscot Bay, 195
  Portland area, 77
  Southern Coast, 30
  Way Down East, 266

C

Cadillac Mountain, *16, 242*
Cufé, The ✕ , *208*
Café This Way ✕ , *232*
Calais, *299–301*
Camden, *171–177*
Camden Deli ✕ , *172*
Camden Harbour Inn ⚑ , *174*
Camden Hartstone Inn ✕⚑ , *172, 174–175*
Camden Hills State Park, *177*
Camden Snow Bowl, *177*
Camping
  Acadia National Park and Mount Desert Island, 227, 249–250, 255, 258
  Blue Hill Peninsula, 217
  Penobscot Bay, 175, 191
  Portland area, 99–100
  Way Down East, 268
Campobello Island, Canada, *292–295*
Canoeing.* ⇨ See *Kayaking and canoeing
Cape Elizabeth, *97–100*
Cape Neddick, *48–50*
Cappy's Chowder House ✕ , *172*
Captain Lord Mansion ⚑ , *67*
Car travel and rentals, *10, 304–305, 308*
  Acadia National Park and Mount Desert Island, 223
  Mid-Coast region, 109
  Penobscot Bay, 156

Portland area, *77–78*
  Southern Coast, 30
  Way Down East, 266
Carriage House Inn ⚑ , *191*
Carriage rides, *246*
Carriage roads, *245, 247*
Casco Bay Islands, *94–95, 97*
Castine, *203–206*
Castle Tucker, *127*
CAT, The (boat excursions), *239*
Caterpillar Hill, *213*
Center for Maine Contemporary Art, *167*
Chapman Cottage ⚑ , *43*
Chapman-Hall House, *137*
Chauncey Creek Lobster Pound ✕ , *34*
Cherryfield, *280*
Cherryfield-Narraguagus Historical Society Museum, *280*
Children's attractions
  Acadia National Park and Mount Desert Island, 228, 229, 231, 236, 239, 240, 241, 243, 256
  Blue Hill Peninsula, 206
  Mid-Coast region, 115, 120, 125, 131, 134, 139–140, 141, 143
  Penobscot Bay, 158, 160, 163, 164, 177, 182, 186–187, 188, 191–192, 193, 198
  Portland area, 79, 80, 85, 100
  Southern Coast, 45, 56, 63–64, 66, 68, 70
  Way Down East, 268, 270, 271, 274–275, 287, 288, 294, 299–300
Children's Museum & Theatre of Maine, *79–80*
Chocolate Museum, *299–300*
Clay Hill Farm ⚑ , *49*
Cleonice Mediterranean Bistro ✕ , *225*
Climate, *25*
Coastal Helicopters, *186–187*
Coastal Maine Botanical Garden, *131*
Cobscook Bay, *289–301*
Cobscook Bay State Park, *295*
Cole Land Transportation Museum, *195*
Colonial Pemaquid Restoration, *139*
Colony, The ⚑ , *67–68*
Columbia Falls, *281–282*
Cook's Lobster House ✕ , *116*
Coveside Bed & Breakfast ⚑ , *122–123*
Craignair Inn ⚑ , *147*
Cranberry Isles, *261*
Crescent Beach, *59*

Crescent Beach State Park, *99*
Crocker House Inn ⚑ , *270–271*
Cuckolds Light, *131*
Cushing Peninsula, *143–151*
Cutler, *288–289*
Cutler Coast Public Reserved Land, *289*

D

Damariscotta, *136–139*
Darby's Restaurant and Pub ✕ , *182*
Deer Isle Granite Museum, *215–216*
Deer Isle Village, *213–214*
Desert of Maine, *100*
Dock Square, *66*
Donnell Pond Public Reserved Land, *268*
Down East Sunrise Trail, *266*
Downeast Salmon Federation, *281*
Drakes Island Beach, *59*

E

Eagle Island, *95*
East Quoddy Head Lighthouse, *293*
East Wind Inn & Meeting House ⚑ , *147*
Eastern Hancock County, *267–268, 270–277*
Eastern Promenade, *83*
Eastport, *295–299*
Echo Lake Beach, *255*
Edgar M. Tennis Preserve, *215*
Edge, The ✕ , *178*
Eggemogin Oceanfront Lodge ⚑ , *212*
El El Frijoles ✕ , *211*
El Rayo Taqueria ✕ , *85*
Elliott Healy Books (shop), *129*
Ellsworth, *225–228*

F

Family Fisheries ✕ , *294*
Farnsworth Art Museum, *15, 18, 158*
Fat Boy Drive-In ✕ , *113–114*
Fawcett's Toy Museum, *143*
Festivals and seasonal events, *26*
  Acadia National Park and Mount Desert Island, 237, 258, 262
  Blue Hill Peninsula, 204, 209
  Mid-Coast region, 115
  Penobscot Bay, 163, 177, 185, 191–192, 197
  Portland area, 102
  Southern Coast, 39, 58

Way Down East, 276, 279, 287, 292
Fiddleheads, 232
Fiddler's Green ✕, 256–257
5th Maine Regiment, 95
Fish House ✕, 151
Fishing, 12–13
Acadia National Park and Mount Desert Island, 226, 247, 259
Penobscot Bay, 192
Southern Coast, 35, 44–45, 50, 55, 59, 68
Way Down East, 299
Five Fifty-Five ✕, 85
Five Gables Inn 🖭, 133
Five Islands Lobster Company ✕, 120–121
Five-O Shore Rd. ✕, 52
Flatbread Company, ✕, 85
Flo's Steamed Hot Dogs ✕, 49
Fore Street ✕, 85–86
Fort Foster, 33
Fort Knox Historic Site, 15, 192–194
Fort McClary, 33
Fort O'Brien State Historic Site, 285
Fort Point State Park & Light-house, 193
Fort Popham, 119
Fourth of July Fireworks, 191
Francine Bistro ✕, 172
Freeport, 100–103
Freeport Historical Society, 100
Frenchboro, 262
Frenchboro Historical Society Museum, 262
Frenchboro Lobster Festival, 262
Frenchman Bay Conservancy Tidal Falls Preserve, 268
Friendship Museum, 143–144

G

General Joshua L. Chamberlain Museum, 113
George B. Dorr Museum of Natural History, 231
Gilbert's Chowder House ✕, 87
Golf, 312
Acadia National Park and Mount Desert Island, 229, 241, 254
Mid-Coast region, 126, 139
Penobscot Bay, 192, 198
Southern Coast, 50, 59
Way Down East, 276, 282
Goose Rocks, 65
Grand Lake Stream, 301
Granite industry, 216

Great Wass Island Preserve, 282
Guinness & Porcelli's ✕, 233

H

Hamilton House, 35, 37–38
Hancock, 268, 270–273
Harbor Fish Market, 79
Harbor House on Sawyer Cove 🖭, 284
Harpswell Inn Bed & Breakfast 🖭, 118
Harpswells, The, 115–116, 118–119
Harraseeket Inn 🖭, 101
Hartstone Inn ✕🖭, 172, 174–175
Havana ✕, 233
Haven by the Sea 🖭, 58
Haystack Mountain School of Crafts, 213
Helicopter tours, 186–187
Herring Cove Provincial Park, 294
Higgins Beach, 99
Hiking and walking, 312
Acadia National Park and Mount Desert Island, 247–248
Blue Hill Peninsula, 210
Mid-Coast region, 126, 136
Penobscot Bay, 169, 187
Portland area, 83
Southern Coast, 45, 61
Way Down East, 279, 288, 289, 295, 298, 301
Historic McCurdy Smokehouse, 290
Holbrook Island Sanctuary, 213
Horseback riding, 248
Horse-drawn carriage rides, 246, 248
Houses of historic interest
Acadia National Park and Mount Desert Island, 225
Blue Hill Peninsula, 204–205, 206–207
Mid-Coast region, 127, 137, 144, 145
Penobscot Bay, 158
Portland area, 80–81, 82
Southern Coast, 33, 35, 37–38, 41, 42, 65, 66
Way Down East, 280, 281, 285–286
Hugo's ✕, 86
Hulls Cove Visitor Center, 243, 245

I

Ice industry, 190
Inland York County, 32–35, 37–39
Inn at Isle au Haut 🖭, 218
Inn at Ocean's Edge 🖭, 179
Inn at Sunrise Point 🖭, 175
Inn at Tanglewood Hall 🖭, 43–44
Inns at Greenleaf Lane 🖭, 133–134
International travelers, tips for, 308–309
Island Inn 🖭, 151
Isle au Haut, 217–218
Islesboro, 180–181
Islesboro Ferry, 180–181
Islesford Historical Museum, 261
Itineraries, 21–24. ⇨ See also specific regions, cities and towns

J

Jeweled Turret Inn 🖭, 184
Jewett, Sarah Orne, 35, 37, 38
Jonesport, 282, 284–285
Jordan Pond, 242–243
Josephine Newman Sanctu-ary, 126

K

Kayaking and canoeing, 312–313
Acadia National Park and Mount Desert Island, 240, 255, 259, 261
Blue Hill Peninsula, 206, 210, 215
Mid-Coast region, 136, 139
Penobscot Bay, 187
Portland area, 97
Southern Coast, 44, 50, 59
Way Down East, 270, 277, 288, 292, 301
Kennebunk, 60–65
Kennebunk Beach, 65
Kennebunk Plains, 65
Kennebunkport, 65–69
Kenebunkport Town Hall, 65
Kennebunks, The, 60–72
King Eider's Pub & Restaurant ✕, 137
Kisma Preserve, 228
Kismet 🖭, 123
Kittery, 32–35
Kittery Historical and Naval Museum, 33

L

L.L. Bean (shop), *14, 102–103*
Lady Pepperell House, *33*
Lamoine State Park, *228*
Landmark, The ✕ , *70*
Lighthouses, *12, 149*
  *Acadia National Park and
    Mount Desert Island, 242*
  *Mid-Coast region, 103, 131,
    129–140, 146, 147–148*
  Penobscot Bay, 160
  Portland area, 97–98
  Southern Coast, 45
  Way Down East, 288, 293
Lily's ✕ , *216*
LimeRock Inn ⌕ , *162*
Lincolnville, *177–180*
Little River Lighthouse, *288*
Lobster Boat Races, *191–192*
Lobster Pound Restaurant ✕ ,
  178
Lobsters, *16, 63, 231*
Longfellow House, *80–81*
Longfellow, Henry Wadsworth,
  80–81
Lord Camden Inn ⌕ , *175*
Lubec, *290–292*
Lucerne Inn ⌕ , *197*

M

Machias, *285–288*
Maine Art Trail, *18*
**Maine Coast Sardine History
  Museum,** *282*
Maine Discovery Museum,
  160, 196
Maine Eastern Railroad, *158*
Maine Lighthouse Museum, *160*
Maine Maritime Museum,
  119–120
**Maine Narrow Gauge Railroad
  Co. & Museum,** *79*
Maine State Aquarium, *131*
**Maine Windjammers Associa-
  tion,** *164*
Marcel's ✕ , *167, 169*
Margaret Todd (schooner), *239*
**Marine Environmental Research
  Institute,** *206*
Mariners Memorial Park, *215*
Maritime Café ✕ , *216*
Marshall Point Lighthouse,
  147–148
Matinicus Island, *165–166*
McClellan Park, *279*
McSeagull's ✕ , *132*
**Meetinghouse Museum and
  Library,** *56*
Merryspring Nature Park, *177*
Mid-Coast region, *8, 106–151*
  *Boothbay and Pemaquid Penin-
    sulas, 130–143*

  *Brunswick to Wiscasset,
    111–129*
  *Cushing and St. George Peninsu-
    las, 143–151*
  *dining, 109, 116, 120–122,
    127–128, 131–132, 137, 140,
    144, 145, 146, 148, 151*
  itineraries, 110
  *lodging, 109, 111, 116, 118,
    122–125, 128–129, 132–135,
    137–138, 140–142, 144, 146,
    147, 148, 150, 151*
  *nightlife and the arts, 115, 125,
    138, 144*
  *shopping, 115, 118–119, 125,
    129, 135, 138–139, 142, 145,
    146, 150*
  *sports and the outdoors, 115,
    117, 119, 126, 135–136,
    139, 143*
  transportation, 108–109
  when to tour, 107–108
Milbridge, *278–279*
Milbridge Historical Museum,
  278–279
Millay, Edna St. Vincent, *174*
Monhegan Island, *18, 150–151*
Monhegan Museum, *150*
Montpelier, *145*
**Moosehorn National Wildlife
  Refuge,** *301*
Morse Mountain Preserve, *126*
Mount Agamenticus Park, *48*
Mount Desert Island. ⇨ *See*
  Acadia National Park and
  Mount Desert Island
Mount Desert Oceanarium, *256*
**Mount Desert Oceanarium &
  Lobster Hatchery,** *231*
**Muscongus Bay Lobster Com-
  pany** ✕ , *141*
Museum of African Culture, *18*
Museums, *18.* ⇨ *See also* Art
  galleries and museums;
  Houses of historic interest
Musical Wonder House, *127*

N

Naskeag Point, *211*
Natalie's ✕ , *173*
Nathan Gates House, *285–286*
**National Historic Waterfront
  District,** *296*
Neal Dow Memorial, *82*
New Harbor, *139–143*
Nickels-Sortwell House, *127*
Nicky's Cruisin' Diner ✕ , *196*
North Atlantic Blues Festival,
  163
North Haven Island, *166*
Northeast Harbor, *250–254*
Norumbega Inn ⌕ , *175–176*

Nott House, *66*
Nubble Light, *45*

O

Oak Gables ⌕ , *138*
Oakland House Seaside Resort
  ⌕ , *212*
Observatories, *82, 193–194*
Ocean House Gallery, *148*
Ocean Park, *69–70*
Ocean Patch Trail, *247*
Oceanside Meadows Inn ⌕ ,
  274–275
Off-Shore Islands, *217*
Ogunquit, *50–55*
Ogunquit Beach, *55*
Ogunquit Heritage Museum, *51*
Ogunquit Trolley, *50–51*
Old Orchard Beach, *18, 69–72*
Old Port, *78–79*
**Old Winterport Commercial
  House,** *193*
Olson House, *144*
Osprey, The ✕ , *121*
Our Place Inn & Cottages ⌕ ,
  166
Owen House ⌕ , *294–295*
Owls Head Lighthouse, *146,
  160*
**Owls Head Transportation
  Museum,** *148, 150*

P

Packing, *311*
Palace Playland, *70*
Park Loop Road, *243*
Parks. ⇨ *See also* Acadia
  National Park and Mount
  Desert Island
  Blue Hill Peninsula, 215, 218
  Mid-Coast region, 120, 126, 143
  Penobscot Bay, 177
  Portland area, 99, 103
  Southern Coast, 39, 48, 55
  *Way Down East, 279, 286, 288,
    293–294, 295, 298, 301*
Parson Fisher House, *206–207*
Passamaquoddy Bay, *289–301*
Peacock House ⌕ , *291*
Peaks Island, *95*
**Peary-MacMillan Arctic
  Museum,** *113*
Pemaquid, *139–143*
Pemaquid Beach Park, *143*
Pemaquid Peninsulas, *130–143*
Pemaquid Point Light, *139–140*
Penobscot Bay, *8, 154–198*
  Belfast to Bangor, 181–198
  *dining, 156, 160–162, 166,
    167, 169, 172–173, 178–179,
    182–183, 189–190, 194, 196*
  itineraries, 161

lodging, 157, 162–163, 166, 169–171, 173–176, 179–180, 183–185, 190–191, 194–195, 196–197
nightlife and the arts, 163, 171, 176, 185, 191–192, 197
Rockland area, 157–158, 160–164
Rockport, Camden and Lincoln-ville, 167–181
shopping, 163–164, 176–177, 180, 186, 198
sports and the outdoors, 164, 165, 171, 177, 186–187, 192, 198
transportation, 155–156, 180–181, 195
when to tour, 155
Penobscot Bay Inn and Res-taurnt ✕⚏ , 184
Penobscot Marine Museum, 188–189
Penobscot Narrows Bridge & Observatory Tower, 15, 193–194
Perkins Cove, 51
Petit Manan National Wildlife Refuge, 278
Pettengill Farm, 100
Pickled Herring ✕ , 296–297
Pilgrim's Inn ⚏ , 214
Pleasant Bay Bed & Breakfast ⚏ , 281–282
Point Lookout Resort ⚏ , 184
Pomegranate Inn ⚏ , 88
Popham Beach Bed & Breakfast ⚏ , 124
Popham Beach State Park, 18, 120
Port Clyde, 147–148, 150
Portland area, 8, 74–103
Arts District, 79–82
climate, 25
dining, 84–87, 95, 98, 101
Eastern Prom Trail, 91
itineraries, 80
lodging, 87–89, 97, 99–99, 101–102
nightlife and the arts, 89–91
Old Port, 78–79
shopping, 75, 91–93, 102–103
side trips, 82, 94–103
sports and the outdoors, 93–94, 99–100, 103
transportation, 75–78, 94
West End, 83–84
when to tour, 75
Portland Fish Exchange, 79
Portland Harbor Museum, 81
Portland Head Light, 15, 97–98
Portland Museum of Art, 18, 81

Portland Observatory, 82
Portsmouth Harbor Inn & Spa ⚏ , 34
Pretty Marsh Picnic Area, 255
Primo ✕ , 160–161

Q
Quoddy Head State Park, 290

R
Railroads
Mid-Coast region, 127, 131
Penobscot Bay, 158
Portland area, 79
Raye's Mustard Mill, 296
Reading Room at the Bar Har-bor Inn & Spa ✕ , 234
Red Sky ✕ , 257
Reid State Park, 18, 126
Rhumb Line ✕ , 189–190
Riverside Inn & Restaurant ✕ , 286
Rock climbing, 241, 248
Rockland and environs, 157–158, 160–166
Rockland Breakwater Light-house, 160
Rockport, 167, 169–171
Rollie's Bar & Grill ✕ , 185
Roosevelt Campobello Interna-tional Park, 293–294
Roque Bluffs State Park, 288
Round Pond, 139–143
Round Pond Fisherman's Coop ✕ , 140
Rowmar Bowling, 131
Ruggles House, 281

S
Sailing, 10, 16, 239–240, 261
St. Croix Island International Historic Site, 300
St. George Peninsula, 143–151
Samoset Resort ⚏ , 170
Sand Beach, 243
Sarah Orne Jewett House, 38
Sargeant Drive, 254
Sayward-Wheeler House, 42
Scarborough Beach State Park, 99
Scarborough March Audobon Center, 99
Scarborough Marsh Nature Center, 72
Scenic Biplane & Glider Rides Over Bar Harbor, 239
Schoodic National Scenic Byway, 272–273
Schoodic Peninsula, 273–277
Seal Cove Auto Museum, 254–255

Sears Island, 189
Searsport, 188–193
Searsport Shores Ocean Camp-ing ⚏ , 191
Seashore Trolley Museum, 66
Sebasco Harbor Resort ⚏ , 124–125
Sedgwick, 210–213
Settlement Quarry, 216
1774 Inn ⚏ , 122
1794 Watchtide . . . by the Sea ⚏ , 190–191
Shackford Head State Park, 298
Shore Acres Preserve, 215
Sips ✕ , 257
Skiing, 177, 246
Snowmobiling, 248
Somesville, 254–255
Somesville Museum, 255
Southern and Inland York County, 32–35, 37–39
Southern Coast, 8, 20–59
dining, 31
itineraries, 32
Kennebunks, 60–72
lodging, 31
nightlife and the arts, 39, 48, 54, 58, 68, 71–72
shopping, 34–35, 41–42, 48, 50, 54, 58, 64, 68
Southern and Inland York County, 32–39
sports and the outdoors, 35, 39, 44–45, 50, 55, 59, 65, 68, 72
transportation, 30-31
when to tour, 29
Yorks, Ogunquit and Wells, 39–59
Southwest Harbor, 256–259
Sow's Ear Winery, 211
Sports and the outdoors, 16, 18–19, 312–313. ➪ See also specific regions, cities and towns
Spring Woods Gallery, 272
Staples Homestead, 193
Starlight Café ✕ , 122
Steuben, 278
Stonehouse Manor of Popham Beach ⚏ , 125
Stonewall Kitchen (shop), 41
Stonington, 215–217
Strand Theatre, The, 158, 160
Swimming. ➪ See Beaches

T
Table ✕ , 208
Tate House, 82
Tenants Harbor, 146–147

Thomaston, *145–146*
Three Tides ✕ , *183*
Thunder Hole, *243*
Thuya Gardens, *251*
Tides Institute & Museum of
 Art, *296*
Tours, *10, 20, 239, 313*
 *Acadia National Park and
  Mount Desert Island, 243*
 Blue Hill Peninsula, 213, 217
 Penobscot Bay, 164, 186
 Portland area, 83, 95, 97
 Southern Coast, 35, 61
 *Way Down East, 270, 279,
  290–291, 301*
Train travel, *10, 305.* ⇨ *See also*
 Railroads
 Mid-Cost region, 109
 Penobscot Bay, 156
 Portland area, 78
 Southern Coast, 30
 Way Down East, 301
Transportation Museum, *160*
Trenton, *228–229*
Trolleys
 *Acadia National Park and
  Mount Desert Island, 243*
 *Southern Coast, 31, 50–51,
  56, 66*
Two Lights State Park, *99–100*

U
Ullikana 🏨 , *237*

V
Valley Cove, *243*
Victoria Mansion, *81–82*
Victorian by the Sea 🏨 , *170*
Vinalhaven, *18, 164–166*
Visitor information
 *Acadia National Park and
  Mount Desert Island, 225,
  228, 230, 242*
 Blue Hill Peninsula, 203
 Mid-Cost region, 107, 130, 137
 *Penobscot Bay, 158, 167, 182,
  188, 195*
 Portland area, 78

*Southern Coast, 33, 45, 51, 56,
 60, 69*
Way Down East, 267

W
Waldoboro, *143–144*
Waldoborough Historical Society Museum, *143*
Waterman's Beach Lobster ✕ ,
 146
Way Down East, *8, 264–301*
*Cobscook and Passamaquoddy
 Bays, 289–301*
*Columbia Falls to Cutler,
 280–282, 284–289*
*dining, 267, 268, 269, 274, 279,
 284, 286, 291, 294, 296–297,
 300*
*Eastern Hancock County,
 267–268, 270–277*
itineraries, 274
*lodging, 267, 270–271,
 274–275, 280, 281–282, 284,
 287, 291, 294–295, 297–298,
 300–301*
*nightlife and the arts, 271, 276,
 279, 284, 287, 292, 298*
*shopping, 271–272, 277–278,
 282, 287–288, 289, 292, 298*
*sports and the outdoors, 270,
 272–273, 277, 278, 279, 282,
 284–285, 288, 289, 292, 295,
 298–299, 301*
Steuben to Cherryfield, 278–280
transportation, 265–266
when to tour, 265
Wedding Cake House, *65*
Wells, *55–59*
Wells Auto Museum, *56*
Wells Beach, *59*
Wells Reserve at Laudholm
 Farm, *56*
Wells Trolley, *56*
Wendell Gilley Museum, *256*
West End (Portland), *83–84*
Western Head Preserve, *289*
Whale watching, *16, 20.* ⇨ *See
 also* Boating and boat tours

*Acadia National Park and
 Mount Desert Island, 241*
Blue Hill Peninsula, 217
Southern Coast, 35, 55
Way Down East, 279, 295, 299
Whale's Tooth Pub & Restaurant
 ✕ , *179*
White Barn Inn ✕ , *62*
White House 🏨 , *185*
Whitehall Inn 🏨 , *176*
Wild Gardens of Acadia, *243*
Wildlife preserves
 *Acadia National Park and
  Mount Desert Island, 228*
 *Blue Hill Peninsula, 213, 215,
  217*
 Mid-Cost region, 126
 Southern Coast, 56, 65, 72
 *Way Down East, 268, 278, 282,
  289, 301*
William M. Nash House, *280*
Williams Pond Lodge 🏨 ,
 194–195
Willowbrook Garden, *268*
Wilson Museum, *204–205*
Windjammer Weekend, *177*
Windjammers, *164, 165, 177*
Wiscasset, *126–129*
Wiscasset Waterville & Farm-
 ington Railway, *127*
Wolfe's Neck Woods State
 Park, *103*
Woodlawn Museum, *225*

X
XYZ ✕ , *257*

Y
York Beach, *45–48*
York Harbor, *42–45*
York Harbor Inn 🏨 , *44*
York Trolley Company, *40*
York Village, *40–42*
York Village Historic District, *41*
Yorks, The, *39–59*
York's Wild Kingdom, *45*
Young's Lobster Pound ✕ , *183*
Youngtown Inn and Restaurant
 ✕🏨 , *180*

Photo Credits: 8, *Jeff Greenberg/Alamy.* 9 (left), *Stock Connection Blue/Alamy.* 9 (right), *Jerry Whaley/
age fotostock.* 12, *Peter Arnold, Inc./Alamy.* 13, *Joy Brown/Shutterstock.* 14 (left), Christina Tisi-Kramer/
Shutterstock. 14 (top right), David Cannings-Bushell/iStockphoto. 14 (bottom right), Aude/wikipedia.
org. 15 (left), Stratosphere/wikipedia.org. 15 (top right), Jeff Greenberg/age fotostock. 15 (bottom right),
Natalia Bratslavsky/iStockphoto. 17 (left), Jeff Greenberg/Alamy. 17 (right), Michael S. Nolan/age fotostock. 19 (left), Jeff Greenberg/age fotostock. 19 (right), Rubens Abbond/Alamy. 20, NA/Alamy.

ABOUT OUR WRITERS

Stephen and Neva Allen have been writing for Fodor's since 1986, with books about Las Vegas, Nevada, Arizona, Idaho, the Rockies, and "American Cities," when they lived in those areas. Since 2000, they have lived with their two cats on the rocky Mid-Coast of Maine.

Former Fodor's production editor **Bethany Cassin Beckerlegge** enjoyed revisiting her favorite vacation destinations for this project. The Connecticut-based writer and editor spends much of her summer in the Mid-Coast region of Maine frequenting her favorite hideaways and searching for new seaside haunts. When not on assignment, Bethany and her husband, Robb, travel the coastal towns of New England with their toddler, Andy.

As a Maine-based freelance writer and editor, **Mary Ruoff** has enjoyed writing articles about Maine travel, among other topics. A graduate of the University of Missouri School of Journalism, she began her writing career as a newspaper reporter. Mary is married to a Mainer, Michael Hodsdon. Along with their son, Dmitry "Dima" Hodsdon, they spend as much time as they can at their family land "Way Down East," where Michael's grandfather was a fisherman.

Laura V. Scheel has spent much of her life in Maine, driving and exploring the state's numerous back roads and small towns. History and travel are two of her favorite subjects, and she has written frequently for Fodor's. When not writing she raises Wellfleet oysters on Cape Cod.

George Semler has been coming to Maine's Blue Hill Peninsula since the summer before he was born. A frequent writer for Fodor's (France, Spain, Cuba, Morocco, Andalusia, Barcelona-to-Bilbao, and Barcelona) as well as for *Saveur, Sky, Forbes*, and other publications, Semler writes about the outdoors, food, travel, and culture.

Maine native **Sarah Stebbins** spent her post-college years as a magazine editor in New York City. She moved home to Portland in 2007, lured by a fellow Mainer (now husband) and the city's low-key way of life. As a freelance writer, Sarah covers home design, travel, and lifestyle topics for *Real Simple, Martha Stewart Living, Every Day with Rachael Ray,* and others. In 2008 she married in true Maine style: There was an island ceremony and reception, a seafood feast—and a hurricane!

Michael de Zayas, who covered the Mid-Coast chapter of this book, has written for dozens of Fodor's guides, including covering turf in New York City, Bahamas, Chile, Mexico, Spain, Bermuda, Vermont, New Hampshire, Miami, and St. Martin. He is based in New York City and owns the clothing Web site Neighborhoodies.com.